ELEMENTARY ACCOUNTING

ELEMENTARY ACCOUNTING

ARNOLD W. JOHNSON, C.P.A.

Professor of Accounting
College of Business Administration
SYRACUSE UNIVERSITY

RINEHART & COMPANY, INC.

Publishers   *New York*

An earlier edition of this work was published
in 1937 under the title

PRINCIPLES OF ACCOUNTING

Ⓡ

PREFACE

IN THE preface to the first edition of this book, it was stated that "accounting, like the dynamic social order of which it is a part, is constantly undergoing change and development." This statement is impressively true today. Accounting, like the professions generally, does not stand still. It changes because of the desire for progress and professional improvement. Without improvement, retrogression sets in. In recent years the profession has rigorously re-examined its thinking on all phases of accounting. In terms of change, the results have been outstandingly progressive. Thus it is that study and progress have gone hand in hand. The study of accounting is, and always must be, a continuous process.

Since the publication of the first edition of this book under the title of *Principles of Accounting*, many changes have taken place in the practices and procedures of accounting. The fundamentals or basic truths of accounting have not changed; it is only that many of the methods and techniques of recognizing the fundamentals have changed, and that shifts have occurred in the objects of emphasis.

The following objectives have guided the preparation of the new edition:

(1) To present the materials for an intensive, undergraduate course in the principles and theories of elementary accounting.

(2) To present these materials in language that is not only understandable but simply and interestingly written.

(3) To present the principles of bookkeeping and accounting in a well-planned arrangement of carefully selected materials. The supporting discussion should be inclusive, thorough, and well illustrated. The modern setting should predominantly govern the point of view.

(4) To present a wide range of tested and realistic problems carefully related to the chapters to which they apply. A sufficient supply of satisfactory problems should be provided so that some can be used for demonstration purposes in the classroom and others for assigned work.

This book continues the use of pedagogical procedures which have stood the test of time. The approach to the study of accounting is therefore made by introducing the recording of bookkeeping processes through the balance sheet. The first six chapters present a complete treatment of the analysis of transactions, after which attention is directed to the more formal forms of the recording process. As the student achieves technical facility, the emphasis of the book shifts increasingly into the analytical, interpretive, and managerial aspects of accounting. The underlying theory of accounting is expounded throughout the book. This emphasis on theory is desirable because all accounting rules and principles develop logically from the foundations of theory. New situations, too, are more easily dealt with when they are examined and solved in the light of accounting theory.

Elementary Accounting embraces procedures and methods that are significantly modern. The work sheet, which is introduced early in the book (Chapter 5), is utilized constantly. Sales discounts are treated as deductions from sales, and purchases discounts as deductions from purchases. Prepaid expenses are current assets. The comprehensive statement of income is used throughout the book. Special debits or credits to surplus are deprecated; the "clean" statement of surplus is advocated. Stress is laid constantly upon the problems of correct accounting valuations with emphasis on the effect of these valuations upon (1) the income statement and (2) the balance sheet. Valuations attendant upon the problems of depreciation, depletion, and manufacturing are discussed fully. The income statement receives an increasing amount of attention as the book develops. In Chapter 30 the dominant position of the statement of income is conclusively stressed.

Business cases, which were introduced in the first edition, are continued in this second edition for the benefit of instructors who find cases valuable. These materials appear as problems following the several chapters to which they relate.

Six practice sets accompany the text. To allow for alternation in use, two practice sets are provided for each type of business: single proprietorship, partnership, and manufacturing corporation. The proprietorship sets emphasize the recording process and are designed for use near the close of the first semester of work. The partnership and corporation sets are more complex and are designed for use in the second semester. The four practice sets for the proprietary and partnership businesses require the preparation of bank reconciliations. All six sets involve social security taxes and withholding income taxes; they also require end-of-the-period adjustments preliminary to the preparation of financial statements.

Elementary Accounting may appear to be rather inclusive as to content. But if it is inclusive, the book should serve the student well, not only in the classroom but also in dealing with accounting problems that may confront him later as a businessman. This is important because the majority of accounting students do not expect to become accountants and their contact with the subject may be limited to the introductory text. *Elementary Accounting* is so planned as to be a flexible book. Instructors should find it easy to select materials according to the needs of their classes and the relative emphases to be given to the bookkeeping, theoretical, managerial, or other aspects of accounting; or to specific topics.

I am indebted to those who have assisted me, directly and indirectly, in the preparation of this book. For their criticisms and recommendations I wish to express my appreciation, particularly, to Professors Ernest A. Heilman of the University of Minnesota, Martin L. Black, Jr., of Duke University, and Daniel Lipsky of Brooklyn College. Helpful suggestions were also received from Mr. V. Lauren Shelton, C.P.A., and Mr. Seymour J. Harris, C.P.A. Mr. George E. Nunn, C.P.A., gave valued assistance in reading the book in proof.

A. W. J.

New Orleans, Louisiana
June, 1946

TABLE OF CONTENTS

TABLE OF CONTENTS

parative balance sheets — Ratios — Current ratio — Acid test ratio — Ratio of accounts receivable to net sales — Ratio of accounts payable to net purchases — Merchandise turnover — Productivity of working capital — Ratio of fixed assets to total assets — Ratio of sales to fixed assets — Net worth ratio — Ratio of net income to net worth — Appraisal of ratio analyses — Financial analysis: an illustration — Statement of source and application of funds — Questions — Problems

Importance of sound accounting valuations — General rules of valuation — *Current assets:* Cash — Accounts receivable — Notes receivable — Marketable securities held as short-term investments — Merchandise inventory — Supplies — *Long-term investments:* Securities — Sinking fund with trustee — *Fixed assets:* Rules of valuation — Buildings — Land — Tools — *Intangibles:* Rules of valuation — Copyrights — Goodwill — Leaseholds — Patents — Trade-marks — *Liabilities:* General rules of valuation — Valuation and the problem of net worth — Questions — Problems

APPENDIXES

ELEMENTARY ACCOUNTING

Chapter 1

INTRODUCTION

ACCOUNTING

Accounting is the master plan for the systematic and significant recording of the effects of business transactions upon the money values of a business. The actual clerical work of recording these facts in the books of a business is known as bookkeeping.

Accounting is the effective summarization of these facts for the purpose of reporting the properties and property rights in an enterprise and for the purpose of reporting and explaining the net income of a business over a period of time. The mediums through which this summarization is expressed are

(1) The statement of financial condition. In practice this statement is generally referred to as the balance sheet.

(2) The statement of operations. In practice this statement is generally referred to as the income statement, or the statement of profit and loss.

Accounting is the interpretation and analysis of recorded transactions, and their summarization by means of a detailed or general examination of all or part of the accounts, or statements, for one or more periods in order to uncover essential information with respect to the operations and financial condition of a business. It is through interpretation and analysis, also, that the trends and tendencies of business activity and financial condition are made known.

Accounting is a service which provides reports by means of which management may more effectively control the operating efficiency and financial solvency of a business. These reports furnish data which make it possible not only to check the results of past operations but also to plan and improve the course of future operations.

In summary, *accounting* may be defined as the collection, compilation, and systematic recording of business transactions in terms of money; the preparation of financial reports; the analysis and interpretation of these reports; and the use of these reports as tools of management.

The following definition of accounting is taken from Accounting Research Bulletin No. 9 (May, 1941) of the American Institute of

Accountants: "Accounting is the art of recording, classifying and summarizing in a significant manner and in terms of money, transactions and events which are, in part at least, of a financial character, and interpreting the results thereof."

THE UTILITIES OF ACCOUNTING

Today more than ever before the ability of a business to earn a net profit and its ability to preserve the capital advanced by owners and creditors depend upon efficient business administration. In support of these objectives, the information provided by a properly designed and operated system of accounting is of fundamental importance. It is through the medium of accounting reports that managements may appraise the performance of those upon whom responsibility has been placed. It is through accounting reports that managements may control operating efficiency and financial solvency. And it is through accounting reports that improvements may be effected in operating techniques and future operations, in part at least, may be budgeted. Accounting, so utilized, is constructive. It is constructive because it provides means for certain effective management controls: control of finances and control of costs.

Conversely, it is through accounting reports that managements themselves may be appraised by the owners who have delegated the functions and responsibilities of management. In these days of large-scale enterprise, of widespread and increasing use of the corporate form of business organization, and of absentee ownership, the stewardship of management is of prime importance. This is but to say that intelligent investment is primarily and fundamentally dependent upon the essential information provided by accounting reports.

The manager of the single proprietorship form of business enterprise, no less than the management of a large corporation, is interested in the following kinds of primary information:

(1) What properties are owned.
(2) What debts are owed.
(3) What the business is worth.
(4) What the profits have been.
(5) How those profits were made.

That this information is important is manifest. Less evident reasons contributing to the importance of such information are as follows: (1) Where more than one person is interested in the profits of a business, the profits must be accurately determined before they can be fairly apportioned and intelligent appraisals of ownership interests made. (2) Where income tax returns must be prepared and substantiated, full and accurate accounting information is required. (3) Where a business is subject to regulation, as the public utilities are, for instance, the proper determination of profits and values is necessary for intelligent regulation.

In broad outline the utilities of accounting may be summarized as follows:

(1) To serve as an instrumentality through which management may seek not only to maintain the integrity of capital but also to make capital productive through the control of operating proficiency.

(2) To present, classify, and evaluate the properties which are controlled by a business; and to present, classify, evaluate, and explain the changes in the claims which exist against these properties.

These are matters of paramount importance to actual and prospective creditors and owners alike. In a broader sense, too, because they affect the public welfare these matters are also the concern of society.

THE FIELDS OF ACCOUNTING

Although all accounting rests on the same fundamentals, it is like other professions in that it exhibits specialization. Distinct fields of accounting have arisen, notably the following:

(1) *Commercial Accounting*, wherein the enterprise seeks to ascertain periodically the profit or loss from operations and also the financial condition of the business. All enterprises which exist for profit employ this kind of accounting.

This type of accounting is used also by nonprofit institutions such as churches, hospitals, chambers of commerce, and so on. The interest of these institutions is not in "profit" but in the control of income and expense and the ascertainment of financial condition.

(2) *Cost Accounting*, wherein the objective is to ascertain the unit cost of goods manufactured for sale. At times cost determination is a complex and difficult procedure.

(3) *Income Tax Accounting*, wherein the objective is essentially the preparation of income tax returns for federal or state authorities. Income tax accounting demands special knowledge of, and acquaintance with, the laws and regulations which underlie the assessment of income taxes.

(4) *Governmental Accounting*, a specialized kind of accounting for municipalities, states, and other governmental bodies. This particular field of accounting has arisen because (a) the administration

of public business is very different from that of private business, and (b) the character of the information to be recorded is different.

(5) *Auditing and Investigations*, a highly specialized field comprising the work of preparing certified statements of profit and loss and of financial condition. *Auditing* dovetails into the work of *Investigations* which may call for the valuation of a business for purposes of sale, merger, new stock issues, and so on, or for critique of the efficiency with which a business is being administered. Analyses and investigations are often exhaustive in character and productive of information for the betterment of operations.

(6) *Budgets and Systems*, the planning and control of operations, a complex procedure demanding a thorough knowledge of accounting. The building and subsequent serviceability of a budget is a field of service whose objective is to guide intelligently the management of a business by setting up in advance a program of estimated operations. Actual results are then compared with expected results.

The adaptation of a system of accounting to the needs of a particular business is the field of *Accounting Systems*. Enterprises are not alike in the kind of information which they require and they must, therefore, be individually fitted with the kind of accounting systems which are appropriate to their needs. While system building is a distinctive field of accounting, it is usually administered by the professional accountant rather than by individuals specializing in system building alone.

THE IMPORTANCE OF ACCOUNTING

From the foregoing discussion it should be apparent, in a more or less general way, that the study of accounting should be worth while not only to the prospective accountant but also to the individual who does not intend to follow the profession of accounting. Business executives, professional men, bankers, creditors, investors, and others, find accounting knowledge useful in understanding the values and limitations of financial reports and in the employment of these reports for the effective administration of their business affairs. No businessman or investor is well equipped unless he is able to understand accounts intelligently and to utilize them for the control of his business or investment program. Accounting cuts across all the fields of business administration, hence its peculiar and fundamental importance in the general field of economic study and activity.

QUESTIONS

Question **1–1.** What is accounting? Differentiate between accounting and bookkeeping.

Question **1–2.** Should a lawyer know accounting? Why?

Question **1–3.** Why should you study accounting when you have no intention of becoming an accountant?

Question **1–4.** May a knowledge of accounting be of service to us when we propose the investment of our savings in stocks, bonds, banks, and other properties or depositories? If so, how?

Question **1–5.** What direct information may accounting reports furnish to the management of a business?

Question **1–6.** Can a progressive company dispense with accounting? Why? Explain in substantial detail.

Question **1–7.** Name some of the several classes of people interested in accounting reports and, in a general way, state the kind of information which is of particular interest to each of these classes.

Question **1–8.** Enumerate some of the utilities of accounting.

Question **1–9.** What are some of the fields in which accounting specialization has been especially prominent?

Question **1–10.** In what ways may accounting usefully serve the following businesses, or lines of business:

Banking	Hospital
Department store	Manufacturing
Farmer	Mining
Garage	Schools
Gas and electric companies	Transportation (air, rail, water)

Chapter 2

FUNDAMENTAL CONCEPTS

THE STATEMENT OF FINANCIAL CONDITION

In Chapter 1 it was pointed out that a businessman wishes to know, among other things, his financial condition as of a given date and also the amount of net income which he has earned over a given period of time. With these two things in mind, assume that Roy Young advises that as of December 31, 1950,

His Business Owns:
Various Properties Costing $30,000.00

His Business Owes:
Various Creditors . . . . $ 5,000.00
Himself, as Owner 25,000.00
$30,000.00

This is obviously a statement of financial condition. While this statement gives some information as to the financial facts of the business, it is deficient because it does not provide information as to

(1) The kinds of properties owned and the valuations attaching to each of these properties, or

(2) The character of the obligations owed and the valuations attaching to each of these obligations.

The statement does not describe the individual properties of the business; it merely states that their group valuation is $30,000.00. It does not give the details of the two groups of obligations; it merely states that their group valuation is also $30,000.00.

A better statement of financial condition for the business of Roy Young on December 31, 1950, would have been as follows:

Roy Young
BALANCE SHEET, DECEMBER 31, 1950

The Business Owns:
Cash $6,700.00
Accounts Receivable:
Birchum & Company $1,000.00
F. A. Collier & Son 3,000.00
John A. Pace Company 4,000.00   8,000.00

6

Merchandise	5,000.00
Store Equipment	2,000.00
Delivery Equipment	1,700.00
Building	5,000.00
Land	1,600.00
	$30,000.00

The Business Owes:
Accounts Payable:

Carl A. Adams	$1,000.00	
Cole & Day, Inc.	2,000.00	$ 3,000.00
Notes Payable		1,000.00
Mortgage Payable (due July 1, 1960)		1,000.00
		$ 5,000.00
Roy Young, Owner		25,000.00
		$30,000.00

This statement is a clear, revealing report upon the status of the finances of the business of Roy Young. The properties owned and the obligations owed are individually described as to kind and as to valuation. There is sufficient cash on hand to pay off the accounts payable, notes payable, and mortgage payable. The accounts payable and notes payable are probably due for payment within the very near future. The real-estate mortgage, however, is not a matter of immediate concern inasmuch as this long-term indebtedness is not due for payment until July 1, 1960. The mortgage payable, unlike the other obligations, has the advantage of being secured by the pledge of specific property.

It is possible to draw further information from the financial statement of Roy Young but, for our immediate purpose, this is not necessary. The important thing to observe is the superiority of the second statement over the first. The second statement is better because of the information which it presents in reasonable, but significant, detail.

THE STATEMENT OF OPERATIONS

A somewhat similar situation exists with respect to the problem of profits. Assume, for example, that when Roy Young began business on January 1, 1950, his investment was $20,000.00; and that twelve months later, December 31, 1950, his investment was $25,000.00. Would it be correct to conclude that Mr. Young had earned a profit of $5,000.00 for the year?

Investment, December 31, 1950 . . . . $25,000.00
Investment, January 1, 1950 . . . .   20,000.00

Profit (?) for the year . . . . $ 5,000.00

If Mr. Young had invested an additional $5,000.00 of cash during the year, it would be erroneous to conclude from the above calculation that $5,000.00 had been earned. For the year 1950, it is even possible that Mr. Young might have earned $8,000.00 and might have withdrawn $3,000.00 of his earnings for personal use, thus leaving but $5,000.00 of the profits in the business. It is possible, further, for the $5,000.00 increase in investment to be explained as the difference between an additional investment of $8,000.00 and an operating loss of $3,000.00 for the year. The above type of calculation, therefore, is not satisfactory. It does not produce a profit figure which can be relied upon as accurate, nor does it reveal how the profits, if any, were earned.

Suppose, instead, that the report of operations for Mr. Young had been as follows:

I sold merchandise for $51,000.00
Which cost me 30,000.00

Leaving a gross profit of $21,000.00
My expenses were 15,000.00

Leaving a net profit on business operations of . . . . $ 6,000.00
Add profit earned on sale of land 2,000.00

Net profit, all sources considered . . . . $ 8,000.00
Investment, January 1, 1950 . . . .   20,000.00

                                                                $28,000.00
Less cash withdrawn for personal use. 3,000.00

Investment, December 31, 1950 . . . . $25,000.00

A statement of this kind reveals not only the amount of net profit for the year but also the way in which the profits were earned and, further, the way in which they were disposed of. The following specific information may be noted:

(1) The volume of sales
(2) The cost of sales
(3) The gross profit
(4) The expenses
(5) The profit from the major operation of business, i.e., merchandising
(6) The profit from the other operations of business

(7) The profit earned from all operations
(8) The profits withdrawn from the business by the owner
(9) The profits left in the business

This statement is a superior statement because it provides accurate information in significant detail.

DEFINITIONS

At this point in our discussion it is well to pause briefly for the purpose of introducing a few of the more common terms of accounting terminology and to become acquainted with their several meanings.

Assets. — An asset is anything of value owned. It is an item of wealth which is satisfactorily measurable in dollars and which is useful in carrying on business enterprise. Legal title to an asset generally resides in the owner. While this is usually the case, exceptions occur. An automobile may be purchased on the installment plan, the contract of purchase specifying that title shall pass when all payments have been made. In cases of this kind, the property is considered to be an asset of the buyer rather than of the seller. This is because — in a business sense — the asset is looked upon, constructively, as the property of the buyer; and because the reservation of title by the seller is simply a protective device to cover his unpaid financial interest in the property sold.

Assets come into the possession of a business by the acts of investment, purchase, conversion, gift, and discovery.

Assets vary in their nature. They may be tangible or intangible, or they may consist of money claims against others. Tangible assets, for example, are cash, merchandise, office equipment, land, buildings. Intangible assets are properties like formulas, franchises, patents, and goodwill. Money claims are those like accounts receivable, notes receivable, and securities. All of these assets have value; and against them exist the claims or property rights of those who have financial interests in these assets. One of the objectives of accounting is to prepare for any given business at any given date a list of the assets owned and the valuations which attach to each of them.

Accounts Receivable. — In its narrower sense the term "accounts receivable" represents the indebtedness of customers for merchandise or equivalent stock in trade (i.e., services) on open account. More broadly the term represents the open account indebtedness of customers for charges of any kind.

Notes Receivable. — Promissory notes and drafts received from debtors are the notes receivable of a business.

Liabilities and Equities. — Anything of economic value is or will be claimed by someone. Therefore, since the assets of a business have economic value, it is obvious that claims must exist against them. Such claims are known as "ownership claims" or as "rights against property" or as "property rights" or as "equities." The claims of the owners of a business are called "proprietorship" or "net worth," while the claims of those who are not owners are called "liabilities." More specifically, liabilities are simply the debts which are owed by a business. They are legally enforceable obligations under which a business is required to deliver — for value received — considerations (usually money) to creditors at fixed or determinable future dates. Until they have been paid, liabilities are legally superior to any and all claims of proprietorship.[1]

As a general rule it may be said that equities explain the sources through which assets have been obtained. The assets of a business are furnished originally by the proprietor or the several owners of a business. Later on, assets may be furnished by individuals who are not owners but creditors. Merchandise, for example, may be purchased on terms of 90 days' credit. While it may be true as a general rule that equities explain where assets have been obtained, some reservation to the complete and unqualified acceptance of this statement appears in order. For instance, a liability like Income Taxes Payable is not in itself to be looked upon as an explanation of where assets came from.

In the statement of financial condition care should be taken to separate clearly the debts of a business from claims which are purely proprietary in nature. This separation is significant inasmuch as the liabilities of a business must be paid in full before it is possible to make any liquidating payment upon a proprietary claim.

Unsecured liabilities are not claims against particular assets but against all unpledged assets generally. For instance, in the statement on page 7, merchandise creditors have a $3,000.00 claim, not against the specific asset merchandise, but against the total of unpledged assets generally. This is true even though these two creditors may have furnished $3,000.00 of the $5,000.00 merchandise which is currently on hand. In making shipment of this merchandise, the vendors automatically made an unconditional transfer of title to Roy Young. In consequence, they have no greater claim against the asset merchandise than against any other unpledged asset.

By way of contrast, the real-estate mortgage of the same state-

---

[1] In terms of these new definitions, the definition of accounting on page 2 may now be made more specific: Accounting is the master plan for the systematic and significant recording of the effects of business transactions upon the assets, liabilities, and net worth of a business.

ment is a secured claim. The mortgage of $1,000.00 is an equity which, by written agreement, is secured by the pledge of the specific asset real estate.

Accounts Payable. — In its narrower sense the term "accounts payable" represents liabilities which have been created by the open account purchase of merchandise and supplies. More broadly the term represents all invoices for merchandise, supplies, services, and so on, which are due for payment within a period of twelve months.

Notes Payable. — Notes payable are the ordinary promissory note and draft liabilities of a business. Notes payable are usually issued in favor of merchandise creditors but, on occasion, they may be issued in favor of one or more banks, or other parties, for the purpose of securing funds.

Profit and Loss Statement. — The profit and loss statement is the statement of operations. The function of this statement is to report the amount of income which has been earned by a business over a specified period of time and to explain, also, how this income was earned.

Balance Sheet. — The balance sheet is the statement of financial condition. It is divided into two major parts, each of which is equal to the other. In one part the assets are listed, valued, and totaled; in the other the equities are listed, valued, and totaled. The balance sheet always applies to a specific date.

The assets on a balance sheet are generally classified into at least three classes:

(1) *Current assets.* Current assets are cash and those assets expected to be converted into cash by the normal operations of business over the next twelve months.

(2) *Fixed assets.* Fixed assets are those tangible assets used in the operation of a business but which are of relatively long life, and which are not intended to be sold. Machinery and buildings are examples.

(3) *Other assets.* The miscellaneous assets of a business are listed under this title.

The liabilities of a business are generally classified into at least two classes:

(1) *Current liabilities.* Current liabilities are those payable within one year.

(2) *Fixed or long-term liabilities.* Fixed liabilities are those payable after one year.

Net Worth — Capital — Investment. — All of these terms have the same meaning. They represent the proprietary interest (or equity) in an enterprise.

THE BALANCE SHEET IS ALWAYS IN BALANCE

Since assets are always balanced by an equal amount of claims against them, it is clear that

$$\text{Assets} = \text{Liabilities} + \text{Net Worth}$$

For a solvent concern this is always true. There can be no change in the total assets of a business without a corresponding change in the amount of the claims (equities), or property rights, existing against these assets. No matter what the character of a business transaction, it cannot disturb the balance of the equation. To show that this is true let us consider the effect of eight new transactions upon the balance sheet of Roy Young:

Roy Young

BALANCE SHEET, DECEMBER 31, 1950

Assets

Current Assets:

Cash		$ 6,700.00
Accounts Receivable:		
Birchum & Company	$1,000.00	
F. A. Collier & Son	3,000.00	
John A. Pace Company	4,000.00	8,000.00
Merchandise		5,000.00
		$19,700.00
Fixed Assets:		
Store Equipment	$2,000.00	
Delivery Equipment	1,700.00	
Building	5,000.00	
Land	1,600.00	10,300.00
		$30,000.00

Liabilities and Net Worth

Current Liabilities:

Accounts Payable:		
Carl A. Adams	$1,000.00	
Cole & Day, Inc.	2,000.00	$ 3,000.00
Notes Payable		1,000.00
		$ 4,000.00

Fixed Liabilities:
    Mortgage Payable, due July 1, 1960 . . . .   1,000.00

          Total Liabilities . . . . $ 5,000.00
Net Worth:
    Roy Young, Capital 25,000.00

                                                    $30,000.00

(1) Roy Young invests additional cash, $5,000.00.

The asset cash is increased $5,000.00. Since the cash was placed in the business by Roy Young, his equity is increased $5,000.00.

This transaction illustrates the increase of an asset and a similar increase in the amount of the proprietor's equity.

(2) A check for $1,000.00 is received from Birchum & Company in payment of their account.

The asset cash is increased $1,000.00 and another asset, the accounts receivable with Birchum & Company, is reduced $1,000.00.

This transaction illustrates the increase of one asset and a decrease of corresponding amount in another asset.

(3) Merchandise is purchased on 60 days' credit from Dale & Son at a cost of $1,300.00.

The asset merchandise is increased $1,300.00. Since Dale & Son furnished the merchandise without requiring immediate cash payment, this particular merchandise creditor has a claim of $1,300.00.

This transaction illustrates the increase of an asset and a corresponding increase in a liability.

(4) A note payable for $1,000.00 is given to Carl A. Adams, a merchandise creditor. The note is given in payment of an open accounts payable of similar amount.

Here a new liability is created to take the place of an old liability. The amount of money owed to Carl A. Adams remains unchanged but the character of the obligation owed has been altered. The liability of notes payable is increased by $1,000.00; and the liability of accounts payable to Carl A. Adams is reduced by the same figure, $1,000.00.

This transaction illustrates the creation (increase) of a liability and the decrease of another liability.

(5) Land costing $600.00 is sold to York & Company for $1,000.00 cash.

Land is reduced $600.00; cash is increased $1,000.00. Total assets have been increased $400.00 by the profit realized on the sale. The proprietor claims that profit, hence the claim (equity) of Roy Young is increased $400.00.

This transaction illustrates the increase of one asset, the decrease of another, and a balancing increase in the amount of the proprietary claim of the owner.

(6) The mortgage payable is paid, $1,000.00.

Cash is reduced $1,000.00; the liability for the mortgage indebtedness is extinguished.

This transaction illustrates the reduction of an asset and a reduction of equal amount in a liability.

(7) Delivery equipment costing $700.00 is sold to F. A. Chester for $400.00 cash.

This transaction is similar to the fifth transaction except that a loss has been realized instead of a profit. Cash is increased $400.00; delivery equipment is reduced $700.00; and the proprietary claim of Roy Young is decreased by the loss of $300.00.

This transaction illustrates the increase of one asset, the decrease of another, and a balancing net decrease in the amount of the proprietary claim of the owner.

(8) Roy Young withdraws $1,000.00 cash for his private use.

Cash is reduced $1,000.00 and the equity of Roy Young is also reduced by $1,000.00.

This transaction illustrates the reduction of an asset and a reduction of equal amount in the proprietary claim of the owner.

The balance sheet of Roy Young, after giving effect to these eight transactions, will be as follows:

Roy Young

BALANCE SHEET, DECEMBER 31, 1950

Assets			Liabilities and Net Worth		
Current Assets:			Current Liabilities:		
Cash		$12,100.00	Accounts Payable:		
Accounts Receivable:			Cole & Day, Inc.	$2,000.00	
F. A. Collier & Son	$3,000.00		Dale & Son	1,300.00	$ 3,300.00
John A. Pace Company	4,000.00	7,000.00			
			Notes Payable		2,000.00
Merchandise		6,300.00			
			Total Liabilities		$ 5,300.00
		$25,400.00			
Fixed Assets:					
Store Equipment	$2,000.00		Net Worth:		
Delivery Equipment	1,000.00		Roy Young, Capital		29,100.00
Building	5,000.00				
Land	1,000.00	9,000.00			
		$34,400.00			$34,400.00

As a matter of technical detail, our discussion may pause briefly for the purpose of directing attention to the heading of a statement of financial condition. A proper heading is illustrated in the balance sheet above. Note that the statement refers to a specific date.

In the illustrative balance sheets on pages 12 and 14, accounts receivable and accounts payable were detailed for teaching purposes. In actual practice it is not customary to show on the balance sheet the details of accounts receivable, accounts payable, notes receivable, or notes payable. Only totals for each of these groups are shown.

The eight transactions presented in the above discussion are examples of nearly every type of business transaction.[2] Although each transaction changed the balance sheet in some particular way or ways, the equilibrium of the balance sheet was not disturbed. This was because each transaction had two equal sides. In the first transaction there was an increase in assets of $5,000.00 and a similar increase in the total of equities; in the fifth transaction there was a net increase in assets of $400.00 and a similar increase in the total of equities. That each transaction had two equal sides is not surprising. This naturally follows because asset values must always be balanced by an equal amount of claims against them. All accounting transactions are characteristically "self-balancing." In our later exposition of accounting method we shall often have occasion to refer to this basic principle.

TEMPORARY VALIDITY OF THE BALANCE SHEET

In the examples above, each transaction resulted in a change in the balance sheet in some particular. A balance sheet must therefore be regarded as a statement of financial condition which is valid for only one given instant of time, and no more; the very next transaction alters the detail of the balance sheet in some degree and brings into being a new statement of financial condition.

FORM OF THE BALANCE SHEET

The balance sheet may be presented in either of two ways, the "report" form or the "account" form. In the report form the assets appear first; below the assets appear the equities. The first two statements of financial condition in this chapter are examples of the

---

[2] Not included in these examples are three types of transactions normally associated with the corporate form of business organization and, for that reason, not illustrated above. These types are as follows:

(1) Liability Increase and Net Worth Decrease. *Example:* A cash dividend is declared out of surplus.

(2) Liability Decrease and Net Worth Increase. *Example:* Bonds are exchanged for stock (capital reorganization).

(3) Net Worth Increase and Net Worth Decrease. *Example:* Directors declare and pay a stock dividend.

report form of balance sheet. A common variation of the report form of balance sheet is the deduction of the liabilities from the assets to leave net worth — in other words, conformity of the balance sheet to the accounting equation of

$$\text{Assets} - \text{Liabilities} = \text{Net Worth}$$

In the account form of balance sheet the assets are placed on the left side and the equities are placed on the right side of the page. The balance sheet of Roy Young on page 14 is an example. The account form of balance sheet is in accordance with the accounting equation of

$$\text{Assets} = \text{Liabilities} + \text{Net Worth}$$

In practice the more common form of balance sheet is the account form. This is especially true with respect to published balance sheets.

In the remainder of this text the account form of balance sheet will be generally employed.

SUMMARY

We are now ready to consider how the assets of a business may be increased or decreased, and what effect, if any, is exerted upon equities when these increases and decreases occur.

Assets may be increased through

 Increasing the equity of

(1) Profits — The owner

(2) The investment of additional assets by a proprietary interest — The owner

(3) The advance of additional assets by creditors — Creditors

Assets may be decreased through

 Decreasing the equity of

(1) Losses — The owner

(2) The withdrawal of assets by a proprietary interest — The owner

(3) The disbursement of assets to creditors — Creditors

A second summary may be prepared to account for changes in net worth. The equity of the owner of a business may be

Increased by

(1) Profits

(2) Personal investment of additional assets

Decreased by

(1) Losses

(2) Personal withdrawal of assets

QUESTIONS

Question **2–1.** *Define:*

Asset	Liability	Balance sheet
Equity	Net worth	Profit and loss statement

Question **2–2.** What essential facts does an owner wish to know about his business? By what accounting statements is this information reported?

Question **2–3.** Assets:

(1) What are they? Illustrate.
(2) Do all businesses employ assets? The same kind of assets? Why?
(3) Are assets temporary or permanent in character? Explain.
(4) What assets might an automobile agency be reasonably expected to possess? A drug store?
(5) Who furnishes the assets with which a business operates?
(6) How are assets increased? Decreased?

Question **2–4.** Equities:

(1) What are they? Illustrate.
(2) Do all businesses have equities? The same kind of equities? Why?
(3) Are equities short term or long term in character? Explain carefully.
(4) How are equities increased? Decreased? Illustrate by using specific transactions. Assume that the proprietor begins business with $10,000.00 cash.

Question **2–5.** Explain why a balance sheet must always be in balance. Will subsequent business transactions affect this equality? Why?

Question **2–6.** For how long is a balance sheet representative of the financial condition of a business?

Question **2–7.** How is the net worth of a business determined?

Question **2–8.** What transactions increase or decrease the net worth of a business?

Question **2–9.** Why are the claims of outsiders shown separately from the net worth claim of a business?

Question **2–10.** A and B are equal partners with capitals of $10,000.00 each. B retires from business. Can settlement be made with B without reducing the assets or equities of the business? If so, explain how. Show the new balance sheet.

Question **2–11.** "Equities explain where assets have been obtained." Do you agree? If so, explain why.

Question **2–12.** A company, at various dates, makes disbursements in payment of

(1) Calendars for distribution to customers
(2) A trade-mark

(3) A franchise

(4) An exclusive distributorship for the Royaltone radio

Are these assets? Why?

PROBLEMS

Problem **2–1.** Clark E. Pace started in business January 1 with an investment of $50,000.00. At the end of the year his balance sheet showed that he was worth $60,000.00. Mr. Pace claimed, therefore, that his profit for the year must have been $10,000.00. Was Mr. Pace correct in his contention? Why?

Problem **2–2.** Show in full detail how the balance sheet of Roy Young on page 14 is developed from the balance sheet on page 12, and succeeding transactions.

Problem **2–3.** The following items comprise the assets and equities of the business of James A. Cardwell on December 31, 19—. Arrange them in balance sheet form.

James A. Cardwell, Capital		$30,000.00
Cash		4,000.00
Accounts Receivable:		
E. A. Crane	$2,500.00	
Fisher & Company	1,100.00	
May & Son	1,400.00	5,000.00
Merchandise		20,000.00
Accounts Payable:		
Acme Supply Company	$4,000.00	
Bell & White	2,000.00	6,000.00
Notes Payable		4,000.00
Securities on Hand		6,000.00
Store Equipment		5,000.00
Supplies		1,000.00
Unpaid Salaries		1,000.00

(1) Do the merchandise creditors have claims against the specific asset merchandise? Explain.

(2) Was the money borrowed on notes payable used to buy merchandise, store equipment, or other specific purpose? Does the balance sheet ordinarily reveal this type of information?

(3) Suppose that the supplies had all been used up but that no other changes occurred in the assets of the balance sheet. Indicate how the balance sheet would be altered.

(4) How would the balance sheet be affected if the securities were sold for a cash price of $7,000.00?

(5) What would have been the effect on the balance sheet if the business had been burglarized to the extent of $300.00 cash and merchandise costing $200.00?

Problem 2-4. The following items constitute the balance sheet of Robert J. Wilcox who operates a business known as the Wilcox Builders Supply Company. Prepare the balance sheet of Mr. Wilcox as of December 31, 19___. Use the "account form" of statement.

Accounts Payable	$·79,489.00
Accounts Receivable	25,582.00
Building	50,000.00
Cash	3,729.00
Due from Officers and Employees.	1,415.00
Land	20,000.00
Merchandise	43,331.00
Miscellaneous Equipment	14,038.00
Notes Receivable	5,000.00
Patents and Trademarks	5,927.00
Securities	13,767.00
Taxes Payable	2,250.00
Wages and Salaries Payable	4,089.00
Warehouse in Process of Construction	12,803.00
Wilcox, Robert J., Capital	109,764.00

Problem 2-5. From the following information prepare the balance sheet of the Starrett Seed Company as of August 31, 19___. Use the "report" form of balance sheet.

Accounts Payable	$17,983.00
Accounts Receivable	16,598.00
Advances to Growers	5,878.00
Automobiles and Trucks	2,211.00
Building	14,027.00
Cash	4,375.00
Land	8,534.00
Machinery and Equipment	15,244.00
Merchandise	32,401.00
Mortgage Payable	6,000.00
Notes Payable to Banks	25,000.00
Notes Receivable	3,046.00
Starrett, L. S., Capital	51,519.00
Sundry Unpaid Expenses	1,812.00

Problem 2-6. Following are the assets and liabilities of Winthrop L. Crane, operating as the Sparkle Soft Drink Company, on December 31, 19___:

Cash	$20,459.00
Notes Receivable	5,000.00
Accounts Receivable	13,312.00
Mortgage Payable	10,000.00
Bottled Soft Drinks and Sundry Products on Hand	19,411.00
Notes Payable	2,000.00
Land	3,932.00
Customers' Refundable Deposits on Cases and Bottles	14,971.00
Buildings, Machinery, and Equipment	31,098.00
Accounts Payable	8,832.00
Cases and Bottles	27,052.00
Trademarks, etc.	1.00

Required:

Prepare a balance sheet December 31, 19— (account form). You are required to determine the net worth.

Problem **2–7.** From the following information prepare a balance sheet (report form) of the Raymond Drug Company as of December 31, 19—:

Accounts Payable	$ 3,569.12
Accounts Receivable	410.80
Building	14,687.41
Cash	809.73
Cigars on Hand	365.61
Deposits Made with Utility Companies	75.00
Fixtures and Equipment	4,130.16
Inventory of Drugs and Drug Sundries	6,867.35
Land	5,000.00
Miscellaneous Supplies	100.00
Mortgage Payable	3,000.00
Notes Payable	5,000.00
J. L. Raymond, Capital	20,888.10
Sales Tax Collections Payable to State Treasurer	96.70
Soda Fountain Supplies	314.29
Taxes Payable	118.64
Water, Light, and Gas Bills Payable	87.79

Problem **2–8.** From the following information construct the balance sheet of the Edwards Packing Company on December 31, 19—:

Automobiles	$ 7,674.00
Buildings	100,000.00
Cash	54,509.00
Accounts Receivable	113,234.00
Accounts Payable	177,011.00
John A. Edwards, Investment	399,769.00
Factory Equipment	136,723.00
Income Taxes Payable	12,046.00
Land	25,000.00
Merchandise	238,446.00
Mortgage Payable on Real Estate	25,000.00
Notes Payable to Banks	100,000.00
Office Equipment	17,448.00
Patents, Formulas, etc.	26,477.00
Property Taxes Payable	2,644.00
Stocks and Bonds	20,000.00
Supplies (current asset)	1,332.00
Wages and Salaries Payable	24,373.00

Problem **2–9.** Following are the items constituting the balance sheet of the New Cubana Sugar Company on July 31, 1952:

Land	$1,641,953.00
Buildings, Machinery, Railroad Rolling Stock, etc.	2,413,512.00
Work Animals, Livestock and Equipment	103,505.00
Pasture Fields	42,509.00
Planted and Growing Cane	33,715.00
Loans to Colonos and Contractors	167,519.00
Materials, Supplies, and Merchandise	162,050.00
Sugar on Hand	521,046.00

Molasses on Hand	12,923.00
Accounts Receivable	46,208.00
Cash	39,182.00
First Mortgage Payable	461,000.00
Accounts Payable	928,981.00
Notes Payable	17,000.00
Unpaid Wages, Interest, Rent, Taxes, and Insurance	9,222.00
Capital Investment	3,767,919.00

Required:

Prepare a balance sheet, using the account form.

Problem **2–10.** Following are the assets and liabilities of the Safeway Paper Cup Company on December 31, 1954:

Thousands of Dollars

Cash	$1,480
Notes and Accounts Receivable	422
Accounts Payable	337
Marketable Securities	112
Inventories of Finished Products, etc.	1,418
Wages and Expenses Payable	82
Taxes Payable	323
Land and Railroad Siding	184
Buildings and Building Equipment	1,717
Machinery and Equipment	2,966
Furniture and Fixtures	133
Automobiles	10
Machinery and Equipment under Construction	125
Patents and Trademarks	145
Notes Payable	500

Required:

From the above information construct a balance sheet (report form). You are required to determine the amount of net worth.

Problem **2–11.** The following items are taken from the balance sheet of the Guaranty Trust Company of New York as of December 31, 19__:

Thousands of Dollars

Cash	$1,044,582
Loans to Customers, etc.	431,135
U.S. Government Obligations	1,137,213
Municipal Bonds, Notes, and Sundry Assets	78,295
Stock of the Federal Reserve Bank	7,800
Sundry Interest and Accounts Receivable.	7,321
Deposits	2,423,224
Bank Building	11,258
Other Real Estate	1,362
Sundry Accounts Payable	18,796

Required:

Reconstruct the balance sheet of the Guaranty Trust Company. You are required to determine the amount of net worth.

Problem **2-12.** The following assets and liabilities are taken from the balance sheet of The Texas Corporation as of December 31, 19___:

	Thousands of Dollars
Cash	$ 65,337
Notes and Accounts Receivable	32,944
Crude and Refined Oil Products	80,821
Accounts Payable	31,267
Materials and Supplies	6,340
Accounts Receivable from Employees	1,624
Notes Payable	7,406
Investments in Companies Operating in the U.S.	30,957
Investments in Companies Operating in Foreign Countries	82,825
Lands, Leases, Wells, and Equipment	286,587
Taxes Payable	13,105
Dividends Payable	5,430
Oil Pipe Lines and Tank Farms	78,447
Refineries and Terminals	163,287
Bonds Payable	111,835
Ships and Marine Equipment	53,549
Sales Stations, Facilities, and Equipment	101,871
Patents	1,341

Required:

Construct a balance sheet of The Texas Corporation as of December 31, 19___. You are to determine the amount of net worth.

Chapter 3

DEBIT AND CREDIT

We now understand that each accounting transaction causes some change in the valuations of the balance sheet. It is apparent, however, that revision of the balance sheet by the method employed in Chapter 2, accurate though it be, is a cumbersome procedure and is especially so if transactions appear in volume. Yet unless daily record is made of each and every accounting transaction, how is it possible for the proprietor of a business to know what assets should be on hand at the end of an accounting period? How is it possible for him to know what liabilities exist against him unless he has made proper record of all the elements by which his liabilities are determined? How is it possible for him to have information with respect to operations unless he has made systematic record of the elements by which operations are explained and net income is calculated?

It follows therefore that, if balance sheets and income statements are to be correct for the dates and periods to which they apply, proper record must have been made of all elements which enter into the determination of financial condition and net income. If this has been done the management is informed not only as to the character and amount of the liabilities of the business but also as to what the assets are and should be. For instance, in Chapter 2, after the balance sheet had been adjusted to give effect to the several transactions of that chapter, it was found that the asset cash had a book value of $12,100.00. This figure represented the amount of cash that should be on hand. If less cash were actually on hand, the proprietor would realize that some cash had been misappropriated or had been improperly disbursed or accounted for.

In attempting improvement of the procedure of Chapter 2, the desideratum would be an arrangement within the framework of the balance sheet whereby changes in assets and liabilities might be recorded, but recorded in such a manner as to preclude the necessity of immediate actual revision of the figures of the original balance sheet. Such an arrangement should permit each transaction to be separately recorded and it should permit, also, a check of the figures if subsequently the new balance sheet, by its failure to balance, discloses the fact that error has occurred. An arrangement of this kind,

23

using the balance sheet and transactions below, is illustrated herewith:

Floyd L. Smith

BALANCE SHEET, NOVEMBER 30, 19—

Assets		Liabilities and Net Worth	
Cash	$3,900.00	Accounts Payable:	
Accounts Receivable:		Harley Sales Co.	$ 200.00
James E. Nelson	300.00		
Securities	1,000.00	Net Worth:	
Office Equipment	1,000.00	Floyd L. Smith, Capital. .	6,000.00
	$6,200.00		$6,200.00

Mr. Smith represents clients in the purchase, sale, and rental of real estate. Assume the following transactions to occur during the month of December. What would be the new balance sheet on December 31, 19—?

(1) Bought an adding machine for cash from the Riley Business Equipment Company, $100.00.

(2) Mr. Smith drew $1,000.00 cash for his private use.

(3) A cash payment was made to the Harley Sales Company in payment of November account, $200.00.

(4) Bought an office safe on credit terms from the Harley Sales Company, $500.00.

(5) The securities were sold for cash, $1,000.00. These securities originally cost $1,000.00.

(6) An automobile for use in the business is purchased from the Bohn Motor Company, $900.00. A down payment of $400.00 is made and the balance is covered by a mortgage note payable in monthly installments of $50.00.

The figures in parentheses, referring to transaction numbers, have been inserted to assist the student in tracing the entries made.

This arrangement has several definite advantages:

(1) Each transaction is recorded individually.

(2) Transactions are recorded by a procedure which does not require immediate revision of the balance sheet.

(3) Transactions may be re-examined and recordings verified if these procedures should become necessary.

(4) The new balance sheet is produced.

But even this arrangement, although much superior to the procedure with which we originally began, is an unwieldy one. This would be especially true if transactions occurred in volume. A further improvement of procedure is evidently required.

ASSETS	BALANCE SHEET NOV. 30	INCREASES IN ASSETS	DECREASES IN ASSETS	BALANCE SHEET DEC. 31
	I	II	III	IV
Cash.	$3,900.00	$ + 1,000.00 (5)	$ − 100.00 (1) − 1,000.00 (2) − 200.00 (3) − 400.00 (6)	$3,200.00
James E. Nelson . . .	300.00			300.00
Securities.	1,000.00		− 1,000.00 (5)	
Office Equipment . . .	1,000.00	+ 100.00 (1) + 500.00 (4)		1,600.00
Automobile		+ 900.00 (6)		900.00
	$6,200.00			$6,000.00

EQUITIES		DECREASES IN EQUITIES	INCREASES IN EQUITIES	
Harley Sales Co. . . .	$ 200.00	− 200.00 (3)	+ 500.00 (4)	$ 500.00
Notes Payable			+ 500.00 (6)	500.00
Floyd L. Smith, Capital	6,000.00	− 1,000.00 (2)		5,000.00
	$6,200.00			$6,000.00

We begin with the following form which is called a "T" account:

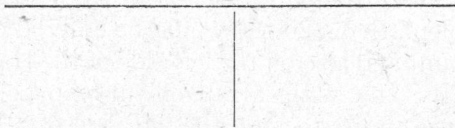

We shall use T accounts to represent the assets and equities of a business; this will be done by using individual T accounts for each kind of asset and equity. One T account will be used for Cash, another for Merchandise, another for Securities, and so on. If we were to record the assets and equities of Floyd L. Smith in T accounts, we would do so by placing the dollar value of each asset on the left side of the T account reserved for that asset, and by placing the dollar value of each equity on the right side of the T account reserved for that equity. The placement of assets on the left side of T accounts, and equities on the right side, parallels the position of assets and equities on the account form of balance sheet, assets being listed on the left side and equities on the right side. The full T-account record of the first balance sheet of Floyd L. Smith would be as follows:

CASH		JAMES E. NELSON		SECURITIES	
3,900.00		300.00		1,000.00	

OFFICE EQUIPMENT		HARLEY SALES CO.		FLOYD L. SMITH, CAPITAL	
1,000.00			200.00		6,000.00

In similar fashion, the dollar value of all new assets subsequently acquired would be added to the left side of the particular T accounts representing such assets, and the dollar value of all new ownership claims incurred would be added to the right side of the particular T accounts representing these equities. For example, if Mr. Smith later invested an additional $5,000.00 of cash in his business, this $5,000.00 would be recorded on the left side of the Cash account and also on the right side of Floyd L. Smith, Capital account.

Conversely, the proper accounting to record the decrease of an asset places the amount of the decrease on the right side of the T account representing that asset and, to record the decrease of an equity, it places the amount of the decrease on the left side of the T account representing that equity. If $200.00 cash were paid to the Harley Sales Company, as in the third transaction of the illustrative problem, then $200.00 would be entered on the right side of the Cash account and also on the left side of the Harley Sales Company account. In so far as the arrangement on page 25 is concerned, and with reference to *assets only*, the left side of T accounts represents

the assets of column I, and
the increases of assets in column II.

Similarly, the right side would represent

the decreases of assets in column III.

Ownership claims or equities, as already stated, are recorded on the right side of accounts in conformity with their position on the right side of the account form of balance sheet. Increases in equities would be added to the right side of the T accounts by which these ownership claims are represented, while decreases would be recorded on the left side. In so far as the arrangement on page 25 is concerned, and with reference to *equities only*, the right side of T accounts represents

> the equities of column I, and
> the increases of equities in column III.

Similarly, the left side would represent

> the decreases of equities in column II.

The foregoing paragraphs may be summarized in the following manner:

(1) On the left side of an account are recorded
    (a) Assets and increases in assets.
    (b) Decreases in equities.
(2) On the right side of an account are recorded
    (a) Equities and increases in equities.
    (b) Decreases in assets.

Using the balance sheet and transactions from page 24, we find that the complete T-account record of the affairs of Floyd L. Smith would be:

CASH		JAMES E. NELSON		SECURITIES	
3,900.00	− 100.00	300.00		1,000.00	− 1,000.00
+ 1,000.00	− 1,000.00				
	− 200.00				
	− 400.00				

OFFICE EQUIPMENT		AUTOMOBILE		HARLEY SALES CO.	
1,000.00		+ 900.00		− 200.00	200.00
+ 100.00					+ 500.00
+ 500.00					

NOTES PAYABLE		FLOYD L. SMITH, CAPITAL	
	+ 500.00	− 1,000.00	6,000.00

To ascertain the amount of cash on hand, the left side of the Cash account is added and the total of the right side deducted; the remainder of $3,200.00 is the balance of the Cash account and the amount of cash on hand. The balances for other accounts are determined in a similar manner except that for equity accounts the computation is reversed, the total of the left side being deducted from that of the right side. The balance of an account is simply the excess of the total of one side over that of the other.

If the left side of an account is larger, the account is said to have a debit balance; if the right side is larger, the account is said to have a credit balance.

DEBIT AND CREDIT

"Debit" and "credit" are two terms commonly used to indicate the manner in which a transaction is to be recorded in the ledger — whether there has been an increase in an asset, an increase in an equity, a decrease in an asset, or a decrease in an equity.

Every entry on the left side of an account is called a *debit*.

Every entry on the right side of an account is called a *credit*.

Another way of explaining the terms "debit" and "credit" is to state that we

DEBIT in order to record

   (1) An asset.
   (2) An increase in an asset.
   (3) A decrease in a liability or net worth claim.

CREDIT in order to record

   (1) A liability or net worth claim.
   (2) An increase in a liability or net worth claim.
   (3) A decrease in an asset.

The two terms "debit" and "credit" should be firmly fixed in mind. Once their meanings are thoroughly understood one should be able to use them without difficulty. Their correct use is illustrated in the following description of the transactions of Floyd Smith:

Transaction	Debit		Credit		Explanation
1	Office Equipment .	100.00			To record increase in asset, office equipment.
			Cash	100.00	To record decrease in asset, cash.
2	Floyd L. Smith, Capital	1,000.00			To record decrease in net worth of Floyd L. Smith.
			Cash	1,000.00	To record decrease in asset, cash.
3	Harley Sales Co. .	200.00			To record decrease in liability, accounts payable.
			Cash	200.00	To record decrease in asset, cash.
4	Office Equipment .	500.00			To record increase in asset, office equipment.
			Harley Sales Co. .	500.00	To record increase in liability, accounts payable.
5	Cash	1,000.00			To record increase in asset, cash.
			Securities	1,000.00	To record decrease in asset, securities.
6	Automobile . . .	900.00			To record increase in asset, automobile.
			Cash	400.00	To record decrease in asset cash.
			Notes Payable . .	500.00	To record increase in liability, notes payable.

DEBITS EQUAL CREDITS

In each of the foregoing six transactions the debit value of the transaction was equal to the credit value. This equality, of course, was to be expected. Since the debit side of a balance sheet is always equal to the credit side, and since this equality is continuous, it follows that the debit side of each transaction must always equal the credit side. No entry in the ledger is complete, therefore, unless the debit entry is equal in value to the credit entry. This is the *rule of double entry*: for every debit there must be a credit of equal value.

Where the accounts of a business are operated in accordance with the rule of double entry, the bookkeeping involved is known as "double-entry bookkeeping."

ANOTHER EXAMPLE

What are the proper debits and credits to record the eight transactions of Roy Young listed on page 13? They are as follows:

Transaction	Debit		Credit	
1	Cash	5,000.00	Roy Young, Capital . .	5,000.00
2	Cash	1,000.00	Birchum & Company .	1,000.00
3	Merchandise	1,300.00	Dale & Son	1,300.00
4	Carl A. Adams	1,000.00	Notes Payable	1,000.00
5	Cash	1,000.00	Land	600.00
			Roy Young, Capital . .	400.00
6	Mortgage Payable . .	1,000.00	Cash	1,000.00
7	Cash	400.00	Delivery Equipment .	700.00
	Roy Young, Capital . .	300.00		
8	Roy Young, Capital . .	1,000.00	Cash	1,000.00

In this example the explanations of the various debits and credits have been omitted. It is recommended that each debit and credit be justified by supplying the explanation which is applicable to each case.

DEFINITIONS

The following three definitions may now be formally considered:

Transaction. — An accounting transaction is any business occurrence which causes a change in any of the valuations of the balance sheet.

Not all business transactions are accounting transactions. For example, a contract is signed by the General Sales Corporation whereby this company leases a business property for a period of five years beginning next January 1, 19—. The annual rental is $6,000.00 payable $500.00 on the first day of each month commencing with January 1, 19—. This contract is not an accounting transaction.

This is because the contract does not change any of the values of the balance sheet.

Account. — An account is an appropriately titled written record representing some specific asset or equity (or subdivision thereof) of the balance sheet. In this written record the value status of the asset or equity is reflected; and increases or decreases in value are systematically recorded during the accounting period.

Ledger. — A collection of accounts representing all the assets and equities of a business constitutes the ledger of that business. The eight accounts in the illustration on page 27 constitute the ledger of Floyd L. Smith.

ACCOUNTS AND THEIR INTERPRETATION

The ledger of Floyd Smith embraced eight accounts, one for each *type* of asset and equity. It is not necessary to open an account with *each* asset of like kind; it is enough to open one account with each class of asset. Floyd Smith may, for example, buy four delivery trucks at $800.00 each. Even though these trucks be purchased at widely separated dates, only one account, not four, will be opened, the acquisitions being shown as follows:

DELIVERY EQUIPMENT

800.00	
800.00	
800.00	
800.00	

The title of an account should be clear, specific, and an exact description of the kind of asset or equity which is represented.

The balance of an account is the excess of debits over credits, or vice versa. Asset accounts have debit balances; liability and net worth accounts have credit balances. The debit balance of an asset account represents the value of the asset on hand. If the Merchandise account, for instance, has a debit balance of $10,300.00, it is understood that, as of the date of the balance in the account, there is merchandise physically on hand worth $10,300.00 Each credit balance of an equity account represents, on the other hand, the claim of a creditor or owner against the assets of a business as of the date that the balance is taken.

QUESTIONS

Question **3–1.** Explain the importance of recording properly and accurately every business transaction.

Question **3–2.** A transaction is to be recorded. How do you determine the proper accounts and how do you determine which sides of the accounts receive the entries?

Question **3–3.** *Define:*

Account	Debit
Balance of an account	Credit
Ledger	

Question **3–4.** Normally, what kind of balance should an asset account have? A liability account?

Question **3–5.** Would the following accounts normally have debit or credit balances?

Cash	Merchandise
Federal Income Tax Payable	Mortgage Payable
Fixtures	Notes Receivable
Fuel	Real Estate
Interest Receivable	Salaries Payable

Question **3–6.** Merchandise worth $1,800.00 is destroyed by fire. Using debits and credits to express your intention, how would you record this fact on the ledger?

Question **3–7.** A machine originally costing $1,000.00 is finally worn out and must be replaced. How should this fact be expressed on the ledger?

Question **3–8.** What is the rule of debit and credit? Of double entry?

Question **3–9.** Would it be possible to have a credit balance in a customer's account? Would it be possible to have a debit balance in a creditor's account? Explain.

Question **3–10.** Why are assets recorded on the left side and equities on the right?

Question **3–11.** Discuss the correctness of the statement that "the balance sheet is the groundwork of accountancy — the origin and terminus of every account."

Question **3–12.** Why should the total debit balances in a ledger equal the total credit balances?

PROBLEMS

Problem **3–1.** What information is revealed by the following accounts drawn from the ledger of John A. Sherman:

ALLEN & CO.		BORDEN & SON, INC.		CASH	
2,000.00	2,750.00	1,220.00	1,500.00	900.00	1,100.00
	1,500.00	1,085.00		1,500.00	440.00
	750.00	2,950.00			
		1,700.00			
		600.00			

FURNITURE AND FIXTURES	MERCHANDISE		SALARIES PAYABLE
2,000.00	8,000.00	650.00	525.00
	5,000.00	3,000.00	

JOHN A. SHERMAN, CAPITAL	SUNDRY SUPPLIES	U.S. TREASURY BONDS
20,000.00	260.00	5,000.00

Problem **3–2.** What accounts should be debited and credited in the following transactions?

(1) W. E. Clark starts in business with cash, $20,000.00.

(2) He buys merchandise from Lewis & Son for cash, $1,000.00.

(3) Store fixtures and equipment are purchased on credit from Rhodes & Stratton, Inc., for $3,300.00.

(4) A cash loan is made to F. M. Ryan, $1,000.00. Mr. Ryan's sixty-day note is received in exchange.

(5) He buys 100 shares of Ray Chemical Company stock from E. C. Scott & Co., brokers, $8,000.00. No cash changes hands in this transaction although arrangements are entered into for a partial payment within the next few days.

(6) He makes a part payment of $1,000.00 on the bill of the third transaction.

(7) He buys a government bond for cash, $1,000.00.

(8) He pays $3,000.00 cash to E. C. Scott & Co., as part payment of the stock purchased in transaction #5.

(9) By agreement a set of fixtures, purchased in transaction #3, is returned to Rhodes & Stratton, Inc., $300.00. There is no cash involved in this transaction.

(10) He withdraws cash for private use, $5,000.00.

(11) A contract is signed for the purchase of land, $1,000.00, and building, $10,000.00, title and consideration to pass on the tenth day of next month.

(12) An adding machine costing $100.00 is stolen from the office.

Problem **3–3.** John A. Ludman opens a business for the servicing of automobiles. His cash investment on June 28, 19__ is $2,000.00. His transactions for the next two days are as follows:

(1) He arranges for the use of a building for his business. The rent is to be $75.00 a month commencing July 1. Mr. Ludman is allowed to occupy the building on June 28–29–30 without charge.

(2) He opens an account at the First National Bank, depositing $2,000.00.

(3) He buys small tools from the Hanes Equipment Company for cash, $110.00.

(4) A customer, H. J. Leonard, brings in a car to have the speedometer repaired. The job is estimated to cost $12.00.

(5) Mr. Ludman sends the speedometer to the local agency of the Stewart-Warner Corporation for repair. On June 30 the speedometer is returned; the bill attached is for $11.00. Mr. Ludman writes a check for $11.00 and records the charge on the bill of H. J. Leonard.

(6) He buys garage equipment from the Wells & Jack Corporation, $900.00. He pays cash, $100.00, and signs a mortgage note for the balance which is payable $100.00 monthly, the first installment payment to be August 1, 19—.

(7) He buys fifty gallons of oil from the Ohio Oil Company on account, $40.00.

(8) He purchases miscellaneous office equipment from the Central Supply Company on account, $60.00.

(9) He arranges for gas, electricity, and water services; and in completing these arrangements he makes a deposit of $25.00 to guarantee payment of bills. This money is refundable when service is discontinued.

(10) An electric advertising sign is completed and attached to the building. This sign was purchased from, and installed by, the City Sign Company at a price of $120.00 for which a note payable was given. The sum $10.00 is to be paid on this note every month, the first payment to be July 10, 19—.

Required:

(1) What are the proper debits and credits to record the above transactions?

(2) Enter the above transactions in a T-account ledger.

(3) Prepare the balance sheet of Mr. Ludman on June 30, 19—.

Problem **3–4.** J. C. Martin, preparatory to active business operations, engages in the following transactions:

(1) He invests cash, $10,000.00.

(2) He buys land for cash from Paul E. Coleman, $2,000.00.

(3) He buys land, $1,000.00, and a building, $10,000.00, from A. B. Lanner, paying $2,000.00 cash immediately and giving a ten-year mortgage for the balance of $9,000.00.

(4) He buys office equipment for cash from Dameron & Curry, $1,000.00.

(5) He pays cash to Ward & Company for an installation of linoleum on his floors, $600.00.

(6) A used typewriter is purchased for cash from the Modern Typewriter Exchange, $70.00.

(7) A neon advertising sign is installed on the building, and paid for, $400.00.

(8) The typewriter, purchased in transaction #6, is returned because

not satisfactory. In its place a new typewriter is purchased for $120.00, the difference of $50.00 being paid in cash.

(9) A contract is signed with the Hoover Protective Agency, Inc. whereby Mr. Martin's property will have special night protection by Hoover private police. This service, to commence on the first day of next month, will cost $10.00 monthly, payable on the tenth of each month.

(10) A cash register is purchased from the National Cash Register Company, $100.00, on terms of $10.00 down, and $10.00 monthly.

Required:

(1) What are the proper debits and credits to record the above transactions? Record these debits and credits in the same form as shown on page 29.

(2) Record these debits and credits in the ledger of Mr. Martin.

(3) Prepare the new statement of financial condition.

Chapter 4

EXPENSE AND INCOME

EXPENSE

Let us reproduce the ledger of Floyd L. Smith as we left it on page 27:

CASH		JAMES E. NELSON		OFFICE EQUIPMENT	
3,200.00		300.00		1,600.00	

AUTOMOBILE		HARLEY SALES CO.		NOTES PAYABLE	
900.00			500.00		500.00

FLOYD L. SMITH, CAPITAL	
	5,000.00

If Mr. Smith now spends $100.00 of cash for advertising purposes, what is the effect of this payment upon the balance sheet? It is clear that cash is reduced $100.00; it is clear also that no new asset is received in exchange; it is clear further that, since total assets have decreased $100.00, total equities must also have been reduced by $100.00. The expenditure [1] is a cost to Mr. Smith; it is debited to his capital account because *his* proprietary claim to the wealth of the business has been reduced. In the language of accounting we may say that the expenditure has resulted in a reduction of the net worth of Floyd L. Smith. All costs and losses operate in this way; they are debits to net worth because they decrease the claim of a proprietary interest.

There are many expenditures similar to the expenditure for advertising. Payments must be made for rent, for the handling of materials, for labor, for taxes, for licenses, for legal costs, for insurance premiums, for repairs, and so on. These expenditures, individually

---

[1] An expenditure may be defined as the disbursement of cash or other asset, or the incurring of an obligation.

and collectively, operate more or less directly to reduce the net worth of a business. In a more practical sense, we may say that these costs reduce the profits of a business and, in this way, result in a reduction of net worth. These are costs *incurred in the production of gross income.* In the accounting sense these expenditures are commonly known as *expenses.*

DEFINITION OF EXPENSE

Assets and services are consumed in producing the gross income of a business. When consumed, these values become expense. To illustrate, an expense

(1) May occur through the physical consumption of an asset.

Example: A tank car of gasoline is purchased. The gasoline is an asset when received but it is converted into an expense as it is consumed.

(2) May occur through the expiration, or lapsing, of a right or privilege.

Example: On January 1, 1950, X paid Y the sum of $2,000.00 for certain patent rights. The patent expired at the end of the year 1950. On December 31, 1950, then, the value of $2,000.00 expired with the expiration of the period for which the patent was valid and valuable. The patent rights have been converted from an asset into an expense.

(3) May be an expenditure for personal services. (As a general rule an expenditure for personal services is an expenditure for expense; to this general rule, however, there are some exceptions.)

Example: Wages of shipping department employees are paid, $300.00.

In all cases, however, *an expense definitely represents the decrease in net worth resulting from the necessary consumption of value for the purpose of producing periodic income.*[2] As a general rule expenses are incurred voluntarily.

This is a broad definition of the term "expense." In general accounting practice, however, it is not interpreted to include the cost of merchandise which has been sold. This is because merchandise is made the subject of separate analysis and control.

---

[2] A loss, on the other hand, is realized when value is consumed or surrendered but not with the intent that income shall be produced. A loss is involuntary and normally of irregular occurrence. A building destroyed by fire, for instance, is a loss, not an expense.

Practically, an expenditure may be considered as an expense rather than as a loss if it is not definitely abnormal.

EXAMPLES OF EXPENSE

(1) Cash is paid for newspaper advertising, $50.00. The expenditure is made for the purpose of creating income. The ledger entries are

DEBIT: Floyd L. Smith, Capital 50.00
CREDIT: Cash 50.00

In this example we debit in order to record a decrease in the proprietary claim of Floyd L. Smith; we credit in order to record a decrease in the asset cash.

(2) Cash is paid out for office salaries, $110.00. Very clearly this is a necessary cost which must be incurred in the creation of income. The ledger entries are

DEBIT: Floyd L. Smith, Capital 110.00
CREDIT: Cash 110.00

In this example we debit in order to record a decrease in the proprietary claim of Floyd L. Smith; we credit in order to record a decrease in the asset cash.

(3) Rent for the current month is paid, $100.00. That this payment constitutes an expense may be made especially clear by observing that when a store pays rent for the space which it occupies, the disbursement is a prerequisite to the creation of income, i.e., if sales are to be made, a place in which to make them is a prerequisite. The ledger entries for the transaction above are

DEBIT: Floyd L. Smith, Capital 100.00
CREDIT: Cash 100.00

In this example we debit in order to record a decrease in the proprietary claim of Floyd L. Smith; we credit in order to record a decrease in the asset cash.

(4) Mr. Smith joins the City Realtors' Association and pays an entrance fee of $40.00. As one of the costs in securing prospects for new business, this disbursement is clearly one of the expenses incurred by a business in the earning of its income. The ledger entries are

DEBIT: Floyd L. Smith, Capital 40.00
CREDIT: Cash 40.00

In this example we debit in order to record a decrease in the proprietary claim of Floyd L. Smith; we credit in order to record a decrease in the asset cash.

An expense does not always mean that cash has actually been paid out. Supplies withdrawn from the stockroom of a garage for repairs on company-owned automobiles would be an expense but the transaction in itself would not involve any cash. This particular transaction would be recorded by the entries

DEBIT: John Doe, Capital   xxx
CREDIT: Supplies   xxx

In this example we debit in order to record a decrease in the proprietary claim of John Doe; we credit in order to record a decrease in the asset supplies.

An expense, further, may even be incurred without either cash or other asset being given in payment. Rent expense, for example, may be incurred for a particular month even though the actual payment for rent may not be made until a later month. Still another example of an expense which does not involve cash is the value lost by the "wearing out" of an asset.

Noncash expenses are further considered in Chapter 14.

INCOME

In the free exchange of goods and services for other goods and services, the increase in net worth resulting from the excess of the values received over the cost of the values surrendered is earned income.

In the interest of making financial statements more informative, accountants generally use the terms "gross income" and "net income" to explain earned income. For the purpose of the moment these two incomes may be broadly defined as follows:

Gross Income. — In free and independent transactions, the considerations received for the sale or use of assets and services constitute gross income. From the viewpoint of the accountant, the considerations received must be measurable in terms of money.

Gross income is earned at the time when an enforceable property right is created against a legal person through his receipt of contractual consideration. The earning of a gross income, however, does not necessarily mean that cash has been collected. It signifies only that, because of a consideration delivered, another consideration has been received or that the right to receive a consideration has been created.

The sale of merchandise on cash or credit terms, the rental earned on properties leased to tenants, fees for personal services, and so on, are examples of various kinds of gross income.

Net Income. — Costs are generally incurred in the production of gross income. These costs embrace the cost of merchandise sold and expenses incurred. After these costs have been deducted from gross income, the remainder is called net income.

EXAMPLES OF INCOME [3]

(5) An adding machine is rented to John Conroy & Son who were taking inventory. Cash of $10.00 is collected as rental. The ledger entries are

DEBIT: Cash 10.00
CREDIT: Floyd L. Smith, Capital 10.00
In this example we debit in order to record an increase
in the asset cash; and we credit in order to record an increase in the proprietary claim of Floyd L. Smith.

(6) A business building is sold for the account of a client. A 5% cash commission is collected on the sale of $20,000.00. The ledger entries are

DEBIT: Cash 1,000.00
CREDIT: Floyd L. Smith, Capital 1,000.00
In this example we debit in order to record an in-
crease in the asset cash; and we credit in order to
record an increase in the proprietary claim of
Floyd L. Smith.

(7) One hundred shares of Ohio Oil Company stock are pur-chased for cash at a total cost of $2,000.00. Shortly thereafter a dividend check for $20.00 is received. The ledger entries are

DEBIT: Securities 2,000.00
CREDIT: Cash 2,000.00
          To record purchase of stock.
DEBIT: Cash 20.00
CREDIT: Floyd L. Smith, Capital 20.00
In the second set of entries we debit in order to
record an increase in the asset cash; and we credit
in order to record an increase in the proprietary
claim of Floyd L. Smith.

(8) A fire insurance policy is sold for the account of the General Fire Insurance Company. Floyd L. Smith, as agent for the insur-ance company, collects a cash commission of $70.00 for his services in making the sale. The ledger entries to record the receipt of the commission check are

DEBIT: Cash 70.00
CREDIT: Floyd L. Smith, Capital 70.00
In this example we debit in order to record an in-
crease in the asset cash; and we credit in order to re-

---

[3] The four expense transactions on pages 37–38 were numbered 1 to 4. The four income transactions of this section are numbered 5 to 8. By use of these transaction numbers the entries in the ledgers on pages 40 and 44 can be easily traced.

cord an increase in the proprietary claim of Floyd L. Smith.

In each of these four income transactions, cash was received. An income transaction, however, should not always be interpreted to mean that cash has been received. For example, a plot of land may have been purchased some years ago at a cost of $20,000.00; today the property is sold for $25,000.00 with payment being received in marketable securities. The gain here, even though no cash is involved, is $5,000.00. Similarly, merchandise may be sold for a price in excess of its original purchase cost; and the sale may be made on credit terms of four months. Even though no cash is currently received, the gross profit on the sale is considered as being earned in the month in which the sale was made. Interest on notes receivable and on bonds owned is actually earned day by day and month by month — that is, it is earned as time goes by. This is true even though there is no collection of interest. Interest on a bond, for example, is earned currently even though the interest coupon may not be collected until a much later date.

Noncash incomes are further considered in Chapter 14.

THE LEDGER OF FLOYD L. SMITH

After giving effect to the foregoing eight expense and income transactions, the ledger of Floyd L. Smith will be as follows:

CASH		JAMES E. NELSON		SECURITIES	
3,200.00	50.00 (1)	300.00		2,000.00	
(5) 10.00	110.00 (2)				
(6) 1,000.00	100.00 (3)				
(7) 20.00	40.00 (4)				
(8) 70.00	2,000.00				

OFFICE EQUIPMENT		AUTOMOBILE		HARLEY SALES CO.	
1,600.00		900.00			500.00

NOTES PAYABLE		FLOYD L. SMITH, CAPITAL	
	500.00	(1) 50.00	5,000.00
		(2) 110.00	10.00 (5)
		(3) 100.00	1,000.00 (6)
		(4) 40.00	20.00 (7)
			70.00 (8)

The new balance sheet of Floyd L. Smith, as prepared from these accounts, will be

Floyd L. Smith

BALANCE SHEET, ———— (DATE) ————

Assets		Liabilities and Net Worth	
Cash	$2,000.00	Accounts Payable:	
Accounts Receivable:		Harley Sales Co.	$ 500.00
James E. Nelson	300.00	Notes Payable	500.00
Securities	2,000.00		
Office Equipment	1,600.00	Total Liabilities . . .	$1,000.00
Automobiles	900.00		
		Net Worth:	
		Floyd L. Smith, Capital.	5,800.00
	$6,800.00		$6,800.00

EXPANSION OF THE CAPITAL ACCOUNT

Up to this point in our discussion of accounting method, expenses have been debited directly to the proprietor's capital account and incomes have been credited directly to the same account. The net change in the balance of the capital account *from such transactions* is the net profit or loss of the business for the period. The proprietor, however, wishes to know not only what the total profits have been but how these profits were earned. He wishes to know all of his sources of income and the amount of gain contributed by each; he wishes to know his various expenses and the amount which has been expended for each of them. This information, however, is not available to him in a practical form if he enters expenses and incomes directly in the Capital account.

To overcome this practical difficulty, *temporary subdivisions* of the Capital account are opened for the separate record of individual items of expense and income. These subdivisions are T accounts; a separate one is opened for each type of expense and income in which the proprietor is interested. For instance, one T account will be opened for Advertising, one for Wages, one for Rent, one for Depreciation, and one for each type of expense about which information is desired.

Suppose that $100.00 is paid out for advertising. Since this is an expenditure properly chargeable to the Capital account of the proprietor, the correct accounting now will be to charge, or debit, the expenditure to that particular subdivision of the Capital account whose function is to reflect reductions of net worth due to advertising expense. The $100.00 disbursement is therefore debited to the Advertising Expense account and credited to the Cash account. A reduction in net worth has been made by means of a debit to the Advertising Expense account.

It follows then that each expense, as it is incurred, is classified as to type of expense and is debited to that subdivision of the Capital account which has the function of representing the particular type of expense in question.

In like manner each type of income will be credited to that particular account, or subdivision of the Capital account, which has the function of representing the type of income in question; one account, for instance, will be opened for Interest Income, one for Dividend Income, one for Commissions Earned, and one for each type of income about which information is desired. When these accounts are credited, each credit means, fundamentally, that an increase in net worth has been recorded by means of a credit to an income account.

Our future accounting will therefore be to enter expenses as debits to individual expense accounts rather than as direct debits to the Capital account; and to enter incomes as credits to individual income accounts rather than as direct credits to the Capital account.

THE LEDGER OF FLOYD L. SMITH

It may be helpful if the discussion of the preceding section is amplified by the use of an example. Before presenting the ledger of Floyd L. Smith as expanded by the new procedure of recording expenses and incomes in separate accounts of their own, we may point out that the proper accounting for the eight expense and income transactions on pages 37 and 39 would now be as follows:

Expense
Transaction

1　　DEBIT:　Advertising Expense . . . .　　50.00
　　　CREDIT:　　　Cash　. . . . .　　　　　　50.00

In this example we debit Advertising Expense in order to record a decrease in the proprietary claim of Floyd L. Smith; we credit in order to record a decrease in the asset cash.

2　　DEBIT:　Office Salaries . . . .　　110.00
　　　CREDIT:　　　Cash . . . .　　　　　110.00

In this example we debit the expense account, Office Salaries, in order to record a decrease in the proprietary claim of Floyd L. Smith; we credit in order to record a decrease in the asset cash.

3　　DEBIT:　Rent Expense . . . .　　100.00
　　　CREDIT:　　　Cash . . . .　　　　　100.00

In this example we debit Rent Expense in order to record a decrease in the proprietary claim of Floyd L. Smith; we credit in order to record a decrease in the asset cash.

| 4 | DEBIT: | General Expense . . . . | 40.00 | |
| | CREDIT: | Cash . . . . | | 40.00 |

In this example we debit General Expense in order to record a decrease in the proprietary claim of Floyd L. Smith; we credit in order to record a decrease in the asset cash.

With respect to the transaction involving supplies withdrawn from the stockroom of a garage for repairs on company owned automobiles, the entry would be

| DEBIT: | Automobile Repairs . . . . | xxx | |
| CREDIT: | Supplies . . . . | | xxx |

In this example we debit Automobile Repairs in order to record a decrease in the proprietary claim of John Doe; we credit in order to record a decrease in the asset supplies.

Income
Transaction

| 5 | DEBIT: | Cash . . . . | 10.00 | |
| | CREDIT: | Miscellaneous Income . . . . | | 10.00 |

In this example we debit in order to record an increase in the asset cash; and we credit Miscellaneous Income in order to record an increase in the proprietary claim of Floyd L. Smith.

| 6 | DEBIT: | Cash . . . . | 1,000.00 | |
| | CREDIT: | Commissions Earned . . . . | | 1,000.00 |

In this example we debit in order to record an increase in the asset cash; and we credit in order to record an increase in the proprietary claim of Floyd L. Smith.

7	DEBIT:	Securities	2,000.00	
	CREDIT:	Cash		2,000.00
		To record purchase of 100 shares of Ohio Oil Company stock.		
	DEBIT:	Cash	20.00	
	CREDIT:	Dividend Income		20.00

In the second set of entries we debit in order to record an increase in the asset cash; and we credit Dividend Income in order to record an increase in the proprietary claim of Floyd L. Smith.

| 8 | DEBIT: | Cash . . . . | 70.00 | |
| | CREDIT: | Commissions Earned . . . . | | 70.00 |

In this example we debit in order to record an increase in the asset cash; and we credit Commissions Earned in order to record an increase in the proprietary claim of Floyd L. Smith.

After all of the foregoing eight expense and income transactions have been recorded, the ledger of Floyd L. Smith would be as follows: [4]

CASH		JAMES E. NELSON	SECURITIES	
3,200.00	50.00 (1)	300.00	2,000.00	Assets
(5) 10.00	110.00 (2)			
(6) 1,000.00	100.00 (3)			
(7) 20.00	40.00 (4)			
(8) 70.00	2,000.00			

OFFICE EQUIPMENT	AUTOMOBILE
1,600.00	900.00

HARLEY SALES CO.	NOTES PAYABLE	
500.00	500.00	Liabilities

FLOYD L. SMITH, CAPITAL	
5,000.00	Capital account

ADVERTISING EXPENSE	GENERAL EXPENSE	OFFICE SALARIES	
(1) 50.00	(4) 40.00	(2) 110.00	Divisions of the debit side of the Capital account

RENT EXPENSE
(3) 100.00

COMMISSIONS EARNED	DIVIDEND INCOME	MISCELLANEOUS INCOME	
1,000.00 (6)	20.00 (7)	10.00 (5)	Divisions of the credit side of the Capital account
70.00 (8)			

[4] In this chapter transactions involving sales of merchandise have been disregarded. Consideration of this type of income transaction is deferred to Chapter 6 because of complexity. The credit part of a transaction for the sale of merchandise involves not only an increase in Capital but a decrease in the asset Merchandise as well. There are, also, certain practical difficulties in ascertaining the values to be assigned to each of the two credits.

A balance sheet prepared from this expanded ledger would be identical with the balance sheet on page 53. The technique of preparing the balance sheet from this ledger is described in detail in the next chapter.

THE RECORDING AND CLASSIFICATION OF EXPENSES AND INCOMES

Expense transactions, as a matter of bookkeeping convenience, are generally debited to expense accounts at the time of their payment rather than at the time of expense incurrence although to this general practice there are exceptions. (See Chapters 14, 15, and 23.) Incomes, too, are normally credited to income accounts at the time of collection rather than at the time when the original income transaction created a new account receivable against a debtor. To this general practice of recording income transactions there also are exceptions. (See Chapters 14 and 15.) An outstanding one is the recording of income which is earned through the sale of merchandise. Whether a sale is for cash or for credit, it is almost universal practice to record the sale as gross income realized on the date when the sale is made.

Sometimes the question may arise as to whether a given expenditure should be debited to an expense account or to an asset account, for example, an expenditure for fuel, gasoline, office supplies, and so on. A good working rule for use in such cases is the following:

Assets which are of small value, or which require frequent replacement, or whose values are short lived, should be debited to expense accounts rather than to asset accounts.

ALL EXPENSES AND INCOMES ARE FINALLY DESTINED FOR THE BALANCE SHEET

Since expense and income accounts are but *temporary* subdivisions of the Capital account, it follows that they will be transferred ultimately to the Capital account. This transferring process, known as "closing the books," is generally done only at the end of an accounting period of twelve months. The majority of businesses operate on a calendar year basis; they therefore "close their books" on December 31.

When all transfers of expense and income accounts have been made, the new balance of the Capital account will be the amount of the owner's proprietary claim as of the end of the accounting period.

QUESTIONS

Question **4–1.** Define (1) expense, (2) income. What is gross income?

Question **4–2.** Why are expenses debited? Why are incomes credited?

Question **4–3.** From the standpoint of the balance sheet, what is the significance of an expenditure for expense?

Question **4–4.** What is the relationship of expense and income accounts to the Capital account of a business?

Question **4–5.** Distinguish between an expense and an warehouse of the Belden Grocery Company burns. Is this an loss, an expenditure, or a disbursement?

Question **4–6.** By what principle would you be guided in deciding upon the number of expense and income accounts to open in a ledger?

Question **4–7.** "An expense means that money has been spent." Do you agree? Why?

Question **4–8.** John Elson increases his investment in the business of which he is the owner. Explain whether or not the money received by the business should be considered as income, and why.

Question **4–9.** Pencils, paper, erasers, ink, and similar supplies are purchased at a total cost of $14.25. What account should be debited for this expenditure? Explain your selection.

PROBLEMS

Problem **4–1.** What are the proper debit and credit accounts to record the following transactions?

(1) E. G. Baker starts in business as a barber with an investment of cash, $1,000.00.
(2) He purchases equipment for cash from E. H. Lanier who was retiring from business, $500.00.
(3) He pays rent for the first month, $50.00.
(4) He issues a check in payment of newspaper advertising announcing the Baker De Luxe Barber Shop, $25.00.
(5) He buys a sterilizer on ten days' credit from the Walker Supply Company, $25.00.
(6) He pays union dues, $10.00; and state license fee, $5.00.
(7) He deposits $12.50 cash with utility companies as a guarantee that gas, electricity, and water bills will be paid.
(8) A traveler's check is cashed for M. G. Anderson, $50.00.
(9) A check is mailed to the Walker Supply Company for the amount owed them (see transaction #5).
(10) A cash register is purchased from the Remington-Rand Company

for $50.00. A down payment of $15.00 is made. The balance is to be paid at the rate of $10.00 monthly.

(11) A trial bottle of Zenith Hair Tonic is purchased for cash from a salesman of the Zenith Company, $1.00.

(12) Magazine and newspaper subscriptions are paid, $21.00.

(13) Collected $65.00 for tonsorial services rendered to customers.

(14) Paid wages to John A. King, as assistant barber, $30.00.

Problem **4-2.** How should the following transactions be recorded?

(1) Employees' salaries are paid, $2,500.00.

(2) Social security taxes on the payroll are paid the federal government, $125.00.

(3) A check for $16.00 is given to the Cardinal Service Station in payment of gasoline purchases for the month.

(4) Trees and bushes are purchased on credit from Wales & Company for $220.00; these trees and bushes are to be used for beautifying the grounds on which the business is located.

(5) Spark plugs costing $5.00 are purchased for cash from the Jackson Motor Company.

(6) Interest of $50.00 is collected on two $1,000.00 par value bonds of the United Drug Company, 5's of 1953.

(7) A credit memorandum for $20.00 is received to correct an error in the pricing of an invoice received from Wales & Company (see transaction #4).

(8) A commission of $25.00 is collected from James Franklin & Sons.

(9) A contract to paint the building is signed, work to commence on the first of next month. The cost of the work is fixed at $700.00.

(10) Rent for the month is paid, $100.00.

(11) Window display materials are purchased for cash, $17.50.

(12) Commissions are paid to salesmen, $314.00.

(13) A bill for a new automobile battery is received from the Belmont Battery Service, $13.00. Payment is made immediately.

(14) A check for $19.00 is paid to the State Treasurer for an automobile license.

(15) A cash register is purchased on six months' credit from the National Cash Register Company, $125.00.

(16) Miscellaneous office supplies are purchased from the Broadway Office Supply Company for cash, $7.50.

(17) A check for $50.00 is given to the Red Cross.

(18) The cash register is short $1.00 at the close of the day's business.

(19) Cash is collected on the account of E. A. Chester & Company covering merchandise sold this company two months ago, $112.00.

(20) Interest of $60.00 is paid on our mortgage payable.

(21) A check for $90.00 is given to *The Daily Times* in payment of advertising.

(22) A check for $200.00 is mailed to Wales & Company in payment of account (see transactions #4 and #7).

(23) An office safe, which is no longer needed, is sold on account to Jordan & Black, Inc., for $210.00. The cost of this safe on the books is $140.00.

(24) The telephone bill is paid, $18.00.

(25) A cash dividend is received on the stock of the American Telephone & Telegraph Company, $90.00.

(26) A bookkeeping system is installed by John R. Chase, accountant; he is paid $50.00.

(27) A subscription to the *United States News* is paid, $4.00.

(28) A loan of cash is made to an employee, Roy H. Knox. The loan is to be repaid in 60 days, $100.00.

(29) A quart of white enamel paint is purchased for cash, $1.00. This paint is to be used for sundry touch-up purposes.

(30) An order is received from E. G. Ainsworth for $1,000.00 of merchandise to be delivered 60 days from now. (Questions: Has an asset been acquired? Has the balance sheet been changed, i.e., is this transaction an accounting transaction?)

Problem **4-3.** What are the proper debit and credit accounts to record the following transactions?

(1) $5,000.00 cash is borrowed from the Marine National Bank. A note for 60 days is signed in favor of the bank.

(2) Office salaries are paid, $2,000.00.

(3) A year's subscription to the *Wall Street Journal* is paid, $18.00.

(4) Office equipment is purchased on credit from Coyle & Dameron, Inc., $300.00.

(5) A check is given to the Community Chest, $10.00.

(6) 100 shares of the common stock of the Buffalo Drug Company is purchased for cash, $10,000.00.

(7) The telephone bill is paid for one month in advance, $11.00.

(8) Wages are paid, $3,000.00.

(9) Commissions are paid to salesmen, $400.00.

(10) Rent for one month in advance is paid, $100.00.

(11) A bus ticket is purchased for cash for the use of one of our salesmen, $17.00.

(12) The account of Coyle & Dameron, Inc. is paid (see transaction #4).

(13) A dividend check of $100.00 is received on the stock of the Buffalo Drug Company.

(14) Social security taxes on the payroll are paid, $200.00.

(15) The bus ticket purchased in transaction #11 is not used. A refund is received for the full purchase price of the ticket.

Problem **4-4.** What are the proper debits and credits to record the following transactions?

(1) John A. Bressler starts in business with cash, $7,000.00, and merchandise, $8,000.00.

(2) Paid rent for one month in advance, $100.00.

(3) Bought office equipment from the Central Office Equipment Company, $500.00. A down payment of $100.00 is made on this purchase. The balance is to be paid in monthly installments of $100.00.

(4) A bill from the Perry Sign Company is paid, $20.00. This bill was for lettering placed on the window.

(5) Three salesmen are hired today at salaries of $200.00 per month each.

(6) The floors are revarnished at a cash cost of $60.00.

(7) A small delivery truck is purchased for cash, $700.00. This was a used truck.

(8) A new speedometer is installed on the truck at a cash cost of $25.00.

(9) A truck license is purchased for cash, $12.00.

(10) Various kinds of office supplies are purchased for cash from the Whitney Office Supplies Company, $33.00. These supplies are estimated to represent one month's requirements.

(11) Newspaper advertising is paid, $39.00.

(12) Collected $1,250.00 in cash for brokerage services rendered to customers.

(13) Office supplies are returned to the Whitney Office Supplies Company, $8.00. They give us credit but no cash.

(14) A cash loan of $500.00 is made to a customer, James L. Briggs. This loan is represented by a note for 60 days.

(15) Wages and salaries are paid, $1,000.00.

Chapter 5

TRIAL BALANCE — CLOSING THE BOOKS — STATEMENTS

In the preceding four chapters we have given emphasis to the fact that the balance sheet must always be in balance, and also to the fact that by the rule of double entry the debit and credit values of a transaction must always be equal to each other. Therefore, since the asset values of a ledger must be balanced by an equal amount of claims against them, it follows that the sum of the debits of a ledger must always equal the sum of the credits; and it follows also that the sum of the debit balances of the accounts of a ledger must always equal the sum of the credit balances of the accounts.

Before closing the books, a bookkeeper usually makes sure that the total debits of his ledger exactly balance the total credits. He does this by ascertaining that the sum of the debit balances is exactly equal to the sum of the credit balances of his accounts. He lists each account on a page which has provision for two columns at the right. If the account has a debit balance, the amount of the debit balance is entered in the first, or debit, column; if the account has a credit balance, the amount of the credit balance is entered in the right, or credit, column. The sums of the two columns should obviously be equal to each other. This test of the mechanical accuracy of the accounts, the equality of debits and credits, is called a "trial balance."

A trial balance is not, per se, an assurance of accurate accounting. The trial balance, for instance, may be in balance even though serious accounting errors have been made in the accounts. A debit value, for example, may have been entered on the debit side of the wrong account. A trial balance proves one thing only: that arithmetically the totals of the debit and credit balances of a ledger are equal to each other.

TRIAL BALANCE OF FLOYD L. SMITH

Turning to the ledger of Floyd L. Smith as we left it on page 44, we find that the trial balance prepared from this ledger will be

Floyd L. Smith

TRIAL BALANCE, —— (DATE) ——

Accounts	Debit Balances	Credit Balances
Cash	$2,000.00	
James E. Nelson	300.00	
Securities	2,000.00	
Office Equipment	1,600.00	
Automobile	900.00	
Harley Sales Co.		$ 500.00
Notes Payable		500.00
Floyd L. Smith, Capital		5,000.00
Advertising Expense	50.00	
General Expense	40.00	
Office Salaries	110.00	
Rent Expense	100.00	
Commissions Earned		1,070.00
Dividend Income		20.00
Miscellaneous Income		10.00
	$7,100.00	$7,100.00

The accounts of this trial balance are listed in the order in which they appear in the ledger. It should be obvious, however, that the equality of a trial balance is not affected by the order in which the accounts may be listed.

In practice, the column headings shown above are omitted from trial balances.

THE PROFIT AND LOSS STATEMENT

After the trial balance has been prepared, the usual order of work is

(1) The preparation of the profit and loss statement

(2) The preparation of the balance sheet

(3) The formal closing of the books (done only at the end of the accounting year)

The purpose of the profit and loss statement is to report the amount of net income which has been earned by a business over a given period of time; and to explain in significant and systematized detail how this net income was earned. Using all of the income and expense accounts of the trial balance, the profit and loss statement of Floyd L. Smith would be as follows:

Floyd L. Smith

PROFIT AND LOSS STATEMENT
FOR THE PERIOD —————

Commissions Earned		$1,070.00
Less Expenses:		
Advertising Expense	$ 50.00	
General Expense	40.00	
Office Salaries	110.00	
Rent Expense	100.00	300.00
Net Income from Operations		$ 770.00
Other Income:		
Dividend Income	$ 20.00	
Miscellaneous Income	10.00	30.00
Net Income		$ 800.00

The period to be covered by a profit and loss statement, in any specific case, may be one month, three months, six months, twelve months, or any other selected period of time. The year is a common period. While profit and loss statements may be prepared for any period of time, the books are usually "closed" but once a year, either as of December 31 or as of the last day of the fiscal period when the latter is not the calendar year. The actual procedure of "closing the books" is described in the later pages of this chapter.

The profit and loss statement sometimes appears under other titles such as "statement of income and expense," "income statement," "income account," "summary of income," "statement of income," and so on. In all of these there is general agreement that gross incomes should be listed first and expenses then deducted.

The title "statement of income" is used by such prominent companies as the American Can Company, General Motors Corporation, and United States Steel Corporation.

THE BALANCE SHEET

The second statement of interest to the proprietor of a business is the balance sheet. In this statement the assets and equities of a business are systematically arranged and totaled. The balance sheet is simply an orderly presentation, in the form of a written report, of the asset, liability, and net worth accounts as they exist on the ledger. The actual preparation of the balance sheet is generally accomplished by working from the trial balance. The balance sheet of Floyd Smith would be as follows:

Floyd L. Smith

BALANCE SHEET, —— (DATE) ——

Assets		Liabilities and Net Worth	
Current Assets:		Current Liabilities:	
Cash	$2,000.00	Accounts Payable:	
Accounts Receivable:		Harley Sales Co.	$ 500.00
James E. Nelson	300.00	Notes Payable	500.00
Securities	2,000.00		
	————		$1,000.00
	$4,300.00		
Fixed Assets:		Net Worth:	
Office Equipment $1,600.00		Floyd L. Smith, Capital . .	5,800.00
Automobile. . . 900.00	2,500.00		
	————		————
	$6,800.00		$6,800.00

This balance sheet is identical with the balance sheet on page 41. It is important to observe that the net worth of Floyd L. Smith in these balance sheets is

The amount of his net worth at the beginning of the period . . .	$5,000.00
Plus the amount of net income earned during the period.	800.00
	————
Net worth as per balance sheet, —— (date) ——	$5,800.00

In more complex cases the net worth at the end of an accounting period may be the balance of the capital account before the books have been closed, plus the net income earned during the period, and less withdrawals of income during the period.

THE WORK SHEET

The profit and loss statement and the balance sheet of the preceding example were prepared by working directly from the trial balance. Income and expense accounts were placed in the income statement; assets, liabilities, and net worth, were placed in the balance sheet. Each item of the trial balance, therefore, was classified as either a profit and loss item or as a balance sheet item.

To speed up the classification of items, and as a convenient and orderly process for expediting the preparation of financial statements, the "work sheet" may be used. In the first pair of columns of the work sheet the trial balance is recorded. In the second pair of columns are placed the items which make up the profit and loss statement; in the third pair of columns are placed the items which make up the balance sheet. The net result, therefore, is to distribute the items of the trial balance into either the profit and loss columns or the balance-sheet columns of the work sheet. The financial statements are prepared from the information contained in these two sets of columns, respectively.

The work sheet does not replace financial statements. It is simply an *auxiliary* device intended to *assist* in the preparation of financial statements.

The work sheet for the Floyd L. Smith problem would be as follows:

Floyd L. Smith

Work Sheet, ——— (date) ———

	TRIAL BALANCE		PROFIT AND LOSS		BALANCE SHEET	
	Dr.	Cr.	Dr.	Cr.	Dr.	Cr.
Cash	2,000.00				2,000.00	
James E. Nelson . . .	300.00				300.00	
Securities	2,000.00				2,000.00	
Office Equipment. . .	1,600.00				1,600.00	
Automobile	900.00				900.00	
Harley Sales Co. . . .		500.00				500.00
Notes Payable		500.00				500.00
Floyd L. Smith, Capital		5,000.00				5,000.00
Advertising Expense .	50.00		50.00			
General Expense . . .	40.00		40.00			
Office Salaries	110.00		110.00			
Rent Expense	100.00		100.00			
Commissions Earned .		1,070.00		1,070.00		
Dividend Income . .		20.00		20.00		
Miscellaneous Income.		10.00		10.00		
	7,100.00	7,100.00				
Net Income to Floyd L. Smith, Capital . . .			800.00			800.00
			1,100.00	1,100.00	6,800.00	6,800.00

The difference between the incomes and expenses listed in the profit and loss columns is the net income of the period, $800.00. Since the income increases the net worth of the proprietor, it is transferred to his capital account by a debit of $800.00 in the profit and loss columns, and a credit in the balance sheet columns. More formally, this transfer reflects the bookkeeping entry closing the Profit and Loss account (see entry, page 57).

GENERAL COMMENTS ON FINANCIAL STATEMENTS

Financial statements are correct only if the account balances of the trial balance are correct, and if these correct account balances are carried into the proper financial statements. For example, the debit for a particular transaction might be placed in the wrong account of the ledger; this error, however, would not throw the trial balance out of balance. It is also possible for the trial balance to be correct, and for the profit and loss statement and balance sheet to be correct *arithmetically*, yet both financial statements may be seriously in error from an *accounting* standpoint. This point may be illustrated as follows:

Assume that the Advertising Expense account of the Floyd L. Smith problem was erroneously considered to be an asset. In this kind of circumstance the net income on the profit and loss statement would be wrongly stated as $850.00. On the balance sheet two errors would be present: Advertising Expense would be included with the assets, and the net worth of Floyd L. Smith would be wrongly stated at $5,850.00. In spite of these two serious errors, however, the balance sheet would be in balance.

Parenthetically, it is proper to direct attention to the desirability of ruling statements and accounts correctly. Correct rulings are shown in the illustrations of this chapter.

CLOSING THE BOOKS

The process of transferring the balances of the temporary divisions of the Capital account to the Capital account itself at the end of the accounting period is called "closing the books." In theory the exact procedure is simply the transfer of the debit balances of expense accounts to the debit side of the Capital account, and the transfer of the credit balances of income accounts to the credit side of the Capital account.

In actual practice, however, these transfers to the Capital account are generally not made in such a direct manner. Instead, the transfers to the Capital account are made by way of the Profit and Loss account, as described in the next paragraph.

PROFIT AND LOSS ACCOUNT

Instead of closing all of the temporary subdivisions of the proprietor's net worth account to the Capital account at the end of the accounting period, additional convenience and information will be attained if these account balances are first transferred to a new subdivision of the Capital account called Profit and Loss account. When all incomes and expenses have been brought together in this account, the balance of the Profit and Loss account will then show the net income or net loss earned by the business for the accounting period. This balance in the Profit and Loss account is then transferred to the Capital account of the proprietor. The use of the Profit and Loss account has two advantages:

(1) A summary account is provided in which all elements of income and expense are gathered together to show the net income or net loss for the period.

(2) The Capital account is not cluttered up with many miscellaneous debits and credits. Only the net income or net loss of an accounting period is transferred to it. The Capital account reflects invested capital. With this function it is therefore proper to limit the entries in the Capital account to those which record significant changes in net worth.

CLOSING THE BOOKS (Continued)

To abide by the rule that for every debit entry there must be a credit entry of equal value, in order to promote accuracy in the accounts, and in order to have "foolproof" features wherever possible, the balances of expense and income accounts are transferred to Profit and Loss by full utilization of the rule of double entry. Thus, when the debit balance of $50.00 in the Advertising Expense account is transferred to the debit side of the Profit and Loss account, the new debit is offset by entering a credit of $50.00 in the Advertising Expense account. Similarly, when the credit balance of $1,070.00 in the Commissions Earned account is transferred to the credit side of the Profit and Loss account, an offsetting debit of $1,070.00 is made in the Commissions Earned account. Other expense and income accounts are transferred to Profit and Loss in a similar manner. When all transfers have been made, all expense and income accounts will have their balances reduced to zero, i.e., these nominal accounts will be "closed."

In closing the books, then, the account with Profit and Loss is debited and expense accounts are credited; each credit cancels out the existing debit balance of an expense account. And income accounts are debited and the account with Profit and Loss is credited; each debit cancels out the existing credit balance of an income account. Technically, these debits and credits may be more formally explained as follows: The debits are made to decrease one or more elements of net worth, and the credits are made to increase one or more elements of net worth.

In the Floyd Smith problem (page 44) the actual transfers to "close the books" will be as follows:

DEBIT: Profit and Loss 50.00
CREDIT: Advertising Expense 50.00
             To transfer balance of latter account to Profit
             and Loss.

DEBIT: Profit and Loss 40.00
CREDIT: General Expense 40.00

To transfer balance of latter account to Profit
and Loss.

DEBIT: Profit and Loss 110.00
CREDIT: Office Salaries 110.00
To transfer balance of latter account to Profit
and Loss.

DEBIT: Profit and Loss 100.00
CREDIT: Rent Expense 100.00

DEBIT: Commissions Earned 1,070.00
CREDIT: Profit and Loss . . . , ...   1,070.00

DEBIT: Dividend Income 20.00
CREDIT: Profit and Loss 20.00

DEBIT: Miscellaneous Income 10.00
CREDIT: Profit and Loss 10.00

In actual practice the seven transfers in the foregoing entries
would usually be expressed in the following condensed manner:

DEBIT: Profit and Loss 300.00
CREDIT: Advertising Expense 50.00
CREDIT: General Expense 40.00
CREDIT: Office Salaries 110.00
CREDIT: Rent Expense 100.00
To transfer balances of expense accounts to Profit
and Loss.

DEBIT: Commissions Earned 1,070.00
DEBIT: Dividend Income 20.00
DEBIT: Miscellaneous Income 10.00
CREDIT: Profit and Loss 1,100.00
To transfer balances of income accounts to Profit
and Loss.

DEBIT: Profit and Loss 800.00
CREDIT: Floyd L. Smith Capital 800.00
To transfer balance of Profit and Loss to Floyd L.
Smith, Capital account.

After the books have been "closed," the ledger of Floyd L.
Smith would be as follows:

CASH		JAMES E. NELSON		SECURITIES	
3,200.00	50.00	300.00		2,000.00	
10.00	110.00				
1,000.00	100.00				
20.00	40.00				
70.00	2,000.00				

OFFICE EQUIPMENT		AUTOMOBILE		HARLEY SALES CO.	
1,600.00		900.00			500.00

NOTES PAYABLE		FLOYD L. SMITH, CAPITAL	
	500.00		5,000.00
			800.00

ADVERTISING EXPENSE		GENERAL EXPENSE		OFFICE SALARIES		RENT EXPENSE	
50.00	50.00	40.00	40.00	110.00	110.00	100.00	100.00

COMMISSIONS EARNED		DIVIDEND INCOME		MISCELLANEOUS INCOME	
1,070.00	1,000.00	20.00	20.00	10.00	10.00
	70.00				
1,070.00	1,070.00				

PROFIT AND LOSS	
50.00	1,070.00
40.00	20.00
110.00	10.00
100.00	
800.00	
1,100.00	1,100.00

The student should observe that after the books have been closed, the only accounts which have balances are those which represent assets and claims against assets. These accounts are obviously the assets and equities which constitute the balance sheet.

REAL AND NOMINAL ACCOUNTS

Real accounts are the assets, liabilities, and net worth of a business at a particular date.

Nominal accounts are those which represent the *temporary* subdivisions of the Capital account, i.e., those which increase or decrease the net income of a business.

Mixed accounts are those which contain both real and nominal elements. For example, the Small Tools account shows a balance of $500.00 on the ledger. A physical inventory shows that only $400.00 worth of tools is actually on hand, the difference of $100.00 having been consumed in production. The Small Tools account, as it stands before correction, represents an asset of $400.00 and an expense of $100.00 — real and nominal elements respectively.

Real accounts are therefore the accounts of the balance sheet; and nominal accounts, the accounts of the profit and loss statement. The real element of a mixed account is carried to the balance sheet; the nominal element is carried to the profit and loss statement.

QUESTIONS

Question **5–1.** What is a trial balance? What is the purpose of a trial balance? Does a trial balance mean that the bookkeeping to date is correct, and that no accounting errors have been made? Explain.

Question **5–2.** What is meant by "closing the books"? Explain fully.

Question **5–3.** What kind of accounts have balances after the books have been closed?

Question **5–4.** What is the purpose of (a) the profit and loss statement and (b) the balance sheet? What is the source of information for each of these statements?

Question **5–5.** For balance sheet purposes at the end of the accounting period, explain how the amount of the proprietor's ownership claim is determined.

Question **5–6.** Distinguish between real, nominal, and mixed accounts. Give examples of each.

Question **5–7.** What kind of accounts

(1) Are employed to construct the profit and loss statement?
(2) Are employed in the balance sheet?
(3) Are found on the ledger before closing the books?
(4) Are found on the ledger after closing the books?

PROBLEMS

Problem **5–1.** Frank A. Hosmer was the owner of a professional football team. On August 1, 19__, his assets were comprised of cash, $80,000.00, and football franchise, $20,000.00. During the ensuing football season, his condensed transactions were as follows:

(1) Gross income collected, $256,000.00. Of this amount $15,000.00 was disbursed for federal taxes, and $80,000.00 was disbursed as guarantees for visiting teams.
(2) Paid salaries, $75,791.00, wages, $6,047.00.
(3) Paid for supplies and materials, $10,951.00.
(4) Paid for telephone, telegraph, and postage, $1,849.00.
(5) Paid for traveling expenses, $16,718.00.

(6) Paid for publications and printing, $5,142.00.

(7) Paid for laundry services, $1,962.00.

(8) Paid for contractual services: insurance premiums, fees of game officials, miscellaneous professional fees, and rentals, $13,881.00.

(9) Paid for miscellaneous expenses, $2,253.00.

(10) Paid for office expenses, $1,724.00, and office salaries, $1,200.00.

Required:

(1) Enter the transactions in a T-account ledger.

(2) Draw off a trial balance, December 31, 19__.

(3) Prepare a statement of income and expense for the five months ending December 31, 19__.

(4) Prepare a balance sheet, December 31, 19__.

Problem **5–2.** The White Laundry operated entirely on a cash basis. On January 1, 19__, its assets were cash, $10,000.00, equipment, $30,000.00, building, $13,000.00, and land, $2,000.00. There were no liabilities. The owner of the business was Daniel E. White.

The condensed transactions of the White Laundry for the next twelve months were as follows:

(1) Collections from customers for laundry services rendered, $54,000.00.

(2) Paid for salaries, $10,000.00, and wages, $25,000.00.

(3) Paid for supplies and materials used in laundry operations, $3,966.00.

(4) Paid for repairs and alterations, $260.00.

(5) Paid the Ideal Press, Inc., for printing bills, notices, etc., $142.00.

(6) Paid the Carnes Insurance Agency for sundry insurance bills, $444.00.

(7) Paid for heat, electricity, and water, $1,842.00.

(8) The bill in the fifth transaction should have been for $124.00. A check for $18.00 is received from the Ideal Press, Inc.

(9) Paid miscellaneous expenses, $410.00.

(10) Paid real estate taxes, $100.00, personal property taxes, $50.00, and social security taxes, $1,000.00.

(11) The cash in the cash registers was short, $76.00.

Required:

(1) Enter the transactions in a T-account ledger.

(2) Draw off a trial balance, December 31, 19__. Record the trial balance on a work sheet, and complete the work sheet.

(3) Prepare a statement of income and expense for the year 19__.

(4) Prepare a balance sheet, December 31, 19__.

(5) Close the books.

Problem **5–3.** Following is the trial balance of the Green Meadow Golf Club at the end of the year 19__:

Cash	$ 21,000.00	
Dues Receivable from Members	5,000.00	
Caddy and Locker House	10,000.00	
Main Building	30,000.00	
Miscellaneous Equipment	10,000.00	
Miscellaneous Supplies	2,000.00	
Cost of Construction of Golf Course	45,000.00	
Accounts Payable		$ 1,000.00
Notes Payable		10,000.00
Membership Capital Investment		100,000.00
Income from Dues		50,000.00
Income from Green Fees, Locker Rents, etc. . . .		15,000.00
Maintenance Expense	6,000.00	
General Expense	20,000.00	
Wages and Salaries	24,000.00	
Taxes Expense	2,000.00	
Interest Expense	1,000.00	
	$176,000.00	$176,000.00

Required:

(1) Prepare a statement of income for the year.

(2) Prepare a balance sheet, December 31, 19—. On the balance sheet place the net income for the year in a special net worth account called Surplus.

Problem **5–4.** Following are the data comprising the financial statements of the American Accounting Association for the year ending December 31, 19—:

Cash	$ 4,750.47	
Dues and Subscriptions Receivable	100.10	
Advertising Accounts Receivable	446.75	
Equipment	22.00	
Accounts Payable.		$ 1,397.88
Miscellaneous Liabilities.		886.75
Net Worth, January 1, 19—		1,269.96
Income from Dues and Subscriptions		6,906.43
Income from Advertising		1,580.00
Cost of publishing the *Accounting Review*	3,692.41	
Expenses of Executive Committee	563.71	
Secretary's Compensation	500.00	
Editor's Compensation	500.00	
Printing, Postage, and Stationery.	364.28	
Expenses of Annual Convention	287.95	
Miscellaneous Expenses	813.35	
	$12,041.02	$12,041.02

Required:

(1) Prepare a statement of income for the year 19—.

(2) Prepare a balance sheet, December 31, 19—.

Problem **5–5.** On December 31, 19—, the following trial balance was prepared from the books of the University Club, a social organization:

Cash	$ 1,455.00	
Dues Receivable	241.00	
Furniture and Furnishings.	2,082.00	
Games and Game Room Equipment	2,500.00	
Kitchen Utensils and Equipment	642.00	
Building.	20,480.00	
Tennis Courts, etc.	1,215.00	
Land	2,000.00	
Accounts Payable		$ 104.00
Mortgage Payable		8,000.00
University Club, Capital.		22,106.00
Income from Membership Dues		4,284.00
Caretaker's Salary	900.00	
Entertainment Expense	382.00	
Insurance Expense	80.00	
Interest Expense	510.00	
Kitchen Expense	78.00	
Laundry Expense.	164.00	
Magazines	76.00	
Maintenance and Repairs	929.00	
Miscellaneous Expense	274.00	
Office Expense	155.00	
Teas, Dinners, and Receptions	331.00	
	$34,494.00	$34,494.00

Required:

(1) Prepare a statement of income for the year 19__.
(2) Prepare a balance sheet, December 31, 19__.

Problem 5–6. L. H. Carter was the publisher of a weekly professional newspaper called the *Business News*. On December 31, 19__, the ledger revealed the following accounts:

Accounts Receivable	$ 3,356.00
Salaries and Wages	25,685.00
Legal Fees	2,000.00
Miscellaneous Equipment.	20,288.00
L. H. Carter, Capital	30,000.00
Freight and Express (expense)	5,160.00
Advertising Income	31,991.00
Subscription Income	50,010.00
Miscellaneous Expense	2,960.00
Office Equipment	3,145.00
Cash	15,316.00
Telephone and Telegraph	654.00
Insurance Expense	111.00
Advertising and Promotion Costs	2,110.00
Taxes Expense	1,024.00
Accounts Payable	12,669.00
Fees, Taxes, Royalties, and Other Miscellaneous Items Payable .	6,393.00
Inventories of Sheets, Paper, Stock, Supplies	11,957.00
Cost of paper, printing, etc. (costs consumed in publishing the newspaper)	33,479.00
Rent Expense	2,000.00
Stationery and Postage Expense	1,818.00

Required:

(1) Take a trial balance.

(2) Prepare a profit and loss statement for the year.

(3) Prepare a balance sheet, December 31, 19___.   Use the account form of statement.

Problem **5–7.**   Mr. Fred L. Sperry was the owner of the Sperry Arms, an apartment house in Colby City, Ohio.   At the end of the calendar year 19___ the books of the Sperry Arms showed the following accounts:

Advertising Expense	$ 462.00
Building	96,000.00
Cash	1,401.00
Electricity Expense	1,012.00
Furniture and Equipment	17,084.00
Garbage Expense	135.00
Gas	964.00
General Expense	451.00
Insurance Expense	610.00
Interest Expense	1,500.00
Labor	2,852.00
Land	10,000.00
Meter Deposits with Utility Companies	200.00
Mortgage Payable	25,000.00
Rents Collected	20,084.00
Repairs	2,701.00
Returnable Cash Deposits of Tenants (covering utilities, etc.)	100.00
Security Furniture Company (unpaid balance due this company on purchase of furniture)	1,635.00
Superintendent's Salary	2,500.00
Supplies Expense	1,068.00
Taxes Expense	2,180.00
Water Expense	702.00
Fred L. Sperry, Capital	?

Required:

(1) Prepare a trial balance from the above information.   You are required to calculate the balance which should be in Mr. Sperry's capital account.

(2) Prepare a profit and loss statement for the year.

(3) Prepare a balance sheet, December 31, 19___.

Problem **5–8.**   Warren S. May was an individual of considerable means. A part of his wealth was invested in preferred and common stocks of selected corporations.   Since the amount of capital invested in this manner was considerable and since, also, there was much work involved in supervising these investments, Mr. May administered his security investments through his own special business organization, the May Investment Company, of which Mr. May was sole owner.

On December 31, 19___, the bookkeeping department of the May Investment Company drew off the following trial balance from the books:

Cash.	$ 192,228.03	
Compensation of Employees	4,825.00	
Dividends Received		$ 152,118.06
Federal and State Taxes (other than Income		
Taxes)	909.58	
Insurance Expense	1,715.35	
Maintenance and Repairs	324.15	
May, Warren S., Capital		2,890,351.09
Miscellaneous Expense	748.59	
Office Equipment	2,826.14	
Office Supplies and Printing Expense	321.38	
Rent.	971.78	
Securities.	2,834,930.02	
Stock Transfer and Register Fees	2,498.00	
Telephone and Telegraph.	171.13	
	$3,042,469.15	$3,042,469.15

Required:

(1) Prepare a well-organized statement showing the net income of the May Investment Company for the year.

(2) Prepare a balance sheet, December 31, 19__.

Problem **5–9.** On January 1, 19__, the condensed balance sheet of Henry G. Anderson was as follows:

Henry G. Anderson

BALANCE SHEET, JANUARY 1, 19—

Assets		Liabilities and Net Worth	
Cash	$ 4,200.00	Accounts Payable	$ 700.00
Supplies	800.00	Income Taxes Payable . .	1,300.00
Equipment	8,000.00	Mortgage Payable.	20,000.00
Hotel Building	45,000.00		
Land	4,000.00	Total Liabilities . . .	$22,000.00
		Net Worth:	
		Henry G. Anderson, Capi-	
		tal	40,000.00
	$62,000.00		$62,000.00

In condensed form, the transactions of Mr. Anderson for the next twelve months were:

(1) Paid all taxes owed as of January 1, 19__; also accounts payable.

(2) Collected rents, $21,700.00.

(3) Paid for miscellaneous repairs, $1,200.00.

(4) Paid for landscaping the hotel grounds, $1,000.00.

(5) Paid for laundry, $2,600.00.

(6) Paid for electricity, gas, water, and telephone, $3,000.00.

(7) Paid for labor, $7,500.00.

(8) Paid social security taxes on payroll, $200.00.

(9) Paid real-estate taxes, $500.00.

(10) Interest on the mortgage was paid, $1,200.00.

(11) All supplies on hand at the beginning of the year were used up.

Required:

(1) Enter the transactions in a T-account ledger.

(2) Draw off a trial balance. Record the trial balance on a work sheet and complete the work sheet.

(3) Prepare a statement of income and expense for the year 19__.

(4) Prepare a balance sheet, December 31, 19__.

(5) Close the books.

Problem **5–10.** On January 1, 19__, John T. Connally, doing business as the Connally Hotel, had the following balance sheet:

Cash	$ 4,758.00	Notes Payable	$ 3,000.00
Hotel Equipment	12,810.00	T. E. Clark.	1,674.00
Land	5,000.00	Leeds Supply Company . .	894.00
Building	40,260.00	Mortgage Payable	15,000.00
		J. T. Connally, Capital . .	42,260.00
	$62,828.00		$62,828.00

For the twelve months following January 1, the condensed transactions of Mr. Connally were as follows:

(1) Paid insurance for the year, $256.00.

(2) Room rent collections, $7,218.00.

(3) Fuel bills were paid, $1,061.00.

(4) Paid the Eckel Steam Laundry for laundry expenses, $394.00.

(5) The notes payable were paid, $3,000.00, and interest, $105.00.

(6) Checks amounting to $1,127.00 were issued in favor of Frey & Hardy, Inc., for office supplies. These supplies were all used up during the current year.

(7) The Eckel Steam Laundry was paid $413.00 for laundry work.

(8) Paid wages, $3,238.00.

(9) Room supplies (towels, soaps, etc.) were purchased on credit from the Leeds Supply Co., $897.00.

(10) Paid $1,000.00 to Harley S. Lynd for the purpose of reducing the mortgage indebtedness.

(11) Paid utility expenses (light, water, gas, etc.), $957.00.

(12) Room rent collections, $7,422.00.

(13) Paid the Leeds Supply Co. their account in full except for $500.00.

(14) Taxes paid amounted to $373.00.

(15) Paid the Eckel Steam Laundry, $510.00.

(16) Gave a check for $174.00 and a two-year note payable to T. E. Clark in settlement of indebtedness to him.

(17) Interest was paid on the mortgage, $870.00.

(18) On December 10, 19__, signed a contract with James C. Bohlman for the remodeling of the hotel lobby at a cost of $3,750.00, work to start January 10, next.

Required:

(1) Open accounts with each asset, liability, and net worth item listed on the balance sheet of January 1, 19__.

(2) Record the transactions of the year in T accounts. For this purpose open all accounts which you may require.

(3) Prepare a trial balance. Record the trial balance on a work sheet and complete the work sheet.

(4) Prepare a profit and loss statement for the year.

(5) Prepare a balance sheet, December 31, 19__.

Problem **5–11.** The following information represents the ledger of the Chamber of Commerce of Meridian City as of December 31, 19__. The figures, properly arranged, constitute a trial balance; you are required to establish the amount of net worth.

Cash on hand was $109,805.00, securities owned were $42,000.00, uncollected dues amounted to $17,170.00. The property and equipment was worth $108,069.00; and miscellaneous assets were $30,021.00. Accounts payable were $1,989.00. Social security taxes payable amounted to $3,822.00; and there was owed to the Collector of Internal Revenue the sum of $1,254.00 for withholding income taxes payable.

Income from dues amounted to $105,086.00; and from miscellaneous sources, $7,226.00.

Operating expenditures during the year were made for the following purposes:

	General and Administrative Costs	Occupancy Costs	Miscellaneous Costs
Building Maintenance		$ 5,490.00	
Dues and Fees to Other Organizations			$ 6,540.00
Entertainment	$ 1,749.00		
Farm Improvement Awards			1,200.00
Insurance	394.00	274.00	
Legislative Expense			784.00
Light, Heat, and Power		2,537.00	
Periodicals and Publications	410.00		
Postage	2,471.00		
Printing and Supplies			323.00
Publicity and Advertising			1,602.00
Salaries	63,856.00	3,559.00	
Social Security Taxes	2,104.00	730.00	
Stationery and Office Supplies	2,069.00		
Telephone and Telegraph.	2,116.00		
Traveling Expense.	1,481.00		
Washington, D.C., National Office.			1,000.00
Weekly News Bulletin (cost of production) . . .			3,045.00
	$76,650.00	$12,590.00	$14,494.00

Required:

(1) Prepare a statement of income for the year.

(2) Prepare a balance sheet, December 31, 19___.

Problem **5–12.** The Franklin City Baseball Club, Inc., was a professional minor league baseball club with membership in the Atlantic Coast League. On December 31, 19___, the general ledger trial balance was:

Cash	$ 20,000.00	
Accounts Receivable	1,400.00	
Investment in Baseball Player Contracts	26,500.00	
Atlantic Coast League Franchise	50,000.00	
Furniture, Fixtures, Equipment	3,500.00	
Notes Payable		$ 25,000.00
Accounts Payable		1,000.00
Taxes Payable		3,400.00
Interest Payable		2,000.00
Net Worth		63,000.00
Collections — Home Games (see note)		52,400.00
Collections — Road Games		30,200.00
Collections — Other Games, Exhibitions, etc.		6,900.00
Concessions		3,200.00
Fence Advertising		3,800.00
Score Cards		2,000.00
Advertising	2,700.00	
Bats, Balls, and Uniforms	1,700.00	
Insurance	2,600.00	
Laundry	300.00	
Legal and Auditing Fees	1,300.00	
Meals (Spring Training)	2,100.00	
Miscellaneous Expense	1,550.00	
Opening Day Expense	125.00	
Payroll Taxes	1,800.00	
Police, Umpires, Announcer	900.00	
Rent of Stadium	5,200.00	
Salaries and Wages	45,900.00	
Sundry Fees and Licenses	1,900.00	
Supplies, Water, Repairs, Electricity, Lighting System, Maintenance	3,500.00	
Taxes	3,505.00	
Tickets and Sundry Supplies	820.00	
Traveling Expense	15,600.00	
	$192,900.00	$192,900.00

Note: Actual home game receipts were $103,200.00. However, $26,000.00 was paid to visiting baseball clubs, $17,600.00 was paid to the U.S. Treasury for amusement taxes, and $7,200.00 was paid to the Atlantic Coast League general fund. After these payments, the net collections remaining were $52,400.00.

Required:

(1) Prepare a statement of income for the year.

(2) Prepare a balance sheet, December 31, 19___.

Problem **5-13.** Richard H. King was the owner and operator of an office building known as the Union Building. On December 31, 19___, the condensed balance sheet of the Union Building was:

Assets		Liabilities and Capital	
Cash	$ 9,175.00	Mortgage Payable	$500,000.00
Cash Deposited with Mortgagee for the Payment of Property Taxes	6,962.00	Richard H. King, Capital .	175,000.00
Fixtures and Equipment . .	8,863.00		
Building	600,000.00		
Land	50,000.00		
	$675,000.00		$675,000.00

During the next twelve months the transactions of the Union Building, as shown by records of cash received and checks issued, were as follows:

CASH RECEIVED

Rents Collected	$118,624.00
Maintenance Supplies Sold (at cost)	114.00
	$118,738.00

CHECKS ISSUED

Maintenance:

Salaries	$ 5,264.00
Elevator Maintenance.	2,220.00
Repairs	3,104.00
Supplies	1,212.00
Miscellaneous	240.00

Operating:

Salaries	24,648.00
Light, Heat, Power	8,276.00
Water	640.00
Supplies	808.00
Miscellaneous	1,460.00

General:

Office Salaries	4,596.00
Office Expense	328.00
Telephone and Telegraph	176.00
Bank Service Charges	140.00
Entertainment	448.00
Interest on Mortgage	30,000.00
Social Security Taxes (expense)	2,104.00
Occupational License	162.00
Insurance	1,124.00

Miscellaneous:

Fixtures and Equipment.	1,764.00
Payment on mortgage	15,000.00
Refund on rents	300.00
Cash deposited with mortgagee for payment of property taxes	15,006.00

Remittances to Collector of Internal Revenue for:
- (a) Social security taxes withheld from the pay checks of employees (debit 15% of this disbursement to Maintenance Salaries, 80% to Operating Salaries, and 5% to Office Salaries) 500.00
- (b) Income taxes withheld from the pay checks of employees (debit 10% of this disbursement to Maintenance Salaries, 65% to Operating Salaries, and 25% to Office Salaries) 3,300.00

$122,820.00

The item of supplies listed in the disbursements above is an expense.

During the year the mortgagee paid property taxes of $18,608.00 from the special cash deposit established with him for the payment of property taxes.

Required:

(1) Prepare a statement of income and expense for the year 19__.

(2) Prepare a balance sheet, December 31, 19__. (For the purpose of this problem, depreciation expense may be disregarded.)

Chapter 6

SALES, PURCHASES, AND COST OF SALES — CLOSING PROCEDURES AND FINANCIAL STATEMENTS

Up to the present time our discussion of accounting method has centered upon the "service" type of business enterprise. Examples of businesses of this kind are many. Among others the following may be mentioned:

Advertising agencies
Apartment houses
Commission merchants
Custom house brokers
Hotels and tourist courts
Instructional and educational services
Insurance agencies
Investment supervision and advisory services
Private watchman and detective organizations
Professional men generally, i.e., doctors, dentists, lawyers, accountants, engineers, business consultants, statisticians, etc.
Radio broadcasting
Realtors
Repair and maintenance concerns
Telephone and telegraph services
Testing laboratories
Theaters
Transportation services of all kinds

In contrast to these "service" organizations stand those businesses which derive their revenues by the purchase and sale of merchandise. In some merchandising concerns it is feasible to determine the exact amount of gross profit [1] which is earned on each unit of sale.[2] As a general rule, in cases of this kind, the unit of sale is high

---

[1] The excess of the selling price of an asset over its net book cost is the "gross profit" realized by the seller. The sale of merchandise for $1,000.00 (original cost, $600.00) involves the earning of a gross profit of $400.00. The terms of sale may be either cash or credit.

[2] This is especially true of businesses engaged in merchandising. However, some of these businesses, and many manufacturing businesses, find it entirely feasible, by use of the method of perpetual inventory, to determine the cost and gross profit on each individual sale. This accounting is described at length in Chapter 25.

in price and the margin of gross profit is large. Examples are auto-mobiles, pianos, refrigerators, household furniture and equipment, industrial and office machines, and real estate.

In most merchandising businesses, however, it is neither expedient nor worth while to calculate the amount of gross profit which has been earned on each sale of merchandise. By a method to be described in this chapter, the average business manager of a trading business is satisfied to learn, *periodically*, the amount of gross profit which has been earned on the *total of all sales*. Between the dates on which these profits are factually determined he does not know, nor is he particularly interested in knowing, the exact gross profits which are being earned on individual sales. During this period, further-more, he does not know, accurately, what amount of gross profit is being earned on the total of his sales although he probably has a manager's *estimate* of what the profits are. These several conditions are especially likely to prevail in businesses engaged in the purchase of merchandise for purpose of resale.

THE SALES ACCOUNT

When merchandise is sold at a price in excess of its cost, the *debit* side of the transaction is

DEBIT: an asset account, Cash, or Accounts Receivable

and the *credit* side of the transaction is, fundamentally,

CREDIT: Merchandise, to record the reduction in the value of this asset, and

CREDIT: an income account, to record the gross profit earned on the sale. One title that might be used for this income account is Gross Profit on Sales.

These two credits are not usually recorded in this manner in actual business practice. Instead, the two credits are combined into one single credit to the Sales account.

In the future, therefore, the following accounting will be used to record *all* sales of merchandise:

DEBIT: Cash (or Accounts Receivable) for the full amount of the sale.

CREDIT: Sales, for the full amount of the sale.

This is the only entry to be made at the time a sales transaction is being recorded. The cost of the merchandise sold on an individual sale is disregarded completely. Later on (at the end of the accounting period), the cost value of *all* merchandise sold is calculated; this cost value for *sales as a group* will become the debit balance of the Cost of Sales account. The two accounts, Sales and Cost of Sales, when read together, will show how much gross profit has been earned on the *total* of the merchandise sales of a period.

Under this new accounting the Sales account is obviously an account for the recording of sales of merchandise *only*. When a credit to the Sales account is analyzed, the credit is found to represent two elements:

(1) The credit to record the reduction in the value of the asset merchandise.

(2) The credit to record the increase in the owner's proprietary claim for the gross profit earned on the transaction.

If the gross profit on a sale were recorded in a separate income account, it would follow that this income account would be closed to Profit and Loss at the end of the accounting period. In place of this income account we have now substituted the Sales and Cost of Sales accounts. Since the income account would have been closed to Profit and Loss, it is logical for these two new accounts also to be closed to Profit and Loss at the end of the accounting period.

THE MERCHANDISE AND PURCHASES ACCOUNTS

It would be possible to operate the Merchandise account in such a way that the balance of the account, at all times, would represent the amount of merchandise which is currently on hand. Every sale and purchase of merchandise would be reflected by a change in the balance of the Merchandise account. But, just as it was inexpedient and unnecessary to calculate gross profits on individual sales (see preceding section), it is similarly inexpedient and unnecessary for most trading concerns to have constantly available the exact value of all merchandise on hand at any and all dates. In fact, ordinary business needs are generally satisfied if the cost value of merchandise on hand is obtained periodically as, for instance, monthly, quarterly, semiannually, or annually. Common business practice is to obtain the value at least once a year.

In the future, therefore, our accounting will give the Merchandise account of a trading business one function only: to represent the value of merchandise on hand *at the end of an accounting period*. The balance in the account will not be changed until the end of the next accounting period, when it will be adjusted to show the value of the merchandise on hand at the end of that period. This adjustment is generally made when the books are being formally closed at the end of an accounting period. As a general rule, no entries will be made in the Merchandise account in the interval between the end of one period and the end of the next succeeding accounting period.

Since the merchandise on hand at the end of the last accounting period is also the merchandise which is on hand at the beginning of the next period, the balance of the Merchandise account *during* a current accounting period may also be thought of as the merchandise on hand at the beginning of the current period.

To care for merchandise which is purchased *during* an accounting period, a subdivision of the Merchandise account is opened. The function of this new account, Purchases, will be that of receiving all debits for the recording of merchandise which is *purchased*.

This accounting means, basically, that the Merchandise and Purchases accounts will now have functions as follows:

(1) The prime function of the Merchandise account will be that of reflecting the amount of merchandise on hand at the end of an accounting period.

(2) The prime function of the Purchases account will be that of reflecting all increases in the asset merchandise because of the purchase of merchandise intended for resale to customers.

At the end of a current accounting period the Merchandise and Purchases accounts are transferred to the Cost of Sales account. Then, in order to record the amount of merchandise actually on hand and to record the cost of all merchandise sold, the Merchandise account is debited and Cost of Sales is credited for the amount of merchandise which is on hand. This accounting is described in detail on the pages which follow.

ILLUSTRATION

This discussion will describe and illustrate the accounting which is to be used henceforth for recording merchandise transactions. To begin with let us assume that the balance sheet of Carl M. Perry on January 1, 1950, was simply:

Carl M. Perry

BALANCE SHEET, JANUARY 1, 1950

Cash	$15,000.00	Carl M. Perry, Capital.	$25,000.00
Merchandise	10,000.00		
	$25,000.00		$25,000.00

Let us assume further that the condensed transactions of Mr. Perry for the year 1950 were:

(1) Sold merchandise for cash, $40,000.00.

(2) Sold merchandise on credit to various customers, $60,000.00.
(3) Purchased merchandise for cash, $20,000.00.
(4) Purchased merchandise on credit from various sellers, $45,000.00.
(5) Collected cash on accounts receivable, $50,000.00.
(6) Paid on accounts payable, $30,000.00.
(7) Paid expenses, $38,000.00.

These seven transactions would be recorded as follows:

Transaction

1	DEBIT:	Cash	40,000.00	
	CREDIT:	Sales		40,000.00
2	DEBIT:	Accounts Receivable	60,000.00	
	CREDIT:	Sales		60,000.00
3	DEBIT:	Purchases	20,000.00	
	CREDIT:	Cash		20,000.00
4	DEBIT:	Purchases	45,000.00	
	CREDIT:	Accounts Payable		45,000.00
5	DEBIT:	Cash	50,000.00	
	CREDIT:	Accounts Receivable		50,000.00
6	DEBIT:	Accounts Payable	30,000.00	
	CREDIT:	Cash		30,000.00
7	DEBIT:	Expenses	38,000.00	
	CREDIT:	Cash		38,000.00

These entries point up a fact which deserves repetitive emphasis: when merchandise sales are recorded, the cost of merchandise sold is disregarded completely.

After giving effect to the seven transactions above, the ledger of Mr. Perry on December 31, 1950, will be:

CASH		ACCOUNTS RECEIVABLE		MERCHANDISE
15,000.00	20,000.00 (3)	(2) 60,000.00	50,000.00 (5)	10,000.00
(1) 40,000.00	30,000.00 (6)			
(5) 50,000.00	38,000.00 (7)			

ACCOUNTS PAYABLE		CARL M. PERRY, CAPITAL		SALES
(6) 30,000.00	45,000.00 (4)		25,000.00	40,000.00 (1)
				60,000.00 (2)

COST OF SALES	PURCHASES	EXPENSES
	(3) 20,000.00	(7) 38,000.00
	(4) 45,000.00	

The trial balance of this ledger will be:

Carl M. Perry

TRIAL BALANCE, DECEMBER 31, 1950

Cash	$ 17,000.00	
Accounts Receivable	10,000.00	
Merchandise	10,000.00	
Accounts Payable		$ 15,000.00
Carl M. Perry, Capital		25,000.00
Sales		100,000.00
Purchases	65,000.00	
Expenses	38,000.00	
	$140,000.00	$140,000.00

The financial statements prepared from this trial balance appear on pages 77 and 78.

The Cost of Sales account is an account whose title is a condensation of the more expressive, but wordy, title of "Cost of the Merchandise Which Has Been Sold." This longer title expresses precisely the function for which the Cost of Sales account exists. The Cost of Sales account, like an expense account, is one of the costs of producing the revenue of a period. Entries affecting the Cost of Sales account will be considered in the next section.

CLOSING ENTRIES FOR COST OF SALES (Illustration continued)

Since financial statements are to be prepared, and the books formally closed on December 31, 1950, the accounts of the ledger must be adjusted so as to show

(1) the cost of the goods which have been sold during 1950, and
(2) the amount of merchandise on hand December 31, 1950.

As the accounts now stand we know

(1) the inventory on hand at the beginning of the period;
(2) the purchases which were made during the period.

The Merchandise and Purchases accounts together show the total amount of merchandise handled during the period and, secondly, the total amount of merchandise to be accounted for. At the end of the accounting period, in order to show this information in one account, the debit balances of the Merchandise and Purchases accounts are transferred to the Cost of Sales account. The actual transfer will be:

(8) DEBIT:	Cost of Sales	75,000.00	
CREDIT:	Merchandise		10,000.00
CREDIT:	Purchases		65,000.00
	To transfer debit balances of latter two accounts to Cost of Sales account.		

If no merchandise is actually on hand at the end of the accounting period, the conclusion follows that *all* of the merchandise to be accounted for must have been sold during the period and that, therefore, $75,000.00 must represent the *cost of the goods which have been sold.* It is ordinarily more likely, however, that some merchandise will still be on hand at the end of an accounting period. In the current illustrative problem the amount of the merchandise on hand December 31, 1950, is $20,000.00. Mr. Perry obtains this value by making a physical count of all merchandise on hand, pricing each item at cost, calculating extensions, and totaling all values.

With the value of the new inventory established at $20,000.00, the *cost of the merchandise which has been sold* must be the difference between $75,000.00 and $20,000.00, or $55,000.00. Accordingly, a credit of $20,000.00 is made to the Cost of Sales account in order to adjust the balance of this account so that it will be equal to the cost of the merchandise which has been disposed of through sale. In order to recognize the asset merchandise on the ledger, a complementary debit of $20,000.00 is made to the Merchandise account. The full entry is therefore

(9) DEBIT: Merchandise 20,000.00
      CREDIT: Cost of Sales 20,000.00
           To record new merchandise inventory.

By this accounting the balance of the Cost of Sales account will now represent the merchandise cost of producing the gross income of a period; and the balance of the Merchandise account will show the value of the inventory on hand at the end of the current accounting period. This is as it should be.

At this point our various merchandise accounts will appear as follows:

MERCHANDISE		SALES	
10,000.00	10,000.00 (8)		40,000.00 (1)
(9) 20,000.00			60,000.00 (2)

COST OF SALES		PURCHASES	
(8) 10,000.00	20,000.00 (9)	(3) 20,000.00	65,000.00 (8)
(8) 65,000.00		(4) 45,000.00	

It is especially important to understand the Cost of Sales account. The balance of $55,000.00 in the account really represents the following information:

Beginning inventory of merchandise $10,000.00
Add merchandise purchased 65,000.00

Total merchandise to be accounted for $75,000.00
Less ending inventory of merchandise 20,000.00

Giving the cost of the merchandise sold as $55,000.00

It is obvious that our several merchandise accounts have informational functions of importance. They serve accounting and also managerial purposes. Management, for example, may compare the volume of purchases over a given period of time (week, month, quarter, etc.) with the volume of goods sold (using sales at cost or estimated cost). This kind of comparison is useful in coordinating and controlling the elements which constitute the merchandising program of a business. Other uses of these accounts should be clear. Proper merchandise accounting should therefore be looked upon as serviceable not only to the accountant but to management as well. It is an important aid in making management's control of business operations more effective.

FINANCIAL STATEMENTS

The following financial statements are prepared from the trial balance on page 75.

The profit and loss statement for the year would be

Carl M. Perry

PROFIT AND LOSS STATEMENT

YEAR ENDING DECEMBER 31, 1950

Sales		$100,000.00
Cost of Sales:		
Inventory, Jan. 1, 1950	$10,000.00	
Purchases . .	65,000.00	
	$75,000.00	
Inventory, Dec. 31, 1950	20,000.00	55,000.00
Gross Profit		$ 45,000.00
Expenses		38,000.00
Net Profit from Operations . .		$ 7,000.00

or the statement may be condensed as follows

Carl M. Perry

PROFIT AND LOSS STATEMENT

YEAR ENDING DECEMBER 31, 1950

Sales	$100,000.00
Cost of Sales	55,000.00
Gross Profit	$ 45,000.00
Expenses	38,000.00
Net Profit from Operations . .	$ 7,000.00

The balance sheet on December 31, 1950, would be

Carl M. Perry

BALANCE SHEET, DECEMBER 31, 1950

Assets		Liabilities and Net Worth	
Cash	$17,000.00	Accounts Payable	$15,000.00
Accounts Receivable . . .	10,000.00	Net Worth:	
Merchandise	20,000.00	Carl M. Perry, Capital.	32,000.00
	$47,000.00		$47,000.00

With financial statements prepared, the books may be formally closed as follows:

(10) DEBIT: Sales 100,000.00
     CREDIT: Profit and Loss 100,000.00
     To transfer credit balance of Sales account to Profit and Loss.

(11) DEBIT: Profit and Loss 55,000.00
     CREDIT: Cost of Sales 55,000.00
     To transfer debit balance of Cost of Sales account to Profit and Loss.

(12) DEBIT: Profit and Loss 38,000.00
     CREDIT: Expenses 38,000.00
     To transfer latter account to Profit and Loss.

(13) DEBIT: Profit and Loss 7,000.00
     CREDIT: C. M. Perry, Capital 7,000.00
     To transfer balance of Profit and Loss to Capital account.

The ledger of Mr. Perry will now appear as follows:

	CASH				ACCOUNTS RECEIVABLE		
	15,000.00	20,000.00	(3)	(2)	60,000.00	50,000.00	(5)
(1)	40,000.00	30,000.00	(6)				
(5)	50,000.00	38,000.00	(7)				

	MERCHANDISE				ACCOUNTS PAYABLE		
	10,000.00	10,000.00	(8)	(6)	30,000.00	45,000.00	(4)
(9)	20,000.00						

CARL M. PERRY, CAPITAL					PROFIT AND LOSS		
		25,000.00		(11)	55,000.00	100,000.00	(10)
		7,000.00	(13)	(12)	38,000.00		
				(13)	7,000.00		
					100,000.00	100,000.00	

	SALES				COST OF SALES		
(10)	100,000.00	40,000.00	(1)	(8)	10,000.00	20,000.00	(9)
		60,000.00	(2)	(8)	65,000.00	55,000.00	(11)
	100,000.00	100,000.00			75,000.00	75,000.00	

	PURCHASES				EXPENSES		
(3)	20,000.00	65,000.00	(8)	(7)	38,000.00	38,000.00	(12)
(4)	45,000.00						
	65,000.00	65,000.00					

ILLUSTRATIVE PROBLEM

A further application of the technique introduced in this chapter, as well as of that introduced in Chapter 5, is to be found in the solution to the extended problem which is presented below. Particular attention should be paid to the new accounts which are employed, namely:

Sales   Merchandise   Profit and Loss
Cost of Sales   Purchases

The student should study each transaction and trace its entry in the ledger. To facilitate study, each entry in the ledger has been cross-indexed to its respective debit or credit by transaction number. Closing entries, to which close attention should be paid, are designated by numbers 36 to 45, inclusive.

Accounts have been arranged in the ledger in the order in which they appear on the balance sheet and on the profit and loss statement, respectively.

For the purpose of this particular problem it has been assumed that it is the wish of Mr. Robinson to have his books closed as of February 28, 1950. In actual practice the books of a business are not closed at the end of each month. Usually they are formally closed but once a year — at the end of the calendar year or other comparable accounting period.

The transactions of L. T. Robinson for the month of February, 1950, are as follows:

(1) L. T. Robinson began business with $12,000.00 cash and $4,000.00 merchandise.
(2) Paid February rent, $300.00.
(3) Bought furniture and fixtures from Ester Supply Company for cash, $1,200.00.
(4) Merchandise is sold for cash to J. M. Barrie for $102.00.

(5) Bought merchandise from James J. Logue, $5,000.00.

(6) Sold merchandise to C. F. Ruble on account, $2,378.00.

(7) A cash sale of $28.00 is made to E. T. Maddox.

(8) Merchandise is purchased from Exley & Son for cash, $700.00.

(9) Sold merchandise on account to Clark R. Morgan, $489.00.

(10) Paid James J. Logue, $5,000.00.

(11) Merchandise is purchased on account from Henry V. Dana, $408.00.

(12) Merchandise is purchased on account from James J. Logue, $1,800.00.

(13) General expenses are paid, $510.00.

(14) Merchandise is sold on account to E. V. Sanders, $867.00.

(15) Bought merchandise on account from F. C. Maxton, $62.00.

(16) A cash sale is made to A. L. Nichols, $51.00.

(17) Merchandise is sold on account to C. F. Ruble, $558.00.

(18) Sundry expenses are paid, $116.00.

(19) Clark R. Morgan returns $100.00 of the merchandise purchased by him in transaction #9 because of inferior quality.

(20) Merchandise is sold on account to H. R. Macy, $599.00.

(21) A check is received from Clark R. Morgan, $389.00.

(22) Merchandise is purchased on account from J. R. Upshaw, $1,800.00.

(23) Merchandise is purchased on account from James J. Logue, $1,530.00.

(24) Merchandise is sold on account to E. V. Sanders, $85.00.

(25) Cash is received from C. F. Ruble to apply on account, $700.00.

(26) Cash is received from E. V. Sanders in payment of merchandise sold him in transaction #24.

(27) Merchandise is sold on account to M. G. Sheldon, $1,311.00.

(28) A check for $62.00 is mailed to F. C. Maxton in payment of merchandise purchased in transaction #15.

(29) L. T. Robinson drew cash for personal use, $200.00.

(30) A check for $1,000.00 is given to James J. Logue in part payment of merchandise previously purchased from him.

(31) L. T. Robinson acts as agent for the Dettle Insurance Company; a policy is sold for which Mr. Robinson receives a check for $63.00.

(32) A check is received from C. F. Ruble, $678.00.

(33) A check is received from E. V. Sanders, $250.00, in part payment of merchandise sold him in transaction #14.

(34) Merchandise is sold on account to Clark R. Morgan, $722.00.

(35) Wages are paid, $231.00.

After these transactions have been recorded, the ledger of L. T. Robinson will be:

LEDGER

CASH

(1)	12,000.00	300.00	(2)
(4)	102.00	1,200.00	(3)
(7)	28.00	700.00	(8)
(16)	51.00	5,000.00	(10)
(21)	389.00	510.00	(13)
(25)	700.00	116.00	(18)
(26)	85.00	62.00	(28)
(31)	63.00	200.00	(29)
(32)	678.00	1,000.00	(30)
(33)	250.00	231.00	(35)

H. R. MACY

(20)	599.00	

CLARK R. MORGAN

(9)	489.00	100.00	(19)
(34)	722.00	389.00	(21)

C. F. RUBLE

(6)	2,378.00	700.00	(25)
(17)	558.00	678.00	(32)

E. V. SANDERS

(14)	867.00	85.00	(26)
(24)	85.00	250.00	(33)

M. G. SHELDON

(27)	1,311.00	

MERCHANDISE

(1)	4,000.00	

FURNITURE AND FIXTURES

(3)	1,200.00	

HENRY V. DANA

	408.00	(11)

JAMES J. LOGUE

(10)	5,000.00	5,000.00	(5)
(30)	1,000.00	1,800.00	(12)
		1,530.00	(23)

F. C. MAXTON

(28)	62.00	62.00	(15)

J. R. UPSHAW

	1,800.00	(22)

L. T. ROBINSON, CAPITAL

(29)	200.00	16,000.00	(1)

SALES

(19)	100.00	102.00	(4)
		2,378.00	(6)
		28.00	(7)
		489.00	(9)
		867.00	(14)
		51.00	(16)
		558.00	(17)
		599.00	(20)
		85.00	(24)
		1,311.00	(27)
		722.00	(34)

PURCHASES

(5)	5,000.00
(8)	700.00
(11)	408.00
(12)	1,800.00
(15)	62.00
(22)	1,800.00
(23)	1,530.00

GENERAL EXPENSE

| (13) | 510.00 |
| (18) | 116.00 |

RENT EXPENSE

| (2) | 300.00 |

WAGES EXPENSE

| (35) | 231.00 |

COMMISSIONS EARNED

| | 63.00 | (31) |

The trial balance, the profit and loss statement, and the balance sheet as prepared from the accounts of L. T. Robinson follow:

L. T. Robinson

TRIAL BALANCE, FEBRUARY 28, 1950

Cash	$ 5,027.00	
H. R. Macy	599.00	
Clark R. Morgan	722.00	
C. F. Ruble	1,558.00	
E. V. Sanders	617.00	
M. G. Sheldon	1,311.00	
Merchandise	4,000.00	
Furniture and Fixtures	1,200.00	
Henry V. Dana		$ 408.00
James J. Logue		2,330.00
J. R. Upshaw		1,800.00
L. T. Robinson, Capital		15,800.00
Sales		7,090.00
Purchases	11,300.00	
General Expense	626.00	
Rent Expense	300.00	
Wages Expense	231.00	
Commissions Earned		63.00
	$27,491.00	$27,491.00

The merchandise on hand at the close of business February 28, 1950, was valued at $10,692.00.

L. T. Robinson

PROFIT AND LOSS STATEMENT FOR THE MONTH OF FEBRUARY, 1950

Sales			$7,090.00
Cost of Sales:			
Merchandise, February 1, 1950	$ 4,000.00		
Purchases	11,300.00		
	$15,300.00		
Merchandise, February 28, 1950	10,692.00	4,608.00	
Gross Profit			$2,482.00

Expenses:
General Expense . . . . $ 626.00
Rent Expense 300.00
Wages Expense 231.00   1,157.00

Net Profit from Operations $1,325.00
Other Income:
Commissions Earned 63.00

Net Income. $1,388.00

L. T. Robinson

BALANCE SHEET, FEBRUARY 28, 1950

Assets			*Liabilities and Net Worth*		
Current Assets:			Current Liabilities:		
Cash		$ 5,027.00	Accounts Payable:		
Accounts Receivable:			Henry V. Dana	$	408.00
H. R. Macy . . .	$ 599.00		James J. Logue		2,330.00
Clark R. Morgan.	722.00		J. R. Upshaw		1,800.00
C. F. Ruble . . .	1,558.00				
E. V. Sanders . .	617.00			$	4,538.00
M. G. Sheldon .	1,311.00	4,807.00	Net Worth:		
			L. T. Robinson, Capital .		17,188.00
Merchandise		10,692.00			
		$20,526.00			
Fixed Assets:					
Furniture and Fixtures. . .		1,200.00			
		$21,726.00			$21,726.00

It should be observed that, with one exception, the values of the assets and liabilities in the trial balance are also the values of the assets and liabilities of the balance sheet. The single exception is merchandise, the value for which is obtained, not from the trial balance, but from a source independent of the trial balance or general ledger, i.e., by *actual* count and valuation.

In order to close his books for the month of February Mr. Robinson would make the following additional entries:

(36) DEBIT: Cost of Sales 4,000.00
     CREDIT: Merchandise 4,000.00
(37) DEBIT: Cost of Sales 11,300.00
     CREDIT: Purchases 11,300.00
(38) DEBIT: Merchandise 10,692.00
     CREDIT: Cost of Sales 10,692.00

At this point the balance of the Cost of Sales account represents the cost of the merchandise sold during the month.

(39) DEBIT: Profit and Loss 4,608.00
      CREDIT: Cost of Sales 4,608.00

(40) DEBIT: Sales 7,090.00
      CREDIT: Profit and Loss 7,090.00

(41) DEBIT: Profit and Loss 626.00
      CREDIT: General Expense 626.00

(42) DEBIT: Profit and Loss 300.00
      CREDIT: Rent Expense. 300.00

(43) DEBIT: Profit and Loss 231.00
      CREDIT: Wages Expense 231.00

(44) DEBIT: Commissions Earned 63.00
      CREDIT: Profit and Loss 63.00

At this point the balance of the Profit and Loss account is the net income of the business for the month of February.

(45) DEBIT: Profit and Loss 1,388.00
      CREDIT: L. T. Robinson, Capital 1,388.00

This entry transfers the net profit to the Capital account of L. T. Robinson.

After the books have been closed, the ledger of L. T. Robinson will appear as follows:

LEDGER

CASH

(1)	12,000.00	300.00	(2)
(4)	102.00	1,200.00	(3)
(7)	28.00	700.00	(8)
(16)	51.00	5,000.00	(10)
(21)	389.00	510.00	(13)
(25)	700.00	116.00	(18)
(26)	85.00	62.00	(28)
(31)	63.00	200.00	(29)
(32)	678.00	1,000.00	(30)
(33)	250.00	231.00	(35)

H. R. MACY

| (20) | 599.00 | |

CLARK R. MORGAN

| (9) | 489.00 | 100.00 | (19) |
| (34) | 722.00 | 389.00 | (21) |

C. F. RUBLE

| (6) | 2,378.00 | 700.00 | (25) |
| (17) | 558.00 | 678.00 | (32) |

E. V. SANDERS

| (14) | 867.00 | 85.00 | (26) |
| (24) | 85.00 | 250.00 | (33) |

M. G. SHELDON

| (27) | 1,311.00 | |

MERCHANDISE

| (1) | 4,000.00 | 4,000.00 | (36) |
| (38) | 10,692.00 | | |

FURNITURE AND FIXTURES

(3)	1,200.00		

HENRY DANA

		408.00	(11)

JAMES J. LOGUE

(10)	5,000.00	5,000.00	(5)
(30)	1,000.00	1,800.00	(12)
		1,530.00	(23)

F. C. MAXTON

(28)	62.00	62.00	(15)

J. R. UPSHAW

		1,800.00	(22)

L. T. ROBINSON, CAPITAL

(29)	200.00	16,000.00	(1)
		1,388.00	(45)

PROFIT AND LOSS

(39)	4,608.00	7,090.00	(40)
(41)	626.00	63.00	(44)
(42)	300.00		
(43)	231.00		
(45)	1,388.00		
	7,153.00	7,153.00	

SALES

(19)	100.00	102.00	(4)
(40)	7,090.00	2,378.00	(6)
		28.00	(7)
		489.00	(9)
		867.00	(14)
		51.00	(16)
		558.00	(17)
		599.00	(20)
		85.00	(24)
		1,311.00	(27)
		722.00	(34)
	7,190.00	7,190.00	

COST OF SALES

(36)	4,000.00	10,692.00	(38)
(37)	11,300.00	4,608.00	(39)
	15,300.00	15,300.00	

PURCHASES

(5)	5,000.00	11,300.00	(37)
(8)	700.00		
(11)	408.00		
(12)	1,800.00		
(15)	62.00		
(22)	1,800.00		
(23)	1,530.00		
	11,300.00	11,300.00	

GENERAL EXPENSE

(13)	510.00	626.00	(41)
(18)	116.00		
	626.00	626.00	

RENT EXPENSE

(2)	300.00	300.00	(42)

WAGES EXPENSE			COMMISSIONS EARNED			
(35)	231.00	231.00	(43) (44)		63.00	63.00 (31)

CLASSIFICATION OF NOMINAL ACCOUNTS

The financial statements of Mr. L. T. Robinson have been constructed so as to emphasize certain kinds of information. With respect to the profit and loss statement, the following specific points deserve mention:

(1) *Sales* is the total of all sales of merchandise.

(2) *Cost of Sales* is the direct cost of the merchandise which has been disposed of through sale.

(3) *Gross profit* is the difference between sales and cost of sales.

(4) The expenses which have been more or less directly incurred in the production of sales are deducted from gross profit.

(5) *Net Profit from Operations* is the net profit realized on sales.

(6) Under *Other Income* (and *Other Expense*) are placed the miscellaneous incomes (and expenses) of doing business. These items tend to recur frequently but, usually, they are not integral to the major activity of merchandising.

(7) *Net Income* is the net income which remains after giving effect to all of the gains, costs, and losses of doing business.

The expenses of a business may be shown on the profit and loss statement under the single heading of Expense. This heading, however, is not satisfactory where there are significant classes of expense. Information is lacking as to the amount of each of these classes of expense. Control of expense expenditures is more difficult.

As a general rule the operating expenses of a merchandising business are divisible into selling expenses and general expenses. Selling expenses are those expenses directly incurred in the sale of merchandise. Advertising, traveling expenses, and sales salaries are examples. General expenses are the miscellaneous expenses incurred in the general operation of a business. Examples are office salaries, insurance, postage, taxes, and utilities expense.

Large businesses require a very detailed analysis of expenses. Accordingly, they have many groups of expenses.

CLASSIFICATION OF ASSETS AND LIABILITIES

In the balance sheet of L. T. Robinson, the assets were arranged so that cash appeared first; and noncash assets were arranged in the order of their expected conversion into cash.

As a general rule, the assets of a business may be divided into three main groups:

(1) *Current Assets*. Cash and those assets which will be converted into cash in the normal operations of a business over a twelve months' period are current assets. The assets of this group are generally arranged in the order of their expected convertibility into cash.

(2) *Fixed Assets*. Broadly speaking, those assets which are long term in nature and are necessary instruments of doing business are called fixed assets. Examples are office equipment, automobiles, buildings, land, and machinery.

(3) *Other Assets*. In this group are placed all assets other than current assets and fixed assets. In later chapters of this book this group will be subdivided into investments, intangibles, and so on.

The liabilities of a business may also be divided into three main groups:

(1) *Current Liabilities*. Liabilities which must be paid within one year are current liabilities.

(2) *Fixed* or *Long-Term Liabilities*. Those liabilities which are long term in nature are called fixed liabilities. An example of a fixed liability is a mortgage payable due ten years from now.

(3) *Other Liabilities*. In this group are placed those miscellaneous liabilities which are not classified as current or fixed.

In the construction of balance sheets it is usual to show current assets first, then fixed assets and other assets. Liabilities follow a similar pattern. By listing current assets first on the asset side, and current liabilities first on the liability side, the balance sheet emphasizes the liquidity of assets and the ability of a business to meet its current obligations.

WORK SHEET

Since all of the accounts of the trial balance are used in the construction of financial statements, and since each of these accounts goes into either the profit and loss statement or the balance sheet, it is quite common for accountants to use the device of the work sheet to aid them in the work of statement preparation.[3]

In the first pair of columns of the work sheet (page 88) the trial balance is recorded. The accounts of the trial balance are then distributed to the proper columns of the work sheet as follows:

---

[3] A very simple form of work sheet was introduced in Chapter 5 (page 54). This work sheet applied to the *service* type of business.

L. T. Robinson

Work Sheet, February 28, 1950

Account	Trial Balance Dr.	Trial Balance Cr.	Cost of Sales Dr.	Cost of Sales Cr.	Profit and Loss Dr.	Profit and Loss Cr.	Balance Sheet Dr.	Balance Sheet Cr.
Cash	5,027.00						5,027.00	
H. R. Macy	599.00						599.00	
Clark R. Morgan	722.00						722.00	
C. F. Ruble	1,558.00						1,558.00	
E. V. Sanders	617.00						617.00	
M. G. Sheldon	1,311.00						1,311.00	
Merchan ise	4,000.00		4,000.00	10,692.00			10,692.00	
Furniture and Fixtures	1,200.00						1,200.00	
Henry V. Dana		408.00						408.00
James J. Logue		2,330.00						2,330.00
J. R. Upshaw		1,800.00						1,800.00
L. T. Robinson, Capital		15,800.00						15,800.00
Sales		7,090.00				7,090.00		
Purchases	11,300.00		11,300.00					
General Expense	626.00				626.00			
Rent Expense	300.00				300.00			
Wages Expense	231.00				231.00			
Commissions Earned		63.00				63.00		
	27,491.00	27,491.00						
Cost of Sales to Profit and Loss				4,608.00	4,608.00			
			15,300.00	15,300.00				
Net Income to L. T. Robinson, Capital					1,388.00			1,388.00
					7,153.00	7,153.00	21,726.00	21,726.00

(1) In the Cost of Sales columns are placed the items which make up the cost of goods sold.

(2) In the Profit and Loss columns are placed the items which make up the profit and loss statement.

(3) In the Balance Sheet columns are placed the items which make up the balance sheet.

When the work sheet has been completed, the formal profit and loss statement is prepared from the profit and loss columns of the work sheet; and the formal balance sheet is prepared from the balance sheet columns of the work sheet.

The work sheet for the L. T. Robinson problem should be studied with understanding. It illustrates the fundamentals to be followed in the construction of a work sheet for a *merchandising* business. Note that the balance of Cost of Sales is transferred to Profit and Loss, and that the balance of Profit and Loss is transferred to Capital, transfers paralleling the entries which are made when the books are being closed at the end of an accounting period. Special attention should be given to the manner in which the new inventory is handled on the work sheet: a debit in the balance sheet columns, and a credit in the cost of sales columns. This debit and credit reflects the entry which would be made on the books to record the new inventory, viz.:

Merchandise 10,692.00
    Cost of Sales 10,692.00
To record amount of new inventory.

QUESTIONS

Question **6–1.** Explain why the accounting of Chapter 6 represents a natural transitional development of the accounting previously employed for the recording of merchandise transactions.

Question **6–2.** In the future how will you proceed to record merchandise sales and merchandise purchases?

Question **6–3.** In the future, what is to be the sole function of the Merchandise account? To what extent, and when, may the Merchandise account receive entries?

Question **6–4.** What is the meaning of a credit to the Sales account?

Question **6–5.** What is the function of the Cost of Sales account? At the end of an accounting period, what information is contained in the Cost of Sales account? When are entries to be made in the Cost of Sales account?

Question **6–6.** The Profit and Loss account: (1) What is its function? (2) When are entries made in it? (3) What disposition is made of its balance?

Question **6–7.** To what extent should detailed debits and credits be made to the Capital account? What is the particular function of the Capital account?

Question **6–8.** Prepare a diagram showing the relationship of the several merchandise accounts to one another and to the Profit and Loss account. Use arrows to indicate the flow of information from one account to another.

Question **6–9.** What important information is reflected by the profit and loss statement? By the balance sheet?

Question **6–10.** On the profit and loss statement

(1) What is meant by the cost of sales?
(2) What particular expenses are deducted from the figure representing gross profit?
(3) What is the difference between "net profit from operations" and "net income"? What is the importance of this distinction?

PROBLEMS

Problem **6–1.** M. H. Williams began business on December 1, 19—, with cash, $4,000.00, merchandise, $6,000.00, store equipment, $2,000.00, and securities, $3,000.00. His summarized transactions for the first month of business were as follows:

(1) Purchased merchandise from Lane & Son on terms of 90 days' credit, $1,400.00.
(2) Paid rent, $80.00.
(3) Sold merchandise to W. H. Gordon on terms of 30 days' credit, $900.00.
(4) Paid various advertising bills amounting to $250.00.
(5) Paid wages and salaries, $100.00.
(6) Sold merchandise to Wells & Co., Inc., on terms of 30 days' credit, $1,600.00.
(7) Paid gas, light, telephone, and water bills amounting to $50.00. (Debit Utilities Expense.)
(8) Sold merchandise to W. H. Gordon on terms of 30 days' credit, $300.00.
(9) Paid advertising bills of $200.00.
(10) Paid wages and salaries, $220.00.
(11) Purchased merchandise from Lane & Son for cash, $400.00.
(12) A dividend check, applicable to the securities owned, is received, $20.00.

Required:

(1) Enter the above transactions in a T-account ledger.

(2) Draw off a trial balance, December 31, 19__.

(3) Prepare a profit and loss statement for the month of December. The inventory of merchandise on December 31, 19__, is $6,100.00.

(4) Prepare a balance sheet, December 31, 19__.

Problem **6–2.** James E. Gayle began business on December 1, 19__, with cash, $10,000.00, merchandise, $7,760.00, and fixtures, $2,240.00. His transactions for the month of December were:

(1) Paid rent, $100.00.

(2) Sold merchandise on credit to May & Co., $2,617.00.

(3) Paid advertising bill of the *Midwest Times*, $320.00.

(4) Sold merchandise on credit to John A. Clark & Co., $1,878.00.

(5) Paid general expenses, $250.00.

(6) Bought merchandise on credit from Fenner & Platt, Inc., $2,904.00.

(7) Bought 100 shares of stock in the General Paper Company for cash, $5,010.00.

(8) Sold merchandise for cash to May & Co., $424.00.

(9) Bought merchandise on credit from L. E. Benton, $1,070.00.

(10) Paid wages and salaries, $444.00.

(11) The invoice of $424.00 to May & Co., in transaction #8, should have been $524.00. On being notified of the error, May & Co. advise they will make payment on January 10.

(12) Paid Fenner & Platt, Inc., $904.00.

(13) An advertising bill of the *Midwest Times* is paid, $270.00.

Required:

(1) Enter the above transactions in a T-account ledger. Among other accounts include the following: Cost of Sales, Merchandise, Profit and Loss, Purchases, and Sales.

(2) Take a trial balance.

(3) Prepare a profit and loss statement for the month of December, 19__. The inventory of merchandise on December 31, 19__, is $8,616.00.

(4) Prepare a balance sheet, December 31, 19__.

(5) Close the books.

Problem **6–3.** John A. Edwards began business on December 1, 19__. with cash, $10,000.00, merchandise, $9,000.00, and fixtures, $3,000.00. His transactions for the first month of business were as follows:

(1) Paid rent to G. E. Marshburn, $100.00.

(2) Sale of merchandise on account to May & Company, $2,600.00.

(3) Paid for advertising in the *Daily News*, $310.00.

(4) Sale of merchandise on account to Roy & Son, $1,800.00.

(5) Paid general expenses, $300.00.

(6) Purchase of merchandise on account from Scott & Company, $2,900.00.

(7) Bought 100 shares of stock in the American Woollen Company for cash, $5,000.00.

(8) Sale of merchandise on account to May & Company, $400.00.

(9) Purchase of merchandise on account from Brent & Son, $1,100.00.

(10) Paid wages, $400.00.

(11) Paid Scott & Company $900.00 as part payment of account.

(12) Paid an advertising bill of the *Daily News*, $290.00.

Required:

(1) Enter the above transactions in a T-account ledger.

(2) Prepare a trial balance.

(3) Prepare a profit and loss statement. Inventory, December 31, 19__, $10,000.00.

(4) Prepare a balance sheet.

(5) Close the books.

Problem 6-4. J. L. Butler began business on January 1, 19__. His transactions for the month were as follows:

(1) Began business with cash, $15,000.00, merchandise, $12,000.00, and fixtures, $5,000.00.

(2) Bought merchandise on account from Eiler & Co., $4,000.00.

(3) Sale of merchandise for cash to H. C. Bennett, $3,110.00.

(4) Paid the *Clarion Times* for advertising, $300.00.

(5) Sale of merchandise on account to Grant & Son, $1,470.00.

(6) Wages and salaries are paid, $690.00.

(7) A check is cashed for H. C. Bennett, $75.00.

(8) Purchased merchandise on account from Jackson & Company, $2,900.00. A down payment of $900.00 was made on this purchase.

(9) Sale of merchandise on account to H. C. Bennett, $1,360.00.

(10) A light delivery truck is accepted from H. C. Bennett in part payment of account, $700.00.

(11) Wages are paid, $890.00.

(12) Cash is received from Grant & Son in part payment of account, $350.00.

Required:

(1) Enter the above transactions in a T-account ledger.

(2) Prepare a trial balance on a work sheet.

(3) Complete the work sheet.

(4) Prepare a profit and loss statement. The merchandise inventory on January 31, 19__, is $15,200.00.

(5) Prepare a balance sheet.

Problem 6-5. Following is the trial balance of J. C. Mayfield on December 31, 19__:

Cash . . . . $ 6,000.00
Clark & Company 1,222.00
Martin & Company. 680.00

Merchandise	7,000.00	
Office Equipment	3,000.00	
Daily & Company		$ 740.00
Notes Payable		5,000.00
J. C. Mayfield, Capital		11,162.00
Sales		25,000.00
Purchases	15,000.00	
General Expense	1,900.00	
Rent Expense	1,000.00	
Utilities Expense	500.00	
Wages and Salaries	5,600.00	
	$41,902.00	$41,902.00

Required:

(1) Record the above trial balance on working papers (i.e., a work sheet).

(2) Complete the working papers. The new inventory is $10,000.00.

(3) Prepare a profit and loss statement for the year.

(4) Prepare a balance sheet, December 31, 19___.

Problem **6–6.** Following is the trial balance of Walter B. Davis, on December 31, 19___.

Cash	$ 4,095.00	
U.S. Treasury Bonds	12,000.00	
Accounts Receivable	11,690.00	
Notes Receivable	800.00	
Inventory	6,201.00	
Delivery Equipment	2,100.00	
Furniture and Fixtures	2,400.00	
Miscellaneous Equipment	3,104.00	
Building	14,000.00	
Land	3,000.00	
Notes Payable		$ 1,000.00
Accounts Payable		1,276.00
Sales Tax Payable		92.00
Social Security Taxes Payable		187.00
Mortgage Payable (due 10 years from now)		6,000.00
Walter B. Davis, Capital		47,750.00
Sales		60,084.00
Purchases	44,300.00	
Advertising	1,329.00	
General Expense	701.00	
Insurance Expense	170.00	
Repairs	176.00	
Salaries	9,000.00	
Taxes (on property)	610.00	
Utilities Expense	663.00	
Warehouse Rent	300.00	
Interest Income		250.00
	$116,639.00	$116,639.00

Required:

(1) Record the above trial balance on a work sheet.

(2) Complete the work sheet. The new inventory is $10,366.00.

(3) Prepare a profit and loss statement for the year ending December 31, 19___.

(4) Prepare a balance sheet, December 31, 19___.

Problem **6–7.** D. C. Elder began business on December 1, 19___, with merchandise, $25,000.00, cash, $15,000.00, building, $8,000.00, and land, $2,000.00. His transactions for the month of December were as follows:

(1) Bought fixtures from the Holmes Fixture Co. for cash, $3,000.00.

(2) Sale of merchandise on account to J. B. Wright, $3,400.00.

(3) Purchase of merchandise on account from L. B. Ainsworth, $1,250.00.

(4) Advertising bills were paid, $100.00.

(5) Sale of merchandise for cash to J. B. Wright, $6,600.00.

(6) Collected $200.00 rent from a tenant occupying one half of the building owned by Mr. Elder.

(7) Paid salaries, $260.00.

(8) Received a check from J. B. Wright to apply on account, $2,400.00.

(9) Purchase of merchandise on account from B. J. Spears, $5,000.00.

(10) Sale of merchandise on account to J. B. Wright, $1,700.00.

(11) Miscellaneous expenses are paid in cash, $350.00.

(12) Because the wrong kind of merchandise was shipped him, J. B. Wright returns the merchandise sold him in transaction #10.

(13) A fixture, which is no longer needed, is sold on account to J. B. Wright at cost, $250.00.

(14) J. B. Wright, being temporarily short of cash, is given a cash loan of $750.00 with the oral understanding that this loan is to be repaid in sixty days. There is no written evidence to support this transaction with the exception of the check written in Mr. Wright's favor.

Required:

(1) Enter the above transactions in T accounts.

(2) Prepare a trial balance on working papers.

(3) Complete the working papers.

(4) Prepare a profit and loss statement for December. The merchandise inventory on December 31, 19___, was $22,080.00.

(5) Prepare a balance sheet.

(6) Close the books.

Problem **6–8.** Following are the transactions of J. L. Smith for the month of December, 19___:

(1) J. L. Smith began business with cash, $18,000.00, and merchandise, $12,000.00.

(2) Paid rent for the month of December to E. L. Burton, $200.00.

(3) Sold merchandise to R. A. Brown on account $2,000.00.

(4) Paid the *Daily Transcript* for advertising, $300.00.

(5) Paid wages, $650.00.

(6) Sold merchandise to J. W. Hanes on account, $1,000.00.

(7) Paid general expenses, $100.00.

(8) Sold merchandise to R. A. Brown for cash, $600.00.

(9) Purchased merchandise on account from Brooks & Co., $1,000.00.

(10) Paid for a neon electric advertising sign, $850.00.

(11) Paid wages, $700.00.

(12) Paid the Parker Office Equipment Company $1,500.00, of which $1,000.00 was for furniture and fixtures, and $500.00 was for an adding machine, typewriter, and other office machines.

(13) Gave a check for $500.00 to Brooks & Co. in part payment of the merchandise purchased in transaction #9.

(14) Purchased land, $3,000.00, and a building, $12,000.00. Paid the seller, John A. White, $5,000.00 cash, and a five-year mortgage payable for $10,000.00.

(15) Sold merchandise to R. A. Brown on account, $2,000.00.

Required:

(1) Record the above transactions in the ledger of J. L. Smith.

(2) Take a trial balance.

(3) Prepare a profit and loss statement for the month of December. Inventory, December 31, 19__, $9,600.00.

(4) Prepare a balance sheet as of December 31, 19__.

(5) Close the books.

Problem **6-9.** Following are the transactions of Mr. J. L. Hughes for the month of December, 19__:

(1) Began business with cash, $12,000.00, and merchandise, $20,000.00.

(2) Paid C. C. Porter for December rent, $105.00.

(3) An advertising bill in favor of the Central Press, Inc., is paid, $250.00.

(4) A check is cashed for J. E. West, $15.00.

(5) Purchase of merchandise on account from Thor & Sharpe, Inc., $1,000.00.

(6) Sale of merchandise on account to May & Co., $2,720.00.

(7) Miscellaneous expenses are paid in cash, $302.00.

(8) Calendars are purchased for cash from the Bayes Printing Company, $100.00. (These calendars were subsequently given away to customers and prospective customers.)

(9) Sale of merchandise for cash to W. C. Cook, $280.00.

(10) The check of transaction #4 is returned by the bank marked "no account." The whereabouts of Mr. West is not known and the check is therefore considered to be worthless.

(11) Received check from May & Co. in part payment of account, $2,000.00.

(12) Purchase of merchandise on account from Stone & Co., Inc., $4,000.00.

(13) Sale of merchandise on account to May & Co., $1,360.00.

(14) J. L. Hughes withdraws $5,000.00 cash because he feels that the business has more cash than it needs.

(15) Twine, wrapping paper, and similar supplies, are purchased for cash from the Cooper Paper Co., $25.00.

(16) Sale of merchandise on account to M. A. Sherrill, $2,070.00.

(17) Wages and salaries are paid, $320.00.

Required:

(1) Enter the above transactions in T accounts.

(2) Prepare a trial balance. Record the trial balance on a work sheet, and complete the work sheet.

(3) Prepare a profit and loss statement for December, 19___. New inventory, $19,586.00.

(4) Prepare a balance sheet, December 31, 19___.

Problem **6–10.** On November 30, 19___, the trial balance of J. R. Lindsay was:

Cash	$ 2,501.00	
Butler & Company	1,654.00	
Gibbs & McKay	2,179.00	
H. C. Scott	1,844.00	
Notes Receivable	1,000.00	
Merchandise	13,462.00	
Equipment and Fixtures	2,159.00	
Building	12,192.00	
Land	3,000.00	
C. M. Nash		$ 2,562.00
Todd & Son		1,489.00
Notes Payable		1,676.00
Mortgage Payable		5,000.00
J. R. Lindsay, Capital		30,962.00
Sales		31,896.00
Purchases	21,749.00	
Delivery Expense	419.00	
General Expense	954.00	
Taxes Expense	149.00	
Utilities Expense	305.00	
Wages Expense	9,768.00	
Interest Expense	250.00	
	$73,585.00	$73,585.00

For the month of December, Mr. Lindsay's transactions were as follows:

(1) Sale of merchandise on account to H. C. Scott, $635.00.

(2) Purchased an adding machine from the Burroughs Adding Machine Company for cash, $140.00.

(3) Paid Chamber of Commerce dues, $25.00.

(4) Sale of merchandise for cash to H. C. Scott, $81.00.

(5) The note receivable is collected, $1,000.00. A check for this amount is received from Butler & Company.

(6) Checks are received to apply on account, Gibbs & McKay, $679.00, H. C. Scott, $500.00.

(7) It is discovered that an item of $39.00 was debited last month to the Equipment and Fixtures account. The debit should have been to General Expense.

(8) A check for $1,676.00 is mailed to W. E. Mayfield in payment of notes payable.

(9) Paid wages and salaries, $1,046.00.

(10) Paid Crane's Service Station for gas, oil, and miscellaneous car expenses, $34.00.

(11) Sale of merchandise on account to Butler & Co., $428.00.

(12) The telephone bill is paid, $18.00.

(13) Purchased merchandise on credit from C. M. Nash, $1,093.00.

(14) Made arrangements with the Daily News Corporation for next year's advertising at a minimum total expenditure of $3,120.00, this advertising to be used at the rate of one $60.00 advertisement in each Friday edition.

(15) Sale of merchandise on account to H. C. Scott, $77.00.

(16) The invoice for the sale in transaction #4 is found to be in error. The correct amount is $91.00.

(17) Sale of merchandise on account to Gibbs & McKay, $184.00.

(18) A stapling machine purchased three weeks ago from the Katz Office Supply Company for $5.00 cash, and charged to General Expense, is returned as unsatisfactory. A check for $5.00 is received covering the return.

Required:

(1) Open T accounts with each account named in the trial balance of November 30, 19__, and insert the proper account balances.

(2) Record the above transactions in your T-account ledger.

(3) Prepare a trial balance. Record the trial balance on working papers.

(4) Complete the working papers.

(5) Prepare a profit and loss statement for the year January 1 to December 31, 19__. New inventory, $19,094.00.

(6) Prepare a balance sheet, December 31, 19__.

Problem **6–11.** The transactions of F. E. Calhoun for the month of December 19__ were as follows:

(1) He commences business December 1 with cash, $5,000.00, merchandise, $6,000.00, and fixtures, $3,000.00.

(2) $20.00 cash is deposited with the Central Gas & Electric Company as a service deposit. This deposit will be refunded when gas and electric service is terminated.

(3) Sale of merchandise on account to Wells & Company, $714.66.

(4) Purchase of merchandise on account from C. C. Brite, $320.00.

(5) A check for $50.20 is given to the Miller Publishing Company for advertising.

(6) Gas, electric, and telephone bills are paid, $48.60.

(7) Sale of merchandise on account to A. L. Ellsworth, $1,407.00.

(8) Sale on account to Wells & Company, $370.00.

(9) Sale of merchandise for cash to C. E. May, $20.00.

(10) Purchase of merchandise on account from C. C. Brite, $417.82.

(11) Due to an error in pricing, the invoice in transaction #8 is found to be incorrect. The correct amount of the invoice is $307.00.

(12) Wages and salaries are paid, $513.00.

(13) Cash is received from A. L. Ellsworth, $800.00.

(14) The check received as payment for the merchandise sold in transaction #9 is found to be worthless.

(15) Sale of merchandise on account to A. L. Ellsworth, $621.01.

(16) A bill for plumbing repairs is paid, $63.00.

(17) A bill for a plate glass window, broken in an unusually violent storm is paid, $400.00.

Required:

(1) Enter the above transactions in a T-account ledger.

(2) Prepare a trial balance.

(3) Prepare a profit and loss statement for the month of December, 19__. Inventory, December 31, 19__, $4,767.82.

(4) Prepare a balance sheet, December 31, 19__.

Problem 6–12. H. F. Taggart's balance sheet of December 31, 19__, is as follows:

Assets		Liabilities and Net Worth	
Cash	$ 4,000.00	Accounts Payable:	
Accounts Receivable:		G. C. Paxton	$ 2,128.00
Cline & Son	4,061.00	H. M. Richards	6,872.00
M. H. Franklin	100.00	Notes Payable	7,821.00
C. E. Hart	2,353.00		
M. S. Lambert	5,586.00	Total Liabilities	$16,821.00
Merchandise	22,000.00		
Securities	5,000.00	H. F. Taggart, Capital . . .	48,279.00
Delivery Equipment	2,000.00		
Miscellaneous Equipment . .	5,000.00		
Land	3,000.00		
Building	12,000.00		
	$65,100.00		$65,100.00

Following are the transactions for the month of January, 19__:

(1) Merchandise is sold for cash, $4,200.00.

(2) Miscellaneous repairs are paid, $160.00.

(3) An office safe, $125.00, and a typewriter, $100.00, are purchased for cash from the Royal Office Supply Company.

(4) Merchandise is sold on account to Cline & Son, $1,077.00.

(5) Merchandise is purchased on account from Stone & Stewart, $2,260.00.

(6) Notes payable of $5,310.00 are paid.

(7) Merchandise is purchased for cash, $800.00.

(8) Merchandise is sold on account to C. E. Hart, $1,862.00.

(9) Cash is received from Cline & Son, $2,061.00.

(10) Merchandise is sold on account to M. S. Lambert, $5,980.00.

(11) An advertising bill of $300.00 is paid.

(12) Cash is paid to G. C. Paxton, $2,128.00.

(13) Wages are paid, $698.00.

(14) A dividend check of $100.00 is received on the stock owned.

(15) Notes payable are paid, $511.00.

(16) Office supplies are purchased for cash from the Royal Office Supply Company, $213.00. (Debit Office Expense.)

(17) Fuel is purchased for cash, $139.00. (Debit General Expense.)

(18) Miscellaneous expenses are paid, $412.00.

(19) Light, water, and gas bills are paid, $73.00.

(20) Merchandise is sold on account to Cline & Son, $1,474.00.

(21) A check for $2,353.00 is received from C. E. Hart.

(22) Gasoline and oil are purchased on account from M. H. Franklin, $60.00.

(23) Merchandise is purchased on account from H. M. Richards, $3,857.00.

(24) An error in pricing is discovered in the bill covering the merchandise purchased in transaction #5. The correct amount of the bill is $2,143.00.

(25) Paid telephone bill, $28.00.

(26) Repairs to delivery equipment are paid, $24.00.

(27) Paid wages and salaries, $1,484.00.

(28) A check for $5,586.00 is received from M. S. Lambert.

(29) Freight of $10.00 is paid. This is freight on a shipment of merchandise to a customer. Mr. Taggart agreed to absorb the transportation charges.

(30) Merchandise is sold for cash, $6,118.00.

(31) A check for $6,872.00 is mailed to H. M. Richards.

(32) Wages and salaries are paid, $2,289.00.

(33) Merchandise is sold for cash, $750.00.

(34) Scrap and other junk items are sold for cash, $50.00.

(35) Merchandise is sold on account to C. E. Hart for $4,422.00.

(36) Received a 60-day note from Cline & Son for the balance of their December account, $2,000.00.

Required:

(1) Record the above transactions in a T-account ledger.

(2) Draw off a trial balance on working papers.

(3) Complete the working papers.

(4) Prepare a profit and loss statement for the month of January. The merchandise inventory on January 31, 19—, is $11,798.00.

(5) Prepare a balance sheet, January 31, 19—.

Problem **6–13.** B. H. Bates began business on October 1, 19—. His condensed transactions for the three months of October, November, and December are given below.

(1) B. H. Bates begins business with $1,500.00 cash, $4,000.00 of merchandise, and $7,000.00 in readily marketable securities.

(2) Rent is paid, $300.00.

(3) Fixtures and equipment costing $1,200.00 are purchased from the General Office Supply Company. $600.00 in cash is immediately paid, with the balance due at the rate of $100.00 a month.

(4) Merchandise is sold on account to Landers & Son, $635.00.

(5) Merchandise is purchased for cash, $470.00.

(6) Merchandise is sold on account to G. A. Brand, $1,400.00.

(7) Sundry expenses are paid, $100.00.

(8) Merchandise is purchased on account from Haney & Company, $1,330.00.

(9) Sold merchandise on account to J. F. Moore, $2,500.00.

(10) An advertising bill is paid, $120.00.

(11) Borrowed $2,000.00 cash from the bank on a 30-day note for the same amount.

(12) A check is received from Landers & Son, $635.00.

(13) Merchandise is purchased on account from G. O. Shipley, $2,200.00.

(14) A check for $700.00 is mailed to Haney & Company.

(15) The telephone bill is paid, $16.00.

(16) Merchandise is sold for cash, $1,800.00.

(17) Merchandise is sold on account to H. E. Hoover, $3,200.00.

(18) Office supplies are purchased for cash from the General Office Supply Company, $90.00.

(19) Various expenses are paid, $110.00.

(20) Merchandise is returned to G. O. Shipley, $600.00, the merchandise not being the kind ordered.

(21) Merchandise is sold on account to H. E. Hoover, $800.00.

(22) Light, water, and gas bills are paid, $60.00.

(23) Wages and salaries are paid, $1,180.00.

(24) Paid Haney & Company, $680.00 (an overpayment of $50.00).

(25) Merchandise is purchased on account from G. O. Shipley for $2,190.00.

(26) A dividend check for $200.00 is received on the stock owned.

(27) Merchandise is sold for cash, $3,240.00.

(28) A payment of $1,000.00 is made on the note at the bank (originally issued in transaction #11). $10.00 interest is also paid to the bank.

(29) Merchandise is purchased on account from G. O. Shipley, $2,810.00.

(30) A check for $100.00 is cashed for L. V. Homer.

(31) Freight of $10.00 is paid. This is freight arising because of Mr. Bates' error in originally shipping merchandise to a wrong destination.

(32) A check for $200.00 is mailed to the General Office Supply Company.

(33) A 60-day note is received from G. A. Brand in settlement of his account, $1,400.00.

(34) The securities are sold for cash, $7,100.00. (Credit the profit on this sale to Miscellaneous Income.)

(35) Bonds are purchased for cash, $8,000.00.

(36) Wages and salaries are paid, $1,210.00.

Required:

(1) Record the above transactions in a T-account ledger.

(2) Prepare a trial balance.

(3) Prepare a profit and loss statement. Inventory, December 31, 19__, $2,790.00.

(4) Prepare a balance sheet, December 31, 19__.

Chapter 7

THE GENERAL JOURNAL —
THE LEDGER ACCOUNT — POSTING

THE GENERAL JOURNAL

Under double-entry bookkeeping the written record which is made of the debit *and* credit elements of a transaction is called the "entry" for the transaction. The sum of the debit accounts of each entry is, of course, equal to the sum of the credit accounts. Accounting experience has proved that the practice of recording entries *directly in the ledger* has certain serious disadvantages. Conversely, accounting experience has also demonstrated that there are important advantages in the practice of first recording all transactions in a preliminary record and then, later, transferring each of these original, or preliminary, entries to the accounts of the general ledger. The function of this chapter is to introduce and explain this "preliminary" record. This new record is called "the general journal" or, more simply, "the journal."

All transactions are *originally* recorded in the journal. The record of each transaction in the journal is called the "journal entry." Each journal entry must show

(1) The date of the transaction
(2) The account to be debited and the amount
(3) The account to be credited and the amount
(4) An adequate explanation of the entry if the meaning is not clear from the formal debits and credits themselves

An entry in the journal may be looked upon as both the official record of, as well as an authorization for, a change in the accounts of a ledger. No debit or credit, therefore, will be made in a ledger account unless the complete entry has first been recorded in the journal.

A standard form of journal, with two transactions entered, follows on page 103.

The following points should be observed:

(1) The year is written in small figures just above the recording of the first month-date. The year-date is written just once to a page

if all entries on the page come within the year-date recorded at the head of the page.

(2) The name of the account to be debited is written close to the date column. The amount is placed in the first, or debit, column.

GENERAL JOURNAL   Page 1

1950					
Oct.	7	Cash	10000 00		
		H. E. Davenport, Capital		10000 00
		Began business today with		
		cash investment of $10,000.00.		
	8	Rent Expense	150 00		
		Cash		150 00
		Paid rent for month		
		ending November 7.		

(3) The name of the account to be credited is written directly below the debit account but indented one-half inch or more. This is done in order to separate the credit account from the debit account. The amount is placed in the second, or credit, money column.

(4) The explanation is written directly below the last credit account.

(5) One line should be left blank between complete journal entries in order to separate transactions from each other.

(6) The small column immediately to the left of the two money columns is a "ledger folio" column. The use of this column is explained in the next section.

THE LEDGER ACCOUNT

In our discussion thus far, T accounts have been used to represent formal ledger accounts, a standard form of which is shown on page 105.

The information to be recorded in each column is indicated by the column headings. (In practice, these headings are omitted.) The item "Ref." is an abbreviation of "Reference." An alternative name for the "reference" column is "folio" column. The use of the reference, or folio, column is explained below.

In actual practice only one account is placed on each ledger leaf. Ledgers are generally loose-leaf rather than bound.

POSTING

The debit and credit values of all transactions recorded in the general journal must sooner or later be transferred to the proper accounts in the ledger. This "transferring" process is called "posting." The detailed procedure of posting is as follows:

(1) The debit member of a journal entry is posted first.

(2) Turn to the ledger account to be debited. On the debit side of this account enter

   (a) The date — year, month, day. For succeeding entries in an account, the year and month should be recorded only if a change has occurred in the year-date or month-date.

   (b) The journal page from which the debit was taken, J1, J2, J3, etc. The recording of the journal page should be made in the "reference" column.

   (c) The amount.

(3) Turn to the journal. In the ledger folio (i.e., reference) column, record the number of the ledger page to which the debit was posted. The ledger and journal are now cross-indexed to each other.

(4) The credit member of a journal entry is transferred to the

NAME OF ACCOUNT

DATE	EXPLANATION	REF.	DEBIT AMOUNT	DATE	EXPLANATION	REF.	CREDIT AMOUNT

ledger in a similar manner. When this has been done, the journal entry has been completely posted.

The "explanation" column of a ledger account

(1) Is used to record the terms of sale, and often the invoice numbers, which apply to debit postings against a customer's account.

(2) Is used in the Profit and Loss account. Each debit and credit to this account should be explained, as General Expense, Wages, etc.

(3) Is usually left blank with respect to other postings. Comments, however, may be made in the explanation column of any account if such comments are of definite value to the user of the account.

Although there is usually no specific time when posting must be done, as a general rule it should be done at least once a month. More frequent postings may be necessary in order to meet the need for up-to-the-minute information. They may also be desirable in order to avoid the accumulation of too great an amount of posting work. Transactions involving debtor and creditor relationships, especially the former, should be posted daily so that the status of these accounts will be up to date and correct at all times. The student will appreciate the importance of such daily postings in the administration of the credit and collection policy of a business.

ADVANTAGES OF THE JOURNAL

The following favorable considerations are observed:

(1) A chronological record of transactions is provided in one place.

(2) Where transactions are recorded directly in the ledger, the process of re-establishing the complete transaction by reference to the accounts involved is normally very difficult. The journal, however, contains a full record of the transaction in one place, and folio references in the ledger make the re-establishment of the complete transaction relatively easy.

(3) Because there is one explanation of the entry in the journal, it is unnecessary to have repetitive explanations accompany each debit and credit in the ledger. Not only is labor saved but the ledger is simplified by being relieved of a great mass of written material.

(4) There is added certainty that the rule of double entry will be observed, and that the ledger will be kept in balance. This is because each journal entry is a complete double entry in itself; and because the journal and ledger are completely cross-indexed to each other in the posting procedure.

. (5) The journal eliminates the necessity of making immediate entry in the ledger of transactions as they take place. Posting to the ledger may be done at any convenient time. For a large business, especially, this is a consideration of great importance.

(6) The journal facilitates the discovery of errors which have been made.

(a) Failure of the trial balance to balance may be due to an error in posting.

(b) If a sale of $100.00 to E. L. Schott is inadvertently debited to the account of E. J. Shore, the error will not be discovered until E. J. Shore refuses to pay the $100.00 charged to his account. The journal must be referred to in order to ascertain to whom the charge properly belongs. The individual ledger account, it will be noted, does not yield this information.

(7) Courts recognize the journal as evidence in proving or disproving claims. This is because the journal is the book wherein transactions are originally recorded. The journal is a book of original entry, whereas the ledger is only a summary, a transcript, of the original record. Courts do not accept unsupported ledger entries.

(8) Since most businesses find it advisable to use several journals, division and economy of labor are made possible. These journals are explained in Chapter 8.

THE JOURNAL AND LEDGER ILLUSTRATED

The books of L. T. Robinson, reproduced below, illustrate

(1) The use of the journal

(a) In recording actual transactions.
(b) In closing the books.

(2) Posting from the journal to the ledger.
(3) The ledger

(a) After all transactions have been recorded therein, and
(b) After the books have been closed.[1]

If the student studies each journal entry, and traces each debit and credit into the ledger, the complete cycle of bookkeeping procedure should be quite clear to him.

The transactions of L. T. Robinson for the month of February, 1950, are as follows:

February

2 — L. T. Robinson began business with $12,000.00 cash, and $4,000.00 merchandise.

3 — Paid February rent, $300.00.

---

[1] The trial balance and statements are drawn up before the books are closed.

3 — Bought furniture and fixtures from Ester Supply Company for cash, $1,200.00.

4 — Merchandise is sold for cash to J. M. Barrie for $102.00, invoice #1.

5 — Bought merchandise from James J. Logue, $5,000.00.

7 — Sold merchandise to C. F. Ruble on account, $2,378.00, invoice #2.

9 — A cash sale of $28.00 is made to E. T. Maddox, invoice #3.

10 — Merchandise is purchased from Exley & Son for cash, $700.00.

12 — Sold merchandise on account to Clark R. Morgan, $489.00, invoice #4.

12 — Paid James J. Logue, $5,000.00, for bill of February 5.

12 — Merchandise is purchased on account from Henry V. Dana, $408.00, and from James J. Logue, $1,800.00.

14 — General expenses are paid, $510.00.

14 — Merchandise is sold on account to E. V. Sanders, $867.00, invoice #5.

16 — Bought merchandise on account from F. C. Maxton, $62.00.

16 — A cash sale is made to A. L. Nichols, $51.00, invoice #6.

17 — Merchandise is sold on account to C. F. Ruble, $558.00, invoice #7.

19 — Sundry expenses are paid, $116.00.

19 — Clark R. Morgan returns $100.00 of the merchandise purchased by him on February 12 because of inferior quality.

20 — Merchandise is sold on account to H. R. Macy, $599.00, invoice #8.

21 — A check is received from Clark R. Morgan, $389.00.

21 — Merchandise is purchased on account from J. R. Upshaw, $1,800.00, and from James J. Logue, $1,530.00.

23 — Merchandise is sold on account to E. V. Sanders, $85.00, invoice #9.

24 — Cash is received from C. F. Ruble to apply on account, $700.00, and from E. V. Sanders, $85.00.

25 — Merchandise is sold on account to M. G. Sheldon, $1,311.00, invoice #10.

25 — A check for $62.00 is mailed to F. C. Maxton in payment of invoice of February 16.

26 — L. T. Robinson draws cash for personal use, $200.00.

26 — A check for $1,000.00 is given to James J. Logue to apply on account.

27 — L. T. Robinson acts as agent for the Dettle Insurance Company; a policy is sold for which Mr. Robinson receives a check of $63.00 as his commission.

27 — Checks are received from C. F. Ruble, $678.00, and E. V. Sanders, $250.00, to apply on account.

28 — Merchandise is sold on account to Clark R. Morgan, $722.00, invoice #11.

28 — Wages are paid, $231.00.

28 — The merchandise on hand at the close of business is valued at $10,692.00.

JOURNAL   Page 1

1950								
Feb.	2	Cash	1	12,000	00			
		Merchandise	7	4,000	00			
		L. T. Robinson, Capital	13			16,000	00	
		Began business today with above investment.						
	3	Rent Expense	21	300	00			
		Cash	1			300	00	
		Paid rent for month of February.						
	3	Furniture and Fixtures	8	1,200	00			
		Cash	1			1,200	00	
		For purchase from the Ester Supply Company.						
	4	Cash	1	102	00			
		Sales	16			102	00	
		For cash sale to J. M. Barrie, invoice #1.						
	5	Purchases	19	5,000	00			
		James J. Logue	10			5,000	00	
		For merchandise purchased on account.						
	7	C. F. Ruble	4	2,378	00			
		Sales	16			2,378	00	
		For merchandise sold on account, invoice #2.						
	9	Cash	1	28	00			
		Sales	16			28	00	
		For cash sale to E. T. Maddox, invoice #3.						
	10	Purchases	19	700	00			
		Cash	1			700	00	
		For cash purchase from Exley & Son.						
	12	Clark R. Morgan	3	489	00			
		Sales	16			489	00	
		For merchandise sold on account, invoice #4.						
	12	James J. Logue	10	5,000	00			
		Cash	1			5,000	00	
		For payment of bill of February 12.						
	12	Purchases	19	2,208	00			
		Henry V. Dana	9			408	00	
		James J. Logue	10			1,800	00	
		For merchandise purchased on account.						
	14	General Expense	20	510	00			
		Cash	1			510	00	
		For sundry expenses paid today.						
	14	E. V. Sanders	5	867	00			
		Sales	16			867	00	
		For merchandise sold on account, invoice #5.						

JOURNAL   Page 2

1950						
Feb.	16	Purchases	19	62 00		
		F. C. Maxton	11		62	00
		For merchandise purchased on account.				
	16	Cash	1	51 00		
		Sales	16		51	00
		For cash sale to A. L. Nichols, invoice #6.				
	17	C. F. Ruble	4	558 00		
		Sales	16		558	00
		For merchandise sold on account, invoice #7.				
	19	General Expense	20	116 00		
		Cash	1		116	00
	19	Returned Sales and Allowances	17	100 00		
		Clark R. Morgan	3		100	00
		For merchandise returned because of inferior quality, originally purchased February 12.				
	20	H. R. Macy	2	599 00		
		Sales	16		599	00
		For merchandise sold on account, invoice #8.				
	21	Cash	1	389 00		
		Clark R. Morgan	3		389	00
		For balance due on invoice February 12.				
	21	Purchases	19	1,800 00		
		J. R. Upshaw	12		1,800	00
		For merchandise purchased on account.				
	21	Purchases	19	1,530 00		
		James J. Logue	10		1,530	00
		For merchandise purchased on account.				
	23	E. V. Sanders	5	85 00		
		Sales	16		85	00
		For merchandise sold on account, invoice #9.				
	24	Cash	1	785 00		
		C. F. Ruble	4		700	00
		E. V. Sanders	5		85	00
		For cash received on above accounts.				
	25	M. G. Sheldon	6	1,311 00		
		Sales	16		1,311	00
		For merchandise sold on account, invoice #10.				
	25	F. C. Maxton	11	62 00		
		Cash	1		62	00
		For payment of invoice of February 16.				
	26	L. T. Robinson, Personal	14	200 00		
		Cash	1		200	00
		For cash withdrawn for personal use.				

JOURNAL   Page 3

1950							
Feb.	26	James J. Logue	10	1,000	00		
		Cash	1			1,000	00
		For check give to apply on account.					
	27	Cash	1	63	00		
		Commissions Earned	23			63	00
		For check received as commission on sale of policy for Dettle Insurance Company.					
	27	Cash	1	928	00		
		C. F. Ruble	4			678	00
		E. V. Sanders	5			250	00
		For cash received on above accounts.					
	28	Clark R. Morgan	3	722	00		
		Sales	16			722	00
		For sale made on account, invoice #11.					
	28	Wages Expense	22	231	00		
		Cash	1			231	00
		For payment of wages for February.					
	28	Cost of Sales	18	15,300	00		
		Merchandise	7			4,000	00
		Purchases	19			11,300	00
		To transfer February 1 inventory, and month's purchases to Cost of Sales.					
	28	Merchandise	7	10,692	00		
		Cost of Sales	18			10,692	00
		To set up inventory as of February 28.					
	28	Profit and Loss	15	4,608	00		
		Cost of Sales	18			4,608	00
		To transfer balance of Cost of Sales to Profit and Loss account.					
	28	Profit and Loss	15	100	00		
		Returned Sales and Allowances	17			100	00
		To close latter account.					
	28	Sales	16	7,190	00		
		Profit and Loss	15			7,190	00
		To close former account.					
	28	Profit and Loss	15	1,157	00		
		General Expense	20			626	00
		Rent Expense	21			300	00
		Wages Expense	22			231	00
		To transfer expenses to Profit and Loss account.					
	28	Commissions Earned	23	63	00		
		Profit and Loss	15			63	00
		To transfer former account to Profit and Loss account.					

JOURNAL   Page 4

1950						
Feb.	28	Profit and Loss	15	1,388	00	
		L. T. Robinson, Capital	13			1,388	00
		To transfer profit to Robinson's capital account.				
	28	L. T. Robinson, Capital	13	200	00	
		L. T. Robinson, Personal	14			200	00
		To transfer balance of Robinson's personal account				
		to capital account.				

LEDGER

CASH   Page 1

1950						1950					
Feb.	2		J1	12,000	00	Feb.	3		J1	300	00
	4		J1	102	00		3		J1	1,200	00
	9		J1	28	00		10		J1	700	00
	16		J2	51	00		12		J1	5,000	00
	21		J2	389	00		14		J1	510	00
	24		J2	785	00		19		J2	116	00
	27		J3	63	00		25		J2	62	00
	27		J3	928	00		26		J2	200	00
							26		J3	1,000	00
							28		J3	231	00

H. R. MACY   Page 2

1950					
Feb.	20		J2	599	00

CLARK R. MORGAN   Page 3

1950						1950					
Feb.	12		J1	489	00	Feb.	19		J2	100	00
	28		J3	722	00		21		J2	389	00

C. F. RUBLE   Page 4

1950						1950					
Feb.	7		J1	2,378	00	Feb.	24		J2	700	00
	17		J2	558	00		27		J3	678	00

E. V. SANDERS   Page 5

| 1950 Feb. | 14 | | J1 | 867 | 00 | 1950 Feb. | 24 | | J2 | 85 | 00 |
| | 23 | | J2 | 85 | 00 | | 27 | | J3 | 250 | 00 |

M. G. SHELDON   Page 6

| 1950 Feb. | 25 | | J2 | 1,311 | 00 | | | | | | |

MERCHANDISE   Page 7

| 1950 Feb. | 2 | | J1 | 4,000 | 00 | 1950 Feb. | 28 | To Cost of Sales | J3 | 4,000 | 00 |
| | 28 | | J3 | 10,692 | 00 | | | | | | |

FURNITURE AND FIXTURES   Page 8

| 1950 Feb. | 3 | | J1 | 1,200 | 00 | | | | | | |

HENRY V. DANA   Page 9

| | | | | | | 1950 Feb. | 12 | | J1 | 408 | 00 |

JAMES J. LOGUE   Page 10

1950 Feb.	12		J1	5,000	00	1950 Feb.	5		J1	5,000	00
	26		J3	1,000	00		12		J1	1,800	00
							21		J2	1,530	00

F. C. MAXTON   Page 11

| 1950 Feb. | 25 | | J2 | 62 | 00 | 1950 Feb. | 16 | | J2 | 62 | 00 |

J. R. UPSHAW   Page 12

					1950					
					Feb.	21		J2	1,800	00

L. T. ROBINSON, CAPITAL   Page 13

1950						1950					
Feb.	28	Drawings	J4	200	00	Feb.	2	Investment	J1	16,000	00
							28	Net Income	J4	1,388	00

L. T. ROBINSON, PERSONAL   Page 14

1950						1950					
Feb.	26		J2	200	00	Feb.	28		J4	200	00

PROFIT AND LOSS   Page 15

1950						1950					
Feb.	28	Cost of Sales	J3	4,608	00	Feb.	28	Sales	J3	7,190	00
	28	Rtd. Sales & Allowances	J3	100	00		28	Commissions Earned	J3	63	00
	28	General Expense	J3	626	00						
	28	Rent Expense	J3	300	00						
	28	Wages Expense	J3	231	00						
	28	To L. T. Robinson, Capital	J4	1,388	00						
				7,253	00					7,253	00

SALES   Page 16

1950						1950				
Feb.	28	To P. & L.	J3	7,190	00	Feb.	4	J1	102	00
							7	J1	2,378	00
							9	J1	28	00
							12	J1	489	00
							14	J1	867	00
							16	J2	51	00
							17	J2	558	00
							20	J2	599	00
							23	J2	85	00
							25	J2	1,311	00
							28	J3	722	00
				7,190	00				7,190	00

RETURNED SALES AND ALLOWANCES   Page 17

1950					1950				
Feb.	19		J2	100 00	Feb.	28	To P. & L.	J3	100 00

COST OF SALES   Page 18

1950					1950				
Feb.	28		J3	4,000 00	Feb.	28		J3	10,692 00
	28		J3	11,300 00		28	To P. & L.	J3	4,608 00
				15,300 00					15,300 00

PURCHASES   Page 19

1950					1950				
Feb.	5		J1	5,000 00	Feb.	28	To Cost of Sales	J3	11,300 00
	10		J1	700 00					
	12		J1	2,208 00					
	16		J2	62 00					
	21		J2	1,800 00					
	21		J2	1,530 00					
				11,300 00					11,300 00

GENERAL EXPENSE   Page 20

1950					1950				
Feb.	14		J1	510 00	Feb.	28	To P. & L.	J3	626 00
	19		J2	116 00					
				626 00					626 00

RENT EXPENSE   Page 21

1950					1950				
Feb.	3		J1	300 00	Feb.	28	To P. & L.	J3	300 00

WAGES EXPENSE   Page 22

1950					1950				
Feb.	28		J3	231 00	Feb.	28	To P. & L.	J3	231 00

COMMISSIONS EARNED   Page 23

1950						1950					
Feb.	28	To P. & L.	J3	63	00	Feb.	27		J3	63	00

The following trial balance is taken from the ledger of L. T. Robinson before the books have been closed:

L. T. Robinson

TRIAL BALANCE, FEBRUARY 28, 1950

Cash	$ 5,027.00	
H. R. Macy	599.00	
Clark R. Morgan	722.00	
C. F. Ruble	1,558.00	
E. V. Sanders	617.00	
M. G. Sheldon	1,311.00	
Merchandise	4,000.00	
Furniture and Fixtures	1,200.00	
Henry V. Dana		$ 408.00
James J. Logue		2,330.00
J. R. Upshaw		1,800.00
L. T. Robinson, Capital		16,000.00
L. T. Robinson, Personal	200.00	
Sales		7,190.00
Returned Sales and Allowances.	100.00	
Purchases	11,300.00	
General Expense	626.00	
Rent Expense	300.00	
Wages Expense.	231.00	
Commissions Earned		63.00
	$27,791.00	$27,791.00

The profit and loss statement and the balance sheet to be prepared from this trial balance will not be illustrated here because the statements will be almost identical with those illustrated in Chapter 6, pages 82 and 83. The only change will be in the profit and loss statement where sales will be shown:

Gross Sales	$7,190.00
Less Returned Sales and Allowances	100.00
Net Sales	$7,090.00

(Returned sales and allowances, and returned purchases and allowances, are also illustrated in the profit and loss statement on page 172.)

NEW ACCOUNTS

Two new accounts are introduced in the L. T. Robinson problem:

(1) *Returned Sales and Allowances.*   (See entry of February 19.) This account, a subdivision of the Sales account, is opened in order to show in one account the amount of

   (a)   Sales returned by customers.
   (b)   Sales rebates.
   (c)   Sales allowances.   Occasionally a customer intending to return merchandise to the seller may be prevailed upon to keep the merchandise provided a reduction is made in the amount of the bill.   A concession of this kind is called an allowance.   A sales allowance by the vendor is a purchase allowance to the vendee.

The function of the Returned Sales and Allowances account, therefore, is to record direct deductions from sales; and that of the Sales account, gross sales only.   At the end of the accounting period when the books are being closed, the Returned Sales and Allowances account, like the Sales account, is transferred directly to the Profit and Loss account.

Conversely, the function of the Returned Purchases and Allowances account would be to record direct deductions from purchases; and of the Purchases account, gross purchases only.   At the end of the accounting period when the books are being closed, the Returned Purchases and Allowances account, like the Purchases account, is transferred directly to the Cost of Sales account.

(2) *L. T. Robinson, Personal.* (See entry of February 26.) Heretofore, the assets withdrawn from a business by the proprietor have been debited to the Capital account in recording the reduction in the amount of his net worth.   It is better practice, however, to record current proprietary withdrawals in a separate withdrawal account. The proprietor's withdrawal account is usually referred to as his Personal account, or as his Drawing account.

When merchandise is withdrawn by a proprietor, his drawing account should be debited at cost, and Purchases credited.

The drawing account of a proprietor should not be debited for withdrawals of invested capital.   Such drawings — large or permanent withdrawals of capital — should be debited to Capital account.

At the end of the accounting period, when the books are being closed, the balance of the proprietor's drawing or personal account should be transferred to his Capital account.[2]

---

[2] In this connection the following alternative accounting is sometimes used: (1) Drawings are debited to Drawing account, (2) the net income of the period is transferred to Drawing account, and (3) the new balance of the Drawing account is trans-

THE STATEMENT OF CAPITAL

At the end of an accounting period, the Capital account of a proprietorship will show

(1) The capital at the beginning of the period.
(2) Increases of capital during the period
    (a) By additional capital investment.
    (b) By the net income earned during the period.
(3) Decreases of capital during the period
    (a) By withdrawals of capital investment, if any.
    (b) By the total of proprietary drawings for the period (i.e., total of proprietor's Drawing account).
    (c) By the net loss for the period.
(4) The capital at the end of the period.

The information in the Capital account may be reported in a statement of capital. For the L. T. Robinson problem this statement would be:

L. T. Robinson

STATEMENT OF CAPITAL, FEBRUARY 1–28, 1950

Capital, February 1, 1950	$16,000.00
Add Net income for February	1,388.00
	$17,388.00
Less Drawings	200.00
Capital, February 28, 1950	$17,188.00

THE ACCOUNTING CYCLE

This chapter carries to completion the description and exposition of fundamental bookkeeping method. It may be of advantage, therefore, to summarize at this point the various steps of the accounting cycle which have been described thus far. In the order of performance these steps are

---

ferred to Capital account. Although the result is the same in the end, the method does not warrant full endorsement for these reasons:

Profits are additions to the net worth of a business. Drawings are deductions from net worth. The Capital account should give full information as to the total added to capital by profits, also the reduction of net worth by withdrawals. The information in the Capital account should parallel that contained in the statement of capital. The Capital account should show increases and decreases in capital, not their net difference. Drawings are simply withdrawals of capital via debits to the Drawing account.

If it were proper to debit the drawings of a period against net profits, it would also appear proper to debit the dividends of a corporation against the net income of a period. The remainder would be transferred to Surplus. Few accountants would approve this corporate accounting.

(1) Journalizing accounting transactions.

(2) Posting journal entries to the ledger.

(3) Preparing the trial balance.

  (*Note:* The work sheet, if used, should be prepared at this point.)

(4) Preparing the profit and loss statement.

(5) Preparing the balance sheet.

(6) Closing the books. This step is generally performed but once a year, at the end of the formal accounting period.

In this order of work it is important to observe that closing entries can be conveniently and quickly prepared through the use of the profit and loss statement. In the transfer of nominal accounts to Profit and Loss, it is well to have the order of the journal entries follow the order of items on the profit and loss statement: that is, the first entry will transfer Sales, and Returned Sales and Allowances, to Profit and Loss; the next entries will transfer Merchandise and Purchases to Cost of Sales; then, after the new inventory has been set up, Cost of Sales will be transferred to Profit and Loss; operating expenses will next be transferred to Profit and Loss, and so on.

Underlying the accounting cycle is the basic principle that business records, in order to be worth while, must be maintained upon the twin fundamentals of honesty and accuracy. Trustworthiness in accounting records is of paramount importance not only to managements, owners, investors, and accountants, but to all who would establish legal rights through the use of accounting information.

QUESTIONS

Question **7–1.** What is the function of the journal? Why must all transactions be recorded in the journal? What are the advantages of the journal?

Question **7–2.** Define, and tell what information is embraced by, a complete journal entry.

Question **7–3.** (1) Define posting. (2) Describe in detail the steps of the posting procedure. (3) When should posting be done? Explain fully.

Question **7–4.** What are the functions of the Sales account? the Returned Sales and Allowances account? the Purchases account? the Returned Purchases and Allowances account?

Question **7–5.** To what account should the balance of the Returned Sales and Allowances account be transferred at the end of the accounting period? the Returned Purchases and Allowances account?

Question **7–6.** Describe the accounting which attaches to the personal and capital accounts of the owner of a business.

Question **7–7.** What is the purpose of the statement of capital? What information is contained in this statement?

Question **7–8.** What are the proper journal entries to record the following transactions of C. M. Harder?

    (1) Sale of merchandise on account to B. J. Gordon, $1,200.00.

    (2) Mr. Harder prepays the freight on the shipment of transaction #1 with the understanding that he is to be reimbursed by Mr. Gordon, $17.00.

    (3) One of the cartons of the Gordon shipment is found to contain merchandise of substandard quality. A credit of $32.00 is accordingly passed to the account of Mr. Gordon.

    (4) Wages and salaries are paid, $1,214.00.

    (5) A note receivable for $685.00 is received from B. J. Gordon.

    (6) Sale of merchandise for cash to B. J. Gordon, $78.00.

    (7) The invoice for the merchandise sold in transaction #6 is later found to be incorrectly totaled. The correct amount of the invoice is $87.00. The additional amount is charged to Mr. Gordon's account in the ledger.

    (8) A check for $500.00 is received from B. J. Gordon.

    (9) A check for $685.00 is received from B. J. Gordon in payment of the note originally received in transaction #5.

    (10) Another check for $15.85 is received from B. J. Gordon in payment of the interest on the note of transactions #5 and #9, $6.85; and $9.00 for the additional charge covered by transaction #7.

Question **7–9.** With respect to the transactions in Question 7–8, what journal entries should be made by Mr. Gordon? (Disregard transaction #4.)

PROBLEMS

Problem **7–1.** L. J. Danvers commenced business on December 1, 19__, with cash, $15,000.00, and merchandise, $5,000.00. His condensed transactions for the month of December were

December

    5 — Purchased merchandise on account from Rice & Redding, $3,000.00.

    9 — Purchased fixtures for cash from Key & Co., Inc., $2,000.00.

    12 — Returned merchandise to Rice & Redding, $50.00. (Credit the Returned Purchases & Allowances account.)

    15 — Sold merchandise on account to Perry & Co., $7,000.00.

    17 — Paid general expenses, $1,500.00.

21 — Sold merchandise on account to Perry & Co., $1,250.00.

25 — Paid advertising, $200.00.

Required:

(1) Record the above transactions in the journal.

(2) Post to the ledger, using formal accounts.

(3) Prepare a trial balance.

(4) Prepare a profit and loss statement. Inventory, December 31, 19__, $1,750.00.

(5) Prepare a balance sheet, December 31, 19__.

(6) Make journal entries to close books and post.

Problem **7–2.** Following is the trial balance of J. G. Royce on December 31, 19__:

Cash	$ 6,031.00	
Lambert & Co.	1,250.00	
R. V. Smith & Son	1,490.00	
Taylor & Ward	724.00	
Notes Receivable	6,000.00	
Merchandise	4,800.00	
Furniture and Fixtures	1,661.00	
Dow & Son		$ 720.00
F. A. Melton		675.00
W. P. Waner & Co.		210.00
J. G. Royce, Capital		19,000.00
Sales		18,402.00
Purchases	10,560.00	
General Expense	752.00	
Rent Expense	600.00	
Wages Expense	5,410.00	
Interest Income		271.00
	$39,278.00	$39,278.00

Required:

(1) Prepare a work sheet. New inventory, December 31, 19__, $5,000.00.

(2) Prepare a profit and loss statement for the year.

(3) Prepare a balance sheet, December 31, 19__.

(4) Make journal entries to close the books.

Problem **7–3.** Following is the trial balance of William B. Elliott on December 31, 19__:

Cash	$ 12,000.00
Accounts Receivable	18,000.00
Securities	20,000.00
Merchandise	16,000.00
Equipment and Fixtures	6,000.00
Land	5,000.00
Building	30,000.00

Accounts Payable		$ 19,000.00
Notes Payable		10,000.00
William B. Elliott, Capital		70,000.00
Sales		64,000.00
Returned Sales	4,000.00	
Purchases	34,000.00	
Returned Purchases		1,000.00
Delivery Expenses	3,000.00	
Insurance Expense	200.00	
Miscellaneous Expense	5,000.00	
Property Taxes	800.00	
Wages Expense	11,000.00	
Dividend Income		1,000.00
	$165,000.00	$165,000.00

Required:

(1) Prepare a work sheet. New inventory, $15,000.00.
(2) Prepare a profit and loss statement for the year 19___.
(3) Prepare a balance sheet, December 31, 19___.
(4) Make journal entries necessary to close the books.

Problem **7–4.** The trial balance of James E. Wilson on December 31, 19___, was as follows:

Cash	$ 3,750.00	
Notes Receivable	3,000.00	
Interest Receivable	50.00	
Robert L. Black	1,750.00	
T. R. Sharp	1,000.00	
John S. Winter	1,000.00	
C. H. Young	4,000.00	
Merchandise	7,000.00	
Delivery Equipment	1,700.00	
Store Equipment	2,500.00	
Land	5,000.00	
Building	15,000.00	
D. E. Hill		$ 3,000.00
G. J. Jackson		6,050.00
Stein & Sons		1,500.00
Taxes Payable		150.00
James E. Wilson, Capital		41,650.00
Sales		38,000.00
Returned Sales	1,200.00	
Purchases	40,000.00	
Returned Purchases		1,050.00
General Expenses	800.00	
Selling Expenses	400.00	
Taxes Expense	300.00	
Traveling Expense	150.00	
Wages and Salaries	3,000.00	
Interest Income		200.00
	$91,600.00	$91,600.00

Required:

(1) Prepare a work sheet. The new inventory on December 31, 19__, was $16,950.00.

(2) Prepare a profit and loss statement for the year 19__.

(3) Prepare a balance sheet, December 31, 19__.

(4) Make journal entries to close the books.

Problem **7-5.** John A. Henderson has the following information before him at the end of the year 19__:

Accounts Payable	$ 20,000.00
Accounts Receivable	26,000.00
Building	37,000.00
Cash	24,000.00
Commissions Earned	1,200.00
Fuel Expense	200.00
General Expense	5,000.00
John A. Henderson, Capital	100,000.00
Interest Receivable	500.00
Interest Income	1,400.00
Land	8,000.00
Merchandise, January 1, 19—	20,000.00
Merchandise, December 31, 19—	22,000.00
Notes Payable	10,000.00
Notes Receivable	23,500.00
Purchases	121,000.00
Rent Expense	1,200.00
Sales	150,000.00
Wages and Salaries	16,200.00

Required:

(1) Record the trial balance on a work sheet. Complete the work sheet.

(2) Prepare a profit and loss statement for the year ending December 31, 19__.

(3) Prepare a balance sheet, December 31, 19__.

(4) Prepare journal entries to close the books.

Problem **7-6.** The following accounts comprise the trial balance of F. L. Clark on December 31, 19__:

Building	$ 30,300.00
A. L. Carson (accounts payable)	7,000.00
R. J. Casey (accounts receivable)	11,000.00
Cash	27,000.00
F. L. Clark, Capital	130,000.00
F. L. Clark, Personal	5,000.00
General Expense	10,000.00
E. A. Gregory (accounts receivable)	9,000.00
Interest Expense	2,500.00
J. M. Kraft & Co. (accounts payable)	8,000.00
Land	5,000.00
Merchandise	40,000.00
Mortgage Payable (due in 10 years)	10,000.00
G. L. Porter (accounts receivable)	10,000.00
Purchases	90,000.00

Returned Purchases.	1,000.00
Returned Sales	1,200.00
Sales	100,000.00
Selling Expense	20,000.00
W. L. Templin & Son (accounts payable)	5,000.00

Required:

(1) Arrange the above information in trial balance form.

(2) Prepare a profit and loss statement for the year 19__. The inventory of merchandise on December 31, 19__, is $70,000.00.

(3) Prepare a balance sheet, December 31, 19__.

Problem **7–7.** Following are the transactions of Arthur C. Kellogg for the month of December 19__:

December

   1 — Began business with cash, $10,000.00, merchandise, $3,000.00, building, $14,000.00, and land, $3,000.00.

   4 — Fixtures and equipment are purchased from Lane & Gay, Inc., for cash, $1,000.00.

   6 — Bought merchandise on account from L. A. Clark, $8,000.00.

   7 — Sold merchandise on account to Todd & Son, $2,050.00.

   7 — Wages and salaries are paid, $80.00.

  10 — Bought merchandise for cash from G. S. Evans & Co., $600.00.

  12 — Traveling expenses are paid, $300.00.

  14 — Wages and salaries are paid, $100.00.

  16 — Sold merchandise on account to J. P. White, $1,000.00.

  17 — A payment of $5,000.00 is made on the purchase of December 6.

  19 — Advertising is paid, $500.00.

  21 — Wages and salaries are paid, $120.00.

  23 — Sold merchandise on account to Todd & Son, $1,470.00.

  24 — General expenses are paid, $100.00.

  25 — Bought merchandise on account from G. S. Evans & Co., $1,600.00.

  26 — Cash is received from J. P. White, $500.00.

  28 — Wages and salaries are paid, $150.00.

Required:

(1) Record the above transactions in the general journal.

(2) Post to the ledger.

(3) Draw off a trial balance.

(4) Prepare a profit and loss statement. Inventory, December 31, 19__, is $10,531.00.

(5) Prepare a balance sheet, December 31, 19__.

(6) Close the books.

Problem **7–8.** The transactions of J. L. Reed for the month of December, 19__, were as follows:

December

1 — J. L. Reed began business with cash, $15,000.00, merchandise, $10,000.00.

2 — Paid rent for the month of December, $400.00.

3 — Bought furniture and fixtures from Beaumont Supply Company for cash, $1,596.00.

5 — Bought merchandise on credit from John T. Norton, $11,704.00.

6 — Sold merchandise on account to Richard E. Patterson, $3,162.74.

10 — Purchased merchandise for cash from Athens & Sherr, Inc., $931.00.

12 — Sold merchandise on account to W. D. Sutton, $2,808.96.

12 — Paid John T. Norton, $6,000.00.

15 — Paid general expenses, $678.30.

17 — Sold merchandise on account to Richard E. Patterson, $3,591.00.

19 — W. D. Sutton returns $100.00 of the merchandise sold him on December 12.

19 — Paid sundry expenses, $154.28.

20 — Purchased merchandise for cash from Goodwin & Company, $2,394.00.

23 — Cash is received from Richard E. Patterson to apply on account, $900.00.

24 — J. L. Reed drew cash for personal use, $300.00.

27 — During the month Mr. Reed sublet a part of his store. A check for $100.00 is received from the tenant in payment of December rent.

31 — Wages for the month are paid, $1,307.23.

Required:

(1) Record the above transactions in the general journal.

(2) Post to the ledger.

(3) Draw off a trial balance.

(4) Prepare a profit and loss statement for the month. Inventory, December 31, 19__, $17,720.36.

(5) Prepare a balance sheet, December 31, 19__.

(6) Close the books.

Problem **7–9.** The transactions of Harry C. Chase for the month of December, 19__, were:

December

1 — Began business with cash, $13,200.00, merchandise, $2,200.00, and marketable securities, $2,600.00.

2 — Paid month's rent, $300.00.

3 — Bought furniture and fixtures from the Wells Supply Company for cash, $1,320.00.

5 — Sold merchandise for cash to C. R. Morgan, $199.10.

7 — Purchased merchandise for cash from Lancey & Son, $770.00.

10 — Sold merchandise on account to C. R. Morgan, $5,380.10.

12 — Paid general expenses, $688.60.

14 — Purchased merchandise on account from J. W. Smith, $7,997.00.

15 — Mr. Chase withdrew cash for personal use, $200.00.

17 — Received a 60-day note from C. R. Morgan to apply on account, $2,000.00.

19 — Purchased merchandise on account from Lancey & Son, $3,663.00.

20 — Mailed to J. W. Smith a check for $4,997.00, and a 90-day note for $3,000.00, in payment of invoice of December 14.

23 — Sold merchandise on account to Massey & Co., $2,229.80.

26 — Returned merchandise to Lancey & Son, $663.00.

27 — Received a check from C. R. Morgan to apply on account, $1,690.05.

28 — Various utility expense bills (gas, light, water, etc.) are paid, $50.60.

29 — Merchandise is returned by Massey & Co. as unsatisfactory, $229.80.

30 — Dividend checks are received on the securities owned, $69.30.

31 — Wages for the month are paid, $354.10.

Required:

(1) Record the above transactions in the journal.

(2) Post to the ledger.

(3) Draw off a trial balance, December 31, 19__.

(4) Prepare a profit and loss statement for the month of December, 19__. New inventory, $8,549.00.

(5) Prepare a balance sheet, December 31, 19__.

(6) Close the books.

Problem **7-10.** The following accounts represent the ledger of E. A. Stuart on December 31, 19__:

Accounts Payable	$11,000.00
Accounts Receivable	12,000.00
Advertising	1,627.00
Building	15,000.00
Cash	7,133.00
Delivery Equipment	3,650.00
General Expense	861.00
Insurance Expense	201.00
Interest Expense	430.00
Interest Income	500.00
Inventory	7,804.00
Land	3,000.00
Mortgage Payable (due 10 years from now)	7,000.00
Notes Payable	5,000.00
Notes Receivable	5,200.00
Office Equipment	3,000.00
Property Taxes	760.00
Purchases	54,702.00
Returned Purchases and Allowances	1,001.00
Returned Sales and Allowances	4,307.00
Sales	80,731.00
Social Security Taxes	369.00

E. A. Stuart, Capital.	50,000.00
E. A. Stuart, Personal	6,000.00
Taxes Payable	1,059.00
Traveling Expense	312.00
U.S. Treasury Bonds	20,000.00
Utilities Expense	719.00
Wages and Salaries	9,216.00

Required:

(1) Record the trial balance on a work sheet.

(2) Complete the work sheet. Inventory, December 31, 19__, $8,211.00.

(3) Prepare a profit and loss statement for the year ending December 31, 19__.

(4) Prepare a balance sheet, December 31, 19__. Show subtotals for current assets, fixed assets, current liabilities, fixed liabilities, and all liabilities.

(5) Prepare a statement of capital for the year ending December 31, 19__.

(6) Prepare journal entries to close the books.

Chapter 8

DIVISION OF THE JOURNAL

BREAKUP OF THE GENERAL JOURNAL INTO SEVERAL JOURNALS

The general journal may be employed to record all business transactions, but to do so results in a mixture of all kinds of transactions. It has been found expedient to divide the general journal into several journals, one for each major type of transaction. The journals most commonly used today are the following:

Sales Journal		Sales Book
Purchases Journal	commonly	Purchases Book
Cash Receipts Journal	known	Cash Receipts Book
Cash Payments Journal	as	Cash Payments Book
General Journal		Journal

The sales book is used to record sales of merchandise only.

The purchases book is used to record purchases of merchandise only.

The cash receipts book is used to record all receipts of cash.

The cash payments book is used to record all disbursements of cash.

The journal is used to record only those transactions which cannot be entered in one of the other journals.

BOOKS OF ORIGINAL ENTRY

Journals are known as "books of original entry" because each is a book of original entry for a certain class of transaction. Postings are made directly to the ledger from each of these books of original entry.

An entry which has been recorded in one of these books must not be recorded also in another journal. For example, a merchandise purchase (on credit) is recorded in the purchases book, and there only; a sale on credit is recorded in the sales book only; cash received is recorded in the cash receipts book only, and cash disbursements are recorded in the cash payments book only.

Some transactions, however, are so complex that they cannot be recorded in their entirety in only one book of original entry. A transaction of this kind should be broken up into its component parts, and each part made the basis of a separate entry in one of the books of original entry. [See examples (C), (D), (E), and (F), pages 136–137.]

SALES BOOK

All merchandise sales on credit are recorded in this journal from an office copy of the sales invoice. The layout of the sales book is not like that of the general journal of the previous chapter, but this difference in form does not involve any breach of the rule of double entry. A typical sales book is as follows:

SALES BOOK   Page 1

Date	Invoice No.	Debit Account of	L.F.	Amount
1950				
Feb. 7	2	C. F. Ruble		2,378 00
12	4	Clark R. Morgan		489 00
14	5	E. V. Sanders		867 00
17	7	C. F. Ruble		558 00
20	8	H. R. Macy		599 00
23	9	E. V. Sanders		85 00
25	10	M. G. Sheldon		1,311 00
28	11	Clark R. Morgan		722 00
28		Sales, Credit		7,009 00

Each sale on account involves

(1) A debit to a customer's account, and
(2) A credit to the Sales account.[1]

This is also the interpretation to be given each entry in a sales book. In the one above there are 8 sales recorded, each representing a debit to a customer's account and a credit to the Sales account. There are 8 debits and 8 credits, but although the 8 debits are posted to as many different accounts, the 8 credits are all posted to the same account, Sales. Why not, instead, post these credits in total, and thus save the labor of 7 postings? If, instead of 8 sales, there were 800 sales, why not post the 800 credits in total, and thus save the labor of 799 postings? Thus the great advantage of a sales book becomes apparent: although debits must continue to be posted individually to customers' accounts, credits are posted in total to the

---

[1] Each entry for a sale is made by authority of an office copy of the sales invoice.

Sales account (at the end of the month). In this way the detailed credit postings which would otherwise be necessary are avoided.

It will be observed that the sales book permits debit items to be posted daily. Credit items are deferred until the end of the month, when they are posted in total.

In the L.F. column of the sales book should be recorded the ledger page to which each item is posted. In the ledger itself reference will be made to S1, meaning that the entry in the ledger account came from the sales book, page 1.

PURCHASES BOOK

All merchandise purchases on credit are recorded in the purchases book from the purchase invoice.[2] Invoices for merchandise, as well as invoices for other expenditures, should be recorded in the books after the invoices have been verified in detail. In large businesses it is quite common to require a responsible approval for each step of the verification process, each invoice being rubber-stamped as follows:

```
Purchase Order No.....     _____
Received O.K.........      _____
Prices O.K............     _____
Terms O.K............      _____
Computations O.K.....      _____
Bill No...............     _____
Entered..............      _____
```

The form of the purchases book is similar to that of the sales book:

PURCHASES BOOK   Page 1

Date [3]		Credit Account of	L.F.	Amount	
1950					
Feb.	5	James J. Logue		5,000	00
	12	Henry V. Dana		408	00
	12	James J. Logue		1,800	00
	16	F. C. Maxton		62	00
	21	J. R. Upshaw		1,800	00
	21	James J. Logue		1,530	00
	28	Purchases, Debit		10,600	00

[2] Other invoices, those for services, supplies, equipment, etc., will, for the time being, be recorded in the simplest way: one recording made at the time of payment.

[3] Purchase invoices are entered in the purchases book under date of the invoice.

Additional columns may be employed to show the following:

(1) Address of creditor.
(2) Bill number, if invoices are numbered as received.
(3) Terms of invoice.

As a general rule, columns of this kind are justified only by the test of genuine serviceability. Even when provided for, they are very often more honored in the breach than the observance of their intended use.

Each purchase on account represents

(1) A debit to the Purchases account, and
(2) A credit to a creditor's account.

The purchases book above records six merchandise purchases on account, and therefore represents

(1) Six debits to the Purchases account, and
(2) Six credits to the several personal accounts named.

But, following the principle employed in posting from the sales book, instead of posting the six debits separately, they are posted in total to the Purchases account at the end of the month. To summarize the posting of the purchases book;

(1) The debits are posted in total to the Purchases account (at the end of the month) to avoid the detailed debit postings which would otherwise be necessary.

(2) The credits are posted individually to creditors' accounts.

The purchases book permits credit items to be posted daily; the posting of the debit total is deferred until the end of the month.

In the L.F. column of the purchases book should be placed the ledger page to which each item is posted. In the ledger, reference

---

The purchases book is usually "held open" for a few days after the close of a month in order to permit the recording of purchases made in the closing days of the month. In case a purchase invoice of one month must be recorded in the purchases book of the next month, the date column should show this fact:

DATE		CREDIT ACCOUNT OF
1950 Dec.	11/25	The Chandler Company . . . . .

The date should be similarly shown in the creditor's account. The reason for showing the date in this way is to establish the month of entry and to facilitate the checking of a creditor's account in case differences arise.

will be made to P1, indicating that the entry in the ledger account came from the purchases book, page 1.

Although the layout of the purchases book does not specifically designate that the Purchases account is to be debited, the fact that a transaction is entered in the purchases book implies a debit to the Purchases account, just as an entry in the sales book implies a credit to the Sales account. At the end of the month these implied debits and credits are formally recognized and posted in total to the ledger.

CASH RECEIPTS BOOK

In this book are recorded all receipts of cash.[4] A simple cash receipts book is as follows:

CASH RECEIPTS BOOK   Page 1

DATE		ACCOUNT CREDITED	EXPLANATION	L.F.	AMOUNT	
1950						
Feb.	2	L. T. Robinson, Capital	Cash investment		12,000	00
	4	Sales	Invoice #1, J. M. Barrie		102	00
	9	Sales	Invoice #3, E. T. Maddox		28	00
	16	Sales	Invoice #6, A. L. Nichols		51	00
	21	Clark R. Morgan	Balance invoice Feb. 12		389	00
	24	C. F. Ruble	On account		700	00
	24	E. V. Sanders	Invoice February 23		85	00
	27	Commissions Earned	For commission on sale of policy for Dettle Insurance Company		63	00
	27	C. F. Ruble	On account		678	00
	27	E. V. Sanders	On account		250	00
	28	Cash, Debit			14,346	00

Each receipt of cash represents

(1) A debit to the Cash account, and
(2) A credit to some other account.

The cash receipts book above records ten receipts of cash, representing, therefore,

(1) Ten debits to the Cash account, and
(2) Ten credits to the several accounts named in the "account credited" column.

---

[4] The authority for a cash receipt entry may be
   (1) The check itself.
   (2) The customer's letter of remittance.
   (3) Credit memorandum from the bank.
   (4) Cash sales tickets.
   (5) Cash register records.
   (6) Cash received tickets. One ticket is prepared for each receipt of cash.

But, again, instead of posting the ten debits individually to the Cash account, we save much time and labor by posting them in total at the end of the month. Posting of the cash receipts book may therefore be summarized thus:

(1) The debits are posted in total to the Cash account (at the end of the month), to avoid the detailed debit postings which would otherwise be necessary.

(2) The credits are posted individually to the accounts named.

The total debit, as stated, is posted to the ledger at the end of the month. Credits may be posted daily, weekly, or monthly. Credits to personal accounts, however, should be posted daily.

In the L.F. column of the cash receipts book should be placed the ledger page to which each item is posted. In the ledger, reference will be made to CR1, indicating that the entry in the ledger account came from the cash receipts book, page 1.

CASH PAYMENTS BOOK

In this book are recorded all payments of cash.[5] A simple cash payments book is as follows:

CASH PAYMENTS BOOK   Page 1

Date		Account Debited	Explanation	L.F.	Amount	
1950						
Feb.	3	Rent Expense	February rent		300	00
	3	Furniture and Fixtures	Bill February 3 from Ester Supply Co.		1,200	00
	10	Purchases	Exley & Son		700	00
	12	James J. Logue	Bill February 5		5,000	00
	14	General Expense			510	00
	19	General Expense			116	00
	25	F. C. Maxton	Bill of February 16		62	00
	26	L. T. Robinson, Personal			200	00
	26	James J. Logue	On account		1,000	00
	28	Wages Expense	February payroll		231	00
	28	Cash, Credit			9,319	00

Each payment of cash represents

(1) A debit to some account other than Cash, and

(2) A credit to the Cash account.

---

[5] The authority for a cash payment entry may be

(1) The checks themselves or carbon copies.
(2) The check book stub.
(3) The voucher (described in a later chapter).
(4) Copy of letter, or form, of remittance.
(5) Debit memorandum from the bank.
(6) Cash payment tickets. One ticket is prepared for each payment of cash.

The cash payments book above records ten payments of cash, representing, therefore,

(1) Ten debits to the several accounts named in the "account debited" column, and

(2) Ten credits to the Cash account.

Posting is facilitated if the credits are posted in total rather than in detail. Complete posting of the cash payments book is as follows:

(1) The debits are posted individually to the accounts named.

(2) The credits are posted in total to the Cash account (at the end of the month) to avoid the detailed credit postings which would otherwise be necessary.

In the L.F. column of the cash payments book should be placed the ledger page to which each item is posted. In the ledger, reference will be made to CP1, indicating that the entry in the ledger account came from the cash payments book, page 1.

JOURNAL

Transactions which cannot be entered in other books of original entry are entered in the journal. The form of the journal, as illustrated in Chapter 7, is not changed.

Adjusting and closing entries, as before, continue to be placed in the journal.

SELECTION OF BOOK OF ENTRY

Occasionally it may be somewhat difficult to decide upon the proper book of original entry for a transaction. The following comments may prove helpful in this regard.

(A) Cash sales may be handled in four ways:

(1) Enter cash sales in the cash receipts book only.

(2) Handle cash sales like credit sales:

    (a) Enter each cash sale in the sales book; debit the customer's account.

    (b) Enter the cash received in the cash receipts book; credit the customer's account.

(3) Cash sales may be handled like credit sales but with this modification in procedure:

    (a) Enter each sale in the sales book; debit all cash sales to the Cash Sales account.

    (b) Enter receipts from cash sales in the cash receipts book; credit all receipts to the Cash Sales account.

Under this method the Cash Sales account is opened and operated just like a customer's account. The method is of advantage where cash is not handled by the book-keeper. It provides a desirable check on cash sales: the cashier's daily report of cash received from cash sales must tally with the daily total of cash sales invoices turned over to the bookkeeper by the billing department. Obviously the Cash Sales account should have a zero balance at the close of each business day.

This method is also to be recommended in cases where it is necessary to classify sales by departments, products, etc., the analysis being made in the sales book at the time of entry.

(4) Cash sales may be entered in the cash receipts book, and also in the sales book.

When this method of recording cash sales is followed, the debit to Cash from the sales book, and the credit to Sales from the cash receipts book, must not be posted. This is because the complete double entry represented by the sales book entry is duplicated by the cash sale entry in the cash receipts book. Obviously, two debits and two credits should not be made for each cash sale transaction; one pair must be omitted. The L.F. columns in the cash receipts book, and sales book, in so far as cash sales are concerned, should be checked ($\sqrt{}$) to indicate the purposeful omission of postings and to prevent duplication of postings.

Of the four methods described, the first and the third are the best.[6]

(B) Cash purchases, too, can be handled in four ways:

(1) Enter cash purchases in the cash payments book only.
(2) Handle cash purchases like credit purchases:
  (a) Enter each cash purchase in the purchases book; credit the seller's account.
  (b) Enter the payment in the cash payments book; debit the seller's account.
(3) Handle cash purchases like credit purchases but with this modification in procedure:
  (a) Enter each purchase in the purchases book; credit all cash purchases to the Cash Purchases account.

---

[6] The application of these four methods to a departmental business is discussed in Chapter 10.

(b) Enter payments for cash purchases in the cash payments book; debit all payments to the Cash Purchases account.

(4) Enter cash purchases in the cash payments book and also in the purchases book.

When this method of recording cash purchases is followed, the debit to Purchases from the cash payments book, and the credit to Cash from the purchases book, must not be posted.

(C) $1,000.00 merchandise is sold to W. C. Morse on terms of 40 per cent down, the balance payable $60.00 monthly. A transaction of this kind should be recorded in two books:

SALES BOOK:	W. C. Morse 1,000.00	
	Sales	1,000.00
	To record the sale.	
CASH RECEIPTS BOOK:	Cash 400.00	
	W. C. Morse	400.00
	To record down payment.	

(D) Conversely, if $1,200.00 merchandise is purchased from W. E. Hall on terms of $500.00 down, the balance payable $70.00 monthly, the transaction would be recorded:

PURCHASES BOOK:	Purchases 1,200.00	
	W. E. Hall	1,200.00
	To record purchase.	
CASH PAYMENTS BOOK:	W. E. Hall 500.00	
	Cash	500.00
	To record down payment.	

(E) Land is purchased from S. G. Vantell for $25,000.00 on terms of $10,000.00 cash, and mortgage of $15,000.00. The proper books of entry would be:

JOURNAL	Land 25,000.00	
	S. G. Vantell	25,000.00
	To record purchase.	
CASH PAYMENTS BOOK:	S. G. Vantell 10,000.00	
	Cash	10,000.00
	To record down payment.	
JOURNAL:	S. G. Vantell 15,000.00	
	Mortgage Payable . . .	15,000.00
	To record mortgage liability on land purchase.	

(F) On February 1, 1950, L. T. Robinson began business with an investment of $12,000.00 cash, and $4,000.00 merchandise. This investment should be recorded as follows:

CASH RECEIPTS BOOK: Cash 12,000.00
                           L. T. Robinson, Capital   12,000.00
                       To record cash investment.
                       (For non-cash investment, see
                       journal, page 1.)
JOURNAL: Merchandise Inventory . . .   4,000.00
                           L. T. Robinson, Capital   4,000.00
                       To record investment of as-
                       sets other than cash. (See
                       cash receipts book, page 1, for
                       cash investment.)

SUMMARY

The division of the general journal into several journals results in a number of advantages:

(1) The different books afford a classification of transactions.

(2) The original record of transactions is simplified. Every entry in the sales book, for example, implies a credit to the Sales account. Constant repetition of the word "Sales" is unnecessary. Explanations are simplified.

(3) Division of labor is made possible. One individual can enter transactions in the sales book, another, transactions in the purchases book, another, cash transactions in the appropriate cash books, and so on.

(4) Because totals and not details are posted, the procedure of posting is measurably simplified with a saving in time and labor.

(5) There is less opportunity for error because of
   (a) Simplified entries.
   (b) Simplified posting.

(6) The ledger is relieved of a mass of detail and becomes, more than ever, a summary of detail.

The most frequently employed books of original entry are sales, purchases, cash receipts, cash payments, and journal. These books are often supplemented by others, common among which are those for returned sales and allowances and for returned purchases and allowances. Whether or not more than five books of original entry should be employed in a given case depends upon circumstances. As a general rule, a separate book of original entry should be used for each type of transaction of frequent occurrence. Economies of the kind illustrated in this chapter are worth realizing whenever possible.

ILLUSTRATIVE PROBLEM

The books of L. T. Robinson, reproduced below, are based upon the transactions of Chapter 7, pages 107 and 108 and illustrate

(1) The employment of five books of original entry.
(2) Posting from these books of original entry to the ledger.
(3) The ledger
  (a) After all transactions have been recorded therein.
  (b) After the books have been closed.

It is recommended that the student examine this problem thoroughly in order to achieve familiarity with the technique employed and to appreciate the superiority of the procedure illustrated.

The trial balance for this problem is identical with that on page 116; the statements are identical with those on pages 82 and 83.

JOURNAL   Page 1

1950					
Feb.	2	Merchandise	7	4,000 00	
		L. T. Robinson, Capital	13		4,000 00
		Began business today with an investment of:			
		$ 4,000.00 merchandise (recorded above)			
		12,000.00 cash (recorded in cash receipts book, page 1)			
		$16,000.00 Total			
	19	Returned Sales and Allowances	17	100 00	
		Clark R. Morgan	3		100 00
		For merchandise returned because of inferior quality; originally purchased February 12, invoice #4.			
	28	Cost of Sales	18	15,300 00	
		Merchandise	7		4,000 00
		Purchases	19		11,300 00
		To transfer latter two accounts to Cost of Sales.			
	28	Merchandise	7	10,692 00	
		Cost of Sales	18		10,692 00
		To set up inventory as of February 28.			
	28	Profit and Loss	15	4,608 00	
		Cost of Sales	18		4,608 00
		To transfer balance of Cost of Sales to Profit and Loss account.			
	28	Profit and Loss	15	100 00	
		Returned Sales and Allowances	17		100 00
		To close latter account.			
	28	Sales	16	7,190 00	
		Profit and Loss	15		7,190 00
		To close former account.			

JOURNAL   Page 2

1950							
Feb.	28	Profit and Loss [7]	15	1,157	00		
		General Expense	20			626	00
		Rent Expense	21			300	00
		Wages Expense	22			231	00
		To transfer expenses to Profit and Loss.					
	28	Commissions Earned	23	63	00		
		Profit and Loss	15			63	00
		To transfer former account to Profit and Loss.					
	28	Profit and Loss	15	1,388	00		
		L. T. Robinson, Capital	13			1,388	00
		To transfer profit to Robinson's capital account.					
	28	L. T. Robinson, Capital	13	200	00		
		L. T. Robinson, Personal	14			200	00
		To transfer balance of Robinson's personal account to capital account.					

SALES BOOK   Page 1

DATE		INVOICE No.	DEBIT ACCOUNT OF	L.F.	AMOUNT	
1950						
Feb.	7	2	C. F. Ruble	4	2,378	00
	12	4	Clark R. Morgan	3	489	00
	14	5	E. V. Sanders	5	867	00
	17	7	C. F. Ruble	4	558	00
	20	8	H. R. Macy	2	599	00
	23	9	E. V. Sanders	5	85	00
	25	10	M. G. Sheldon	6	1,311	00
	28	11	Clark R. Morgan	3	722	00
	28		Sales, Credit	16	7,009	00

PURCHASES BOOK   Page 1

DATE		CREDIT ACCOUNT OF	L.F.	AMOUNT	
1950					
Feb.	5	James J. Logue	10	5,000	00
	12	Henry V. Dana	9	408	00
	12	James J. Logue	10	1,800	00
	16	F. C. Maxton	11	62	00
	21	J. R. Upshaw	12	1,800	00
	21	James J. Logue	10	1,530	00
	28	Purchases, Debit	19	10,600	00

---

[7] A journal entry which embraces more than two accounts is called a compound journal entry. Compound entries to the Cost of Sales account, and to the Profit and Loss account, should be posted in detail. Note, for example, the detail in the Profit and Loss account illustrated on page 143.

CASH RECEIPTS BOOK   Page 1

Date		Account Credited	Explanation	L.F.	Amount	
1950						
Feb.	2	L. T. Robinson, Capital	Cash investment	13	12,000	00
	4	Sales	Invoice #1, J. M. Barrie	16	102	00
	9	Sales	Invoice #3, E. T. Maddox	16	28	00
	16	Sales	Invoice #6, A. L. Nichols	16	51	00
	21	Clark R. Morgan	Balance invoice Feb. 12	3	389	00
	24	C. F. Ruble	On account	4	700	00
	24	E. V. Sanders	Invoice Feb. 23	5	85	00
	27	Commissions Earned	For commission on sale of policy for Dettle Insurance Company	23	63	00
	27	C. F. Ruble	On account	4	678	00
	27	E. V. Sanders	On account	5	250	00
	28	Cash, Debit		1	14,346	00

CASH PAYMENTS BOOK   Page 1

Date		Account Debited	Explanation	L.F.	Amount	
1950						
Feb.	3	Rent Expense	February rent	21	300	00
	3	Furniture and Fixtures	Bill February 3 from Ester Supply Company	8	1,200	00
	10	Purchases	Exley & Son	19	700	00
	12	James J. Logue	Bill February 5	10	5,000	00
	14	General Expense		20	510	00
	19	General Expense		20	116	00
	25	F. C. Maxton	Bill February 16	11	62	00
	26	L. T. Robinson, Personal		14	200	00
	26	James J. Logue	On account	10	1,000	00
	28	Wages Expense	February payroll	22	231	00
	28	Cash, Credit		1	9,319	00

In bound books the cash receipts and cash payments are generally recorded on opposite pages, the left and right pages, respectively. In loose-leaf books, the cash receipts and cash payments are generally recorded on separate pages which are filed in individual cash receipts and cash payments post binders.

LEDGER

CASH   Page 1

1950							1950					
Feb.	28			CR1	14,346	00	Feb.	28			CP1	9,319	00

H. R. MACY   Page 2

1950										
Feb.	20	S1	599	00						

CLARK R. MORGAN   Page 3

1950					1950				
Feb.	12	S1	489	00	Feb.	19	J1	100	00
	28	S1	722	00		21	CR1	389	00

C. F. RUBLE   Page 4

1950					1950				
Feb.	7	S1	2,378	00	Feb.	24	CR1	700	00
	17	S1	558	00		27	CR1	678	00

E. V. SANDERS   Page 5

1950					1950				
Feb.	14	S1	867	00	Feb.	24	CR1	85	00
	23	S1	85	00		27	CR1	250	00

M. G. SHELDON   Page 6

1950										
Feb.	25	S1	1,311	00						

MERCHANDISE   Page 7

1950					1950					
Feb.	2	J1	4,000	00	Feb.	28	To Cost of			
	28	J1	10,692	00			Sales	J1	4,000	00

FURNITURE AND FIXTURES   Page 8

1950										
Feb.	3	CP1	1,200	00						

HENRY V. DANA   Page 9

						1950				P1	408	00
						Feb.	12			P1	408	00

JAMES J. LOGUE   Page 10

1950			CP1	5,000	00	1950	5			P1	5,000	00
Feb.	12		CP1	5,000	00	Feb.	5			P1	5,000	00
	26		CP1	1,000	00		12			P1	1,800	00
							21			P1	1,530	00

F. C. MAXTON   Page 11

1950			CP1	62	00	1950	16			P1	62	00
Feb.	25		CP1	62	00	Feb.	16			P1	62	00

J. R. UPSHAW   Page 12

						1950				P1	1,800	00
						Feb.	21			P1	1,800	00

L. T. ROBINSON, CAPITAL   Page 13

1950						1950						
Feb.	28	Drawings	J1	200	00	Feb.	2	Investment	J1	4,000	00
							2	Investment	CR1	12,000	00
							28	Net Income	J2	1,388	00

L. T. ROBINSON, PERSONAL   Page 14

1950			CP1	200	00	1950			J2	200	00
Feb.	26		CP1	200	00	Feb.	28		J2	200	00

PROFIT AND LOSS Page 15

1950						1950					
Feb.	28	Cost of Sales	J1	4,608	00	Feb.	28	Sales	J1	7,190	00
	28	Rtd. Sales &					28	Commissions			
		Allowances	J1	100	00			Earned	J2	63	00
	28	General Expense	J2	626	00						
	28	Rent Expense	J2	300	00						
	28	Wages Expense	J2	231	00						
	28	To L. T. Rob-									
		inson, Capital	J2	1,388	00						
				7,253	00					7,253	00

SALES Page 16

1950						1950					
Feb.	28	To P. & L.	J1	7,190	00	Feb.	4		CR1	102	00
							9		CR1	28	00
							16		CR1	51	00
							28		S1	7,009	00
				7,190	00					7,190	00

RETURNED SALES AND ALLOWANCES Page 17

1950						1950					
Feb.	19		J1	100	00	Feb.	28	To P. & L.	J1	100	00

COST OF SALES Page 18

1950						1950					
Feb.	28	Merchandise	J1	4,000	00	Feb.	28	Merchandise	J1	10,692	00
	28	Purchases	J1	11,300	00		28	To P. & L.	J1	4,608	00
				15,300	00					15,300	00

PURCHASES Page 19

1950						1950					
Feb.	10		CP1	700	00	Feb.	28	To Cost of			
	28		P1	10,600	00			Sales	J1	11,300	00
				11,300	00					11,300	00

GENERAL EXPENSE   Page 20

1950						1950					
Feb.	14		CP1	510	00	Feb.	28	To P. & L.	J2	626	00
	19		CP1	116	00						
				626	00					626	00

RENT EXPENSE   Page 21

1950						1950					
Feb.	3		CP1	300	00	Feb.	28	To P. & L.	J2	300	00

WAGES EXPENSE   Page 22

1950						1950					
Feb.	28		CP1	231	00	Feb.	28	To P. & L.	J2	231	00

COMMISSIONS EARNED   Page 23

1950						1950					
Feb.	28	To P. & L.	J2	63	00	Feb.	27		CR1	63	00

QUESTIONS

Question **8–1.** Why is it advisable to divide the journal into several books of original entry? Explain fully.

Question **8–2.** What is meant by books of original entry?

Question **8–3.** What is the authority for an entry in the sales book? in the purchases book? in the cash receipts book? in the cash payments book?

Question **8–4.** Explain three ways of handling cash sales. Which of these ways would you recommend for (1) a department store doing a business of $10,000.00 per day, 70% of which is cash; and (2) an automobile manufacturer whose parts sales to his 1,500 master dealers are nearly all on a credit basis, only 10% being cash?

Question **8–5.** What are the advantages and disadvantages of the four methods of handling cash sales as described on page 134?

Question **8-6.** Where would you record the following:

(1) A credit memorandum for returned sales? for returned purchases?
(2) Merchandise shipped C.O.D. parcel post?
(3) A delivery truck purchased for $1,000.00 on terms of $400.00 down, the balance payable in twelve equal monthly installments? (How would this transaction be recorded on the seller's books?)
(4) A cash purchase?

Question **8-7.** Explain how you would determine the proper number of books of original entry for a given business. Can you name ten books of original entry?

Question **8-8.** How should compound journal entries to the Cost of Sales account, and the Profit and Loss account, be posted? Why?

Question **8-9.** An automobile, carried on your books at $250.00, is traded in on a new car costing $1,000.00. You receive a trade-in allowance of $300.00. In addition you give the dealer, C. H. Miles & Company, a check for $200.00 and agree to pay the balance of the purchase price in ten equal monthly installments without interest.

State specifically what book, or books, of original entry you would employ, and the entry, or entries, you would make in each.

PROBLEMS

Problem **8-1.** The transactions of Fred J. Longmire for the month of December, 19__, were as follows:

December

1 — Began business with cash, $5,000.00, merchandise, $3,000.00, and fixtures, $2,000.00.
1 — Paid rent for the month, $200.00.
5 — Purchased merchandise on account from Fisher & Son, $3,450.00.
7 — Sale of merchandise on account to Wilson & Co., $2,750.00.
9 — Purchased merchandise for cash from Fisher & Son, $803.00.
13 — Personal household bills of Mr. Longmire are paid, $204.00.
16 — Paid general expenses, $488.00.
17 — Purchased merchandise on account from E. A. Garrett, $2,716.00.
20 — Sale of merchandise on account to Lee & Landis, $1,849.00.
23 — Sale of merchandise for cash to Wilson & Co., $200.00.
26 — Received check from Wilson & Co., to apply on account, $750.00.
28 — Sale of merchandise on account to Lee & Landis, $301.00.
31 — Paid payroll for December, $501.00.

Required:

(1) Enter above transactions in five books of original entry.
(2) Post to formal ledger accounts.
(3) Prepare a trial balance.

(4) Prepare a profit and loss statement for December. Inventory, December 31, 19__, $6,300.00. The use of a work sheet is optional.

(5) Prepare a balance sheet, December 31, 19__.

(6) Close the books.

Problem **8–2.** Following are the transactions of J. K. Roy for the month of January, 19__:

January

2 — J. K. Roy begins business with cash, $5,000.00, merchandise, $3,000.00.

3 — Fixtures and equipment are purchased for cash, $1,250.00.

5 — Merchandise is purchased on credit from J. L. Snider, $750.00.

6 — Sale of merchandise on credit to A. W. Brady, $912.00.

8 — Sale of merchandise on credit to L. E. White, $1,800.00.

10 — Merchandise is purchased on credit from E. V. Latt & Son, $412.00.

11 — Cash is received from A. W. Brady, $700.00.

13 — Sale of merchandise for cash to Greer & Company, $50.00.

15 — Sale of merchandise on credit to C. A. Kenney for $1,614.00.

18 — Some of the merchandise purchased from E. V. Latt & Son on January 10 proving to be inferior, a claim is made. An allowance of $42.00 in the form of a credit memorandum is received today from E. V. Latt & Son in settlement of our claim.

19 — Rent for the month of January is paid, $100.00.

20 — Merchandise is purchased on credit from R. S. Jones, $1,300.00.

21 — Cash is received from L. E. White, $800.00.

22 — A check for $370.00 is mailed to E. V. Latt & Son.

24 — Sale of merchandise on credit to L. E. White, $355.00.

25 — General expenses are paid, $239.00.

26 — Merchandise is purchased on account from R. S. Jones, $200.00.

27 — Cash is received from A. W. Brady, $212.00.

28 — Merchandise is purchased for cash from Caton & Company, $186.00.

29 — A check for $500.00 is mailed to R. S. Jones to apply on account.

31 — Wages are paid, $400.00.

Required:

(1) Enter the above transactions in the following books of original entry: purchases, sales, cash receipts, cash payments, and journal.

(2) Post these transactions to the ledger.

(3) Draw off a trial balance.

(4) Prepare a work sheet. Inventory, January 31, 19__, $2,115.00.

(5) Prepare a profit and loss statement for the month of January.

(6) Prepare a balance sheet, January 31, 19__.

Problem **8–3.** Following are the transactions of Thomas M. Farley for the month of December, 19__:

December

1 — Thomas M. Farley begins business with $8,000.00 cash.

2 — Store equipment is purchased for cash from the Standard Store Equipment Company, $1,500.00.

3 — Merchandise is purchased on credit from P. J. Curran, $1,427.00.

4 — Rent for the month is paid, $150.00.

5 — Sale of merchandise on account to M. J. Cruise, $1,675.00.

6 — Merchandise is purchased for cash from James & Company, $2,203.00.

8 — Sale of merchandise on account to H. C. Perry, $3,168.00; and to John F. Royce, $123.00.

9 — Expenses for cleaning, painting, and miscellaneous repairing are paid, $184.00.

10 — Merchandise is purchased on account from Sherwood & Company, $756.00.

11 — A check for $500.00 is received from H. C. Perry.

12 — The Pennsylvania Railroad is paid $14.00 for the freight on the Sherwood purchase of December 10. The contract of purchase for this merchandise specified that the freight was to be prepaid and absorbed by Sherwood & Company.

13 — Cash is received from M. J. Cruise, $1,275.00.

15 — Wages are paid, $210.00.

16 — Sale of merchandise for cash to John F. Royce, $46.00.

17 — Merchandise is purchased on credit from Long & Company, $2,388.00; and from P. J. Curran, $1,001.00.

18 — Cash is received from H. C. Perry, $668.00.

19 — Sale of merchandise on account to E. H. Reed, $2,964.00.

20 — A check for $732.00 is mailed to Sherwood & Company.

22 — Sale of merchandise on account to H. C. Perry, $482.00.

23 — Various expenses are paid, $393.00.

24 — Merchandise is purchased on account from Long & Company, $411.00.

26 — Cash is received from M. J. Cruise, $400.00.

26 — Cash is paid to Long & Company, $2,000.00.

28 — Cash is received from John F. Royce, $124.00.

28 — Various expenses are paid, $324.00. Wages are paid, $312.00.

31 — Social security taxes are paid, $15.00.

Required:

(1) Enter the above transactions in the following books of original entry: purchases, sales, cash receipts, cash payments, and journal.

(2) Post these transactions to the ledger.

(3) Draw off a trial balance.

(4) Prepare a work sheet. Inventory, December 31, 19__, $2,026.00.

(5) Prepare a profit and loss statement for the month of December.

(6) Prepare a balance sheet, December 31, 19__.

(7) Close the books.

Problem **8–4.** Following is the trial balance of the Belmont Trading Company on December 31, 19___:

Cash	$ 24,900.00	
Securities	10,000.00	
Accounts Receivable	11,000.00	
Merchandise	9,000.00	
Fixtures and Miscellaneous Equipment	12.000.00	
Accounts Payable		$ 8,000.00
Notes Payable		10,000.00
Charles A. Belmont, Capital		50,000.00
Charles A. Belmont, Personal	6,000.00	
Sales		84,302.00
Returned Sales	3,000.00	
Purchases	62,000.00	
Returned Purchases		5,000.00
Advertising Expense	1,300.00	
Delivery Expense	800.00	
Freight Out (expense)	500.00	
Miscellaneous General Expense	1,900.00	
Miscellaneous Sales Expense	1,600.00	
Rent	1,800.00	
Salaries and Wages, General	4,600.00	
Sales Salaries	5,680.00	
Social Security Taxes	302.00	
Supplies Expense	500.00	
Traveling Expense	600.00	
Utilities Expense	520.00	
Dividends Received		400.00
Interest Earned		300.00
	$158,002.00	$158,002.00

Required:

(1) Prepare a work sheet. Inventory, December 31, 19___, $10,101.00.

(2) Prepare a profit and loss statement for the year.

(3) Prepare a balance sheet, December 31, 19___.

(4) Make journal entries to close the books.

Problem **8–5.** Following are the transactions of Lee J. Daniels for the period December 20–31, 19___:

December

20 — Lee J. Daniels began business with cash, $10,000.00, merchandise, $2,000.00, and delivery truck, $1,000.00. Purchased land, $1,000.00, and building, $5,000.00, from A. E. Wilson, paying cash of $2,000.00 and giving a mortgage payable of $4,000.00. Purchased merchandise on account from Dott & Wiley, $2,500.00.

21 — Issued checks for city license tax, $25.00, gasoline and oil, $10.00, grease and wash of delivery truck, $2.00. Sales on account: W. H. Carson, $400.00, Roberts & Co., $100.00, J. T. Sears, $500.00. Cash sales, $200.00.

23 — Sale of merchandise to Roberts & Co., receiving in payment therefore a 60-day note for $500.00.

26 — Issued checks for janitor supplies, $11.00, miscellaneous expenses, $40.00, delivery truck repairs, $7.00. Sale on account to J. T. Sears, $100.00. Cash sales, $410.00. Purchased merchandise on account from Bruce & Milton, Inc., $3,000.00, Dott & Wiley, $500.00.

27 — Received checks from W. H. Carson, $400.00, J. T. Sears, $100.00. Sale on account to Roberts & Co., $601.00.

28 — Purchase of merchandise on account from Dott & Wiley, $2,000.00. Sales on account: W. H. Carson, $300.00, J. T. Sears, $800.00.

29 — Issued checks for garage bill, $10.00, property taxes, $75.00, installation of electric sign on building, $500.00. Mailed check to Dott & Wiley for $1,000.00.

31 — Issued checks for office salaries, $400.00, wages, $320.00. Sale on account to Roberts & Co., $1,187.00. Cash sales, $102.00.

Required:

(1) Enter above transactions in five books of original entry.
(2) Draw off a trial balance. Enter the trial balance on a work sheet.
(3) Complete the work sheet.
(4) Prepare a profit and loss statement. Inventory, December 31, 19__, $6,000.00.
(5) Prepare a balance sheet.

Problem **8–6.** The transactions of Mr. Henry M. Rittler for the month of December, 19__, were as follows:

1 — Began business with the following assets:

Cash	$8,615.00	Interest Receivable	$ 385.00
Merchandise	9,000.00	Building	10,000.00
Notes Receivable	7,000.00	Land	2,000.00

1 — Paid rent for the month of December, $500.00.

1 — Purchased furniture, fixtures, and equipment from the Business Equipment Company for cash, $2,664.00.

2 — Sale of merchandise on account to H. E. Brown, $1,846.00, J. W. Mason, $2,106.00, and J. F. Foley, $1,011.00.

3 — Purchase of merchandise on account from J. D. Burnett, $4,941.00, and G. A. Brill, $4,405.00.

4 — Purchase of merchandise for cash from J. D. Burnett, $117.00.

5 — Sale of merchandise on account to J. F. Foley, $1,322.00, and C. J. Stevens, $760.00.

6 — Paid J. D. Burnett on account, $2,941.00.

7 — J. F. Foley returns unsatisfactory merchandise, $33.00.

9 — Various general expenses are paid, $627.00.

10 — Purchased merchandise on account from Hexter & Son, $1,302.00.

11 — A Ford delivery truck is purchased from the Renton Agency, Inc.,

for $1,015.00, with a down payment of $315.00, the balance payable $50.00 monthly.

11 — A check is received from H. E. Brown in full payment of account to date.

12 — Sale of merchandise for cash to John A. Reed, $99.00.

13 — Sale of merchandise on account to H. E. Brown, $1,818.00, and C. J. Stevens, $1,482.00.

14 — A check for $200.00 is given to *The Daily Herald* in payment of advertising.

15 — Paid wages and salaries for the first half of December, $874.00.

16 — Sale of merchandise on account to J. H. Kline, $847.00.

17 — A credit memorandum for $130.00 is received from G. A. Brill as an allowance on the merchandise purchased from him on December 3. One lot of this merchandise proved to be of inferior grade; rather than have the merchandise returned, Mr. Brill offered the credit of $130.00 if Mr. Rittler would keep the full shipment. This Mr. Rittler agreed to do.

18 — Purchase of merchandise from J. D. Burnett for cash, $280.00, and from Hexter & Son on account, $1,251.00.

19 — Cash is received from J. F. Foley, $500.00.

20 — Mr. Rittler withdraws merchandise for his personal use, $50.00. (Credit Purchases.)

24 — Purchase of merchandise on account from G. A. Brill, $649.00.

24 — A check is received from G. A. Brill for $130.00 to cover his credit memorandum of December 17.

26 — Sale of merchandise to H. E. Brown for $2,071.00 with a cash down payment of $500.00.

27 — A machine for stamping and sealing envelopes, purchased on December 1 from the Business Equipment Company for $64.00, is returned for credit with their permission. A check is received in payment.

28 — Merchandise is returned to G. A. Brill for credit, $84.00.

30 — Various expenses are paid:

Automobile license . .	$18.00	Gasoline and oil	$16.00
Telephone bill	14.00	Office supplies	32.00
Electricity and gas . .	29.00	Postage stamps	10.00
Water	7.00	Lettering on window . .	20.00

30 — A 90-day note is given to J. D. Burnett in full settlement of account.

30 — Personal bills of Mr. Rittler are paid, $44.00.

31 — A check for $7,420.00 is received in payment of notes receivable of $7,000.00, and all interest to date, $420.00.

31 — Paid wages and salaries for the second half of December, $996.00.

Required:

(1) Enter the above transactions in the appropriate books of original entry.

(2) Post to the ledger.

(3) Take a trial balance.

(4) Prepare a profit and loss statement for the month of December. The inventory of merchandise on hand December 31, 19__, was $12,011.00.

(5) Prepare a balance sheet as of December 31, 19__.

(6) Close the books.

Problem **8-7.** The following transactions describe the operations of James T. Barrett for the month of December, 19__:

December

1 — James T. Barrett began operations by buying out the business of John T. Cady & Son. The following assets and liabilities were taken over:

Assets:		*Liabilities:*	
Merchandise . . .	$22,364.00	Dill & Brock	$ 2,850.35
Allen & Company	577.30	Ever-ready Supply House	16,892.15
Brace & Brace . .	918.10	Fellway & Carp	6,487.50
Cary & Son . . .	453.60	Notes Payable	1,000.00
Equipment	8,000.00		
Building	20,000.00		
Land	3,000.00		

1 — Mr. Barrett adds $11,917.00 cash to his investment.

1 — Sale of merchandise on account to Allen & Company, $2,873.99.

2 — A check is sent to the Ever-ready Supply House in payment of invoice of November 26 for $1,799.60.

2 — Cash is received from Cary & Son, $453.60.

3 — Purchase of merchandise on account from Dill & Brock, $1,342.99.

3 — Sale of merchandise for cash to Brace & Brace, $577.19.

3 — $300.00 is paid to Bennett & White, certified public accountants, who made an audit of the accounts of John T. Cady & Son for Mr. Barrett.

3 — Mr. Barrett enters into a cooperative advertising agreement with Charles R. Coleman. Mr. Barrett agrees to pay all advertising invoices that may be incurred with the understanding, however, that he is to be reimbursed by Mr. Coleman for 50% of the total advertising expense.

4 — Wages are paid for the week ending today, $264.00.

4 — Sale of merchandise on account to Brace & Brace, $1,450.42.

5 — Merchandise is returned to Dill & Brock, $202.50.

5 — Cash is received from Allen & Company, $1,273.99.

6 — Sale of merchandise on account to Cary & Son, $1,342.98.

6 — Selling expenses are paid, $784.12.

8 — Paid the Ever-ready Supply House for bill of November 24, $1,705.59.

8 — Sale of merchandise on account to Allen & Company, $993.81.

9 — Purchase of merchandise on account from the Ever-ready Supply House, $1,912.41.

10 — Cash is received from Allen & Company, $2,493.81.

10 — Sale of merchandise on account to Cary & Son, $2,148.77.

10 — General expenses are paid, $714.21.

11 — Cash is received from Brace & Brace, $918.10.

11 — Wages are paid for the week ending today, $280.00.

11 — Sale of merchandise on account to Brace & Brace, $1,316.12.

11 — Purchase of merchandise on account from Fellway & Carp, $1,289.26.

11 — A rebate of $174.57 is received in the form of a credit memorandum from the Ever-ready Supply House to apply on the purchase of December 9.

12 — Sale of merchandise for cash to Fred J. Burnett, $770.00.

12 — Selling expenses are paid, $728.05.

12 — A check is received from Cary & Son in full payment of invoice of December 6.

13 — A check for $1,208.68 is mailed to Fellway & Carp for bill of November 12.

15 — Sale of merchandise on account to Allen & Company, $1,692.16.

15 — Freight of $24.11 is prepaid for the account of Allen & Company.

16 — A check is drawn in favor of the Ever-ready Supply House in payment of a note payable for $1,000.00. This is the note payable included in the liabilities assumed by Mr. Barrett on December 1.

16 — Sale of merchandise on account to Cary & Son, $805.79.

17 — A check for $3,411.18 is mailed to Fellway & Carp in payment of their bill of November 30.

17 — Sale of merchandise on account to Allen & Company, $2,001.05.

17 — General expenses are paid, $641.00.

18 — Allen & Company return $107.44 of the merchandise purchased by them on December 15. A credit memorandum is issued in their favor.

18 — Wages are paid for the week ending today, $275.00.

18 — A bill from the Times Press Corporation for advertising is paid, $304.00. Mr. Coleman's share of this bill is 50%.

19 — Sale of merchandise on account to Brace & Brace, $1,508.60.

19 — A check for $1,342.99 is mailed to Dill & Brock in payment of their bill of December 3.

20 — Cash of $1,692.16 is received from Allen & Company in payment of our invoice of December 15.

20 — Cary & Son return $53.72 of the merchandise purchased by them on December 16. A credit memorandum is issued in their favor.

20 — Cash of $1,450.42 is received from Brace & Brace in payment of our invoice of December 4.

22 — Equipment is sold for $1,200.00 cash to the Central Equipment Company. There is no gain or loss on this sale.

23 — A credit memorandum for $38.81 is mailed to Brace & Brace as a special allowance on our invoice of December 11.

23 — Sale of merchandise on account to Allen & Company, $241.74.

24 — A check is received from Allen & Company for the balance of their account.

25 — Wages are paid for the week ending today, $314.00.

25 — Cary & Son pay the balance due on our invoice of December 16.

25 — Purchase of merchandise on account from the Ever-ready Supply House, $682.75.

25 — A check for $152.00 is received from Charles R. Coleman to cover his share of the advertising bill of December 18.

26 — Sale of merchandise on account to Brace & Brace, $1,075.00.

26 — $10,000.00 cash is borrowed from the First National Bank. A note is issued in favor of the bank for this amount.

28 — Except for $3,000.00, the account of the Ever-ready Supply House is paid in full.

29 — Purchase of merchandise on account from Dill & Brock, $1,745.88, and from the Ever-ready Supply House, $3,411.67.

29 — A check for $1,000.00 is received from Cary & Son to apply on account.

30 — Dill & Brock are paid $4,392.73.

30 — Paid $800.00 to the Underwood Typewriter Company for a new bookkeeping machine.

31 — Sale of merchandise on account to Brace & Brace, $2,471.10, and from Cary & Son, $2,011.58.

31 — A note for $2,156.90, without interest, and due in sixty days, is given to Fellway & Carp.

31 — Wages are paid for the week ending today, $253.00.

Required:

(1) Enter the above transactions in the appropriate books of original entry.

(2) Post to the ledger.

(3) Take a trial balance.

(4) Prepare a profit and loss statement. The value of the merchandise on hand December 31, 19—, is $15,576.73.

(5) Prepare a balance sheet.

(6) Close the books.

Chapter 9

ACCOUNT TECHNIQUE AND MISCELLANEOUS

ACCOUNT TECHNIQUE

Nominal Accounts. — The proper ruling of accounts is best described by the use of examples. The first example will illustrate the ruling of a nominal account at the end of the year:

RENT

1950					1950				
Jan.	1	CP1	300 00		Dec.	31	To Profit &		
Feb.	1	CP3	300 00				Loss	J39	3,600 00
Mar.	1	CP7	300 00						
Apr.	1	CP9	300 00						
May	1	CP12	300 00						
June	1	CP14	300 00						
July	1	CP17	300 00						
Aug.	1	CP22	300 00						
Sept.	1	CP26	300 00						
Oct.	1	CP29	300 00						
Nov.	1	CP32	300 00						
Dec.	1	CP36	300 00						
			3,600 00						3,600 00

Real Accounts. — The Cash account, shown on the next page, will illustrate how a real account may be ruled off at the end of the year. Real accounts, it should be remembered, are never formally "closed," but they may, on occasion, be "balanced."

It is not necessary to balance real accounts, but it is often advantageous to do so, especially where the debit and credit items are many. Balancing a real account is usually done at the end of the year although, if desired, an account may be balanced at intervals as well.

The credit of $4,678.11 shown in the Cash account on page 155 is offset by a debit below the double ruled lines. It is important to remember to maintain this equality of debit and credit. The √ mark serves as a cross reference within the account since no journal entry is involved.

The very small figures which appear in the debit and credit

money columns are cumulative subtotals (recorded in pencil). The figures which appear in the debit explanation column represent the debit balances of the account at the end of the months indicated and are recorded there for trial balance purposes.

CASH

1950						1950					
Jan.	31	3,368.31	CR1	5,846	42	Jan.	31		CP2	2,478	11
Feb.	28	3,277.94	CR4	1,612	87	Feb.	28		CP5	1,703	24
				7,459	29					4,181	35
Mar.	31	3,939.15	CR7	2,482	40	Mar.	31		CP9	1,821	19
				9,941	69					6,002	54
Apr.	30	5,053.89	CR9	3,614	21	Apr.	30		CP12	2,499	47
				13,555	90					8,502	01
May	31	4,309.13	CR12	3,102	44	May	31		CP15	3,847	20
				16,658	34					12,349	21
June	30	3,909.37	CR14	2,949	86	June	30		CP18	3,349	62
				19,608	20					15,698	83
July	31	3,063.45	CR16	3,001	41	July	31		CP22	3,847	33
				22,609	61					19,546	16
Aug.	30	2,144.37	CR17	1,621	99	Aug.	31		CP24	2,541	07
				24,231	60					22,087	23
Sept.	30	2,382.57	CR20	2,448	55	Sept.	30		CP27	2,210	35
				26,680	15					24,297	58
Oct.	31	3,032.19	CR23	2,956	04	Oct.	31		CP31	2,306	42
				29,636	19					26,604	00
Nov.	30	3,336.66	CR26	3,107	11	Nov.	30		CP36	2,802	64
				32,743	30					29,406	64
Dec.	31	4,678.11	CR30	3,982	86	Dec.	31		CP42	2,641	41
				36,726	16					32,048	05
							31	Balance	√	4,678	11
				36,726	16					36,726	16
1951											
Jan.	1		√	4,678	11						

Credit balances are placed in the credit explanation columns of accounts.

The technique of the two preceding paragraphs, it should be understood, is applicable to nominal as well as to real accounts.

Both real and nominal accounts, of course, should be adequately detailed as to posting references and dates. The omission of the year date when a transaction is recorded and posted, for example, may later prove to be an omission of consequence to many an account user, even the professional auditor.

Note the following points in the *personal* account below:

(1) Except for the item of June 22, all debits represent charges for sales.
(2) On June 17 a credit memorandum was issued for merchandise returned by Clark & Company, Inc.

(3) On June 30 a check was received in payment of the invoice of June 19. A √ mark is placed opposite the $87.16 debit and also the $87.16 credit to show that these items offset each other.

(4) At the end of June the balance of the account was $438.30. This balance was paid July 10; at the time of this entry √ marks were placed opposite the credit of $438.30, and the several debits which were paid.

The single-line rulings indicate the points at which the account is in balance. The new unpaid balance of the account ($192.63) is composed of the unchecked items below the single-line rulings. Notice that the July debit total is the sum of the items below the ruled line.

Personal Accounts. —

CLARK & COMPANY, INC.

1950							1950						
June	4		S21	√	174	11	June	17	C/m	RS6	√	11	82
	11		S21	√	212	82		30	Ck	CR15	√	87	16
	16		S22	√	41	10	July	10	Ck	CR16	√	438	30
	19		S22	√	87	16						537	28
	22	Ppd. freight	CP38	√	4	07							
	72	438.30	S23	√	18	02		25	Ck	CR17	√	61	17
					537	28							
July	2		S24		114	02							
	7		S25		25	10							
	16		S26		43	24							
	20		S26	√	61	17							
	31	192.63	S27		10	27							
					253	80							

The explanation columns of a personal account may be used to record the terms of the invoice or other significant information.

If, for credit purposes, it is desired to have a customer's account show whether or not cash discounts are being taken, and assuming that this information is not otherwise readily available, the required information may be obtained by

(1) Posting the cash and the cash discount separately in the account, or

(2) Posting one amount, prefacing it with the letter *d* in the explanation column to indicate that the cash discount was taken.

In addition to the name, the heading of a customer's account may provide for information such as address, credit limit, page number, and other general data.

Correction of Errors. — Erasures should not be made in an account or in a book of original entry. Erasures not only tend to detract from the appearance of a page but they also tend to suggest that the records may have been tampered with. In a lawsuit erasures may greatly weaken the importance of the books of account as evidence.

When a figure has been incorrectly recorded, the wrong figure should have a single line drawn through it, and the correct figure written just above it, thus:

480.27
~~408.27~~

If an entry has been made in the wrong account

(1) The wrong posting may be ruled out and the posting made to the proper account, or

(2) The correction may be made by journal entry, thus:

Interest Expense 47.16	
Interest Earned	47.16

To correct debit posting made to the Interest Earned account in error; should have been made to the Interest Expense account.

The Three-Column Account. — The following form of account, which is especially adapted to mechanical bookkeeping, is often employed because it gives the balance of the account after each posting. When bookkeeping machines are used, the account balances are automatically computed.

CLARK & COMPANY, INC.

DATE		EXPLANATION	REF.	DEBIT		CREDIT		BALANCE	
1950									
June	4		S21	174	11			174	11
	11		S21	212	82			386	93
	16		S22	41	10			428	03
	17	C/m	RS6			11	82	416	21
	19		S22	87	16			503	37
	22	Prepaid freight	CP38	4	07			507	44
	27		S23	18	02			525	46
	30	Ck	CR15			87	16	438	30
July	2		S24	114	02			552	32
	7		S25	25	10			577	42
	10	Ck	CR16			438	30	139	12
	16		S26	43	24			182	36
	20		S26	61	17			243	53
	25	Ck	CR17			61	17	182	36
	31		S27	10	27			192	63

Bookkeeping machines and the three-column account, although adapted to all the accounts of a business, are especially used in connection with accounts receivable. Some bookkeeping machines prepare the customer's statement, the ledger account record, and the book of original entry record, all at one impression.

MONTHLY STATEMENTS

At the end of the month a statement of account is sent to each customer. This statement usually shows

The balance unpaid at the beginning of the month.
The debits made to the customer's account during the month.
The credits made to the customer's account during the month.
The balance unpaid at the end of the month.

The following statement is made up from the ledger account of the Bremerton Trading Company (see PROBLEM 9–1 at the end of this chapter):

THE CHANDLER–GORDON COMPANY
500 First Avenue South
SEATTLE WASHINGTON

Statement of Account   December 31, 1950

Bremerton Trading Company,
  Bremerton, Wash.

Nov. 30 Balance	23.54	
Dec. 4	42.81	
6	26.10	
12	114.77	
15	22.65	
22	17.43	
29	9.04	256.34
Credits		
Dec. 14	181.23	
18	22.65	203.88
		52.46

RECONCILIATION OF THE BANK ACCOUNT

It is the usual practice on the part of a bank to furnish each depositor with a monthly statement of account. This statement, usually rendered as of the last day of the month, shows

The balance at the beginning of the month.
The deposits made during the month.
The checks paid by the bank during the month.
Miscellaneous debits and credits for the month.
The balance at the end of the month.

When the depositor receives his statement, he also receives the canceled checks charged to his account during the month by the bank, and the debit or credit memoranda in support of miscellaneous debits and credits to his account.

The depositor should reconcile the balance reported by the bank with the balance shown by his Cash account.[1] Usually a difference will exist because some checks issued by the maker will not have found their way to the bank for payment by the last day of the month. When these unpaid checks have been taken into account, the bank balance and Cash account balance should be equal if there are no other adjustments. To illustrate:

The balance of the Cash account of L. T. Robinson as of February 28, 1950, is the result of the following detail:

CASH RECEIPTS			CASH PAYMENTS			
1950			1950		*Check No.*	
Feb. 2	. . . .	.$12,000.00	Feb. 3	. . . .	1	. . . . $ 300.00
4	. . . .	102.00	3	. . . .	2	. . . . 1,200.00
9	. . . .	28.00	10	. . . .	3	. . . . 700.00
16	. . . .	51.00	12	. . . .	4	. . . . 5,000.00
21	. . . .	389.00	14	. . . .	5	. . . . 510.00
23	. . . .	85.00	19	. . . .	6	. . . . 116.00
24	. . . .	700.00	25	. . . .	7	. . . . 62.00
27	. . . .	63.00	26	. . . .	8	. . . . 200.00
27	. . . .	678.00	26	. . . .	9	. . . . 1,000.00
27	. . . .	250.00	28	. . . .	10	. . . . 231.00
		$14,346.00				$9,319.00

The statement on page 161 is received from the bank as of the close of business February 28, 1950.

Upon receipt of this statement, Mr. Robinson proceeds to arrange his canceled checks in numerical order. He finds checks #7 and #10 missing. They are outstanding because they have not yet been presented to the bank for payment. Mr. Robinson's reconciliation is as follows:

---

[1] It is assumed that all cash receipts are deposited in the bank, preferably daily, and that all disbursements of cash are made by check.

Bank balance, February 28, 1950 . . . . $5,320.00
Less outstanding checks:

#7	$ 62.00	
#10	231.00	293.00

Balance per Cash account in general ledger . . . . $ 5,027.00

Occasionally other factors influence the reconciliation:

(1) Certain debits or credits made by the bank may not be recorded on the depositor's books. For example:

Debits: Collection charges
　　　　Payment of depositor's note by authority of maker
　　　　Printing special checks
　　　　Service charges
Credits: Draft collections

These debits and credits should be recorded in the depositor's cash payments and cash receipts books, respectively, for the month covered by the bank statement. After the cash books have been posted, the new balance of the Cash account will be the figure to which the bank account will be reconciled. If the debits and credits under consideration cannot be entered in the cash books of the month covered by the bank statement — because the cash books have already been closed — they should be entered in the cash books of the next succeeding month.

(2) Debits made by the depositor may not appear on the bank statement. For example:
Deposits in transit
Drafts deposited with the bank for collection if recorded by the depositor as deposits. (The bank, however, does not credit the depositor until collection has been made.)

When debit items of this general character *are* actually cash, they should be added to the bank balance when the bank account is reconciled. Such items are cash if there is proof that they have been almost immediately credited to the account of the depositor by the bank. When these debit items *are not* actually cash, they should be deducted from the balance of the Cash account.

Occasionally, too, a bank may incorrectly debit or credit a depositor's account. When this occurs the bank should be notified immediately and the reported bank balance increased or decreased, as the case may be, by the amount of the error.

L. T. Robinson,
412 Pine St.
Hudson, N. Y.

In Account with
THE CENTRAL NATIONAL BANK
HUDSON, N. Y.

Date	Checks in Detail		Date	Deposits ☞	Date	New Balance
	BALANCE BROUGHT FORWARD		Feb 2 '50	12,000.00	Feb 2 '50	12,000.00*
			Feb 4 '50	102.00	Feb 4 '50	12,102.00*
Feb 5 '50	300.00–	1,200.00–			Feb 5 '50	10,602.00*
			Feb 9 '50	28.00	Feb 9 '50	10,630.00*
Feb 13 '50.	700.00–	5,000.00–			Feb 13 '50	4,930.00*
Feb 16 '50	510.00–		Feb 16 '50	51.00	Feb 16 '50	4,981.00*
					Feb 16 '50	4,471.00*
Feb 21 '50	116.00–		Feb 21 '50	389.00	Feb 21 '50	4,860.00*
					Feb 21 '50	4,744.00*
			Feb 24 '50	785.00	Feb 24 '50	5,529.00*
Feb 27 '50	1,000.00–	200.00–	Feb 27 '50	991.00	Feb 27 '50	6,520.00*
					Feb 27 '50	5,320.00*

CC = Certified check   DM = Debit memo   EX = Exchange   MBC = Minimum balance charge
CL = Collection   EC = Error corrected   LST = List   RTD = Returned item

Please examine at once. If no error is reported in ten days the account will be considered correct to close of business.
FEBRUARY 28, 1950.

The following example is an outline of the general procedure to be followed in complex cases of bank reconciliation:

John A. Blank

RECONCILIATION OF ACCOUNT WITH FIRST NATIONAL BANK AUGUST 31, 19—

Cash account, balance per books	$xxx xx	Bank statement, balance. . . .		$xxx xx
Add		*Add*		
Bank credits appearing on bank statement but not recorded in Cash Receipts book:		Cash receipts not recorded on bank statement:		
(detailed)	xxx xx	(detailed)		xxx xx
	$xxx xx			$xxx xx
Less		*Less*		
Bank debits appearing on bank statement but not recorded in Cash Payments book:		Outstanding checks: No. xx	$xxx xx	
		xx	xxx xx	
(detailed)	xxx xx	xx	xxx xx	xxx xx
True cash	$xxx xx	True cash		$xxx xx

The true cash is the amount of cash which should appear on the balance sheet. In short, an effective bank reconciliation works toward the balance sheet figure for cash.

RECIPROCAL ACCOUNTS

The principles involved in the reconciliation of the bank account are applicable, also, in the reconciliation of reciprocal accounts generally. Such accounts include the account receivable of the vendor and the account payable of the vendee, home office and branch accounts, and so on. The debits in the account receivable on the books of the vendor, for example, would be compared with the credits in the account payable on the books of the vendee; credits would be compared with the debits, respectively; and, from these comparisons, a summary would be prepared of the items comprising the difference between the balances of the two accounts.

In actual practice, a reconciliation of this kind is usually made by comparison of the vendor's account on the books of the vendee with a detailed transcript or statement of account furnished by the vendor.

CASH DISCOUNTS

A cash discount is a special concession, or rebate, granted by a seller to a purchaser in consideration of the buyer's early payment of an invoice. The discount is generally expressed as a certain per cent of the amount of an invoice. The cash discount is allowed if the customer makes payment on or before a date designated by the terms of the invoice being paid.

Example: The expression 2/10, n/30 ("2% ten days, net thirty days") means that a 2% cash discount may be taken by the purchaser if payment is made within 10 days from the date of the invoice. If the bill is not paid within 10 days, it is due for payment 30 days from the date of the invoice, and no cash discount is allowed.

Cash discount should always be computed on the amount of a bill less any returns or allowances applicable thereto. A cash discount, however, applies only to merchandise; it does *not* apply to such invoice items as freight, postage, tax, insurance, and so on. These items are payable net, i.e., without deduction of discount.

Cash discounts relate to cash settlements only. They do not relate to noncash considerations, like a note settlement, unless the payee of the note specifically allows the discount.

Cash discount should be allowed on the partial payment of an invoice within the discount period. This is proper because one invoice could be divided into two or more invoices; and one of these invoices could be paid within the discount period with benefit of cash discount. Therefore if the purchaser of merchandise covered by an invoice for $1,020.40 (terms 2/10, n/30) sends the seller a check for $500.00 within the discount period, the credit for partial payment should be $510.20. ($500.00 ÷ 98% = $510.20.) The entry for the cash receipt would be

```
Cash  . . . . . . . . . . . . . . . . . . . . . . .   500.00
Sales Discounts  . . . . . . . . . . . . . . . . . .    10.20
    Accounts Receivable  . . . . . . . . . . . . . .            510.20
To record check of $500.00, and cash discount applicable
thereto.
```

In other words, this entry means that one half of the invoice, $510.20, is settled by a check for $500.00. [$510.20−(2% × $510.20) = $500.00.]

TRADE DISCOUNTS

A trade discount is a percentage deduction from the list price of an article for some purpose other than to encourage the payment of an invoice on or before a fixed or determinable date. More specifically, trade discounts are used for the purpose of determining prices, for example,

(a) To reduce list prices to real prices, i.e., present market prices. (The list price of an article is the price which is listed or quoted by the catalog of the jobber, wholesaler, or manufacturer.) Catalogs of sellers commonly show items at list prices which are seldom, if ever, real selling prices. Real prices are obtained by deducting trade discounts from list prices; and real prices are changed by varying the percentages of trade discounts.

(b) To give favorable or preferential prices to present or prospective customers where price differentials between customers are legally warranted. This is done by varying the discounts offered in price quotations. (Price differentials may be warranted by the class of customer, for example, wholesaler, restaurant, or institution, or by *quantity* purchases wherein lower prices are justified by reduced or differential costs to the seller.)

If more than one trade discount applies to an article, the first discount is applied against list price, the second discount against list price reduced by the first discount, and so on successively. After all trade discounts have been deducted, the dollar value which remains is the real price at which an article will be charged to the account of a customer and cash settlements made. Trade discounts are not entered on the books.

Cash discounts and trade discounts are illustrated in the following example:

List price of an article.	$1,000.00

Less trade discounts of 40%, 10%, and 5%:

$$40\% \times \$1,000.00 = \$400.00$$
$$10\% \times \ \ \$600.00 = \ \ \ 60.00$$
$$5\% \times \ \ \ \$540.00 = \ \ \ 27.00 \qquad 487.00$$

Net price at which article is billed on invoice; and price at which article is ordinarily recorded on the books of seller and purchaser. $ 513.00
If the cash discount terms are 2/10, n/30, the cash discount allowed for payment within the discount period is 2% × $513.00, or . .   10.26

Check required to pay invoice in full within ten days of date of invoice . . . . $ 502.74

On the statement of profit and loss, accounting theory requires that sales discounts should be deducted from sales; and purchases discounts from purchases. This handling and interpretation of cash discounts is in accord with the following reasoning:

(1) Sales and purchases should be stated in the profit and loss statement at their cash values, or cash equivalents.

(2) The true effective price of merchandise is the least amount of cash which will settle a transaction for merchandise. Both seller and purchaser look at this net cash price as the real price of the merchandise which is changing hands.

(3) Income is realized by the sale and not by the purchase of

goods. Purchases discounts are not income but an offset to Purchases.

(4) Sales discounts are not expense but an offset to Sales. Customers are expected to take their discounts. Further, to label sales discounts as expense is tantamount to stating that there is extra expense involved in the handling of accounts which pay promptly as contrasted with those which do not.

Cash discounts are further discussed in Chapter 30.

FREIGHT IN

Merchandise may be received by a purchaser on a "freight collect" basis. This means that the purchaser pays the carrier for the transportation charges at the time the goods are received. On the other hand, the merchandise may be received "freight prepaid." This means that the seller pays the carrier for the freight charges at the time the goods are shipped.

Sales are billed to customers on one of the following bases for freight:

(1) F.o.b. shipping point, freight collect.
(2) F.o.b. shipping point, freight prepaid. Freight charges paid by the seller are debited to the account of the buyer.
(3) F.o.b. destination, freight prepaid.
(4) F.o.b. destination, freight collect. Freight charges paid by the buyer are debited to the account of the seller.

F.o.b. means "free on board." Merchandise shipped f.o.b. shipping point means that the purchaser absorbs transportation charges from shipping point forward as his expense. He debits Freight In for freight costs incurred. The purchaser looks upon these transportation bills as directly increasing the cost of merchandise purchases. On the profit and loss statement, therefore, the Freight In account is placed in the Cost of Sales section as an addition to the cost of Purchases.

Merchandise shipped f.o.b. destination means that the seller absorbs transportation charges to destination of shipment. He debits Freight Out (a selling expense) for freight costs incurred on sales.

As a general rule it is customary for a purchaser to absorb transportation costs on purchases of merchandise.

When does title pass on shipments made according to the various freight terms described above? This is an important question for accountants. As a general rule it may be stated that under terms of

"F.o.b. shipping point" title passes when the seller delivers the
goods to the carrier.[2]

"F.o.b. destination" title passes when goods arrive at destination.[2]

TRIAL BALANCE ERRORS

A trial balance is a bookkeeping device to prove the balance of
the general ledger. Total debit balances must equal total credit
balances before the bookkeeper can proceed to the work of preparing
statements and closing the books.

Trial balance errors are of five kinds:

(1) The original entry for a transaction may be incorrect. The
Buildings account, for instance, may have been debited instead of
Taxes Expense. Errors of this kind are difficult to detect because,
although they are in the trial balance, they do not throw it out of
balance. It is very desirable, however, that they be discovered if
possible, because they affect the accuracy of the profit and loss statement and the balance sheet. The detection of such errors is the work
of a qualified accountant, who must critically analyze the original
entries.

(2) Errors may result because of incorrect postings. For example,

(a) Posting the wrong amount.
(b) Posting a debit to the credit side of an account, or vice
versa.
(c) Posting the same item twice.
(d) Failure to post at all.

(3) Original books of entry may be incorrectly footed.

(4) Errors may be the result of incorrectly computing account
balances, either in

(a) Adding the debits,
(b) Adding the credits, or
(c) In taking the difference between the two.

---

[2] The following excerpts are taken from the Uniform Sales Act, Section 19:

"Rule 4. (2) Where, in pursuance of a contract to sell, the seller delivers the goods
to the buyer, or to a carrier or other bailee (whether named by the buyer or not) for the
purpose of transmission to or holding for the buyer, he is presumed to have unconditionally appropriated the goods to the contract, except in the cases provided for in
the next rule and in Section 101. This presumption is applicable although by the terms
of the contract the buyer is to pay the price before receiving delivery of the goods, and
the goods are marked with the words collect on delivery or their equivalent.

"Rule 5. If the contract to sell requires the seller to deliver the goods to the buyer,
or at a particular place, or to pay the freight or costs of transportation to the buyer,
or to a particular place, the property does not pass until the goods have been delivered
to the buyer or reached the place agreed upon."

(5) Errors may occur in drawing up the trial balance proper:

    (a) A balance may be incorrectly copied in the trial balance.

    (b) A debit may be placed in the credit column, or vice versa.

    (c) A balance may be entirely omitted.

    (d) One or both columns of the trial balance may be incorrectly footed.

In practice errors are bound to occur. Obviously their discovery is not made easier by the numerous sources of their origin. The following suggestions may prove helpful in assisting the student to trace errors.

Locating Errors. —

(1) An error of 1, 10, 100, etc., is usually due to an error in addition or subtraction.

(2) The difference between the two sides of a trial balance may be due to the omission of an entire debit or credit.

(3) If the difference is divisible by 2, look for a figure equal to the quotient which may be either

    (a) A posting made to the wrong side of an account.

    (b) A debit balance placed in the credit column of the trial balance, or vice versa.

(4) If the difference is divisible by 9,

    (a) A one-column transposition may be the cause of error.

Examples:

Correct	Transposed	Difference	
54	45	9	$\div 9 = 1$
87	78	9	$\div 9 = 1$
75	57	18	$\div 9 = 2$
97	79	18	$\div 9 = 2$
130	103	27	$\div 9 = 3$
85	58	27	$\div 9 = 3$
85,132	58,132	27,000	$\div 9 = 3,000$
74,111	47,111	27,000	$\div 9 = 3,000$

In the first example, 1 is the difference between the digits transposed; in the second example, 2; and in the third example, 3. Obviously, if one suspects a transposition, attention should be confined to those adjacent digits whose difference is 1, 2, or 3, as the case may be.

In the fourth example, the three zeros indicate that the three right-hand columns are correct as they stand. The error is in the fourth and fifth columns, and the difference between the transposed

digits is 3. In searching for the error, one's attention should be confined to those figures of 10,000 and over; figures such as 67,132,
86,000, and 19,121, should be disregarded because their differences
of 1, 2, and 8, respectively, for the significant figures are at variance
with the objective difference of 3. In other words, the search should
be centered upon 5-digit figures whose fourth- and fifth-column
digits have a difference of 3.

　　　(b) The error may be due to a slide of one place.

Example:

	Difference	
25.00 written as 2.50	22.50	÷ 9 = 2.50

The quotient is the figure incorrectly written in the trial balance.

(5) If the difference is divisible by 99,

　　　(a) A two-column transposition may be the cause of error.

Examples:

Correct	*Transposed*	*Difference*	
514	415	99	÷ 99 = 1
735	537	198	÷ 99 = 2
981	189	792	÷ 99 = 8

The difference between the digits transposed is 1, 2, and 8, respectively. Attention should therefore be confined to digits in the
first and third columns whose differences are 1, 2, and 8, as the case
may be.

　　　(b) The error may be due to a slide of two places.

Example:

	Difference	
250.00 written as 2.50	247.50	÷ 99 = 2.50

The quotient is the figure incorrectly written in the trial balance.
This type of error is very common because of the tendency to think
of or call $250.00 as "two-fifty" and to write it $2.50.

(6) If the difference is divisible by 999,

　　　(a) A three-column transposition may be the cause of error.

Example:

Correct	*Transposed*	*Difference*	
5,006	6,005	999	÷ 999 = 1

(b) The error may be due to a slide of three places.

Example:

	Difference	
2,500.00 written as 2.50	2,497.50	÷ 999 = 2.50

Again, the quotient is the figure incorrectly written in the trial balance.

These special suggestions for locating trial balance errors are about the only ones of this type that are really serviceable. If they do not prove helpful, the only recourse is to check the work of the period systematically — footings of books of original entry, postings, account balance, the transcript and footings of the trial balance.

As a last resort, the bookkeeper may prepare T accounts in which are placed the account balances as of the date of the last trial balance. To these are posted the transactions of the period after which account balances are determined. Comparison of these balances with the balances of the formal general ledger trial balance should reveal wherein the latter are incorrect.

Trial balance difficulties give emphasis to the desirability of careful and accurate work on the books at all times. The reward of work well done is (1) neatness and legibility, and (2) a real saving of time and energy, to which should be added the favorable psychology of steady accomplishment.

PROFIT AND LOSS STATEMENT

As progress is made in the study of accounting, it will be necessary to center an increasing amount of attention upon the profit and loss statement. Some of the problems underlying its construction will now be discussed. The prime function of the profit and loss statement is to show the net income (or net loss) of a business over a specified period of time, and to show how or why that income was earned. If this function is to be performed, the profit and loss statement must be arranged so that it will show certain major types of information.

Net Sales. — The difference between gross sales, and deductions for sales returns and allowances, and sales discounts is called net sales. This figure measures the amount of merchandise "permanently" sold to customers in terms of the minimum amount of cash which would settle these sales. By the standard of cash, it represents the real volume of business transacted in an accounting period.

Cost of Sales. — The cost of sales is the cost of the merchandise sold during an accounting period. Cost of sales is comprised of

The beginning inventory of merchandise

plus   Purchases (net)

minus   Purchases discounts

plus   Transportation costs incurred on purchases, and

minus   The ending inventory of merchandise.

Transportation charges are included in cost of sales because they increase the cost of merchandise. On the profit and loss statement, therefore, Freight In is added to Purchases in order to show the full cost of all merchandise purchased during the accounting period (see illustration on page 172). By analogous reasoning, the full cost of an inventory is the cost of merchandise plus a proper allowance for transportation charges.

When the books are being closed, the Freight In account should be closed to the Cost of Sales account. Purchases discounts, also, should be closed to this account.

Insurance paid on merchandise is usually looked upon as an expense rather than as an addition to the purchase cost of goods.

Gross Profit. — Gross profit is the difference between net sales and cost of sales.

Operating Expenses. — Operating expenses, generally divided into selling expenses and general expenses, are those incurred in the production of the main income stream of a business.

Net Profit from Operations. — The net profit from operations is gross profit minus operating expenses. It represents the amount of profit realized from the main function for which a business was organized as, for example, merchandising.

Other Income. — Under the heading of "Other Income" are placed those incomes more or less regularly realized from sources outside the regular operations of a business. Examples are incomes derived from dividends, interest, and rents.

Other Expense. — Under the heading of "Other Expense" are placed those expenses more or less regularly incurred as nonoperating costs. These miscellaneous expenses are not looked upon as direct costs of producing the income represented by Net Profit from Operations. Examples are interest expense, and taxes on idle property.

On the profit and loss statement the figure for Other Expense is deducted from the sum of net-profit-from-operations and other-income. In the absence of other items of gain or loss (of special character), the remainder is called

Net Income. — This figure is the net income from all of the transactions of a business over an accounting period.

Accountants do not agree as to whether or not losses, and so-called "extraordinary" or "abnormal" costs and gains, should be placed in the profit and loss statement. Some accountants would restrict the profit and loss statement to the showing of net-profit-from-operations plus other-income and minus other-expense; and they would handle "abnormal" items as direct debits or credits to Capital account (or Surplus account, for a corporation). Modern advanced accounting thought, however, heavily favors the inclusion of all so-called abnormal items in the profit and loss account, and in the profit and loss statement. On the income statement these extraordinary items would be shown as follows:

Net Profit from Operations	$xxx xx
Other Income	xxx xx
	$xxx xx
Other Expense	xxx xx
	$xxx xx
Special Income Credits:	
Profit on Sale of Land	xxx xx
	$xxx xx
Special Income Debits:	
Storm Damage	xxx xx
Net Income before Income Taxes	$xxx xx
Provision for Income Taxes	xxx xx
Net Income	$xxx xx

In this manner the "net income" figure for an accounting period is made fully inclusive in every sense of the word. It would be defined as follows:

Net Income. — The amount of net income earned by a business over a period of time is the excess of net worth at the end of the period over the net worth at the beginning of the period excluding, however, any increases in realized net worth during the period due to investments or donations of capital, and making allowance, also, for any distributions of earned or invested capital.

Under this modern philosophy of accounting for business income, the capital account of a business would receive entries for the following items *only*:

(1) Transfer of the balance of the Profit and Loss account to capital account (or Surplus, for a corporation).

(2) Additions or withdrawals of capital.

(3) Transfer of the balance of a proprietary drawing account to capital account.

ILLUSTRATION

The following profit and loss statement will illustrate the correct placement of certain types of information.

John A. Blank

PROFIT AND LOSS STATEMENT, YEAR ENDING DECEMBER 31, 19—

Gross Sales			$46,000.00
Less Returned Sales and Allowances		$ 1,400.00	
Sales Discounts		600.00	2,000.00
Net Sales			$44,000.00
Cost of Sales:			
Merchandise, January 1, 19—		$10,000.00	
Purchases	$21,100.00		
Less Returned Purchases			
and Allowances	$ 800.00		
Purchases Discounts	300.00	1,100.00	20,000.00
Freight In		1,000.00	
		$31,000.00	
Merchandise, December 31, 19—		13,000.00	18,000.00
Gross Profit			$26,000.00
Selling Expenses:			
Advertising	$ 1,400.00		
Sales Salaries	5,000.00		
Traveling Expenses	2,000.00	$ 8,400.00	
General Expenses:			
Miscellaneous Expenses	$ 3,000.00		
Office Salaries	8,600.00		
Utilities Expense	1,000.00	12,600.00	21,000.00
Net Profit from Operations			$ 5,000.00
Other Income:			
Interest Income			1,200.00
			$ 6,200.00
Other Expense:			
Interest Expense			200.00
			$ 6,000.00
Special Income Credits:			
Profit on Sale of Land			2,000.00
			$ 8,000.00
Special Income Debits:			
Contribution — Civic Center Memorial Fund			1,000.00
Net Income before Income Taxes			$ 7,000.00

Provision for Income Taxes 2,000.00

Net Income . . . . $ 5,000.00

QUESTIONS

Question **9-1.** A sales invoice is posted to the credit side of a customer's account in error. How should the correction be made? Would your answer be different if the posting had been made to the wrong account? If so, explain.

Question **9-2.** Your bank balance, after all outstanding checks have been deducted, does not equal your cash account balance. What are the possible causes of disagreement?

Question **9-3.** The bank balance should be reconciled monthly. Why?

Question **9-4.** Who, in your opinion, should be responsible for the work of reconciling the bank account?

Question **9-5.** An article is quoted at $100.00 list, less trade discounts of 30-20-10-5. What is the invoice price of the article?

Question **9-6.** The difference between your trial balance totals is 180. Suggest several possibilities as to the cause of error.

Question **9-7.** Your trial balance does not balance. Outline, in order, the steps that you would take to uncover the error, or errors, made.

Question **9-8.** X received the following quotations on the same article of merchandise:

From Y: $2.00 per unit, less 40%, 10%, and 5%.
         Cash discount, 2%.
From Z: $2.00 per unit, less 50%, and 5%.
         Cash discount, 1%.

X accepted the best offer, purchasing 100 units, f.o.b. destination. The freight, which the shipper failed to prepay, was paid by X and amounted to $4.05. X paid for the merchandise within the discount period, deducting the freight of $4.05 in making his remittance.
What are the proper entries to record X's transactions?

Question **9-9.** J. W. Crain owes Martin & Son $614.76 for merchandise purchased August 1 on terms of 3/10, 1/20, n/60. On August 10 Mr. Crain writes a check for $500.00 in favor of Martin & Son in part payment of account. What entry should Mr. Crain make?

Question **9-10.** X, in Chicago, buys merchandise from Y, in New York, for $733.00 less discounts of 30-10-5. Terms 2/10, n/60, f.o.b. Chicago. X pays freight of $10.00. X returns unsatisfactory merchandise, receiving a credit memorandum of $38.70 therefor.
X pays the bill within the cash discount period, taking all deductions

to which he is entitled. What is the amount of his check? What entry should be made to record the disbursement?

Question **9–11.** On March 1, 19__, John A. Adams purchased merchandise from Brent & Co., in Chicago for $1,060.00, less discounts of 30, 10, and 10. Terms, f.o.b. destination, and 3/10, n/60. Mr. Adams paid freight of $13.16. On March 7 he received a credit memorandum for goods returned, $30.00. On March 10 Mr. Adams sent a check to Brent & Co. for $346.73, after taking all deductions to which he was entitled. On April 30 he remitted for the balance due.

What entries should be made by Mr. Adams on March 10 and April 30?

Question **9–12.** Merchandise costing $1,261.60 is purchased from Y on terms of 5/10, n/60. What are the proper entries to be made if the invoice is paid within the cash discount period by a note for $630.80 and a check for the balance due? a check for $630.80 and a note for the balance due?

Assume cash discount to be earned only on the amount of cash actually exchanging hands.

What would your entries have been if, within the cash discount period, a check for $500.00 had been given in partial payment of the invoice, and the balance of the invoice had been paid at the end of the 60-day credit period?

Question **9–13.** The following transactions occurred on the dates indicated:

October

1 — J. L. Dunn purchased merchandise from Perry & Son for $1,000.00 less discounts of 30–10–10. Terms f.o.b. shipping point, and 3/10, n/30.

2 — Dunn paid freight of $17.00 when the merchandise arrived.

7 — On this date Mr. Dunn received a credit memorandum from Perry & Son for $50.00, covering merchandise returned.

10 — Dunn mailed a check of $307.49 to Perry & Son.

31 — Dunn mailed a check for the balance due to Perry & Son.

What entries should be made on October 10 and 31?

Question **9–14.** Indicate whether or not the following errors will be revealed by failure of the trial balance to balance:

(1) A debit which is not posted.
(2) A debit posted to the debit side of the wrong account.
(3) A credit which is not posted.
(4) A credit posted to the Sales account should have been to the Purchases account.
(5) A debit posted to the credit side of the correct account.
(6) An entry which is posted twice.
(7) An entry in which the postings are made as $105.00 instead of $150.00.
(8) An entry which is entirely omitted in posting.

(9) An entry journalized as:

| Wages Expense . . . . | 100.00 | |
| Cash . . . . | | 100.00 |

which should have been:

| Wages Payable . . . . | 100.00 | |
| Cash . . . . | | 100.00 |

(10) An entry journalized as:

| Freight Expense . . . . | 100.00 | |
| Cash . . . . | | 100.00 |

which should have been:

| Simmons & Company . . . . | 100.00 | |
| Cash . . . . | | 100.00 |

(11) An error in computing the balance of an account.

(12) An account balance incorrectly copied upon the trial balance.

(13) An account balance omitted from the trial balance.

(14) A debit balance placed in the credit column of the trial balance.

(15) A debit balance of $450.00 copied as $550.00 on the trial balance; and a credit balance computed as $1,613.00 and so copied on the trial balance, but which in reality is $1,513.00.

(16) Errors in footing the trial balance.

(17) Error in footing the purchases book.

(18) Error in footing a columnar cash receipts book.

PROBLEMS

Problem **9-1.** You are the bookkeeper of the Chandler-Gordon Company. On January 7, 1951, a letter is received from a customer, the Bremerton Trading Company, stating that it cannot reconcile with its books the balance of $52.46 shown as unpaid on the Chandler-Gordon statement of December 31, 1950. According to its records it owes:

Invoice November 17	. . . .	$ 5.47
" November 25	. . . .	16.05
" December 22	. . . .	17.43
" December 29	. . . .	9.04
		$47.99

With the letter is a transcript of the Chandler-Gordon account as it appears on the Bremerton Trading Company's books:

	Debits			*Credits*	
Oct. 19	. . . .	78.16	Oct. 10	. . . .	78.16
23	. . . .	100.00	22	. . . .	123.11
30	. . . .	130.25	27	. . . .	107.14

Debits		Credits	
Nov. 14	27.50	Nov. 1	27.50
18	180.26	12	165.14
23	423.20	12	15.12
22	72.14	15	423.20
27	52.15	17	5.47
30	2.45	19	114.29
Dec. 12	181.23	27	10.00
18	22.65	Dec. 11/25	16.05
		4	42.81
		6	26.10
		12	114.77
		15	22.65
		22	17.43
		29	9.04

Your account with the Bremerton Trading Company is as follows:

BREMERTON TRADING COMPANY

1950						1950					
Oct.	10	2/10, n/30	S	78	16	Oct.	20		CR	78	16
	22	2/10, n/30	S	123	11		25		CR	100	00
	27	2/10, n/30	S	107	14	Nov.	1		CR	130	25
Nov.	1	2/10, n/30	S	27	50		15		CR	26	95
	12	2/10, n/30	S	165	14		20		CR	179	95
	12	Freight prepaid	CP	15	12		22	C/m (invoice			
	15	5/10, n/30	S	423	20			11/15)	J	72	14
	17	2/10, n/30	S	5	47		24		CR	419	59
	19	2/10, n/30	S	114	29		29	Invoices 11/19,			
	25	Net	S	16	05			11/27	CR	52	15
	27	2/10, n/30	S	10	00		30	C/m (invoice			
Dec.	4	2/10, n/30	S	42	81			11/1)	J	2	45
	6	2/10, n/30	S	26	10	Dec.	14	Invoices 12/4,			
	12	2/10, n/30	S	114	77			12/6, 12/12	CR	181	23
	15	2/10, n/30	S	22	65		18	C/m (invoice			
	22	2/10, n/30	S	17	43			12/15)	J	22	65
	29	2/10, n/30 (52.46)	S	9	04					1265	52
				1317	98						

Prepare an itemized statement, or letter of explanation, showing how, and why, you consider your balance of $52.46 correct.

Problem **9-2.** Prepare a reconciliation of the bank account from the following information:

Bank statement balance, August 31, 19—.	$13,246.00
Cash account balance, August 31, 19—	14,862.00
Collection and exchange charged by bank.	6.84
Checks outstanding and not yet charged to our bank account by bank	2,314.00
Cash in our cash drawer, recorded in our cash receipts book of August 31, but deposited in the bank on September 1	817.00
Securities purchased for us by bank, cost of same being debited to our bank account by bank. Debit memorandum for this purchase accompanied the canceled checks which the bank returned with its August 31 statement	3,106.16

What entries should be placed on the books to reflect the above information?

Problem **9-3.** On October 31, 19___, Mr. Clyde L. Farrar began the reconciliation of his bank account with the following information before him:

Balance on bank statement, October 31, 19— $12,076.10
Balance of Cash account, October 31, 19— 5,977.69
Checks outstanding 2,025.22
Deposit made October 31 but not appearing on October bank
statement 812.16
Included with the canceled checks returned by the bank is one
check for $114.65 signed by Clark L. Farrar. This is not a check
of Mr. Clyde L. Farrar.
The bank statement also shows a deposit of $5,000.00. This represents a loan procured from the bank on October 17 on a note payable of $5,000.00 for 60 days. This loan has not been recorded on the books of Mr. Farrar.

Required:

(1) Reconcile the bank account.

(2) From the information contained in your bank reconciliation construct the entries which should be placed on the books.

Problem **9-4.** L. M. Roberts commenced business on June 2, 19___. His cash book for the month of June was:

CASH RECEIPTS			CASH PAYMENTS		
				Check No.	
June 2	Investment	10,000.00	June 3	. . . . 1	301.00
5	. . . .	202.00	3	. . . . 2	1,214.00
11	. . . .	128.00	10	. . . . 3	710.00
16	. . . .	57.00	12	. . . . 4	2,344.00
21	. . . .	389.00	14	. . . . 5	2,510.00
23	. . . .	486.00	19	. . . . 6	261.00
24	. . . .	200.00	20	. . . . 7	162.00
27	. . . .	50.00	25	. . . . 8	17.00
28	. . . .	878.00	26	. . . . 9	204.00
28	. . . .	244.00	28	. . . . 10	1,000.00
30	. . . .	310.00	29	. . . . 11	220.00
		12,944.00			8,943.00

His bank statement for June was:

BANK STATEMENT

	Charges	*Deposits*	*Balance*
June 2		10,000.00	10,000.00
5	301.00	202.00	9,901.00
7	1,214.00		8,687.00
11		128.00	8,815.00
15	2,344.00		6,471.00
17		57.00	6,528.00
18	710.00		5,818.00

	Charges	Deposits	Balance
June 19	261.00		5,557.00
22		389.00	5,946.00
25	2,510.00	686.00	4,122.00
27	162.00	50.00	
	1,000.00		3,010.00
29		1,122.00	4,132.00
30	50.00		4,082.00

Required:

(1) Reconcile the bank account. The charge of $50.00 in the bank statement covers a "hot check," i.e., one originally deposited by Mr. Roberts but which could not be collected by the bank. The check is signed by a customer, E. A. Atlee. Mr. Roberts expects that the check will be collected ultimately.

(2) Make the entry to take up the "hot check" on the books of Mr. Roberts.

Problem **9-5.** On October 31, 19___, Mr. W. C. Willard reconciled his bank account as follows:

```
Balance per bank statement . . . . . . . . . . . . . .      $841.22
Less: Outstanding checks:
    Oct.  2  . . . . . . . . . . . . . . . .   $ 2.00
          25  . . . . . . . . . . . . . . . .      3.15
          29  . . . . . . . . . . . . . . . .     37.20
          31  . . . . . . . . . . . . . . . .      7.85       50.20
                                                            --------
Balance per Cash account  . . . . . . . . . . . . . .      $791.02
```

Mr. Willard's cash books, and bank statement, for the month of November were:

CASH RECEIPTS BOOK		CASH PAYMENTS BOOK		BANK STATEMENT			
					Charges	Deposits	Balance
Nov. 3 . .	207.12	Nov. 1 . .	6.53	Nov. 1			841.22
4 . .	106.25	1 . .	45.15	1	37.20		804.02
6 . .	297.36	1 . .	2.91	4	45.15		758.87
7 . .	75.00	1 . .	8.74	5	3.15	313.37	1,069.09
8 . .	101.09	2 . .	6.12	5	7.21		1,061.88
10 . .	191.41	2 . .	2.30	7	2.91	297.36	1,356.33
30 . .	99.00	2 . .	11.89	9	6.12		1,350.21
		2 . .	7.21	9	6.53		1,343.68
	1,077.23	5 . .	2.75	9	8.74		1,334.94
		10 . .	25.00	9	7.85		1,327.09
		14 . .	6.01	9	2.30	176.09	1,500.88
		17 . .	3.00	12	50.00		1,450.88
		19 . .	3.80	12	2.00	191.41	1,640.29
		21 . .	6.77	15	6.01		1,634.28
		28 . .	26.23	23	6.77		1,627.51
				29	11.89		1,615.62
			164.41	30	2.75		1,612.87

Required:

Reconcile the bank account, November 30. The $50.00 charge in the bank statement is found to be a counter check drawn by Mr. W. C. Willard on November 12 when he needed some cash in a hurry.

Problem 9-6. Continuing into the next month, the cash books of L. T. Robinson for the month of March are:

CASH RECEIPTS		CASH PAYMENTS		
1950		1950	Check No.	
Mar. 2	$ 87.00	Mar. 1 . . . 11 . . .	$ 300.00	
5	210.00	2 . . . 12 . . .	50.00	
10	599.00	4 . . . 13 . . .	200.00	
10	722.00	6 . . . 14 . . .	75.00	
10	617.00	8 . . . 15 . . .	20.00	
15	500.00	10 . . . 16 . . .	408.00	
19	72.00	10 . . . 17 . . .	2,330.00	
24	500.00	10 . . . 18 . . .	1,800.00	
24	110.00	12 . . . 19 . . .	200.00	
28	1,311.00	15 . . . 20 . . .	150.00	
		16 . . . 21 . . .	300.00	
	$4,728.00	19 . . . 22 . . .	1.50	
		22 . . . 23 . . .	30.00	
		24 . . . 24 . . .	200.00	
		26 . . . 25 . . .	807.00	
		31 . . . 26 . . .	120.00	
			$6,991.50	

Mr. Robinson's bank statement for the month ending March 31, 1950, was as follows:

Date	Charges			Deposits	Balance
Mar 1 '50					5,320.00
Mar 1 '50	231.00 —				5,089.00
Mar 2 '50				87.00	5,176.00
Mar 2 '50	300.00 —				4,876.00
Mar 5 '50				210.00	5,086.00
Mar 5 '50	200.00 —	50.00 —			4,836.00
Mar 8 '50	62.00 —				4,774.00
Mar 10 '50				1,938.00	6,712.00
Mar 10 '50	3.00 —				6,709.00
Mar 12 '50	408.00 —	75.00 —	2,330.00		3,896.00
Mar 15 '50				500.00	4,396.00
Mar 15 '50	200.00 —	1,800.00 —			2,396.00
Mar 17 '50	150.00 —	300.00 —			1,946.00
Mar 19 '50				72.00	2,018.00
Mar 24 '50				610.00	2,628.00
Mar 24 '50	150.00 —				2,478.00
Mar 28 '50				1,311.00	3,789.00
Mar 28 '50	807.00 —				2,982.00

Included with the canceled checks returned by the bank is a debit memorandum, dated March 10, 1950, for $3.00 covering a charge for special checks furnished to Mr. Robinson by the bank. All other debits in the bank statement are for checks and are correct as charged. No checks have been issued by Mr. Robinson in March other than checks No. 11 to 26, inclusive.

Prepare a reconciliation of Mr. Robinson's bank account as of March 31, 1950. (In preparing this reconciliation, you may find that reference to Mr. Robinson's bank reconciliation of February 28, 1950, is helpful; see page 160.)

The balance of Mr. Robinson's cash account on February 28, 1950, was $5,027.00.

Problem **9–7.** On January 11, 1952, the accounts of Harris & Barnes were being audited by a firm of public accountants. One of the auditors assembled the following information preparatory to a reconciliation of the bank account with the cash book:

	Check No.	CASH BOOK Receipts	CASH BOOK Payments	BANK STATEMENT Charges	BANK STATEMENT Deposits	BANK STATEMENT Balance
1951						
Dec. 31 Balance		3,620.00				3,474.00
1952						
Jan. 2		800.00			640.00	4,114.00
.....1 ..	1		212.00			
.....2 ..	2		20.00	290.00		3,824.00
3		614.00			800.00	4,624.00
.....3 ..	3		87.00			
.....4 ..	4		90.00	212.00		4,412.00
4		300.00			614.00	5,026.00
.....5 ..	5		140.00			
.....6 ..	6		10.00			
5		710.00			300.00	5,326.00
.....7 ..	7		300.00	140.00		
				180.00		
				20.00		4,986.00
6		1,200.00			710.00	5,696.00
.....8 ..	8		62.00			
.....9 ..	9		404.00	78.00		5,618.00
7		313.00			1,200.00	6,818.00
.....10 ..	10		100.00	10.00		
				404.00		6,404.00
9		950.00			313.00	6,717.00
.....11 ..	11		162.00	7.00		6,710.00
10		2,200.00			950.00	7,660.00
.....12 ..	12		480.00	300.00		
.....13 ..	13		1,600.00	24.00		7,336.00
.....14 ..	14		844.00			
.....15 ..	15		98.00			
10 Balance			6,098.00			
		10,707.00	10,707.00			

Jan. 11 Balance 6,098.00

The detailed debits and credits of the bank statement have been checked and found correct. The $7.00 charge on January 9 was for bank service charges, collection and exchange fees, etc. All other charges are represented by canceled checks. Each bank deposit represented the firm's total cash receipts for the preceding business day.

Three checks, one for $24.00, one for $180.00, and one for $290.00, were outstanding in the bank reconciliation of December 31, 1951.

Prepare the bank reconciliation as of the close of business January 10, 1952. The check for $78.00, on examination, is found to be Check No. 3, of January 3, 1952.

Problem 9–8. On October 31, 19___, John A. Chamberlain reconciled his bank account as follows:

Balance per bank statement.			$ 73.40
Add: Unrecorded deposits:			
October 30		$ 9.39	
October 31		40.69	50.08
			$123.48
Less: Outstanding checks:			
October 5		$ 3.04	
12		3.00	
29		26.45	
30		2.00	
31		15.00	49.49
Balance per Cash account in ledger			$ 73.99

Mr. Chamberlain's cash book for November and his bank statement for the month were as follows:

		CASH BOOK		BANK STATEMENT		
		Receipts	*Payments*	*Charges*	*Deposits*	*Balance*
Nov.	1					73.40
		. . . .	2.25		9.39	82.79
		. . . .			40.69	123.48
	2	. . 298.00 . .	50.00	26.45		97.03
	3	. . . .	45.00	3.04		93.99
	5	. . . .	151.00		298.00	391.99
		. . . .	11.05	45.00		
		. . . .		15.00		
		. . . .		2.00		329.99
	6	. . . .	6.55	11.05		318.94
	8	. . . .		151.00		167.94
	9	. . 100.00 . .		2.25		
		. . . .		3.00		162.69
	10	. . . .			100.00	262.69
	15	. . . .	32.07	50.00		
		. . . .		6.55		206.14
	16	. . 12.00 . .				
	17	. . 46.17 . .			12.00	218.14
	20	. . . .	16.24		36.17	254.31
	22	. . . .		12.00		242.31
	29	. . 121.02 . .	78.20	16.24		226.07
	30	. . . .			121.02	347.09
	30'	. . 116.14 . .		1.00		346.09

Usually cash receipts of one day were deposited in the bank on the following day. On November 17, however, $10.00 in cash was taken out of the cash receipts of that day for the purchase of stamps and the balance of $36.17 was deposited in the bank. The $1.00 bank debit on November 30 was a charge for Mr. Chamberlain's failure to keep a minimum balance of $100.00 on deposit throughout October. The debit of $12.00 on November 22 was for an N.S.F. check (i.e., bad check). This check, which was deposited on November 17, was signed by R. H. Wiggins, a customer.

Required:

(1) Prepare the bank reconciliation of November 30, 19___.

(2) From the information contained in your bank reconciliation construct the entries which should be placed on the books.

Problem **9–9.** On August 31, 19___, the bookkeeper of Roy H. Goodwin prepared a bank reconciliation as follows:

Balance per bank statement		$2,062.11
Balance per cash account		1,663.42
Difference		$ 398.69
Explanation of difference:		
Collection and sundry service fees		$ (7.12)
Outstanding checks:		
#598	$ 12.14	
#604	75.00	
#605	184.16	
#609	39.82	
#613	94.69	405.81
Total		$398.69

Give an intelligent criticism of this type of bank reconciliation.

Problem **9–10.** On October 22, 19___, E. M. Fleming purchased merchandise which was covered by an invoice for $10,000.00, 2/10, n/90. This merchandise was expected to be sold during the Christmas season on credit terms calling for cash payments by customers on the 10th of the month following date of sales invoice.

On November 1, 19___, Mr. Fleming was confronted with the choice of making payment by borrowing funds at the bank in order to pay the invoice with deduction of cash discount, or of forfeiting the cash discount and paying the invoice in full on January 20.

Although Mr. Fleming had about $1,200.00 cash in the bank, this cash was not actually available for payment of the invoice. It was needed for other general business purposes, payrolls, and so on. Mr. Fleming, however, could borrow money from the bank for 90 days at 6%. The bank required a borrower to maintain a minimum balance of 20% of the loan in his bank account. Mr. Fleming stated that his existing bank balance would take care of one-half of this bank requirement of 20%.

Required:

(1) Should Mr. Fleming have borrowed money at the bank for 90 days? Produce figures to prove that the loan should or should not have been made.

(2) Assume the terms of the invoice to have been 1/10, n/90. Under these conditions should Mr. Fleming have procured a loan on November 1?

Chapter 10

MULTIPLE-COLUMN BOOKS OF ORIGINAL ENTRY — DEPARTMENTAL ACCOUNTS AND STATEMENTS

The advantages of using specialized books of original entry were described in Chapter 8. With the exception of the general journal, each of these books of original entry contained one money column only.

In order to realize important additional advantages, it is generally desirable to expand one or more of the books of original entry from a book of one column into one containing two, three, four, five, or even more money columns. Because of the many columns which they sometimes employ, these "multiple-column" books of original entry may appear to be rather complex. In reality, however, these books are quite simple in their basic structure. The extra columns of these books of original entry are intended to speed up the placement of debits and credits in the accounts of the ledger. They aid greatly in the rapid recording and classification of transactions. They specify more clearly what accounts are to be debited or credited; and they expedite the posting process.

As a general rule, the extra or special columns in books of original entry are intended

(1) To permit certain transactions to be recorded completely on one line of one book of original entry.

(2) To permit the posting of column totals rather than the details of these totals.

(3) To expedite the proper classification of accounting transactions.

The balance of this chapter will discuss and illustrate the advantages which attend the use of special columns in the books of original entry.

MULTIPLE-COLUMN CASH RECEIPTS BOOK

If a sale on account for $1,000.00 were made to L. A. Jones on terms of 2/10, n/30, and if the invoice were collected within the cash discount period, two entries would be necessary to record the settlement:

```
CASH RECEIPTS BOOK: Cash . . . . . . . . . . .   980.00
                         L. A. Jones . . . . . .          980.00
                       To record the cash received.

JOURNAL:               Sales Discounts . . . . . .   20.00
                         L. A. Jones . . . . . . .           20.00
                       To credit L. A. Jones with 2%
                       cash discount.
```

Were the two entries combined, the compound entry would be:

```
Cash . . . . . . . . . . . . . . . . . . . . . . . . .   980.00
Sales Discounts . . . . . . . . . . . . . . . . . . .    20.00
     L. A. Jones . . . . . . . . . . . . . . . . . .            1,000.00
To record cash received in payment of sales invoice of —,
less 2% cash discount.
```

In order (1) to facilitate the recording of transactions of this type, and (2) to avoid the necessity of making entries in two books of original entry, and (3) to record all the required debits and credits in one place, the cash receipts book is provided with special columns in which are recorded *all* the required debits and credits, thus:

CASH RECEIPTS BOOK   Page 1

Date	Account Credited	Explanation	L.F.	Credit Accounts Receivable	Debit Sales Discounts	Cash
1950 Dec. 1	L. A. Jones			1,000 00	20 00	980 00

This entry in the cash receipts book is equivalent to the compound entry above.

Frequently, however, accounts other than those of customers must be credited because of cash received. Another column is therefore provided in which to record the amounts of these miscellaneous credit accounts. The cash receipts book would then appear:

CASH RECEIPTS BOOK   Page 1

DATE	ACCOUNT CREDITED	EXPLANATION	L.F.	CREDIT Miscellaneous	L.F.	Accounts Receivable	DEBIT Sales Discounts	Cash
1950								
Dec. 10	G. R. Kinsey	November account			27	212 00	2 12	209 88
10	M. G. Honting	November account			17	48 09	96	47 13
10	May & May	November account			32	462 25	9 25	453 00
10	R. G. Wood	November account			65	129 47	2 59	126 88
17	Notes Receivable	Field & Son	42	118 30				118 30
17	Interest Income	On Field note	20	1 18				1 18
19	J. J. Jackson	November account			22	99 17		99 17
23	Sales — Dept. A	B. L. Cole	80	29 80				29 80
26	E. L. Lang	Invoice Dec. 8			27	42 10	84	41 26
28	Sales — Dept. B	H. G. Wright	81	38 10				38 10
31	Bonds	Gillette 5's, 1950	9	2,000 00				2,000 00
				2,187 38		993 08	15 76	3,164 70
							(83)	(12)

The cash receipts book would be posted as follows:

DEBIT (at the end of the month):

Cash, for column total $3,164.70
Sales Discounts, for column total 15.76

CREDIT:

Each customer's account with the amount in the accounts receivable column. These postings are made daily. Total credit postings for the month would be equal. . . . . $ 993.08

Each account indicated in the "Account Credited" column with the amount recorded in the miscellaneous column. Postings may be made either at the end of the month or, if desired, more or less regularly throughout the month. Total miscellaneous postings for the month would equal 2,187.38

ADVANTAGES OF A MULTIPLE-COLUMN CASH RECEIPTS BOOK

The advantages of a multiple-column cash receipts book may be summarized as follows:

(1) Collections covering sales invoices paid within the cash discount period are *completely* recorded on one line of the cash receipts book.

(2) Each of these cash settlements requires but one posting, not two, to a customer's account.

(3) Instead of each receipt of cash being posted, only the total of the cash column is posted to the debit of the Cash account in the

ledger. Similarly, only the total of the sales discounts column is posted to the Sales Discounts account.

(4) The principle of posting only column totals may be extended to other accounts frequently used in the recording of transactions in the cash receipts book. This is illustrated in the example on page 191.

(5) Because of fewer entries and fewer postings, time and space are saved and accuracy is increased.

MULTIPLE-COLUMN CASH PAYMENTS BOOK

In similar manner, special columns have their place in the cash payments book. The four-column cash payments book is a good example of the multiple-column disbursements record. In the illustration below three common types of disbursements have been entered.

CASH PAYMENTS BOOK

| Date | | Account Debited | Explanation | L.F. | Debit | | | Credit | | |
					Miscellaneous	L.F.	Accounts Payable	Purchases Discounts	Cash	
19__										
May	1	Advertising Expense	Day Sales Co.		100 00				100 00	
	10	A. E. Ames & Co.	April account				500 00	10 00	490 00	
	31	Wages Expense	May payroll		1,000 00					
		Withholding Income								
		Taxes Payable			(140 00)					
		Social Security								
		Taxes Payable			(10 00)				850 00	

In this particular example, the total of the cash column would be posted to the credit side of the Cash account in the ledger. The total of the Purchases Discounts column would be posted in a similar manner. The items in the other columns would be posted in detail. The items in parentheses are credits.

The convenience of recording payments involving cash discounts on purchases on one line of the cash payments book should be obvious.

The cash payments book often has more than four columns. The extra columns are used because of the variety of accounts to be debited and because of the fact that some types of transactions recur with considerable frequency. The following example illustrates a cash payments book of this general type.

CASH PAYMENTS BOOK

Date	Account Debited	Explanation	L.F.	Miscellaneous	L.F.	Accounts Payable	Wages and Salaries	Freight In	Purchases Discounts	Cash
1950 Dec. 1	Freight In	Baltimore & Ohio	42					2 14		2 14
4	Office Expense	Royal Supply Co.		22 10						22 10
7	Freight In	Baltimore & Ohio						3 10		3 10
8	Wages & Salaries	Week ending Dec. 7					42 50			42 50
9	Emory A. Adams	November a/c			4	412 16			8 24	403 92
9	Briggs & Briggs	November a/c			10	115 10			2 30	112 80
9	L. S. Mortimer	November a/c			38	510 72			25 54	485 18
9	M. J. Rorty	November a/c			51	13 70			27	13 43
10	Notes Payable	First National Bank	41	1,000 00						1,000 00
10	Interest Expense	First National Bank	19	20 00						20 00
15	Wages & Salaries	Week ending Dec. 14					152 10			152 10
18	Freight In	Baltimore & Ohio						4 07		4 07
19	Purchases — Dept. A	W. M. Borah	70	211 50						211 50
22	Wages & Salaries	Week ending Dec. 21					37 60			37 60
22	Freight In	Baltimore & Ohio						4 20		4 20
28	Young & Company	Bill Dec. 23			67	389 41			19 47	369 94
29	Wages & Salaries	Week ending Dec. 28					165 14			165 14
31	Freight In	Baltimore & Ohio						3 71		3 71
				1,253 60		1,441 09	397 34	17 22	55 82	3,053 43
							(61)	(14)	(73)	(12)

Debit: Miscellaneous, L.F., Accounts Payable, Wages and Salaries, Freight In

Credit: Purchases Discounts, Cash

This cash payments book would be posted as follows:

DEBIT:

Each account as indicated in the "Account Debited" column with the amount recorded in the miscellaneous column. Postings may be made either at the end of the month or, if desired, more or less regularly throughout the month. Total miscellaneous postings for the month would equal $1,253.60

Each creditor's account with the amount in the accounts payable column. These postings are made daily. Total debit postings for the month would equal. 1,441.09

Wages and Salaries, for column total 397.34

Freight In, for column total 17.22

The last two postings are made at the end of the month.

CREDIT (at the end of the month):

Purchases Discounts, for column total. . . . . $ 55.82

Cash, for column total 3,053.43

ADVANTAGES OF A MULTIPLE-COLUMN CASH PAYMENTS BOOK

These advantages are:

(1) Disbursements covering purchases invoices paid within the cash discount period are *completely* recorded on one line of the cash payments book.

(2) Each of these cash payments involves but one posting, not two, to a creditor's account.

(3) Instead of each payment of cash being posted, only the total of the cash column is posted to the credit of the Cash account in the ledger. Similarly, only the total of the purchases discounts column is posted to the Purchases Discounts account.

(4) The principle of posting only column totals may be extended to other accounts frequently used in the recording of transactions in the cash payments book. For example, the totals of the columns for wages and salaries and freight in (on page 188) are posted to the debit side of the accounts for Wages and Salaries and Freight In.

(5) Because of fewer entries and fewer postings, time and space are saved and accuracy is increased.

HOW MANY COLUMNS?

Most of the special columns generally employed in the cash books of business have been illustrated in this chapter. In many cases, however, the principle of columnar utilization is extended to include even more columns. Determination of the proper number of columns to employ in any given book of original entry is a question whose answer is contingent upon the characteristics of the business to which the columns are to apply. Individual needs vary widely.

Some businesses require more columns than others, some require columns for one purpose, and some for another. For example, where occasion demands, the cash receipts book might even be constructed to include additional *debit* columns — for bank charges, freight allowed, interest expense, and so on.

As a general rule, a special column — in any book of original entry — should be employed whenever its use leads to economies in the recording and posting of transactions. Typical of the possibilities in this direction are the two cash books on page 191.

All of the columns in these cash books are posted in total except accounts receivable, accounts payable, and miscellaneous, which are posted in detail.[1]

It should be observed that even in columnar records as complex as these last two cash books, the rule of double entry is carefully observed. The only difference is a change in the form by which the double-entry equation is recorded and given recognition.

Before the totals of any columnar book are posted, the bookkeeper should determine that the sum of the debit totals of each book is equal to the sum of the credit totals. This is a check of great importance and should never be omitted.

If a business has two or more bank accounts, the cash column in each cash book should be replaced by one column for each bank account. An alternative arrangement in the cash receipts book would be to use one cash column; and one *memorandum* column for each bank to be used for the recording of deposits. The cash payments book, similarly, would have one cash column; and one *memorandum* column for each bank for the recording of checks drawn.

THE MULTIPLE-COLUMN JOURNAL

In the preceding pages extra columns have been generously employed to expand the cash receipts and cash payments books. Extra columns may also be used to expand the general journal but, for this particular book, expansion is sometimes not as essential as for the other books of original entry. Indeed, for many businesses, the two-column journal is entirely satisfactory. In other business, however, it is likely that controlling accounts will be used and, where they are employed, the journal in all probability will be a four- or a six-column one. This type of journal, illustrated on page 220, will not be considered further until Chapter 11, "Controlling Accounts."

In still other cases the journal may be expanded so as to repre-

---

[1] When controlling accounts are employed for accounts receivable and accounts payable, the only columns posted in detail to the general ledger are the miscellaneous ones. See Chapter 11, "Controlling Accounts."

CASH RECEIPTS BOOK

						CREDIT				DEBIT	
DATE	ACCOUNT CREDITED	EXPLANATION	L.F.	Miscellaneous	L.F.	Accounts Receivable	Interest Income	Notes Receivable	Sales	Sales Discounts	Cash

CASH PAYMENTS BOOK

						DEBIT								CREDIT	
DATE	ACCOUNT DEBITED	EXPLANATION	L.F.	Miscellaneous	L.F.	Accounts Payable	Advertising	Freight In	Interest Expense	Notes Payable	Purchases	Wages & Salaries	Traveling Expense	Purchase Discounts	Cash

sent a consolidation of all of the books of original entry into one single book of original entry called the Cash Journal. This type of record, which may employ as many as twenty or thirty columns, is rather widely used. In this text the cash journal is formally considered in Chapter 11.

DEPARTMENTAL ACCOUNTS AND STATEMENTS

When a business is divided into departments, it is important to know the amount of business transacted by, and the relative profitability of, each of these departments. If the accounting department is to have the responsibility of preparing financial reports containing this kind of information, it will be necessary to open

Sales
Returned Sales and Allowances
Purchases
Returned Purchases and Allowances
Freight In
Merchandise Inventory and
Cost of Sales

accounts for each department. Thus, each department will be handled as if it were a separate business. At the end of each accounting period the accounts for each department will be summarized and closed in the same manner that the accounts of L. T. Robinson were closed in Chapter 8. The merchandise accounts of department A, for instance, will be closed as follows:

Cost of Sales — Department A	xxx xx	
Merchandise Inventory — Department A		xxx xx
Cost of Sales — Department A	xxx xx	
Returned Purchases and Allowances — Dept. A	xxx xx	
Purchases — Department A		xxx xx
Freight In — Department A		xxx xx
Merchandise Inventory — Department A	xxx xx	
Cost of Sales — Department A		xxx xx
To record new inventory.		
Profit and Loss — Department A	xxx xx	
Cost of Sales — Department A		xxx xx
Sales — Department A	xxx xx	
Returned Sales and Allowances — Department A . .		xxx xx
Profit and Loss — Department A		xxx xx

Merchandise accounts for each of the other departments of a business will be closed in similar fashion.

DEPARTMENTAL EXPENSES AND NET PROFITS

After departmental gross profits have been determined, departmental net profits should be computed by allocating direct and indirect expenses to each department. Expenses, necessarily, must be recorded on the books, as far as it is practicable to do so, on a departmental basis:

Traveling Expense — Department A
Traveling Expense — Department B
Traveling Expense — Department C

In many cases, however, it is not practicable to distribute expenses to departments as they are incurred. Examples of such expenses are advertising, donations, executive salaries, experimental expenses, rent, taxes, and so on. In such cases, the entire expense is charged to a single expense account and, at the end of the month, the balance of the account is distributed to departments upon some equitable basis. The following examples illustrate three bases of expense apportionment:

Insurance should be prorated to departments in the ratio of insurable values within each department.
Rent may be distributed to departments in the ratio of floor space occupied by each department.
Taxes should be distributed to departments on the basis of tax valuations within each department.

Some indirect expenses, for which satisfactory distribution bases cannot be found, may often be apportioned to departments in the ratio of

(1) Total expenses already debited to the several departments, or
(2) Sales by departments.

These ratios can be recommended only (1) when they are the best ratios available, and (2) when they are considered as reasonably representative distribution bases. Sales, for instance, do not always afford a satisfactory basis for the distribution of expenses because expenses in the several departments may not have been incurred in proportion to sales.

ILLUSTRATION

Two expense distributions, one direct, the other indirect, will illustrate the bookkeeping procedure involved:

(1) Profit and Loss — Department A 380.00
    Profit and Loss — Department B 822.00
    Profit and Loss — Department C 85.00
        Traveling Expense — Department A 380.00
        Traveling Expense — Department B 822.00
        Traveling Expense — Department C 85.00
    To close departmental traveling expense accounts to de-
        partmental profit and loss accounts.

(2) Profit and Loss — Department A 194.40
    Profit and Loss — Department B 158.80
    Profit and Loss — Department C 46.80
        Rent Expense 400.00
    To distribute rent expense between departments as per
        the following calculation:

	Floor Space in Each Department	Ratios	Rent Expense Apportioned by Floor Space Ratios
A	10,687 sq. ft.	48.6%	$194.40
B	8,743 sq. ft.	39.7%	158.80
C	2,570 sq. ft.	11.7%	46.80
	22,000 sq. ft.	100.0%	$400.00

When all the expenses have been distributed to departments by entries such as these, the Profit and Loss accounts for the several departments will show departmental net profits from merchandising, i.e., net operating profits by departments. The balances of the departmental Profit and Loss accounts are then transferred to Profit and Loss — General. This account is the summary profit and loss account for the business as a whole.

Many concerns do not compute departmental net profits. They maintain that the computations cannot be accurately made since many of their expenses cannot be accurately apportioned to departments. And without accurate apportionment there can be no such thing as complete accuracy and utility in the figures which purport to represent net profits.

Some of these concerns which do not compute departmental net profits content themselves with the next best procedure:

(1) The determination of gross profits by departments, and

(2) The determination of "direct costs" of making sales by departments. Such direct costs are known as selling expenses, or as costs of distribution, and are so classified on the profit and loss statement. The difference between the gross profit and selling expenses is the "selling profit" on sales. This remainder measures the direct yield from sales and, therefore, becomes an important departmental index of profitability.

Blank & Company

PROFIT AND LOSS STATEMENT

FOR MONTH ENDING JANUARY 31, 19__

	DEPT. A		DEPT. B		DEPT. C		TOTAL	
Gross Sales	$8,233	00	$12,014	00	$4,954	00	$25,201	00
Less Returned Sales and Allowances; and Sales Discounts . . .	65	00	117	00	32	00	214	00
Net Sales	$8,168	00	$11,897	00	$4,922	00	$24,987	00
Cost of Sales	$5,490	00	$ 6,880	00	$3,622	00	$15,992	00
Gross Profit	$2,678	00	$ 5,017	00	$1,300	00	$ 8,995	00
Selling Expenses:								
Advertising	$ 380	00	$ 822	00	$ 85	00	$ 1,287	00
Delivery Expense	339	00	339	00	170	00	848	00
Depreciation on Delivery Equipment	46	00	46	00	23	00	115	00
Freight Out	42	00	29	00	26	00	97	00
Salaries	500	00	1,070	00	280	00	1,850	00
Traveling Expense	218	00	395	00	103	00	716	00
Total Selling Expense	$1,525	00	$ 2,701	00	$ 687	00	$ 4,913	00
Selling Profit	$1,153	00	$ 2,316	00	$ 613	00	$ 4,082	00
General Expenses:								
Bad Debts	$ 55	00	$ 105	00	$ 9	00	$ 169	00
Insurance	43	00	89	00	30	00	162	00
Miscellaneous	68	00	208	00	34	00	310	00
Office Salaries	225	00	681	00	106	00	1,012	00
Taxes	72	00	299	00	48	00	419	00
Telephone and Telegraph	6	00	20	00	11	00	37	00
Total General Expense	$ 469	00	$ 1,402	00	$ 238	00	$ 2,109	00
Net Profit from Operations	$ 684	00	$ 914	00	$ 375	00	$ 1,973	00
Other Income:								
Interest Earned							29	00
							$ 2,002	00
Other Expense:								
Taxes on Idle Land							51	00
Net Income							$ 1,951	00

However, net profits by departments should be computed whenever they can be determined with reasonable accuracy because net profit figures, in the last analysis, are the proof of successful merchandising. Scientific exactness is not necessarily required to make net profit figures of value to the management of a business, for the figures will be of genuine serviceability if they reveal the trends and tendencies of business activity.

DEPARTMENTAL PROFIT AND LOSS STATEMENT

At this point it is well to state, parenthetically, that the benefits of departmental analyses may be obtained without having these analyses completely incorporated in the detail of the formal accounts of the ledger. If the books provide the *primary* information required, the bookkeeping may continue to be of the simplest type, i.e., the closing of *all* nominal accounts into departmental cost of sales accounts and *one* profit and loss account. The required departmental analysis may be limited to the profit and loss statement alone. As an illustration of what is meant, the profit and loss statement on page 195 is suggested as being adequately serviceable for a business with three departments.

COLUMNAR SALES AND PURCHASES BOOKS

In order that departmental merchandise accounts may be established without too much bookkeeping labor, special columns are employed in the sales and purchases books for the purpose of classifying merchandise transactions at the time of entry. The sales book, for example, might appear as follows:

SALES BOOK   Page 1

DATE	INVOICE No.	DEBIT ACCOUNT OF	L.F.	DEBIT		CREDIT		
				Accounts Receivable	Sales Dept. A	Sales Dept. B	Sales Dept. C	
1950								
Dec. 1	187	G. R. Kinsey	24	342 50	187 50	155 00		
5	188	M. D. Honting	17	104 67			104 67	
8	189	E. L. Lang	27	42 10	27 14	10 06	4 90	
11	190	R. G. Wood	65	207 00	54 00		153 00	
15	191	Homer & Son	12	188 42		188 42		
19	192	R. G. Wood	65	19 21	19 21			
21	193	Payne & Company	48	414 90	200 02	117 88	97 00	
26	194	G. R. Kinsey	24	382 12	273 98		108 14	
27	195	May & May	32	16 07			16 07	
29	196	J. J. Jackson	22	598 71		598 71		
31	197	Homer & Son	12	122 11			122 11	
				2,437 81	761 85	1,070 07	605 89	
					(80)	(81)	(82)	

The sales book would be posted as follows:

DEBIT (daily):
Each customer's account as indicated; total debit postings for
the month would equal $2,437.81

CREDIT (at the end of the month):
Sales — Department A, for column total . . . . $ 761.85
Sales — Department B, for column total 1,070.07
Sales — Department C, for column total 605.89

Ledger pages to which the column totals have been posted are
shown in parentheses.

The purchases book would be similarly constructed:

PURCHASES BOOK   Page 1

| | | | CREDIT | DEBIT | | |
Date	CREDIT ACCOUNT OF	L.F.	Accounts Payable	Purchases Dept. A	Purchases Dept. B	Purchases Dept. C
1950						
Dec. 7	C. T. Williams	59	428 15	103 12	98 22	226 81
12	Emory A. Adams	4	300 77		300 77	
17	L. S. Mortimer	38	721 36	214 77	404 70	101 89
19	Briggs & Briggs	10	111 80	27 10		84 70
23	Young & Company, Inc.	67	389 41	148 98		240 43
27	Emory A. Adams	4	27 22		27 22	
31	Hugh A. McNeil	35	212 20	57 14		155 06
			2,190 91	551 11	830 91	808 89
				(70)	(71)	(72)

The purchases book would be posted as follows:

DEBIT (at the end of the month):
Purchases — Department A, for column total . . . . $ 551.11
Purchases — Department B, for column total 830.91
Purchases — Department C, for column total 808.89

CREDIT (daily):
Each seller's account as indicated; total credit postings for the
month would equal $2,190.91

Merchandise returns and allowances require similar departmental
analysis. If separate books are kept for transactions of this kind,
they should be planned in accordance with the columnar principles
illustrated above.

CASH SALES FOR A DEPARTMENTAL BUSINESS

With respect to a departmental business, the four ways of handling cash sales, as described in Chapter 8, require brief comment:

(1) Enter cash sales in the cash receipts book only. When this method is used, the cash receipts book should have one cash sale column for each department. If there are very many departments, however, the cash receipts book may become so wide that it is unwieldy, and it may be better to use one of the other methods.

(2) and (3) Handle cash sales like credit sales. Both of these methods, especially the third, are excellent ways of accounting for departmental cash sales.

(4) Enter cash sales in the cash receipts book and also in the sales book. The debits to Cash from the sales book and the credits to Sales from the cash receipts book are not posted. When this method is used it is advisable to open a separate column in the sales book for the debits to Cash; and to open a separate column in the cash receipts book for the credits to Sales, thus:

SALES BOOK   Page 1

| Date | Debit Account of | L.F. | Debit | | Credit | |
			Accounts Receivable	Cash[2]	Sales Dept. A	Sales Dept. B

CASH RECEIPTS BOOK   Page 1

| Date | Account Credited | Explana-tion | L.F. | Credit | | | Debit | |
				Miscel-laneous	L.F.	Accounts Re-ceivable	Sales[2]	Sales Dis-counts	Cash

A complete set of books with multiple-column books of original entry is illustrated in Chapter 11.

---

[2] This column is not posted, either in detail or in total.

QUESTIONS

Question **10–1.** What is the purpose of departmentalizing the accounts of a business? Outline the technique of departmental accounting.

Question **10–2.** Consider the largest department store in your community. If you were in charge of the company, to what extent would you provide for departmental information? Explain fully.

Question **10–3.** To what extent do you believe it feasible to departmentalize the accounts of the Campbell Soup Company? an agency of the Ford Motor Company? a wholesale grocery?

Question **10–4.** Is it possible to allocate accurately the following expenses to departments? If so, state the bases of allocation.

Advertising	Rent
Delivery Expense	Taxes
Executive Salaries	Traveling Expense
Indirect Labor	Utilities Expense (electricity, gas,
Insurance	water, telephone and telegraph)
Office Expense	Warehouse Expense
Office Salaries	

Question **10–5.** Prepare a form to illustrate a columnar returned sales and allowances book (3 departments). How should this book be posted?

Question **10–6.** Draw up forms of four-column cash receipts and cash payments books. How should these books be posted?

Question **10–7.** Refer to the cash book forms on pages 186, 188, and 191. Can you explain why the L.F. columns for miscellaneous items are not used for accounts receivable and accounts payable? Separate L.F. columns, it will be noticed, are carried for accounts receivable and accounts payable.

Question **10–8.** What are the advantages of columnar books of original entry?

Question **10–9.** How would you handle cash sales for a business with two products? twelve products? Under similar conditions how should cash purchases be handled?

Question **10–10.** Describe and explain the principal divisions into which a profit and loss statement is divided.

PROBLEMS

Problem **10–1.** On a certain quantity of small electric drills which he was expecting to purchase, Mr. Whiting, president and manager of the Whiting Hardware Company, received the following quotations, and entered into the transactions indicated:

October   *List*   *Discounts*

1 — Quotations from:

Gray & Company $1,000.00   40–10–10

Allen & Son 1,200.00   50–20

1 — The purchase of drills was made from the firm giving the best price. Additional terms of purchase were: f.o.b. destination, and 3/5, 2/10, n/60.

3 — Received the merchandise and invoice (dated October 1). The invoice also showed an extra charge for insurance of $1.27, which was correct.

3 — Paid collect freight on the above merchandise, $19.70.

5 — Sent a check for $300.00 in part payment of account. The recording of this check took into consideration a proper allowance for cash discount.

11 — Sent a check for $80.30. The amount of this check was calculated at $100.00 less deduction of $19.70 freight, or net of $80.30. The recording of this check took into consideration a proper allowance for cash discount.

November

30 — Sent a check for the balance required to settle the vendor's account.

Required:

Make the journal entries to record the above transactions. Show the date of each entry.

Problem **10–2.** F. H. Melton has the following information before him at the end of the year:

Advertising Expense	$ 5,216.00
S. E. Bell (customer)	6,464.00
B. L. Brown (creditor)	36,014.00
Building	20,000.00
Cash	9,681.00
Commissions Earned	2,000.00
Freight In	3,000.00
General Expense	6,111.00
S. J. Hadley (creditor)	23,672.00
Land	7,000.00
F. H. Melton, Capital	80,000.00
F. H. Melton, Personal	3,780.00
Merchandise, January 1, 19__	30,000.00
Merchandise, December 31, 19__	77,000.00
Miscellaneous Equipment	12,000.00
Mortgage Payable	5,000.00
Notes Payable	5,000.00
Notes Receivable	619.00
Office Expense	1,862.00
Purchases	125,000.00
Returned Purchases.	6,000.00
M. H. Ronald (customer)	4,116.00
Sales	100,000.00

Traveling Expense	3,800.00
Wages and Salary Expense	13,218.00
W. A. Wood (customer)	5,819.00

Required:

(1) Draw off a trial balance on working papers.

(2) Complete the working papers.

(3) Prepare a profit and loss statement for the year ending December 31, 19__.

(4) Prepare a balance sheet, December 31, 19__.

(5) Make journal entries to close books.

Problem **10-3.** The following information is taken from the financial statements of C. C. Fleming:

Advertising Expense	$ 849.00
Cash	5,881.00
Delivery Equipment	1,915.00
Delivery Expense	326.00
W. P. Drake (creditor)	3,020.00
C. C. Fleming, Capital	35,847.00
C. C. Fleming, Personal	3,417.00
Freight In	806.00
General Expense	922.00
Harold & Hanley (customer)	3,685.00
Jackson & Son (creditor)	7,186.00
Merchandise, January 1, 1950	11,891.00
Merchandise, December 31, 1950	19,515.00
Miscellaneous Equipment	4,636.00
Notes Payable	7,368.00
Notes Receivable	7,829.00
Office Expense	586.00
W. H. Page Company (customer)	3,827.00
Purchases	33,810.00
Purchases Discounts	647.00
Rent Expense	1,000.00
Returned Purchases and Allowances	1,196.00
Returned Sales and Allowances	3,361.00
Sales	43,123.00
Sales Discounts.	151.00
Selling Expenses (miscellaneous)	301.00
C. W. Stanley (customer)	8,352.00
Traveling Expense	1,158.00
Utilities Expense	461.00
Wages and Salaries	3,223.00

Required:

(1) Draw off a trial balance on working papers.

(2) Complete the working papers.

(3) Prepare a profit and loss statement for the year ending December 31, 1950.

(4) Prepare a balance sheet, December 31, 1950.

Problem **10-4.** James A. Wiley began business on December 1, 19__, with cash, $5,000.00, merchandise, $4,000.00, securities, $5,000.00, and fixtures, $2,000.00. His transactions for the month were as follows:

December

1 — Paid December rent, $150.00.

2 — Purchased merchandise on account from Hart & Co., Inc., $3,000.00, 2/10, n/30.

5 — Sale of merchandise on account to L. H. Freeman, $1,300.00, 1/10, n/30.

7 — Paid the Valley Press Inc. for advertising, $80.00.

11 — Purchased merchandise on account from Dale & Son, $1,100.00, 3/10, n/60.

12 — Paid Hart & Co., bill of December 2, less cash discount.

15 — Received check from L. H. Freeman in payment of invoice of December 5, less cash discount.

17 — Sale of merchandise on account to Gerald & Shield, $3,400.00, 2/10, n/60.

20 — Paid general expenses, $335.00.

21 — Paid Dale & Son bill of December 11, less cash discount.

22 — Purchased merchandise on account from Dale & Son, $1,000.00, n/30.

24 — Sale of merchandise for cash to Robert E. Payne, $416.00, net.

27 — Received check from Gerald & Shield in payment of $3,000.00 of their account, less 2%. This is approved by Mr. Wiley.

29 — Received a dividend check on the securities owned, $25.00.

31 — Paid wages and salaries, $607.00.

Required:

(1) Enter the above transactions in five books of original entry. Use single-column sales and purchases books, and four-column cash books.

(2) Post to the ledger and take a trial balance.

(3) Prepare a profit and loss statement for the month of December. New inventory, $5,264.00.

(4) Prepare a balance sheet, December 31, 19__.

Problem **10–5.** Following are the accounts entering into the profit and loss statement of Merrill P. Clark for the year 19__:

Sales — Department A		$36,554.00
Sales — Department B		73,342.00
Returned Sales — Department A	$ 1,288.00	
Returned Sales — Department B	1,519.00	
Merchandise, January 1, Department A	10,022.00	
Merchandise, January 1, Department B	15,996.00	
Purchases — Department A	28,016.00	
Purchases — Department B	56,263.00	
Returned Purchases — Department A		1,078.00
Returned Purchases — Department B		3,644.00
Freight In — Department A	701.00	
Freight In — Department B	1,173.00	
Advertising	5,714.00	
Delivery Expense	3,765.00	

Depreciation Expense — Delivery Equipment . . .	510.00	
Depreciation Expense — Miscellaneous Equipment .	402.00	
Sales Salaries.	8,645.00	
Traveling Expense	3,180.00	
Bad Debts Expense	750.00	
Insurance Expense	724.00	
Miscellaneous General Expense	1,736.00	
Office Salaries	4,494.00	
Taxes	1,860.00	
Utilities Expense	764.00	
Sales Discounts.	912.00	
Purchases Discounts		2,302.00

The new inventories on December 31, 19—, are Department A, $15,074.00, Department B, $25,491.00.

Required:

Prepare a departmental profit and loss statement for the year. Allocate expenses to departments as follows:

	Dept. A	*Dept. B*
Advertising	In ratio of net sales	
Delivery Expense	In ratio of net sales	
Depreciation Expense — Delivery Equipment	In ratio of net sales	
Depreciation Expense — Miscellaneous Equipment . . .	50%	50%
Sales Salaries.	33⅓%	66⅔%
Traveling Expense	33⅓%	66⅔%
Bad Debts Expense	33⅓%	66⅔%
Insurance Expense	30%	70%
Miscellaneous General Expense	50%	50%
Office Salaries	40%	60%
Taxes	30%	70%
Utilities Expense	40%	60%
Sales Discounts.		100%
Purchases Discounts	33⅓%	66⅔%

For the purpose of this problem, show only round dollars in the profit and loss statement.

Problem 10–6. On December 1, 19—, Glenn A. Walsh began business by purchasing the business of Dodge & Gray. Mr. Walsh acquired the following assets at the prices indicated: $3,000.00 of auto parts and accessories, $4,000.00 of tires, tubes, and related items, and $2,000.00 of equipment. The transactions of Mr. Walsh for December were:

December

1 — He invested cash, $3,000.00.

1 — Paid December rent, $165.00.

2 — Sale on account to Jessup & Wilson, $407.00 (parts $209.00, tires and tubes, $198.00), 1/10, n/30.

5 — Gave the *Daily Tribune* a check for advertising, $148.00.

9 — Purchase on account from the City Auto Supply Co., $699.00 (parts, $425.00, tires and tubes, $274.00), 5/10, n/60.

10 — Sale on account to Price-Melton, Inc., $800.00 (parts, $420.00, tires and tubes, $380.00), 1/10, n/30.

12 — Received check from Jessup & Wilson for invoice of December 2, less cash discount.

15 — Cash sale to Price-Melton, Inc., $501.00 (tires and tubes).

17 — Purchase on account from the Stanley Tire Co., $200.00 (tires and tubes), 5/10, n/60.

19 — Paid City Auto Supply Company for bill of December 9, less cash discount.

20 — Received check from Price-Melton, Inc., covering invoice of December 10, less cash discount.

22 — Cash purchase from Daly & Sund, $104.00 (parts, $70.00, tires and tubes, $34.00).

23 — Sale on account to Jessup & Wilson, $1,648.00 (parts, $519.00, tires and tubes, $1,129.00), 1/10, n/30.

24 — Purchase on account from the Stanley Tire Co., $465.00 (tires and tubes), 5/10, n/60.

26 — Sale on account to Jackson Motor Co., $387.00 (tires and tubes), n/30.

27 — Paid Stanley Tire Company for bill of December 17, less cash discount.

28 — Paid general expenses, $240.00, and selling expenses, $181.00.

28 — Jackson Motor Co. file a claim for $7.00 covering freight which they paid on merchandise shipped them December 26. Their claim is found to be correct and a credit of $7.00, accordingly, is passed to their account.

29 — Sale on account to Price-Melton, Inc., $1,214.00 (parts, $844.00, tires and tubes, $370.00), 1/10, n/30.

31 — Paid Glenn A. Walsh $78.00 as reimbursement for freight bills paid by him on the merchandise purchases of the month (parts, $28.00, tires and tubes, $50.00).

31 — Paid wages and salaries for December, $804.00.

31 — Purchase on account from the City Auto Supply Company, $122.00 (parts, $105.00, tires and tubes, $17.00), 5/10, n/30.

Required:

(1) Enter the above transactions in five multiple-column books of original entry. Mr. Walsh desires the accounts to be kept in a manner which will permit the computation of gross profits, but not net profits, by departments. Do not departmentalize cash discounts; handle purchases discounts as other income and sales discounts as other expense.

(2) Post to the ledger and take a trial balance.

(3) Prepare a profit and loss statement for December showing gross profits by departments. Inventories on December 31, 19—, amounted to auto parts, $2,513.00, tires and tubes, $3,289.00.

(4) Prepare a balance sheet, December 31, 19—.

Problem **10–7.** A. E. Ward analyzed all his merchandise transactions by product in order to determine the relative profitability of the two lines which he merchandised. His two classes of merchandise were product A and product B, respectively.

His balance sheet of October 31, 19__, was as follows:

A. E. Ward

BALANCE SHEET, OCTOBER 31, 19—

Cash	$ 3,196.00	T. Y. Tyler	$ 1,000.00
O. A. Alexander	1,200.00	J. X. Verdy	5,000.00
S. J. Burt	2,900.00	R. Z. Wellman	1,500.00
L. E. Carter	3,000.00	Wages Payable	114.00
Notes Receivable	800.00		
Merchandise — Product A	4,450.00	A. E. Ward, Capital	18,634.00
Merchandise — Product B	2,702.00		
Other Assets	8,000.00		
	$26,248.00		$26,248.00

His November transactions were as follows:

November

2 — Sold L. E. Carter on account, product A, $2,700.00.

2 — A cash sale of product A is made to O. A. Adams for $250.00.

3 — Product A is purchased on account from J. X. Verdy, $1,000.00.

4 — Office expenses are paid, $60.00.

5 — Product A is purchased on account from T. Y. Tyler, $1,350.00.

6 — Cash is received from L. E. Carter in payment of his October account, $3,000.00, less 1%.

7 — A check is drawn in favor of T. Y. Tyler in payment of October account, $1,000.00, less 2%.

9 — Product B is purchased on account from R. Z. Wellman, $400.00.

10 — Product A is sold to O. A. Alexander on account, $1,400.00.

10 — A check is given to R. Z. Wellman in payment of October account, $1,500.00, less 2%.

11 — Product A is purchased for cash from L. K. Tener & Son for $200.00.

12 — Cash is received in payment of L. E. Carter note, $800.00; and interest, $8.00.

13 — November rent is paid, $250.00.

14 — Sold Morten Drury on account, product A, $300.00.

16 — General expenses are paid, $190.00.

17 — Wages due October 31 are paid, $114.00.

18 — O. A. Alexander pays $400.00 on account.

19 — A check for $3,000.00 is given to J. X. Verdy to apply on account.

20 — A special consignment of merchandise is sold for T. Y. Tyler; there is a commission of $120.00 due Mr. Ward for making this sale; a debit memorandum is sent to Mr. Tyler for this amount.

21 — Cash is received from S. J. Burt in payment of October 31 invoice for $2,500.00, less 2%.

23 — A cash sale of product B is made to V. A. Gant for $70.00.

24 — Cash is received from O. A. Alexander to apply on account, $600.00; also a 30-day note, dated November 21, 19__, for $1,000.00.

25 — Morten Drury pays invoice of November 14, less 2%.

27 — Sold S. J. Burt on account, product A, $250.00, and product B, $1,000.00.

28 — Wages are paid, $312.00, and selling expenses, $582.00.

Required:

(1) Enter the above transactions in appropriate columnar books of original entry. Use four-column cash receipts and cash payments books. Do not attempt to distribute expenses between departments. Do not departmentalize cash discounts; handle purchases discounts as other income and sales discounts as other expense.

(2) Post to the ledger.

(3) Take a trial balance.

(4) Prepare a profit and loss statement showing sales, cost of sales, and gross profits for each department, and for all departments together. Do not attempt to distribute expenses between departments. November 30 inventories are product A, $4,310.00, and product B, $2,395.00.

(5) Prepare a balance sheet as of November 30, 19___.

(6) Close the books.

Problem **10–8.** On December 1, 19___, R. G. Franklin entered into business for himself by buying the following assets from Samuel H. Gardner, who was retiring from business:

Merchandise:
Department A	$ 8,110.17
Department B	1,636.95
Office Furniture and Equipment	1,570.00
Miscellaneous Equipment	3,800.00
Goodwill	10,000.00

In addition to these assets, Mr. Franklin invested $9,882.88 in cash.

Mr. Franklin's transactions for the month of December are given below. Unless otherwise stated, terms for purchases and sales are no cash discount, net thirty days.

December

1 — Paid rent for the month of December, $425.00.

2 — Sold merchandise to C. N. Duncan for $2,672.14 (department A); 2/10, n/30.

2 — Sold merchandise for cash to A. H. Gumaer for $911.71 (department A, $900.42, department B, $11.29).

3 — Received purchase invoice from Wm. K. Henry for $8,215.39 (department A, $3,111.14, department B, $5,104.25).

3 — Sold merchandise on account to E. B. Meyer, $1,641.12 (department A), 2/10, n/30.

3 — Sold merchandise for cash to J. J. Sullivan for $215.32 (department A).

4 — Purchased merchandise on account from Collins & Company, $3,312.64 (department B), 2/10, n/30.

5 — Office expenses are paid, $309.14.

5 — Sold merchandise for cash to W. P. Raine, $601.47 (department A).

5 — Paid freight on merchandise purchased from Collins & Company, $12.14.

5 — Sold merchandise on account to H. W. Hess, $881.00 (department B), 1/10, n/30.

6 — Received bill dated December 3, for merchandise purchased on account from T. J. Grayson, $4,902.99 (department A), 2/10, n/30.

6 — Paid advertising bill in favor of the *Post-Gazette* for $312.14. Divide equally between departments A and B.

6 — Received check from C. N. Duncan in payment of invoice of December 2, less 2%.

8 — A check is given to A. H. Gumaer in payment of merchandise returned, originally purchased December 2, $11.29 (department B).

9 — R. G. Franklin invested additional cash, $1,000.00.

9 — Paid traveling expenses, $297.56 (department A, $214.07, department B, $83.49).

9 — Sold merchandise on account to H. W. Hess, $1,734.13 (department A, $549.41, department B, $1,184.72).

10 — Sold merchandise on account to:

	Amount	Dept. A	Dept. B
Parker & Son	$3,138.71	$1,621.46	$1,517.25
H. S. Cossard, 2/10, n/30 . . .	1,430.09	565.92	864.17
E. M. Shelley	6,548.92	5,277.04	1,271.88

11 — Paid Collins & Company for bill of December 4, less 2%.

11 — Sold merchandise on account to W. D. Gordon, $876.73 (department B).

12 — Received check from E. B. Meyer for bill of December 3, less 2%.

12 — Received check from H. W. Hess for bill of December 5, less 1%.

13 — Paid $4,000.00 to Wm. K. Henry to apply on bill of December 3.

13 — Sold merchandise to E. B. Meyer, $775.07 (department A, $371.32, department B, $403.75).

15 — Merchandise is returned to Wm. K. Henry, $160.76 (department A).

15 — Received check for $1,000.00 from E. M. Shelley to apply on account.

16 — Credits are passed to the following accounts for merchandise returned:

	Amount	Dept. A	Dept. B
C. N. Duncan	$ 89.80	$ 89.80	
Parker & Son	165.66	128.14	$37.52

16 — Received purchase invoice dated December 12 from Sutton & Company, $6,039.60 (department A, $2,148.71, department B, $3,890.89).

17 — Received check from H. S. Cossard in payment of invoice of December 10, less 2%.

17 — Received check from E. M. Shelley to apply to account, $2,000.00.

18 — Paid T. J. Grayson for invoice of December 3, less 2%.

18 — Sold merchandise on account to R. L. Shields, $7,682.15 (department A, $3,510.17, department B, $4,171.98); and to E. M. Shelley, $927.44 (department A).

19 — Merchandise is returned by E. B. Meyer, $29.30 (department A).

19 — Received invoice from Wm. K. Henry for merchandise purchased on December 17, $1,429.03 (department A).

20 — Sale on account to E. M. Shelley, $1,940.81 (department A).

22 — Paid Merchants' Delivery, Inc., $150.00. (Debit Delivery Expense.)

22 — Received bill dated December 19 for merchandise purchased from Collins & Company, $1,021.77 (department A), 2/10, n/30.

23 — Received bill dated December 22, for merchandise purchased from T. J. Grayson, $406.17 (department A, $6.00, department B, $400.17).

23 — Received check from R. L. Shields to apply on account, $1,000.00.

24 — Sold merchandise for cash to E. B. Meyer, $911.31 (department A, $279.94, department B, $631.37).

24 — Purchased merchandise on account from Sutton & Company, $2,385.61 (department A).

26 — Paid various office expenses, $171.00.

26 — Paid Collins & Company's bill of December 19, less 2%.

26 — Freight is paid on the Sutton & Company purchase, $36.90.

27 — Paid Dillig & Jones $250.00 for a report on the business of Weldorf Specialties, Inc., which is being considered for purchase by Mr. Franklin.

28 — Paid $165.00 for a radio to be awarded as a prize to high man in a sales contest being conducted this month by department A.

29 — Paid the *Post-Gazette* for advertising, $384.14. This bill is to be apportioned 60% to department A, 40% to department B.

30 — Received a $100.00 check as a prize award for best display in its class at Merchants' Exposition.

31 — Gas and electricity bills are paid, $37.25.

31 — A 60-day note, dated today, is received from E. M. Shelley in payment of the balance of his account.

31 — Paid traveling expenses, $652.00 (department A, $217.00, department B, $435.00).

31 — A 15-day note, dated today, is given to Sutton & Company, $6,039.60.

31 — Paid Merchants' Delivery, Inc., $117.00.

31 — Paid telephone bill, $74.90, and telegraph bill, $101.99.

31 — Salaries and wages for the month are paid:

Sales Salaries and Wages — Department A	$ 895.80
Sales Salaries and Wages — Department B	1,214.27
Office Salaries	532.00
Total	$2,642.07

31 — Paid Community Chest Fund, $100.00.

Required:

(1) Enter the above transactions in the appropriate columnar books of original entry. Do not departmentalize cash discounts; handle purchases discounts as other income and sales discounts as other expense.

(2) Post to the ledger.

(3) Take a trial balance.

(4) Prepare a departmental profit and loss statement.

    (a) Inventories December 31 are department A, $7,334.61, and department B, $6,160.25.

    (b) Delivery expense should be allocated to departments according to gross sales ratios.

    (c) Rent should be apportioned according to floor space: department A, 63 %, department B, 37 %.

    (d) All other indirect operating expenses should be prorated to departments in the average ratio that direct expenses have been absorbed by departments at the time of original entry.

(5) Prepare a balance sheet.

(6) Close the books. A separate cost of sales account should be employed for each department. Only *one* profit and loss account, however, should be opened on the books.

Chapter 11

CONTROLLING ACCOUNTS — THE CASH JOURNAL

As a business grows there comes also an increase in

(1) The number of customers served.
(2) The number of creditor relationships.
(3) The kinds and types of information needed to govern and administer the business intelligently.

These increases necessitate the use of hundreds, often thousands, of accounts for a single enterprise. A separate account is required for each customer, each creditor, and each kind of accounting information.

Obviously any increase in the number of accounts employed occasions also an increase in

(1) The size of the general ledger.
(2) The amount of bookkeeping labor required.

Under such circumstances it may be found desirable to subdivide the ledger; otherwise it may become too unwieldy a record for practical use. The ledger, for instance, might be divided into three sections:

(1) The accounts receivable ledger.
(2) The accounts payable ledger.
(3) The general ledger. This would contain all the accounts of a business except those with customers and merchandise creditors.

Merely subdividing a bulky general ledger does not, however, overcome certain difficulties:

(1) Sectionalizing a ledger does not reduce its over-all size. With no reduction in the number of accounts included in the full ledger, the general ledger trial balance must of necessity be very long.
(2) Sectionalizing does not reduce the size of the trial balance. A long trial balance, and the preparation of statements therefrom, is a tedious process even when no errors occur. The longer the trial balance, the greater is the likelihood of error. The location of errors then becomes increasingly difficult and laborious.

Delay in obtaining a trial balance of the general ledger will also delay

(1) The mailing of monthly statements to customers. This, in turn, may delay collections.

(2) The preparation of the profit and loss statement and the balance sheet. Much of the value of these statements is found in their timeliness, and delay in their preparation may lessen their value.

These difficulties — the drag of detail upon progress — are circumvented, in part at least, through the use of controlling accounts.

ACCOUNTS RECEIVABLE CONTROLLING ACCOUNT

Suppose that all customers' accounts are taken out of the general ledger and that in their place is substituted a single account called Accounts Receivable:

ACCOUNTS RECEIVABLE

3,600.00	

Suppose also that the accounts removed from the general ledger are placed in a separate subsidiary ledger as follows:

R. D. ANDERSON		J. H. BAKER		FRANK COX	
100.00		400.00		700.00	

JOHN DOYLE		J. E. EATON		C. C. FIELDS	
300.00		600.00		200.00	

R. P. GREGG		ROY O. HALL	
800.00		500.00	

This, the accounts receivable ledger, is a subsidiary ledger in which are kept all accounts with customers. The total of these detailed accounts is equal to the balance of the Accounts Receivable account on the general ledger.

The Accounts Receivable account on the general ledger

(1) Shows the total amount due from all customers and in this way represents the subsidiary ledger on the general ledger.

(2) "Controls" the subsidiary ledger in the sense that the total of all balances in the subsidiary ledger must equal the balance in the Accounts Receivable account.

Definition: A controlling account is a summary account, the balance of which is explained in detail in a subsidiary ledger.

POSTING

Since the total of the balances in the accounts receivable ledger must be equal to the balance of the Accounts Receivable controlling account on the general ledger, it follows logically, to maintain this equality, that whenever postings are made to the subsidiary ledger, postings must also be made to the controlling account on the general ledger, and vice versa. At first sight this would appear to involve a great deal of extra posting work but, as a matter of fact, the posting work of the general ledger bookkeeper is greatly reduced. In place of posting details to customers' accounts, he posts, instead, summaries of detail (i.e., column totals) to the one account, Accounts Receivable. For example, if a thousand sales were debited to various customers' accounts during a given month by an assistant bookkeeper, only one debit posting, the sum of the thousand sales, would be made to the controlling account by the general ledger bookkeeper. This posting would be made at the end of the month as part of the following entry:

```
Accounts Receivable . . . . . . . . . . . . . . . .   xx xxx xx
    Sales . . . . . . . . . . . . . . . . . . . . . .         xx xxx xx
```

This entry is the complete general ledger record of the sales book. Only two postings to the general ledger are required; without the device of the controlling account, a thousand and one postings to the general ledger would have been necessary.

The work of posting, when an Accounts Receivable controlling account is employed, may be summarized thus:

(1) The general ledger bookkeeper will ordinarily merely post column totals to the Accounts Receivable controlling account. He will not post the details which make up these totals.

(2) The subsidiary ledger bookkeeper will post the details of column totals to individual customers' accounts.

(3) If debits or credits are made to customers' accounts from

books of original entry which do not contain special columns for accounts receivable, it will be necessary to post each item twice, once to the Accounts Receivable account in the general ledger, and once to the individual customer's account in the subsidiary ledger.

If a column total must be posted to two accounts, the debit ledger reference may be shown at the left of the amount, the credit reference at the right, thus:

SALES BOOK   Page 1

Date	Invoice No.	Debit Account of	L.F.	Amount	
1950					
Feb. 7	2	C. F. Ruble	√	2,378	00
12	4	Clark R. Morgan	√	489	00
14	5	E. V. Sanders	√	867	00
17	7	C. F. Ruble	√	558	00
20	8	H. R. Macy	√	599	00
23	9	E. V. Sanders	√	85	00
25	10	M. G. Sheldon	√	1,311	00
28	11	Clark R. Morgan	√	722	00
				7,009	00
				(1)	(17)

Postings to personal accounts are commonly indicated by √ marks, instead of by page numbers, in the L.F. columns of the books of original entry. This is because accounts in the subsidiary ledger are usually maintained alphabetically, and because the addition of new accounts and the dropping of others make impracticable the use of page numbers for a current customers' ledger.

The reference (i.e., folio) column of a customer's account may be variously utilized:

(1) The reference column may be used to record the page of the book of original entry from which the posting was made. This is its customary usage.

(2) The reference column may be used to record invoice numbers and similar information. This is the use to which the reference column is often put under machine bookkeeping — the statement, account, and sales book being prepared simultaneously. Credits are referred to as "cash" or as "c/m." Miscellaneous debits and credits are explained by other symbols.

(3) Where personal accounts are arranged alphabetically, the reference column may be used to identify the posting source, as in the paragraph above, or, less preferably, it may be left blank as a

general rule. When the latter practice is employed, postings to customers' accounts are usually made directly from sales invoices which, after posting, are filed alphabetically, by dates, for ready reference. (Other source materials, such as cash tickets, would be filed in a similar manner.) [1]

To sum up: every posting to a subsidiary ledger must be reflected in a posting to the related controlling account, and vice versa.

ACCOUNTS PAYABLE

If there are many creditors' accounts, an Accounts Payable controlling account may be established in the general ledger with the detailed accounts kept in a subsidiary accounts payable ledger. The bookkeeping technique to be followed is similar to that for accounts receivable.

PROVING THE SUBSIDIARY LEDGER

To prove the subsidiary ledger requires the preparation of a schedule listing all account balances in the subsidiary ledger. If the total of this schedule is equal to the balance in the related controlling account, the subsidiary ledger is said to have been proved or reconciled. Mathematically, the two have been proved to be equal.

This proof will not reveal incorrect postings such as, for instance, a debit made to the account of Johnson & Company which should have been made to the account of Johnston & Son. Balances in both personal accounts will be incorrect, but the incorrect balances will not be discovered by a mere proving of the subsidiary ledger.

The subsidiary ledger, as a general rule, should be reconciled with its related controlling account at the end of each month. However, if it is expedient, there is no objection to making these reconciliations more frequently.

It may be observed that the balance of a controlling account may ordinarily be considered to be correct if the general ledger trial balance is in balance.

---

[1] Posting directly from invoice to account virtually eliminates the sales book as a needed reference medium for the subsidiary ledger. Many concerns have, in consequence, discontinued the entry of sales in detail in the sales book. Instead they record merely a summary of the sales of each day. If there were 26 sales days in a month, there would be 26 entries in the sales book for the month (each entry representing a collective debit to Accounts Receivable and a credit to Sales). It would be possible for these 26 summary entries to represent hundreds, if not thousands, of invoices. At the end of each month the sales book is footed and totals are posted to the general ledger.

ILLUSTRATIVE PROBLEM

The transactions of L. T. Robinson for the month of February, 1950, revised to allow for cash discounts and for two merchandise departments are given on pages 215–217. The books of Mr. Robinson, reproduced below, are based upon these transactions and illustrate

(1) The use of multiple-column books of original entry.

(2) Posting from these books of original entry to the ledger.

(3) The general ledger.

(4) The use of controlling accounts for accounts receivable and accounts payable.

(5) Subsidiary ledgers for accounts receivable and accounts payable.

The accounts in the general ledger follow the same order used in earlier illustrations of the L. T. Robinson problem. Accounts are arranged in the order in which they appear on the financial statements — balance sheet accounts first, then profit and loss accounts. Cash, as the most liquid of assets, appears first because it is first in the balance sheet. Noncash current assets are arranged in the order in which they are expected to be converted into cash in the normal operation of business. Then appear accounts representing, in order, fixed assets, current liabilities, and net worth. Nominal accounts follow in the order of their appearance on the statement of profit and loss.

Attention is also directed to the manner in which single- and double-line rulings are used in the accounts and books of original entry.

February

2 — L. T. Robinson began business with $12,000.00 cash and $4,000.00 merchandise (department A, $2,400.00, department B, $1,600.00).

3 — Paid February rent, $300.00.

3 — Bought furniture and fixtures from Ester Supply Company for cash, $1,200.00.

4 — Merchandise is sold for cash to J. M. Barrie for $102.00 (department A, $61.90, department B, $40.10), invoice #1.

5 — Bought merchandise from James J. Logue, $5,000.00 (department A, $3,740.00, department B, $1,260.00). Terms 5/10, n/30.

7 — Sold merchandise to C. F. Ruble on account, $2,378.00 (department A, $1,498.14, department B, $879.86), invoice #2. Terms n/30.

9 — A cash sale of $28.00 (department A) is made to E. T. Maddox, invoice #3.

10 — Merchandise is purchased from Exley & Son for cash, $700.00, less 5% (department A, $300.00, department B, $400.00).

12 — Sold merchandise on account to Clark R. Morgan, $489.00 (department A, $180.93, department B, $308.07), invoice #4. Terms 1/10, n/30.

12 — Paid James J. Logue, $5,000.00, less 5%, for bill of February 5.

12 — Merchandise is purchased on account from Henry V. Dana, $408.00 (department A, $262.96, department B, $145.04); and from James J. Logue, $1,800.00 (department B). Terms n/60.

14 — General expenses are paid, $510.00.

14 — Merchandise is sold on account to E. V. Sanders, $867.00 (department A, $312.42, department B, $554.58), invoice #5. Terms n/30.

16 — Merchandise is purchased on account from F. C. Maxton, $62.00 (department B). Terms 5/10, n/30.

16 — A cash sale is made to A. L. Nichols, $51.00, less 1% (department A), invoice #6.

17 — Merchandise is sold on account to C. F. Ruble, $558.00 (department A), invoice #7. Terms n/30.

19 — Sundry expenses are paid, $116.00.

19 — Clark R. Morgan returns $100.00 of the merchandise purchased by him on February 12 because of inferior quality (department A, $38.17, department B, $61.83).

20 — Merchandise is sold on account to H. R. Macy, $599.00 (department A), invoice #8. Terms n/30.

21 — A check is received from Clark R. Morgan, $389.00, less 1%, in payment of balance due on bill of February 12.

21 — Merchandise is purchased on account from J. R. Upshaw, $1,-800.00 (department A, $867.14, department B, $933.86); and from James J. Logue, $1,530.00 (department A, $723.89, department B, $806.11). Terms n/60.

23 — Merchandise is sold on account to E. V. Sanders, $85.00 (department B), invoice #9. Terms 1/10, n/30.

24 — Cash is received from C. F. Ruble to apply on account, $700.00; also from E. V. Sanders, $85.00, less 1%.

25 — Merchandise is sold on account to M. G. Sheldon, $1,311.00 (department A, $409.00, department B, $902.00), invoice #10. Terms n/30.

25 — A check is mailed to F. C. Maxton in payment of invoice of February 16, less 5%.

26 — L. T. Robinson draws cash for personal use, $200.00.

26 — A check for $1,000.00 is given to James J. Logue to apply on account.

27 — L. T. Robinson acts as agent for the Dettle Insurance Company; a policy is sold for which Mr. Robinson receives a check of $63.00 as his commission.

27 — Checks are received from C. F. Ruble, $678.00, and E. V. Sanders, $250.00, to apply on account.

28 — Merchandise is sold on account to Clark R. Morgan, $722.00 (department B), invoice #11.   Terms n/30.

28 — Wages are paid, $231,00.

28 — The merchandise on hand at the close of business is valued at $10,692.00 (department A, $5,800.00, department B, $4,892.00).

SALES BOOK   Page 1

Date	Invoice No.	Debit Account of	L.F.	Debit Accounts Receivable	Credit Sales Dept. A	Credit Sales Dept. B
1950						
Feb. 7	3	C. F. Ruble	✓	2,378 00	1,498 14	879 86
12	4	Clark R. Morgan	✓	489 00	180 93	308 07
14	5	E. V. Sanders	✓	867 00	312 42	554 58
17	7	C. F. Ruble	✓	558 00	558 00	
20	8	H. R. Macy	✓	599 00	599 00	
23	9	E. V. Sanders	✓	85 00		85 00
25	10	M. G. Sheldon	✓	1,311 00	409 00	902 00
28	11	Clark R. Morgan	✓	722 00		722 00
				7,009 00	3,557 49	3,451 51
				(2)	(10)	(11)

PURCHASES BOOK   Page 1

Date	Credit Account of	L.F.	Credit Accounts Payable	Debit Purchases Dept. A	Debit Purchases Dept. B
1950					
Feb. 5	James J. Logue	✓	5,000 00	3,740 00	1,260 00
12	Henry V. Dana	✓	408 00	262 96	145 04
12	James J. Logue	✓	1,800 00		1,800 00
16	F. C. Maxton	✓	62 00		62 00
21	J. R. Upshaw	✓	1,800 00	867 14	932 86
21	James J. Logue	✓	1,530 00	723 89	806 11
			10,600 00	5,593 99	5,006 01
			(6)	(16)	(17)

CASH RECEIPTS BOOK

Date	Account Credited	Explanation	L.F.	Miscellaneous	✓	Accounts Receivable	Sales Dept. A	Sales Dept. B	Sales Discounts	Cash
1950 Feb. 2	L. T. Robinson, Capital	Cash investment	7	12,000 00						12,000 00
4	Sales	Invoice #1, J. M. Barrie					61 90	40 10		102 00
9	Sales	Invoice #3, E. T. Maddox					28 00			28 00
16	Sales	Invoice #6, A. L. Nichols					51 00		51	50 49
21	Clark R. Morgan	Balance invoice Feb. 12			✓	389 00			3 89	385 11
24	C. F. Ruble	On account			✓	700 00				700 00
24	E. V. Sanders	Invoice February 23			✓	85 00			85	84 15
27	Commissions Earned	For commission on sale of policy for Dettle Insurance Company	21	63 00						63 00
27	C. F. Ruble	On account			✓	678 00				678 00
27	E. V. Sanders	On account			✓	250 00				250 00
				12,063 00		2,102 00	140 90	40 10	5 25	14,340 75
						(2)	(10)	(11)	(23)	(1)

218

CASH PAYMENTS BOOK

Date	Account Debited	Explanation	L.F.	Debit Miscellaneous	✓	Debit Accounts Payable	Credit Purchases Discounts	Credit Cash
1950 Feb.								
3	Rent Expense	February rent	19	300 00				300 00
3	Furniture and Fixtures	Bill February 3 from Ester Supply Company	5	1,200 00				1,200 00
10	Purchases — Dept. A } Purchases — Dept. B }	Exley & Son	16 17	300 00 400 00			35 00	665 00
12	James J. Logue	Bill of February 5	18		✓	5,000 00	250 00	4,750 00
14	General Expense		18	510 00				510 00
19	General Expense		18	116 00				116 00
25	F. C. Maxton	Bill of February 16		✓		62 00	3 10	58 90
26	L. T. Robinson, Personal		8	200 00				200 00
26	James J. Logue	On account		✓		1,000 00		1,000 00
28	Wages Expense	February payroll	20	231 00				231 00
				3,257 00		6,062 00	288 10	9,030 90
						(6)	(22)	(1)

219

JOURNAL

| | DEBIT | | | | | | CREDIT | |
Accounts Payable	Accounts Receivable	General Ledger	DATE		L.F.	General Ledger	Accounts Receivable	Accounts Payable
		2,400 00	1950 Feb. 2	Merchandise — Dept. A	3			
		1,600 00		Merchandise — Dept. B	4			
				L. T. Robinson, Capital	7	4,000 00		
				Began business today with an investment of:				
				$ 4,000.00 cash (recorded in cash receipts book, page 1).				
				12,000.00 merchandise				
				$16,000.00 Total investment.				
		38 17	19	Returned Sales & Allowances — Dept. A	12			
		61 83		Returned Sales & Allowances — Dept. B	13			
				Clark R. Morgan	✓		100 00	
				For merchandise returned because of inferior quality; originally purchased February 12, invoice #4.				
		8,293 99	28	Cost of Sales — Dept. A	14			
				Merchandise — Dept. A	3	2,400 00		
				Purchases — Dept. A	16	5,893 99		

28			
3	Merchandise — Dept. A	5,800 00	
14	Cost of Sales — Dept. A		5,800 00
	To record new inventory.		
28			
15	Cost of Sales — Dept. B	7,006 01	
4	Merchandise — Dept. B		1,600 00
17	Purchases — Dept. B		5,406 01
28			
4	Merchandise — Dept. B	4,892 00	
15	Cost of Sales — Dept. B		4,892 00
	To record new inventory.		
28			
9	Profit and Loss	4,608 00	
14	Cost of Sales — Dept. A		2,493 99
15	Cost of Sales — Dept. B		2,114 01
	To transfer balances of Cost of Sales accounts to Profit and Loss account.		
28			
9	Profit and Loss	100 00	
12	Returned Sales & Allowances — Dept. A		38 17
13	Returned Sales & Allowances — Dept. B		61 83
	To close latter two accounts.		

JOURNAL

	DEBIT		DATE		L.F.	CREDIT		
Accounts Payable	Accounts Receivable	General Ledger				General Ledger	Accounts Receivable	Accounts Payable
			1950 Feb. 28	Sales — Dept. A	10			
		3,698 39		Sales — Dept. B	11			
		3,491 61		Profit and Loss	9	7,190 00		
				To close sales accounts.				
			28	Profit and Loss	9			
		1,157 00		General Expense	18	626 00		
				Rent Expense	19	300 00		
				Wages Expense	20	231 00		
				To transfer expenses to Profit and Loss.				
			28	Commissions Earned	21			
		63 00		Purchases Discounts	22			
		288 10		Profit and Loss	9	351 10		
				To transfer other income to Profit and Loss.				

Date	L.F.	Account	Debit		Credit	
28	9	Profit and Loss	5	25		
	23	Sales Discounts			5	25
		To transfer other expense to Profit and Loss.				
28	9	Profit and Loss	1,670	85		
	7	L. T. Robinson, Capital			1,670	85
		To transfer profit to Robinson's capital account.				
28	7	L. T. Robinson, Capital	200	00		
	8	L. T. Robinson, Personal			200	00
		To transfer balance of Robinson's personal account to capital account.				
			45,374	20	45,274	20
					100	00

(2)

GENERAL LEDGER

CASH   Page 1

1950						1950					
Feb.	28		CR1	14,340	75	Feb.	28		CP1	9,030	90

ACCOUNTS RECEIVABLE   Page 2

1950						1950					
Feb.	28		S1	7,009	00	Feb.	19		J2	100	00
							28		CR1	2,102	00

MERCHANDISE — DEPT. A   Page 3

1950						1950					
Feb.	2		J1	2,400	00	Feb.	28		J1	2,400	00
	28		J1	5,800	00						

MERCHANDISE — DEPT. B   Page 4

1950						1950					
Feb.	2		J1	1,600	00	Feb.	28		J1	1,600	00
	28		J1	4,892	00						

FURNITURE AND FIXTURES   Page 5

1950											
Feb.	3		CP1	1,200	00						

ACCOUNTS PAYABLE   Page 6

1950						1950					
Feb.	28		CP1	6,062	00	Feb.	28		P1	10,600	00

L. T. ROBINSON, CAPITAL   Page 7

1950						1950					
Feb.	28	Drawings	J2	200	00	Feb.	2	Investment	J1	4,000	00
							2	Investment	CR1	12,000	00
							28	Net Income	J2	1,670	85

L. T. ROBINSON, PERSONAL   Page 8

1950						1950					
Feb.	26		CP1	200	00	Feb.	28		J2	200	00

PROFIT AND LOSS
Page 9

1950						1950					
Feb.	28	Cost of Sales — Dept. A	J1	2,493	99	Feb.	28	Sales — Dept. A	J2	3,698	39
	28	Cost of Sales — Dept. B	J1	2,114	01		28	Sales — Dept. B	J2	3,491	61
	28	R. S. & A. — Dept. A	J1	38	17		28	Commissions Earned	J2	63	00
	28	R. S. & A. — Dept. B	J1	61	83		28	Purchases Discounts	J2	288	10
	28	General Expense	J2	626	00						
	28	Rent Expense	J2	300	00						
	28	Wages Expense	J2	231	00						
	28	Sales Discounts	J2	5	25						
	28	To L. T. Robinson, Capital	J2	1,670	85						
				7,541	10					7,541	10

SALES — DEPT. A
Page 10

1950						1950				
Feb.	28	To P. & L.	J2	3,698	39	Feb.	28	S1	3,557	49
							28	CR1	140	90
				3,698	39				3,698	39

SALES — DEPT. B
Page 11

1950						1950				
Feb.	28	To P. & L.	J2	3,491	61	Feb.	28	S1	3,451	51
							28	CR1	40	10
				3,491	61				3,491	61

RETURNED SALES AND ALLOWANCES — DEPT. A
Page 12

1950					1950					
Feb.	19	J1	38	17	Feb.	28	To P. & L.	J1	38	17

RETURNED SALES AND ALLOWANCES — DEPT. B
Page 13

1950					1950					
Feb.	19	J1	61	83	Feb.	28	To P. & L.	J1	61	83

COST OF SALES — DEPT. A   Page 14

1950						1950					
Feb.	28	Old inventory	J1	2,400	00	Feb.	28	New inventory	J1	5,800	00
	28	Purchases	J1	5,893	99		28	To P. & L.	J1	2,490	99
				8,293	99					8,293	99

COST OF SALES — DEPT. B   Page 15

1950						1950					
Feb.	28	Old inventory	J1	1,600	00	Feb.	28	New inventory	J1	4,892	00
	28	Purchases	J1	5,406	01		28	To P. & L.	J1	2,114	01
				7,006	01					7,006	01

PURCHASES — DEPT. A   Page 16

1950						1950					
Feb.	10		CP1	300	00	Feb.	28	To Cost of			
	28		P1	5,593	99			Sales	J1	5,893	99
				5,893	99					5,893	99

PURCHASES — DEPT. B   Page 17

1950						1950					
Feb.	10		CP1	400	00	Feb.	28	To Cost of			
	28		P1	5,006	01			Sales	J1	5,406	01
				5,406	01					5,406	01

GENERAL EXPENSES   Page 18

1950						1950					
Feb.	14		CP1	510	00	Feb.	28	To P. & L.	J2	626	00
	19		CP1	116	00						
				626	00					626	00

RENT EXPENSE   Page 19

1950						1950					
Feb.	3		CP1	300	00	Feb.	28	To P. & L.	J2	300	00

WAGES EXPENSE   Page 20

1950 Feb.	28		CP1	231	00	1950 Feb.	28	To P. & L.	J2	231	00

COMMISSIONS EARNED   Page 21

1950 Feb.	28	To P. & L.	J2	63	00	1950 Feb.	27		CR1	63	00

PURCHASES DISCOUNTS   Page 22

1950 Feb.	28	To P. & L.	J2ʳ	288	10	1950 Feb.	28		CP1	288	10

SALES DISCOUNTS   Page 23

1950 Feb.	28		CR1	5	25	1950 Feb.	28	To P. & L.	J2	5	25

ACCOUNTS RECEIVABLE LEDGER

H. R. MACY

1950 Feb.	20		S1	599	00						

CLARK R. MORGAN

1950 Feb.	12		S1	489	00	1950 Feb.	19		J1	100	00
	28		S1	722	00		21		CR1	389	00

C. F. RUBLE

1950 Feb.	7		S1	2,378	00	1950 Feb.	24		CR1	700	00
	17		S1	558	00		27		CR1	678	00

E. V. SANDERS

1950 Feb.	14		S1	867	00	1950 Feb.	24		CR1	85	00
	23		S1	85	00		27		CR1	250	00

M. G. SHELDON

1950												
Feb.	25			S1	1,311	00						

ACCOUNTS PAYABLE LEDGER

HENRY V. DANA

						1950				P1	408	00
						Feb.	12					

JAMES J. LOGUE

1950			CP1	5,000	00	1950			P1	5,000	00
Feb.	12		CP1	1,000	00	Feb.	5		P1	1,800	00
	26						12		P1	1,530	00
							21				

F. C. MAXTON

1950			CP1	62	00	1950			P1	62	00
Feb.	25					Feb.	16				

J. R. UPSHAW

						1950				P1	1,800	00
						Feb.	21					

L. T. Robinson

TRIAL BALANCE, FEBRUARY 28, 1950

Cash	$ 5,309.85	
Accounts Receivable	4,807.00	
Merchandise Inventory — Department A	2,400.00	
Merchandise Inventory — Department B	1,600.00	
Furniture and Fixtures	1,200.00	
Accounts Payable		$ 4,538.00
L. T. Robinson, Capital		16,000.00
L. T. Robinson, Personal	200.00	
Sales — Department A		3,698.39
Sales — Department B		3,491.61
Returned Sales and Allowances — Department A . .	38.17	
Returned Sales and Allowances — Department B . .	61.83	
Purchases — Department A	5,893.99	

Purchases — Department B	5,406.01	
General Expenses	626.00	
Rent Expense	300.00	
Wages Expense	231.00	
Commissions Earned		63.00
Purchases Discounts		288.10
Sales Discounts	5.25	
	$28,079.10	$28,079.10

L. T. Robinson

PROFIT AND LOSS STATEMENT,
MONTH ENDING FEBRUARY 28, 1950

	DEPT. A	DEPT. B	TOTAL
Gross Sales	$3,698.39	$3,491.61	$ 7,190.00
Less Returned Sales and Allowances . . .	38.17	61.83	100.00
Net Sales	$3,660.22	$3,429.78	$ 7,090.00
Cost of Sales:			
Merchandise, February 2, 1950	$2,400.00	$1,600.00	$ 4,000.00
Purchases	5,893.99	5,406.01	11,300.00
	$8,293.99	$7,006.01	$15,300.00
Merchandise, February 28, 1950	5,800.00	4,892.00	10,692.00
Cost of Sales	$2,493.99	$2,114.01	$ 4,608.00
Gross Profit	$1,166.23	$1,315.77	$ 2,482.00
Expenses:			
General Expense			$ 626.00
Rent Expense			300.00
Wages Expense			231.00
Total Expenses			$ 1,157.00
Net Profit from Operations			$ 1,325.00
Other Income:			
Commissions Earned			$ 63.00
Purchases Discounts			288.10
			$ 351.10
			$ 1,676.10
Other Expense:			
Sales Discounts			5.25
Net Income			$ 1,670.85

L. T. Robinson

BALANCE SHEET, FEBRUARY 28, 1950

Assets		*Liabilities and Net Worth*	
Current Assets:		Current Liabilities:	
Cash	$ 5,309.85	Accounts Payable . . .	$ 4,538.00
Accounts Receivable .	4,807.00		
Merchandise	10,692.00	Net Worth:	
	$20,808.85	L. T. Robinson, Capital	17,470.85
Fixed Assets:			
Furniture and Fixtures.	1,200.00		
	$22,008.85		$22,008.85

L. T. Robinson

SCHEDULES SHOWING PROOF OF SUBSIDIARY LEDGERS,
FEBRUARY 28, 1950

Accounts Receivable Ledger:		Accounts Payable Ledger:	
H. R. Macy	$ 599.00	Henry V. Dana	$ 408.00
Clark R. Morgan. . . .	722.00	James J. Logue	2,330.00
C. F. Ruble	1,55 .00	J. R. Upshaw	1,800.00
E. V. Sanders	617.00		$4,538.00
M. G. Sheldon	1,311.00		
	$4,807.00		

COMMENTARY

In the statement of profit and loss for L. T. Robinson (page 229), purchases discounts are shown as other income; and sales discounts as other expense. This handling of cash discounts is very common in actual practice although, as already stated on page 164, accounting theory dictates that cash discounts are deductions from sales and purchases, respectively. (See also illustrations on pages 172 and 195.)

However, the segregation of cash discounts between departments can only be made with considerable difficulty. To attain this segregation, the cash discount on each cash settlement would have to be divided between departments. And to record the division, two sales discounts columns would be required in the cash receipts book; and two purchases discounts columns in the cash payments book. A very good example of the difficulty of apportioning cash discounts by departments is afforded by the analysis required in the remittance of Clark R. Morgan on February 21:

	Department A	Department B	Total
Invoice February 12	$180.93	$308.07	$489.00
Credit memo February 19	38.17	61.83	100.00
	$142.76	$246.24	$389.00
Sales discount	$ 1.43	$ 2.46	$ 3.89
Amount of check			$385.11

Because of the practical difficulties of apportioning cash discounts between departments, many businesses, as a matter of bookkeeping *convenience*, handle cash discounts in the manner illustrated by the L. T. Robinson problem of this chapter. But even though the practical difficulties of apportioning cash discounts between departments be admitted, it is still true that it would be better, and definitely in accord with theory, if accounting practice generally would handle sales discounts as deductions from sales, and purchases discounts as deductions from purchases. Still better would be that accounting wherein all sales and purchases are recorded in the books at net cash prices. In this latter respect invoices to customers might be patterned so as to show net cash prices in the same manner as bills for electricity: gross———   discount———   net———

SUBDIVISION OF CONTROLLING ACCOUNTS

If accounts with customers are numerous, several controlling accounts may be established as, for example,

Accounts Receivable Control — A to E
Accounts Receivable Control — F to L
Accounts Receivable Control — M to R
Accounts Receivable Control — S to Z

Each controlling account represents a separate, subsidiary ledger. The use of several controls makes it possible to reconcile each group of customers' accounts independently. This is a consideration of much importance to firms which have many accounts receivable.

When controlling accounts are subdivided, recognition of this fact must be made in the books of original entry. The sales book, for example, would be:

SALES BOOK   Page 1

DATE	INVOICE No.	DEBIT ACCOUNT OF	L.F.	DEBIT ACCOUNTS RECEIVABLE				CREDIT SALES
				A — E	F — L	M — R	S — Z	

OPENING A CONTROLLING ACCOUNT

If a new set of books is being opened, controlling accounts may be employed from the start. For every controlling account incorporated in the new accounting system there should be a supporting subsidiary ledger.

Controlling accounts may, however, be desired for an accounting system which has not previously used such controls. Suppose, for example, that an Accounts Receivable control is desired; the procedure outlined below should be followed:

(1) Remove all customers' accounts from the general ledger.

(2) In their place substitute one controlling account called Accounts Receivable, thus:

ACCOUNTS RECEIVABLE

1950 Oct.	1	Balance	J37	3,600	00				

(3) Record this substitution by a memorandum in the journal as follows:

Oct. 1   Customers' accounts were today transferred to a subsidiary ledger. On the general ledger these accounts were replaced by a single account called Accounts Receivable. The accounts transferred are[2]

R. D. Anderson	$ 100.00
J. H. Baker	400.00
Frank Cox	700.00
John Doyle	300.00

[2] If the number of accounts is very large, a typewritten list may be prepared instead and permanently filed to support the memorandum in the journal.

J. E. Eaton	600.00
C. C. Fields	200.00
R. P. Gregg	800.00
Roy O. Hall	500.00
	$3,600.00

Reference to the journal should be made in the newly established Accounts Receivable control. No formal postings are necessary because the journal record is an explanation and not a formal double entry. The purpose of the journal memorandum is to have a permanent record of the transfer in a book of original entry.

USE OF CONTROLLING ACCOUNTS

Controlling accounts should be employed when a group of like accounts are important, and when it is easier to keep these accounts in a controlling account than to add them up individually.

ADVANTAGES OF CONTROLLING ACCOUNTS

(1) The size of the general ledger is reduced. There is less probability of error in the general ledger.

    (a) There are fewer general ledger accounts; one account replaces a group of accounts.

    (b) There are fewer postings and these are commonly column totals checked by the rule of double entry.

(2) The general ledger trial balance is shortened and more easily balanced. Time is saved.

(3) The preparation of financial statements is expedited.

(4) Errors are localized:

    (a) If the general ledger trial balance is *in balance,* the failure of a subsidiary ledger to agree with its related controlling account normally indicates an error in the subsidiary ledger. The controlling account provides a predetermined total for the accounts of the subsidiary ledger.

    (b) If the general ledger trial balance is *not in balance,* and the subsidiary ledgers agree with their respective controls, error is indicated to exist in the general ledger accounts other than the controlling accounts.

(5) Totals of a group of (subsidiary) accounts are quickly available.

(6) Work can be divided and responsibility fixed.

CONTROLLING ACCOUNTS: THEIR FURTHER APPLICATION

The most common examples of controlling accounts are those which represent accounts receivable and accounts payable. There are, however, many other controlling accounts, among which may be mentioned the following:

(1) *Branch Accounts:*

The Royal Tire and Rubber Company maintains its head office in New York City. Branches are located throughout the United States. On the home office books one account is carried with each branch; these accounts are debited with the money, merchandise, fixtures, equipment, and so on, advanced to the branches by the home office. The balance of each branch account represents the home office investment in the branch; the balance is explained in detail by the branch office records.

(2) *Capital Stock:*

On December 31, 1944, the Westinghouse Electric Corporation was owned by 48,362 persons. It would obviously be impractical for the Westinghouse Electric Corporation to open a capital account with each shareholder on its general ledger. Instead, two controlling accounts were employed:

(a) CAPITAL STOCK — COMMON...................... $156,329,050
      which account represents all the common stock
      ownership of the company.

(b) CAPITAL STOCK — PREFERRED .... $ 3,998,700
      which account represents all the preferred stock
      ownership of the company.

Each of these accounts is supported in detail by subsidiary stock-holders' ledgers. These ledgers have accounts showing the interest of each shareholder of the company.

(3) *Notes Receivable:*

Where note transactions are frequent, it is advisable to open a Notes Receivable controlling account on the general ledger and to keep explanatory detail in a subsidiary ledger. This subsidiary ledger, commonly called a notes receivable register, is illustrated in Chapter 12.

In similar fashion, where volume warrants, a controlling account and subsidiary note register may be kept for notes payable.

(4) *Selling Expenses:*

All selling expenses are charged to this controlling account on the general ledger and are classified in detail in a subsidiary selling expense ledger.

(5) *Administrative Expenses:*

All administrative expenses are charged to this controlling account on the general ledger and are classified in detail in a subsidiary expense ledger.

(6) *Factory Ledger:*

This account is found in a manufacturing business. All details of factory accounting are kept in a subsidiary ledger. This ledger is represented on the general ledger by a controlling account called "factory ledger."

The subsidiary factory ledger, in turn, may carry controlling accounts of its own. Typical are the following:

Raw Materials	Manufacturing Expense
Work in Process	Machinery
Finished Goods	Factory Equipment

Each of these accounts is supported by a subsidiary record which reveals in detail the makeup of each controlling account balance.

THE PRIVATE LEDGER

Occasionally a business may desire to keep certain information confidential, as, for instance,

Investment	Management salaries
Loans	Profits

This information may be kept confidential by placing it in a private ledger. This ledger will be represented on the general ledger by an account called Private Ledger. Conversely, the nonconfidential information of the general ledger will be represented on the private ledger by an account called General Ledger. Together, the two ledgers comprise the general ledger.

Because it is used infrequently in business and because it is not very important in the study of elementary accounting, the private ledger will not be further discussed in this chapter. Its further consideration is the content of Appendix A of this book.

THE CASH JOURNAL (OR SYNOPTIC JOURNAL, OR COMBINED CASH BOOK AND JOURNAL)

In this chapter and preceding ones emphasis has been given to the fact that there are many important advantages to be realized through the proper use of unit journals, multiple-column records, and controlling accounts. These advantages, in so far as they are a product of the accounting methods just mentioned, are naturally as

CASH BOOK

Accounts Payable	Posted	Accounts Receivable	Cash	General Expense	Purchases Dept. A	Purchases Dept. B	Sales Discounts	Selling Expense	Miscellaneous	Date	L.F	Account Debit — Credit
			12,000.00							1950 Feb. 2	9	Cash
									2,400.00		10	Merchandise In-
									1,600.00		18	L. T
									300.00	3	15	Rent Expense
			102.00						1,200.00	3	7	Furniture and
										4		Cash — Sales
					3,740.00	1,260.00				5		James
	√	2,378.00								7		C. F. Ruble
			28.00							9		Cash — Sales
	√	489.00								10		Purchases —
5,000.00	√ √				300.00	400.00				12		Clark R. Mor-
										12		James J. Logue
					262.96	145.04				12		Henry
						1,800.00				12		James
				510.00						14		General Expense
	√	867.00								14		E. V. Sanders
						62.00				16		F. C.
			50.49				.51			16		Cash — Sales
	√	558.00								17		C. F. Ruble
				116.00						19		General Expense
									38.17	19	16	Rtd. Sales &
									61.83		17	Clark Rtd. Sales &
	√	599.00								20		H. R. Macy
			385.11				3.89			21		Clark
					867.14	932.86				21		J. R.
					723.89	806.11				21		James
	√	85.00								23		E. V. Sanders
			700.00							24		C. F.
			84.15				.85			24		E. V
	√	1,311.00								25		M. G. Sheldon
62.00	√									25		F. C. Maxton
									200.00	26	19	L. T Robinson
1,000.00	√									26		James J. Logue
			63.00							27	4	Com-
			678.00							27		C. F.
			250.00							27		E. V.
	√	722.00								28		Clark R. Mor-
									231.00	28	23	Wages Expense
6,062.00		7,009.00	14,340.75	626.00	5,893.99	5,406.01	5.25		6,031.00			
(1)		(2)	(3)	(8)	(12)	(13)	(22)					

available to one business as to another for the reason that the methods themselves are freely available. These methods, however, do not have the same value for all types of businesses. When they are considered either individually or collectively, it is clear that they are worth more to some enterprises than to others. Multiple-column records, and others, are admittedly of much more importance to the large enterprise than to the small one. This greater serviceability is directly due to the fact that for the large enterprise transactions not only appear in volume but generally tend to be more complex as well.

Small concerns are often disinclined, for one reason or another, to use accounting records which are even as complex as those which have been illustrated in this chapter and preceding ones. Such disinclination, whether rightly or wrongly carried into practice, need not necessarily mean forfeiture of the right to benefit by the several advantages which attach to the so-called more "elaborate" systems of record keeping. Where the transactions of a business are relatively simple, as in a club or in a small retail store, it is possible to use but one book of original entry, a journal, but a journal embracing as many as twelve, fourteen, or even more, columns. This kind of

AND JOURNAL

TITLES	EXPLANATION	CREDIT							
		Miscellaneous	Accounts Payable	Posted	Accounts Receivable	Cash	Purchases Discounts	Sales Dept. A	Sales Dept. B
ventory — Dept. A	Cash investment								
ventory — Dept. B	Merchandise investment								
Robinson, Capital	Merchandise investment	16,000.00							
	February rent					300.00			
Fixtures	Bill Feb. 3, Ester Supply Co.					1,200.00			
	Invoice #1, J. M. Barrie							61.90	40.10
J. Logue	Invoice #2		5,000.00	✓				1,498.14	879.86
	Invoice #3, E. T. Maddox							28.00	
Cash	Exley & Son					665.00	35.00		
gan	Invoice #4							180.93	308.07
	Bill February 5					4,750.00	250.00		
V. Dana			408.00	✓					
J. Logue			1,800.00	✓					
— Cash						510.00			
	Invoice #5							312.42	554.58
Maxton	Invoice #6, A. L. Nichols		62.00	✓				51.00	
	Invoice #7							558.00	
— Cash						116.00			
Allces. — Dept. A	Merchandise returned,								
Allces. — Dept. B	originally billed Feb. 12								
R. Morgan				✓	100.00				
	Invoice #8							599.00	
R. Morgan	Balance on invoice Feb. 12			✓	389.00				
Upshaw			1,800.00	✓					
J. Logue			1,530.00	✓					
	Invoice #9								85.00
Ruble	On account			✓	700.00				
Sanders	Invoice Feb. 23			✓	85.00				
	Invoice #10							409.00	902.00
	Bill of February 16					58.90	3.10		
Personal						200.00			
	On account					1,000.00			
missions Earned	Dettle Insurance Company	63.00							
Ruble	On account			✓	678.00				
Sanders	On account			✓	250.00				
gan	Invoice #11								722.00
	February payroll					231.00			
		16,063.00	10,600.00		2,202.00	9,030.90	288.10	3,698.39	3,491.61
		(1)			(2)	(3)	(14)	(20)	(21)

journal is essentially a consolidation of all the multiple-column books of original entry which might otherwise be used; it is generally given the name "combined cash book and journal" or the name "cash journal." One example of this kind of synoptic record is illustrated on pages 236–237; the transactions used are those found on page 215. The accounts, trial balance, and statements to be prepared from this *single* book of original entry are identical with those prepared from the more complex records illustrated in the earlier part of this chapter (see pages 228 ff.).

For our present purpose it will not be necessary to discuss the synoptic journal further inasmuch as the structure, advantages, and general applicability of this type of record will be made apparent by a careful study of the illustration.

QUESTIONS

Question **11–1.** Define a controlling account.

Question **11–2.** Describe the procedure of posting when controlling accounts are used. Assume that special columns for controlling accounts are used in the books of original entry (the journal excepted), and that the journal is the ordinary two-column journal.

Question **11–3.** Freight is prepaid for the account of a customer. In which columns of an ordinary four-column cash payments book would this disbursement be entered? What postings would be made?

Question **11–4.** For every debit and credit in a subsidiary ledger, there must be a duplicate debit and credit in the related controlling account. Explain why this duplication does not throw the general ledger trial balance out of balance. In your answer distinguish between double entry and double postings.

Question **11–5.** Considering the total time and labor involved in operating controlling accounts and subsidiary ledgers, is any time actually saved by the employment of such accounts and ledgers? If so, how? Where? If not, why are they employed at all?

Question **11–6.** Explain what is meant by proving a subsidiary ledger. Why is this necessary? How often should this be done?

Question **11–7.** Explain how you would install an accounts receivable controlling account

(1) In a new set of books.
(2) In a set of books which had been operated for some time.

Question **11–8.** Suppose that the general ledger trial balance is out of balance by a substantial amount. The balance of the Accounts Receivable controlling account is computed as $78,416.00; the correct balance, however, is $78,316.00. The subsidiary ledger totals $78,316.00. What is the significance of this situation before and after reconciliation of the subsidiary ledger with the general ledger control?

Question **11–9.** What are the advantages of controlling accounts?

Question **11–10.** Give several examples which illustrate the application of the principle of controlling accounts.

Question **11–11.** Explain (1) the meaning of the balance of the Private Ledger account on the general ledger, and (2) the meaning of the balance of the General Ledger account on the private ledger.

Question **11–12.** Are the Private Ledger and General Ledger accounts true controlling accounts? Explain.

Question **11–13.** Enumerate the criticisms, favorable as well as unfavorable, which may apply to the synoptic journal.

PROBLEMS

Problem **11–1.** J. C. Wells began business on January 1, 19—, with cash, $20,000.00, inventory, $10,000.00, and fixtures, $5,000.00. His condensed transactions for the calendar year were as follows:

Sales on credit:

Lynn & Co.	$5,000.00
Corbin & Son	7,000.00
E. M. Dunn	3,000.00
J. H. Todd	4,000.00
M. C. Dale	5,000.00
Corbin & Son	6,000.00

Cash collections:

Lynn & Co., $1,000.00, less 1%
E. M. Dunn, $3,000.00, less 2%
Corbin & Son, $2,000.00, net

Miscellaneous:

A note receivable for $3,000.00
was received from Corbin & Son.

Purchases on credit:

J. R. Dean	$4,000.00
Rice & Co.	5,000.00
Neal & Son	3,000.00
J. R. Dean	4,000.00

Cash payments:

J. R. Dean, $1,000.00, less 1%
Neal & Son, $3,000.00, less 5%
J. R. Dean, $1,000.00, net

General expenses	$10,000.00
Freight in	1,000.00
Freight bill, to be charged to Rice & Co.	100.00
Freight bill, to be charged to J. H. Todd	50.00

Required:

(1) Enter transactions in books of original entry.

(2) Post to a T-account general ledger, employing control accounts for accounts receivable and accounts payable.

(3) Post to subsidiary ledgers.

(4) Draw off a trial balance.

(5) Prepare a profit and loss statement for the year. The new inventory is $12,000.00.

(6) Prepare a balance sheet, December 31, 19__.

(7) Prepare reconciliation schedules for each control account.

Problem **11–2.** E. W. Reynolds began business on December 1, 19__, with cash, $5,000.00, merchandise, $7,000.00, fixtures and equipment, $3,000.00, building, $10,000.00, and land, $2,000.00. In summary form, his condensed transactions for December were as follows:

Sales of merchandise on account, 1/10, n/30:

L. E. Adams	$ 400.00
E. M. Clark	1,100.00
Dott & Son	500.00
Baker & Co.	800.00
E. M. Clark	900.00
Eaton & Co.	1,700.00
L. E. Adams	600.00
Dott & Son	1,300.00
Baker & Co.	700.00
Eaton & Co.	300.00
Dott & Son	700.00
Eaton & Co.	1,000.00
	$10,000.00

Purchases of merchandise on account, 2/10, n/60:

| L. B. Sherman | $ 300.00 |
| Riley & Son | 1,100.00 |

Lewis & Co. 300.00
J. M. Terry & Co. 900.00
L. B. Sherman 700.00
Riley & Son 100.00
Lewis & Co. 700.00
L. B. Sherman 400.00
J. M. Terry & Co. 1,800.00

                                                                      $6,300.00

Cash received from customers to apply on account:

L. E. Adams   . . . . $ 400.00, less 1%
Eaton & Co. . . . .   1,700.00, less 1%
E. M. Clark . . . .   900.00, less 1%
Dott & Son . . . .   700.00, less 1%
Baker & Co. . . . .   1,000.00, less 1%

Cash payments:

J. M. Terry & Co. . . . . $ 900.00, less 2% ⎫
Riley & Son . . . .   100.00, less 2% ⎪ These payments
L. B. Sherman . . . .   400.00, less 2% ⎬ to apply on
Lewis & Co. . . . .   200.00, less 2% ⎭ account
Expenses 3,735.00
Freight prepaid on merchandise shipped
   to Eaton & Co., this freight to be re-
   paid by customer 50.00

Miscellaneous:

Merchandise returned by Eaton & Co. . . . . $ 50.00
Merchandise returned to Lewis & Co. 100.00

Required:

(1) Enter the above transactions in the proper books of original entry. The cash books should be four-column books.

(2) Post to a T-account general ledger and, as necessary, to T-account subsidiary ledgers with accounts receivable and accounts payable.

(3) Take a trial balance.

(4) Prepare a profit and loss statement for the month. Inventory, December 31, 19__, $8,000.00.

(5) Prepare a balance sheet, December 31, 19__.

(6) Prepare schedules showing reconciliation of subsidiary ledgers with general ledger.

Problem **11–3.** On July 31, 19__, John Gay had the following balance sheet:

Cash . . . . $10,000.00   John Gay, Capital. $10,700.00
Accounts Receivable:
   Earl Dailey. . . . $ 90.00
   Ewing & Company   110.00
   J. E. Griffith . . .   300.00
   A. L. Hunt   . . .   200.00   700.00

                                   $10,700.00 $10,700.00

Mr. Gay's summarized transactions for the month of August are given below:

August

  1 — Sale to J. M. Adkins, $100.00.
      Purchase from Scott & Scott, $500.00.
      Borrowed $1,000.00 cash, issuing note payable for same amount.
      Expenses paid, $100.00.
  3 — Purchase from Xenlon's, Inc., $750.00.
      Cash sale, $200.00.
  5 — Sale to Frye & Moore, $300.00.
      Purchase from T. J. Varner, $100.00.
  6 — Cash received from J. M. Adkins, $100.00, less 2%.
  7 — Sale to Benson & Son, $200.00.
      Purchase from H. L. Zakary, $175.00.
      Paid Scott & Scott, $500.00, less 5%.
  9 — Sale to J. E. Griffith, $400.00.
      Purchase from Xenlon's, Inc., $200.00.
      Cash received from Benson & Son, $200.00, less 2%.
      Cash paid to T. J. Varner, $100.00, less 5%.
 12 — Purchase from Wade & Company, $300.00.
 13 — Sale to L. G. Craig, $300.00.
      Purchase from Roy Young, $125.00.
      Cash sale, $100.00.
      Cash paid to Xenlon's, Inc., $200.00, less 5%.
 15 — Sale to A. L. Hunt, $600.00.
      Purchase from Scott & Scott, $500.00.
 16 — Sale to Earl Dailey, $200.00.
      Purchase from T. J. Varner, $150.00.
      Cash received from L. G. Craig, $300.00, less 2%.
      Wages paid, $150.00.
 17 — Purchase from Xenlon's, Inc., $225.00.
      Cash paid to Wade & Company, $300.00, less 5%.
 19 — Sale to J. M. Adkins, $500.00.
      Purchase from Scott & Scott, $360.00.
      Cash paid to Roy Young, $125.00.
 22 — Purchase from Wade & Company, $100.00.
      Sale to Ewing & Company, $100.00.
      Cash purchase, $200.00.
 23 — Sale to Benson & Son, $400.00.
      Purchase from Roy Young, $370.00.
      Cash received from J. M. Adkins, $500.00, less 2%.
      Cash paid to Scott & Scott, $500.00, less 5%.
 24 — Sale to Frye & Moore, $200.00.
      Purchase from Scott & Scott, $690.00.
 26 — Sale to L. G. Craig, $100.00.
      Purchase from Xenlon's, Inc., $110.00.
      Cash received from Earl Dailey, $200.00, less 2%.

Cash paid to Xenlon's, Inc., $225.00.

27 — Sale to J. E. Griffith, $700.00.

28 — Purchase from Roy Young, $200.00.

Cash paid to Wade & Company, $100.00, less 5%.

30 — Sale to Earl Dailey, $200.00.

Purchase from H. L. Zakary, $100.00.

Cash received from Frye & Moore, $300.00.

Expenses paid, $932.00.

31 — Sale to A. L. Hunt, $300.00.

Purchase from Wade & Company, $300.00.

Paid H. L. Zakary, $275.00.

Wages paid, $150.00.

Required:

(1) Enter the above transactions in the appropriate columnar books of original entry. Unless otherwise stated, all purchase and sale transactions are on account. Two controlling accounts are to be employed, one for accounts receivable and one for accounts payable.

(2) Post to a T-account ledger.

(3) Take a trial balance.

(4) Prepare schedules showing agreement of subsidiary ledgers with controlling accounts.

Problem **11-4.** The books of A. C. Wells for the month of December, 19__, are given below.

JOURNAL

Dec.	1	Inventory	7,000	00		
		Furniture and Fixtures	2,200	00		
		Delivery Equipment	1,100	00		
		A. C. Wells, Capital			10,300	00
		To record noncash investment.				
	10	Sales Returns and Allowances	160	00		
		Accounts Receivable (Allen & Co.)			160	00
		Unsatisfactory merchandise returned.				
	25	Accounts Payable (I. J. Goode & Son)	110	00		
		Purchases Returns and Allowances			110	00
		Allowance for damaged goods.				
	26	Sales Discounts	10	00		
		Accounts Receivable (N. A. Ford)			10	00
		For additional cash discount on collection of December 15.				
	29	Freight In	81	00		
		Accounts Payable (I. J. Goode & Son) . .			81	00
		For prepaid freight on December 22.				

SALES BOOK				PURCHASES BOOK			
Dec.	2	Allen & Co. . .	1,000 00	Dec.	6	L. E. Adamson .	1,500 00
	5	N. A. Ford . .	4,000 00		10	R. C. Kinsey. .	2,000 00
	11	Hales & Kane .	890 00		17	K. O. Ellison. .	1,900 00
	17	S. T. Jackson .	2,000 00		22	I. J. Goode &	
	23	N. A. Ford. . .	101 00			Son	2,200 00
	30	S. T. Jackson .	1,010 00				
							7,600 00
			9,001 00				

CASH RECEIPTS BOOK

			CREDIT		DEBIT	
			Misc.	Accounts Receivable	Sales Discounts	Cash
Dec.	1	A. C. Wells, Capital	Investment	3,000 00			3,000 00
	10	Allen & Co.	On account		700 00	14 00	686 00
	15	N. A. Ford	On account		2,800 00	46 00	2,754 00
	19	Hales & Kane	On account		800 00	16 00	784 00
	23	Commission Income	Dale lease	105 00			105 00
	26	S. T. Jackson	On account		1,600 00	32 00	1,568 00
	31	Sales	Invoice #7	5,000 00			5,000 00
				8,105 00	5,900 00	108 00	13,897 00

CASH DISBURSEMENTS

				DEBIT		CREDIT	
				Misc.	Accounts Payable	Purchases Discounts	Cash
Dec.	16	L. E. Adamson	On account		1,500 00	45 00	1,455 00
	20	R. C. Kinsey	On account		1,200 00	36 00	1,164 00
	26	Utilities Expense		60 00			60 00
	27	K. O. Ellison	On account		1,700 00	51 00	1,649 00
	29	I. J. Goode & Son	On account		1,000 00	30 00	970 00
	31	Wages and Salaries	December payroll	600 00			600 00
		Delivery Expense	A. C. Express Co.	250 00			250 00
		Purchases	D. Y. Lane Co.	2,000 00			2,000 00
				2,910 00	5,400 00	162 00	8,148 00

Required:

(1) Post to the general ledger and two subsidiary ledgers. Terms on credit sales are 2/10, n/30, on purchases, 3/10, n/60.

(2) Take a trial balance, December 31, 19__.

(3) Prepare a profit and loss statement for December, 19__. New inventory, $3,892.00.

(4) Prepare a balance sheet, December 31, 19__. Include supporting schedules for accounts receivable and accounts payable.

Problem **11–5**. Clark E. Campbell began business on June 1, 19__, with the following assets:

Cash	$ 5,000.00
Merchandise	6,289.00
Furniture, Fixtures, and Equipment	2,929.00
Delivery Equipment	1,782.00
	$16,000.00

Transactions for the month of June were as follows:

June

1 — Purchase from J. R. Cresswell, $672.00.
    Sale to T. A. Clark, $135.00.

3 — Purchase from Emerson & Son, $1,008.00.

4 — Cash sale to W. P. Knox, $268.00.
    Purchase from J. L. Haney, $127.00.
    Sale to Grant & Grant, $403.00.

5 — Cash is received from T. A. Clark in payment of invoice June 1, $135.00, less 2%.

6 — Purchase from Ward & Company, $237.50.
    Sale to Jones & Company, $268.00.

7 — Sale to Mead & McKay, $537.00.
    Paid J. R. Cresswell for bill of June 1, $672.00, less 5%.

8 — Cash is received from Jones & Company in payment of invoice June 6, $268.00, less 2%.
    Purchase from Emerson & Son, $269.00.

10 — Sale to Payne & Company, $410.00.
    Purchase from J. E. Winter, $415.00.
    Cash is paid to J. L. Haney for bill of June 4, $127.00, less 5%.

11 — Cash is paid to Emerson & Son for bill of June 8, $269.00.
    Purchase from Price & Powell, $169.00.

12 — Sales to Sharp & Company, $278.00, and to H. C. Riggs, $672.40.
    Purchase from J. L. Haney, $484.00.

13 — Cash is paid to Price & Powell for bill of June 11, $169.00, less 5%.

14 — Paid administrative expenses, $145.33, and sales expenses, $190.70.

15 — Purchase from Emerson & Son, $295.00.

17 — Paid J. L. Haney for bill of June 12, $484.00, less 5%.
    Purchase from J. R. Cresswell, $201.60.

19 — We failed to deduct the discount on our remittance to Emerson & Son on June 11. Following our claim for credit, a check for 5 % discount on $269.00 is today received from Emerson & Son in settlement.

Cash purchase from Frank Haines, $162.00.

Sale to Mead & McKay, $128.00.

20 — Purchase from J. E. Winter, $139.00, and from Ward & Company, $497.00.

Cash is received from Grant & Grant for invoice of June 4, $403.00, less 1 %.

21 — Purchase from Emerson & Son, $927.30.

Sale to T. A. Clark, $274.10.

Cash is received from H. C. Riggs for invoice of June 12, $672.40, less 2 %.

24 — Sale to Grant & Grant, $143.00.

Purchase from Ward & Company, $157.00.

A credit memorandum for $2.10 is received from Emerson & Son for error in their bill of June 21.

25 — Purchase from Price & Powell, $264.00.

Sale to Jones & Company, $954.20.

Freight of $18.10 is prepaid for the account of Jones & Company.

26 — Cash is paid to Emerson & Son, $1,008.00, less 3 %, for bill of June 3.

27 — Purchase from J. R. Cresswell, $138.00.

Sale to Sharp & Company, $272.00.

Cash is paid to J. E. Winter for bill of June 10, $415.00, less 5 %.

28 — Purchase from Price & Powell, $408.25.

Sale to Grant & Grant, $412.10.

Cash is received from Sharp & Company for invoice of June 12, $278.00, less 2 %.

29 — Paid administrative expenses, $131.10, sales expenses, $154.00.

Sales to Jones & Company, $537.00, and to J. C. Trenton, $1,152.00.

A credit of $18.00 is passed to the account of Sharp & Company for merchandise damaged because of faulty packing in shipment of June 27.

Required:

(1) Enter the above transactions in the appropriate columnar books of original entry. Unless otherwise stated, all purchases and sales are on account. Two controlling accounts are to be employed, one for accounts receivable, and one for accounts payable

(2) Post to a T-account ledger.

(3) Take a trial balance.

(4) Prepare a profit and loss statement for the month of June. Merchandise inventory June 30, 19__, $7,084.68.

(5) Prepare a balance sheet, June 30, 19__.

(6) Prepare schedules showing agreement of subsidiary ledgers with balances of controlling accounts.

Problem **11–6.** A. L. Bennett had the following balance sheet as of April 30, 19__:

Cash	$ 3,174.00	Accounts Payable	$ 2,605.00
Accounts Receivable . . .	3,248.00		
Merchandise	4,301.00	A. L. Bennett, Capital . .	12,000.00
Furniture, Fixtures, and			
Equipment	3,882.00		
	$14,605.00		$14,605.00

Subsidiary ledger schedules follow:

Accounts Receivable:

Roy Anderson	$ 204.00
Brett & Brett	813.00
R. W. Houston	479.00
G. J. McCoy	419.00
B. W. Rietz	387.00
The Royal Company . .	321.00
H. L. Scherr	415.00
West & Company . . .	210.00
	$3,248.00

Accounts Payable:

C. F. Joliffe	$ 472.00
Chas. E. Nigh	867.00
Raymond's, Inc.	235.00
J. D. Sisler	212.00
Yorke & Son	819.00
	$2,605.00

Mr. Bennett's transactions for the month of May were as follows:

May

1 — Sale to Roy Anderson, $106.00.
    Purchase from Raymond's, Inc., $529.00.
3 — Purchase from Chas. E. Nigh, $794.00.
4 — Cash sale to T. D. Nixon, $211.00.
    Purchase from George Lowe, $100.00.
    Sale to H. L. Scherr, $317.00.
5 — Cash is received from Roy Anderson in payment of April account, $204.00.
6 — Purchase from Yorke & Son, $187.00.
    Sale to Brett & Brett, $211.00.
7 — Sale to R. W. Houston, $423.00.
    Cash is received from Brett & Brett in payment of April account, $813.00, less 2%.
    Purchase from Chas. E. Nigh, $211.00.
8 — Paid all bills owed as of April 30, less 2%.
10 — Purchase from J. D. Sisler, $326.00.
    Sale to G. J. McCoy, $332.00.
    Checks in payment of April accounts were received today from R. W. Houston, $479.00, B. W. Rietz, $387.00, The Royal Company, $321.00, H. L. Scherr, $415.00, West & Company, $210.00 — all checks less 2%.
11 — At request of Roy Anderson, a credit memorandum for $4.08 is

sent him covering discount which he failed to take in his remittance of May 5.

Purchase from C. F. Joliffe, $133.00.

12 — Purchase from George Lowe, $381.00.

Sales to Dee Crane, $529.00, and to West & Company, $219.00.

13 — Sale to B. W. Rietz, $315.00.

Merchandise is returned to J. D. Sisler, $22.00.

14 — Cash is paid to C. F. Joliffe for bill of May 11, $133.00, less 1%.

Paid general expenses, $114.00, and selling expenses, $150.00.

15 — Purchase from Chas. E. Nigh, $232.00.

17 — Cash is paid to George Lowe for bill of May 12, $381.00, less 2%.

Purchase from Raymond's, Inc., $158.00.

19 — Sale to R. W. Houston, $100.00.

Cash purchase from T. C. Worden, $127.00.

A credit memorandum for $11.00 is received from Chas. E. Nigh because of an error in pricing his bill of May 15.

20 — Cash is received from H. L. Scherr for invoice of May 4, $317.00, less 2%.

Purchases from J. D. Sisler, $109.00, and from Yorke & Son, $391.00.

21 — Sale to Roy Anderson, $215.00.

Purchase from Chas. E. Nigh, $730.00.

Cash is received from Dee Crane for invoice of May 12, $529.00, less 2%.

24 — Purchase from Yorke & Son, $123.00.

Sale to H. L. Scherr, $112.00.

A credit for $12.00 is passed to the account of Dee Crane for merchandise returned from sale of May 12.

25 — Sales to Brett & Brett, $236.00, and to The Royal Company, $515.00.

Purchase from C. F. Joliffe, $207.00.

Freight of $14.10 is prepaid on the shipment to The Royal Company (debit Accounts Receivable — The Royal Company).

26 — Cash is paid to Chas. E. Nigh for bill of May 3, $794.00, less 3%; and to Dee Crane for credit memorandum of May 24, $12.00, less 2%.

A note for $419.00 is received from G. J. McCoy in payment of his April account.

27 — Cash is paid to J. D. Sisler for bill of May 20, $109.00, less 1%.

Sale to West & Company, $214.00.

Purchase from Raymond's, Inc., $108.00.

28 — Cash is received from West & Company for invoice of May 12, $219.00, less 2%.

Sales to H. L. Scherr, $124.00, and to B. W. Rietz, $202.00.

Purchase from C. F. Joliffe, $417.00.

31 — Paid general expenses, $103.00, and selling expenses, $124.00.

Sales to Brett & Brett, $423.00, and to The Royal Company, $592.00.

Required:

(1) Enter the above transactions in the appropriate columnar books of original entry. Unless otherwise stated, all purchases and sales are on account. Two controlling accounts are to be employed, one for accounts receivable, and one for accounts payable.

(2) Post to a T-account ledger.

(3) Draw off a trial balance.

(4) Prepare a profit and loss statement for the month of May. Merchandise inventory, May 31, 19__, $4,863.00.

(5) Prepare a balance sheet, May 31, 19__.

(6) Prepare schedules showing agreement of subsidiary ledgers with balances of controlling accounts.

Problem **11–7.** The transactions of J. K. Lane for the month of June, 19__, are to be entered in a sixteen-column journal using the following column headings:

Debit Columns	*Credit Columns*
Accounts Payable	Accounts Payable
Accounts Receivable	Accounts Receivable
Cash	Cash
General Expense	Purchases Discounts
Purchases	Sales
Rent	Miscellaneous
Sales Discounts	
Selling Expense	
Wages and Salaries	
Miscellaneous	

Expenses will be charged to one of the five expense accounts indicated above. Purchases and sales, unless otherwise indicated, are for merchandise. At the end of the month prepare a trial balance directly from the totals of the columns of the journal. Then prepare a statement of profit and loss for the month, and a balance sheet as of June 30, 19__.

June

1 — J. K. Lane began business by investing cash, $8,000.00, and merchandise, $12,000.00.

1 — Purchased sundry items of fixtures and equipment for cash from the Edwards Equipment Company, $1,019.00.

2 — Purchase from E. J. Smithers, terms 2/10, n/60, $1,450.00.

2 — Purchase from M. O. Morrow, terms 3/10, n/60, $1,500.00.

3 — Sale to J. K. Weston, terms 3/10, n/60, $785.00.

3 — Paid the Herald Printing Company for an advertising bill, $35.00.

3 — Paid rent for the month of June, $125.00.

4 — Sale to John Samuels, terms 3/10, 2/20, n/60, $940.00.

5 — Purchase from the Spencer Co., terms 2/10, n/30, $1,850.00.

5 — Sale to Wm. Johnson, terms 2/10, n/30, $165.00.

7 — Purchase from Walker & Co., terms 3/10, n/60, $980.00.

8 — Sale to Henry Stevens, terms 2/10, n/30, $198.00.

9 — Paid E. J. Smithers for purchase of June 2.

9 — By agreement with M. O. Morrow, we give him our note for ninety days at 8 % in payment of our purchase of June 2, less the cash discount.

10 — Paid general expenses, $112.00.

12 — J. K. Weston sent in his check for $485.00 in partial payment of his purchase on June 3 ($500.00 less 3 %).

13 — John Samuels is given a credit of $40.00 for merchandise returned from his purchase of June 4.

14 — Wm. Johnson paid his account today, less discount.

15 — Paid wages and salaries for month to date, $245.00.

15 — Purchase from Watson & Son, terms 2/10, n/30, $1,950.00.

15 — In part payment of our purchase of June 5, we send the Spencer Company a check for $1,470.00 after taking the cash discount to which we are entitled.

16 — A cash sale is made to J. K. Barnes, $1,410.00.

17 — Paid Walker & Co., for our purchase of June 7.

20 — Paid general expenses, $249.77, and advertising, $26.50.

23 — Received cash from John Samuels for balance due on invoice of June 4, less discount.

25 — Sale to J. K. Weston, terms 3/10, n/60, $1,800.00.

27 — Purchase from M. O. Morrow, terms 3/10, n/60, $1,350.00.

29 — Sale to John Samuels, terms 2/10, n/30, $350.00.

30   Paid wages and salaries for period June 16–30, $364.20.

30 — Merchandise inventory on hand, $17,000.00.

Chapter 12

NOTES RECEIVABLE

DEFINITION

The Uniform Negotiable Instruments Act defines a promissory note as "an unconditional promise in writing made by one person to another signed by the maker, engaging to pay on demand or at a fixed or determinable future time a sum certain in money to order, or to bearer."

Example:

Due_____ Chicago, Ill., July 31, 1950.	$1,000.00

Sixty days **after date,** I **promise to pay to the order of**_____

Henry E. Field _____ at_____

One Thousand and no/100 _____ Dollars.

For value received, with interest from date at the rate of 6%.

Irving J. Bush

WHY NOTES ARE USED

Notes are used for the following reasons:

(1) They represent a written acknowledgment of the debt by the debtor. As such they are better evidence than an open account.

(2) Funds may be obtained in advance of the maturity of the note by discounting (i.e., selling) the note with a bank, or other party. It is much easier to obtain funds against notes receivable than against open accounts receivable.

(3) They often serve to procure longer credit terms.

(4) They frequently earn interest.

CHARACTERISTICS OF A NOTE

The essential characteristics of a note are these:

(1) It must be in writing.
(2) It must contain an unconditional promise to pay.
(3) It must be for a definite amount.
(4) It must be made out "to order."
(5) It must have a definite due date.
(6) It must be signed by the maker in favor of the payee.

ENDORSEMENTS

The ownership of a negotiable instrument is transferred by

(1) *Delivery* where the instrument is made payable to bearer.
(2) *Endorsement* in all other cases.

Endorsements may be classified as

    (1) *Unqualified:*
       A. W. Johnson
          (or)
       Pay to the order of
       W. F. Manning.
         A. W. Johnson

    (2) *Qualified:*
       Pay to the order of
       W. F. Manning without
       recourse.
         A. W. Johnson

The words "without recourse" mean that A. W. Johnson disclaims any liability for the note in the event of nonpayment.

    (3) *Restrictive:*
       Pay to the order of
       W. F. Manning only.
         A. W. Johnson
          (or)
       Pay to the order of the
       First National Bank for
       collection.
         A. W. Johnson

The maker should state on the back of a note or other negotiable instrument (in the space above the first endorsement) exactly what is being paid. Endorsement then constitutes legal acknowledgment by the payee that the item or items enumerated are paid.

PRESENTMENT FOR PAYMENT

When a note falls due it should be presented to the drawee for payment. If the note specifies a certain bank as the place of payment, the bank will usually pay the note on presentation and charge the amount of the payment to the account of the drawee.

Presentment is necessary in order to hold the endorsers of a note liable for its payment. In the event that a note is not paid when due, the holder of a note should immediately notify endorsers of this fact; failure to do so will have the effect of releasing endorsers from their liability for payment. If the holder and endorser reside in the same place, notice of dishonor must reach the endorser by the next business day after dishonor. If the endorser lives in a place different from that of the holder, notice of dishonor must be in the mail by the next business day following dishonor.[1]

Notice of nonpayment may be rendered formally by filing a "notice of protest." This procedure is as follows:

(1) A written statement is made by the holder of the note that the instrument is due and has not been paid.

(2) The notary public attempts collection of the note. Upon his failure to do so he writes "protested" across the face of the note, with notation as to date, and reason for protest.

(3) Notices of protest are sent to the maker of the note and to each endorser.

The expenses of protesting a note are known as protest fees.

DUE DATE OF A NOTE

A note may fall due

(1) On demand.

(2) Upon a specified date.

---

[1] The Uniform Negotiable Instruments Act provides:

"Where the parties reside in the same place, notice must be given within the following times:

(1) If given at the place of business of the person to receive notice, it must be given before the close of the business hours of the day following.

(2) If given at his residence, it must be given before the usual hour of rest on the day following.

(3) If sent by mail, it must be deposited in the post office in time to reach him in the usual course on the day following.

"Where the parties reside in different places:

(1) If sent by mail, it must be deposited in the post office in time to go by mail the day following the day of dishonor or, if there be no mail at a convenient hour on that day, by the next mail thereafter.

(2) If given otherwise than through the post office, then within the time that notice would have been received in due course of mail, if it had been deposited in the post office within the time specified in the last subdivision."

(3) After a certain period of time:
    (a) "Sixty days after date (July 31)"

August	31 days
September	29 days
	60 days

Due date: 60 days after July 31, or September 29.
    (b) "Two months after date (July 25)"
        Due date: September 25.
      "Two months after date (July 31)"
        Due date: September 30.
        This particular due date is explained by the fact that
an instrument, dated on the 31st and due X months
after date, is due on the last day of the month in which
it matures.
    (c) "One year after date (July 31, 1950)"
        Due date: July 31, 1951.

Thus, if the term of a note is given in days, count the number of
days from the date of the note to find the due date. If the term of
the note is given in months, from the date of the note to the corresponding date of the next month is one month, to the corresponding
date of the second month is two months, to the corresponding date of
the third month is three months, and so on.

The Uniform Negotiable Instruments Act, Section 85, provides:
"Every negotiable instrument is payable at the time fixed therein
without grace. When the day of maturity falls upon Sunday, or a
holiday, the instrument is payable on the next succeeding business
day. Instruments falling due on Saturday are to be presented for
payment on the next business day, except that instruments payable
on demand may, at the option of the holder, be presented for payment before twelve o'clock noon on Saturday when that entire day
is not a holiday."

INTEREST

Interest may be defined as a payment made for the use of money.
It is better, however, to define interest as the increase of an indebtedness which occurs because of the passage of a period of time.

As a general rule note transactions involve interest. Some notes
are "with interest" and some are "without interest." If the cash
repayment, or total of cash payments, made by the maker of a note
is more than the amount of cash originally received by him, the difference is interest.

Some notes do not involve interest. This is because the amount paid at maturity is the same as the amount received when the loan was made.

Notes may be issued without cash consideration. A note may be issued — with or without interest — in settlement of the balance of an account or as the immediate means of settlement of a merchandise transaction. In this latter respect trade acceptances do not generally carry interest.

Interest is commonly computed upon the basis of a 360-day year (12 months of 30 days each).

The period for which interest is computed varies. For instance, if a note is payable "two months after date (July 31)."

(1) A bank will compute interest for the exact number of days elapsed, i.e., 61 days, whereas

(2) Business practice is to compute the interest for two months (60 days).

INTEREST CALCULATIONS

Problem: Find the interest on $1,000.00 for 60 days at 6%.
Solution: $6/100 \times \$1,000.00 \times 60/360 = \$10.00$

Problem: Find the interest on $1,000.00 for 6 days at 6%.
Solution: $6/100 \times \$1,000.00 \times 6/360 = \$1.00$

The same results may be obtained by taking the principal figures and pointing off 2 places to the left and 3 places to the left, respectively.

This coincidence introduces the well-known "6% rule" for the computation of interest:

(1) To find the interest on a sum of money for 60 days, at 6%, point off 2 places to the left.

(2) To find the interest on a sum of money for 6 days, at 6%, point off 3 places to the left.

Examples:

Problem: Find the interest on $1,724.87 for 60 days at 6%.
Answer (pointing off 2 places): = $17.25

Problem: Find the interest on $1,724.87 for 6 days at 6%.
Answer (pointing off 3 places): = $1.72

Problems:

Find the interest at 6% on $615.23 for

6 days . . . . = $0.62

11 days.....2 × $0.61523 = $1.23046 = 12 days
                         − .10254 = − 1 day
                         ───────
                                                        = $1.13
18 days.....3 × $0.61523........................... = $1.85
30 days....½ × $6.1523........................... = $3.08
45 days....½ × $6.1523   = $3.076   = 30 days
                            1.538   = 15 days
                           ───────
                                                        = $4.61
46 days....½ × $6.1523   = $3.0761   = 30 days
                            1.5381   = 15 days
            ⅙ × $0.61523 =   .1025   =   1 day
                           ───────
                                                        = $4.72
54 days.................$6.1523   = 60 days
                      − .6152   = − 6 days
                       ───────
                                                        = $5.54
3 months...............$6.1523   =   2 months
                       3.0761   =   1 month
                       ───────
                                                        = $9.23

If the interest rate is 7%, these answers should be increased by ⅙; if the interest rate is 5% they should be decreased by ⅙. Other rates may be obtained by similar computations.

If it is desired to compute the interest upon the basis of a 365-day year, the answers should be decreased by $\frac{1}{73}$. In other words, to obtain the interest on a sum of money on a 365-day basis, compute the interest on a 360-day basis, then deduct $\frac{1}{73}$ (because $\frac{1}{360}$ is $\frac{73}{72}$ of $\frac{1}{365}$).

ACCOUNTING FOR NOTES RECEIVABLE

Due_____   New York, N. Y., March 1, 1950. $1,000.00

Four months after date, I promise to pay to the order of _____

William E. Trent_____ at_____

One Thousand and no/100_____ Dollars.

For value received.

                            Lloyd J. Martin

The entries to be made on the books of William E. Trent in connection with this note, as illustrated below, will embrace several of the accounting problems encountered in recording notes receivable. Parallel columns are used, one to show the entries on the assumption that the note is "without interest," and the other to show the entries on the assumption that the note is "with interest at 6%." Entries involving cash are, of course, to be made in the cash receipts book, all others in the journal. For convenience, however, all entries have been prepared in journal entry form.

THE NOTE IS RECEIVED

On March 1, 1950, William E. Trent receives a note from Lloyd J. Martin for $1,000.00, due in four months.

Without Interest			*With Interest at 6%*		
Mar. 1 Notes Receivable . .	1,000.00		Mar. 1 Notes Receivable . .	1,000.00	
Lloyd J. Martin .		1,000.00	Lloyd J. Martin .		1,000.00
To record receipt of four-month note, dated today.			To record receipt of four-month note, dated today, with interest at 6%.		

In lieu of an interest-bearing note, Mr. Martin might have given his note for $1,020.00, the face of the note including $20.00 interest to maturity. This, of course, would not have carried running interest. Mr. Trent would make the following entry on receipt of this note:

Mar. 1 Notes Receivable	1,020.00	
Interest Earned		20.00
Lloyd J. Martin		1,000.00
To record receipt of four-month note, dated today, interest of $20.00 included in face of note.		

When the note is collected in cash, the entry would be:

July 1 Cash	1,020.00	
Notes Receivable		1,020.00
To record payment of Lloyd J. Martin note of March 1, 1950.		

Notes receivable, whether interest-bearing or not, are always recorded on the books at face value. This bookkeeping means, of course, that note instruments are valued on two valuation bases: interest-bearing notes are valued at present value and noninterest-bearing notes are valued at maturity value.

THE NOTE IS PAID AT MATURITY

On July 1, 1950, Lloyd J. Martin pays his note of March 1, 1950, in full.

Without Interest

July 1 Cash 1,000.00
    Notes Receivable .   1,000.00
To record payment of
Lloyd J. Martin note of
March 1, 1950.

With Interest at 6%

July 1 Cash 1,020.00
    Notes Receivable .   1,000.00
    Interest Earned. .   20.00
To record payment of
Lloyd J. Martin note of
March 1, 1950, with in-
terest at 6%.

THE NOTE IS DISHONORED AT MATURITY

On July 1, 1950, Lloyd J. Martin refused payment on his four-month note to William E. Trent, dated March 1, 1950.

Without Interest

July 1 Lloyd J. Martin . . . 1,000.00
    Notes Receivable .   1,000.00
To charge account of
Lloyd J. Martin with
dishonored note.

With Interest at 6%

July 1 Lloyd J. Martin . . . 1,020.00
    Notes Receivable .   1,000.00
    Interest Earned. .   20 00
To charge account of
Lloyd J. Martin with
dishonored note and in-
terest.

The dishonored note is debited to Martin's personal account for the reason that his account should show the fact of dishonor. The debit in Martin's account for the dishonored note is a valuable bit of credit information.

THE NOTE IS PARTLY PAID AT MATURITY

On July 1, 1950, Lloyd J. Martin paid $450.00 on his four-month note to William E. Trent, dated March 1, 1950, and gave a new sixty-day note for the balance.

Without Interest

July 1 Cash 450.00
    Notes Receivable . .   450.00
To record part payment of
Lloyd J. Martin's note of
March 1, 1950.

July 1 Lloyd J. Martin 550.00
    Notes Receivable . .   550.00
To charge account of Lloyd
J. Martin with unpaid portion of his note of March 1,
1950.

July 1 Notes Receivable 550.00
    Lloyd J. Martin . . .   550.00
To record receipt of new
sixty-day renewal note.

With Interest at 6%

July 1 Cash 470.00
    Interest Earned . .   20.00
    Notes Receivable . .   450.00
To record part payment of
Lloyd J. Martin's note of
March 1, 1950, and 6% in-
terest in full to date.

July 1 Lloyd J. Martin 550.00
    Notes Receivable . . .   550.00
To charge account of Lloyd
J. Martin with unpaid portion of his note of March 1,
1950.

July 1 Notes Receivable 550.00
    Lloyd J. Martin . . .   550.00
To record receipt of new
sixty-day renewal note with
interest at 6%.

By the above accounting it is not to be inferred that Martin's status, at any time, reverts to that of an open account debtor. The unpaid balance on the first note is run through Martin's account for the reason that his account should show, as a matter of credit information, the added time required by Martin to effect a full settlement of his indebtedness.

THE NOTE IS DISCOUNTED

On April 26, 1950, William E. Trent endorses the note of Lloyd J. Martin and discounts it at the bank, receiving cash.

Without Interest			*With Interest at 6%*	
April 26 Cash	989.00		April 26 Cash	1,008.78
Interest Expense . . .	11.00		Interest Earned	8.78
Notes Receivable			Notes Receivable	
Discounted . .		1,000.00	Discounted .	1,000.00
To record note of Lloyd			To record note of Lloyd	
J. Martin, discounted			J. Martin, discounted	
today.			today.	

The cash received on these notes is computed as follows:

Value of note at maturity . .	$1,000.00	Value of note at maturity . .	$1,020.00
Less discount (interest)[2] on maturity value of note for 66 days (April 26 to July 1) . .	11.00	*Less* discount (interest)[2] on maturity value of note for 66 days (April 26 to July 1). .	11.22
Cash proceeds of note	$ 989.00	Cash proceeds of note	$1,008.78

In the event that a note is not paid at maturity any endorser can be held liable for its payment. This contingent liability is recognized in the entries above by the crediting of a new account called Notes Receivable Discounted.

The two entries above are recorded in the cash receipts book as follows:

CASH RECEIPTS BOOK

DATE		ACCOUNT CREDITED	EXPLANATION	L.F.	CREDIT		DEBIT	
					Miscellaneous	Accounts Receivable	Sales Discounts	Cash
1950 Apr.	26	Notes Rec. Disctd.	L. J. Martin note Mar. 1		1,000 00			
		Interest Expense	66 days' discount		(11 00)			989 00
	26	Notes Rec. Disctd.	L. J. Martin note Mar. 1		1,000 00			
		Interest Earned			8 78			1,008 78

The item in parentheses indicates a debit entry.

---

[2] The discount rate is the bank's interest rate. In the examples above, the bank rate is assumed to be 6%.

With respect to the interest-bearing note which is discounted in the above illustration, it may be observed that the true interest earned for the period over which the note was held, 56 days, is $9.33. It is permissible, therefore, to credit Interest Earned for $9.33 and to debit Discount Expense for $0.55. While this is sound theory, accounting practice finds it expedient simply to credit Interest Earned for the net figure, $8.78, as is done in the example.

"Discounting" commercial paper with a bank is a practice of common commercial occurrence. Discounting is very important from an accounting standpoint, and it is a practice of business with which one should be thoroughly familiar. In this respect a summary of the steps to be followed in determining the cash proceeds of a note which is being discounted may be helpful:

(1) Determine the value of the note as of its maturity date. By maturity value is meant the number of dollars required to be paid when the note falls due.

(2) Determine the due date of the note.

(3) Determine the number of days the note has yet to run. The date on which the note is given is *not* counted; the date on which the note is due *is* counted.

(4) Calculate the bank discount by applying the discount rate against the maturity value of the note for the number of days as determined in the third step.

(5) The difference between the values as determined in the first and fourth steps is the cash value, or bank proceeds, of the note.

In following these steps of discounting, correct calculations of interest and discount are necessary. In these calculations it is well to remember that

As to interest, if the term of a note is given in days, use a 360-day year for the calculation of interest. If the term of a note is given in months, use a 12 months' year for the calculation of interest. A 2 months' note, or a 60-day note, for example, is an interest period of one-sixth of a year.

As to discount, if the discount period is stated in days, use a 360-day year. If stated in months, use a 12 months' year.

THE DISCOUNTED NOTE IS PAID BY THE MAKER AT MATURITY

On July 1, 1950, Lloyd J. Martin paid the First National Bank in full for his note in favor of William E. Trent, dated March 1, 1950.

Without Interest				*With Interest at 6%*		
July 1	Notes Receivable Discounted	1,000.00		July 1	Notes Receivable Discounted	1,000.00
	Notes Receivable .		1,000.00		Notes Receivable .	1,000.00
	To record payment by maker of Lloyd J. Martin note.				To record payment by maker of Lloyd J. Martin note.	

When the maker pays his note at maturity it is obvious that the act of payment has the effect of releasing each endorser from his contingent liability for the payment of the note. The purpose of each of the two entries above is to remove this contingent liability from the books of account. These entries may be made as soon as the period in which an endorser must be notified (of nonpayment) has expired. If no notice of nonpayment is received, it is in order to assume that the note has been paid.

THE DISCOUNTED NOTE IS DISHONORED AT MATURITY

On July 1, 1950, Lloyd J. Martin refused to pay the First National Bank the amount due on his note of March 1, 1950, in favor of William E. Trent. Protest fees, $1.53. William E. Trent thereupon took up the note, paying the bank the amount due.

Without Interest				*With Interest at 6%*		
July 1	Lloyd J. Martin . . .	1,001.53		July 1	Lloyd J. Martin . . .	1,021.53
	Cash		1,001.53		Cash	1,021.53
	To record payment of dishonored note, and protest fees of $1.53.				To record payment of dishonored note, together with protest fees, $1.53, and interest, $20.00.	
July 1	Notes Receivable Discounted	1,000.00		July 1	Notes Receivable Discounted	1,000.00
	Notes Receivable .		1,000.00		Notes Receivable .	1,000.00
	To extinguish contingent liability set up when Martin note was discounted. This note was paid by us July 1 on account of dishonor.				To extinguish contingent liability set up when Martin note was discounted. This note was paid by us July 1 on account of dishonor.	

NOTES RECEIVABLE ON THE BALANCE SHEET

One way of showing notes receivable on the balance sheet is as follows:

Notes Receivable	$100,000.00	
Less Notes Receivable Discounted	40,000.00	$60,000.00

This method shows the net amount of notes receivable on hand as an asset, and it also shows the contingent liability existing for unmatured notes which have been discounted.

Current accounting practice prefers, however, to show among the assets of a balance sheet only the notes which are actually on hand, thus:

Notes Receivable $60,000.00

and to show the discounted notes as a memorandum on the balance sheet. This may be done by a footnote to the balance sheet as follows:

Note: The company is contingently liable, December 31, 1950, for notes receivable discounted in the amount of $40,000.00.

In place of a footnote, the memorandum may be placed in the body of the balance sheet as follows:

Liabilities and Net Worth

Current Liabilities:		
Accounts Payable		$200,000.00
Taxes Payable		50,000.00
		$250,000.00
Long-Term Liabilities:		
Mortgage Payable		100,000.00
Contingent Liabilities:		
Notes Receivable Discounted	$40,000.00	
Total Liabilities		$350,000.00
Net Worth:		
Alden J. Coffman, Capital		150,000.00
		$500,000.00

NOTES RECEIVABLE REGISTER

Where many notes are received, it will be advantageous to record them in a separate book of original entry. Such a book is shown on pages 262–263.

At the end of each month the totals of the debit and credit columns of the notes receivable register are posted to the general ledger as is done with the column totals of any other book of original entry. The total of all open items in the notes receivable register should equal the difference between the balances of the Notes Receivable and Notes Receivable Discounted accounts.

An alternative method for recording notes receivable in the notes receivable register is as follows: One or more pages of the notes receivable register are reserved for each month in which notes mature. Each note, as received, is entered on the page of the month in which it matures. Thus notes received in January, and due in

January will be entered on the January page.

NOTES RECEIVABLE
Month of

DATE			DEBIT Notes Receivable		L.F.	CREDIT Accounts Receivable	To Be Paid By (Fill in only when drawee differs from name credited)
Received		Of Note					
1950 Aug.	2	1950 July	31	1,000	00		Irving J. Bush	
	6	Aug.	5	846	42		Chas. E. Moore	
	10		10	500	00		Henry S. Marshall	George E. Palmer

February will be entered on the February page.
March will be entered on the March page.
April will be entered on the April page.

At the end of each month the notes received in that month are totaled, and the totals transferred to a summary page, from which the grand total is posted to the general ledger.

The advantage of this method is that it groups notes according to maturities. In this way, note collections are easily followed, and the amount of cash collections from notes for each month can be estimated.

A notes receivable register is not convenient to use where notes receivable are payable in installments, as for instance, in credit automobile sales. In such cases it is better to open a separate notes receivable account with each customer and to record all payments in these accounts. In other words, this arrangement constitutes a subsidiary ledger whose controlling account is the Notes Receivable account on the general ledger. The notes receivable register, as the original book of entry, would be simplified accordingly.

An even better arrangement is to separate the subsidiary note accounts into two groups, one for notes receivable, and one for notes receivable discounted, each governed by a controlling account.

The contingent liability on installment paper which has been discounted is easily ascertainable if regular reports of collections are obtained from the banks or discount companies with which discount business is transacted. The collections reported by these agencies should be recorded in the appropriate notes receivable discounted accounts.

REGISTER
August, 1950

Time		Due													Interest Rate	Date		Re-marks
Mo.	Days	Year	J	F	M	A	M	J	J	A	S	O	N	D		Paid	Dis-counted	
3	60	1950							29						6%			
	60										9		5		7%			

QUESTIONS

Question **12–1.** Draw up an example of a promissory note.

Question **12–2.** Why should not a dishonored note be charged to an account called Notes Receivable Dishonored rather than to the account of the maker of the note?

Question **12–3.** What is meant by discounting a note? How is the cash value of a note determined?

Question **12–4.** When a note is discounted, what is the object of crediting Notes Receivable Discounted instead of Notes Receivable? How and when is the Notes Receivable Discounted account cleared?

Question **12–5.** When a note is partly, or fully renewed, what is the object of entries such as the following?

Harry T. Bradford	750.00	
Notes Receivable		750.00
Notes Receivable	750.00	
Harry T. Bradford		750.00

After these entries have been posted, the balances of the two accounts named are the same as they were before posting.

Question **12–6.** How should notes receivable, and notes receivable discounted, be shown on the balance sheet? Explain and illustrate.

Question **12–7.** What is a notes receivable register? When and how is it used?

Question **12–8.** If you were a furniture or motor car dealer with most of your business done on credit, how would you account for the notes which you take in?

PROBLEMS

Problem **12–1.** What are the due dates of the following notes?

Dated	Term	Dated	Term
February 28	2 months	May 5	60 days
March 25	60 days	July 31	60 days
April 30	90 days	July 31	2 months

Problem **12–2.** What is the interest on $814.10?

(1) for 10	days	@ 6%? 5%? 4%?	At 6½%? 7%? 8%?
(2) for 14	days	@ 6%? 5%? 4%?	At 6½%? 7%? 8%?
(3) for 27	days	@ 6%? 5%? 4%?	At 6½%? 7%? 8%?
(4) for 30	days	@ 6%? 5%? 4%?	At 6½%? 7%? 8%?
(5) for 43	days	@ 6%? 5%? 4%?	At 6½%? 7%? 8%?
(6) for 59	days	@ 6%? 5%? 4%?	At 6½%? 7%? 8%?
(7) for 2	months	@ 6%? 5%? 4%?	At 6½%? 7%? 8%?
(8) for 3½	months	@ 6%? 5%? 4%?	At 6½%? 7%? 8%?
(9) for 4	months and 8 days	@ 6%? 5%? 4%?	At 6½%? 7%? 8%?
(10) for 6	months	@ 6%? 5%? 4%?	At 6½%? 7%? 8%?

If interest were to be computed on the basis of a 365-day year, how should the preceding answers be corrected?

Problem **12–3.** Prepare the entries to be made on the books of the payee for the following note transactions. The bank rate, where required, may be assumed to be 6%. All notes are received in payment of accounts receivable.

DATE OF NOTE		MAKER	TERM	INTEREST	AMOUNT	TRANSACTION
Oct.	10	J. H. Huebner	2 months		$1,000.00	Oct. 11 = The note is received. Maturity = The note is paid.
	14	T. W. Andrews	30 days	6%	608.70	Oct. 14 = The note is received. Maturity = The note is paid.
	15	J. W. Weimer	60 days		211.10	Oct. 17 = The note is received. Maturity = The note is dishonored.
	16	C. T. Baer	90 days	7%	412.00	Oct. 17 = The note is received. Maturity = The note is dishonored.
	19	H. L. Scherr	45 days		610.00	Oct. 19 = The note is received. Maturity = Received $310.00 cash and new 30-day note for balance due.
	19	E. M. DuBois	60 days	6%	714.25	Oct. 19 = The note is received. Maturity = Received cash, $314.25 and interest, also new 30-day note for balance due.
	19	D. C. Ewing	60 days	6%	700.00	Oct. 20 = The note is received. Maturity = Received cash to apply on principal, $300.00, and new 45-day 6% note for balance due.
	21	H. C. Riggs	2 months		125.10	Oct. 22 = The note is received. 29 = The note is discounted at the First National Bank. Maturity = The note is paid.
	22	W. L. Fairfield	2 months	8%	543.11	Oct. 22 = The note is received. Nov. 2 = The note is discounted at the First National Bank. Maturity = The note is paid.
	22	D. K. Merritt	120 days	7%	1,236.88	Oct. 23 = The note is received. Jan. 9 = The note is discounted at the First National Bank. Bank rate 8%. Maturity = The note is paid.
	23	W. D. Lee	90 days		500.00	Oct. 23 = The note is received. Nov. 20 = The note is discounted at the First National Bank. Maturity = The note is dishonored. Protest fees, $1.78.
	25	F. L. Jones	3 months	6%	450.00	Oct. 26 = The note is received. Nov. 29 = The note is discounted at the First National Bank. Bank rate 8%. Maturity = The note is dishonored. Protest fees, $1.78.

DATE OF NOTE	MAKER	TERM	INTEREST	AMOUNT	TRANSACTION
26	R. A. Knapp	30 days		200.00	Oct. 27 = The note is received. Maturity = The note is renewed in full for another 30 days.
26	C. J. Merck	30 days	6%	250.00	Oct. 26 = The note is received. Maturity = The note is renewed in full; no cash is received.
28	J. J. Eaton	3 months	6%	200.00	Oct. 28 = The note is received. Nov. 28 = The note is transferred to John Norton, a creditor. Maturity = The note is paid.
29	G. B. Sharpe	60 days	9%	100.00	Oct. 30 = The note is received. Dec. 1 = The note is transferred to John Norton, a creditor. The note is endorsed "without recourse." Maturity = The note is not paid.

Problem **12–4.** Payment on the account of W. J. Gray is four months overdue on the date that a note is received from him in settlement. The note is for $520.00: $500.00 is the balance of his account, and $20.00 is the interest on $500.00 for six months. What entry should be made to record the receipt of the note?

Problem **12–5.** A note receivable is dated July 1, 1950, runs for three months, carries no interest, and has a face value of $1,012.00. On August 17 the note is discounted at the bank at the rate of 8%. What entry should be made to record the discounting transaction?

Problem **12–6.** What entry should be made on the books of the payee when the following note receivable is discounted?

> Date　　　　　　　　 = January 17, 19__
> Term　　　　　　　　 = Ninety days
> Amount　　　　　　　 = $843.77
> Running interest = 8%
> Discounted　　　　 = February 27, at 6%.

Problem **12–7.** What entry should be made on the books of the payee when the following note receivable is discounted?

> Date　　　　　　　　 = October 17, 19__
> Term　　　　　　　　 = Ninety days
> Amount　　　　　　　 = $1,423.00
> Running interest = 7%
> Discounted　　　　 = November 28, at 5%.

Problem **12–8.** What entry should be made on the books of the payee when the following note receivable is discounted?

> Date　　　　　　　　 = July 14, 19__
> Term　　　　　　　　 = Ninety days
> Amount　　　　　　　 = $1,286.14
> Running interest = $6\frac{1}{2}$%
> Discounted　　　　 = August 29, at 8%.

Problem **12–9.** What entry should be made on the books of the payee when the following note receivable is discounted?

Date	= June 16, 19__
Term	= Three months
Amount	= $5,275.00
Running interest	= 6%
Discounted	= July 8, at 4%.

Problem **12–10.** What entry should be made on the books of the payee when the following note receivable is discounted?

Date	= October 9, 19__
Term	= Due on following January 1
Amount	= $900.00
Running interest	= 10%
Discounted	= October 13, at 6%.

Problem **12–11.** Included among the notes receivable of the ABC Company is one from W. L. Gordon, dated October 22, for $786.27, with interest at 7%, and due in 90 days. On November 20 the note was discounted at the bank rate of 6%. At maturity the note was dishonored; protest fees amounted to $2.50. What entries should be made by the ABC Company on November 20, and the date of note maturity?

Problem **12–12.** Prepare entries on the books of the payee for the following note transactions on the dates indicated. The bank rate, where required, is 6%. All notes have been received in payment of accounts receivable.

DATE OF NOTE		MAKER	TERM	INTEREST	AMOUNT	TRANSACTIONS
July	7	L. J. White	60 days	6%	$ 812.10	Maturity = Received cash to apply on principal, $500.00, and new 60-day note for the balance due.
Aug.	1	S. B. Hackett	60 days	6%	998.88	Maturity = Received cash to apply on interest and principal, $608.87, and new 60-day note for the balance due.
July	10	L. B. Fritts	2 months		500.00	July 18 = The note is discounted.
Aug.	4	F. K. Hunt	60 days		615.00	Aug. 12 = The note is discounted.
July	19	G. R. Maxon	90 days	8%	1,824.00	July 19 = The note is received. The face of the note includes 8% interest on a balance overdue by 60 days.
Aug.	17	B. R. Bailey	90 days	8%	1,994.04	Aug. 30 = The note is discounted.
July	26	A. F. Stead	3 months	7%	1,250.00	Sept. 10 = The note is discounted. Maturity = The note is dishonored. Protest fees, $4.00.
Aug.	30	J. J. Rhyn	3 months	7%	3,000.00	Oct. 15 = The note is discounted (bank rate, 8%). Maturity = The note is dishonored. Protest fees, $4.00.

Chapter 13

NOTES PAYABLE AND DRAFTS

ACCOUNTING FOR NOTES PAYABLE

Due_____ New York, N. Y., March 1, 1950. $1,000.00

Four months after date, I promise to pay to the order of _____

William E. Trent_____ at _____

One Thousand and no/100 _____ Dollars

For value received.

Lloyd J. Martin

This note is a note receivable to William E. Trent, and a note payable to Lloyd J. Martin. As with notes receivable, notes payable are entered upon the books at face value.

Chapter 12 illustrated the proper accounting for this as a "note receivable." The proper accounting for it from the viewpoint of the debtor rather than the creditor, i.e., as a "note payable," is described by the entries which follow.

THE NOTE IS ISSUED IN FAVOR OF A MERCHANDISE CREDITOR

On March 1, 1950, Lloyd J. Martin gave his four-month note to William E. Trent in part payment of his account.

Without Interest			*With Interest at 6%*		
Mar. 1 William E. Trent . . 1,000.00			Mar. 1 William E. Trent . . 1,000.00		
Notes Payable .		1,000.00	Notes Payable .		1,000.00
To record issuance of four-month note.			To record issuance of four-month, 6%, note.		

If, in lieu of the interest-bearing note, Mr. Martin had given a note for $1,020.00 (the face of the note including $20.00 interest to maturity), his entry for the issuance of the note would have been:

Mar. 1	William E. Trent.	1,000.00	
	Interest Expense	20.00	
	Notes Payable		1,020.00
	To record issuance of four-month note, interest of $20.00 included in face of note.		

The entry to record the payment of the note would be:

July 1	Notes Payable	1,020.00	
	Cash		1,020.00
	Paid William E. Trent for note of March 1, 1950.		

Banks, in making loans to customers, often use notes whose face values include interest to maturity.

THE NOTE IS ISSUED IN FAVOR OF A BANK

On March 1, 1950, Lloyd J. Martin obtained a loan at the First National Bank for which he gave his four-month note. (The note would be identical with the one illustrated above except that the payee would be the First National Bank.) The bank discount rate is 6%.

Without Interest				*With Interest at 6%*		
Mar. 1 Cash	980.00			Mar. 1 Cash	1,000.00	
Interest Expense . . .	20.00			Notes Payable .		1,000.00
Notes Payable . .		1,000.00		To record four-month		
To record four-month				6% note to First Na-		
note to First National				tional Bank.		
Bank.						

The cash received on the first note is computed as follows:

Value of note at maturity	$1,000.00
Less discount on maturity value for 4 months, at 6%	20.00
Cash proceeds of note	$ 980.00

Theoretically, the amount of cash to be received on the second note would be computed as follows:

Value of note at maturity . . . . : . .	$1,020.00
Less discount on maturity value for 4 months, at 6%	20.40
Theoretical cash proceeds of note	$ 999.60

In this particular kind of case, however, banking practice deviates from strict theory. The bank will advance the face value of the note if the interest rate in the note of the borrower is the same as the discount rate of the bank. Therefore, in this second example, the cash proceeds will be $1,000.00, *not* $999.60.

The two notes payable would be recorded in the cash receipts book as follows:

CASH RECEIPTS BOOK

DATE		ACCOUNT CREDITED	EXPLANATION	L.F.	CREDIT		DEBIT	
					Miscellaneous	Accounts Receivable	Sales Discounts	Cash
1950								
Mar.	1	Notes Payable	First Nat'l Bank		1,000 00			
		Interest Expense			(20 00)			980 00
	1	Notes Payable	First Nat'l Bank		1,000 00			1,000 00

The item in parentheses, as before, indicates a debit entry.

Accounting practice finds it expedient to debit the discount of $20.00 direct to the Interest Expense account. According to accounting theory, however, the proper debit for the interest of $20.00 is Discount on Notes Payable rather than Interest Expense. This is because true interest expense can be realized only after the passage of a period of time. In the example above the real amount borrowed was $980.00 and not $1,000.00. At the end of each month the interest expense for the month would be recognized by the following entry:

Interest Expense 5.00
    Discount on Notes Payable. 5.00
    To record this month's interest expense, ¼ of $20.00 = $5.00.

On the balance sheet the Discount on Notes Payable account would be a valuation account; it would be deducted from Notes Payable.

This section may be concluded by observing that "discounting a note at a bank" is a term rather indiscriminately used to apply to two distinct kinds of note transactions: (1) transferring to a bank a note receivable by endorsing the note in favor of the bank and (2) borrowing funds from a bank by executing a note payable in favor of the bank. In both cases the cash advanced by the bank will be the maturity value of the note less the amount of discount for the period of time which the note has yet to run.

THE NOTE IS PAID AT MATURITY

On July 1, 1950, Lloyd J. Martin paid William E. Trent (or First National Bank) in full for his note of March 1, 1950.

Without Interest	*With Interest at 6%*
July 1 Notes Payable 1,000.00	July 1 Notes Payable 1,000.00
Cash 1,000.00	Interest Expense . . . 20.00
Paid W. E. Trent for	Cash 1,020.00
note dated March 1,	Paid W. E. Trent for
1950.	note dated March 1,
	1950, and interest at
	6%.

THE NOTE IS PARTLY PAID AT MATURITY

On July 1, 1950, Lloyd J. Martin paid $450.00 on his four-month note to William E. Trent, dated March 1, 1950, and gave a new sixty-day note for the balance.

Without Interest				*With Interest at 6%*		
July 1 Notes Payable	450.00		July 1 Notes Payable	450.00	
Cash		450.00		Interest Expense	20.00	
For part payment of note				Cash		470.00
to Wm. E. Trent dated				For part payment of note		
March 1, 1950.				to Wm. E. Trent, dated		
				March 1, 1950, with 6%		
				interest in full to date.		
July 1 Notes Payable	550.00		July 1 Notes Payable	550.00	
Notes Payable . . .		550.00		Notes Payable . . .		550.00
To record issuance of new				To record issuance of new		
sixty-day note for unpaid				sixty-day, 6%, note for un-		
balance on Wm. E. Trent				paid balance on Wm. E.		
note of March 1, 1950.				Trent note of March 1,		
				1950.		

THE NOTE IS DISHONORED AT MATURITY

No entry is necessary. The debt is still an outstanding note payable.

NOTES PAYABLE REGISTER

As with notes receivable, a special book of original entry may, if desired, be used to record notes payable. In form, the notes payable register is very much like the notes receivable register, and hence it need not be specifically illustrated here.

DRAFTS

A draft is defined by the Uniform Negotiable Instruments Act as "an unconditional order in writing addressed by one person to another, signed by the person giving it, requiring the person to whom it is addressed to pay on demand or at a fixed or determinable future time a sum certain in money to order or to bearer."

Example:

No.__Due__   Seattle, Wash., May 10, 1950. $2,000.00

Sixty days after date, pay to the order of _____

Robert L. Cassell _____

Two Thousand and no/100 _____ Dollars

Value received, and charge to the account of

To: Stanley T. Webb   *Richard T. Child*

WHY DRAFTS ARE USED

Drafts are used

(1) To speed collections of open accounts.

(2) To ship goods on a C.O.D. basis.

(3) To ship goods on a "note" rather than on an open account basis. The purchaser, in order to get his merchandise, must accept the draft, which document, along with an order bill of lading, is in the hands of his local bank.

(4) To obtain a written acknowledgment of the debt by the debtor.

(5) To obtain a negotiable instrument which, like any note receivable, may be discounted by the holder to procure funds.

CHARACTERISTICS OF A DRAFT

A draft is a negotiable instrument. The essential characteristics of a note are therefore also the essential characteristics of a bill of exchange (draft). These requisites have already been described (see page 251), and hence they need not be repeated here. New features only require mention.

Broadly speaking, drafts are of two kinds:

(1) Sight drafts ("at sight") in which immediate payment is ordered.

(2) Time drafts ("30 days after sight [or] date") which are payable after the lapse of a designated period of time.

In practice, drafts often appear under other names, such as bank checks, bank drafts, cashier's checks, acceptances.

There are three parties to a draft:

(1) The drawer, or maker, of the draft.
(2) The drawee, or the person upon whom the draft is drawn, the one who will pay the instrument.
(3) The payee, or the person to whom the money is payable. The payee is often the same person as the drawer.

The drawer orders the drawee to pay the payee.

Obviously, the drawee cannot be made to pay unless he has agreed to do so. A draft, therefore, is not a binding obligation until it has been agreed to, or "accepted," by the drawee. Acceptance

(1) Of a sight draft is evidenced by drawing a check in payment.
(2) Of a time draft is evidenced by writing across the face of the draft the following acceptance:

Accepted
May 12, 1950.
Stanley T. Webb (signature)

ACCOUNTING FOR DRAFTS

To all intents and purposes an accepted time draft is an ordinary promissory note. To the payee a draft is a note receivable; to the drawee a draft is a note payable. From the accounting standpoint, also, drafts are to be regarded either as notes receivable, or as notes payable, as the case may be. It should be emphasized, however, that acceptance by the drawee *must*, in all cases, precede formal accounting entries for drafts.[1]

The time draft on page 271 is the basis of the following illustrative entries:

THE TIME DRAFT IS ACCEPTED

On the books of Robert L. Cassell, payee:

Notes Receivable 2,000.00
    Richard T. Child 2,000.00
To record acceptance of sixty-day draft, dated May 10,
1950, by Stanley T. Webb, Richard T. Child, maker.

---

[1] This does not preclude the maintenance of a memorandum record to provide information as to drafts outstanding.

On the books of Stanley T. Webb, drawee:

Richard T. Child	2,000.00	
Notes Payable		2,000.00

To record acceptance of sixty-day draft, dated May 10, 1950, drawn by Richard T. Child, favor Robert L. Cassell.

On the books of Richard T. Child, drawer: [2]

Robert L. Cassell	2,000.00	
Stanley T. Webb		2,000.00

To record acceptance of sixty-day draft, dated May 10, 1950, drawn on Stanley T. Webb, favor Robert L. Cassell.

This entry debits Robert L. Cassell to record the payment made to him and credits Stanley T. Webb for making the payment.

THE SIGHT DRAFT IS ACCEPTED

If the draft above had been payable "at sight," its acceptance would have been evidenced by its immediate payment. Hence the entries

On the books of Robert L. Cassell, payee:

Cash	2,000.00	
Richard T. Child		2,000.00

To record sight draft paid by Stanley T. Webb and drawn by Richard T. Child.

On the books of Stanley T. Webb, drawee:

Richard T. Child	2,000.00	
Cash		2,000.00

To record payment of sight draft drawn by Richard T. Child, favor Robert L. Cassell.

On the books of Richard T. Child, drawer:

Robert L. Cassell	2,000.00	
Stanley T. Webb		2,000.00

To record payment of sight draft by Stanley T. Webb, favor Robert L. Cassell.

---

[2] If it is desired to recognize the drawer's contingent liability upon this draft, the entries will be:

Notes Receivable	2,000.00	
Stanley T. Webb		2,000.00

To record acceptance of sixty-day draft, dated May 10, 1950, favor Robert L. Cassell.

Robert L. Cassell	2,000.00	
Notes Receivable Discounted		2,000.00

To record transfer to Robert L. Cassell of accepted sixty-day draft, dated May 10, 1950, Stanley T. Webb, drawee.

ENTRIES FOR TWO-NAME DRAFTS

Sometimes the same individual is both the payee and the maker of a draft. If, in the illustration on page 271, the payee were Richard T. Child, then payee and maker would be identical. The entries would be:

The time draft is accepted   *The sight draft is accepted*

On the books of Richard T. Child:

Notes Receivable . .	2,000.00		Cash	2,000.00	

Notes Receivable . . 2,000.00
    Stanley T. Webb   2,000.00
To record acceptance
of sixty-day draft,
dated May 10, 1950,
drawn on Stanley T.
Webb, favor ourselves.

Cash 2,000.00
    Stanley T. Webb   2,000.00
To record payment of
sight draft by Stanley
T. Webb, favor our-
selves.

On the books of Stanley T. Webb:

Richard T. Child . . 2,000.00
    Notes Payable .   2,000.00
To record acceptance
of sixty-day draft,
dated May 10, 1950,
drawn by Richard T.
Child, in favor of him-
self.

Richard T. Child . . 2,000.00
    Cash 2,000.00
To record payment of
sight draft drawn by
Richard T. Child, in
favor of himself.

DRAFT REGISTER

Where a large amount of business is transacted by shipping merchandise under order bills of lading, sight or time drafts attached, the shipments may be recorded in the regular sales book. Much better, however, is the maintenance of a separate sales book called the draft register, in which all draft shipments are recorded.[3] This book is operated as a second book of original entry for sales; the debit posting, however, is to Drafts Receivable rather than to Accounts Receivable. This is for the purpose of drawing a line of demarcation between the two kinds of receivables. As each draft is taken up, the date of its acceptance is noted opposite the entry of the draft in the draft register. The total of the open items in the draft register is equal to the balance of the Drafts Receivable account in the general ledger. This practice is followed by the Ford Motor Company in accounting for sight drafts.

In lieu of a draft register, or a memorandum record for the recording of outstanding drafts (page 272), some companies — as a

---

[3] If both sight drafts and time drafts are employed, a sight draft register and a time draft register should be used with a general ledger controlling account for each register.

matter of bookkeeping convenience — record outgoing sight and time draft shipments as if they were ordinary credit sales. When the draft is accepted, Cash or Notes Receivable is debited, and Accounts Receivable credited. If the draft is not accepted and the shipment returned, the original entry is reversed.

When financial statements are being prepared at the end of an accounting period, Accounts Receivable and Sales must be adjusted with respect to outstanding, unaccepted drafts covering shipments on which title has not passed. Such merchandise-and-draft shipments are not sales. They must be eliminated from Sales and Accounts Receivable when financial statements are being prepared. This merchandise should be included as a part of the ending inventory and should be priced at cost. Without these adjustments, it is obvious that the net income of the period would be distorted.

QUESTIONS

Question **13–1.** When a note payable is partly paid, or is dishonored, at maturity, should the note be transferred to the creditor's personal account? Why?

Question **13–2.** What is a draft? Illustrate. Distinguish between a sight draft and a time draft.

Question **13–3.** Why are drafts used?

Question **13–4.** What s meant by "acceptance" and what is its accounting significance?

Question **13–5.** If a draft is not paid at maturity by the drawee, does the payee have any claim against the drawer? If so, how should this contingency be provided for by the drawer?

Question **13–6.** The Ford Motor Company sends out hundreds of sight drafts each day. Most of these drafts are promptly honored but a few are more or less delayed in payment, sometimes as much as two or three weeks or more. What kind of record should be made of these drafts? Explain fully. Is your record an integral part of the complete accounting system? Should it be?

Question **13–7.** What would be your accounting procedure for sales for a company which sends only about 10 % of its shipments C.O.D. (parcel post, express, and freight)?

PROBLEMS

Problem **13–1.** Prepare the entries to be made on the books of the maker for the following note transactions. Unless otherwise indicated, notes payable are issued in payment of accounts payable. The bank discount rate, where required, may be assumed to be 6 %.

Date of Note		Payee	Term	Interest	Amount	Transaction
April	4	J. L. Hayman	30 days		$ 300.00	April 4 = The note is issued. Maturity = The note is paid.
	5	W. E. Hunter	2 months	8%	148.12	April 5 = The note is issued. Maturity = The note is paid.
	6	First National Bank	60 days		1,000.00	April 6 = The note is issued. Maturity = The note is paid.
	7	First National Bank	90 days	6%	1,500.00	April 7 = The note is issued. Maturity = The note is paid.
	8	First National Bank	2 months	8%	2,000.00	April 8 = The note is issued. Bank rate 8%. Maturity = The note is paid.
	9	E. R. Gibson	60 days		882.86	April 9 = This note is issued in payment of an invoice for $874.12, due today. The face of the note is $874.12 plus 6% interest for 60 days. Maturity = The note is paid.
	10	F. D. Weston	45 days		500.00	April 10 = The note is issued. Maturity = Paid $300.00 cash, and gave new 30-day note for balance due.
	14	M. A. Stone	60 days	6%	500.00	April 14 = The note is issued. Maturity = Paid $300.00 cash and interest; balance on new 30-day, 6%, note.
	15	R. B. Forbes	72 days	6%	500.00	April 16 = The note is issued. Maturity = Paid $350.00 to apply on principal; gave new 30-day 6% note for balance due.
	16	E. D. Young	3 months		100.00	April 16 = The note is issued. Maturity = The note is not paid.
	17	Wm. O. Laird	84 days	10%	900.00	May 20 = The note is issued in payment of invoice due for payment April 17.
	20	L. E. Sears	60 days		828.21	April 20 = The note is issued in payment of merchandise bought today, $836.74, less 2% for immediate cash payment. By arrangement with the seller, the invoice is paid net, $820.01, with a note whose face is this net amount plus interest for 60 days at 6%.

DATE OF NOTE		PAYEE	TERM	INTEREST	AMOUNT	TRANSACTION
April	22	Lee & Evans, Inc.	18 days	8%	309.19	April 22 = This note is issued in payment of invoice of April 12, terms 5% 10 days, net 60 days. Lee & Evans Inc., accept the note at face value and allow the full cash discount.
						Maturity = The note is paid.
	25	Davis & Company	3 months		1,258.56	April 24 = This note is issued in payment of Davis & Company invoice of April 15 for $1,324.80, terms 5% 10 days, net 30 days. Davis & Company accept the note for its cash value at their bank as of April 25 and allow cash discount as justified by the cash value of the note.
						Maturity = The note is paid.

Problem 13–2. On April 1, 19__, X discounted his own note (without interest, dated April 1, 19__ and due July 1, 19__) for $3,000.00, with the Fremont National Bank (whose discount rate was 6%). X paid the note at maturity. Give all entries for X.

How would your entries have been altered if this note had carried 6% running interest?

Problem 13–3. Prepare the entries to be made on Z s books for the following:

Jan. 2 — X draws a 60-day, 7% draft, dated today, for $1,296.00 on Y in favor of Z.

  4 — Y accepts the draft.

  22 — Z discounts the draft at the First National Bank whose discount rate is 6%.

Mar. 3 — The draft is paid.

Problem 13–4. Prepare entries for the following:

July 2 — Merchandise is shipped to L. E. Titus under sight draft bill of lading, $1,214.11.

  3 — A similar shipment is forwarded to Cort & Cort, $732.50.

  5 — Merchandise is purchased from Mead & Company, $514.25, under terms of a 30-day acceptance, which is taken up.

  7 — The bank notifies us that the L. E. Titus draft has been collected. Also that Cort & Cort have refused to pay their draft.

8 — Merchandise is shipped to the Welch Manufacturing Company under terms of a 60-day trade acceptance, $899.76.

10 — The Welch draft is accepted.

10 — The bank charges our bank account for June collection fees, $10.99.

Problem **13–5.** X drew a $1,000.00 draft on Y in favor of Z, payable at 60 days' sight. The draft was dated August 14, 1950, and was accepted by Y on August 26, 1950. At maturity Y rendered his check in payment. Show all entries on the books of X, Y, and Z.

Problem **13–6.** X drew a sight draft dated August 1, 1950, on Y, in favor of Z, for $1,600.00. The draft was accepted August 6. Show all entries for X, Y, and Z.

Problem **13–7.** X drew a 30-day sight draft, dated March 28, 1950, on Y in favor of himself for $1,400.00. The draft was accepted April 1. The draft was not paid when due. Give the entries for X and Y.

Problem **13–8.** Piper & Co. drew a draft for $1,284.06 on F. M. Walters in favor of Baker & Co., Inc. The draft was dated April 12, due August 1, and carried $6\frac{1}{2}\%$ running interest. The draft was accepted April 30 and was discounted June 28, bank rate 7%.

Give the entry to record the discounting transaction on the books of Baker & Co., Inc.

Problem **13–9.** On October 1, 19___, X drew a 90-day sight draft for $1,200.00 on Y in favor of Z. Y accepted this draft on November 1, 19___. Z discounted the draft with the Fremont National Bank on December 1, 19___, bank rate 6%. The draft was paid at maturity. Give the entries for X, Y, and Z.

Problem **13–10.** A draft for $1,000.00, dated September 1, 19___, and due December 1, 19___, drawn by X, on Y, in favor of Z, was accepted September 5. Z discounted this draft November 2 with the First National Bank. Y failed to pay the draft at maturity and Z was therefore obliged to reimburse the bank. X, in turn, gave his check to Z in exchange for the dishonored draft. Give the entries for X, Y, and Z.

Problem **13–11.** Purchase invoice of the X Company for $1,000.00 is payable by the 10th of the month following date of invoice, less 5% cash discount. When the 10th of the month arrives, we are temporarily short of cash but, not wishing to lose the cash discount, we offer X our 90-day note, without interest, in settlement. X replies that a note settlement will be satisfactory provided the face of the note is an amount large enough to net X $950.00 by immediate discount of the note at X's bank. (Bank rate 6%.) What entry should be made on our books to record the issuance of the note?

Problem **13–12.** On June 30, 19__, the books of Henry P. Guthman included the following accounts:

RAY C. KRAMER

May 1	2/10, n/60	568.14	
June 28	2/10, n/30	1,209.62	

BEN A. ADLER

	June 26	5/10, n/30	1,407.60
	June 29	n/60	492.40

With respect to the above accounts the following transactions occurred on the dates indicated:

July 5 — Borrowed funds from the First National Bank by giving a non-interest-bearing note, due September 1, for $1,500.00. Bank rate, 7%.

  6 — Gave Mr. Adler a check for $1,140.00 in part payment of invoice of June 26, this payment including an allowance for cash discount.

  8 — Received a 30-day 6% note, dated today from Mr. Kramer in payment of invoice of June 28, less 2%.

  8 — Discounted the Kramer note at the bank. Rate, 6%.

Aug. 7 — The Kramer note, due today, was not paid. Mr. Guthman paid the amount due and received the note from the bank.

Sept. 1 — The note payable at the bank is paid.

Oct. 1 — Drew two drafts, dated today, on Mr. Kramer. The first draft was a sight draft for $700.00 in favor of Mr. Adler. The second was a 30-day 10% sight draft in favor of Guthman; the face of this draft was the balance due in Kramer's account plus 10% interest on overdue amounts for the periods over which such amounts have been delinquent. Both drafts were immediately accepted.

  31 — The Kramer 30-day sight draft is paid.

Required:

Make the required entries on each of the above dates on the books of Mr. Guthman.

Problem **13–13.** Following are the transactions of T. R. Jones in his first month of business:

January

  2 — Began business with a cash capital of $50,000.00. Purchased from S. J. Bassett a store building at a cost of $30,000.00, and land, $6,000.00. This realty was paid for by giving a mortgage for

$14,000.00 and a check for the balance due. To equip the store Mr. Jones buys store fixtures, $3,000.00, and office equipment, $2,000.00, all for cash from the Fred C. Clarke Company.

3 — Purchase of merchandise on account from the Allen Importing Company, $28,000.00.

4 — Paid $500.00 cash for stationery and postage.

5 — Sale of merchandise on account to the Bell Company, $8,400.00.

9 — Gave a check to the General Sign Company for signs and sundry advertising, $300.00.

10 — Sale of merchandise to Darby & Company on sight draft, $800.00. The draft is honored.

12 — Purchase of merchandise on account from the Carr Company, $11,000.00. Paid freight on this purchase, $34.00. This freight should have been paid by the Carr Company.

14 — Cash is paid out for salesmen's salaries, $1,300.00, office salaries, $1,100.00, warehouse wages, $800.00, general expenses, $800.00.

17 — Sale of merchandise to Darby & Company on account, $15,000.00.

18 — A 6% 30-day note, dated today, is received from the Bell Company, $8,000.00.

19 — The Allen Importing Company is given a check for $11,200.00 less 5% cash discount; and a 30-day note for $16,800.00.

20 — Sale of merchandise on account to M. C. Enfield for $17,000.00.

21 — A credit memorandum is mailed to M. C. Enfield covering error in sales invoice of January 20, $100.00.

23 — Purchase of merchandise on account from the Allen Importing Company, $20,100.00.

24 — Sale of merchandise on account to the Bell Company, $11,200.00. Received a non-interest-bearing note, dated today and due March 10, from M. C. Enfield, $10,000.00.

26 — Received cash from Darby & Company, $10,000.00, less 2%.

27 — Paid for miscellaneous repairs on building, $920.00.

28 — Paid salesmen's salaries, $2,000.00, office salaries, $2,100.00, warehouse wages, $2,600.00, general expenses, $800.00.

30 — The Bell Company note is endorsed and turned over to the Carr Company in part payment of account. (See January 18.)

31 — Discounted the Enfield note (of January 24) at the bank whose rate is 5%. Freight and express bills on merchandise purchases amount to $880.22 for the month; these bills are all paid in cash.

Required:

(1) Enter these transactions in the appropriate books of original entry. Maintain controlling accounts for accounts receivable and accounts payable.

(2) Take a general ledger trial balance.

(3) Prepare a profit and loss statement for the month of January. Inventory of merchandise January 31, 19__, $21,800.00.

(4) Prepare a balance sheet, January 31, 19__.

(5) Reconcile the subsidiary ledgers.

Problem **13–14.** From the books, statements, and other information presented below (1) prepare a reconciliation of the bank account as of December 31, 1950, and (2) make entries in the January cash books to correct the account "Cash in The Valley National Bank" which, on December 31, 1950, had a balance of $776.64.

Herbert J. Knox

RECONCILIATION OF ACCOUNT WITH THE VALLEY NATIONAL BANK
NOVEMBER 30, 1950

Balance, per bank statement		$686.44
Add deposit in transit		142.68
		$829.12
Less outstanding checks: #48	$ 2.60	
#60	42.12	
#61	75.17	119.89
		$709.23
Balance, per Cash account in ledger		$731.73
Less charge for printing checks	$ 2.50	
check drawn by Allen B. Hays deposited and charged back by the bank because of insufficient funds . .	20.00	22.50
		$709.23

CASH RECEIPTS BOOK

1950			MISC.	ACCTS. REC.	CASH	DEPOSITS
Dec.	1	Herbert E. Ashlock		120.40	120.40	
	3	Tony & Hughes		212.18	212.18	
	5	Delivery Equipment	25.00		25.00	
	7	Sales	489.62		489.62	847.20
	11	Allen B. Hays. This check covers N.S.F. check given in November		20.00	20.00	
	12	Notes Payable to Bank	200.00		200.00	
	13	George T. Blum		84.62	84.62	
	14	Sales	586.20		586.20	890.82
	17	Sewell, Emery, & Co.		620.40	620.40	
	21	Sales	418.06		418.06	1,038.46
	25	Henry A. Brown		208.65	208.65	
	26	Herbert E. Ashlock		250.70	250.70	
	28	Sales	405.10		405.10	864.45
	30	Roy Akerson		30.62	30.62	
	31	Sales	250.71		250.71	281.33
			2,374.69	1,547.57	3,922.26	3,922.26

CASH PAYMENTS BOOK

1950	CHECK No.			MISC.	ACCTS. PAY.	BANK
Dec. 2	63	General Sales Co.			350.00	350.00
4	64	Advertising Expense		35.08		35.08
7	65	Wages Expense		120.20		120.20
10	66	Thor Manufacturing Co.			720.42	720.42
12	67	General Expense		76.95		76.95
14	68	Wages Expense		176.14		176.14
16	69	The Byrd Company			847.21	847.21
19	70	Advertising Expense		125.60		125.60
21	71	Wages Expense		150.74		150.74
24	72	Sloan & Son			605.20	605.20
25	73	General Expense		205.30		205.30
26	74	General Sales Co.			80.40	80.40
28	75	Wages Expense		162.24		162.24
29	76	Advertising Expense		36.17		36.17
30	77	General Sales Co.			140.00	140.00
31	78	General Expense		45.70		45.70
				1,134.12	2,743.23	3,877.35

BANK STATEMENT

Herbert J. Knox in account with The Valley National Bank

1950	CHECKS				DEPOSITS	BALANCE
Dec. 1	Balance					686.44
1	75.17				142.68	753.95
3	350.00	42.12				361.83
8	35.08	120.20			847.20	1,053.75
12	720.42				200.00	533.33
16	847.21	176.14			690.82	200.80
23	150.74	125.60			1,038.46	962.92
27	80.40	605.20	205.30		40.40	112.42
30	162.42	140.00	202.67		864.45	471.78
31	3.12	76.95				391.71

The charge for $202.67 on December 30 is for a $200.00 note owed the bank, plus interest for 60 days at 8 %. The charge for $3.12 on December 31 is for sundry bank service charges. All other charges are for checks. The deposit of $40.40 on December 27 represents the face value of a note receivable, $40.00, and interest, $0.40, collected by the bank for Mr. Knox. All items on the bank statement are correct.

Chapter 14

PERIODIC ADJUSTMENT OF THE LEDGER

WHY CURRENT ACCOUNTS OF THE LEDGER NEED ADJUSTMENT

The preparation of statements and the closing of the ledger at the end of each accounting period would be relatively simple matters if the accounts of the ledger could be accepted as they stand. This, however, cannot usually be done. Invariably it is necessary for certain adjustments to be made before the balances of accounts can be accepted as accurate. After these adjustments have been made, it is then in order for financial statements to be prepared, and the books closed. Examples of these adjustments follow:

(1) The Merchandise Inventory account, before adjustment, reflects the value of the inventory on hand at the beginning of the period. This value, however, is not the value of the inventory on hand at the end of the accounting period. Therefore, in order to show the value of the inventory on hand at the *end* of the period, the Merchandise Inventory account must be "adjusted" by clearing away the old value and replacing it with the new. This adjustment is one with which the student is already familiar.

(2) Fixed assets, such as automobiles, fixtures, or machinery, are constantly and continuously becoming less and less valuable because of depreciation. The accounts which represent these assets must be "adjusted" at least annually in order to reflect the lessened dollar value of these properties. The reduced value of the asset reflects the reduced amount of service yet to be received from the asset.

(3) Assets such as accounts receivable are recorded in the books of original entry at face values. However, on balance sheet dates, accounts receivable are usually appraised as being worth a little less than the total of their face values. Accounts receivable are considered as being worth less than face value because of the expectation that some debts will not be collected. Where these conditions prevail, an "adjustment" of the value of accounts receivable is necessary. The purpose of this adjustment is to bring the book value of accounts receivable into agreement with cash values, i.e., the amount of cash expected to be realized by collections of accounts receivable. Similar comments apply to notes receivable.

(4) Expense and income accounts commonly require correction

283

because their balances frequently do not represent the true expense
or income of a period. One explanation of this condition relates to
the fact that the incurring of an expense does not necessarily coincide
with the date of payment. The expense may be incurred

> before the period in which payment is made,
> during the period in which payment is made, or
> after the period in which payment is made,

but, commonly, the debit to expense is made only at the time of payment. Consequently, when financial statements are to be prepared
and the nominal accounts of a ledger closed, expense accounts must
first be "adjusted" so that the current period is charged with all expenses incurred, paid or not paid, and relieved of expenses which
properly belong to future accounting periods. Expense accounts,
after adjustment, show the correct amount of expense applicable to
the period covered by the statement of profit and loss.

Similarly, the earning of an income does not necessarily coincide
with the date of its receipt in cash. The actual "earning" of an income may occur

> before the period in which collection is made,
> during the period in which collection is made, or
> after the period in which collection is made,

but, frequently, the credit to income is made only at the time of its
receipt in cash. Consequently, when financial statements are to be
prepared and the nominal accounts of the ledger closed, income accounts must first be "adjusted" so that the current period is credited
with all income earned, even though not yet received in cash, and
relieved of income which properly belongs to future accounting
periods. Income accounts, when thus corrected, will show the true
income applicable to the period to be covered by the statement of
profit and loss.

These four examples illustrate the necessity for the adjustment
of account balances at the end of an accounting period. It should be
apparent that adjustments *must* be made before it is possible to prepare profit and loss statements and balance sheets which are *accurate*.

DEPRECIATION

Fixed assets, like building, machinery, and equipment, do not
last forever. They have definite lives. When they are no longer
useful, the investment in them is gone. The investment has been
used up in the operations of business, i.e., *it has been converted into
expense*. The name of this expense is Depreciation Expense. Whether

a fixed asset has been used for 5 or 25 years is not as important as the fact that the investment in the asset has been converted into an expense applicable to this 5- or 25-year period of life; and that part of this expense applies to *each* of the years of life.

Depreciation is the decline in the dollar value of an asset which comes about because of shrinkage in the amount of services receivable. As the services of the asset are used up, expense occurs. The dollar value of a delivery truck, for example, declines as the services of the truck are used up. By dollar value here is meant not market value but going-concern value, i.e., services receivable expressed in terms of the owner's investment in the asset. Depreciation expense is measured in terms of the original dollar cost of the depreciable asset.

Depreciation expense is one of the inescapable costs involved in the ownership of fixed assets. Obviously it is also one of the inescapable costs involved in the operation of a business which owns fixed assets. If the balance sheet of this business is to be correct, and if periodic income is to be stated correctly, the books must be adjusted periodically in order to reflect

(1) The expense of depreciation, and
(2) The lessened book value of the depreciable asset.

This adjustment is illustrated in the following example.

Example:

New automobiles for the use of salesmen were purchased on January 1, 1950, at a cost of $8,000.00. Their useful life was estimated to be four years. On December 31, 1950, therefore, the automobiles had depreciated 25% in value, or $2,000.00. Their new value was $6,000.00. The following entry records the decrease in value:

```
Depreciation Expense — Automobiles . . . . . . . .   2,000.00
     Automobiles  . . . . . . . . . . . . . . . . . .             2,000.00
     To record depreciation expense on salesmen's automo-
     biles for the year 1950.
```

Although this entry records the expense of depreciation, and also the reduced value of the asset, it is almost universal accounting practice to place the *credit* member of this type of depreciation entry in a *separate* account called Reserve for Depreciation. The above entry therefore should be revised. The proper journal entry would be accordingly,

```
Depreciation Expense — Automobiles . . . . . . . .   2,000.00
     Reserve for Depreciation — Automobiles.  . . . .             2,000.00
     To record depreciation expense on salesmen's automo-
     biles for the year 1950.
```

When the books are being closed at the end of an accounting period, the Depreciation Expense account is transferred to Profit and Loss just as other expenses are.

The Reserve for Depreciation account measures the shrinkage which has taken place in the book value of an asset. On the balance sheet the reserve account should be deducted from the asset account in the following manner:

Automobiles	$8,000.00	
Less Reserve for Depreciation	2,000.00	$6,000.00

A separate reserve for depreciation account should be maintained for each group of depreciable fixed assets. There will be a reserve for depreciation account for automobiles, one for buildings, one for machinery, and so on.

Each reserve for depreciation account is a real account. It has a balance as long as the depreciable asset is carried in the balance sheet. The balance of any particular reserve for depreciation account is not closed until the related depreciable asset is retired or sold.

Adjusting entries to recognize depreciation are very important, for without such adjustment

(1) The expenses of the period would be understated,
(2) The net profit would be overstated, and
(3) The balance sheet would be incorrect because of the overvaluations attached to depreciable assets.

BAD DEBTS

Many concerns have found through experience that debts are not 100% collectible. Because of this fact, accounts receivable (and often notes receivable) are considered to be worth something less than full face value. The amount of the loss to be taken can be closely approximated by the use of a percentage developed upon the basis of past experience. The estimated loss for a period may be expressed

(1) As a percentage of the net sales for the period. This method is widely used. However, where the ratio of credit sales to cash sales varies significantly from period to period, it is better that the bad debts percentage be applied against the credit sales alone.

(2) As a percentage of the accounts receivable at the end of the accounting period. This method is not ordinarily to be recommended because of certain inaccuracies which may ensue when a fixed percentage is applied against fluctuating periodic accounts receivable figures.

(3) As the result of careful classification and analysis of past-due accounts. This method, although excellent, is burdensome, and is especially so when hundreds of accounts are involved.

Clearly, the loss from uncollectible accounts is a loss chargeable to the period in which the sales were made. In order to set up the bad debts expense which is considered to apply to a current period, and also in order to have the books show the real value which is considered to be present in accounts receivable, the following entry is made at the end of each accounting period:

Bad Debts Expense . . . . xxx xx
   Reserve for Bad Debts . . . .   xxx xx

The credit member of this entry should theoretically be Accounts Receivable, but this account cannot be immediately credited because, at the time of the above entry, it is not known which particular accounts are going to prove uncollectible. Hence the credit is placed temporarily in a separate account called Reserve for Bad Debts, to remain there until the uncollectible accounts have been definitely ascertained. As specific accounts are determined to be worthless, they should be removed from the books by the following entry:

Reserve for Bad Debts . . . . xxx xx
   Accounts Receivable . . . .   xxx xx

Current accounts receivable which are worthless should be removed immediately from the books by the same kind of entry. This write-off is made in anticipation of the reserve to be set up at the end of the accounting period. Before this reserve is set up it is quite possible, in consequence, for the Reserve for Bad Debts account to have a debit balance.

Recognition of bad debts expense at the end of an accounting period is important because without adjustment therefor

(1) The expenses of the period would be understated,
(2) The net profit would be overstated, and
(3) The balance sheet would be incorrect because of the overvaluation of accounts receivable.

Example:

During 1950, the Jordan-Field Company, a department store, had sales of $1,000,000.00. Past experience of the store has shown that the average annual loss from uncollectible accounts has been about 2% of net sales. Accordingly, on December 31, 1950, the following entry is made:

```
Bad Debts Expense  . . . . . . . . . . . . . .    20,000.00
    Reserve for Bad Debts . . . . . . . . . . .                20,000.00
To record estimated bad debts for the year 1950.
```

During the year, accounts receivable (arising out of 1950 sales) of $17,228.00 have proven uncollectible. They are written off the books as follows:

```
Reserve for Bad Debts . . . . . . . . . . . . .   17,228.00
    Accounts Receivable . . . . . . . . . . . .                17,228.00
To write off uncollectible accounts receivable as fol-
lows: ____ (detail) . . . .
```

The balance of the Bad Debts Expense account is closed to the Profit and Loss account, and the balance of the Reserve for Bad Debts account is carried to the balance sheet as a valuation account for accounts receivable as follows:

```
Accounts Receivable  . . . . . . . . . . . . .   $112,700.00
Less Reserve for Bad Debts. . . . . . . . . . .     2,772.00   109,928.00
                                                 _____
```

The credit of $20,000.00 to the Reserve for Bad Debts account is an *estimate* of the amount of uncollectible 1950 sales. Subsequent to December 31, 1950, the actual loss for 1950 will be determined to be more than, or less than, $20,000.00. The difference between the amount of actual expense and the estimated expense of $20,000.00 is the amount by which the original estimate was wrong. In order to correct the 1950 provision and to avoid distortion of the value of outstanding accounts receivable on December 31, 1951, the difference in question is placed on the books by adjusting the Reserve for Bad Debts account, and debiting or crediting a nominal account of suitable title. If the difference is small, however, there is no practical objection to its retention in the Reserve for Bad Debts account, which is the usual practice.

If the difference is large, the 1950 provision is shown to have been inadequate, or excessive, with corresponding distortion to the 1950 financial statements. Such errors are particularly undesirable.

One should understand that while a rate of 2% may represent the average rate of loss over a period of years, it is possible for this rate to be inapplicable to a specific year. The correct percentage for such a year might be more or less than 2%. This is but another way of saying that the yearly provision for bad debts expense is not purely a matter of mechanical determination. Judgment must always govern the decision establishing the amount of the provision for bad debts. The test in every case should be: Is the amount of the provision, as viewed from all information available, an adequate measure of the probable loss from bad debts for the period?

Recoveries. — If an account receivable once written off is partially or fully collected in a later accounting period, the collection should be recorded by the following entries:

```
Accounts Receivable — L. L. Dutton . . . . . . . . . .   104.17
    Bad Debts Collected  . . . . . . . . . . . . . . .              104.17
To reinstate the account of L. L. Dutton which was written
off as uncollectible on December 31, 19__.

Cash . . . . . . . . . . . . . . . . . . . . . . . . .   104.17
    Accounts Receivable — L. L. Dutton . . . . . . . .              104.17
To record cash received.
```

The collection is handled through accounts receivable in order to have the account of L. D. Dutton complete in its historical detail. The Bad Debts Collected account is an income of the period of collection.

PREPAID EXPENSES

Prepaid expenses are expenses already entered upon the books but which are only partially consumed at the end of an accounting period. They comprise materials and services, purchased but not yet actually consumed, which will become expense in the normal course of future business operations. Prepaid expenses are assets; they are inventories of expense commodities or services receivable.

Although expenditures may have been charged to expense, only that portion of the material or service purchased which has been consumed by the current period should be considered as an expense of the period. The unused portion should be taken out of expense and carried forward to the next period as prepaid expense. In giving expression to this principle of accounting for prepaid expenses, it is obvious that the unused portion of an expenditure is placed in the balance sheet as an asset. The amount of this unused portion, in the case of materials, is usually determined by taking a physical inventory and, in the case of services, by valuing the unused portion on a time basis. In summary, therefore, when materials or services have not all been used up at the end of an accounting period, the unconsumed portion should be taken out of expense and set up as an asset. Expense accounts are credited with the amount to be deferred; the debits may be either to separate asset accounts (Prepaid Rent, Prepaid Taxes, Prepaid Interest, and the like) or to one summary account called "Prepaid Expenses."

Example:

During the year 1950, coal was purchased and debited to the Fuel Expense account, $1,000.00. On December 31, 1950, a physical inventory revealed that there was $150.00 worth of coal still on hand. In order that the expense account will show the true expense for the year of $850.00, and in order to place the asset of $150.00 on the books, the following adjusting entry is necessary:

```
Prepaid Expenses . . . . . . . . . . . . . . . . . . .    150.00
    Fuel Expense  . . . . . . . . . . . . . . . . . .              150.00
    To record inventory of coal, December 31, 1950.
```

The balance of the Fuel Expense account may now be closed to Profit and Loss.

After the ledger has been closed, the adjusting entry should be reversed. The asset will become an expense in the future normal operation of business; for this reason it is returned immediately to the Fuel Expense account of the new accounting period. When the reversing entry has been posted, the ledger accounts will appear as follows:

PREPAID EXPENSES

1950 Dec.	31		J72	150	00	1951 Jan.	1		J1	150	00

FUEL EXPENSE

1950						1950					
Jan.	1		CP1	250	00	Dec.	31		J72	150	00
Apr.	1		CP11	250	00		31	To P. & L.	J74	850	00
July	1		CP20	250	00						
Oct.	1		CP32	250	00						
				1,000	00					1,000	00
1951 Jan.	1	Prepaid	J1	150	00						

Other examples of prepaid expenses are prepaid advertising, insurance, interest, and rent as well as unused supplies of various kinds.

The necessity for adjusting entries to care for prepaid expenses should be evident, for without such adjustments

(1) The expenses of the period would be overstated,

(2) The net income would be understated, and

(3) The balance sheet would be incorrect because of the omission from its assets of prepaid expenses.

ACCRUED EXPENSES

At the end of an accounting period there is often no record on the books of certain expenses which have been incurred. Wages, for example, are normally recorded only at the time of payment, although it is clearly apparent that wages expense is an expense applicable to all the days of the wage period and not to the single day on which payment happens to be made. Wages expense is typical of that class of expenses which accrue day by day but which are inconvenient to record daily. However, when the books are closed between wage-payment dates the accounts must be made factually correct; it is therefore necessary to record the wages expense incurred up to the date the books are closed, and also to record the liability for wages owed to workmen even though the payroll may not be immediately due for payment. In such an adjustment we see this principle involved: Expense which has been incurred, but which has not been recorded on the books at the end of an accounting period, should be added to the expense account of the current period and placed in the balance sheet as a liability item.

Accrued liabilities are liabilities which usually must be paid off in cash. They are set up on the books by debits to appropriate expense accounts, and by credits either to separate liability accounts (Wages Payable, Interest Payable, and so on) or to one summary account for all accrued expenses called Accrued Liabilities. The expense accounts, after adjustment, may then be closed to Profit and Loss, while the account with Accrued Liabilities is carried to the balance sheet as a current liability.

Example:

During 1950, $10,000.00 was paid for labor and the expenditure debited to Wages Expense. On December 31, 1950, when the books are being closed, additional wages have been earned by workmen amounting to $250.00; these wages, however, are not due for payment until the next payday, January 4. In order to show the true labor cost for the year of $10,250.00 in the Wages Expense account, and in order to show on the books the liability for wages owed of $250.00, the following adjusting entry is necessary:

```
Wages Expense  . . . . . . . . . . . . . . . . . . . . . 250.00
    Accrued Liabilities  . . . . . . . . . . . . . . . .        250.00
    To record unpaid wages as of December 31, 1950.
```

After this entry has been posted, the balance of the Wages Expense account is closed to Profit and Loss.

After the ledger has been closed, the adjusting entry above should be reversed. The reason for this will be explained. The ledger accounts, after the reversing entry has been posted, would appear as follows:

ACCRUED LIABILITIES

1951 Jan.	1		J1	250	00	1950 Dec.	31		J72	250	00

WAGES EXPENSE

1950 Dec.	31	Balance		10,000	00	1950 Dec.	31	To P. & L.	J74	10,250	00
	31	Accrued	J72	250	00						
				10,250	00					10,250	00
						1951 Jan.	1	Accrued	J1	250	00

Assume that on payday, January 4, $440.00 is paid to workmen. This payment would represent the discharge of a wage liability of $250.00 already on the books (the credit balance in the Wages Expense account), and the payment of $190.00 labor expense of the new period. The entire $440.00 should be charged to the Wages Expense account:

WAGES EXPENSE

1951 Jan.	4		CP1	440	00	1951 Jan.	1	Accrued	J1	250	00

The balance of the account, $190.00, is the correct wage expense for the new period to date.

Other examples of accrued expenses are commissions, interest, rent, salaries, taxes on real and personal property, social security taxes (on employer), premiums on workmen's compensation insurance, and the utility services (gas, electricity, telephone, and water).

Adjusting entries for accrued expenses are necessary, for, without such adjustments:

(1) The expenses of the period will be understated,
(2) The net income would be overstated, and
(3) The balance sheet would be incorrect because of the omission of accrued expenses from its liability side.

DEFERRED INCOME

Some incomes may be recorded on the books before they are earned. Suppose, for instance, that an insurance company credits

Insurance Income for an initial ánnual premium of $2,400.00, which it receives on December 1 from a new policyholder. When the books are closed December 31, it would not be correct to consider all the $2,400.00 as income earned in the period ending that date. This is because the insurance protection is rendered not for one month but for twelve months. It follows that since $\frac{1}{12}$ of the insurance protection is rendered during December, $\frac{1}{12}$ of the income, or $200.00, should be credited to that month. The remaining $\frac{11}{12}$, or $2,200.00, should be credited to the income of the new year.

A statement of principle may therefore be made: Income which has been recorded on the books but which is, in whole or in part, unearned income at the end of an accounting period, should be removed from the income account of the current period and included with the liabilities of the balance sheet as unearned, or deferred, income. The accounting entries are as follows:

Income accounts are debited with the amount to be deferred, and the credits are made either to separate liability accounts — one account for each type of deferred income — or to one summary account called Deferred Income. The latter method is ordinarily to be preferred. Unless more adjustments are necessary, the income accounts are closed to Profit and Loss, and the account with Deferred Income is carried to the balance sheet as a liability. It is a liability because it is an obligation which is payable, not in cash, but in services.

Example:

On October 1, 1950, X agreed to lease a certain property to the Blue and White Chain Stores for an annual rental of $7,200.00 payable in advance. A check for that amount was accordingly received and credited to Rent Income. On December 31, 1950, X closes his books. In order to have his Rent Income account show the true earned income applicable to 1950 of $1,800.00, and in order to defer the balance to 1951, the following adjusting entry is necessary:

Rent Income 5,400.00
    Deferred Income 5,400.00
To set up unearned rent income.

After this entry has been posted, the balance of the Rent Income account is closed to Profit and Loss. The account with Deferred Income remains open as a liability representing the obligation of X to execute his part of the contract for the nine months which remain.

After the ledger has been closed, this adjusting entry should be reversed in order to place the deferred income in the Rent Income account of 1951. This is because the deferred income will gradually become earned Rent Income in 1951. For convenience the whole amount is returned to income at one time. The ledger accounts on January 1, 1951, would be as follows:

DEFERRED INCOME

1951			J1	5,400	00	1950			J72	5,400	00
Jan.	1					Dec.	31				

RENT INCOME

1950						1950			CR20	7,200	00
Dec.	31		J72	5,400	00	Oct.	1				
	31	To P. & L.	J74	1,800	00						
				7,200	00					7,200	00
						1951					
						Jan.	1	Deferred	J1	5,400	00

Other examples of deferred incomes are profits on installment sales, interest, subscriptions, tickets, scrip good for merchandise, services, and so on.

The importance of adjusting entries to recognize deferred incomes on the books should be apparent, for without such adjustments

(1) Incomes of the period would be overstated,
(2) The net income would be overstated, and
(3) The balance sheet would be incorrect because of the omission of the liability represented by deferred incomes.[1]

ACCRUED INCOME

At the end of an accounting period there is often no record on the books of income which has been earned (i.e., accrued day by day) but which has not yet been received. Bond interest is an example. If, for instance, X owns a $1,000.00, 6% bond, interest payable April 1 and October 1, three months' interest, or $15.00, will have been earned up to the date his books are closed, December 31. This income is not on the books. An adjustment is therefore necessary in order to place the accrued interest in the income account of the current period.

---

[1] Of its total equities of $122,283,255 on June 30, 1945, the Fidelity-Phenix Fire Insurance Company reported $22,343,122 to be unearned income. In their balance sheets for December 31, 1944, the Commercial Credit Company showed a liability for deferred income of $9,522,767, and Time, Inc., a similar liability for $14,901,525.

Income of this kind is recorded on the books by a debit to each type of accrued income, or preferably, to one summary account called Accrued Income Receivable. Offsetting credits are made to appropriate income accounts. Unless more adjustments are necessary, income accounts may then be closed to Profit and Loss. The Accrued Income Receivable account is an asset account, a value to be collected later, and is accordingly included with the assets of the balance sheet.

In summary, therefore, adjustments for accrued income are made in order to give effect to the following principle: Income which has been earned, but which has not been recorded on the books at the end of an accounting period, should be added to the income account of the current period and placed in the balance sheet as an asset item.

Example:

On April 1, 1950, X purchased a $1,000.00, 6% bond, interest payable April 1 and October 1. On October 1, 1950, six months' interest was collected in cash and credited to Bond Interest Income.

On December 31, 1950, when the books are closed, the accrued income on the bond is recognized by the following entry:

```
Accrued Income Receivable . . . . . . . . . . . . . . . . .   15.00
     Bond Interest Income   . . . . . . . . . . . . . . . . .          15.00
     To record three months' accrued bond interest.
```

When this entry has been posted, the Bond Interest Income account will show the true bond interest earned for the period:

BOND INTEREST INCOME

				1950				CR18	30	00
				Oct.	1			J72	15	00
				Dec.	31					

The balance of the account may now be closed to Profit and Loss. The account with Accrued Income Receivable remains open as an asset representing the right to three months' interest.

After the ledger has been closed, this adjusting entry should be reversed. The propriety of this entry will be made clear by an examination of the accounts as they stand April 1, 1951, when six months' interest is collected on the bond and credited to Bond Interest Income:

ACCRUED INCOME RECEIVABLE

1950			J72	15	00	1951			J1	15	00
Dec.	31					Jan.	1				

BOND INTEREST INCOME

1950 Dec.	31	To P. & L.	J74	45	00	1950 Oct. Dec.	1 31		CR18 J72	30 15	00 00
				45	00					45	00
1951 Jan.	1	Accrued	J1	15	00	1951 Apr.	1		CR10	30	00

The balance of the Bond Interest Income account, $15.00, represents the true bond interest income applicable to the new period up to April 1, 1951.

Other examples of accrued incomes are commissions, interest, rent, royalties, and the like.

Adjusting entries to recognize accrued incomes are necessary, for without them

(1) Incomes of the period would be understated,
(2) Net income would be understated, and
(3) The balance sheet would be incorrect because of the omission from its assets of accrued incomes receivable.

OTHER UNRECORDED EXPENSES AND INCOMES

Expense invoices are usually debited to expense accounts at the time of payment. At the end of the accounting period, certain of these expense bills are unpaid and unrecorded. In order to bring these expenses into the period to which they apply, and not to bring them into the period in which they are paid, and in order to record the liability which they represent, unpaid expenses, at the end of the accounting period [2] are recorded as follows:

Expense Accounts (detailed) . . . . xxx xx
  Accounts Payable . . . . xxx xx
To record unpaid expense bills.

At the beginning of the new period this entry is reversed.

Adjusting and reversing entries like these are not required in cases where the purchases book is expanded to include purchases of all kinds — merchandise, supplies, and services. This accounting is discussed in Chapter 23, "The Voucher System."

Unrecorded incomes, if any, should be recorded at the end of the period in a manner similar to that used for placing unrecorded expenses on the books.

---

[2] If monthly accounting reports are prepared, these entries should be made monthly.

REVERSING ENTRIES

In the accounting which has been described and illustrated thus far in this chapter, reversing entries have been made — after the books have been closed — for all adjustments except those for merchandise, depreciation expense, and bad debts expense.

Some accountants, however, prefer to omit reversing entries altogether. After adjusting entries have been recorded, and the books closed, the entries of these accountants in the *new* period would be

As to prepaid expenses: At the *end* of the *new* accounting period the balances of prepaid expense accounts would be adjusted through expense accounts so as to be left with balances reflecting the values for the new inventories of prepaid expenses.

As to accrued expenses: When accrued expenses of the old period are paid in the new period, each of these disbursements would be debited to the correct liability account. All other expense disbursements would be debited to appropriate expense accounts. At the end of the new accounting period, adjusting entries for unrecorded accrued expenses would be placed on the books in the usual manner.

As to deferred incomes: At the end of the new accounting period, the balances of deferred income accounts would be adjusted through income accounts so as to be left with correct new balances.

As to accrued incomes: When accrued incomes of the old accounting period are collected in the new period, the collections would be credited to asset accounts, like Interest Receivable, Rent Receivable, and so on. All other collections of income would be credited to appropriate income accounts. At the end of the new accounting period, adjusting entries for unrecorded accrued incomes would be placed on the books in the usual manner.

As to unrecorded expense invoices: The entries to record disbursements for these items are similar to those described above for the payment of accrued expenses.

QUESTIONS

Question **14-1.** Define and distinguish among

Current entries   Closing entries
Adjusting entries   Reversing entries

When and why are adjusting and reversing entries used? Illustrate.

Question **14-2.** Define depreciation. Why must it be recognized at the end of the accounting period?

Question **14–3.** Bad debts expense:

(1) How is its amount determined?
(2) How is it recorded on the books?

Question **14–4.** Reserve for Bad Debts:

(1) What is the proper interpretation to be placed upon this account?
(2) Does it appear on the profit and loss statement, or on the balance sheet? Explain its placement.
What debits and credits are made to this account?

Question **14–5.** Three years ago an account receivable was written off the books because it was considered worthless. Today the account is collected. What is the proper accounting to record the collection?

Question **14–6.** Define and illustrate

Prepaid expenses	Deferred incomes
Accrued expenses	Accrued incomes

From the standpoint of the profit and loss statement, and the balance sheet, explain why proper provision must be made on the books for each of these four items.

Question **14–7.** What journal entries should be made to reflect prepaid expenses, accrued expenses, deferred incomes, and accrued incomes?

Question **14–8.** Why do prepaid expenses appear in the balance sheet as assets?

Question **14–9.** The various automobile manufacturers of the United States spend large sums of money each year in preparing models for the production of the next year. Are these expenditures expenses of the year in which they occur, or are they prepaid expenses? Explain.

Question **14–10.** Why does the deferred income of a business appear on the balance sheet as a liability?

Question **14–11.** What disposition would you make on December 31, 19__, of the following unrecorded information

(1) Federal income taxes for the current year are estimated at $5,000.00.
(2) There is on hand an unpaid bill of Jay C. Cambias, dated December 17, 19__, for $500.00, covering work performed in painting and redecorating the office.
(3) There is on hand an unpaid bill of the Standard & Poor Corporation of New York, dated December 27, 19__, for $180.00. This bill is an invoice covering the Trade & Securities Service for next year.

Question **14–12.** What adjusting entries should be made on December 31, 19__, to care for the following unrelated data?

(1) Interest accrued on notes receivable, $300.00.
(2) Interest accrued on notes payable, $100.00.

(3) Interest collected but not yet earned, $200.00, recorded in the Interest Income account.

(4) Rent collected for January, February, and March of next year, $750.00, recorded in the Rent Income account.

(5) Rent due from one of our tenants for the months of November and December is unrecorded and uncollected, $200.00.

(6) Of the balance in the Insurance Expense account, unexpired insurance premiums amount to $900.00.

(7) Bad debts are estimated at 1% of the year's sales of $200,000.00.

(8) The account receivable of Carl F. Glenn is uncollectible, $374.18.

(9) The year's depreciation expense on delivery equipment is estimated at $500.00.

(10) The amount of the accrued payroll for the office and sales department is $4,200.00.

(11) Building cost $100,000.00, estimated life 25 years, no scrap value. No depreciation expense recorded on the books for this year.

(12) Estimated property taxes owed to date but not yet recorded on the books, $700.00.

(13) Advertising supplies on hand, $300.00. (All invoices for advertising supplies have been debited to Advertising Expense.)

(14) A commission of $900.00 is due one of our salesmen on a special order which he obtained. The merchandise was shipped and billed to the customer on December 30, 19—.

(15) A bill, dated December 27, 19—, from Ferry's Garage for repairs to automobiles used in the shipping department, is unrecorded and unpaid, $174.11.

(16) A note for $1,032.24 arrived in this morning's mail from Harry J. Reed, a customer. This note covered a past due account receivable of $1,012.00 and interest for November and December of $10.12, and also interest in advance for January and February for an additional $10.12.

(17) On December 7, 19—, a check for $1,000.00 was received from a customer as a deposit on an order for $10,000.00. The merchandise is to be shipped to him not later than the following March 31, 19—. The bookkeeper credited the cash received to the Sales account.

PROBLEMS

Problem **14-1.** On January 1, 1950, the Superior Bakeries, Inc., purchased a building for $100,000.00, and land, $15,000.00. It was estimated that the building would have a probable useful life of 25 years.

On January 1, 1951, a fleet of motor trucks was purchased at a cost of $20,000.00. Depreciation was estimated at 25% per year.

What entries for depreciation expense should be made in 1950 and **1951?**

Problem **14–2.** Following are certain transactions of the Safeway Furniture Company on the dates indicated:

December 31, 1950 — Bad debts expense for the year 1950 is estimated at 5 % of the year's net sales of $100,000.00.

July 14, 1951 — The account receivable with Reed & Banes for $500.00 is written off as uncollectible. (A 1950 account receivable.)

July 31, 1951 — The account receivable with Frank A. McCall for $400.00 is written off because this customer is in bankruptcy. (A 1951 account receivable.)

December 31, 1951 — The credit balance remaining in the 1950 Reserve for Bad Debts account is $201.00. All present accounts receivable are from 1951 sales. The bad debts expense for 1951 is estimated at 4½ % of the year's net sales of $110,000.00.

July 1, 1953 — A check for $500.00 is received from Reed & Banes in payment of account written off July 14, 1951.

Required:

What entries should be made on each of the above dates?

Problem **14–3.** The following accounts are taken from the ledger, before adjustment, of the Prentice Hardware Company on December 31, 1950:

Accounts Receivable	$100,000.00	
Bad Debts Expense	0.00	
Reserve for Bad Debts		$ 16,000.00
Sales		600,000.00

All of the outstanding accounts receivable are from sales made in 1950. The bad debts expense for the year 1950 is estimated at 2 % of sales.

Required:

(1) Make the adjusting entry, or entries, required by the above information.

(2) How should accounts receivable appear on the balance sheet of December 31, 1950?

Problem **14–4.** After the adjusting entry for bad debts expense had been posted, the balances of five accounts were:

Accounts Receivable	$112,000.00	
Bad Debts Expense	16,000.00	
Reserve for Bad Debts		$ 18,642.00
Returned Sales and Allowances	40,000.00	
Sales		840,000.00

Explain why the balance in the Reserve for Bad Debts account is larger than the balance in the Bad Debts expense account.

The Accounts Receivable account includes accounts from the sales of the current year only. Of these accounts, however, $4,284.00 are worthless and should be written off.

What will be the amount of bad debts expense in the profit and loss statement for the year? What will be the amount of the reserve for bad debts in the balance sheet?   What additional entries should be placed on the books?

Problem **14–5.** Warren B. Taylor began business on January 1, 1950. On December 31, 1950, his ledger included the following accounts:

Accounts Receivable	$71,224.90
Sales	$346,804.69
Returned Sales and Allowances	12,062.87

Bad debts expense for 1950 was estimated at 4 % of net sales.

In 1951, collections on 1950 accounts receivable amounted to $65,362.73; and $5,862.17 of 1950 accounts receivable were uncollectible.

Sales in 1951 amounted to $378,400.55, and returned sales and allowances, $10,074.16. Collections on 1951 sales amounted to $288,044.90; and $1,214.17 of 1951 accounts receivable were uncollectible.

Bad debts expense for 1951 was estimated at 3 % of net sales.

Required:

(1) Make all entries, in 1950 and 1951, affecting the Bad Debts Expense account, and the Reserve for Bad Debts account.

(2) Present accounts receivable on the balance sheets of December 31, 1950, and December 31, 1951.

Problem **14–6.** On December 1, 1950, a company paid $864.00 as premium on a three-year fire insurance policy on its property. The books of the company were closed December 31, 1950.

Required:

(1) Make the adjusting entry.
(2) Make the closing entry.
(3) Make the reversing entry of January 1, 1951.
(4) Give a complete transcript of the Insurance Expense account.

Problem **14–7.** The Advertising account of the Cordell Department Store appeared as follows:

ADVERTISING

1950											
Nov.	1	Balance			14,012	00					
	12		CP32		830	00					
Dec.	10		CP35		1,820	00					

The books were closed on December 31, 1950. The December sales volume of the company was accompanied by a heavy advertising program; the amount owed on December 31 for the month's advertising was $2,814.00. This amount was due for payment on January 10, 1951.

Required:

(1) Make the adjusting entry.
(2) Make the closing entry.

(3) Make the reversing entry of January 1, 1951.

(4) Give a complete transcript of the Advertising account.

Problem **14–8.** The debit balance of the Salesmen's Commission account on December 31, 1950, was $15,102.00. This balance did not include commissions of $1,898.00 earned by the company's salesmen on December sales. The books were closed December 31, 1950.

Required:

    (1) Make the adjusting entry.

    (2) Make the closing entry.

    (3) Make the reversing entry of January 1, 1951.

    (4) Give a complete transcript of the Salesmen's Commission account.

Problem **14–9.** The General Magazine Company launched a new magazine on October 1, 19__. During October, 1,114 yearly subscriptions at $2.00 each were received; in November, 1,640 subscriptions; and in December, 2,818 subscriptions. All subscription collections were credited to Subscription Sales. October subscriptions began with the October issue of the magazine, November subscriptions with the November issue, and so on.

Required:

    (1) What adjusting, closing, and reversing entries should be made when the books are being closed December 31, 19__?

    (2) What amounts will appear in the profit and loss statement for the three months ending with December 31, 19__, and in the balance sheet of December 31, 19__?

Problem **14–10.** The balance of the Sales account of J. G. Larimore on December 31, 19__, was made up as follows:

Wholesale merchandise sales	$190,000.00
Merchandise shipped December 31, 19__, on sight draft order bill of lading; this draft was accepted January 9, 19__	10,000.00
Retail merchandise sales	125,000.00
2% sales tax collections on December sales and which must be remitted to State Treasurer in January	500.00
Balance of Sales account	$325,500.00

Required:

What adjusting entries are called for by the above information?

Problem **14–11.** As of December 31, 1950, the Quality Cleaners were three months behind on their rent. Their Rent Expense account showed a debit balance of $540.00 representing the rent paid for the first 9 months of the year.

Required:

    (1) Make the adjusting entry.

    (2) Make the closing entry.

    (3) Make the reversing entry on January 1, 1951.

    (4) Give a complete transcript of the Rent Expense account.

(5) Make the entry on January 31, 1951, when all rent to date was paid, $240.00.

Problem **14–12.** The Rent Income account of the lessor of the premises occupied by the Quality Cleaners shows a credit balance of $540.00, representing the collection of rent for the first 9 months of 1950. The books are closed December 31, 1950.

Required:

(1) Make the adjusting entry.
(2) Make the closing entry.
(3) Make the reversing entry on January 1, 1951.
(4) Give a complete transcript of the Rent Income account.
(5) Make the entry on January 31, 1951, when all rent to date was collected, $240.00.

Problem **14–13.** On January 1, 1950, the Advertising Expense account had a zero balance. During January, 1950, various advertising bills of 1949 were paid and debited to Advertising Expense, $3,426.00. These bills were completely overlooked when the books were being closed in 1949. During 1950 various 1950 advertising bills were paid, amounting to $15,142.00. On December 31, 1950, there were unrecorded advertising bills of $1,116.00.

What adjusting, closing, and reversing entries should be made when the books are being closed at the end of 1950?

Problem **14–14.** On November 30, 1950, a finance company made a loan and received in exchange a six months' non-interest-bearing note for $10,000.00. Discount rate 6%.

What entry should be made to record the loan? What adjusting, closing, and reversing entries should be made when the books of the finance company are being closed on December 31, 1950?

Problem **14–15.** On December 31, 1949, the balance sheet of Barrett & Company included the following items:

Wage Advances to Employees (asset) . . . . $ 500.00
Wages Payable (liability) 6,041.00

During 1950 the company disbursed $108,778.00 in payment of wages. On December 31, 1950, the balance sheet showed:

Wages Payable $12,088.00

What was the amount of wages expense for 1950?

Problem **14–16.** A balance sheet at the end of 1949 showed

Accrued Interest Receivable $2,350.00
Deferred Interest Income 680.00

During 1950 $5,140.00 cash interest was received.
The balance sheet at the end of 1950 showed

Accrued Interest Receivable $1,820.00
Deferred Interest Income 980.00

What was the amount of true interest income for 1950?

Problem **14–17.** The bookkeeper of the Parker Ferry Stove Company prepared the following condensed statement of profit and loss for the year ending December 31, 19__:

Sales		$58,726.00
Cost of Sales		32,401.00
Gross Profit		$26,325.00
Office Expense	$ 1,280.00	
General Expense	2,416.00	
Insurance Expense	414.00	
Wages Expense	16,000.00	20,110.00
Net Profit		$ 6,215.00

On investigation you find that the following items were not considered by the bookkeeper:

Wages owed but not yet due for payment	$187.00
Stationery and supplies on hand	30.00
Prepaid insurance	214.00
Accrued taxes payable	750.00
Estimated uncollectible accounts	142.00

Required:

Correct the profit and loss statement so as to show the true profit for the year.

Problem **14–18.** On December 31 X owned three notes receivable:

Face	Interest	Remarks as of December 31
$1,000.00	6%	There is no discount, or interest receivable, on this note.
1,000.00	6%	There is accrued interest receivable of $25.00 on this note.
1,000.00	none	There is $30.00 discount on this note. (X today loans $970.00 cash and in return receives a note for $1,000.00.)

As of the same date X owed three notes payable:

Face	Interest	Remarks as of December 31
$600.00	6%	There is no discount, or interest payable, on this note.
600.00	6%	There is accrued interest payable of $12.00 on this note.
600.00	none	There is $6.00 prepaid interest on this note. (X today gives his note payable for $600.00 and in return receives cash proceeds of $594.00.)

(1) What will be the interest and discount items appearing in the balance sheet for December 31?

(2) Assuming these notes not to have matured, what adjusting entries should be made preparatory to a balance sheet as of the close of business February 28?

(3) What will be the interest items appearing in the balance sheet for February 28?

Chapter 15

ALTERNATIVE METHOD OF ACCOUNTING FOR ACCRUALS AND DEFERMENTS

"CASH" AND "ACCRUAL" ACCOUNTING

Books are said to be kept on a "cash" basis when expenses are recorded as expenses of the periods in which they are paid, and when incomes are recorded as incomes of the periods in which collections of income are made. In strict theory, accrued and deferred items are not recognized under "cash" accounting. They are disregarded in statements of profit and loss and when the books are being closed. In strict theory, further, a disbursement to pay for any asset which will ultimately be used up in operations is an expense of the period of disbursement.

In actual practice, the application of the "cash" method of accounting is generally not so severe. In the interest of greater accuracy in calculating periodic net income, the cash method is usually modified to permit the inclusion of

Inventories
Sales and purchases made on credit terms
A provision for bad debts expense (consisting only of specific uncollectible accounts), and
A provision for depreciation expense.

Although the factor of simplicity weighs heavily in its favor, the cash method of accounting is defective because usually it does not establish the amount of net income correctly. This is because the cash method of accounting fails to allocate properly revenues and revenue-costs to the periods to which they apply.

The "accrual" method of accounting is any accounting which endeavors to include in a given period all revenues earned, and all costs incurred, in that period.

For the ordinary private commercial business, "accrual" accounting is always to be preferred over "cash" accounting. The latter is patently defective. If the net income of a business is to be determined and reported with any degree of accuracy, it should be clearly evident that the accrual basis of accounting *must* be used. The accrual method of accounting is generally employed in actual business practice, and it is the method exclusively used in this text.

Two so-called "methods" are used to reflect the accrual system of accounting. One of these methods or procedures was described in Chapter 14, and the other will be described in this chapter. This method is an alternative one of accounting for prepaid and accrued expenses, and for deferred and accrued incomes. It is a method of especial usefulness to businesses which require frequent financial statements as, for example, monthly.

In any particular system of accounts it is not to be inferred that one or the other of these methods of accrual accounting will be used to the exclusion of the other. Actually it is probable that both methods might be used in a single set of books. For any specific expense or income account the first method might be best, for another account the method of this chapter would be more natural. In any given case, the choice depends primarily upon the amount of the accrual or deferral, and the frequency of entries.

The alternative method of accounting for accruals and deferments will now be described.

PREPAID EXPENSES

Instead of being debited to an expense account, prepaid expenses are debited to an appropriate prepaid expense account at the time of payment. At the end of each month the expense applicable to that month is transferred from each prepaid expense account and debited to the related expense account.

Example:

On October 1, 1950, the Blue and White Chain Stores leased a certain property for an annual rental of $7,200.00 payable in advance. Their entries would be

```
1950
Oct.  1 Prepaid Rent . . . . . . . . . . . . . . . . .   7,200.00
           Cash  . . . . . . . . . . . . . . . . . .               7,200.00
             For 12 months' rent paid in advance.
      31 Rent Expense  . . . . . . . . . . . . . . . .    600.00
           Prepaid Rent . . . . . . . . . . . . . . .                 600.00
             For rent applicable to October.
Nov. 30 Rent Expense  . . . . . . . . . . . . . . . .     600.00
           Prepaid Rent . . . . . . . . . . . . . . .                 600.00
             For rent applicable to November.
Dec. 31 Rent Expense  . . . . . . . . . . . . . . . .     600.00
           Prepaid Rent . . . . . . . . . . . . . . .                 600.00
             For rent applicable to December.
```

On December 31, 1950, after the books have been closed, the two rent accounts would appear as follows:

PREPAID RENT

1950					1950					
Oct.	1		CP87	7,200	00	Oct.	31		J50	600	00
						Nov.	30		J57	600	00
						Dec.	31		J65	600	00

RENT EXPENSE

1950						1950					
Oct.	31		J50	600	00	Dec.	31	To P. & L.	J68	1,800	00
Nov.	30		J57	600	00						
Dec.	31		J65	600	00						
				1,800	00					1,800	00

ACCRUED EXPENSES

At the end of each month accrued expenses are recognized by the debiting of appropriate expense accounts and the crediting of related accrued liability accounts. When these expenses are paid, the payments are debited not to expense but to the appropriate accrued liability accounts.

Example:

Durant & Durant have a $25,000.00 6% mortgage on their property, interest payable January 1 and July 1. At the end of each month they make the following entry:

Interest Expense 125.00
    Mortgage Interest Payable 125.00
To record monthly accrual of interest.

The mortgage interest payments on January 1, 1950, and July 1, 1950, are recorded as follows:

Mortgage Interest Payable 750.00
    Cash 750.00
To record semiannual payment of interest.

On December 31, 1950, the two interest accounts would appear as follows:

MORTGAGE INTEREST PAYABLE

1950						1950					
Jan.	1		CP18	750	00	Jan.	1	Balance	✓	750	00
July	1		CP40	750	00		31		J4	125	00
Dec.	31	Balance	✓	750	00	Feb.	28		J7	125	00
						Mar.	31		J10	125	00
						Apr.	30		J14	125	00
						May	31		J17	125	00
						June	30		J19	125	00
						July	31		J22	125	00
						Aug.	31		J26	125	00
						Sept.	30		J29	125	00
						Oct.	31		J31	125	00
						Nov.	30		J33	125	00
						Dec.	31		J37	125	00
				2,250	00					2,250	00
						1951					
						Jan.	1	Balance	✓	750	00

INTEREST EXPENSE

1950						1950					
Jan.	31		J4	125	00	Dec.	31	To P. & L.	J40	1,500	00
Feb.	28		J7	125	00						
Mar.	31		J10	125	00						
Apr.	30		J14	125	00						
May	31		J17	125	00						
June	30		J19	125	00						
July	31		J22	125	00						
Aug.	31		J26	125	00						
Sept.	30		J29	125	00						
Oct.	31		J31	125	00						
Nov.	30		J33	125	00						
Dec.	31		J37	125	00						
				1,500	00					1,500	00

Other accrued expenses would be handled in a similar manner. In each case care should be taken to see that the total of accrual credits for the period equals the exact liability for the year.

In some cases — taxes, for instance — the monthly accrual must be the month's pro rata share of the *estimated* taxes for the year. When the actual tax liability has been determined, the account balances should be adjusted to conform to it, and subsequent book entries modified accordingly.

ACCRUED INCOME

At the end of each month accrued incomes are recognized by the debiting of appropriate accrued income accounts and the crediting of related income accounts. When this income is received in cash, the receipt should be credited to the appropriate accrued income account.

Example:

The Elliott Mortgage Loan Company holds the mortgage of $25,000.00 on the property of Durant & Durant. At the end of each month it makes the following entry:

```
Mortgage Interest Receivable. . . . . . . . . . . . . .   125.00
     Interest Income  . . . . . . . . . . . . . . . . .             125.00
     To record monthly accrual of interest.
```

The interest payments of January 1, 1950, and July 1, 1950, would be recorded thus:

```
Cash . . . . . . . . . . . . . . . . . . . . . . . . . .   750.00
     Mortgage Interest Receivable. . . . . . . . . . .             750.00
     To record semiannual collection of interest.
```

On December 31, 1950, the two interest accounts would appear as follows:

MORTGAGE INTEREST RECEIVABLE

1950						1950					
Jan.	1	Balance	√	750	00	Jan.	1		CR1	750	00
	31		J5	125	00	July	1		CR20	750	00
Feb.	28		J11	125	00	Dec.	31	Balance	√	750	00
Mar.	31		J17	125	00						
Apr.	30		J25	125	00						
May	31		J30	125	00						
June	30		J36	125	00						
July	31		J41	125	00						
Aug.	31		J47	125	00						
Sept.	30		J54	125	00						
Oct.	31		J60	125	00						
Nov.	30		J66	125	00						
Dec.	31		J84	125	00						
				2,250	00					2,250	00
1951											
Jan.	1	Balance	√	750	00						

INTEREST INCOME

1950						1950				
Dec.	31	To P. & L.	J88	1,500	00	Jan.	31		J5	125	00
						Feb.	28		J11	125	00
						Mar.	31		J17	125	00
						Apr.	30		J25	125	00
						May	31		J30	125	00
						June	30		J36	125	00
						July	31		J41	125	00
						Aug.	31		J47	125	00
						Sept.	30		J54	125	00
						Oct.	31		J60	125	00
						Nov.	30		J66	125	00
						Dec.	31		J84	125	00
				1,500	00					1,500	00

The principle that the total of credits for accrued income should equal the total accrued income actually earned during a period, as illustrated by the Interest Income account, should be self-evident.

DEFERRED INCOME

Income which is unearned at the time of its receipt in cash is credited to an appropriate deferred income account. At the end of each month the income earned in that month is transferred from each deferred income account and credited to the related income account.

Example:

On October 1, 1950, X leased a certain property to the Blue and White Chain Stores for an annual rental of $7,200.00 payable in advance. X's entries would be

```
1950
Oct.   1 Cash  . . . . . . . . . . . . . . . . . . . . . .   7,200.00
            Unearned Rent . . . . . . . . . . . . . . . . .              7,200.00
         For 12 months' rent received in advance.

Oct. 31 Unearned Rent . . . . . . . . . . . . . . . . .       600.00
            Rent Income . . . . . . . . . . . . . . . . . .                600.00
         For rent earned in October.

Nov. 30 Unearned Rent . . . . . . . . . . . . . . . . .       600.00
            Rent Income . . . . . . . . . . . . . . . . . .                600.00
         For rent earned in November.

Dec. 31 Unearned Rent . . . . . . . . . . . . . . . . .       600.00
            Rent Income . . . . . . . . . . . . . . . . . .                600.00
         For rent earned in December.
```

On December 31, 1950, the two rent accounts would appear as follows:

UNEARNED RENT

1950					1950				
Oct.	31	J61	600	00	Oct.	1		CR20	7,200	00
Nov.	30	J66	600	00					
Dec.	31	J72	600	00					

RENT INCOME

1950							1950				
Dec.	31	To P. & L.	J74	1,800	00		Oct.	31		J62	600	00
							Nov.	30		J66	600	00
							Dec.	31		J72	600	00
				1,800	00						1,800	00

DISTRIBUTION RECORDS

In order to facilitate the booking of entries such as those illustrated in the pages above, memorandum records are frequently maintained. One example of this type of record is illustrated on page 312.

Example:

X has recorded his various leases thus:

1950

LEASE REGISTER

Date of Lease		Lessee	Term	Amount Received in Advance				Distribution of Income												Balance Carried Forward to 1951
					Jan.	Feb.	Mar.	Apr.	May	June	July	Aug.	Sept.	Oct.	Nov.	Dec.	
1950 Oct.	1	Blue & White Chain Stores	12 mo.	7,200 00										600 00	600 00	600 00	5,400 00
	15	A. E. Webb	6 "	240 00										20 00	40 00	40 00	140 00
	31	Bishop & Son	12 "	1,200 00											100 00	100 00	1,000 00
Nov.	10	Corley's Haberdashery	3 "	180 00											40 00	60 00	80 00
	30	Ching's Laundry	3 "	60 00												20 00	40 00
Dec.	15	Fortney's Business College	12	2,400 00												100 00	2,300 00
				11,280 00										620 00	780 00	920 00	8,960 00

X's monthly entries would be:

1950

Oct. 31 Unearned Rent 620.00
              Rent Income 620.00
              To record rent earned in October.
Nov. 30 Unearned Rent 780.00
              Rent Income 780.00
              To record rent earned in November.
Dec. 31 Unearned Rent 920.00
              Rent Income 920.00
              To record rent earned in December.

In similar manner, the entries for 1951 would be based upon the monthly column totals of the 1951 lease register. The 1951 register, of course, would be opened by bringing forward the unearned balance of $8,960.00 in the last column of the 1950 lease register.

Distribution records are often used in distributing prepaid insurance premiums, and deferred subscription incomes, to the months of the accounting year.

ACCRUAL ACCOUNTING: COMPARISON OF METHODS

Accrual accounting, under each of the two methods which have been described, may be compared and summarized as follows:

By the Method Described in Chapter 14	By the Alternative Method Described in This Chapter
ACCRUED EXPENSES	
(1) At the end of the accounting period, the amount of the unrecorded accrued expense should be debited to an expense account and credited to a liability account (i.e., accrued expense liability).	(1) Same as contra.
(2) Close the balance of the expense account to the Profit and Loss account.	(2) Same as contra.
(3) After the books have been closed, reverse the adjusting entry made in (1) above. When the accrued expense is paid, debit the expense account.	(3) No reversing entry is required. When the accrued expense is paid, debit the liability account.
PREPAID EXPENSES	
(1) At the time of original entry, the expenditure should be debited to an expense account.	(1) At the time of original entry, the expenditure should be debited to an asset account (i.e., prepaid expense).
(2) At the end of the accounting period, such recorded expense as may still be prepaid should be debited to an asset account (i.e., prepaid expense) and credited to an expense account.	(2) At the end of the accounting period, the expired part of the asset established by the entry above should be debited to an expense account and credited to the asset account.

By the Method Described in Chapter 14	By the Alternative Method Described in This Chapter
(3) Close the balance of the expense account to the Profit and Loss account.	(3) Close the balance of the expense account to the Profit and Loss account.
(4) After the books have been closed, reverse the adjusting entry made in (2) above.	(4) No reversing entry is required.

ACCRUED INCOMES

(1) At the end of the accounting period, the amount of the unrecorded accrued income should be debited to an asset account (i.e., accrued income receivable) and credited to an income account.	(1) Same as contra.
(2) Close the balance of the income account to the Profit and Loss account.	(2) Same as contra.
(3) After the books have been closed, reverse the adjusting entry made in (1) above. When the accrued income is collected, credit the collection to an income account.	(3) No reversing entry is required. When the accrued income is collected, credit the collection to the asset established in (1) above.

DEFERRED INCOMES

(1) Credit all income collections to income accounts.	(1) At the time of its receipt, credit unearned income to a liability account (i.e., deferred or unearned income).
(2) At the end of the accounting period such recorded income as may yet be unearned should be debited to an income account and credited to a liability account (i.e., deferred or unearned income).	(2) At the end of the accounting period such unearned income as may have become earned income should be debited to the liability account established in (1) above and credited to an income account.
(3) Close the balance of the income account to the Profit and Loss account.	(3) Close the balance of the income account to the Profit and Loss account.
(4) After the books have been closed, reverse the adjusting entry made in (2) above.	(4) No reversing entry is required.

ADVANTAGES OF THE ALTERNATIVE METHOD OF ACCRUAL ACCOUNTING

(1) The practice of adjusting the books to an accrual basis at the end of an accounting period is a practice which is best adapted to time periods of one year. On the other hand, the alternative method of accrual accounting is not only well adapted to accounting periods of one year but is also especially adapted to interim periods as well. In the latter respect the alternative method is much superior. By requiring less bookkeeping labor and by requiring a less complex work sheet, the alternative method of accrual accounting measurably facilitates the work of preparing interim financial statements.

(2) Monthly account balances for expense and income accounts

are cumulatively correct for the time period represented by such accounts. Monthly accretions correctly represent each monthly period. On the other hand, accounts which are kept on the cash basis, and adjusted yearly, are correct at the end of the year only.

(3) No reversing entries are required after the close of the accounting period.

The student should understand that expenses incurred and paid for in the month to which they apply, and incomes earned and collected in the month in which they are earned, continue to be debited directly to expense and credited to income. Under the alternative method of accrual accounting only those items which carry over into another month, or period, are required to be passed through the deferred expense and income accounts.

QUESTIONS

Question **15–1.** Explain in adequate detail the meaning of the terms "cash accounting" and "accrual accounting."

Question **15–2.** Evaluate each of these two types of accounting. Include in your appraisal favorable as well as unfavorable criticisms.

Question **15–3.** Describe briefly the two methods by which the books of a business may give effect to the accrual system of accounting.

Question **15–4.** At the end of a fiscal period would there be any difference in the balances of accounts which are adjusted only at the end of the period, as compared with the balances of these accounts kept under the alternative method of accrual accounting?

Question **15–5.** Explain how a monthly provision for property taxes might be recorded on the books. Suppose that at the end of the year the books show a liability for property taxes of $1,200.00; and that sixty days later the tax bill is received showing the actual liability as $1,284.60. What entry, or entries, should be made when the tax bill is paid on March 10?

Question **15–6.** What is the purpose of a distribution record or register? Name four kinds of information for which such a record might be serviceable.

Question **15–7.** When would you recommend the use of the "alternative" method of accrual accounting? What are the advantages of this method?

Question **15–8.** Describe in adequate detail the accounting you would use in properly recording the subscription income of *The Saturday Evening Post*. Describe the accounting you would use if financial statements were prepared for each month of the year.

PROBLEMS

Problem **15–1.** The condensed profit and loss statement of John A. Bearly for the year ending December 31, 19__, was as follows:

Sales	$86,014.22
Cost of Sales	48,229.81
Gross Profit.	$37,784.41
Expenses	30,770.19
Net Profit	$ 7,014.22
Other Income	1,512.87
Net Income	$ 8,527.09

This statement was prepared under the so-called "cash method" of accounting. Mr. Bearly wonders what the net income figure would have been if the statement had been prepared by the "accrual method" of accounting. You are asked to prepare such a statement taking into account

Prepaid expenses at beginning of period.	$1,042.88
Accrued expenses at beginning of period	3,180.99
Deferred income at beginning of period	782.53
Accrued income at beginning of period	101.22
Prepaid expenses at the end of period .	732.40
Accrued expenses at the end of period	4,009.72
Deferred income at the end of period	812.67
Accrued income at the end of period	312.04

Required:

(1) Prepare a profit and loss statement under the accrual method of accounting.

(2) Assuming that the books are henceforth to be operated by the alternative method of accrual accounting (as described in Chapter 15), what adjusting entry or entries should be placed on the books December 31, 19__?

Problem **15–2.** From the following information construct profit and loss statements which will show the net income of James E. Henderson for the year 19__ under (a) accrual accounting and (b) cash accounting (as generally followed in actual business practice.)

Cash received from customers	$60,001.00
Sales invoices written for merchandise delivered	76,024.00
Purchases incurred.	60,927.00
Payments made on purchases	50,704.00
Expenses paid	15,804.00
Expenses not paid as of January 1, 19__	3,310.00
Expenses not paid as of December 31, 19__	1,211.00
Expenses prepaid as of January 1, 19__	684.00
Expenses prepaid as of December 31, 19__	1,429.00
Inventory of merchandise, January 1, 19__	26,101.00
Inventory of merchandise, December 31, 19__	30,608.00

Problem **15–3.** The following information constitutes a condensed description of the business of Leslie J. Stimson for two successive years:

	1st Year	2d Year
Sales (all credit)	$38,000.00	$50,000.00
Accounts receivable found worthless	500.00	3,500.00
Wages and salaries paid	8,000.00	11,000.00
Fixed assets purchased on credit during the year. For the purpose of this problem, assume these purchases to have been made on January 1 of each year	1,000.00	2,000.00
Cash disbursed in partial payment of fixed assets .	700.00	1,800.00
Cash received from customers	32,000.00	46,250.00
Cash interest received on bonds owned		300.00
Property taxes paid	200.00	
Miscellaneous expenses paid	3,000.00	7,000.00
On December 31 of each year there existed:		
Accrued interest on bonds owned	300.00	
Accrued wages and salaries	1,000.00	200.00
Accrued property taxes		300.00
Accrued miscellaneous expenses	1,500.00	700.00

Mr. Stimson ordinarily operated on the assumption that 5% of his credit sales would not be collected.

Of the miscellaneous expenses paid in the second year, $500.00 were expenses applicable to the next succeeding accounting period.

Fixed assets were estimated to depreciate at the annual rate of 10%.

Cost of sales may be considered as 60% of sales.

Required:

What is the net income of Mr. Stimson for each year under the accrual basis of accounting? under cash accounting (as generally followed in actual business practice)? Prepare four profit and loss statements as your solution to this problem.

Problem **15–4.** During 1952 *The Companion Digest,* a monthly magazine, received the following twelve-month subscriptions:

January	$ 5,004.00	July	$ 9,000.00
February	7,080.00	August	10,440.00
March	18,000.00	Setembper	12,000.00
April	10,200.00	October	14,400.00
May	16,800.00	November	11,028.00
June	12,000.00	December	20,640.00

Assuming that all subscriptions are received on the first day of each month, that magazines are immediately placed in the mails, and that the books are kept on the "alternative" basis of accrual accounting

(1) What entry should be made each month to record the subscriptions received in that month?

(2) Prepare a distribution record suitable to the needs of *The Companion Digest.* From this distribution record prepare the monthly entries which would be made for the distribution of income.

Problem **15–5.** The Easton Hardwood Lumber Company took out the following fire insurance policies last year:

Date	Policy Number	Company	Term	Premium Paid
Jan. 1	4112	Hanover Fire Insurance Company	3 years	$450.00
Apr. 1	19478	Rossia Insurance Company	1 year	108.00
Aug. 15	88068	Fidelity-Phenix Fire Insurance Co.	3 years	630.00

Required:

(1) Make the entries to record the premium payments.
(2) Prepare an insurance distribution record.
(3) Make monthly insurance entries for the past calendar year.

Problem **15–6.** J. R. Alexander owns the following four notes receivable:

Dated	Amount	With Interest at	Due in
Jan. 1	$1,000.00	6%	6 months
Feb. 28	4,080.00	5%	12 months
Apr. 15	3,000.00	8%	10 months
July 15	2,000.00	4½%	8 months

Required:

(1) Draw up a distribution register for the monthly apportionment of the interest earned on notes receivable. This register should be for the first calendar year only.

(2) What entry should be made on the books July 31? The books are kept on the monthly accrual basis of accounting.

(3) What entry should be made when the first note is collected on July 1?

Problem **15–7.** Following are certain transactions of Dean & Co., Inc.:

July

1 — Rent for twelve months is paid, $2,400.00.
15 — A three-year fire insurance premium is paid, $648.00.
31 — Interest of $25.00 is earned in July on a note which is held against A. E. Huston.

August

1 — Cash is received from A. E. Huston in payment of July interest.
1 — Funds are borrowed from the First National Bank on a $5,000.00 note for four months. The bank charges 6% interest payable in advance.
15 — A check for $50.00 is received from A. E. Huston in payment of interest for the months of August and September.
31 — Warehouse space is sublet to Quinn & Boden for a period of three months. A check for $300.00 is received as full payment of the rent for the period.

Required:

(1) What are the proper entries to record the above transactions, the books being kept on the monthly accrual basis?

(2) What entries should be made on July 31 and August 31 to adjust the books?

Chapter 16

THE WORK SHEET

The preparation of statements and the work of adjusting and closing the books at the end of an accounting period are facilitated by the use of a "work sheet." This is especially true if there are many accounts involved and if there are many adjusting and closing entries to be made. The work sheet is not, however, a part of the permanent records of a business, and its use therefore cannot be said to be obligatory.

PURPOSE OF THE WORK SHEET

The work sheet is a device designed to

(1) Prove the mechanical accuracy of adjusting and closing entries outside the books. It assures accuracy in the formal closing of the books.

(2) Serve as a guide in the making of formal adjusting and closing entries.

(3) Summarize the results of the period on a single sheet.

(4) Ascertain quickly and verify the net profit or loss before the books are closed.

(5) Facilitate the preparation of statements, both yearly and interim.

PREPARATION OF THE WORK SHEET

The twelve-column form of work sheet is as follows:

Account	Trial Balance Before Adjustment		Adjustments		Trial Balance After Adjustment		Cost of Sales		Profit and Loss		Balance Sheet	
	Dr.	Cr.	Dr.	Cr.	Dr.	Cr.	Dr.	Cr.	Dr.	Cr.	Dr.	Cr.

This form demonstrates clearly the steps necessary to the preparation of the work sheet:

(1) In the first pair of columns is entered the general ledger trial balance before adjusting and closing entries have been given effect.

(2) In the second pair of columns are entered all adjusting entries.

(3) In the third pair of columns is entered the trial balance after giving effect to adjusting entries. The detail of this trial balance is distributed to the remaining six columns of the work sheet in the manner prescribed by steps (4), (5), and (6).

(4) In the fourth pair of columns are placed those nominal accounts used in calculating the cost of merchandise sold.

(5) The balance of the Cost of Sales columns and all other nominal accounts are distributed to the Profit and Loss columns.

(6) The balance of the Profit and Loss columns and all real accounts are carried to the columns labeled "Balance Sheet."

In the pages which follow two examples of problems involving work sheets are given. The first work sheet is simple in nature, the second somewhat more complex.

First Example:

The trial balance of John L. Davis on December 31, 19__, is shown in the first two columns of the work sheet. For the purpose of adjusting this trial balance, the following information is applicable:

(1) Unexpired insurance amounted to $500.00.
(2) Accrued rent receivable amounted to $1,000.00.
(3) Uncollectible accounts receivable were estimated at $5,000.00.
(4) Depreciation expense for the year was estimated at $3,000.00.
(5) Accrued wages and salaries were $4,000.00.
(6) Of the rent income already on the books, $500.00 was applicable to the next accounting period.
(7) The new inventory of merchandise was $100,000.00.

In this first example only the work sheet will be given. In the second example the work sheet, financial statements, and bookkeeping entries will be given.

The new inventory is handled in the same manner as it was on the work sheet on page 88, i.e., by a debit in the balance sheet columns, and a credit in the cost of sales columns. This debit and credit reflects the entry which would be made if the new inventory were recorded on the books, viz.:

```
Merchandise . . . . . . . . . . . . . . . . . .    100,000.00
    Cost of Sales . . . . . . . . . . . . . . . . .              100,000.00
    To record amount of new inventory.
```

The treatment of the new inventory in the work sheet is an important detail which should be thoroughly understood.

As an *alternative* method, some accountants record the new inventory by incorporating the above journal entry in the adjustments

John L.

WORK SHEET, DE

	TRIAL BALANCE BEFORE ADJUSTMENT			ADJUSTMENTS				TRIAL AFTER	
Cash	12,100	00						12,100	00
Accounts Receivable	60,000	00						60,000	00
Reserve for Bad Debts			100	00			(3) 5,000	00		
Merchandise	70,000	00						70,000	00
Building	100,000	00						100,000	00
Reserve for Depreciation — Building			6,000	00			(4) 3,000	00		
Accounts Payable			30,000	00						
John L. Davis, Capital			200,000	00						
Sales			500,000	00						
Purchases	400,000	00						400,000	00
Insurance Expense	1,000	00					(1) 500	00	500	00
Taxes	4,000	00							4,000	00
Wages and Salaries	96,000	00		(5) 4,000	00				100,000	00
Rent Income			7,000	00	(6) 500	00	(2) 1,000	00		
	743,100	00	743,100	00						
Prepaid Insurance					(1) 500	00			500	00
Accrued Rent Receivable					(2) 1,000	00			1,000	00
Bad Debts Expense					(3) 5,000	00			5,000	00
Depreciation Expense					(4) 3,000	00			3,000	00
Wages and Salaries Payable							(5) 4,000	00		
Deferred Rent Income							(6) 500	00		
					14,000	00	14,000	00	756,100	00
Cost of Sales to Profit and Loss										
Net Income to John L. Davis, Capital										

column of the work sheet. The debit member of this adjusting entry is carried to the balance sheet columns, the credit member to the cost of sales columns. The final result is the same under either method.

Davis

CEMBER 31, 19—

Balance Adjustment		Cost of Sales				Profit and Loss				Balance Sheet			
										12,100	00		
										60,000	00		
5,100	00	70,000	00	100,000	00					100,000	00	5,100	00
										100,000	00		
9,000	00									9,000	00		
30,000	00									30,000	00		
200,000	00									200,000	00		
500,000	00	400,000	00					500,000	00				
						500	00						
						4,000	00						
						100,000	00						
7,500	00							7,500	00				
										500	00		
										1,000	00		
						5,000	00						
						3,000	00						
4,000	00											4,000	00
500	00											500	00
756,100	00												
				370,000	00	370,000	00						
		470,000	00	470,000	00								
						25,000	00					25,000	00
						507,500	00	507,500	00	273,600	00	273,600	00

Second Example:

L. A. Roberts

Trial Balance, December 31, 1950

Cash	$ 14,000.00	
Bonds	2,000.00	
Notes Receivable	12,000.00	
Accounts Receivable	28,000.00	
Reserve for Bad Debts		$ 647.00
Merchandise	24,000.00	
Delivery Equipment	3,600.00	
Reserve for Depreciation — Delivery Equipment		1,700.00
Furniture and Fixtures	8,000.00	
Reserve for Depreciation — Furniture and Fixtures		2,200.00
Store Equipment	4,000.00	
Reserve for Depreciation — Store Equipment		1,000.00
Buildings	30,000.00	
Reserve for Depreciation — Buildings		6,000.00
Land	12,000.00	
Accounts Payable		20,000.00
Notes Payable		25,000.00
L. A. Roberts, Capital		69,000.00
L. A. Roberts, Personal	8,000.00	
Sales		178,350.00
Returned Sales and Allowances	1,600.00	
Sales Discounts	700.00	
Purchases	128,000.00	
Returned Purchases and Allowances		4,000.00
Purchases Discounts		2,400.00
Freight In	1,000.00	
Advertising	6,000.00	
Miscellaneous Selling Expense	1,700.00	
Salesmen's Salaries	11,000.00	
General Expense	5,600.00	
General Salaries	4,000.00	
Insurance Expense	1,200.00	
Taxes	2,897.00	
Interest Expense	1,000.00	
	$310,297.00	$310,297.00

The following information is available for adjusting and closing the books:

Merchandise inventory, December 31, 1950 . . . . $21,000.00

Depreciation Expense:
Buildings, 4% of cost
Delivery Equipment, 20% of cost
Furniture and Fixtures, 10% of cost
Store Equipment, 10% of cost

Bad Debts Expense:
Estimated at 1% of net sales.

Prepaid Expenses:

    Advertising expense applicable to 1951 . . . . 2,000.00

    Prepaid insurance. 200.00

Accrued Expenses:

    General salaries owed but not yet due 100.00

    Interest on notes payable 700.00

    Salesmen's salaries owed but not yet due 350.00

    Taxes accrued but not yet due 300.00

Deferred Income:

    Included in sales are $750.00 in gift certificates sold to customers for use as Christmas gifts to their friends. These certificates are redeemable in merchandise of the recipient's selection.

Accrued Income:

    Interest earned on bonds 60.00

    Interest earned on notes receivable 300.00

The above information, with one exception, is reflected in the entries of the adjustments columns of the work sheet. This one exception, to which attention has already been directed, relates to the manner in which the new inventory of merchandise is recorded: a debit in the balance sheet columns and a credit in the cost of sales columns.

L. A.

WORK SHEET DE

Account	Trial Balance Before Adjustment Dr.	Cr.	Adjustments Dr.	Cr.	Trial After Dr.
Cash	14,000 00				14,000 00
Bonds	2,000 00				2,000 00
Notes Receivable	12,000 00				12,000 00
Accounts Receivable	28,000 00				28,000 00
Reserve for Bad Debts		647 00		(E) 1,753 00	
Merchandise	24,000 00				24,000 00
Delivery Equipment	3,600 00				3,600 00
Reserve for Depreciation — Delivery Equipment		1,700 00		(B) 720 00	
Furniture and Fixtures	8,000 00				8,000 00
Reserve for Depreciation — Furniture and Fixtures		2,200 00		(C) 800 00	
Store Equipment	4,000 00				4,000 00
Reserve for Depreciation — Store Equipment		1,000 00		(D) 400 00	
Buildings	30,000 00				30,000 00
Reserve for Depreciation — Buildings		6,000 00		(A) 1,200 00	
Land	12,000 00				12,000 00
Accounts Payable		20,000 00			
Notes Payable		25,000 00			
L. A. Roberts, Capital		69,000 00			
L. A. Roberts, Personal	8,000 00				8,000 00
Sales		178,350 00	(L) 750 00		
Returned Sales and Allowances	1,600 00				1,600 00
Sales Discounts	700 00				700 00
Purchases	128,000 00				128,000 00
Returned Purchases and Allowances		4,000 00			
Purchases Discounts		2,400 00			
Freight In	1,000 00				1,000 00
Advertising	6,000 00			(F) 2,000 00	4,000 00
Miscellaneous Selling Expense	1,700 00				1,700 00
Salesmen's Salaries	11,000 00		(J) 350 00		11,350 00
General Expense	5,600 00				5,600 00
General Salaries	4,000 00		(H) 100 00		4,100 00
Insurance Expense	1,200 00			(G) 200 00	1,000 00
Taxes	2,897 00		(K) 300 00		3,197 00
Interest Expense	1,000 00		(I) 700 00		1,700 00
	310,297 00	310,297 00			
Depreciation Expense — Buildings			(A) 1,200 00		1,200 00
Depreciation Expense — Delivery Equipment			(B) 720 00		720 00
Depreciation Expense — Furniture and Fixtures			(C) 800 00		800 00
Depreciation Expense — Store Equipment			(D) 400 00		400 00
Bad Debts Expense			(E) 1,753 00		1,753 00
Deferred Expenses			(F) 2,000 00 (G) 200 00		2,200 00
Accrued Liabilities				(H) 100 00 (I) 700 00 (J) 350 00	
Deferred Income				(K) 300 00 (L) 750 00	
Accrued Income Receivable			(M) 60 00 (N) 300 00		360 00
Interest Income				(M) 60 00	
				(N) 300 00	
Cost of Sales to Profit and Loss					
Net Income to L. A. Roberts, Capital					
				9,633 00	9,633 00	316,980 00

Roberts

CEMBER 31, 1950

Balance Adjustment Cr.	Cost of Sales Dr.	Cost of Sales Cr.	Profit and Loss Dr.	Profit and Loss Cr.	Balance Sheet Dr.	Balance Sheet Cr.
					14,000 00	
					2,000 00	
					12,000 00	
					28,000 00	
2,400 00						2,400 00
	24,000 00	21,000 00			21,000 00	
					3,600 00	
2,420 00						2,420 00
					8,000 00	
3,000 00						3,000 00
					4,000 00	
1,400 00						1,400 00
					30,000 00	
7,200 00						7,200 00
					12,000 00	
20,000 00						20,000 00
25,000 00						25,000 00
69,000 00						69,000 00
					8,000 00	
177,600 00				177,600 00		
			1,600 00			
			700 00			
	128,000 00					
4,000 00		4,000 00				
2,400 00		2,400 00				
	1,000 00					
			4,000 00			
			1,700 00			
			11,350 00			
			5,600 00			
			4,100 00			
			1,000 00			
			3,197 00			
			1,700 00			
			1,200 00			
			720 00			
			800 00			
			400 00			
			1,753 00			
					2,200 00	
1,450 00						1,450 00
750 00						750 00
					360 00	
360 00				360 00		
		125,600 00	125,600 00			
			12,540 00			12,540 00
316,980 00	153,000 00	153,000 00	177,960 00	177,960 00	145,160 00	145,160 00

The net income figure in the work sheet is determined by the excess of credits over debits in the profit and loss columns. Since it is an item of proprietorship, the net income figure is transferred to the credit side of the balance sheet columns. Total balance sheet credits should then equal total balance sheet debits, thus proving the mathematical accuracy of the work sheet. When this proof has been secured:

(1) The profit and loss statement should be prepared from the detailed information of the profit and loss columns of the work sheet.

(2) The balance sheet should be prepared from the information contained in the balance sheet columns.

(3) Finally, the formal adjusting and closing entries should be recorded on the books. In this recording process the work sheet should be of invaluable assistance.

These steps will be illustrated below in a continuation of the L. A. Roberts problem.

THE PROFIT AND LOSS STATEMENT

L. A. Roberts

PROFIT AND LOSS STATEMENT
YEAR ENDING DECEMBER 31, 1950

Gross Sales			$177,600.00
Less Returned Sales and Allowances		$ 1,600.00	
Sales Discounts		700.00	2,300.00
Net Sales			$175,300.00
Cost of Sales:			
Merchandise, January 1, 1950		$ 24,000.00	
Purchases	$128,000.00		
Less Returned Purchases			
and Allowances ... $4,000.00			
Purchases Discounts 2,400.00	6,400.00		
	$121,600.00		
Freight In	1,000.00	122,600.00	
		$146,600.00	
Merchandise, December 31, 1950		21,000.00	125,600.00
Gross Profit			$ 49,700.00
Selling Expenses:			
Advertising	$ 4,000.00		
Depreciation — Delivery Equipment	720.00		
Depreciation — Store Equipment	400.00		
Miscellaneous Selling Expense	1,700.00		
Salesmen's Salaries	11,350.00	$ 18,170.00	

General Expenses:

Bad Debts Expense.	$ 1,753.00		
Depreciation Expense — Buildings . . .	800.00		
Depreciation Expense — Furniture and Fixtures	1,200.00		
General Expense	5,600.00		
General Salaries	4,100.00		
Insurance	1,000.00		
Taxes	3,197.00	17,650.00	35,820.00

Net Profit from Operations	$ 13,880.00
Other Income:	
Interest Income	360.00
	$ 14,240.00
Other Expense:	
Interest Expense	1,700.00
Net Income	$ 12,540.00

THE BALANCE SHEET

L. A. Roberts

BALANCE SHEET, DECEMBER 31, 1950

Assets

Current Assets:

Cash		$ 14,000.00
Bonds		2,000.00
Notes Receivable		12,000.00
Accrued Interest Receivable		360.00
Accounts Receivable	$ 28,000.00	
Less Reserve for Bad Debts	2,400.00	25,600.00
Merchandise		21,000.00
Prepaid Expenses		2,200.00
		$ 77,160.00

Fixed Assets:

	Cost	Reserve for Depreciation	Net Book Value	
Buildings	$30,000.00	$ 7,200.00	$22,800.00	
Delivery Equipment . . .	3,600.00	2,420.00	1,180.00	
Furniture and Fixtures . .	8,000.00	3,000.00	5,000.00	
Store Equipment	4,000.00	1,400.00	2,600.00	
Land	12,000.00		12,000.00	
	$57,600.00	$14,020.00	$43,580.00	43,580.00
				$120,740.00

Liabilities and Net Worth

Current Liabilities:

Notes Payable		$ 25,000.00
Accounts Payable		20,000.00
Accrued Expenses		1,450.00
Deferred Income		750.00
		$ 47,200.00

Net Worth:

L. A. Roberts, Capital		$ 73,540.00
		$120,740.00

ADJUSTING AND CLOSING ENTRIES

Depreciation Expense — Buildings	1,200.00	
Reserve for Depreciation — Buildings		1,200.00

To record depreciation expense on buildings.

Depreciation Expense — Delivery Equipment	720.00	
Reserve for Depreciation — Delivery Equipment		720.00

To record depreciation expense on delivery equipment.

Depreciation Expense — Furniture and Fixtures	800.00	
Reserve for Depreciation — Furniture and Fixtures		800.00

To record depreciation expense on furniture and fixtures.

Depreciation Expense — Store Equipment	400.00	
Reserve for Depreciation — Store Equipment		400.00

To record depreciation expense on store equipment.

Bad Debts Expense	1,753.00	
Reserve for Bad Debts		1,753.00

To record estimated bad debts for 1950.

Deferred Expenses	2,200.00	
Advertising		2,000.00
Insurance		200.00

To record prepaid advertising and insurance.

General Salaries	100.00	
Interest Expense	700.00	
Salesmen's Salaries	350.00	
Taxes	300.00	
Accrued Expenses		1,450.00

To record accrued expenses.

Sales	750.00	
Deferred Income		750.00

To record liability on gift certificates, original credit having been made to the Sales account.

Accrued Income	360.00	
Interest Income		360.00

To record accrued interest income.

```
Cost of Sales  . . . . . . . . . . . . . . . . . . . . . . . .    125,600.00
Merchandise . . . . . . . . . . . . . . . . . . . . . . . .      21,000.00
Returned Purchases and Allowances  . . . . . . . . . .           4,000.00
Purchases Discounts  . . . . . . . . . . . . . . . . . .         2,400.00
      Merchandise . . . . . . . . . . . . . . . . . . . .                      24,000.00
      Purchases . . . . . . . . . . . . . . . . . . . . . .                    128,000.00
      Freight In . . . . . . . . . . . . . . . . . . . . . .                     1,000.00
To record new merchandise inventory of $21,000.00; and to
close latter five accounts into Cost of Sales.

Profit and Loss  . . . . . . . . . . . . . . . . . . . . . .    125,600.00
      Cost of Sales  . . . . . . . . . . . . . . . . . . . .                    125,600.00
To close latter account into Profit and Loss.

Sales . . . . . . . . . . . . . . . . . . . . . . . . . . .     177,600.00
      Returned Sales and Allowances  . . . . . . . . . . .                       1,600.00
      Sales Discounts  . . . . . . . . . . . . . . . . . . .                       700.00
      Profit and Loss  . . . . . . . . . . . . . . . . . . .                   175,300.00
To close first three accounts into Profit and Loss.

Profit and Loss  . . . . . . . . . . . . . . . . . . . . . .     18,170.00
      Advertising  . . . . . . . . . . . . . . . . . . . . .                     4,000.00
      Depreciation Expense — Delivery Equipment  . . . . .                         720.00
      Depreciation Expense — Store Equipment . . . . . . .                         400.00
      Miscellaneous Selling Expense . . . . . . . . . . . .                      1,700.00
      Salesmen's Salaries . . . . . . . . . . . . . . . . .                     11,350.00
To close selling expenses into Profit and Loss.

Profit and Loss  . . . . . . . . . . . . . . . . . . . . . .     17,650.00
      Bad Debts Expense  . . . . . . . . . . . . . . . . .                       1,753.00
      Depreciation Expense — Buildings . . . . . . . . . .                         800.00
      Depreciation Expense — Furniture and Fixtures . . . .                      1,200.00
      General Expense . . . . . . . . . . . . . . . . . . .                      5,600.00
      General Salaries . . . . . . . . . . . . . . . . . . .                     4,100.00
      Insurance . . . . . . . . . . . . . . . . . . . . . .                      1,000.00
      Taxes . . . . . . . . . . . . . . . . . . . . . . . .                      3,197.00
To close general operating expenses into Profit and Loss.

Interest Income . . . . . . . . . . . . . . . . . . . . . .         360.00
      Profit and Loss  . . . . . . . . . . . . . . . . . . .                       360.00
To close other income into Profit and Loss.

Profit and Loss  . . . . . . . . . . . . . . . . . . . . . .      1,700.00
      Interest Expense . . . . . . . . . . . . . . . . . . .                     1,700.00
To close other expense into Profit and Loss.

Profit and Loss  . . . . . . . . . . . . . . . . . . . . . .     12,540.00
      L. A. Roberts, Capital. . . . . . . . . . . . . . . .                     12,540.00
To transfer net income to capital account.

L. A. Roberts, Capital  . . . . . . . . . . . . . . . . . .       8,000.00
      L. A. Roberts, Personal . . . . . . . . . . . . . . .                      8,000.00
To transfer balance of personal account of L. A. Roberts to
capital account.
```

REVERSING ENTRIES

For reference purposes the student may desire to have the L. A. Roberts problem completed by a presentation of the reversing entries which would be made on January 1, 1951. These entries follow:

Advertising	2,000.00	
Insurance Expense	200.00	
Deferred Expenses		2,200.00

To reverse adjusting entry of December 31, 1950.

Accrued Expenses.	1,450.00	
General Salaries		100.00
Interest Expense		700.00
Salesmen's Salaries		350.00
Taxes		300.00

To reverse adjusting entry of December 31, 1950.

Deferred Income	750.00	
Sales		750.00

To reverse adjusting entry of December 31, 1950.

Interest Income	360.00	
Accrued Income		360.00

To reverse adjusting entry of December 31, 1950.

ADVANTAGES OF THE WORK SHEET

(1) The mathematical accuracy of the accounts is established before the books are formally closed.

(2) It is a valuable guide in making the formal adjusting and closing entries on the books.

(3) It serves as a source of information in the preparation of the profit and loss statement.

(4) It serves as a source of information in the preparation of the balance sheet.

(5) The net income of a period can be determined quickly, and statements prepared, without going through the lengthy and laborious work of formally closing the books.

(6) For the preparation of interim financial statements, the work sheet is invaluable. It is not necessary to close the books in order to have the use of interim statements.

The highest degree of accuracy is not always demanded in interim financial statements.   In some cases managements are satisfied with the relative accuracy of statements prepared, for example, upon the basis of estimated, or computed, inventories.   The degree of accuracy to be incorporated in interim statements depends, of course, upon individual preferences and upon the requirements of those who are to use the statements.

PROFIT AND LOSS ACCOUNT

After the closing entries of the L. A. Roberts problem have been posted, the Profit and Loss account will appear:

PROFIT AND LOSS

1950					1950				
Dec.	31	Cost of Sales	125,600	00	Dec.	31	Sales	177,600	00
	31	Rtd. Sales &							
		Allces.	1,600	00		31	Other Income:		
		Sales Discounts	700	00			Interest Income	360	00
	31	Selling Expenses:							
		Advertising	4,000	00					
		Deprec. Exp.:							
		Delivery							
		Equipment	720	00					
		Store Equip-							
		ment	400	00					
		Misc. Selling							
		Expense	1,700	00					
		Salesmen's Sal-							
		aries	11,350	00					
	31	General Expenses:							
		Bad Debts	1,753	00					
		Deprec. Exp.:							
		Buildings	800	00					
		Furn. & Fix-							
		tures	1,200	00					
		General Exp.	5,600	00					
		General Salaries	4,100	00					
		Insurance Exp.	1,000	00					
		Taxes	3,197	00					
	31	Other Expenses:							
		Interest *B*xpense	1,700	00					
	31	Net Income to							
		L. A. Roberts,							
		Capital	12,540	00					
			177,960	00				177,960	00

The Profit and Loss account is a summary account [1] in which all elements of loss and gain are gathered together to show the net gain or loss of an accounting period. While postings to the Profit and Loss account may be made in detail, as in the illustration, the modern tendency is to post to the account by *group totals* only. With details contained in statements of profit and loss, and work sheets,

---

[1] At the end of the accounting period certain accounts like Profit and Loss are opened to summarize the information of several accounts. The net balance of each consolidated account is transferred to some other account. Those which function in this manner are known as "summary accounts," or as "clearing accounts." The Cost of Sales account, departmental summary accounts, and the Profit and Loss account are all examples of summary accounts.

The following illustrates a further kind of serviceability to which summary accounts may be put:

Company X transfers all expenses, such as depreciation, taxes, repairs, supplies, light, etc., which have to do with its Building account, to an account called Building Expense account. The balance of the Building Expense account gives the "rent"

there is no longer the necessity present in former years for showing details in the Profit and Loss account.

The Profit and Loss account is not an account for current entry. Direct debits and credits to Profit and Loss, during an accounting period, are contrary to the purpose of the Profit and Loss account, and they are likely to result in the overlooking of significant information.

ARRANGEMENT OF THE PROFIT AND LOSS STATEMENT

An improved form of the profit and loss statement is illustrated in the L. A. Roberts problem. This statement is arranged to show

(1) *Gross Sales.* — Gross sales is the total invoice price of all merchandise sold during the accounting period.

(2) *Returned Sales and Allowances.* — Returns and allowances merit careful attention because they reduce profits by reducing sales. They also cause a not inconsiderable rehandling expense. Reasons for excessive returns and allowances should be ascertained and measures taken to correct their causes.

(3) *Net Sales.* — Net sales is the difference between gross sales and returned sales and allowances, and sales discounts. It is the revenue from sales before deducting any of the costs of producing such revenue.

(4) *Cost of Sales.* — Cost of sales is the cost of the merchandise which has been sold.

(5) *Gross Profit.* — Gross profit is the difference between net sales and the cost of merchandise sold. It is the profit existing before deducting any of the operating expenses incurred in the production of such profit.

(6) *Selling Expenses.* — Selling expenses represent the direct costs of distribution — sales and delivery expenses. Note that depreciation of delivery equipment and of store equipment is classified as a selling expense.

(7) *General Expenses.* — General expenses comprise all the *operating* expenses of a business other than manufacturing expenses and selling expenses.

(8) *Net Profit from Operations.* — Net profit from operations shows the profitability of the regular and major activities of business operation. In the words of Professor Powelson, "a business cannot

---

which the company pays on its *owned* property. The company may thus compare the cost of occupancy under its own ownership with the cost that would be incurred were the property occupied on an outright rental basis.

The balance of the Building Expense account is transferred to Profit and Loss, or it may be distributed to other accounts in the interest of further statistical information — departmental summary accounts, for example.

long be maintained in a healthy condition unless it is *operating* at a profit."

(9) *Other Income.* — Income which is received from the miscellaneous but ordinary activities of a business is called other income.

(10) *Other Expense.* — Costs which are not properly includible in the direct operating expenses (manufacturing, selling, and general) of a business constitute other expense.

Other incomes and expenses represent the miscellaneous rather than the major activities of business operation. They are usually the secondary gains and losses of business operation as distinguished from those which are primary.

(11) *Net Income.* — This is the net ncome from all of the transactions of a business over an accounting period.

As stated before, accountants are not agreed as to whether or not so-called extraordinary or nonrecurring items should be placed in the profit and loss statement. Modern accounting thought, however, is very definitely in favor of including *all* of the gains and losses of a period in the profit and loss statement. The profit and loss statement is made inclusive by adding new sections called Special Income Credits and Special Income Debits, respectively, to care for unusual items of gain or loss. The final figure on this comprehensive statement of income is called simply Net Income. (See illustration, page 629.)

The comprehensive statement of income is discussed further in Chapter 30, and in Chapters 24 and 25 of the author's *Intermediate Accounting.*

ARRANGEMENT OF THE BALANCE SHEET

The balance sheet of the L. A. Roberts problem illustrates some of the advantages to be attained by a proper classification of items. In their order of presentation the principal balance sheet groupings are as follows:

Assets

(1) *Current Assets.* Current assets are cash, and other assets which, within the next twelve months of normal business operations, are expected to be (a) realized in cash or (b) used up in the production of income. Examples are notes receivable, accounts receivable, marketable securities, inventory, and so on. Current assets should be listed in the balance sheet in the order of their expected conversion into cash.

(2) *Fixed Assets.* Fixed assets are tangible assets of rather "permanent" character required in the operation of a business. They are generally long in life. They are not intended for sale. Examples are land, building, machinery, and delivery equipment.

(3) *Other Assets.* Assets not falling within either of the above groups may be placed under the classification of Other Assets. At a later date this classification will be subdivided. (See Chapter 31.)

While some accountants place prepaid expenses under the grouping of Other Assets, and other accountants place them under the independent heading of Prepaid Expenses, they are classified as current assets in this book. Since current assets constitute *working* capital, it is proper for this classification to include prepaid expenses. Prepaid expenses are further discussed in Chapter 31, page 663.

Liabilities and Net Worth

(1) *Current Liabilities.* Liabilities which are payable within one year of the date of the balance sheet are current liabilities. Examples are taxes payable, wages payable, accounts payable, and so on.

(2) *Fixed Liabilities.* Liabilities which mature after one year from the balance sheet date are fixed liabilities. A mortgage is an example. (The L. A. Roberts balance sheet has no fixed liabilities.)

(3) *Other Liabilities.* Under the heading of Other Liabilities are listed all other liabilities.

(4) *Net Worth.* Net worth embraces the proprietary claims of a business.

QUESTIONS

Question **16–1.** Explain the construction of the work sheet.

Question **16–2.** How is the net profit, or loss, determined in the work sheet?

Question **16–3.** Why is the owner's personal account transferred to the balance sheet columns of the work sheet?

Question **16–4.** Explain how the merchandise inventories are handled in the work sheet.

Question **16–5.** The work sheet: (1) What is its purpose? (2) When should it be used? (3) What are its advantages?

Question **16–6.** The balance sheet columns of a work sheet do not balance. What would you do?

Question **16–7.** "The work sheet is a device by which the accuracy of the accounts is assured." Is this true? Explain.

Question **16–8.** Point out why the financial statements of the L. A. Roberts problem are superior in form to the financial statements heretofore employed.

Question **16–9.** Define:

Current assets   Fixed assets
Current liabilities   Fixed liabilities

Question **16–10.** What are interim statements? How are they prepared? Are the books closed after each interim statement? Explain.

PROBLEMS

Problem **16–1.** The condensed trial balance of W. K. Barnes on December 31, 19__, was:

Cash	$ 40,000.00	
Accounts Receivable	25,000.00	
Merchandise	20,000.00	
Building	60,000.00	
Reserve for Depreciation — Building		$ 10,000.00
Land	5,000.00	
Accounts Payable		40,000.00
W. K. Barnes, Capital		100,000.00
Sales		100,000.00
Purchases	70,000.00	
General Expenses	12,000.00	
Wages Expense	18,000.00	
	$250,000.00	$250,000.00

Additional Information

(1) Depreciation expense on the building, $3,000.00.
(2) Uncollectible accounts receivable are estimated at $1,000.00.
(3) Unpaid wages, $2,000.00.
(4) Merchandise on hand, December 31, 19__, $30,000.00.

Required:

(1) Prepare a work sheet.
(2) Prepare a profit and loss statement for the year.
(3) Prepare a balance sheet, December 31, 19__.

Problem **16–2.** Before closing, the trial balance of John E. Davis as of December 31, 19__, is as follows:

Cash	$ 2,700.00	
Accounts Receivable	7,500.00	
Merchandise	10,000.00	
Equipment	6,000.00	
Reserve for Depreciation — Equipment		$ 1,500.00

Building	10,000.00	
Reserve for Depreciation — Building		1,000.00
Land	2,000.00	
Accounts Payable		10,000.00
John E. Davis, Capital		25,000.00
Sales		30,000.00
Purchases	20,000.00	
Advertising Expense	1,500.00	
General Expense	2,000.00	
Wages Expense	5,800.00	
	$67,500.00	$67,500.00

Additional Information

(1) There is on hand an unrecorded and unpaid advertising bill, $500.00.

(2) Depreciation expense for the year is estimated at building, $300.00, equipment, $500.00.

(3) Accrued wages amount to $200.00.

(4) Uncollectible accounts receivable are estimated at $500.00.

(5) The new inventory of merchandise is $13,000.00.

Required:

(1) Prepare a twelve-column work sheet.

(2) Prepare a profit and loss statement for the year ending December 31, 19—.

(3) Prepare a balance sheet, December 31, 19—.

Problem **16–3.** On December 31, 1950, the trial balance of John L. Kane was

Cash	$ 40,000.00	
Accounts Receivable	100,000.00	
Bonds of the Case Corporation	20,000.00	
Merchandise	80,000.00	
Accounts Payable		$ 20,000.00
6% Notes Payable		30,000.00
John L. Kane, Capital		154,000.00
Sales		500,000.00
Purchases	300,000.00	
Selling Expense	94,000.00	
General Expense	20,000.00	
Wages Expense.	50,000.00	
	$704,000.00	$704,000.00

Other Information

(1) The sales figure includes a $3,000.00 sales invoice, the merchandise for which, it is found, is still in the warehouse and included in the new inventory of merchandise. Title to this merchandise has not yet passed to the customer.

(2) The bad debts expense for the year is estimated at 5 % of sales.

(3) Accounts receivable include $5,000.00 of known uncollectible accounts.

(4) The new inventory of merchandise is $100,000.00.

(5) The accrued payroll is $6,000.00.

(6) The notes payable are for six months and are dated October 1, 1950; no interest has been paid on these notes.

(7) There are miscellaneous general supplies on hand amounting to $1,000.00.

(8) The Case bonds were acquired January 1, 1950. They carry interest at the rate of 5 % per year, payable July 1 and January 1. None of the interest on these bonds for the year 1950 has been collected. This interest, it is expected, will be collected within the next several days.

Required:

(1) Prepare a work sheet.

(2) Prepare a profit and loss statement for the year 1950

(3) Prepare a balance sheet, December 31, 1950.

Problem **16-4.** Following is the trial balance of J. B. Elwell on December 31, 19__, before adjusting entries:

Cash	$ 6,000.00	
Accounts Receivable	3,000.00	
Merchandise	10,000.00	
Delivery Equipment	2,500.00	
Reserve for Depreciation —		
Delivery Equipment		$ 500.00
Accounts Payable		2,000.00
Notes Payable		5,000.00
J. B. Elwell, Capital		14,080.00
J. B. Elwell, Personal	4,000.00	
Sales		61,000.00
Sales Discounts	1,000.00	
Purchases	43,000.00	
Returned Purchases		1,000.00
Purchases Discounts		820.00
Freight In	3,000.00	
Advertising Expense	2,100.00	
Delivery Expense	1,500.00	
Insurance Expense	100.00	
Miscellaneous Expense	2,200.00	
Salaries and Wages	6,000.00	
	$84,400.00	$84,400.00

Additional Information

(1) Bad debts are estimated at $100.00.

(2) The new inventory of merchandise on December 31, 19__, is $13,575.00.

(3) Accrued wages and salaries amount to $500.00.

(4) Advertising paid in advance, $100.00.

(5) The notes payable are dated October 20, 19——. Although these notes carry interest at the rate of 7 %, no interest has yet been paid on these notes for the period October 20 — December 31, 19——.

(6) Delivery equipment should be depreciated at the annual rate of 20 %.

(7) Insurance premium paid in advance, $25.00.

(8) There is on hand a letter from a creditor advising that we took $20.00 too much cash discount on a recent remittance. On investigation we find that the creditor is correct. The cashier is instructed to make payment of this amount on January 10.

Required:

(1) Construct a work sheet.

(2) Prepare a profit and loss statement for the year.

(3) Prepare a balance sheet, December 31, 19——.

Problem **16–5.**

R. L. Clarkson

TRIAL BALANCE, DECEMBER 31, 19——

Cash	$ 33,400.00	
Accounts Receivable	50,000.00	
Reserve for Bad Debts		$ 100.00
Notes Receivable	25,000.00	
Notes Receivable Discounted		10,000.00
Merchandise	40,000.00	
Prepaid Insurance	1,200.00	
Miscellaneous Equipment	10,000.00	
Reserve for Depreciation — Miscellaneous Equipment		3,000.00
Buildings	90,000.00	
Reserve for Depreciation — Buildings		7,300.00
Land	15,000.00	
Accounts Payable		36,000.00
Interest Payable		1,100.00
Mortgage Payable		40,000.00
R. L. Clarkson, Capital		160,000.00
Sales		210,000.00
Purchases	125,000.00	
Purchases Discounts		3,000.00
Freight In	10,000.00	
Miscellaneous Sales Expense	18,600.00	
Sales Salaries	29,000.00	
Miscellaneous General Expense	8,000.00	
General Salaries	14,000.00	
Interest Income		1,000.00
Interest Expense	2,300.00	
	$471,500.00	$471,500.00

Other Information

(1) Merchandise inventory, December 31, 19___, $50,000.00.
(2) Interest accrued on notes receivable, $300.00, on mortgage, $1,200.00. Interest received in advance, $100.00.
(3) Accrued payroll: sales salaries, $2,000.00, general salaries, $1,000.00.
(4) Annual depreciation rates: buildings, 3 %, miscellaneous equipment, 10 %.
(5) Unexpired insurance premium, $500.00. Insurance premiums, as paid, have been debited to Prepaid Insurance.
(6) The bad debts expense for the year is estimated at 1 % of net sales.

Required:

(1) Construct a work sheet of ten or twelve columns.
(2) Prepare a profit and loss statement for the year.
(3) Prepare a balance sheet, December 31, 19___.

Problem **16–6.** Following is the trial balance of B. J. Coleman at the end of the year 19___:

Cash	$ 4,850.00	
Accounts Receivable	12,000.00	
Reserve for Bad Debts	220.00	
Notes Receivable	3,000.00	
Notes Receivable Discounted		$ 800.00
Merchandise	6,300.00	
Miscellaneous Equipment	4,000.00	
Reserve for Depreciation — Miscellaneous Equipment		2,000.00
Accounts Payable		5,000.00
Notes Payable		3,000.00
B. J. Coleman, Capital		13,000.00
Sales		55,000.00
Returned Sales	4,000.00	
Sales Discounts	1,000.00	
Purchases	36,000.00	
Returned Purchases		300.00
Purchases Discounts		700.00
Freight In	1,200.00	
Selling Expense	1,500.00	
General Expense	5,400.00	
Insurance Expense	180.00	
Interest Income		50.00
Interest Expense	200.00	
	$79,850.00	$79,850.00

Additional Information

(1) New inventory of merchandise, $5,470.00.
(2) Accrued general expenses, $75.00.
(3) Accrued interest on notes payable, $40.00.
(4) Accrued interest on notes receivable, $54.00.
(5) Unexpired insurance premium, $50.00.

(6) Prepaid interest on notes payable, $25.00.
(7) Stamps on hand, $20.00.
(8) Bad debts are estimated at 2 % of net sales.
(9) Depreciation is estimated at 10 % per year on fixed assets.

Required:

(1) Prepare a twelve-column work sheet.
(2) Prepare a profit and loss statement for the year.
(3) Prepare a balance sheet, December 31, 19___.

Problem **16–7.** Following is the trial balance of E. L. Evans before adjusting and closing the books for the year ending December 31, 19___:

Cash	$ 12,817.00	
Accounts Receivable	35,000.00	
Reserve for Bad Debts		$ 11.00
Notes Receivable	10,000.00	
Notes Receivable Discounted		3,000.00
Merchandise	30,000.00	
Miscellaneous Equipment	11,000.00	
Reserve for Depreciation — Misc. Equipment		1,000.00
Building	40,000.00	
Reserve for Depreciation — Building		4,000.00
Accounts Payable		36,620.00
Notes Payable		7,000.00
E. L. Evans, Capital		84,000.00
E. L. Evans, Personal	4,000.00	
Sales		102,480.00
Returned Sales	3,580.00	
Purchases	68,414.00	
Purchases Discounts		2,340.00
Freight In	3,020.00	
Advertising	4,000.00	
Sales Salaries	10,000.00	
Office Salaries	5,800.00	
Miscellaneous Office Expense.	2,400.00	
Interest Income		210.00
Interest Expense	630.00	
	$240,661.00	$240,661.00

Additional Information

(1) Merchandise inventory December 31, 19___, $36,114.00.
(2) Accrued payroll: sales salaries, $300.00, office salaries, $200.00.
(3) Accrued interest on notes receivable, $280.00.
(4) Annual depreciation rates: building, 3 %, miscellaneous equipment, 10 %.
(5) Bad debts are estimated at 1 % of net sales.
(6) There is on hand an unrecorded and unpaid purchases invoice for merchandise, $284.00. This merchandise, however, is included in the new inventory.
(7) It is ascertained that one of the notes receivable discounted in the

face value of $600.00 has been paid. This payment has not been recorded on the books.

There are office supplies on hand amounting to $250.00.

Required:

(1) Prepare a twelve-column work sheet.
(2) Prepare a profit and loss statement for the year.
(3) Prepare a balance sheet, December 31, 19__.

Problem 16–8. Following is the trial balance of John A. Hall on December 31, 19__.

Cash	$ 3,134.00	
Notes Receivable	2,220.00	
Notes Receivable Discounted		$ 620.00
Accounts Receivable	12,210.00	
Merchandise	6,938.00	
Delivery Equipment	2,120.00	
Accounts Payable		5,556.00
Notes Payable		4,000.00
John A. Hall, Capital		16,000.00
John A. Hall, Personal	3,415.00	
Sales		57,721.00
Sales Returns	1,690.00	
Sales Discounts	1,031.00	
Purchases	38,854.00	
Purchases Returns		183.00
Purchases Discounts		632.00
Freight In	1,443.00	
Advertising	1,022.00	
Delivery Expenses	1,388.00	
General Expense	2,220.00	
Insurance Expense	105.00	
Wages and Salaries	6,796.00	
Interest Income		52.00
Interest Expense	178.00	
	$84,764.00	$84,764.00

Additional Information

(1) New inventory of merchandise, $3,400.00.
(2) Unexpired insurance, $42.00.
(3) Stamps and office supplies on hand, $76.00.
(4) Accrued wages and salaries, $114.00.
(5) Accrued interest on notes receivable: six months at 6 % per annum.
(6) Accrued interest on notes payable: $3,000.00 for 72 days at 6 % per annum.
(7) Prepaid interest on $1,000.00 of notes payable, $20.00.
(8) Uncollectible accounts are estimated at 1 % of net sales.
(9) Delivery equipment is estimated to depreciate at the annual rate of 20 %.

Required:

(1) Prepare a twelve-column work sheet.
(2) Prepare a profit and loss statement for the year.
(3) Prepare a balance sheet, December 31, 19__.

Problem **16-9.** Before adjustment, the trial balance of W. C. Logan on December 31, 19__, is as follows:

Cash	$ 93,685.00	
Accounts Receivable	35,450.00	
Notes Receivable	14,270.00	
Merchandise	70,770.00	
Prepaid Advertising	1,623.00	
Prepaid Insurance	1,065.00	
Prepaid Taxes	1,530.00	
Delivery Equipment	10,000.00	
Reserve for Depreciation — Delivery Equipment		$ 2,000.00
Miscellaneous Equipment	21,350.00	
Reserve for Depreciation — Miscellaneous Equipment		3,000.00
Building	70,000.00	
Reserve for Depreciation — Building		7,000.00
Land	20,000.00	
Accounts Payable		20,579.00
Notes Payable		60,000.00
Mortgage Payable		50,000.00
W. C. Logan, Capital		200,000.00
Sales		243,061.00
Purchases	211,600.00	
General Expenses	13,090.00	
Wages and Salaries	18,548.00	
Interest Earned		1,185.00
Interest Expense	3,844.00	
	$586,825.00	$586,825.00

The following adjustment data are given:

(1) Merchandise inventory, December 31, 19__, $101,960.00.
(2) Annual depreciation rates: building, 2 %, delivery equipment, 20 %, miscellaneous equipment, 10 %.
(3) A reserve for bad debts amounting to 8 % of the accounts receivable should be established in order to care for the estimated uncollectible accounts.
(4) The true amount of prepaid expenses on December 31, 19__, is advertising, $250.00, insurance, $300.00, taxes, $375.00.
(5) Unpaid and unrecorded payroll as of December 31, 19__, $1,254.00.
(6) Accrued interest payable on notes payable and mortgage payable, $2,908.00.
(7) $15.00 of the $1,185.00 interest income on the books is prepaid.
(8) There is unrecorded interest income of $212.00 on the notes receivable. This interest, while earned, is not yet due for payment.

Required:

(1) Prepare a twelve-column work sheet.

(2) Prepare a profit and loss statement for the year ending December 31, 19__.

(3) Prepare a balance sheet, December 31, 19__.

Problem 16–10. The following trial balance is taken from the books of J. T. Morton for the year ending December 31, 19__:

Cash	$ 16,400.00	
Accounts Receivable	34,600.00	
Notes Receivable	14,600.00	
Merchandise	12,340.00	
Delivery Equipment	3,120.00	
Furniture and Fixtures	6,200.00	
Store Equipment	8,070.00	
Accounts Payable		$ 40,000.00
Notes Payable		10,000.00
J. T. Morton, Capital		38,000.00
J. T. Morton, Personal	3,000.00	
Sales		144,000.00
Purchases	106,700.00	
Purchases Discounts		1,200.00
Advertising	3,400.00	
Delivery Expense	1,160.00	
Salesmen's Salaries	10,600.00	
Traveling Expense	3,027.00	
Heat and Light	450.00	
Office Salaries	4,200.00	
Rent	5,000.00	
Stationery and Printing	200.00	
Interest Income		139.00
Interest Expense	272.00	
	$233,339.00	$233,339.00

The following information is available for adjusting and closing the books:

(1) The merchandise on hand is valued at $10,480.00.

(2) The account of L. M. Wilson, $250.00, is considered worthless. All other accounts are considered fully collectible.

(3) Depreciation expense is to be provided for as follows:

Delivery Equipment = 25 %
Furniture and Fixtures = 10 %
Store Equipment = 10 %

(4) Advertising paid in advance, $500.00.

(5) Gasoline and oil on hand, $67.00.

(6) There is $100.00 interest accrued, but not yet due for payment, on notes payable.

(7) Of the Interest Income account $20.00 is applicable to the next accounting period.

(8) There is $61.00 interest accrued, but not yet due for payment, on notes receivable.

(9) Unpaid traveling expenses, per salesmen's reports, amount to $410.00.

Required:

(1) Prepare a twelve-column work sheet.

(2) Prepare a profit and loss statement for the year ending December 31, 19__.

(3) Prepare a balance sheet, December 31, 19__.

Problem **16–11.** The unadjusted trial balance of Edward A. Stone on December 31, 19__, was as follows:

Cash	$ 20,751.00	
Accounts Receivable	47,663.00	
Notes Receivable	3,000.00	
Merchandise	23,414.00	
Building	50,000.00	
Reserve for Depreciation — Building		$ 7,270.00
Delivery Equipment	4,000.00	
Reserve for Depreciation — Delivery Equipment		1,014.00
General Equipment	3,500.00	
Reserve for Depreciation — General Equipment		352.00
Land	10,000.00	
Accounts Payable		26,726.00
Notes Payable		12,000.00
Edward A. Stone, Capital		75,000.00
Edward A. Stone, Personal	5,000.00	
Sales		207,736.00
Purchases	129,811.00	
Selling Expense	18,912.00	
General Expense	13,792.00	
Interest Income		144.00
Interest Expense	399.00	
	$330,242.00	$330,242.00

The following information should be taken into account in preparing the annual financial statements:

(1) Merchandise inventory, December 31, 19__, $21,512.00.

(2) The account receivable with Davis & Son, $411.00, is considered worthless. All other accounts receivable are considered good.

(3) Depreciation expense for the year is estimated at buildings, $1,030.00, delivery equipment, $986.00, general equipment, $315.00.

(4) Wages and salaries accrued, but not yet due for payment, are $624.00. This cost is to be apportioned 1/3 to selling expense, and 2/3 to general expense.

(5) Unrecorded interest receivable amounts to $72.00.

(6) Unrecorded interest payable amounts to $200.00.

(7) Of the interest expense already recorded on the books, $49.00 represents interest paid in advance.

(8) Of the interest income already recorded on the books, $16.00 represents unearned interest.

(9) There is on hand a purchase invoice, received after the purchase book was closed, amounting to $3,287.00. This merchandise is included in the new merchandise inventory of $21,512.00.

Required:

(1) Prepare a work sheet.

(2) Prepare a profit and loss statement for the year 19___.

(3) Prepare a balance sheet, December 31, 19___.

Problem **16–12.** The trial balance of C. F. Rogers on December 31, 1952, is as follows:

Cash	$ 12,400.00	
Accounts Receivable	24,900.00	
Reserve for Bad Debts		$　　520.00
Notes Receivable	10,600.00	
Bonds	2,000.00	
Merchandise	21,310.00	
Delivery Equipment	3,200.00	
Reserve for Depreciation, Delivery Equipment	- -	1,500.00
Furniture and Fixtures	7,000.00	
Reserve for Depreciation, Furniture and Fixtures		1,900.00
Store Equipment	3,500.00	
Reserve for Depreciation, Store Equipment		800.00
Buildings	26,000.00	
Reserve for Depreciation, Buildings		4,700.00
Land	10,600.00	
Accounts Payable		17,700.00
Notes Payable		22,000.00
C. F. Rogers, Capital		61,500.00
C. F. Rogers, Personal	6,000.00	
Sales		158,464.00
Returned Sales and Allowances	1,420.00	
Sales Discounts	1,604.00	
Purchases	113,600.00	
Returned Purchases and Allowances		3,490.00
Purchase Discounts		2,140.00
Freight In	900.00	
Advertising	5,300.00	
Miscellaneous Selling Expense	1,500.00	
Salesmen's Salaries	9,800.00	
General Expense	5,010.00	
General Salaries	3,550.00	
Insurance Expense	1,060.00	
Taxes	2,600.00	
Interest Expense	860.00	
	$274,714.00	$274,714.00

The following information is available for adjusting and closing the books:

Merchandise inventory, December 31, 1952 . . . . $18,600.00
Depreciation expense:
    Buildings, 4%
    Delivery Equipment, 20%
    Furniture and Fixtures, 10%
    Store Equipment, 10%
Bad debts are estimated to be 1% of net sales. The $520.00 credit balance
  in the Reserve for Bad Debts account in the trial balance is the unused
  balance of the reserve set up December 31, 1951. As of December 31,
  1952, there are no 1951 accounts receivable outstanding.
Advertising paid for in 1952 but applicable to 1953 . . . . 1,800.00
Insurance paid for in 1952 but applicable to 1953 . . . . 175.00
General salaries accrued but not yet due for payment 100.00
Interest accrued on notes payable 600.00
Salesmen's salaries accrued but not yet due for payment 300.00
Taxes accrued but not yet due for payment 250.00
The figure for sales includes $644.00 of standard merchandise which has
  been contracted for by a customer. The contract provides that delivery
  is to be made in February, 1953, payment to be made 2/10, n/30 follow-
  ing date of delivery. This merchandise is on hand and is included in the
  merchandise, inventory of December 31, 1952, at a correct valuation.
Interest accrued on bonds but not yet due for collection 50.00
Interest accrued on notes receivable but not yet due for collection 260.00
There is on hand an unrecorded invoice of the Business Machines Company
  amounting to $100.00. This invoice, covering typewriter repairs and
  overhauls, will be paid in January.

Required:

    (1) Prepare a twelve-column work sheet.
    (2) Prepare a profit and loss statement for the year 1952.
    (3) Prepare a balance sheet, December 31, 1952.

Problem **16-13.** The books of Andrew J. Price were kept on a monthly
accrual basis. His trial balance on December 31, 1952, was as follows:

Cash	$ 24,908.26	
U.S. Treasury Bonds	25,000.00	
Bond Interest Receivable	260.42	
Accounts Receivable	30,411.99	
Reserve for Bad Debts		$ 2,060.30
Notes Receivable	11,660.00	
Notes Receivable Discounted		11,660.00
Inventory	18,607.00	
Prepaid Advertising.	2,640.00	
Prepaid Insurance	220.00	
Delivery Equipment	3,520.00	
Reserve for Depreciation — Delivery Equipment .		2,295.34
Furniture and Fixtures	7,700.00	
Reserve for Depreciation — Furniture and Fixtures		2,795.84
Store Equipment	3,850.00	
Reserve for Depreciation — Store Equipment . .		1,232.91
Building	28,600.00	
Reserve for Depreciation — Building		6,218.66
Land	12,000.00	
Accounts Payable		20,470.00
Notes Payable		24,000.00
Interest Payable		522.50
Taxes Payable		637.50

Deferred Sales		700.00
Andrew J. Price, Capital		80,000.00
Andrew J. Price, Personal	6,000.00	
Sales		191,602.00
Returned Sales and Allowances	1,502.00	
Sales Discounts	1,764.00	
Purchases	123,601.00	
Returned Purchases and Allowances		3,839.00
Purchases Discounts		2,354.00
Freight In	1,874.00	
Advertising	4,190.00	
Depreciation Expense — Delivery Equipment . .	645.34	
Miscellaneous Selling Expense	1,852.00	
Sales Salaries	15,780.00	
Bad Debts Expense	1,488.30	
Depreciation Expense — Building	1,048.66	
Depreciation Expense — Furniture and Fixtures .	705.84	
Depreciation Expense — Store Equipment . . .	352.91	
General Expense	5,571.00	
General Salaries	8,905.00	
Insurance Expense	946.00	
Taxes, Property	2,873.75	
Taxes, Social Security	1,015.00	
Interest Income		572.92
Interest Expense	1,468.50	
	$350,960.97	$350,960.97

The following information was available for adjusting and closing the books:

Inventory of merchandise, December 31, 1952 . . . . . $21,604.00.

Annual depreciation expense rates: building, 4 %, delivery equipment, 20 %, furniture and fixtures, 10 %, store equipment, 10 %.

Bad debts expense for the year is estimated at 1 % of net sales (before deduction of sales discounts). Net sales for the month of December were $41,270.00.

Accounts receivable now on the books and ascertained to be worthless amount to $811.04.

The credit balance in the Reserve for Bad Debts account includes $327.01 of the credit balance in this account at the close of business December 31, 1951. Since there are no 1951 accounts receivable presently outstanding, the $327.01 should be removed from the Reserve for Bad Debts account.

The account with Deferred Sales represents unredeemed coupons out of coupon books sold to customers for cash. These coupons, redeemable only in trade, are acceptable at face value in payment of merchandise.

Advertising applicable to 1953	$2,000.00
Insurance premium applicable to 1953.	175.00
Sales salaries owed but not yet due for payment	500.00
General salaries owed but not yet due for payment	200.00
Property taxes accrued in December	262.50

(Note: Accrued social security taxes are already correctly reflected in the account with Taxes Payable.)

Interest accrued in December on notes payable 137.50
Interest accrued in December on U.S. Treasury, 2½% bonds, of
1972 (interest payable January 1 and July 1) . . . . ?

There is on hand an invoice, dated December 31, 1952, of the Standard Glass Company covering the replacement of a broken plate-glass window, $163.00. This bill is scheduled for payment in January.

Required:

(1) Prepare a work sheet.
(2) Prepare a profit and loss statement for the year 1952.
(3) Prepare a balance sheet, December 31, 1952.
(4) Prepare adjusting entries to be placed on the books, December 31, 1952.

Problem **16–14.**

John E. Wellman

BALANCE SHEET, DECEMBER 31, 1950
Assets

Current Assets:
Cash $17,400.00
Inventory 8,000.00
Accounts Receivable $28,000.00
    Reserve for Bad Debts 1,000.00   27,000.00

Prepaid Office Supplies 400.00 $52,800.00

Fixed Assets:
Building $40,000.00
    Reserve for Depreciation 17,200.00 $22,800.00

Equipment 16,000.00
    Reserve for Depreciation 11,200.00   4,800.00   27,600.00

  $80,400.00

Equities

Current Liabilities:
Accounts Payable . . . . $ 8,100.00
Accrued Wages Payable 7,000.00
Accrued Expenses Payable 5,000.00 $20,100.00

Other Liabilities:
Deferred Interest Income 300.00

Net Worth:
John E. Wellman, Capital 60,000.00

  $80,400.00

John E. Wellman

STATEMENT OF PROFIT AND LOSS
YEAR ENDED DECEMBER 31, 1950

Sales		$208,000.00	
Sales Returns		8,000.00	$200,000.00
Cost of Sales:			
Inventory, January 1, 1950	$ 16,000.00		
Purchases	120,000.00	$136,000.00	
Inventory, December 31, 1950		8,000.00	128,000.00
Gross Profit			72,000.00
Expenses:			
Wages		$ 28,000.00	
Office Supplies		800.00	
General Expenses		40,000.00	
Bad Debts Expense		1,000.00	
Depreciation Expense — Building.		1,200.00	
Depreciation Expense — Equipment		3,200.00	74,200.00
Net Loss on Operations		$ 2,200.00	
Interest Income		1,200.00	
Net Loss		$ 1,000.00	

In preparing the work sheet from which the above statements were made, the accountant took the following supplementary information into consideration:

(a) Bad debts are estimated at ½% of net sales.
(b) Annual depreciation rates: building 3%; equipment 20%.
(c) Accrued wages, $7,000.00.
(d) Deferred office supplies expense, $400.00.
(e) Deferred interest income, $300.00.
(f) Accrued expenses payable, $5,000.00.

Required:

Construct the trial balance from which the accountant prepared his work sheet. In establishing this trial balance, reconstruct the work sheet.

Problem **16–15.**

James E. Kent

ADJUSTED TRIAL BALANCE
DECEMBER 31, 1950

Cash	$ 16,920.00	
Notes Receivable	22,000.00	
Notes Receivable Discounted		$ 8,000.00
Accrued Interest Receivable	200.00	
Accounts Receivable	30,000.00	
Reserve for Bad Debts		5,500.00
Merchandise Inventory, January 1, 1950	75,000.00	
Prepaid Insurance	1,000.00	
Prepaid Advertising.	1,500.00	

Store Fixtures	9,800.00	
Reserve for Depreciation — Store Fixtures		1,870.00
Office Equipment	3,200.00	
Reserve for Depreciation — Office Equipment		900.00
Store Building	60,000.00	
Reserve for Depreciation — Store Building		14,000.00
Land	10,000.00	
Notes Payable		12,000.00
Accounts Payable		36,000.00
Bond Interest Payable		750.00
Accrued Salaries Payable		400.00
Accrued Taxes Payable		1,200.00
Mortgage Payable, due January 1, 1960		25,000.00
Deferred Interest Income		100.00
James E. Kent, Capital		100,000.00
James E. Kent, Personal	4,500.00	
Sales		360,000.00
Sales Discounts . . . , ...	7,100.00	
Sales Returns and Allowances	6,000.00	
Purchases	225,000.00	
Purchases Returns		2,000.00
Purchases Discounts		2,400.00
Freight In	2,500.00	
Advertising Expense	18,500.00	
Depreciation Expense — Store Building and Fixtures . . .	3,980.00	
Miscellaneous Selling Expense	7,600.00	
Sales Salaries	35,000.00	
Depreciation Expense — Office Equipment.	320.00	
Miscellaneous General Expense	2,300.00	
Office Expense	8,200.00	
Office Salaries	19,000.00	
Interest Income		1,500.00
Interest Expense	2,000.00	
	$571,620.00	$571,620.00

Required:

(1) Prepare a well-organized profit and loss statement for the year. New merchandise inventory, December 31, 1950, $60,000.00.

(2) Prepare a well-classified balance sheet, December 31, 1950.

Chapter 17

PARTNERSHIPS: INTRODUCTORY CONSIDERATIONS

DEFINITION

The Uniform Partnership Act defines a partnership as "an association of two or more persons to carry on, as co-owners, a business for profit." This definition refers to living persons only. It follows therefore that a corporation cannot be a member of a partnership.

WHY PARTNERSHIPS ARE FORMED

The partnership form of business organization makes it possible to combine the capital, ability, and experience of two or more persons. Collectively the partners feel that they have a stronger organization than they could have individually.

Partnerships are common to smaller types of business enterprise, and to enterprises wherein the element of personal service is important (accounting, brokerage, and the law, for example). As a general rule, the larger the enterprise, the less likely is the partnership form of business organization to be employed.

NATURE OF PARTNERSHIP

A partnership has no legal existence. When the partnership is sued, all the partners must be named as defendants. If the partnership wishes to bring action, it must sue in the names of all the partners as individuals.

Each partner of an ordinary partnership is individually liable for all the debts of the partnership. His only recourse is against the other partners. In the event of his withdrawal from partnership, a partner is not relieved of his liability for partnership debts outstanding as of the date of his withdrawal unless written releases have been procured from creditors.

A special type of partnership called "limited partnership" is provided for by the statutes of most states. In a limited partnership certain partners (but not all partners) are permitted to limit their personal liability to the amounts which they have contributed to the

capital of the partnership.   A limited partnership must be formed
and operated in compliance with the provisions of the Limited Partnership Act of the state in which the partnership operates.   The
partnership, for instance, must have at least one general partner of
unlimited liability, must file for public record in the manner specified
by the Limited Partnership Act an informative certificate of limited
partnership, must advertise that it is a limited partnership, and so
on.   If a limited partner leads creditors to believe he is a general
partner or if he takes an active part in the management, he automatically becomes liable as a general partner.

Each member of an ordinary partnership is a principal as well as
an agent.   Acting for the firm, and within the scope of its business,
the acts of each are binding upon all partners.[1]   Transactions by a
partner outside the usual course of the partnership business are not
binding upon the other partners unless they consent to be bound;[2]
such acts are, for example,

(1)   The sale of the partnership name.[3]
(2)   Guarantees or accommodation endorsements.[4]
(3)   The transfer of a partner's interest.[5]
(4)   Any act that would make it impossible to carry on the ordinary business of the partnership.[6]

A partnership is easily dissolved.   The most common causes of
partnership dissolution are

(1)   By agreement of the partners to dissolve.
(2)   Expiration of the term for which the partnership was formed.
(3)   Completion of the enterprise.
(4)   Impossibility of continuing the enterprise.
(5)   Retirement or admission of a partner.
(6)   Death of a partner.
(7)   Incompetency of a partner (i.e., insanity, bankruptcy, mis-
conduct, and so on).   Dissolution under these circumstances may be
effected by court decree.

---

[1] "Every member of an ordinary partnership is its general agent for the transaction of its business in the ordinary way, and the firm is held responsible for whatever
is done by its partners when acting for the firm within the limits of the authority con-
ferred by the nature of the business it carries on.   Every person is entitled to assume
that each partner is impowered to do for the firm whatever is necessary for the transaction of its business, in the way in which that business is ordinarily carried on by
other people." — *Pooley* v. *Whitmore* (57 Tenn. 629).
[2] 20 R. C. L. 884–885.
[3] 20 R. C. L. 872; 908–909.
[4] 20 R. C. L. 899; 903.
[5] 20 R. C. L. 983.   47 C. J. 1020.
[6] 20 R. C. L. 908–909.   47 C. J. 832–833.

FORMATION OF THE PARTNERSHIP

Partnerships may be formed by oral contract, by written contract, or by implied action of the partners. It is better, however, to have the partnership organized upon the basis of a written contract, complete in all details, and signed by all partners.

THE PARTNERSHIP CONTRACT

Among the important points to be covered in the articles of partnership are the following:

Organization. —

(1) Name of the partnership.

(2) Partners, names and duties. May partners engage in outside business activities and, if so, to what extent?

(3) Duration of partnership contract.

(4) Nature of business.

(5) Place of business.

(6) Amount of capital to be contributed by each partner. The valuations to be attached to noncash assets contributed by partners.

(7) Apportionment of future capital contributions, if capital increases become necessary.

Operation. —

(1) Salaries, if any, to be allowed each partner, and their accounting.

(2) Withdrawals to be allowed each partner; time and amount.

(3) Profits and losses. A fixed or determinable ratio should be provided for their division between partners. (In the absence of agreement, profits and losses are divided equally.)

(4) The accounting period.

(5) Shall interest be allowed on capital? If so, at what rate, and when shall it be recorded on the books? Definition of capital.

(6) Treatment of over- and undercontributions of capital.

(7) Treatment of undrawn salaries and profits. Shall they be added to Capital accounts?

(8) Treatment of excess drawings.

(9) Provision for arbitration of disputes.

Dissolution. —

(1) Procedure to be followed in the event of the retirement or death of a partner.

(2) How shall goodwill be valued? How shall the assets be valued and by whom?

(3) How shall settlement of the capital account of a retired or deceased partner be made?

(4) Procedure to be followed when the business is to be liquidated and dissolved.

PARTNERSHIP ACCOUNTING

Partnership accounting introduces three new features:

(1) A capital account is maintained with each partner.

(2) A personal account is maintained with each partner.

(3) Profits and losses must be accurately apportioned to partners in order to establish correctly their respective capital interests.

In other respects partnership accounting is similar to accounting for the single proprietorship.

OPENING THE BOOKS OF A PARTNERSHIP

Each partner is given a capital credit equal to the net assets he has contributed.

Example:

A. C. Bryce and E. K. Burger decide that it will be mutually advantageous to consolidate their businesses under the name of Bryce & Burger. The opening entries on the partnership books are as follows (all valuations having been accepted by both partners):

JOURNAL   Page 1

1950					
Apr.	1	Building	20,000 00		
		Land	10,000 00		
		Mortgage Payable		7,000 00	
		A. C. Bryce, Capital		23,000 00	
		To record the assets (except cash) and liabilities contributed to the partnership of Bryce and Burger formed today.			
	1	Accounts Receivable	40,000 00		
		(in detail)			
		Delivery Equipment	1,500 00		
		Furniture and Fixtures	2,000 00		
		Merchandise	25,000 00		
		Accounts Payable		35,000 00	
		(in detail)			
		E. K. Burger, Capital		33,500 00	
		To record the assets (except cash) and liabilities contributed to the partnership of Bryce and Burger formed today.			

Note: The cash contributed by the partners was:

A. C. Bryce $25,000.00
E. K. Burger 10,000.00

which amounts are recorded in the cash receipts book.

The following is a summary of the articles of partnership of Bryce & Burger (detail):

CASH RECEIPTS BOOK   Page 1

				CREDIT			DEBIT		
DATE	ACCOUNT CREDITED	EXPLANATION	L.F.	Miscellaneous	L.F.	Accounts Receivable	Sales Discounts	Cash	
1950									
Apr. 1	A. C. Bryce, Capital	Cash investment		25,000 00				25,000 00	
1	E. K. Burger, Capital	Cash investment		10,000 00				10,000 00	

DRAWING ACCOUNTS

The more or less regular withdrawals of cash or merchandise by partners should be debited to the partners' personal accounts or, as they are more commonly called in partnership accounting, their drawing accounts. The function of partners' drawing accounts is identical with that of the personal account of the owner of a single proprietorship. The personal accounts of partners are debited with

(1) Withdrawals of cash, merchandise, or other assets.

(2) Partners' salaries paid.

(3) Payment by the partnership of partners' personal obligations.

(4) Partnership funds collected and retained by partners. (Rare.)

They are credited with

(1) Partners' salaries owed. (This should be done regularly at the end of each month. The offsetting debit in each case is to the expense account Partners' Salaries.)

(2) Partnership obligations assumed or paid by partners.

(3) Partners' personal funds collected and retained by the partnership. (Rare.)

At the end of each accounting period the balances of partners' drawing accounts should be transferred to their related capital accounts. If these balances are to be withdrawn in the very near future, the drawing accounts of partners might remain open without strong objection.

A debit balance in a partner's drawing account, if greater than the partner's share of net income, or if in excess of allowable drawings as specified in the partnership contract, as a general rule should be made good by the partner in question. Reimbursement, however, may not materialize satisfactorily in actual practice. It is very desirable, as was indicated on page 355, that the partnership agreement clearly specify the rights and obligations of partners when drawings are excessive.

In the solution of problems calling for partnership balance sheets, debit or credit balances in partners' drawing accounts should be consolidated with partners' capital accounts (unless the problem clearly specifies otherwise). Closing entries, if called for, should be in harmony with such consolidation.

Withdrawals of merchandise by partners should be charged to partners' drawing accounts at cost and credited to Purchases (or Cost of Sales). Sometimes, in order to handle these charges expeditiously, they are recorded in the sales book in the manner of ordinary sales. The inaccuracy which would be injected into the sales figure by this accounting would normally not be significant because usually, in comparison with total sales, the amount of merchandise withdrawn by partners is not important. When this accounting is followed, the bookkeeper should open special accounts with each partner in the accounts receivable ledger. At the end of each month, these partners' accounts receivable should be settled by cash collections, or their balances should be transferred to the regular draw-ing accounts of partners in the general ledger.

PARTNERS' ADVANCES

In addition to their specified capital investments, partners may contribute further funds to a business. Such advances may be credited in one of three ways:

(1) To Capital account if such funds constitute additional capi-tal investment.

(2) To a Partners' Loan Payable account as a loan to the part-nership.

(3) To a Partners' Notes Payable account if the advance is evi-denced by a note signed by all of the partners. The regular Notes Payable account should not be credited because this account repre-sents note claims of those outside the partnership. The books should differentiate between the two kinds of note claims since in all cases liabilities take precedence over proprietary claims.

Whether or not interest is to be paid on the loan which a partner-ship receives from one of its members and if so, how much, is a matter for agreement between the parties to the loan contract. If the par-ties have not expressed themselves, the general rule is "to allow interest upon the advances, although there was no express agreement by the firm to pay it, in the absence of some agreement to the con-trary, express or implied. The right to interest . . . is to be implied in such cases without any express promise, as in like transactions be-tween parties holding no partnership relations to each other." [7] In-terest paid on partners' loans should be debited to Interest Expense.

Profits left by a partner with the firm are not entitled to interest except by consent of the partners of the firm.[8]

PARTNERS' BORROWINGS

A partnership may advance funds to one or more of its members. Such advances may be debited in one of three ways:

(1) To Capital account, if the withdrawal constitutes a perma-nent withdrawal of capital.

(2) To a Partners' Loan Receivable account as a receivable to be later collected.

(3) To a Partners' Notes Receivable account if the advance is evidenced by a note.

---

[7] *Rodgers* v. *Clement* (162 N. Y. 422). See also *Mack* v. *Engel* (165 Mich. 540) and *Hodges* v. *Parker* (17 Vt. 242).

[8] *Winchester* v. *Glazier* (152 Mass. 316).

Whether or not interest is to be charged on loans made to partners is a matter for mutual arrangement and agreement. Unless there is an understanding to the contrary between the firm and the borrowing partner, as when a note is executed, interest may not be charged on the indebtedness of a partner to the firm.[9]

PARTNERS' SALARIES

Partners are not entitled to salaries unless salaries are specifically provided for by the articles of partnership.

Partners may expressly agree that salaries shall be allowed without indicating their purpose or their accounting, or that salaries shall be allowed for the purpose of dividing profits. In either event, salaries are purely a device of profit apportionment. (See Chapter 18, page 375.) If monthly salaries are specified, debits should be made regularly to Partners' Salaries with offsetting credits to Cash or to Partners' Drawing accounts. At the end of the accounting period, the Partners' Salaries account should be closed to Profit and Loss — not as an expense but as a partial distribution of profit.

Partners' salaries are not true business expenses. They do not affect the net income of a partnership. True economic gain or loss cannot be the result of transactions between proprietary interests.

Although it does not represent sound theory, one view on partners' salaries is quite interesting. This view holds that partners' salaries called for by the articles of partnership are expenses of doing business (i.e., a cost of management). Like any other *expense* account, therefore, Partners' Salaries should be included with the expenses of the statement of profit and loss; and closed to the Profit and Loss account.

Those who hold to this point of view argue that it accords with the thinking of practical businessmen: that reasonable partners' salaries are expense because partners' salaries are wages of management. Further, in an incorporated business, salaries of this kind are an expense of operation. It is not consistent, they say, to regard the costs of management for a partnership as a distribution of net income and to regard the costs of management for a corporation as an expense.

It is also stated that failure to regard salaries as other than operating expense is to take exception to the usual commercial concept of net profit, i.e., as that profit which remains after all expenses have been provided for, management costs included. Net profit is profit on investment and is not inclusive of earnings on services.

---

[9] *Holden* v. *Peace* (39 N. C. 223); *Snell* v. *Taylor* (182 Ill. 473); *Sweeney* v. *Neeley* 53 Mich. 421).

Were he to accept the foregoing definition of net profit, the accountant unquestionably would often have difficulty in satisfactorily applying it to specific statements of profit and loss. Partners' salaries are sometimes fixed at values which are not the sound values of managerial services but which, instead, are related to the profit-earning ability of the business or, indeed, to the personal financial needs of partners. In the interest of establishing sound accounting values on financial statements, it would appear incumbent on the accountant to establish the economic worth of the services of partners to a business. This might not be an easy thing to do; and it might also often be embarrassing. It would be futile to hope that this task of appraisal would ever become easier when it is considered that the economic worth of partners' services is constantly being subjected to change. These difficulties, as well as expediency, support the accountant who goes no further than to determine the net income of a business, exclusive of partners' salaries. The determination of the economic net income of a business is left to the partners themselves, or to others who may be interested.

It should be fixed firmly in mind that partners' salaries do not represent the usual employer-employee contractual relationship. They do not represent disbursements to legal persons outside the partnership. They are not even the result of a contract between partners and nonpartners. And they are not preferred claims in the event of partnership liquidation. It is pertinent to repeat again that true accounting gain or loss cannot be the result of transactions between proprietary interests.

From the foregoing it should be clear that there is no valid reason why an accountant should do other than hold to sound accounting theory. He will handle partners' salaries as distributions of net income. He will *not* handle them as operating expense.

CLOSING THE BOOKS OF A PARTNERSHIP

The procedure which is followed in adjusting and closing the books of a single proprietorship is also the procedure for adjusting and closing the books of a partnership.

The balance of the Profit and Loss account is distributed to the partners in accordance with the provisions of the partnership contract.

Example:

Profit and Loss	8,000.00	
A. C. Bryce, Capital		4,000.00
E. K. Burger, Capital		4,000.00

To distribute profit to partners according to their profit and loss ratios (50% to each).

```
A. C. Bryce, Capital  . . . . . . . . . . . . . .      3,000.00
E. K. Burger, Capital . . . . . . . . . . . . . .      1,200.00
    A. C. Bryce, Drawing  . . . . . . . . . . . .                  3,000.00
    E. K. Burger, Drawing  . . . . . . . . . . .                   1,200.00
To transfer drawing account balances to partners' capital
accounts.
```

INTEREST ON PARTNERS' LOANS AND DRAWINGS

It is important to understand the true nature of interest which is debited or credited on partners' loans or drawings. Assume, for example, that A and B, sharing profits and losses equally, have the following balance sheet on December 31, 1949:

```
Assets . . . . . . . . . .   $50,000.00   A, Capital  . . . . . . . .   $25,000.00
                                          B, Capital  . . . . . . . .    25,000.00

                             $50,000.00                                 $50,000.00
```

On January 1, 1950, B, with the consent of A, converted one half of his capital credit to the status of a 6% loan payable. During 1950 operations of the firm — excluding interest on B's loan of $12,500.00 — yielded neither profit nor loss, i.e., the firm "broke even." There were no drawings, or changes in capital investments, during the year. On the basis of this data the preliminary balance sheet on December 31, 1950, would be

```
Assets . . . . . . . . . .   $50,000.00   A, Capital  . . . . . . . .   $25,000.00
                                          B, Capital  . . . . . . . .    12,500.00
                                          B, Loan  . . . . . . . . .     12,500.00

                             $50,000.00                                 $50,000.00
```

To recognize the interest on B's loan, the following entry may be made:

```
Interest Expense  . . . . . . . . . . . . . . . . . .   750.00
    B, Personal. . . . . . . . . . . . . . . . . . .                750.00
To record one year's interest on B's loan.
```

The Interest Expense account would be closed to Profit and Loss, the balance of the latter account being distributed as follows:

```
A, Capital . . . . . . . . . . . . . . . . . . . . . .   375.00
B, Capital . . . . . . . . . . . . . . . . . . . . . .   375.00
    Profit and Loss . . . . . . . . . . . . . . . . .               750.00
To distribute balance in latter account.
```

After giving effect to this entry the balance sheet will be:

Assets	$50,000.00	A, Capital	$24,625.00
		B, Capital	12,875.00
		B, Loan	12,500.00
	$50,000.00		$50,000.00

In view of the above accounting may it be concluded from the Profit and Loss account that the net loss for the year has been $750.00? That this is *not* the case may be proven by

(1) The fact that the net assets have remained unimpaired at $50,000.00. The evidence of a loss would be a reduction of $750.00 in net assets.

(2) The fact that the same balance sheet would have been produced if interest had been recognized by the following sole entry:

A, Personal.	375.00	
B, Personal.		375.00
To record interest on B's loan.		

This entry means, basically, that one half of the $750.00 interest cost is paid by A to B, and that the other one half is absorbed by B privately.

From the foregoing discussion we may conclude that

(1) True accounting net income or loss does not arise as the result of transactions between purely proprietary elements.

(2) True net income or loss is evidenced by a corresponding increase or decrease of net assets.

(3) Interest debits or credits on partners' loan or drawing accounts, and interest or penalties on deficiencies or excesses in partners' capital accounts, are purely and simply devices to equalize the relationships existing between the partners.

(4) Transactions between partners, and transactions with non-partners, are different in character.

This summary may be concluded by stating that interest adjustments between partners are normally handled through the Profit and Loss account and, normally, also appear on the profit and loss statement. While unsound theoretically, the practice is defended primarily on the grounds of accounting convenience and expediency. The desirability of this practice will be especially appreciated in cases where there are more than two partners or where the profit and loss ratios of partners are unequal. Although the "net income" figure of the profit and loss statement will not be correct when it includes interest (debited or credited to partners' accounts), it can be accepted by understanding the true nature of such interest items and the practical considerations which cause them to find placement on the profit and loss statement.

PARTNERSHIP FINANCIAL STATEMENTS

The form of the profit and loss statement for a partnership is the same as that for a single owner in the same line of business. The partnership profit and loss statement, if desired, may include a schedule showing the distribution of net income for the period, thus:

A and B

PROFIT AND LOSS STATEMENT
JANUARY 1 — DECEMBER 31, 1953

Sales	$60,000.00
Cost of Sales	39,000.00
Gross Profit.	$21,000.00
Expenses	12,000.00
Net Profit from Operations	$ 9,000.00

Net profit distributed as follows:

	A	B	TOTAL
In profit and loss ratios	$4,500.00	$4,500.00	$ 9,000.00

The balance sheet of a partnership, likewise, is similar to that of a single proprietorship in the same line of business, the only difference being that instead of one capital account, there will be one for each partner. On the partnership balance sheet, the capital accounts of partners should be totaled to show partnership net worth.

Partners may desire to have an explanation of the decrease or increase in their capital accounts at the end of the period as compared with that at the beginning. This information is furnished by a statement of capital.

Example:

X and Y

STATEMENT OF CAPITAL FOR THE YEAR ENDING DECEMBER 31, 19__

	X	Y	TOTAL
Capital, January 1, 19__	$20,000.00	$25,000.00	$45,000.00
Add:			
Capital additions in 19__	10,000.00		10,000.00
Profit for 19__	4,500.00	4,500.00	9,000.00
Total credits	$34,500.00	$29,500.00	$64,000.00

Less:

Capital withdrawals in 19__	$ 2,500.00		$ 2,500.00
Drawings	3,600.00	$ 3,000.00	6,600.00
Total debits	$ 6,100.00	$ 3,000.00	$ 9,100.00
Capital, December 31, 19__.	$28,400.00	$26,500.00	$54,900.00

A statement of capital furnishes partners with information which is not readily or advantageously includible on the profit and loss statement or the balance sheet. As a general rule only the net balance of each partner's capital account appears on the balance sheet.

QUESTIONS

Question **17–1.** What are the distinctive features of the partnership form of business organization?

Question **17–2.** Explain how a partnership may be formed.

Question **17–3.** You are called upon to draw up a partnership contract for A, B, and C. What specific provisions would you incorporate in such an agreement?

Question **17–4.** Name the distinctive features of partnership accounting.

Question **17–5.** Explain two ways of recording merchandise withdrawals by partners. Which method do you prefer? Why?

Question **17–6.** It is suggested that withdrawals of merchandise by partners be charged to Profit and Loss. Give your opinion of this suggestion.

Question **17–7.** "Drawings should be charged to Profit and Loss." Do you agree? Why?

Question **17–8.** Why is it desirable to keep partners' loans in separate accounts, i.e., why not include them with Accounts or Notes Receivable; or with Accounts or Notes Payable, as the case may be?

Question **17–9.** Explain two ways of accounting for partners' salaries. In a given case how would you proceed in deciding which method to use?

Question **17–10.** A bookkeeper is directed to charge the salaries of each partner, as due, against the capital account of each partner entitled to such salary. Explain whether or not you agree with these instructions, and why.

Question **17–11.** C and D are partners receiving monthly salaries of $400.00 each although their services to the firm are hardly worth more than $200.00 each. How would you, as an independent accountant, handle the item of partners' salaries in preparing the annual statements of the partnership?

PROBLEMS

Problem **17–1.** A and B, conducting like businesses, decide that a consolidation of their affairs will prove to be of mutual advantage. Their condensed balance sheets December 31, 1950, are:

	A	B
Cash	$ 20,000.00	$ 40,000.00
Notes Receivable	4,000.00	5,000.00
Accounts Receivable	42,000.00	38,000.00
Merchandise	29,000.00	35,000.00
Delivery Trucks	6,000.00	5,000.00
Fixtures and Racks	1,000.00	3,000.00
Office Furniture and Equipment	1,000.00	1,200.00
	$103,000.00	$127,200.00
Accounts Payable	$ 18,000.00	$ 16,000.00
Notes Payable	25,000.00	15,000.00
A, Capital	60,000.00	
B, Capital		96,200.00
	$103,000.00	$127,200.00

In organizing the new partnership A and B agree that the above balance sheet values are to be taken, except for the following revaluations of certain of A's assets:

Accounts Receivable	$38,000.00
Merchandise	24,000.00
Fixtures and Racks	nil

Required:

Make the opening entries for the books of the new partnership.

Problem **17–2.** The books of X and Y have been closed except for the following accounts which have the balances indicated:

X — Drawing	$ 6,000.00	
Y — Drawing	6,000.00	
Partners' Salaries	15,000.00	
Profit and Loss		$45,000.00

Required:

(1) Prepare the remaining closing entries. X and Y share profits equally. Salaries of partners are to be considered as a business expense.

(2) Prepare a statement of capital for X and Y for the year. At the beginning of the year each partner had a capital credit of $100,000.00.

Problem **17–3.** Interpret the following account:

F. H. MITCHELL, DRAWING

1950		1950	
Jan. 10	100.00	Jan. 31	250.00
31	150.00	Feb. 28	250.00
Feb. 28	250.00	Mar. 31	250.00
Mar. 20	300.00	Apr. 30	250.00
June 30	700.00	May 31	250.00
July 31	250.00	June 30	250.00
Aug. 31	250.00	July 31	250.00
Sept. 12	250.00	Aug. 31	250.00
		Sept. 30	250.00
		Oct. 31	250.00
		Nov. 30	250.00
		Dec. 31	250.00

How should the balance of this account be reflected in the balance sheet?

Problem **17–4.** On July 1, 19__, X loaned the partnership of X and Y $50,000.00. On December 31, 19__, when the books were being closed, X demanded a credit on his loan at the rate of 6 % per annum. Y objected, pointing out that there was no agreement to pay interest, and further, the hardship such a credit would work, the Profit and Loss account having, as the result of a difficult year, a credit balance of only $2,000.00. What would have been your decision?

Problem **17–5.** C and D formed a partnership, each agreeing to contribute $50,000.00 of capital. It was agreed, also, that if any partner's actual capital was less than $50,000.00, a charge should be made against the personal account of the partner for an amount equal to 10 % of the capital deficiency.

At the end of the first year it was found that the actual capital investments were: C, $50,000.00, and D, $40,000.00.

What accounting should be placed on the books to record the 10 % charge against D? Is this item genuine income to the partnership?

Problem **17–6.**

Doyle & Scott

PROFIT AND LOSS STATEMENT

YEAR ENDING DECEMBER 31, 19__

Sales		$100,000.00
Cost of Sales		50,000.00
Gross Profit		$ 50,000.00
Operating Expenses	$25,000.00	
Partners' Salaries	20,000.00	45,000.00
Net Profit from Operations		$ 5,000.00

Doyle & Scott

PROFIT AND LOSS STATEMENT

YEAR ENDING DECEMBER 31, 19___

Sales	$100,000.00
Cost of Sales	50,000.00
Gross Profit	$ 50,000.00
Operating Expenses	25,000.00
Net Profit from Operations	$ 25,000.00

Required:

(1) If the services of the two partners are reasonably worth $10,000.00 each, which of the two statements above is correct? Why?

(2) If you appraise the services of the partners as being reasonably worth $5,000.00 each, although the partners actually drew $10,000.00 each, what should the profit and loss statement be?

Problem **17–7.** The following trial balance is taken from the books of A and B on December 31, 19___:

Cash	$ 12,000.00	
Merchandise	10,000.00	
Miscellaneous Assets	29,000.00	
Sales		$ 56,000.00
Purchases	35,000.00	
General Expenses	12,000.00	
Partners' Salaries (A, $3,000.00; B, $5,000.00)	8,000.00	
A — Capital		24,000.00
A — Drawing	5,000.00	
B — Capital		26,000.00
B — Drawing		5,000.00
	$111,000.00	$111,000.00

Required:

(1) Make the entries to close the books of A and B. The new inventory of merchandise is $15,000.00.

(2) Prepare a statement of capital. During the year no changes have occurred in the balances of partners' capital accounts.

Problem **17–8.** Following is the trial balance of Frantz & Wilcox on December 31, 19___, giving effect to adjusting entries:

Cash	$ 5,838.00	
Accounts Receivable	13,000.00	
Notes Receivable	2,900.00	
Notes Receivable Discounted		$ 900.00
Merchandise Inventory	20,000.00	
Delivery Equipment	3,000.00	
Reserve for Depreciation — Delivery Equipment		1,250.00

Office Equipment	4,300.00	
Reserve for Depreciation — Office Equipment		1,000.00
Building (new)	12,000.00	
Land	3,000.00	
Prepaid Expenses	450.00	
Accounts Payable		16,550.00
Accrued Liabilities		900.00
Notes Payable		1,000.00
Mortgage Payable		5,000.00
J. N. Frantz, Capital		15,000.00
J. N. Frantz, Personal	4,200.00	
A. L. Wilcox, Capital		28,600.00
A. L. Wilcox, Drawings	8,000.00	
Sales		142,000.00
Returned Sales	2,000.00	
Sales Discounts	2,000.00	
Purchases	114,000.00	
Returned Purchases		1,400.00
Purchases Discounts		5,000.00
Freight In	1,000.00	
Advertising Expense	1,000.00	
Delivery Expense	600.00	
Depreciation Expense — Delivery Equipment	750.00	
Depreciation Expense — Office Equipment	430.00	
General Expense	700.00	
General Salaries	6,000.00	
Miscellaneous Sales Expense	2,500.00	
Sales Salaries	7,200.00	
Taxes	600.00	
Traveling Expense	2,400.00	
Utilities Expense	750.00	
Interest Income		438.00
Interest Expense	420.00	
	$219,038.00	$219,038.00

Additional Information

(1) The partnership contract calls for these annual salaries to the partners: Frantz, $3,000, and Wilcox, $5,000. These salaries, to be
handled as managerial expense on the statement of profit and
loss, have not yet been recorded on the books.

(2) After allowance of 8% interest per annum on capital investments
at the beginning of the accounting period, profits are to be shared
as follows: Wilcox, 60%, Frantz, 40%.

(3) The new inventory of merchandise on December 31, 19__, is
$32,000.

Required:

(1) Prepare a profit and loss statement for the year 19__.

(2) Prepare a balance sheet, December 31, 19__.

(3) Prepare a statement of capital, including itemized showing of distribution of income.

(4) Make the entries to close books.

Chapter 18

PARTNERSHIPS: DIVISION OF PROFITS AND LOSSES

The profits and losses of a partnership may be divided according to any one of the following bases:

(1) *Equally.* If the partnership contract is silent concerning the profit and loss ratio, it is the presumption of the law that profits and losses are to be divided equally.

(2) *According to agreed ratios.*

(3) *According to capital ratios.*

(4) *Interest on capital at an agreed per cent; remaining profits split equally, or as agreed.*

(5) *Salaries to partners, interest on capital, balance of profits split equally, or as agreed.*

The partnership contract should definitely state the method by which profits and losses are to be divided. The examples which follow illustrate the division of profits according to each of the several methods listed above. In each case the illustration begins with the following condensed ledger of A and B for the year ending December 31, 19—:

CASH		A, CAPITAL		A, DRAWING	
53,700.00			30,000.00	2,400.00	

B, CAPITAL		B, DRAWING		PROFIT AND LOSS	
	20,000.00	2,100.00			8,200.00

PROFITS DIVIDED EQUALLY

Closing entries under this method would be

Profit and Loss	8,200.00	
A, Capital		4,100.00
B, Capital		4,100.00
To divide the profits equally.		

A, Capital	2,400.00	
B, Capital	2,100.00	
A, Drawing		2,400.00
B, Drawing		2,100.00

To transfer drawing account balances to capital accounts.

PROFITS DIVIDED ACCORDING TO AGREED RATIOS

If A and B had agreed to share profits 70% and 30%, respectively, the closing entries would be

Profit and Loss	8,200.00	
A, Capital		5,740.00
B, Capital		2,460.00

To divide the profits, 70% to A, and 30% to B.

A, Capital	2,400.00	
B, Capital	2,100.00	
A, Drawing		2,400.00
B, Drawing		2,100.00

To transfer drawing account balances to capital accounts.

PROFITS DIVIDED ACCORDING TO CAPITAL RATIOS

The division of profits according to capital ratios implies that profits are realized chiefly through capital. The word "capital" may mean

(1) Original capital investment.
(2) Capital at the beginning of the accounting period.
(3) Capital at the end of the accounting period.
(4) Average capital invested during the accounting period.

Four capital ratios are therefore possible, each of which is illustrated herewith.

I. *Profits divided in ratio of original capital investments*

If, under this method, A and B had started in business with capitals of $24,000.00 and $16,000.00, respectively, they would have shared profits as follows:

Profit and Loss	8,200.00	
A, Capital		4,920.00
B, Capital		3,280.00

To divide the profits, $^{24}/_{40}$ to A, $^{16}/_{40}$ to B.

A, Capital	2,400.00	
B, Capital	2,100.00	
A, Drawing		2,400.00
B, Drawing		2,100.00

To transfer drawing account balances to capital accounts.

II. *Profits divided in ratio of capitals at beginning of period*

On January 1, 19—, A and B had capital credits of $25,000.00

and $20,000.00 respectively. On December 31, 19—, accordingly, the profits would be apportioned

Profit and Loss	8,200.00	
A, Capital		4,555.56
B, Capital		3,644.44

To divide the profits $^{25}/_{45}$ to A, and $^{20}/_{45}$ to B.

A, Capital	2,400.00	
B, Capital	2,100.00	
A, Drawing		2,400.00
B, Drawing		2,100.00

To transfer drawing account balances to capital accounts.

III. *Profits divided in ratio of capitals at end of period*

Under this plan closing entries would be

Profit and Loss	8,200.00	
A, Capital		4,920.00
B, Capital		3,280.00

To divide the profits, $^{30}/_{50}$ to A, and $^{20}/_{50}$ to B.

A, Capital	2,400.00	
B, Capital	2,100.00	
A, Drawing		2,400.00
B, Drawing		2,100.00

To transfer drawing account balances to capital accounts.

IV. *Profits divided according to average capitals invested during period*

To divide profits according to this method, the average capital employed in the business by each partner during the year must be computed. Assume that the capital accounts of A and B for 19— were as follows:

A, CAPITAL				B, CAPITAL			
19__		19__		19__		19__	
Jan. 31	10,000.00	Jan. 1 Bal.	25,000.00	Feb. 1	2,000.00	Jan. 1 Bal.	20,000.00
		June 30	5,000.00	June 30	10,000.00	Apr. 30	4,000.00
		July 31	8,000.00	Aug. 31	2,000.00	Nov. 30	10,000.00
		Nov. 1	2,000.00				

A's average capital would be computed as follows:

Capital Invested		Months Investment Remained Unchanged	Equivalent Investment for One Month
January 1 to January 31	$25,000.00	1	$ 25,000.00
February 1 to June 30	15,000.00	5	75,000.00
July 1 to July 31	20,000.00	1	20,000.00
August 1 to October 31	28,000.00	3	84,000.00
November 1 to December 31 . .	30,000.00	2	60,000.00
Number of months in period		12	
Total equivalent investment for one month			$264,000.00

Average investment for the year = $264,000.00 ÷ 12 = $22,000.00

B's average capital would be (computation condensed):

$$
\begin{aligned}
\$20{,}000.00 \times 1 &= \$\ 20{,}000.00 \\
18{,}000.00 \times 3 &= \ \ 54{,}000.00 \\
22{,}000.00 \times 2 &= \ \ 44{,}000.00 \\
12{,}000.00 \times 2 &= \ \ 24{,}000.00 \\
10{,}000.00 \times 3 &= \ \ 30{,}000.00 \\
20{,}000.00 \times 1 &= \ \ 20{,}000.00 \\
\hline
12\ )\ &\$192{,}000.00
\end{aligned}
$$

$$\$\ 16{,}000.00 = \text{Average capital}$$

Based upon these calculations, closing entries to distribute the profit of the year would be as follows:

Profit and Loss	8,200.00	
A, Capital		4,747.37
B, Capital		3,452.63

To divide the profits in average capital ratios, $^{22}/_{38}$ to A, $^{16}/_{38}$ to B.

A, Capital	2,400.00	
B, Capital	2,100.00	
A, Drawing		2,400.00
B, Drawing		2,100.00

To transfer drawing account balances to capital accounts.

The student should observe that the same allocation of profit would have resulted if the ratios $^{264,000}/_{456,000}$ and $^{192,000}/_{456,000}$ had been applied against the $8,200.00 profit figure. It is not necessary, therefore, to calculate the average capitals in order to obtain the correct average capital ratios for the year.

Where withdrawals and additions of capital are made during a month, it is more accurate to calculate the average investment on the basis of days rather than months. That is, each investment is multiplied by the number of days it remains unchanged; total day-dollars divided by total days gives the average investment for the period.

PROFITS DIVIDED BY ALLOWING INTEREST ON CAPITAL: BALANCE DIVIDED ACCORDING TO AGREEMENT

This method divides a part of the profits according to capital ratios and the remaining part according to agreement.

A and B agree to divide profits 60% and 40%, respectively, after 6% interest has been allowed on the balances of capital accounts at the beginning of the fiscal period.

To expedite consideration of this and later problems, the ledger of A and B on December 31, 19—, is reproduced from page 370:

CASH		A, CAPITAL		A, DRAWING	
53,700.00			30,000.00	2,400.00	

B, CAPITAL		B, DRAWING		PROFIT AND LOSS	
	20,000.00	2,100.00			8,200.00

The entries of A and B on December 31, 19—, would be

Profit and Loss	2,700.00	
A, Capital		1,500.00
B, Capital		1,200.00

To credit partners' capital accounts with 6% interest on capital investments at beginning of period (see p. 372).

Profit and Loss	5,500.00	
A, Capital		3,300.00
B, Capital		2,200.00

To distribute remaining balance in Profit and Loss account, 60% to A, and 40% to B.

A, Capital	2,400.00	
B, Capital	2,100.00	
A, Drawing		2,400.00
B, Drawing		2,100.00

To transfer drawing account balances to capital accounts.

Special Case (1):

Suppose that instead of a credit balance of $8,200.00, the Profit and Loss account carried a credit balance of only $1,200.00. This balance is less than 6% interest on the combined capitals. How shall the profits be divided? The correct entries would be

Profit and Loss	2,700.00	
A, Capital		1,500.00
B, Capital		1,200.00

To credit partners' capital accounts with 6% interest on capital investments at beginning of period.

A, Capital	900.00	
B, Capital	600.00	
Profit and Loss		1,500.00

To distribute remaining balance (debit) in Profit and Loss account, 60% to A, and 40% to B.

A, Capital	2,400.00	
B, Capital	2,100.00	
A, Drawing		2,400.00
B, Drawing		2,100.00

To transfer drawing account balances to capital accounts.

In other words, the net effect of the above entries is to distribute the net profit of $1,200.00: $600.00 to A, and $600.00 to B.

Special Case (2):

Suppose that operations for the year had resulted in a debit balance in the Profit and Loss account of $1,600.00. The entries to be made in this case, following the procedure above, are as follows:

Profit and Loss	2,700.00	
A, Capital		1,500.00
B, Capital		1,200.00

To credit partners' capital accounts with 6% interest on capital investments at beginning of period.

A, Capital	2,580.00	
B, Capital	1,720.00	
Profit and Loss		4,300.00

To distribute remaining balance (debit) in Profit and Loss account, 60% to A, and 40% to B.

A, Capital	2,400.00	
B, Capital	2,100.00	
A, Drawing		2,400.00
B, Drawing		2,100.00

To transfer drawing account balances to capital accounts.

In other words, the net effect of the above entries is to distribute the net loss of $1,600.00: $1,080.00 to A, and $520.00 to B.

Although interest in these three illustrations has been computed upon capital balances at the beginning of the period, it might have been calculated on any one of the three other capital bases:

(1) Original capital investment.
(2) Capital at the end of the accounting period.
(3) Average capital invested during the accounting period.

Obviously, the partnership contract should define the capital base upon which interest is to be computed. In the absence of such definition, the average capital base would be the most logical one to use.

The debit which is made to Profit and Loss to record the interest allowed to partners on their respective capitals must not be considered as an operating expense of the business. It is purely and simply a *partial distribution of profit*. This point must be clearly and definitely understood.

PROFITS DIVIDED BY ALLOWING SALARIES TO PARTNERS, INTEREST ON CAPITALS, AND BALANCE DIVIDED ACCORDING TO AGREEMENT

An excellent application of this method is to fix each salary at a level commensurate with the worth of each partner's services to the business, to allow a reasonable rate of interest on partners' capitals to compensate for unequal investments and then, having provided compensation for unequal personal services and unequal investments of capital, to divide all remaining profits equally. For example:

A and B, in their partnership contract, agree that annual profits and losses are to be divided as follows:

(1) Annual salaries: A, $2,700.00, B, $1,500.00.

(2) 6% interest on capital investments at the beginning of the period.

(3) Remaining balance in the Profit and Loss account to be divided equally.

In accordance with these provisions, the entries of A and B on December 31, 19—, would be

Profit and Loss	8,200.00	
A, Capital		4,850.00
B, Capital		3,350.00

To divide the net profit of the year as follows:

	Apportionment of profit to A	B	Profit
Salaries	2,700.00	1,500.00	
Interest on capital	1,500.00	1,200.00	
Balance of profit	650.00	650.00	
	4,850.00	3,350.00 =	8,200.00

A, Capital	2,400.00	
B, Capital	2,100.00	
A, Drawing		2,400.00
B, Drawing		2,100.00

To transfer balances of drawing accounts to capital accounts.

PROFIT AND LOSS ACCOUNT

The Profit and Loss account should exhibit a clear line of demarcation between the net income for the period and the distribution of that income. For instance:

PROFIT AND LOSS

			Credits			
Debits	xx xxx	xx	Credits	xx xxx	xx
in	x xxx	xx	in	x xxx	xx
detail	xxx	xx	detail	xxx	xx
Net Income ✓	8,200	00			
	212,000	00		212,000	00
Distribution of Net Income:			Net Income ✓	8,200	00
Salaries:					
A	2,700	00			
B	1,500	00			
Interest on Capital:					
A	1,500	00			
B	1,200	00			
Remainder:					
A — 50%	650	00			
B — 50%	650	00			
	8,200	00		8,200	00

The section of the Profit and Loss account in which the net income is distributed to partners' accounts is called the "distribution" or "appropriation" section of the Profit and Loss account.

QUESTIONS

Question **18–1.** The net assets of the partnership of A and B are $50,000.00. A's capital is $30,000.00, B's, $20,000.00. Upon the sale of the business for $60,000.00, A contends that since a capital profit has been realized, the $10,000.00 profit should be divided according to the capital ratios of the partners, and not equally, as periodic net income has been divided. Is A correct in his contention? Explain.

Question **18–2.** C and D, in partnership, have capitals of $20,000.00 and $5,000.00, respectively. Since the partnership agreement does not specify the basis upon which profits are to be divided, the partners turn to you for an opinion upon the question. How would you answer them?

Question **18–3.** Would you, in the above case, recommend a written agreement between the partners to divide profits according to their capital ratios?

Question **18–4.** What do you understand by the term "capital ratio"? Which capital ratio do you prefer, and why?

Question **18–5.** What is the purpose of allowing interest on capital?

What rate of interest should be used? Upon what capital base may interest be computed? Which base do you consider best? Why?

Question **18–6.** Is interest on capital an operating expense? Explain why it is debited to the Profit and Loss account.

Question **18–7.** X and Y agreed

(1) To furnish $20,000.00 capital each.
(2) To charge 10 % interest on any capital deficiency.
(3) To credit 6 % interest on any capital excess.

During the first year of operation, X actually furnished $16,000.00, and Y, $25,000.00. Their bookkeeper made the following interest entries at the end of the year:

X, Drawing	400.00	
Y, Drawing		400.00
To charge X with 10% interest on his capital deficiency of $4,000.00.		
X, Drawing	300.00	
Y, Drawing		300.00
To credit Y with 6% interest on his capital excess of 5,000.00.		

Are the entries correct? If you disagree with them, give the entries that you think should have been made.

Question **18–8.** A and B have equal capital accounts but share profits 60 % and 40 %, respectively. B proposes that the partnership agreement be amended to provide for 6 % interest on capital. What will be the effect of such a provision on the division of profits between A and B?

Question **18–9.** C and D have unequal capital investments but equal profit and loss ratios. Which partner will benefit by a provision to allow interest on capitals?

Question **18–10.** X and Y divide profits equally after 6 % interest has been allowed on capitals. The bookkeeper debits Interest Expense and credits each partner for his proportionate credit. Do you agree? Explain.

Question **18–11.** Distinguish between drawings and partners' salaries. When are partners' salaries to be regarded as distributions of profit and when as operating expenses?

Question **18–12.** As compensation for his management of the partnership of C and D, it is agreed that C shall receive 40 % of the net profits of the business. The profits for the year before providing for C's compensation are $8,400.00. C computes his bonus to be $3,360.00 but D computes it to be $2,400.00. Which figure is correct? Why?

Question **18–13.** A and B are partners. A proposes that $10,000.00 of the undrawn profits standing to the credit of his capital account be converted to a loan account with 6 % interest. B opposes the conversion, stating that the partnership has ample funds, enough, in fact, to permit the withdrawal of the entire $10,000.00 in cash should A desire to do so. What considerations are raised by A's proposal?

Question **18–14.** In 1948 A and B divided profits of $10,000.00 on a 70–30 basis. In 1949 they divided profits of $16,000.00 on a 60–40 basis. In 1950, when the profit and loss ratio was 50–50, it was discovered that the December 31, 1948, inventory was overstated $2,000.00 because of an error in the calculation of inventory. By means of journal entries show what adjustments should be made in the partners' capital accounts.

Question **18–15.** During the past calendar year X withdrew the following amounts from the partnership of X and Y:

$200.00 on the last day of each month, except November, when $350.00 was withdrawn.
$3,000.00 on August 7.

To what account, or accounts, should these withdrawals be debited?

PROBLEMS

Problem **18–1.** A and B share profits according to their average capital ratios. Their ledger accounts for the year just ended are:

A, CAPITAL

19__			19__		
June 1		4,000.00	Jan. 1 Balance		22,000.00
Sept. 1		5,000.00	Mar. 1		6,000.00
			Oct. 1		6,000.00

B, CAPITAL

19__			19__		
May 1		8,000.00	Jan. 1 Balance		50,000.00
July 1		2,000.00	Oct. 1		15,000.00
Sept. 1		5,000.00			

By means of journal entries distribute the profit for the year, $10,537.50.

Problem **18–2.** What is the average capital of the following account?

M. G. HILL, CAPITAL

19__			19__		
July 7		5,000.00	Jan. 1 Balance		18,000.00
Aug. 10		1,000.00	Feb. 14		2,000.00
			Oct. 11		10,000.00

Problem **18–3.** Following is the trial balance of a partnership doing business as the Coronation Trading Company:

Coronation Trading Company

TRIAL BALANCE, DECEMBER 31, 1950

Cash	$ 33,000.00	
Accounts Receivable	68,000.00	
Merchandise	37,900.00	
Accounts Payable		$ 6,800.00
A. B. Anderson, Capital		40,000.00
L. T. Bowman, Capital		50,000.00
G. S. Clark, Capital		60,000.00
A. B. Anderson, Drawing	7,000.00	
L. T. Bowman, Drawing	7,500.00	
G. S. Clark, Drawing	13,000.00	
Sales		491,500.00
Purchases	352,770.00	
Freight In	12,850.00	
Selling Expenses	71,080.00	
General Expenses	43,040.00	
Sales Discounts	2,160.00	
	$648,300.00	$648,300.00

The inventory of merchandise on December 31, 1950, is $25,800.00. The partnership agreement provides that profits shall be divided as follows:

(1) Interest at the rate of 5 % per annum on the opening balances in partners' capital accounts.

(2) Salaries of $5,000.00 each to Bowman and Clark; $10,000.00 to Anderson.

(3) Remaining profit to be divided: 1/6 to Anderson, 1/3 to Bowman, and 1/2 to Clark.

Required:

Prepare a balance sheet, December 31, 1950.

Problem **18–4.** A and B share profits 60 % and 40 %, respectively. The books have been closed for the year ending December 31, 19__, with the exception of providing for partners' salaries, and interest on capital. The only open accounts on the ledger are:

Sundry Assets	$85,200.00	
Liabilities		$15,000.00
A — Loan		10,000.00
A — Capital		20,000.00
A — Drawing	1,000.00	
A — Salary	3,000.00	
B — Capital		30,000.00
B — Drawing	3,000.00	
Profit and Loss		17,200.00
	$92,200.00	$92,200.00

Prepare the balance sheet for December 31, and also all necessary journal entries preliminary thereto. The following information should be considered:

(1) Each partner is entitled to a salary of $300.00 per month. Partners' salaries are to be considered as a device for the division of profits.

(2) In addition to salaries, partners are each permitted to make withdrawals against expected profits of $200.00 per month.

(3) Interest is to be allowed on capital at the annual rate of 6%.

Problem **18–5.** (a) If, in the trial balance of the preceding problem, the balance of the Profit and Loss account had been $8,200.00, what entries should be made to close the books for the year? (Under this set of conditions the balance of the Sundry Assets account will be $76,200.00.) What will be the new balance sheet?

(b) Suppose, instead, that operations for the year had resulted in a loss; and that the debit balance of the Profit and Loss account in the trial balance was $4,800.00. What entries should be made to close the books for the year? What will be the new balance sheet?

Problem **18–6.** Following is the condensed trial balance of the A, B, C partnership on December 31, 19__:

Miscellaneous Assets	$111,000.00	
Liabilities		$ 22,000.00
A — Capital		38,000.00
B — Capital		30,000.00
C — Capital		32,000.00
A — Drawing	5,000.00	
B — Drawing	3,000.00	
C — Drawing	4,000.00	
Sales		92,000.00
Merchandise	10,000.00	
Purchases	45,000.00	
Selling Expense	11,000.00	
Miscellaneous Expense	9,000.00	
Management Salaries (A, $3,000.00, B, $4,000.00, C, $5,000.00).	12,000.00	
Purchases Discounts		1,000.00
Fire Damage to Building	5,000.00	
	$215,000.00	$215,000.00

Required:

(1) Prepare a profit and loss statement for the year. New inventory, $11,000.00.

(2) Prepare a balance sheet, December 31, 19__. *Note:* It was mutually agreed that 5% interest was to be allowed on partners' end-of-the-year capitals of A, $38,000.00, B, $30,000.00, and C, $32,000.00. The profit and loss sharing ratios of the partners were A, 40%, B, 30%, and C, 30%.

(3) Prepare a statement of partners' capitals. During the year, A withdrew $12,000.00 of capital in addition to personal drawings of $5,000.00.

Problem **18–7.** The condensed ledger of A, B, and C at the end of 1950 was as follows:

ASSETS		LIABILITIES		PROFIT AND LOSS	
100,000.00			18,550.00		10,200.00

A, CAPITAL				B, CAPITAL			
May 1	12,000.00	Jan. 1	37,000.00	Apr. 1	5,000.00	Jan. 1	57,000.00
				Sept. 1	9,750.00	July 1	4,000.00

The partners agreed that profits and losses were to be divided as follows:

(1) Interest at 6 % was to be allowed on average capitals.
(2) Salaries were to be A, $3,600.00, B, $2,400.00, C, $1,200.00.
(3) Remaining profits were to be divided equally.

Prepare the final balance sheet for the year, also all journal entries preliminary thereto.

If, under other circumstances, the closing of the books had resulted in a debit balance in the account with C, indicate how you would have placed this item on the balance sheet.

Problem **18–8.** With the exception of providing for interest on B's loan, the accounts of A and B have been closed for the year ending December 31, 19__, as follows:

A, CAPITAL				B, CAPITAL			
Sept. 1	5,000.00	Jan. 1	40,000.00	June 1	5,000.00	Jan. 1	20,000.00
Oct. 31	10,000.00	July 15	25,000.00	Sept. 1	2,500.00	Apr. 1	15,000.00
						July 1	10,000.00
						Oct. 1	7,500.00

A, DRAWING		B, DRAWING	
3,000.00	2,000.00		2,000.00

MANAGEMENT SALARIES		ASSETS	
4,000.00		? ? ?	

PROFIT AND LOSS		B, LOAN	
	19,830.00		July 1 25,000.00

The partnership contract provides that

(1) Partners' salaries shall be $3,000.00 per year each. Salaries may be drawn by partners in equal monthly installments.

(2) In addition to their salary allowances, partners may draw against profits at the rate of $100.00 per month.

(3) Interest at the rate of 6 % shall be allowed on loans by partners to the firm.

(4) Interest at 8 % shall be allowed on average capitals employed during the accounting period.

(5) Except as provided above, profits and losses are to be shared, A, 60 %, and B, 40 %.

Required:

(1) Make journal entries to close the books.

(2) Prepare a balance sheet, December 31, 19__.

Problem **18–9.** On January 1, 1952, a partnership was formed whose articles of copartnership contained, among other things, the following provisions:

	Capitals	Salaries to be Allowed as Business Expense	Interest to be Allowed on Capitals	Profit and Loss Ratios
A	$100,000.00	$10,000.00	5%	33 $\frac{1}{3}$%
B	50,000.00	6,000.00	5%	26 $\frac{2}{3}$%
C	50,000.00	5,000.00	5%	20 %
D	40,000.00		5%	20 %

Before profits are apportioned in profit and loss ratios, D is to receive a special share of profit which, with his interest on capital, will total $10,000.00.

Required:

What profit must be earned by the partnership, before deductions for salaries and interest, to permit partner A to receive a total return from the partnership of $20,000.00?

Problem **18–10.** A and B were partners under an agreement that the profits were to be equally divided and that A was to furnish one fourth and B three fourths of the capital actually used during each calendar year, interest at 6 % per annum to be charged or credited on any differences.

Examine the following transcripts of their capital accounts and ascertain whether or not the entries at the end of the year were correctly made.

A, CAPITAL

1950			1950		
Sept. 1	Withdrawal	3,000.00	Jan. 1		10,000.00
Dec. 31	Interest on above for		Dec. 31	P & L	4,400.00
	4 months	60.00			

B, CAPITAL

1950				1950			
July	1	Withdrawal	2,000.00	Jan.	1		30,000.00
Dec.	31	Interest on above for		Dec.	31	P & L	4,400.00
		6 months	60.00				

Chapter 19

PARTNERSHIPS: PROBLEMS OF FORMATION AND DISSOLUTION

A partnership is legally dissolved upon any change in its personnel. The books, therefore, should be immediately closed (unless otherwise provided for by the articles of partnership) in order to determine each partner's capital interest *as of the date of dissolution*.

The legal dissolution of a partnership does not necessarily mean a break in the continuity of business operations. This may be avoided if new articles of partnership are immediately formed and signed. The books of the old partnership may, if desired, be continued as the books of the new partnership, provided a line of demarcation is established between the old and the new organizations.

PROBLEMS OF FORMATION

The entries to be made upon the books of a partnership when a new partner is admitted depend upon the terms under which a new partner receives entry to the business. These terms may be classified into the following accounting situations:

I. *Where capital is not contributed to the partnership by the new partner*

    CASE I–1: The new partner receives a share in the profits only.

    CASE I–2: The new partner purchases part, or all, of the interest of one of the old partners.

II. *Where capital is contributed to the partnership by the new partner*

    CASE II–1: No allowance is made for goodwill.

    CASE II–2: Goodwill may be credited either to
        (a) The old partners, or to
        (b) The new partner.

    CASE II–3: Instead of crediting any of the partners with goodwill, a capital bonus may be credited either to
        (a) The old partners, or to
        (b) The new partner.

Illustrations of each of these cases will now be given. Each example begins with the assumption that A and B, in partnership, have capitals of $9,000.00 and $15,000.00, respectively, and that profits and losses are shared equally.

CASE I–1: *The new partner receives a share in the profits only*

A and B admit C to partnership. C is to receive one third of the profits. Although C is not required to make any investment of capital, he is entitled to leave part, or all, of his profits in the business and thereby build up a capital interest.

No accounting entries are necessary here. It is well, however, to make a memorandum in the journal to the effect that a new partnership has been formed, and to describe the accounting features of the new agreement.

CASE I–2: *The new partner purchases part, or all, of the interest of one of the old partners*

B, with the consent of A, sells his interest in the business to C.

This is a purely personal transaction between B and C. Irrespective of the consideration which C pays to B, the books will show only that B's capital interest has now become the capital interest of C:

B, Capital	15,000.00	
C, Capital		15,000.00
To record the purchase of B's interest by C.		

In these two examples, CASE I–1 and CASE I–2, the amount of capital invested in the business does not change. In the examples which follow, the capital invested in the business is *increased*.

CASE II–1: *No allowance is made for goodwill*

A and B admit C to a one-third interest in the business by the investment of $12,000.00 cash. Total capital to be $36,000.00.

Since the total capital of the new partnership is to be $36,000.00, and since A and B together have $24,000.00, or two thirds, C's capital credit is obviously the amount of his contribution:

Cash	12,000.00	
C, Capital		12,000.00
To record investment by new partner, C, for a one-third interest in the capital and profits of the partnership.		

CASE II–2–(a): *Goodwill is credited to the old partners*

Successful operation of a business may provide it with a sales value in excess of its net assets. This excess is called goodwill. It is an intangible asset obviously belonging to those who have developed it.

A and B admit C to a one-third interest in the business by the investment of $15,000.00. Total capital to be $45,000.00.

In this case it is clear that C is entitled to a capital credit of one third of $45,000.00:

Cash	15,000.00	
C, Capital		15,000.00

To record investment by new partner, C, for a one-third
interest in the capital and profits of the partnership.

At this point the net assets of the partnership, as represented by the partners' capital accounts, are

A	$ 9,000.00	
B	15,000.00	
C	15,000.00	$39,000.00
which means that the goodwill must be		6,000.00
if the total capital is to be		$45,000.00

In other words, the business of A and B, which was capitalized at $24,000.00, is really worth more, i.e., $30,000.00. This difference, goodwill, belongs to A and B and is divided according to their profit and loss ratios:

Goodwill	6,000.00	
A, Capital		3,000.00
B, Capital		3,000.00

To credit A and B with the goodwill of their business.

After this entry has been posted, the capital accounts of the partners, as finally adjusted, will be

A, CAPITAL	B, CAPITAL	C, CAPITAL	TOTAL AGREED CAPITAL
9,000.00	15,000.00	15,000.00 =	$45,000.00
3,000.00	3,000.00		

CASE II–2–(b): *Goodwill is credited to the new partner*

A and B admit C to a one-third interest by the investment of $9,000.00. Total capital to be $36,000.00.

In this case C is entitled to a capital credit of one third of $36,000.00, or $12,000.00. The difference between this figure and C's cash contribution of $9,000.00 is the measure of the additional value, the goodwill, brought into the business by C. The correct entry to record C's admission to partnership is

```
Goodwill . . . . . . . . . . . . . . . . . . . . . . . .    3,000.00
Cash . . . . . . . . . . . . . . . . . . . . . . . . . . .  9,000.00
        C, Capital . . . . . . . . . . . . . . . . . . . .              12,000.00
```
To record investment by new partner, C, for a one-third
interest in the capital and profits of the partnership.

After this entry has been posted, the capital accounts of the partners will be:

A, CAPITAL	B, CAPITAL	C, CAPITAL	TOTAL AGREED CAPITAL
9,000.00	15,000.00	12,000.00	= $36,000.00

CASE II–3–(a): *A capital bonus is allowed the old partners*

A and B admit C to a one-third interest in the business by a cash investment of $15,000.00. Total capital to be $39,000.00.

This is virtually the same as CASE II–2–(a). The difference is that, instead of a total capital of $45,000.00, the capital is to be $39,000.00, the amount of the net tangible assets of the partnership. This means, in turn, that goodwill is not to be placed upon the books.

C is entitled to a capital credit of one third of $39,000.00, or $13,-000.00. He therefore pays $15,000.00 cash for a $13,000.00 interest in the partnership. The difference of $2,000.00 is a bonus to the old partners. The entry to admit C is

```
Cash . . . . . . . . . . . . . . . . . . . . . . . . . .  15,000.00
        A, Capital . . . . . . . . . . . . . . . . . . .               1,000.00
        B, Capital . . . . . . . . . . . . . . . . . . .               1,000.00
        C, Capital . . . . . . . . . . . . . . . . . . .              13,000.00
```
To record $15,000.00 investment by new partner, C;
$2,000.00 to be credited as bonus to A and B. C to have
an interest of one third in the capital and profits of the
partnership.

After this entry has been posted, the capital accounts of the partners will be

A, CAPITAL	B, CAPITAL	C, CAPITAL	TOTAL AGREED CAPITAL[1]
9,000.00	15,000.00	13,000.00	= $39,000.00
1,000.00	1,000.00		

---

[1] Another way of looking at this problem is to reason that if C is willing to pay $15,000.00 for a one-third interest in the business, the whole business must be worth $45,000.00. Since the tangible assets total $39,000.00, the goodwill must be $6,000.00,

CASE II–3–(b): *A capital bonus is allowed the new partner*

A and B admit C to a one-third interest in the business by a cash investment of $9,000.00. Total capital to be $33,000.00.

C's cash contribution is recorded as

Cash	9,000.00	
C, Capital		9,000.00
To record investment by new partner, C.		

a value belonging to A and B. If the goodwill were recognized on the books by the entry

Goodwill	6,000.00	
A, Capital		3,000.00
B, Capital		3,000.00
To credit A and B with the goodwill of their business.		

the accounts of the partnership would be

GOODWILL	OTHER ASSETS
6,000.00	39,000.00

A, CAPITAL	B, CAPITAL	C, CAPITAL
9,000.00 3,000.00	15,000.00 3,000.00	15,000.00

But the partners, being conservative, do not desire to have the uncertain asset of goodwill to remain permanently on the books. It is accordingly removed — written off as a loss to A, B, and C, because the write-off represents the eradication of an asset owned by the new partnership. After the following entry has been posted,

A, Capital	2,000.00	
B, Capital	2,000.00	
C, Capital	2,000.00	
Goodwill		6,000.00
To write off the asset goodwill.		

the accounts of the partnership will be:

GOODWILL		OTHER ASSETS
6,000.00	6,000.00	39,000.00

A, CAPITAL		B, CAPITAL		C, CAPITAL		TOTAL AGREED CAPITAL
2,000.00	9,000.00 3,000.00	2,000.00	15,000.00 3,000.00	2,000.00	15,000.00	= $39,000.00

The balances of these accounts are identical with those of the first solution to this problem.

But C should have a capital credit of one third of $33,000.00, or $11,000.00, and A and B together should have capital credits of two thirds of $33,000.00, or $22,000.00. The additional credit to C constitutes a loss to A and B, viz.:

A, Capital	1,000.00	
B, Capital	1,000.00	
C, Capital		2,000.00

To credit C with capital bonus. C is to have a one-third interest in the capital and profits of the partnership.

In effect, therefore, A and B are paying C $2,000.00 to join them in business.[2] After the above entries have been posted, the capital accounts of the partners will be

A, CAPITAL		B, CAPITAL		C, CAPITAL		TOTAL AGREED CAPITAL[3]
1,000.00	9,000.00	1,000.00	15,000.00		9,000.00	= $33,000.00
					2,000.00	

Addendum. — It is important to observe that in each of the problems above complete information was had on each of the following points:

(1) The total capital of the new partnership.
(2) The capitals of the old partners.
(3) The new partner's capital contribution and his capital credit.

Occasionally, a problem may be encountered where information on these points is not complete. The following problem, as an illustration, therefore permits two solutions:

---

[2] It would have been incorrect to have recorded the $2,000.00 bonus thus:

Goodwill	2,000.00
C, Capital	2,000.00

The capital accounts of the partners would then be:

A, CAPITAL	B, CAPITAL	C, CAPITAL
9,000.00	15,000.00	9,000.00
		2,000.00

giving a total capital of $35,000.00, which is contrary to the terms agreed to.

[3] This case is similar to CASE II–2–(b). Instead of a total capital of $36,000.00, the capital here is $33,000.00, the sum of the net tangible assets. This, of course, indicates that goodwill is not to be placed on the books.

If goodwill is written off in the problem in CASE II–2–(b), as we left it, the account balances will be identical with those presented in CASE II–3–(b).

A and B admit C to a one-third interest in the business by a cash investment of $15,000.00.

Solution (1):

$24,000.00 + $15,000.00 = $39,000.00 = Net Assets = Total Capital

C is to have a capital credit of one third of $39,000.00, or $13,000.00.

Entry (explanation omitted):

Cash	15,000.00	
A, Capital		1,000.00
B, Capital		1,000.00
C, Capital		13,000.00

Solution (2):

If a one-third interest is worth $15,000.00, the total capital must be three times that figure or $45,000.00.

Entries (explanations omitted):

Goodwill	6,000.00	
A, Capital		3,000.00
B, Capital		3,000.00
Cash	15,000.00	
C, Capital		15,000.00

In the absence of further information, either solution must be accepted as correct.

PROBLEMS OF DISSOLUTION

Consideration will now be given to some of the problems of accounting which arise in connection with partnership dissolution, i.e., those occasioned by

(1) The sale of the business.
(2) The retirement or the death of a partner.
(3) Liquidation of the business.

Sale of Partnership Business. — If the business is sold for a lump sum, any profit or loss on the sale should be distributed to the partners in their normal profit and loss ratios. For example,

A and B have the following balance sheet:

Cash	$ 2,000.00	Accounts Payable . . .	$ 6,700.00
Accounts Receivable . .	25,000.00		
Merchandise	8,000.00	A, Capital	16,000.00
Delivery Equipment . .	1,000.00	B, Capital	14,000.00
Office Equipment . . .	700.00		
	$36,700.00		$36,700.00

A and B sell their business, exclusive of cash, to John Doe for $30,000.00. The entries to record the sale, and close the books, are:

John Doe	30,000.00	
Accounts Payable	6,700.00	
Accounts Receivable		25,000.00
Merchandise		8,000.00
Delivery Equipment		1,000.00
Office Equipment		700.00
Profit on Sale of Business		2,000.00

To charge John Doe with net assets sold to him for a lump sum price of $30,000.00.

Profit on Sale of Business	2,000.00	
A, Capital . . . . : . .		1,000.00
B, Capital		1,000.00

To distribute profit to partners.

Cash	30,000.00	
John Doe		30,000.00

To record cash settlement.

A, Capital	17,000.00	
B, Capital	15,000.00	
Cash		32,000.00

To liquidate partners' capital accounts.

If the assets of a partnership have been appraised individually, the new valuations may be placed on the books through one or more adjusting entries. This is not general practice, however. Instead, the individual appraisals are incorporated into the explanatory data supporting the entry of sale. The difference, if any, between the price charged the purchaser and the book value of the net assets sold is a profit or loss on the sale. It should be distributed to partners in their profit and loss ratios. To illustrate:

Suppose that the assets of A and B had been individually appraised as follows:

	Book Value	Sales Value
Accounts Receivable.	$25,000.00	$24,000.00
Merchandise	8,000.00	10,000.00
Delivery Equipment	1,000.00	1,000.00
Office Equipment	700.00	700.00
Goodwill	0.00	1,000.00
	$34,700.00	$36,700.00

The entries to record the sale, and close the books, are as follows:

John Doe	30,000.00	
Accounts Payable	6,700.00	
Accounts Receivable		25,000.00
Merchandise		8,000.00

Delivery Equipment	1,000.00
Office Equipment	700.00
Profit on Sale of Business	2,000.00

To charge John Doe with net assets sold to him for a
price of $30,000.00, detailed as follows:

	Sales Price
Accounts Receivable	$24,000.00
Merchandise	10,000.00
Delivery Equipment	1,000.00
Office Equipment	700.00
Goodwill	1,000.00
	$36,700.00
Accounts Payable	6,700.00
	$30,000.00

Profit on Sale of Business	2,000.00	
A, Capital		1,000.00
B, Capital		1,000.00

To distribute profit to partners.

Cash	30,000.00	
John Doe		30,000.00

To record cash settlement.

A, Capital	17,000.00	
B, Capital	15,000.00	
Cash		32,000.00

To liquidate partners' capital accounts.

Conversion of Partnership to Corporation. — If a partnership is converted into a corporation, the conversion represents the sale of the net assets to the corporation. The partnership will record the sale, and close its books, in the manner illustrated above. Instead of cash, however, the partnership generally receives stock in the corporation. This asset will be debited to an account like "Stock in AB Corporation," for example. The liquidation of partners' capital accounts will be recorded by debits to partners' capital accounts and a credit to the asset account, "Stock in the AB Corporation."

An illustration of the accounting underlying the conversion of a partnership to a corporation is presented in Chapter 20.

Retirement or Death of a Partner. — The accounting procedure to be followed here is very similar to that which has just been described. The steps to be taken may be summarized thus:

(1) The books should be closed as of the date of dissolution (unless otherwise provided by the contract of partnership).

(2) Entries should be placed upon the books to record any revaluation of assets necessary to determine the capital claim of the

retiring partner, or the estate of the deceased partner. These revaluations, of course, must have been provided for by the articles of partnership. Gains or losses arising through revaluation should be credited or debited to the partners in their profit and loss ratios. When these revaluations are established, market or present values govern unless the articles of partnership provide otherwise.

With respect to the actual recording of asset revaluations, a conservative practice is to record only the increment or decrement belonging to the retiring partner. The only goodwill to be recorded, for instance, would be the amount actually credited to the capital account of the retiring partner. A conservative valuation is thus placed upon an asset whose value, at best, is problematical.

(3) The adjusted credit balance in the capital account of the retired, or deceased, partner's capital account should be transferred to a special accounts payable, or notes payable, account as the case may be. The liability thus set up will be discharged as provided for in the articles of partnership or, in lieu thereof, as otherwise agreed.

Liquidation of the Business. — Extreme care is necessary in distributing the cash of a partnership which is being liquidated. As a general rule, liabilities should be paid off first, then loans of partners, and, lastly, partners' capital accounts. Partners' unpaid salaries do not rank as preferred claims, there being no bona fide employer-employee relationship. Express partners' salaries, however, like other express and so-called "liabilities" to partners, take precedence over other kinds of partners' claims.

In no case, however, should any cash be paid to partners until all profits and losses have been distributed to capital accounts and the right of offset has been applied. Thus, a debit balance in a partner's capital account would be applied against the credit balance in his loan or salary account; only the difference would be disbursed.

Example:

A and B, sharing profits and losses equally, have the following balance sheet:

Cash	$ 2,000.00	Accounts Payable . . .	$ 6,700.00
Accounts Receivable . .	25,000.00		
Merchandise	8,000.00	A, Capital	16,000.00
Delivery Equipment . .	1,000.00	B, Capital	14,000.00
Office Equipment . . .	700.00		
	$36,700.00		$36,700.00

A and B decide to dissolve business. They realize the following amounts from the sale of their assets:

Accounts Receivable	$22,000.00
Merchandise	5,000.00
Delivery Equipment	1,200.00
Office Equipment	500.00

The accounting to care for the realization of assets and liquidation of liabilities is illustrated by the following entries:

Cash	28,700.00	
Accounts Receivable		22,000.00
Merchandise		5,000.00
Delivery Equipment		1,200.00
Office Equipment		500.00
To record cash received for assets sold.		
Dissolution Profit and Loss	6,000.00	
Delivery Equipment	200.00	
Accounts Receivable		3,000.00
Merchandise		3,000.00
Office Equipment		200.00
To transfer gains and losses to Dissolution Profit and Loss account.		
A, Capital	3,000.00	
B, Capital	3,000.00	
Dissolution Profit and Loss		6,000.00
To transfer loss to partners in their profit and loss ratios.		
Accounts Payable	6,700.00	
Cash		6,700.00
To record payment of liabilities.		
A, Capital	13,000.00	
B, Capital	11,000.00	
Cash		24,000.00
To liquidate partners' capital accounts.		

A number of specialized accounting problems arise where partnership liquidation is slow and where it is desired to disburse periodically such cash as may have been collected. Because of the care necessary in such situations, and the responsibilities involved, the liquidator should be thoroughly familiar with the best procedure of liquidation. For this information reference should be made to Chapter 31 of the author's *Advanced Accounting.*

QUESTIONS

Question **19–1.** B dies. Explain when and why the partnership books of A and B should be closed.

Question **19–2.** Explain why A and B might admit C to partnership under terms of no capital contribution but a share in the profits of the business.

Question **19–3.** B, whose capital interest in the partnership of A and B is $50,000.00, sells 40% of his interest to C for $30,000.00. What entry should be made on the partnership books? What will the new profit and loss ratios be?

Question **19–4.** What is the relationship between goodwill and capital bonus? Illustrate.

Question **19–5.** Goodwill of $12,000.00 is set up on the books just prior to

(1) The admittance of C as partner.
(2) The sale of the entire business to X, Y, and Z.

In each case, how should the goodwill be divided between A and B?

Question **19–6.** For what reasons may a partnership be dissolved?

Question **19–7.** How should profits and losses upon the sale of partnership assets be divided between the partners? Why?

Question **19–8.** A partner dies. How would you proceed to determine the amount of the claim of his estate?

Question **19–9.** What considerations should guide you in distributing the cash of a partnership which is being dissolved and liquidated?

PROBLEMS

Problem **19–1.** X and Y are partners, sharing profits and losses in the ratios of 60% and 40%, respectively. X has a capital credit of $25,200.00, and Y, $10,800.00. In each of the problems which follow (1) prepare all necessary journal entries, and (2) set up the final capital credit of each partner. Each problem should be considered independently, i.e., beginning with X's capital of $25,200.00, and Y's capital of $10,800.00.

(1) Z is admitted to partnership and a 20% share in the profits in return for his services but no capital investment.
(2) Z buys one half of X's interest in the business for $15,000.00 cash.
(3) X and Y admit Z to a one-third interest in the business by investing, and receiving credit for, $20,000.00 cash.
(4) X and Y admit Z to a one-third interest in the business by a cash investment of $15,000.00. Total capital to be $51,000.00.
(5) X and Y admit Z to a one-third interest by a cash investment of $15,000.00. Total capital to be $54,000.00.
(6) X and Y admit Z to a one-third interest by a cash investment of $20,000.00. Total capital to be $57,000.00.
(7) X and Y admit Z to a one-third interest by a cash investment of $24,000.00. Total capital to be $72,000.00.
(8) X and Y admit Z to a one-third interest in the business by a cash investment of $18,000.00.
(9) X and Y admit Z to a one-third interest by a cash investment of $18,000.00. Total capital to be $45,000.00. X, Y, and Z agree

that the capital interest of each partner in the new partnership shall be exactly equal to the new profit and loss interest of each partner. (After allowing for Z, X and Y are to continue sharing profits in the ratio of 60–40.)

(10) X and Y admit Z to a one-third interest in the business by a cash investment of $20,100.00. Two solutions.

(11) If Z's interest in the profits were to be $33\frac{1}{3}\%$, what profit and loss ratios would you allocate to X and Y?

Problem 19–2. A and B, whose capitals are $20,000.00 and $40,000.00, respectively, admit C to a 25% interest in the business upon payment of $12,000.00. Total capital of the new partnership is to be $72,000.00. The following entry is made:

Cash	12,000.00	
Goodwill	6,000.00	
C, Capital		18,000.00

Do you agree? Explain.

Problem 19–3. X and Y are partners with capitals of $65,000.00 and $55,000.00, respectively. They share profits in a 60–40 ratio.

X and Y admit Z to a one-third interest in the net assets, and profits, of the partnership with the understanding that

(1) Z is to pay $60,000.00 cash for his interest.
(2) All partners are to have equal capitals of $40,000.00 each; net assets of the firm to be $120,000.00.
(3) Profits and losses of the new partnership are to be shared equally.
(4) No goodwill account is to be opened.

Required:

(1) Make the entry to record the admittance of Z to the partnership.
(2) Make the entry showing the disbursement of cash to X and Y.

Problem 19–4. The balance sheet of A and B on January 1, 1955, is

Assets	$70,000.00	A, Loan	$10,000.00
		A, Capital	38,000.00
		B, Capital	22,000.00
	$70,000.00		$70,000.00

A and B admit C to a one-third interest in the partnership by an investment of $38,000.00 cash which is credited to his capital account. Record this on the books and set up the new balance sheet.

They agree further that

(1) Interest at 6% is to be allowed on average capital employed during the year.
(2) Salaries are to be allowed: A, $2,680.00; B, $3,600.00; and C, $5,060.00.

(3) Profits are to be shared equally.

As of December 31, 1955, operating profits, before salaries and interest, are $24,000.00. The general ledger is:

ASSETS		ACCOUNTS PAYABLE	
150,000.00			6,000.00

PROFIT AND LOSS		A, LOAN	
	24,000.00		10,000.00

A, CAPITAL

May 1	36,000.00	Jan. 1 Balance	46,000.00

B, CAPITAL

Sept. 1	10,000.00	Jan. 1 Balance	30,000.00
Nov. 1	10,000.00	July 1	30,000.00

C, CAPITAL

		Jan. 1 Balance	38,000.00
		July 1	22,000.00

Required:

(1) Distribute the $24,000.00 profit to the partners. Set up the new balance sheet.

(2) Prepare a statement of capital for the partners for the year ending December 31, 1955.

Problem **19–5.** The partnership agreement of X, Y, and Z specifies capital contributions and profit and loss ratios as given below. It further provides that in the event a partner's average capital is less than his agreed contribution, he is to be charged 8% interest on his deficiency; if more, he is to be credited with 6% interest on his excess.

Annual salaries are also provided for: X, $2,000.00, Y, $3,000.00, and Z, $5,000.00. Salaries may be drawn in quarterly installments, but no interest is to be allowed on undrawn salaries. During the year the following actual payments of salary were made: X, $2,000.00, Y, $2,000.00, and Z, $2,400.00.

The actual average capital investments of the partners for the past calendar year were

| P & L Ratio | Agreed Investment | Actual Average Capital Investment for Three Months Ending | | | |
		March 31	June 30	Sept. 30	Dec. 31
X 20%	$20,000.00	$20,000.00	$16,000.00	$26,000.00	$22,000.00
Y 30%	30,000.00	20,000.00	25,000.00	28,000.00	30,000.00
Z 50%	50,000.00	20,000.00	30,000.00	34,000.00	43,000.00

The net profit of the partnership for the year as reflected by the balance of the Profit and Loss account was $9,436.00. The capital account balances of the partners on December 31 before giving effect to interest, salaries, and profits, were X, $22,000.00, Y, $30,000.00, and Z, $43,000.00.

You are requested to prepare the balance sheet of the partnership as of December 31. There were no liabilities.

Problem **19–6.** X and Y have the following balance sheet:

Cash	$ 3,000.00	Accounts Payable . . .	$10,000.00
Accounts Receivable . .	37,500.00		
Merchandise	12,000.00	X, Capital	25,000.00
Delivery Equipment . .	1,500.00	Y, Capital	20,000.00
Office Equipment . . .	1,000.00		
	$55,000.00		$55,000.00

X and Y sell their business, except cash, to Z and Z for $60,000.00. Z and Z take over the business immediately and one month later give their check for $60,000.00 to X and Y in settlement of purchase.

Required:

(1) Present the entries to close the books of X and Y.

(2) What would your closing entries have been if the assets had been appraised as follows: accounts receivable, $35,000.00, merchandise, $15,-000.00, delivery equipment, $1,200.00, office equipment, $800.00, and goodwill, $18,000.00? What entry should be made to open the books of Z and Z?

Problem **19–7.** A and B established a partnership in which A invested a building valued at $50,000.00, and land valued at $30,000.00. B invested cash of $25,000.00 in the partnership bank account. B was to act as manager. Profits and losses were to be divided equally.

During the night of the first twenty-four hours of the partnership, the building was burned to the ground. Since the building was not insured, the loss was heavily felt. The partners decided that it was purposeless for them to start operations anew. With this decision, A took back his land, and the $25,000.00 of cash was disbursed.

Required:

Make the entry showing the disbursement of the cash.

Problem **19–8.** The balance sheet of Lee & Ellison on December 31, 19___, was as follows:

Cash	$ 5,000.00	Accounts Payable	$ 38,000.00
Accounts Receivable . $10,000.00			
Less Reserve for Bad Debts . . 2,000.00	38,000.00	A. N. Lee, Loan	30,000.00
Merchandise	40,000.00	A. N. Lee, Capital	20,000.00
Fixed Assets	75,000.00	G. R. Ellison, Capital . . .	70,000.00
	$158,000.00		$158,000.00

Profits and losses have been shared, Lee, 40 %, and Ellison, 60 %. The partnership was dissolved as of December 31, 19___. The accounts receivable were subsequently sold for $30,000.00, the merchandise for $33,000.00, and the fixed assets for $50,000.00. All cash was paid to those entitled to receive it. Frame all journal entries to wind up the partnership.

Problem **19–9.** A, B, and C have the following balance sheet on December 31, 19___:

Cash	$ 2,000.00	Accounts Payable . . .	$10,000.00
Accounts Receivable . .	30,000.00		
Merchandise	10,000.00	A, Capital	12,000.00
Delivery Equipment . .	2,000.00	B. Capital	12,000.00
Office Equipment . . .	1,000.00	C. Capital	11,000.00
	$45,000.00		$45,000.00

C dies on January 27 of the next year. It is ascertained that operating profits for the period, January 1 to January 27, amount to $372.00.

The assets are appraised as follows:

	Book Value, January 27	Appraised Value, January 27
Cash	$ 3,200.00	$ 3,200.00
Accounts Receivable	26,000.00	25,100.00
Merchandise	12,000.00	15,000.00
Delivery Equipment.	2,000.00	1,400.00
Office Equipment	1,000.00	1,000.00
Goodwill . . . . . :	nil	6,000.00
	$44,200.00	$51,700.00

The liabilities of the partnership, as of the close of business January 27, amount to $8,828.00.

Required:

Close the books of the partnership. The business is continued under the name of A and B. C's claim is to be liquidated over a period not to exceed two years.

Problem **19–10.** The condensed balance sheet of a partnership is as follows:

Assets	$65,000.00	R, Capital	$20,000.00
		S, Capital	20,000.00
		T, Capital	20,000.00
		T, Loan	5,000.00
	$65,000.00		$65,000.00

T subsequently died. The liability to T's estate as determined in accordance with the articles of partnership was as follows:

Capital	$20,000.00
Share of net income for period	2,500.00
Share of revaluation of assets (not including goodwill)	3,000.00
Share of goodwill (the asset goodwill was not carried on the books).	2,000.00
Loan	5,000.00
	$32,500.00

Through arrangements made with R and S, X enters the partnership of R and S by assuming and paying the liability of the partnership to the estate of T. The total capital of the new partnership was to be $87,500.00 of which X's share was $32,500.00. R, S, and X were to share profits and losses equally.

What entries should be made on the books of the partnership?

Problem **19–11.** Following is the balance sheet of A, B, and C:

Assets	$80,000.00	Accounts Payable . . .	$25,000.00
		A, Loan Payable . . .	12,500.00
			P & L
			Ratios
		A, Capital . . . 40%	7,500.00
		B, Capital . . . 20%	15,000.00
		C, Capital . . . 40%	20,000.00
	$80,000.00		$80,000.00

The partners decide to dissolve their partnership. The assets realize $60,000.00 cash.

Required:

Make the journal entries to close the books of the partnership.

Problem **19–12.** Following are the open accounts on the ledger of the partnership of W, X, Y, and Z:

Cash . . . . . :	$ 2,600.00	
Noncash Assets	66,000.00	
Accounts Payable		$18,000.00
W, Loan Payable		10,000.00
W, Capital		5,000.00

X, Capital		15,000.00
Y, Capital		20,000.00
Z, Capital		5,000.00
Z, Drawing	4,400.00	
	$73,000.00	$73,000.00

The profit and loss sharing ratios of the partners were: W, 30%, X, 20%, Y, 40%, and Z, 10%.

In the dissolution of the business, the noncash assets were converted into $42,000.00 cash.

Required:

By means of journal entries, distribute the cash on hand to those who are entitled to receive it. (There is no accrued interest on W's loan. Z has no property other than his interest in the partnership.)

Problem 19-13. The balance sheet of Raye & Wilson on January 1, 19—, was:

Cash		$ 10,000.00	Accounts Payable		$ 25,000.00
Accounts Re-			Notes Payable		15,000.00
ceivable . .	$21,000.00				
Rsv. for				*P & L*	
Bad Debts	1,000.00	20,000.00	*Partners*	*Ratios*	
			J. C. Raye	56¼%	50,000.00
Merchandise		50,000.00	John F. Wilson . .	33¾%	40,000.00
Real Estate		60,000.00	Roy S. Wilson . .	10 %	10,000.00
		$140,000.00			$140,000.00

Real estate costing $40,000.00 is sold for cash, $60,000.00. Roy S. Wilson then retires from partnership, receiving cash for his interest.

After the retirement of Roy S. Wilson, the remaining partners decided to liquidate their business. The accounts receivable were sold for $15,000.00, and the merchandise for $40,000.00, all cash. The remaining real estate was sold for $30,000.00 to the holder of the note payable, who paid $15,000.00 cash, and canceled the note payable of $15,000.00. All cash on hand was then paid out to the proper parties.

Required:

(1) Make the entry to record the cash settlement with Roy S. Wilson.

(2) After the retirement of Roy S. Wilson, what will be the equitable profit and loss ratios of the remaining two partners?

(3) Make the entries to disburse the cash to J. C. Raye and John F. Wilson.

Problem 19-14. On June 30, 19—, the trial balance of XYZ was:

Cash	$ 24,500.00	
Accounts Receivable	19,000.00	
Notes Receivable	7,000.00	
Reserve for Bad Debts		$ 3,000.00

Merchandise	43,000.00	
Miscellaneous Equipment	30,000.00	
Reserve for Depreciation — Miscellaneous Equipment		15,000.00
Delivery Equipment	2,500.00	
Reserve for Depreciation — Delivery Equipment		1,000.00
Accounts Payable		11,000.00
X — Capital		20,000.00
Y — Capital		50,000.00
Z — Capital		50,000.00
X — Drawing	5,000.00	
Y — Drawing	5,000.00	
Z — Drawing	5,000.00	
Sales		200,000.00
Purchases	151,000.00	
Selling Expenses	38,000.00	
General Expenses	20,000.00	
	$350,000.00	$350,000.00

As of the date of this trial balance, X was to take over the business of the partnership. Preliminary to this change-over, it was mutually agreed

(1) To close partners' drawing accounts.
(2) To close the partnership books as of June 30, 19___.
(3) To liquidate the old partnership.
(4) To pay all partnership liabilities.

To complete the formal closing of the books of the partnership, the following information is applicable:

(1) Bad debts: estimated at 1 % of sales.
(2) Annual depreciation rates: miscellaneous equipment, 10 %, delivery equipment, 20 %.
(3) New inventories at cost were: merchandise, $54,000.00, sales supplies, $1,000.00, office supplies, $500.00.

X's purchase of the partnership assets was based on the following mutually accepted sales values:

Accounts receivable (net)	$ 14,000.00
Notes receivable	7,000.00
Merchandise	60,000.00
Miscellaneous equipment (net)	10,000.00
Delivery equipment (net)	500.00
Sales supplies	1,000.00
Office supplies	500.00
Goodwill	7,000.00
	$100,000.00

Payment by X for the total of the assets taken over by him was made by

(1) Cash in the amount of $20,000.00 from the private funds of X.
(2) Application of the balance in X's capital account to the purchase price, and

(3) Two notes payable each for one half of the balance due. One of these notes was due in one year, the other in two years.

Required:

(1) Make the journal entries to close the books of the partnership.

(2) Make the entries to open a new set of books for X.

(3) Prepare the balance sheet of X, giving effect to all of the foregoing transactions. In addition X invested cash of $12,166.68 in his business.

Problem 19-15. Following is the balance sheet of X, Y, and Z:

Assets	$55,000.00	Accounts Payable	$ 8,250.00
		X, Loan	5,500.00
		X, Capital	20,630.00
		Y, Capital	13,748.00
		Z, Capital	6,872.00
	$55,000.00		$55,000.00

The partners share profits and losses equally.

In the dissolution of the business, the assets realize $40,000.00 in cash.

Required:

(1) Show all entries necessary to wind up the books of the partnership. Z has no assets other than his investment•in the partnership.

(2) Suppose the assets had realized cash of (a) $21,880.00, (b) $17,-860.00, (c) $6,700.00. What accounting should have been followed in each case?

In case (b) assume that, when the cash is disbursed, there is some doubt as to whether Y will be able to make good the debit balance in his account. Then assume, further, that thirty days later, a check is received from Y covering the amount of his deficiency.

Problem 19-16.

Clark, Jones, & Husen

BALANCE SHEET, DECEMBER 31, 1952

Cash	$13,000.00	Accounts Payable			$18,000.00
Accounts Receivable	15,000.00		*P & L*		
Merchandise	17,000.00		*Ratios*		
Fixed Assets	10,000.00	L. A. Clark, Capital	20%		10,000.00
		S. M. Jones, Capital	30%		12,000.00
		A. R. Husen, Capital	50%		15,000.00
	$55,000.00				$55,000.00

Desiring to go into business for himself, Mr. Clark retires from partnership and offers to settle his capital claim for $9,200.00 cash if payment is made immediately. This offer is accepted and a check is issued to Mr. Clark for $9,200.00. Jones and Husen agree that they will continue to share the profits of the business in the same ratio as heretofore.

At the end of 1953, net income for the year is found to be $5,600.00. On December 31, 1953, the assets were cash, $4,400.00, accounts receivable, $16,000.00, merchandise, $18,600.00, and fixed assets (after reserve for depreciation, $1,000.00), $9,000.00.

Neither of the partners added assets to or withdrew assets from the business during the year.

Because of their low cash position, the partners decided that a reorganization was necessary. They accordingly admitted K. M. Wilford to partnership by accepting from him the following assets and liability: cash, $10,000.00, accounts receivable (after a reserve of $3,000.00), $12,000.00, merchandise, $7,000.00, and accounts payable, $9,000.00.

It was further agreed that Jones and Husen were to be granted a goodwill of $5,000.00, and that Jones and Husen were each to contribute sufficient cash to bring their capital account balances up to $20,000.00 and $25,000.00, respectively.

The new profit and loss ratios were: Jones, 30%, Husen, 40%, and Wilford, 30%.

It was further agreed that goodwill was to be written off before the new partnership commenced actual operations.

Required:

(1) Prepare the balance sheet of the new partnership of Jones, Husen, and Wilford.

(2) Make the entries to record the above transactions. The books of the first partnership were continued in use by the new partnerships.

Chapter 20

CORPORATIONS: INTRODUCTORY CONSIDERATIONS

DEFINITIONS

A corporation has been defined by Chief Justice Marshall as "an artificial being, invisible, intangible, and existing only in contemplation of law." [1] More recently the United States Supreme Court has defined a corporation as "an association of individuals united for some common purpose and permitted by law to use a common name and to change its members without a dissolution of the association."

WHY CORPORATIONS ARE FORMED

The corporate form of business organization is widely used. The main advantages claimed are these:

(1) The corporation may operate indefinitely. In the majority of states it is possible to procure charters of perpetual life.

(2) The liability of each proprietary interest is limited. As a general rule creditors of a corporation may levy only against business assets, i.e., those owned by the corporation.

(3) Ownership of the corporation may be centralized or widely diffused.

(4) The corporate form of business organization is especially well adapted to businesses which require large investments of capital.

---

[1] "A corporation is an artificial being, invisible, intangible, and existing only in contemplation of law. Being the mere creature of law, it possesses only those properties which the charter of its creation confers upon it, either expressly or as incidental to its very existence. These are such as are supposed best calculated to effect the object for which it was created. Among the most important are immortality, and, if the expression may be allowed, individuality; properties by which a perpetual succession of many persons are considered as the same and may act as a single individual. They enable a corporation to manage its own affairs, and to hold property without the perplexing intricacies, the hazardous and endless necessity of perpetual conveyances for the purpose of transmitting it from hand to hand. It is chiefly for the purpose of clothing bodies of men, in succession, with these qualities and capacities that corporations were invented and are in use. By these means a perpetual succession of individuals are capable of acting for the promotion of the particular object, like one immortal being." — *Dartmouth College* v. *Woodward*, 4 Wheaton (U.S.) 518 (1819).

(5) The corporate form of business organization encourages the formation of new businesses.

(6) Ownership interests may be transferred readily without affecting the life or the business of the corporation.

(7) The corporation possesses greater flexibility for purposes of financing than do other forms of business organization.

(8) To some extent the corporation has an advantage in achieving mobility, flexibility, and efficiency in its management and, as a corollary, in the administration of its internal affairs as well.

These advantages are important but they are offset by some disadvantages. Whether or not it is true that corporations have sometimes been guilty of economic waste and of practices which are unethical and antisocial, they are subject to considerable public regulation, inquiry, and interference with their affairs. This burden is one of heavy expense. Corporations, further, are subject to special fees and taxes (like franchise taxes), as well as especially high rates of income taxation.

It is not advisable for the purpose of this text to attempt a full description and discussion of the corporate form of business organization. For a detailed presentation of this subject, a standard text on corporate finance and business organization should be consulted.

NATURE OF THE CORPORATION

A corporation is a legal entity. It is distinct and separate from its owners, the stockholders. All transactions with the corporation must be in the name of the corporation. No stockholder, as such, may act for the corporation or for other stockholders. A stockholder is *not* an agent of either the corporation or its stockholders.

Title to the assets of the business rests in the corporation and not in the names of those who own it. Legal proceedings must be brought in the name of the corporation. In the eyes of the law the corporation is a legal individual.

No liability, either to the corporation or to its creditors, attaches to stockholders who have paid par for their stock or, in the case of no par stock, who have paid their capital stock subscriptions in full. Creditors may attach corporate assets only.[2] The capital of a cor-

---

[2] An exception to this rule is the double liability which has rested upon stockholders of banking corporations by state and federal laws. This meant that a purchaser of $1,000.00 par value bank stock was liable for another $1,000.00 for the benefit of creditors of the bank.

The Banking Act of 1935 provided that double liability with respect to stockholders of national banks would cease on and after July 1, 1937. Repeal of double liability became a practical reality on and after July 1, 1937, provided that the banking laws of the several states were amended to permit such repeal. New York, by enactment of May 29, 1936, made such an amendment. Double liability in New York ended July 1, 1937, provided published notice was given by banks six months in advance.

poration, therefore, is expected to remain for the protection of creditors; in a partnership this is not required.

A corporation possesses continuous existence. Dissolution occurs by

(1) Voluntary surrender of charter by stockholders.

(2) Expiration of the period for which the corporation was formed.

(3) Order of court.

(4) Breach of corporation laws.

The life of a corporation, consequently, is not affected by changes in the personnel of its ownership.

Dividends are payable to stockholders if earned, and only by formal declaration of the board of directors. Proprietary drawing accounts do not exist.

Management is centralized, responsibility is fixed. A partnership, on the other hand, often has its lines of authority divided, to the detriment of unified policy and responsible leadership.

FORMATION OF THE CORPORATION

The steps to form a corporation are briefly as follows:

(1) A charter application, signed by three or more incorporators, and notarized, is filed with the secretary of the state in which the business is to be incorporated. This application covers such information as

(a) Name and address of the corporation.

(b) Kind of business.

(c) Capital stock. Amount and number of shares for each class of stock.

(d) Incorporators; names and addresses.

(e) Period for which formed.

(f) Names and addresses of subscribers to the corporation's capital stock. Shares subscribed for by each.

(g) Number of directors. Names and addresses of directors until first meeting of stockholders.

(h) That incorporators are of age, that two thirds of them are U. S. citizens, etc.

(2) Upon approval by the Secretary of State, and the payment of filing fees, the application becomes the company's charter, its authority to operate as a corporation.

(3) The stockholders meet to elect directors and to adopt bylaws to govern the internal administration of the corporation.

(4) The directors meet and appoint the officers of the company.

CAPITAL STOCK

The authorized capital for which a company is incorporated is known as its "authorized capital stock." Capital stock, representing the legal ownership of a corporation, is divided into "shares" of ownership. Each share is equal in value, which may be anywhere from $1.00 to $1,000.00.

Example:

The X Corporation is capitalized for $100,000.00. The capital stock is divided into 1,000 equal parts of $100.00 each, each such part being called a "share" and representing a $\frac{1}{1000}$ ownership interest in the corporation.

Each share is an ownership right to participate ratably in the

(1) Management through the exercise of voting rights.
(2) Profits when declared as dividends.
(3) Assets upon dissolution of the corporation.
(4) New *issues* of capital stock to the extent necessary to protect the privileges named in (1), (2), and (3).

These shares of ownership have their physical evidence in the form of stock certificates issued by the corporation to the owner. For instance, a purchaser of eight shares of stock of the X Corporation would receive a stock certificate for eight shares of stock as evidence of his $\frac{8}{1000}$ ownership of the corporation.

Stock certificates are numbered serially and have two pen-and-ink signatures in addition to the printed signatures of the secretary and president of the corporation. The pen-and-ink signatures are those of

(1) The registrar, whose signature certifies that the certificate is genuine.
(2) The transfer agent, whose signature indicates that the certificate is made out in the name shown as the owner on the records of the corporation.

In smaller companies the functions of registrar and transfer agent may be exercised by officers of the company. In this case the only two signatures on certificates of stock will be the pen-and-ink signatures of the secretary and the treasurer of the corporation.

Stock certificates are transferred by endorsement. In order to record the change of ownership on the books of a corporation, the certificate sold must be surrendered, the transfer of ownership recorded, and a new certificate issued in the name of the new owner.

STOCKHOLDERS' LEDGER

On December 31, 1944, the Packard Motor Car Company was owned by 111,012 stockholders. It would be obviously impractical for the Packard Motor Car Company to have, on its general ledger, a capital stock account with each stockholder. Instead, a controlling account called Common Stock is maintained on the general ledger, with supporting detail carried in a subsidiary stockholders' ledger.

An account with each shareholder is carried in this subsidiary ledger. Each account shows the number of shares owned, along with information as to dates and certificate numbers. Credits are made for shares acquired, and debits made for shares disposed of. All accounts, being proprietary in nature, are credit balance accounts.

A corporation which has more than one class of stock will have one controlling account for each class of stock, together with supporting subsidiary ledgers.

SUBSCRIBERS' LEDGER

Subscriptions to the capital stock of a corporation, if numerous, or if payable in installments, may be recorded in a subsidiary ledger, an account being maintained with each subscriber. This subsidiary ledger would be governed by a controlling account in the general ledger called Subscribers or Subscriptions Receivable.

Subscriptions are debts (written promises to pay for stock) payable to the corporation at dates specified by the subscription contract. On the balance sheet, subscriptions to capital stock should be shown as a deduction from capital stock subscribed. Some accountants, however, classify subscriptions to capital stock as assets (see page 420).

According to *Hawley* v. *Upton* (102 U. S. 314), a subscriber to capital stock is legally a stockholder even though his subscription has not been paid.

STOCK CERTIFICATE BOOK

This book is similar to a checkbook in principle. Each page of a new stock certificate book consists of a blank certificate with stub attached. Whenever a stock certificate is issued to a stockholder, the certificate is detached and suitable notation is made on the certificate stub.

Certificates which are surrendered to the corporation are canceled and attached to their respective stubs. The open stubs therefore represent outstanding certificates.

TRANSFER REGISTER

The function of this book is to record, chronologically, all stock transferred from one person to another. It contains the following transfer information:

Date	Date . . . .
Number of old certificate	Number of new certificate . . . .
Number of shares	Number of shares . . . .
Surrendered by	Issued to . . . .

Postings are made to the stockholders' ledger from the transfer register, one form of which is as follows:

Date	Trans-ferred By	Certifi-cate No.	Number of Shares	L. F.	Trans-ferred To	Certifi-cate No.	Number of Shares

Many large corporations, with thousands of stockholders and transfers of stock, turn their transfer register and stockholders' ledger over to independent transfer agents (trust companies and banks, for example). Thus a company might have its head office and manufacturing operations in Detroit; but its transfer ledger and subsidiary stock records would be with a trust company in New York.

MINUTE BOOK

This book contains a record of all meetings of the board of directors and of the stockholders. It is the official record of the company. It is important to the accountant because it is the original authority for many entries.

CORPORATION ACCOUNTING

Corporation accounting is distinctive because of its treatment of net worth. The net worth of a corporation is represented by

(1) One or more Capital Stock accounts — one account for each class of stock. These accounts represent the amount of capital actually paid in to the corporation by stockholders.[3] The balance of each

---

[3] While this is the general interpretation to be given to capital stock accounts, the interpretation, in many cases, must be considerably modified. The many factors which make it possible for variances to exist between the credit to Capital Stock and the amount of paid-in capital are described in Chapters 21 and 22.

capital stock account must not exceed the authorized capitalization for that class of stock as fixed by the certificate of incorporation.

(2) One or more Surplus accounts to record that part of net worth not represented by capital stock accounts.

Aside from the accounting connected with capital stock and surplus accounts, corporation accounting is, as a general rule, similar to the accounting which is used for the single proprietorship and the partnership forms of business organization.

CONSIDERATION FOR CAPITAL STOCK

The capital stock of a corporation may be paid for in cash, in property, or in services. Noncash considerations are received by a corporation at values determined by its board of directors. These values are final. They can be set aside only by proof of fraud in their establishment. Such proof is generally a very difficult legal task.

The history of corporate finance is replete with examples wherein corporations have issued stock in payment of assets which they have acquired at inflated values. Corporation X, for example, may take over Corporations Y and Z for the purpose of reducing or eliminating competition. Corporation X may issue $1,000,000.00 of its par value stock in payment of the net assets of Corporations Y and Z, even though the fair market value of these assets may be only $750,000.00. These assets may be placed on the books of Corporation X at $1,000,000.00; or at $750,000.00 with a further debit to goodwill of $250,000.00.

On the other hand, a corporation may be formed to promote a patent, or to develop a mining claim. In exchange for the patent or mining claim, the corporation may issue stock in an amount in excess of the fair market value of the properties received.

When the book values of assets are inflated, the capital stock of a corporation is said to be watered.

The use of a goodwill account to cover up an overissue of stock, as in the example above, is untenable finance. It represents not only a misconception of the nature of goodwill but also of the fundamental constituents of value. Although the asset values acquired in such financing may not be satisfactory to him, the accountant generally must accept them. He does so on the basis of full disclosure of the valuation base in financial reports.

COMMON STOCK AND PREFERRED STOCK

Up to this point all capital stock has been assumed to be common stock. There are, however, several classes of capital stock, the most common kinds being preferred stock and common stock. Often these two classes of stock are divided into First Preferred Stock, Second Preferred Stock, Class A Common Stock, Class B Common Stock, and so on. Each class of stock is represented on the general ledger by a controlling account of that name.

Preferred stock possesses certain preferential rights over common stock. Usually it has preference as to dividends and as to assets in the event of the dissolution of the corporation. Occasionally preferred stock possesses conversion rights. The preferences and rights which attach to a particular issue of preferred stock should be stated in the charter or in the bylaws, as well as in the certificates of preferred stock.[4]

Preferred stock may be cumulative or noncumulative as to dividends. A 6% cumulative preferred stock is entitled to an annual dividend of 6% before any dividend payment may be made to the holders of common stock. Moreover, if the preferred dividends are not paid in a given year, the preferred dividends "accumulate." These accumulations must be paid off in full before any dividend payments may be made upon the common stock. Unless expressly contracted otherwise, preferred stock is, by the weight of judicial authority, both cumulative and voting.[5]

Up to 1930 there was a growing tendency on the part of the courts of the various states to regard noncumulative preferred stock as having a preferential right to dividends to the extent that dividends had been earned. Thus if in a given case and year there were no earnings, dividends rights for that year would be forfeited permanently. On the other hand, if $4 of a $6 dividend had been earned, the noncumulative preferred stock was considered to have a preferred right to a dividend of $4 and to lose forever all right to the balance of $2 which was not earned. The state courts also held that when earnings were sufficient to pay part, or all, of the full dividend rate on the noncumulative preferred stock, but these earnings were not disbursed, the unpaid "earned" dividends accumulated in favor

---

[4] The following are a few of the provisions of the $5, cumulative, convertible, preference stock of the Gillette Safety Razor Company, Inc.:

  (1) Preferred as to dividends only. A full year's dividends must be set aside for the preferred stock before any dividend may be paid on the common stock.
  (2) In liquidation it shares ratably with the common stock.
  (3) Callable after November 1, 1935, at 105.
  (4) Has one vote per share.
  (5) Is convertible into common stock, share for share.
  (6) Certain other protective provisions, such as protection of conversion privilege against dilution.

[5] *Hazel Atlas Glass Co.* v. *Van Dyke & Reeves* (8 Fed. [2d] 716 [1925]). 7 R. C. L. 287 and 7 R. C. L. 345.

of the preferred stock and were required to be paid off in full before dividends could be paid on the common stock.

This developing dividend theory of the state courts was significantly rejected in an outstanding decision of the federal court in 1930. In *Wabash Ry.* v. *Barclay* (280 U. S. 197) the United States Supreme Court held that holders of noncumulative preferred stock were not entitled to preferential dividends for those years in which net profits were earned but applied in good faith to capital improvements. The court indicated its agreement with "the common understanding of lawyers and business men" that "noncumulative stock is only entitled to a dividend if declared out of annual profits" and that "if those profits are justifiably applied by the directors to capital improvements, and no dividend is declared within the year, the claim for that year is gone and cannot be asserted at a later date."

Massachusetts followed this case in 1931 (*Joslin* v. *Boston & Maine R.R.* [274 Mass. 551]). In New Jersey, however, dividends on noncumulative preferred stock have been declared cumulative to the extent that profits have been earned and that profits remain after they have been applied against an earned deficit arising out of the operations of prior years.[6]

Preferred stock n ay also be participating. In the absence of specific information to the contrary, this means that the preferred stock is entitled to the same dividend rate as is paid on the common stock if this rate is higher than the regular rate on the preferred stock, i.e., if 8% is paid on the common stock, 8% must also be paid on the 7% preferred. The preferred stock of the Westinghouse Electric Corporation is of this character. Preferred stock, according to the weight of judicial authority, is not participating stock unless contractually agreed to the contrary. This is the rule of the federal courts and the courts of Maine, Maryland, and New York; Georgia, Indiana, and Pennsylvania hold the preferred to be fully participating; the supreme courts of other states have not passed upon the point.[7]

---

[6] *Cintas* v. *American Car & Foundry Company*, 131 N.J. Eq. 419 (1942). *Lich* v. *U. S. Rubber Co.*, 123 F. 2d 145 (1942). *National Newark & Essex Banking Co. of Newark* v. *Durant Motor Co. of New Jersey*, 1 A. 2d 316, 124 N.J. Eq. 213.

[7] *England.* — In England it has been definitely decided that preferred shareholders have no right to share in the distribution of any surplus so long as they have been paid the dividend stipulated in their contract. *Will* v. *United Lankant Plantations Co.* ([1914] A. C. 11, 83 L. J. Ch. [N.S.] 195), affirming the decision of the Court of Appeals (1912) 2 Ch. 571.

Canada. — Canada follows the English rule. In *Ramsey* v. *Steel Company of Canada, Limited*, the court said: "Where the preference shares, duly created and issued, are declared to be entitled to a fixed cumulative preferential dividend at a certain rate per annum, any further participation in the profits of the company is impliedly negatived, and if the right to any further participation is to be granted it must be distinctly so stated."

Example:

A corporation has a capitalization of

$100,000.00   5% Preferred Stock ($100.00 par), cumulative and participating
200,000.00   Common Stock ($100.00 par)

and profits available for distribution as dividends of $21,000.00. This amount would be apportioned to the preferred and common stocks as follows:

United States. — In *Niles* v. *Ludlow Valve Mfg. Co.* (202 Fed. 141 [1913]) the U. S. court said: "The common shareholders bear substantially all the losses of adversity and are entitled to the gains of prosperity. A contract that they should assume all the risk with no corresponding advantage should be clearly established. We find nothing in the law or the certificates or in the past action of the defendant to indicate that anyone connected with the business supposed that the preferred stockholders were to share equally with the common stockholders in the division of surplus earnings."

Georgia. — In *Coggeshall* v. *Georgia Land and Investment Company* (14 Ga. App. 637 [1914]), the Georgia Supreme Court stated: "Preferred stock takes a multiplicity of forms but usually possesses certain distinctive characteristics. The dividend may be either cumulative or noncumulative; and unless the contract provides otherwise, preferred stockholders participate in the surplus profits after the preferred dividend has been declared on the preferred stock, and an equal dividend on the common stock."

Indiana. — In *Star Publishing Company* v. *Ball* (192 Ind. 158 [1922]), the Indiana Supreme Court said: "The preferred stockholder is just as much a party to this venture as the common stockholders, and is entitled to all the rights of the common stockholders, except as modified by statute and contract."

Maine. — In *Stone* v. *United States Envelope Company* (119 Maine, 394 [1920]), the Maine Supreme Court said: "We put the decision, however, upon the ground that, where nothing to the contrary appears, the creation of preferred stock prima facie implies that the preferential rights of the stockholders are given in lieu of and to the exclusion of the equality in participation which would otherwise exist," and "Surely the phrase 'preferred stock' holds out to the ear of the ordinary investor no promise of participation in earnings beyond his preferential dividend. That this is true has been recognized by the authorities."

Maryland. — In *James F. Powers Foundry Co.* v. *Miller et al.* (171 A. 842 [1934]), the Court of Appeals said: "Preferred dividends are limited to the rate prescribed by the charter of the issuing corporation and stated in the certificate, and that they are not cumulative unless that is provided."

New York. — From (a) Section 5 of the Stock Corporation Law, 1923, and (b) *People ex rel. Siegel* v. *Lyons* (201 App. Div. N. Y. 530 [1922]) and (c) *Lockwood* v. *General Abrasive Co.* (205 N. Y. Supp. 511 [1924]), affirmed 210 App. Div. 141 (1924), it appears that New York courts would not give holders of preferred stock any rights not specifically granted in the certificate of incorporation. To permit preferred stock to participate would be to "read into that instrument [the certificate of incorporation] words which it does not contain."

Pennsylvania. — In *Fidelity Trust Co.* v. *Lehigh Valley R. Co.* (215 Pa. 610 [1906]), the Pennsylvania Supreme Court said: ". . . when each class of stock had been paid ten per cent they were equal and equally entitled to partake of whatever remained in the fund applicable for dividend purposes." In 1909, *Sternbergh* v. *Brock* (225 Pa. 279), the court said: "Where there is no stipulation in the contract to the contrary, the weight of authority clearly favors the right of preferred stockholders to share with the common stockholders in all profits distributed, after the latter have received an amount equal to the stipulated dividend on the preferred stock." These views were reaffirmed in *Sterling* v. *H. F. Watson Co.* (241 Pa. 105 [1913]) and *Englander* v. *Osborne* (261 Pa. 366 [1918]).

DIVIDEND ON

	PREFERRED STOCK	COMMON STOCK	TOTAL
Regular dividend at rate of 5%	$5,000.00		$ 5,000.00
Dividend on common stock at 5% . .		$10,000.00	10,000.00
Additional dividend of 2% on each share of preferred and common stock . . .	2,000.00	4,000.00	6,000.00
Total dividend of 7%	$7,000.00	$14,000.00	$21,000.00

As before stated, this is the type of participation which is usually considered as being applicable to participating preferred stock. However, there are other types of participating preferred stock, the degree of participation varying widely. Because of this variance, a participating preferred stock should be defined as one which receives a share in profits in excess of its regular rate of dividend after the common stock has received a dividend equal to the rate on the preferred stock, or at some other stipulated rate. For a full description of participating preferred stocks, reference should be made to standard texts on corporation finance.

To conclude this section it may be stated that, unless otherwise specified, preferred stock is

preferred as to dividends   not callable
preferred as to assets   not convertible
cumulative   not participating
voting

SURPLUS

Broadly speaking, surplus is the excess of net worth over capital stock. In a more specific sense, it is common accounting practice to divide realized surplus into capital surplus and earned surplus. These surplus accounts will now be defined.

Capital surplus is invested capital in excess of that represented by accounts with capital stock. Capital surplus is debited only for bona fide withdrawals of invested capital, and is credited only for bona fide additions to the capital investment of a business. These debits and credits to capital surplus are only for debits and credits which may not be placed properly in accounts with capital stock.

Earned surplus is all realized surplus other than capital surplus. From another point of view, earned surplus is that amount of cumulative income which has not been capitalized, consumed by losses, or distributed as property dividends.

Earned surplus is credited with the net income of an accounting period. This income includes

(1) Compensation earned for the furnishing of capital or services

(less such costs as may have been incurred in the earning of such compensation), and

(2) Gains of *any* kind. Generally these gains will have been realized by the concurrent exchange of assets or services for considerations of greater value, i.e., values in excess of the net book cost, if any, of the assets or services surrendered.

Earned surplus is debited with the net loss of an accounting period. This loss includes

(1) Costs in excess of the compensation received for the furnishing of capital or services.

(2) Net book costs in excess of the considerations received in the concurrent exchange of assets.

(3) Losses of *any* kind.

Earned surplus is debited also with disbursements of earned income and with transfers to capital stock.

Broadly speaking, earned surplus receives all debits and credits to realized surplus other than those to capital surplus.

At the end of the corporate accounting period, the balance of the Profit and Loss account is closed out in the following manner:

Profit and Loss . . . .   xxx xx
    Earned Surplus . . . .   xxx xx
To transfer net income for the year ending December 31, 19__,
to earned surplus.

OPENING THE BOOKS OF A CORPORATION

The procedure to be followed in opening the books of a corporation can best be described by the use of an illustration.

Example:

The Conn Manufacturing Company is incorporated April 15, 1950, for an authorized capital stock of $100,000.00, consisting of 1,000 shares of common stock of $100.00 par value per share. Subscriptions at a price of 100 are received for 750 shares as follows:

110 shares, $11,000.00, payable immediately. Cash is received.

640 shares, $64,000.00, payable 25% down, the balance payable monthly in equal installments. The entries to be made are

1950
April 15   The Conn Manufacturing Company was organized under the laws of the
            State of Delaware with an authorized capital stock of $100,000.00 divided into
            1,000 shares common stock of $100.00 par value per share.

(This memorandum of organization is placed in the general jour-

nal. In the general ledger a similar memorandum is placed in the
Capital Stock account to the effect that the total authorized capital
stock of the company is $100,000.00, consisting of 1,000 shares of
common stock of $100.00 par value per share.)

April 15	Cash	11,000.00	
	Common Stock		11,000.00
	To record sale of 110 shares of stock at par for cash.		
15	Subscriptions Receivable	64,000.00	
	Common Stock Subscribed		64,000.00
	To record subscriptions to 640 shares of stock at par.		
15	Cash	16,000.00	
	Subscriptions Receivable		16,000.00
	To credit subscribers for down payments of 25% on their subscriptions to common stock.		
May 15	Cash	16,000.00	
	Subscriptions Receivable		16,000.00
	To record collection of second subscription installment.		
June 15	Cash	16,000.00	
	Subscriptions Receivable		16,000.00
	To record collection of third subscription installment.		
July 15	Cash	16,000.00	
	Subscriptions Receivable		16,000.00
	To record collection of fourth and final subscription installment.		
15	Common Stock Subscribed	64,000.00	
	Common Stock		64,000.00
	To record the issuance of fully paid stock certificates covering 640 shares of stock.		

When all installments have been collected, the stock subscription
contracts become paid in full; certificates of capital stock are then
issued. This is illustrated by the second journal entry on July 15.

If subscriptions to more than one kind of stock were received by
a company, separate accounts should be opened as, for example,

> Subscriptions Receivable — Common Stock
> Subscriptions Receivable — Preferred Stock
> Common Stock Subscribed
> Preferred Stock Subscribed

When stock certificates are issued, the latter accounts are debited
and Common Stock and Preferred Stock are credited, respectively.

If all subscription contracts to capital stock had been paid in full
on April 15, 1950, the only entry necessary would have been

April 15	Cash	75,000.00	
	Common Stock		75,000.00
	To record collection of subscriptions to 750 shares of capital stock at par; and the issuance of stock certificates.		

The function, then, of the Common Stock account is to show the amount of common stock which has been issued. Common stock is issued to subscribers when they have paid the amounts called for by their stock subscription contracts.

Debits and credits to accounts with Common Stock and with Common Stock Subscribed are always for the par values of the shares being recorded.

The amount of unsubscribed common stock can be easily obtained at any time by deducting the sum of the accounts for Common Stock and Common Stock Subscribed from the total authorized capitalization for common stock.[8]

Accounting for capital stock which has been subscribed for on the

---

[8] Some accountants would prefer the following entries to open the books of the Conn Manufacturing Company:

1950

April 15	Unissued Stock.	100,000.00	
	Capital Stock		100,000.00
	To record authorized capital stock.		
15	Cash	11,000.00	
	Unissued Stock.		11,000.00
	To record sale of 110 shares of stock at par for cash.		
15	Subscribers	64,000.00	
	Unissued Stock Subscribed		64,000.00
	To record capital stock subscriptions.		
15	Cash	16,000.00	
	Subscribers		16,000.00
	To record 25% cash payment.		
May 15	Cash	16,000.00	
	Subscribers		16,000.00
	To record payment of second subscription installment.		
June 15	Cash	16,000.00	
	Subscribers		16,000.00
	To record payment of third subscription installment.		
July 15	Cash	16,000.00	
	Subscribers		16,000.00
	To record payment of final subscription installment.		
15	Unissued Stock Subscribed	64,000.00	
	Unissued Stock.		64,000.00
	To record the issuance of fully paid stock certificates covering 640 shares of stock.		

Commentary. — These entries may be used because of the statistical information which they give. It should be noted, however, that the first entry does not represent either a business or an accounting transaction. Unissued stock is not an asset. The Capital Stock account, in turn, is a fiction: — it is not the capital stock outstanding but merely the authorization to issue capital stock. Authorization is merely legal permission by the state for the corporation to secure capital for its capital stock if it can. It is not clear why these accounts should be opened, especially since the information which they contain is easily obtained without their use.

installment plan of payment raises the question of proper interpretation of balances in the Subscriptions Receivable and Common Stock Subscribed accounts. Because subscriptions to capital stock constitute contracts which are legally enforceable against reputably responsible parties, some accountants handle stock subscription contracts as a special class of bona fide receivables, and capital-stock-subscribed accounts as intermediate or provisional, but nonetheless real, constituent parts of net worth. From this point of view it follows that any debit balance in the subscriptions receivable account should be shown in the balance sheet as an asset, distinctively labeled and that the credit balance in the capital-stock-subscribed account should be shown as a part of corporate net worth.

Other accountants favor a more conservative placement of subscriptions receivable and capital-stock-subscribed accounts in the balance sheet. These accountants take the view that debit balances in accounts with subscribers to capital stock represent an amount of capital which is yet to be collected rather than as capital already available to the corporation. From this point of view, subscriptions receivable should be placed on the balance sheet as a deduction from capital stock subscribed. The difference between the balances of the two accounts represents the actual amount of capital paid in to the corporation on stock subscription contracts payable over a period of time.

This second classification is usually to be preferred.

UNCOLLECTIBLE SUBSCRIPTIONS

The entries to be made in the event of a corporation's inability to collect a stock subscription depend primarily upon statutory law, and secondarily upon the original accounting used to record the stock subscription. If the payments made by a subscriber are forfeited in favor of the corporation, the uncollectible balance may be written off as follows:

Capital Stock Subscribed	1,000.00	
Subscribers		410.00
Capital Surplus		590.00

To record the forfeiture of subscription to $1,000.00 par value common stock, and on which $590.00 had been paid.

The forfeited payments are credited to Capital Surplus because they do not represent earnings realized through the sale of an asset nor do they constitute compensation for the furnishing of capital or services.

Some states require a refund to the defaulting subscriber of the amount paid, less expenses and discount incident to the resale of the stock, thus:

Capital Stock Subscribed	1,000.00	
Subscribers (original purchaser)		1,000.00
To record forfeited stock subscription.		

Subscribers (original purchaser)	50.00	
Subscribers (second purchaser)	950.00	
Capital Stock Subscribed		1,000.00
To record resale of stock for $950.00; and to charge original subscriber with discount of $50.00 on resale.		

Cash	950.00	
Subscribers (second purchaser)		950.00
To record cash received in payment of subscription to stock.		

Subscribers (original purchaser)	540.00	
Cash		540.00
To record refund of balance due to original subscriber.		

DISCOUNT ON CAPITAL STOCK

Where the law of a state permits, capital stock may be sold at a discount from par. If $10,000.00 par value common stock were sold for $8,800.00, the entry would be:

Cash	8,800.00	
Discount on Common Stock	1,200.00	
Common Stock		10,000.00
To record sale of 100 shares common stock at $88.00 per share, par value being $100.00 per share.		

If the stock had been sold on the installment plan of payment, the entry would have been:

Subscriptions Receivable	8,800.00	
Discount on Common Stock	1,200.00	
Common Stock Subscribed.		10,000.00
To record subscription contracts for 100 shares of common stock at $88.00 per share, par value being $100.00 per share. Payment for this stock to be on installment basis.		

In both cases the account with common stock is set up at par. The balance in the Discount on Stock account should be written off as quickly as possible. This write-off is not compulsory but is desirable in order to remove a balance whose accounting utility fades rather rapidly. The write-off should be against surplus, preferably Capital Surplus, and not against current profit and loss. Discount on Stock is not a cost of revenue.

While the Discount on Stock account is sometimes shown on the balance sheet as a deferred charge, this treatment is not accurate. Discount on stock is not an asset. It is correct accounting to handle the account as a negative element of net worth in the manner shown in the illustration on page 449.

A stockholder who purchased his stock from the corporation at a price below par is liable for the discount to creditors of the corporation only; and his liability relates only to corporate debts contracted during the period of his ownership of stock. On resale of this stock, the new purchaser is not liable for the discount unless he makes the purchase with constructive knowledge that the stock is not fully paid. This might be indicated by omission of the words "fully paid" from the certificate of capital stock. The liability of the original stockholder for discount on stock which is subsequently transferred applies to a time period which varies with the laws of the several states. In New York the transferor remains liable for a period of two years after the date of the disposition of his stock.

If the corporation writes off the Discount on Stock account, one doctrine holds that the stock then becomes fully paid. In support of this doctrine, it would be desirable for the minute book of the corporation to show that directors formally approved the write-off of stock discount for the purpose of extinguishing the discount liability of stockholders.

PREMIUM ON CAPITAL STOCK

Less frequent are the instances wherein a corporation successfully sells its stock at a price in excess of par. The consideration which is received in excess of par value is credited to the Capital Surplus account thus:

```
Cash . . . . . . . . . . . . . . . . . . . . . . . .  11,000.00
    Common Stock . . . . . . . . . . . . . . .                10,000.00
    Capital Surplus . . . . . . . . . . . . . . .                 1,000.00
To record the sale of 100 shares of common stock
($100.00 par) at a price of 110.
```

Sometimes the premium received is placed in a temporary statistical account called Premium on Stock. This account is later closed to Capital Surplus.

If the above stock had been subscribed for on the installment plan of payment, the initial entry would have been:

```
Subscriptions Receivable . . . . . . . . . . . . .  11,000.00
    Common Stock Subscribed. . . . . . . . . . .                10,000.00
    Capital Surplus Subscribed . . . . . . . . . .                 1,000.00
To record subscription contracts for 100 shares of com-
mon stock ($100.00 par) at a price of 110.
```

When the subscription contracts have been collected, the Capital Surplus Subscribed account would be closed thus:

Capital Surplus Subscribed 1,000.00
    Capital Surplus 1,000.00
To record realization of capital surplus through full col-
lection of subscription contracts for 100 shares of stock
at 110.

PARTNERSHIP TO CORPORATION

The accounting steps necessary to convert a partnership into a
corporation may be summarized thus:

On the Books of the Partnership

(1) Close the books in the pattern of any normal closing of the
nominal accounts of a period.

(2) Debit the corporation for the net assets transferred to it.
The amount of this debit will be the price at which the net assets
have been sold to the corporation. It will also be the amount of
capital stock to be received by the partnership.

Debit the individual liability accounts in order to close out their
balances.

Credit the individual asset accounts in order to close out their
balances. (This credit will include the cash adjustment, if any,
called for in the third step below.)

Any difference between the debit to the corporation and the book
value of the net assets transferred is a profit or loss on the sale and
should be recorded in an account like "Profit on Sale of Business."

(3) Distribute the profit or loss on the sale of the business to the
partners in their profit-and-loss-sharing ratios.

After these entries have been posted, the balances in the partners' capital accounts should equal the amount of capital stock to be
received by them. To secure these balances, small cash adjustments
may be necessary.

(4) Debit an asset account, and credit the corporation, for the
stock received in payment of the net assets transferred.

(5) Distribute the stock to the partners. This entry will close
the capital accounts of partners.

On the Books of the Corporation

On the books of the corporation the only entry will be:

Assets (in detail) . . . .   xxx xx
    Liabilities (in detail). . . . .   xxx xx
    Capital Stock . . . .   xxx xx
To record issuance of stock in payment of net assets purchased
from _____.

ILLUSTRATION

The following problem illustrates the conversion of a partnership to a corporation.

After one year of operation, A. C. Bryce and E. K. Burger have the following balance sheet:

Cash	$ 18,000.00	Accounts Payable	$ 60,800.00
Accounts Receivable	76,000.00	Mortgage Payable	7,000.00
Merchandise	48,000.00		
Delivery Equipment	2,000.00	A. C. Bryce, Capital	57,000.00
Furniture and Fixtures	1,800.00	E. K. Burger, Capital	50,000.00
Building	19,000.00		
Land	10,000.00		
	$174,800.00		$174,800.00

The partners decide to incorporate their business under the name of Bryce & Burger, Inc. A corporation is organized with an authorized capital stock of $200,000.00 common stock, par value per share, $100.00. It is agreed that the assets of the partnership are fairly valued as follows:

	BOOK VALUE	SALE VALUE
Cash	$ 18,000.00	$ 18,000.00
Accounts Receivable	76,000.00	72,580.00
Merchandise	48,000.00	48,000.00
Delivery Equipment	2,000.00	2,000.00
Furniture and Fixtures	1,800.00	1,800.00
Building	19,000.00	25,000.00
Land	10,000.00	15,000.00
Goodwill	0.00	7,200.00
	$174,800.00	$189,580.00

The entries to be made upon the books of the partnership are:

Bryce & Burger, Inc.	121,800.00	
Accounts Payable	60,800.00	
Mortgage Payable	7,000.00	
Cash		18,020.00
Accounts Receivable		76,000.00
Merchandise		48,000.00
Delivery Equipment		2,000.00
Furniture and Fixtures		1,800.00
Building		19,000.00
Land		10,000.00
Profit on Sale of Business		14,780.00

To charge Bryce & Burger, Inc., for assets sold this company for a price of $121,800.00, detailed as follows:

Sales Price

Cash	$ 18,020.00	
Accounts Receivable	72,580.00	
Merchandise	48,000.00	
Delivery Equipment	2,000.00	
Furniture and Fixtures	1,800.00	
Building	25,000.00	
Land.	15,000.00	
Goodwill	7,200.00	
	$189,600.00	
Accounts Payable . . .	$60,800.00	
Mortgage Payable . .	7,000.00	67,800.00
	$121,800.00	

Profit on Sale of Business	14,780.00	
A. C. Bryce, Capital		7,390.00
E. K. Burger, Capital		7,390.00
To distribute profit to partners.		
Cash	20.00	
A. C. Bryce, Capital		10.00
E. K. Burger, Capital		10.00
For cash received to equalize balances of partners' capital accounts with par value of stock to be received from Bryce & Burger, Inc.		
Stock of Bryce & Burger, Inc.	121,800.00	
Bryce & Burger, Inc.		121,800.00
For 1,218 shares common stock received in payment of net assets transferred to Bryce & Burger, Inc.		
A. C. Bryce, Capital	64,400.00	
E. K. Burger, Capital	57,400.00	
Stock of Bryce & Burger, Inc.		121,800.00
To record distribution of stock to partners.		

The entries on the books of the corporation will be simply:

Bryce & Burger, Inc.,
organized under the laws of the State of New York with an authorized capital stock of $200,000.00 divided into 2,000 shares of common stock, par value $100.00 per share.

Cash	18,020.00	
Accounts Receivable	76,000.00	
Merchandise	48,000.00	
Delivery Equipment	2,000.00	
Furniture and Fixtures	1,800.00	
Building	25,000.00	
Land.	15,000.00	
Goodwill	7,200.00	
Reserve for Bad Debts		3,420.00
Accounts Payable		60,800.00
Mortgage Payable		7,000.00
Common Stock		121,800.00

For 1,218 shares of common stock issued to A. C. Bryce and E. K. Burger in payment of net assets purchased from them.

In this entry the accounts receivable are recorded at their sale valuation of $72,580.00 by showing their gross valuation of $76,000.00 and a valuation reserve of $3,420.00. This is done in order to maintain the agreement of the accounts receivable control with its subsidiary ledger.

STOCK BONUS

A corporation may offer a block of five shares of preferred stock with a bonus of one share of common stock for a group price of $500.00. The entry for the sale of such a block of stock might be

Cash	500.00	
Bonus Stock Expense	100.00	
Preferred Stock		500.00
Common Stock		100.00

To record sale of block of 5 shares preferred stock and 1 share common stock at group price of $500.00.

The bonus in this kind of transaction is in reality nothing but discount on stock. The bonus, therefore, should be debited to the account Discount on Common Stock. Stock issued at a discount of 100% may rightly be regarded by the purchaser as a somewhat dubious kind of "bonus," especially in the light of his liability to corporate creditors for the full amount of stock discount. To overcome this objection, a corporation sometimes will offer common treasury stock instead of unissued stock as the bonus.

If in the above example the preferred stock could have been sold separately at 98, the entry above would have been revised to read

Cash	500.00	
Discount on Preferred Stock	10.00	
Discount on Common Stock	90.00	
Preferred Stock		500.00
Common Stock		100.00

To record sale of block of 5 shares preferred stock and 1 share common stock at group price of $500.00, cash value of the preferred stock being $98.00 per share.

This entry describes exactly the conditions of stock issuance. An entry of this kind, although superior, cannot be made in cases where it is not possible to obtain the market value for either of the stocks in question.

QUESTIONS

Question 20-1. What are the advantages and disadvantages of the corporate form of business organization?

Question 20-2. Describe the essential characteristics of a corporation.

Question **20–3.** What are the steps in forming a corporation?

Question **20–4.** What is the function of each of the following: stockholders' ledger, subscribers' ledger, stock certificate book, transfer register, minute book?

Question **20–5.** What accounts represent the net worth of a corporation?

Question **20–6.** What types of considerations may be accepted in payment of capital stock? At what values are noncash assets brought upon the books?

Question **20–7.** What is watered stock? How may the water in stock be eliminated?

Question **20–8.** Describe the general characteristics of preferred stock.

Question **20–9.** What is surplus?

Question **20–10.** Distinguish between earned surplus and capital surplus.

Question **20–11.** Interpret the following balance sheet:

Cash	$124,077.80	Accounts Payable	$220,760.00
Noncash Assets	295,358.11	Common Stock, $100.00 par.	300,000.00
Surplus	101,324.09		
	$520,760.00		$520,760.00

Question **20–12.** How would you record the authorized capital stock of a corporation upon the books?

Question **20–13.** What is the function of the Capital Stock account? What is the distinction, if any, between the terms "capital" and "capital stock"?

Question **20–14.** How would you ascertain the amount of unsubscribed stock?

Question **20–15.** By the use of pro forma journal entries describe how the books of a corporation are opened, assuming that capital stock is to be paid for on the installment plan.

Question **20–16.** What are stock subscriptions? How should the debit and credit parts of a stock subscription transaction be shown on the balance sheet?

Question **20–17.** How should discount on stock be accounted for? Where should it be placed on the balance sheet?

Question **20–18.** Describe the accounting procedure incident to the conversion of a partnership to a corporation.

PROBLEMS

Problem **20-1.** Cordway Products, Inc., is incorporated on July 1, 19__, with an authorized capital stock of

$100,000.00 7 % cumulative preferred stock, $100.00 par.
$500,000.00 common stock, $100.00 par.

The preferred stock is sold at par for cash.
Common stock in the par value of $50,000.00 is sold at par for cash.
Common stock in the par value of $400,000.00 is subscribed for at par, payable 25 % cash, the balance in three equal monthly installments. These installments are paid on their due dates.
Prepare the entries to record these transactions.

Problem **20-2.** The ABC Corporation was organized on May 1, 19__, with an authorized capital stock of 1,000 shares of 7 % preferred stock, $100.00 par, and 5,000 shares of common stock, $100.00 par. During May the following transactions were entered into:

(1) One hundred shares of preferred stock were sold at par for cash.
(2) Received subscriptions for 500 shares of common stock at par.
(3) Received subscriptions for 600 shares of preferred stock at par.
(4) Received subscriptions for 1,500 shares of common stock at par.
(5) Three hundred shares of preferred stock are sold for cash at a price of 110.
(6) Received $20,000.00 cash as partial payments on the subscriptions of transaction #3.
(7) Received subscriptions for 1,000 shares of common stock at 105.
(8) Received $200,000.00 cash on the subscriptions of transactions #2 and #4.
(9) Received $40,000.00 cash on the subscriptions of transaction #3.
(10) Received $105,000.00 cash on the subscriptions of transaction #7.

Required:

(1) Record the above transactions in journal entry form.
(2) Post to a T-account ledger.
(3) Prepare a balance sheet, May 31, 19__.

Problem **20-3.** The charter of the Ohio Plastics Corporation gave the company the right to issue

1,000 shares of 6 % preferred stock, par value $100.00
10,000 shares of common stock, par value $100.00

The first 5,000 shares of common stock were contracted for as follows:

(1) 1,000 shares were issued to A at par for cash, $100,000.00.
(2) 1,000 shares were issued to B at par in payment of certain patents, formulas, and processes, $100,000.00.
(3) 1,000 shares were subscribed for at par by C. Of the purchase price 20 % was paid immediately and C agreed to pay the bal-

ance in four equal monthly installments. At the end of the second month two of these installments had been paid.

(4) 1,000 shares were subscribed for at par by D. Of the purchase price 10 % was paid immediately and D agreed to pay the balance in nine equal monthly installments. At the end of the second month D had failed to pay either of the first two installments. His stock claim was accordingly forfeited, the corporation retaining the 10 % original down payment.

(5) 1,000 shares (those forfeited by D) are sold to E for cash, $94,000.00.

(6) 1,000 shares are issued to F at 95 for cash, $95,000.00.

At the end of the second month, 100 of the shares originally issued to B are reacquired by the corporation at par for cash.

The company also sold 750 shares of its preferred stock at par for cash.

Required:

(1) Prepare a balance sheet at the end of the second month, showing as much detail as the problem will allow. For the purpose of this problem it may be assumed that active operations of the company have not yet commenced. Your balance sheet should show, among other things, the amount of (a) authorized stock, (b) unissued stock, (c) issued stock, (d) fully paid stock, (e) outstanding stock, (f) treasury stock, (g) partly paid stock.

(2) Basing your answers wholly upon the information provided by the problem, decide whether the preferred stock is (a) preferred as to dividends? (b) preferred as to assets? (c) cumulative? (d) participating? (e) convertible? (f) callable? (g) voting?

Problem 20–4. C. W. Morse and George Simpson decide to combine their businesses under the name of Morse & Simpson, Inc. A corporation is formed with an authorized capital stock of $100,000.00 6 % cumulative preferred stock, and $100,000.00 common stock, both stocks of $100.00 par value. Preferred stock is issued in payment of net assets based on the following balance sheet values:

Assets	*C. W. Morse*	*George Simpson*
Cash	$ 8,116.00	$ 3,624.00
Accounts Receivable	38,027.00	18,408.00
Notes Receivable	5,000.00	
Merchandise	20,000.00	16,118.00
Delivery Equipment	3,200.00	1,800.00
Furniture and Fixtures	2,000.00	1,000.00
Building	10,000.00	
Land	5,000.00	
Securities		4,000.00
	$91,343.00	$44,950.00

Liabilities and Net Worth		
Accounts Payable	$30,114.00	$10,642.00
Notes Payable		5,000.00
Mortgage Payable	4,000.00	

C. W. Morse, Capital 57,229.00
George Simpson, Capital 29,308.00

$91,343.00 $44,950.00

C. W. Morse and George Simpson withdraw cash from their respective businesses sufficient to equalize their capital accounts to 572 and 293 shares of preferred stock, respectively. Thirty-five shares of preferred stock at 104 are sold for cash to R. S. Power.

In addition, subscriptions for 600 shares common stock at 100 are received, payable in 30 days. Twenty-five shares common stock at par are sold for cash.

Required:

(1) Make the entries to record the above transactions.

(2) Prepare a balance sheet as of date of organization (assuming that subscriptions were taken as of that date).

(3) Make the entries closing the books of C. W. Morse.

Problem **20–5.**

Lowe & Bell

BALANCE SHEET, JULY 1, 1950

Assets

Cash		$ 6,000.00
Accounts Receivable	$ 9,000.00	
Less Reserve for Bad Debts	1,000.00	8,000.00
Merchandise		10,000.00
Miscellaneous Equipment.	$ 3,000.00	
Less Reserve for Depreciation	1,000.00	2,000.00
Building	$20,000.00	
Less Reserve for Depreciation	4,000.00	16,000.00
Land.		1,000.00
Prepaid Advertising		300.00
		$43,300.00

Liabilities and Net Worth

Accounts Payable		$ 4,500.00
Notes Payable		2,000.00
Total Liabilities		$ 6,500.00
Net Worth:		
J. C. Lowe, Capital	$16,400.00	
R. G. Bell, Capital	20,400.00	36,800.00
		$43,300.00

The two partners had previously made application for a charter to operate as The Lowell Corporation. On June 30, 1950, the charter was approved and authority granted to issue 1,000 shares of common stock of the par value of $50.00 per share.

On July 1, 1950, the new corporation took over all of the assets and liabilities of the partnership at balance sheet values except as follows:

(1) Accounts receivable are expected to yield total collections of $7,500.00.

(2) The inventory is to be valued at current replacement cost, $11,-000.00.

(3) The Reserve for Depreciation — Building account should be adjusted so as to have a balance of $5,000.00.

(4) No value is given to the asset of prepaid advertising.

The new corporation also sold 80 shares of common stock at par for cash to A. L. Strong, one of the incorporators of the new company.

Required:

(1) Make the journal entries on the books of the partnership to record

(a) The sale of the net assets to the corporation.
(b) The receipt of stock from the corporation.
(c) The dissolution of the partnership.

(2) Make the journal entries on the books of the corporation to record the assets received from Lowe, Bell, and Strong.

(3) Prepare a balance sheet of the corporation, July 1, 1950.

Problem **20–6.** W. H. Beal and Clark & Clark were competing retail drugstores in an Eastern city of 40,000 population. The two stores were located on diagonally opposite corners at the intersection of Third Avenue and Hudson Street. The Clark store was a partnership comprised of Henry L. Clark and his brother, Arthur J. Clark. Henry L. Clark acted as manager and possessed the larger capital investment. They shared profits in the ratio of 7–3, respectively.

The condensed balance sheets of the two businesses on December 31, 19__, were as follows:

	W. H. Beal	Clark & Clark
Cash	$ 211.32	$ 897.87
Accounts Receivable	14.77	1,748.17
Merchandise	6,220.31	7,760.63
Fixtures and Equipment	3,822.40	7,214.20
Prepaid Expenses	121.18	386.42
	$10,389.98	$18,007.29
Accounts Payable	$ 1,784.26	$ 4,668.55
Notes Payable		5,000.00
Accrued Liabilities	399.99	348.17

W. H. Beal, Capital	8,205.73	
Henry L. Clark, Capital		5,590.56
Arthur J. Clark, Capital		2,400.01
	$10,389.98	$18,007.29

After long consideration of their respective interests, Mr. Beal and Mr. Clark decided that it would be mutually advantageous for their enterprises to be consolidated. They agreed, therefore, to combine their businesses in a new corporation to be known as the Union Drug Company. The new corporation was formed and assumed the assets and liabilities of the two drugstores at book values after giving effect to the following merger terms, which were mutually agreed upon:

(1) The authorized capital of the new corporation was to be $20,000.00 of 7% cumulative nonvoting preferred stock, $100.00 par; and $30,000.00 of common stock, $100.00 par.

(2) The accounts receivable of Clark & Clark were conservatively estimated to be worth $1,250.00, the merchandise at $6,000.00, and the fixtures and equipment at $5,000.00.

(3) The net assets of W. H. Beal were to be taken over by the corporation at a lump sum value of $10,000.00.

(4) Before turning their net assets over to the corporation, Henry L. Clark and Arthur J. Clark were to make additional capital investments in cash sufficient to bring their capital account credits up to $5,000.00 and $2,000.00, respectively.

Upon assuming the assets and liabilities of the two enterprises, January 1, 19—, the Union Drug Company issued its common stock at par in payment for the net assets received. Organization expenses were privately absorbed by the incorporators.

Arthur J. Clark subscribed to $3,000.00 of the preferred stock of the Union Drug Company at par, making an immediate cash payment of $1,000.00 and agreeing to pay the balance of $2,000.00 on or before July 1, 19—.

Required:

Construct the opening balance sheet of the Union Drug Company.

Chapter 21

CORPORATIONS: PAR VALUE
STOCK (Continued) — SURPLUS

ORGANIZATION EXPENSES

Organization expenses are the reasonable costs incurred in bringing a corporation into existence. They are the initial costs of establishing the corporate entity. These costs are items like fees, taxes, and licenses, and the cost of stock certificates and accounting records.[1] These costs are debited to the Organization Expense account.

Accountants have generally approved the practice of writing off rapidly the balance of the Organization Expense account, the period of write-off being confined to a period of five years or less. Write-offs of organization expenses have been debited directly to any available surplus. Debits to current profit and loss have been avoided on the ground that the write-offs were not revenue costs of the periods in which the write-offs were made. On the balance sheet Organization Expense has been classed as a deferred charge.

This accounting has been defended by its advocates upon the grounds of bookkeeping convenience as well as upon the grounds of having the balance sheet show only conservative, i.e., so-called "real," values.

Accounting theory, however, clearly indicates that organization expenses are revenue costs and not debits to surplus.

Over the entire period in which it operates as a going concern, it

---

[1] The following excerpt is taken from the prospectus of the Barium Steel Corporation, organized August 3, 1933, under the laws of the State of Ohio:

"The Corporation has entered into a contract, whereby J. A. Sisto & Co., for their services to the Corporation and for agreeing to endeavor to find purchasers for the 5,000 shares now being offered at $45.00 per share, will receive the stock from the Corporation at $40.00 per share, upon the consummation of any and all sales. The differential in price to J. A. Sisto & Co. represents their compensation for services and covers all expenses incurred by them, including legal and other fees, advertising, printing of prospectuses, etc. . . .

"The estimated expenses to be borne by the Corporation in connection with its organization and the sale of the shares being offered, in addition to the price concession to J. A. Sisto & Co., are the following: expenses of organization and of the issue, printing, engraving and exchange of securities, including Federal original issue taxes, $1,200.00; legal fees, $500.00; appraisers' fees, $2,500.00; miscellaneous expenses, $4,500.00."

is obvious that a corporation can earn no net income unless its costs, including organization costs, have been recovered through revenues. Since true initial organization expenses like legal fees, charter filing fees, and so on, are compulsory costs of the right to exist, it is logical for these costs to be debited to the fiscal years which constitute the period of corporate existence. It is sound accounting, therefore, to write off organization expenses over the life of the corporation, the amount of each equal annual write-off being a debit against current profit and loss.

By similar reasoning, the costs of stock certificates, accounting records, and other reasonable organization expenses of limited life are costs of the particular accounting periods in which these items are used up. These specific organization expenses, therefore, should be written off against the gross incomes of the periods in which they are consumed.

From the standpoint of accounting theory, the propriety of writing off organization expenses against periodic income cannot be questioned. It is in the application of theory to practice that difficulties arise. The amount of the periodic write-off, for example, may not be correct because the factors of time and consumption have not been established accurately. The amount of the periodic write-off, further, may be of such negligible proportion that the worth-whileness of the entry may be questioned. These practical difficulties, however, do not invalidate the theory of accounting for organization expenses.

As a matter of fact, the discussion of the three preceding paragraphs actually does lend some support to the general practice of writing off organization expenses over a short period of time (i.e., three to five years or less). The point of major import is that the write-offs should be debited against income and not against surplus. This accounting is reinforced additionally by recognition of the fact that subsequent expenditures for maintenance or improvement of corporate organization are consistently and properly debited to expense.

On the balance sheet the unamortized balance of the Organization Expense account should be placed at or near the bottom of the group for intangible assets.

CASH DIVIDENDS

A dividend may be paid upon the outstanding capital stock of a corporation provided (1) that the dividend has been authorized by formal declaration of the board of directors and (2) that the dividend has been declared as payable from the *earnings* of the corporation.

The payment of an unearned dividend is illegal because the payment would result in an impairment of the *capital* of the corporation. This is not to say that dividends declared in one period must be earned in that period; they may be declared out of the undistributed earnings of past periods. The general principle is simply that dividends are usually limited by the amount of realized earned surplus.[2]

A dividend is declared payable at a certain future date, usually quarterly or semiannually,[3] at a certain rate or amount per share, to stockholders of a certain future date, thus:

The Royal Sugar Company

June 1, 19___

The Board of Directors has this day declared a quarterly dividend of one dollar ($1.00) per share on the common stock of this Company, payable July 1, 19___, to stockholders of record at the close of business June 15, 19___.

JOHN A. ANDERSON, *Secretary*

Directors are not obligated to declare dividends.[4] Even if profits have been earned, directors may decide to withhold dividends in

---

[2] But this statement is subject to the following exception: in the absence of statute or charter provision to the contrary, dividends may legally be paid from the capital surplus account of a corporation *MacIntosh* v. *Flint and Pere Marquette Railway Co.* (34 Fed. 582, 601) and from paid-in surplus (14 Corpus Juris, 806). In the MacIntosh case the court stated:

"Income is not limited to the gain which results from business and labor, but it includes as well the proceeds derived from the use or sale of property.

"Also, . . . the court is unable to understand upon what principle the receipts . . . derived from the surplus land assets are to be distinguished from other income or earnings of the company applicable to the payment of dividends."

In no case should dividend payments impair the capital stock of a corporation. *Williams* v. *Western Union Tel. Co.* (93 N. Y. 162, 192); *Berryman* v. *Bankers' Loan Insurance Co.* (117 App. Div. 730, 102 N. Y. S. 695); *Miller* v. *Bradish* (28 N. W. 594 [Iowa]). In New Jersey, however, it is not unlawful to pay dividends out of profits even though the capital be in fact impaired. *Goodnow* v. *American Writing Paper Co.* (73 N. J. Eq. 692, 69 A. 1014). Such dividend payments must not, on the other hand, operate to impair the rights of creditors. *Williams* v. *Boice* (38 N. J. Eq. 364, 370).

[3] In this connection the following excerpt from the 1932 Annual Report of the Commercial Solvents Corporation is of interest:

"The number of small share-holdings continued steadily to increase at such a rate that the substantial cost (approximately 12 cents each) of preparing and distributing dividend checks reach — in thousands of instances — excessive proportions in relation to the amount of the dividend involved. On June 30th more than 4,000 checks, in amounts of less than $1.00, were mailed to stockholders.

"To effect the considerable saving of time and money to the Corporation, made possible by less frequent dividend periods, a semiannual instead of a quarterly period for dividend distributions was fixed on August 24th, . . ."

[4] "When a corporation has a surplus, whether a dividend shall be made, and if made, how much it shall be, and when and where it shall be payable, rest in the fair and honest discretion of the directors uncontrollable by the courts." — *Williams* v. *Western Union Tel. Co.* (93 N. Y. 162, 192).

order to conserve or build up working capital. Moreover, directors often "reserve" a part of earned surplus in specially earmarked surplus accounts; by this practice the surplus actually available for dividends is less than the amount theoretically available. Furthermore, the ability of directors to declare dividends may be restricted by an insufficient amount of liquid assets. A low cash balance would have a direct and adverse affect upon the ability of a company to pay a dividend. Dividends depend not only upon an adequate balance in the Earned Surplus account; they depend also upon an adequate amount of liquid assets for their payment. In other words, the availability of surplus for dividend purposes is directly correlated to the degree to which corporate assets are liquid.

As soon as a dividend is declared, it becomes a liability [5] of the corporation and should be so recorded:

```
19__
Mar. 10  Earned Surplus [6] . . . . . . . . . . . . . . . . .     5,535.00
              Dividends Payable, Preferred Stock. . . . . . .                 1,750.00
              Dividends Payable, Common Stock  . . . . . .                    3,785.00
         To record quarterly dividends declared today, 1¾%
         on preferred stock, and 1% on common stock.  Payable
         April 1, 19__, to stock of record March 20, 19__.
```

When the dividend is paid, the only entry necessary is

```
April 1  Dividends payable, Preferred Stock  . . . . . . . .    1,750.00
         Dividends Payable, Common Stock  . . . . . . . .       3,785.00
              Cash . . . . . . . . . . . . . . . . . . . .                    5,535.00
         To record payment of dividends.
```

In the absence of dividend declarations, arrearages of dividends on preferred stocks are not liabilities. On the balance sheet these dividend arrearages should be mentioned in the form of a footnote or parenthetical notation.

STOCK DIVIDENDS

The declaration of a dividend payable in cash reduces the net worth of a corporation. The declaration of a dividend payable in capital stock, however, does not affect the net worth. A stock dividend merely transfers a part of the Surplus account to the Capital Stock account.

A stock dividend may be declared for one or more of the following reasons:

(1) To consolidate more of the net worth of the corporation in the permanent capital stock account. This gives official record to

---

[5] *Bryan* v. *Welch* (74 F. [2d] 964 [1935]).

[6] An alternative procedure is to debit Dividends Paid. At the end of the accounting period the balance of this account is closed into Surplus.

the fact that this transferred surplus is "permanently invested" in assets.

(2) To reduce the pressure for dividends by reducing the balance of earned surplus.

(3) To increase the total dividend payment without increasing the dividend rate. The old rate may be applied to the increased amount of capital stock.

(4) To lower prices of the company's stock to better trading levels on stock exchanges.

(5) To reduce the amount of earnings per share.

(6) To conserve working capital.

Example:

The Z Corporation has a net worth consisting of $100,000.00 common stock (par value, $100.00), and surplus, $120,000.00. The directors declare a 60% stock dividend:

```
Earned Surplus. . . . . . . . . . . . . . . . . . .  60,000.00
    Stock Dividend Payable  . . . . . . . . . .              60,000.00
To record declaration of 60% stock dividend.
```

At this point the stock dividend might be placed on the balance sheet in either of two ways:

```
(1) Net Worth:
      Common Stock, $100.00 par . . . . . . .  $100,000.00
      60% Stock Dividend Payable. . . . . . .    60,000.00
      Earned Surplus  . . . . . . . . . . . .    60,000.00   $220,000.00


(2) Net Worth:
      Common Stock, $100.00 par . . . . . . .  $100,000.00
      Earned Surplus:
        60% Stock Dividend Payable  $60,000.00
        Free Surplus . . . . . . .   60,000.00   120,000.00   $220,000.00
```

The means of payment for a stock dividend is common stock unless the dividend declaration specifies the use of preferred stock. The common stock to be used as the dividend comes out of previously unissued stock, or treasury stock. This is true because the total of outstanding common stock must not exceed the amount of stock authorized by the charter of the corporation.

When the dividend is paid, the entry is

```
Stock Dividend Payable  . . . . . . . . . . . . .  60,000.00
    Capital Stock  . . . . . . . . . . . . . . . .             60,000.00
To record payment of stock dividend.
```

A stockholder who owned 100 shares of stock would receive a stock certificate for an additional 60 shares as his dividend. The dividend, however, does not change his proportion of ownership. Before the dividend the shareholder owned $^{100}/_{1000}$ of the company; after the dividend, the shareholder owned $^{160}/_{1600}$ of the company. In both cases his proportion of ownership is 10%.

If the company maintains the same annual dividend rate, say 12%, it will disburse $19,200.00 in dividends as compared with $12,000.00 disbursed previously.

A stock dividend may be declared by a corporation whose capitalization consists of both preferred and common stock. Under such circumstances the stock dividend is usually paid to the holders of common stock, the preferred stock dividend requirements having been previously satisfied through the declaration of cash dividends.

In general it may be said that the right of preferred stock to participate in stock dividends is no different from its right to participate in cash dividends.[7] In Virginia, however, it has been held that " . . . when there are two kinds of stockholders, one preferred and the other common, when there is no difference in their status under the corporate charter except a preference as to dividends, and none under the statute law, the sale of stock to common stockholders at par, without giving the preferred stockholders an opportunity to purchase their proportionate part under the same conditions, or the issuance of a stock dividend to the common stockholders to the exclusion of the preferred stockholders, is an impairment of the rights of the latter which entitles them to relief in equity if the stock has not been delivered, or to damages for breach of a contract obligation if it has." — *Riverside & Dan River Cotton Mills* v. *Thomas Branch & Company* (137 S. E. 620, 52 A. L. R. 213 [1917]).

The Virginia rule is also the rule in Pennsylvania. *Stirling* v. *H. F. Watson Co.* (241 Pa. 105 [1913]).

TREASURY STOCK

Stock which has been issued, and fully paid for at a price at least equal to par, and which is reacquired by the issuing corporation is called treasury stock.

---

[7] *Tennant* v. *Epstein* (356 Ill. 26 [1934]).

Niles v. *Ludlow Valve Mfg. Co.* (202 Fed. 141 [1913]); writ of certiorari denied (231 U. S. 748). In this case the court ruled adversely to the right of the preferred shareholders to share in a 100% stock dividend by stating that "when the preferred stockholders received the large interest of 8% provided for in the contract, they received all to which they are entitled from the income of the corporation." (See also footnote on this case, page 415.)

Note: The question of the participation rights of preferred stock in cash and stock dividends has come before few of the state supreme courts. The cases cited in this chapter represent all the leading adjudications on this question to date.

Treasury stock, being fully paid, may be issued as bonus stock or it may be resold. Regardless of the price of resale, no liability attaches to the purchaser of treasury stock. In all other respects treasury stock is similar to unissued stock.

Because of its special character, treasury stock is usually recorded at its par value in a special Treasury Stock account. This account is simply a subdivision of the debit side of the Capital Stock account. The function of the Capital Stock account is that of reflecting the amount of par value stock which has been issued; and the function of the Treasury Stock account is that of reflecting the par value of fully paid stock reacquired by the issuing corporation.

When a corporation acquires some of its own stock, and this particular stock has never been fully paid for up to its par value, the debit should be to Reacquired Stock rather than to Treasury Stock. This should be done in order to show the technical difference between the two classes of stock, one of which may carry a discount liability to the purchaser, the other not.

Yet another exception to the above accounting occurs where a corporation acquires some of its own stock for the purpose of effecting a formal and permanent retirement of the shares in question. In this case the debit should be made to the account with Capital Stock.

From the foregoing three paragraphs it follows that the amount of capital stock outstanding at any given date may be obtained by deducting the sum of the balances of the Treasury Stock and Reacquired Stock accounts from the balance of the account with Capital Stock.

DONATED TREASURY STOCK

For the purpose of raising working capital, stockholders may donate pro rata a portion of their fully paid stock to the corporation. The sale of this stock supplies the corporation with funds. To illustrate:

The XYZ Corporation, capitalized for 100,000 shares common stock (par value $1.00), issues all of its authorized stock in payment for the rights to a certain patent. In order to supply the corporation with funds for the development of the commercial possibilities of the patent, the incorporators donate 25,000 shares to the corporation. These shares are sold by the corporation for cash, $18,000.00. These transactions are recorded as follows:

Treasury Stock	25,000.00	
Capital Surplus		25,000.00

To record donation of 25,000 shares, par value $1.00 per share.

Cash	18,000.00	
Capital Surplus	7,000.00	
Treasury Stock		25,000.00

To record sale of 25,000 shares of treasury stock at $0.72 per share.

Sometimes stock is donated to a corporation for the purpose of creating a surplus for a specific purpose, such as, for instance, the write-down of an inflated asset.

TREASURY STOCK PURCHASED

A corporation may acquire treasury stock through the act of purchase. The entries are similar to those for donated treasury stock.

Example (1):

Shortly after the sale of 25,000 shares of treasury stock for cash, the XYZ Corporation purchased 1,000 shares of treasury stock from a stockholder at a cost of $600.00. These shares were later resold by the corporation for $710.00. The entries are:

Treasury Stock	1,000.00	
Cash		600.00
Capital Surplus		400.00

To record purchase of 1,000 shares, par value $1.00 per share.

Cash	710.00	
Capital Surplus	290.00	
Treasury Stock		1,000.00

To record sale of 1,000 shares of treasury stock at $0.71 per share.

Example (2):

At another date the XYZ Corporation purchased 1,000 shares of treasury stock at a cost of $1,100.00 and subsequently sold them for $990.00. The entries are:

Treasury Stock	1,000.00	
Capital Surplus	100.00	
Cash		1,100.00

To record purchase of 1,000 shares, par value $1.00 per share.

Cash	990.00	
Capital Surplus	10.00	
Treasury Stock		1,000.00

To record sale of 1,000 shares of treasury stock at $0.99 per share.

When treasury stock is acquired at less than par value, the discount is credited to Capital Surplus;[8] when the stock is acquired at more than par value the excess over par is debited to Capital Surplus. Reference to definitions of income, profit, asset, and earned surplus will make clear that treasury stock transactions cannot involve gain or loss. Earned surplus therefore cannot be affected by treasury stock transactions. Debits and credits to surplus for treasury stock transactions must always be to Capital Surplus.

Where no Capital Surplus exists, or where the balance in the Capital Surplus account is inadequate to absorb fully debits arising from treasury stock transactions, expediency would sanction the substitution of such other surplus as may be available. While this accounting is not sound in theory, it may have to be used where surplus information on the ledger is not divided between earned and capital surplus accounts, or where the breakdown of an existing surplus account into types of surplus would not be worth the cost.

TREASURY STOCK ON THE BALANCE SHEET

Because treasury stock results, temporarily at least, in a reduction of the amount of the proprietary interest in a corporation, it should be shown as a deduction from the capital stock account on the balance sheet:

Common Stock, $100.00 par value:

Authorized stock	10,000 shares . .	$1,000,000.00
Less unissued stock . .	1,000 " . .	100,000.00
Issued stock	9,000 " . .	$ 900,000.00
Less treasury stock . .	500 " . .	50,000.00
Outstanding	8,500 shares		$850,000.00

Treasury stock should never be shown as an asset in the balance sheet. This classification would overstate the total of assets and misrepresent the amount of outstanding capital stock.

Treasury stock does not conform to the definition of an asset, i.e., anything of value owned. Treasury stock is not an asset even though cash or some other asset has been expended in its acquisition. The effect of this kind of transaction is not the acquisition of an asset but the reduction of an equity, specifically, the reduction of net worth. Intention to reissue or not to reissue the stock does not alter the effect of the transaction. The excess cash of a corporation, for

---

[8] A corporation which purchases shares of its own stock for less than the sum for which it was issued and then retires the stock may have benefited by the transaction in a sense, but the real gain is by its remaining stockholders and not by the corporation as such. The change effected is merely a change in the capital structure. *Eisner* v. *Macomber*, 252 U. S. 189.

example, may be invested in noncash assets, or it may be used to reduce liabilities or capital stock. If liabilities were reduced, it does not follow that cash has been invested in an asset. It would be ridiculous to contend, when a note payable is paid, that the paid note is an asset of the corporation merely because it could be reissued. There is no recordable asset, obviously, until funds are actually received by reissue of the note payable to a legal person.

By similar reasoning, treasury stock is not an asset but merely one channel through which assets may be acquired. Treasury stock is not capital in itself but, like unissued stock, may be used to procure capital. That treasury stock is not an asset may also be demonstrated by the fact that it has no realizable value when a corporation is being liquidated.

In this discussion two principles have been emphasized: (1) treasury stock which is purchased is accounted for as a stock retirement, and (2) the reissue of stock is accounted for in the same manner as an original issue of stock. This accounting is appropriate because it recognizes the withdrawal of capital by one proprietary interest and the investment of capital by a new proprietary interest — two entirely independent transactions, no matter how temporary the period of acquisition and reissue may be. *Acquisition of treasury stock is an independent transaction. Reissue of the stock is another independent transaction.*

EARNED DEFICIT

Corporations may realize losses as well as gains. If these losses should be large enough in the aggregate, it would be possible for them to wipe out the credit balance in the Earned Surplus account and create a debit balance. A debit balance in the Earned Surplus account would mean that the capital of the corporation has been impaired. It would be advisable, in cases of this kind, to transfer the debit balance of the Earned Surplus account to an account called Earned Deficit. This would not only correctly label the debit but it would tend also to avoid the possible misinterpretation which uninformed readers might draw from seeing a debit balance in the Earned Surplus account on the balance sheet.

DEBITS AND CREDITS TO SURPLUS

According to the accounting philosophy of past years, losses and gains which cannot be identified with the regular operations of a business should be transferred directly to Earned Surplus. This philosophy has been based upon the theory that the function of the profit and loss statement, and the Profit and Loss account, is to gather together only those elements which, in the aggregate, measure the regular operations of a business for a period.

Even if the practice of debiting "nonregular" items directly to Earned Surplus were deserving of sanction, the worth-whileness of the practice would be doubtful. Expediency and common sense would dictate the propriety of placing these items in the current Profit and Loss account [9] instead of in Earned Surplus. Especially would this be true if the effect upon the amount of periodic net income were insignificant. In other cases the inclusion of extraneous expense items in the current Profit and Loss account of a period would be well justified upon the grounds that irregular or extraordinary expenses recur regularly year after year. In other words, these irregular costs, when considered as a group, are just as regular an expense of periodic operations as any of the more commonly accepted expense groups. Similar comments apply to irregular or extraordinary items of income.

Accounting practice of the past has generally abided by the *custom* of placing so-called abnormal or extraneous gains and losses in the Surplus account. Modern thought and practice, however, reasons that it is better accounting to place *all* of the gains and losses of a period in the account with current Profit and Loss. In this way the balance of the Profit and Loss account will be made inclusive of *all* of the nominal elements of the accounting transactions of a period. By this accounting it also follows that the only entries to be placed in Earned Surplus will be those for the recording of the net income (or net loss) of a period, cash dividends, stock dividends, and certain transactions affecting earned surplus reserves.

This new concept of the function of the Profit and Loss account obviously embraces the statement of profit and loss. This statement will include extraneous gains under the heading of "special income credits," and extraneous losses and costs, as "special income debits." The final figure on the profit and loss statement will be simply "net income" for the period. Net income becomes thus, simply and understandably, "net income after everything." This type of all-inclusive income statement is illustrated in Chapter 30, page 629.

SURPLUS AND SURPLUS RESERVES

Surplus is generally divided into accounts with Earned Surplus and Capital Surplus, definitions for which were given on page 416.

Surplus accounts often appear under other names, especially with

---

[9] This does not mean direct entry in the Profit and Loss account but entry in some other appropriately titled nominal account.

respect to earned surplus which is not available for dividends. Surplus of this nature is often found under such titles as

> Reserve for Contingencies
> Reserve for Plant Expansion
> Reserve for Preferred Stock Dividends
> Reserve for Retirement of Preferred Stock
> Reserve for Sinking Fund
> Reserve for Treasury Stock
> Reserve for Undivided Profits

Many accounts which are not surplus accounts have titles similar to these. It is therefore incumbent upon the reader of the balance sheet to interpret accounts carefully in order to distinguish surplus accounts from those which are not. A reserve account, for example, may be

(1) A valuation account, that is, an account used to arrive at the true value of an asset (or a liability). *Example:* Reserve for Bad Debts.

(2) A liability account. *Example:* Reserve for Income Taxes.

(3) A surplus account. *Example:* Reserve for Contingencies.

When reserve accounts have been determined to be surplus accounts, it would also be in order to determine whether they are earned surplus or capital surplus and whether they are free or restricted appropriations of surplus.

An appropriation of surplus is a special reservation of net worth created by the following type of entry:

Earned Surplus	xxx xx	
Reserve for Treasury Stock.		xxx xx
To create a restricted surplus account equal to cost of treasury stock purchased.		

An appropriation of surplus is not a reservation of specific assets. However, a fund may be established to correspond with appropriations of surplus. Thus, the balance sheet of the American Bank Note Company, December 31, 1944, shows on the asset side,

Investments of Appropriated Surplus:		
Securities	$1,200,801.00	
Cash in Banks	267,462.00	$1,468,263.00

and, on the liability side,

Appropriated Surplus:	
For Employees' Pensions.	$1,468,263.00

In a similar manner, the balance sheet of Standard Brands Incorporated on December 31, 1944, shows, on the asset side,

Post-War Rehabilitation and Other Contingencies Fund:
U.S. Treasury Certificates and Cash $4,025,000.00

and, on the liability side,

Reserves:
Post-War Rehabilitation and Other Contingencies $4,025,000.00

The balance sheet of the Canadian Pacific Railway on December 31, 1944, shows an appropriation of surplus for purpose of self-insurance. This reservation of surplus is matched, on the asset side, by an insurance fund of equal amount. A similar illustration is found in the balance sheet of the United Fruit Company, December 30, 1944. The balance sheet of the American Sugar Refining Company on December 31, 1944, shows a pension fund of $3,036,-883.87 and, on the credit side, a pension fund reserve of equal amount.

Thus, in summary, the net worth of a corporation is the sum of one or more capital stock accounts and one or more surplus accounts (some of whose titles, however, may not include the word "surplus").

STATEMENT OF SURPLUS

The statement of surplus for a corporation is comparable to the statement of capital for a proprietorship or partnership. To illustrate:

Chester Foods Corporation
STATEMENT OF EARNED SURPLUS
FOR THE YEAR ENDING DECEMBER 31, 1950

Balance, December 31, 1949		$1,000,000.00
Net Income for the year 1950		200,000.00
		$1,200,000.00
Dividends:		
Preferred Stock	$ 20,000.00	
Common Stock	100,000.00	120,000.00
Balance, December 31, 1950		$1,080,000.00

The following examples are taken from the annual reports of the companies named:

The Pure Oil Company

STATEMENT OF SURPLUS

FOR THE YEAR ENDED DECEMBER 31, 1943

	Paid-in Surplus	Earned Surplus
Balance, December 31, 1942	$28,207,088	$43,646,358
Add net income for the year		13,874,517
	$28,207,088	$57,520,875
Deduct cash dividends declared on:		
Preferred shares		$ 3,908,607
Common shares		2,985,765
		$ 6,894,372
Balance, December 31, 1943	$28,207,088	$50,626,503

The foregoing two illustrations are surplus statements of the "clean" or modern style. The next two illustrations are surplus statements of the older style.

Owens-Illinois Glass Company

CONSOLIDATED EARNED SURPLUS ACCOUNT

FOR THE YEAR ENDED DECEMBER 31, 1943

Surplus, December 31, 1942		$31,771,564.24
Add: Net profit for the year ended December 31, 1943		9,478,296.82
		$41,249,861.06
Less: Cash dividends paid — $2.00 per share.		5,322,408.00
		$35,927,453.06

Add: Adjustments applicable to years 1929 to 1942, inclusive, to conform with the principles followed by the Bureau of Internal Revenue in determining the Company's tax liability for the years 1929 to 1936, inclusive:

Excess depreciation taken		$2,430,805.50
Property losses disallowed (now charged to Reserve for Depreciation) and other property adjustments		1,104,264.71
		$3,535,070.21

Less: Federal income and excess profits taxes paid and accrued, not previously provided for $155,280.75

Interest paid and accrued on federal income and excess profits taxes (less reduction in current federal excess profits taxes applicable thereto).	45,990.57	201,271.32	
		$3,333,798.89	
Write off of intangibles		693,208.60	2,640,590.29
Surplus, December 31, 1943			$38,568,043.35

The Davison Chemical Company

STATEMENT OF SURPLUS, YEAR ENDING JUNE 30, 1932

Surplus, July 1, 1931		$5,854,295.47
Less:		
Net loss for year ended June 30, 1932	$1,564,317.69	
Uncollectible receivables written off and provision therefor, applicable to period prior to July 1, 1931 .	1,556,842.76	
Discounts and allowances and provision for abnormal collection expenses to be incurred in connection with receivables originating prior to July 1, 1931 .	77,518.28	
Provision for loss on accounts due from former officer of subsidiary company (including charges of $138,310.69 resulting from litigation)	303,557.13	
Provision for loss in realization of advances to president of company and interest thereon	705,284.32	
Provision for loss in realization of advances to The Silica Gel Corporation	1,916,800.98	
Reduction of book value of investment in capital stock of the Silica Gel Corporation to market value	291,138.38	
Loss on sale of stock held under officials' and employees' stock purchase plan	322,222.70	
Dividends paid by subsidiary companies	7,576.00	
Other surplus adjustments — net	140,451.10	
	$6,885,709.34	
Less portion of loss of subsidiaries for the year applicable to minority interests	203,938.48	6,681,770.86
Deficit, June 30, 1932		$ 827,475.39

The importance of the statement of surplus is that it explains those changes in net worth which are not explained by the statement of profit and loss. For many corporations the statement of surplus must be read, along with the profit and loss statement, in order to obtain a complete review of the operations of a period. The stockholders of the Davison Chemical Company, upon reviewing the statement of surplus reproduced above, must have found this observation to be painfully true.

When the profit and loss statement is truly comprehensive in nature, i.e., when it is inclusive of *all* of the gains and losses of a period, the result is to reduce greatly the importance of the statement of surplus. As a general rule, the only items which would be placed in a statement of earned surplus would be those for net income and dividends declared. To illustrate, the earned surplus statement of the Standard Oil Company of New Jersey for 1942 is simply:

Balance at December 31, 1941	$104,833,548.00
Add Net Income for the year ending December 31 1942 . .	88,907,077.00
	$193,740,625.00
Deduct Dividends paid in cash — $2.00 per share	54,557,332.00
Balance December 31, 1942	$139,183,293.00

The earned surplus statements of General Motors Corporation for 1942 and 1943 were similarly constructed.

Many companies using the comprehensive statement of income go one step further: to the statement of income they add the statement of earned surplus. The result is a combination income-and-surplus statement. (See illustration on page 629.)

CAPITAL STOCK AND SURPLUS ON THE BALANCE SHEET

The several elements comprising the net worth of a corporation may be presented as follows on the balance sheet:

Net Worth:

Preferred Stock, 7% cumulative, par $100.00, authorized and outstanding	1,000 shares			$100,000.00
Common Stock, par $100,00:				
Authorized	5,000 shares		$500,000.00	
Less: Unissued stock	1,000 shares	$100,000.00		
Reacquired stock	15 shares	1,500.00		
Treasury stock	200 shares	20,000.00		
	1,215 shares		121,500.00	
Issued and outstanding	3,785 shares			378,500.00
Capital Stock Subscribed	350 shares		$ 35,000.00	
Less Stock Subscriptions Receivable			15,000.00	20,000.00
Capital Surplus				$ 10,000.00
Earned Surplus:				
Reserve for Preferred Stock Dividends		$ 7,000.00		
Unappropriated		33,000.00	40,000.00	
Total Surplus			$ 50,000.00	
Less Discount on Stock			28,000.00	22,000.00
				$520,500.00

449

QUESTIONS

Question **21–1.** What is the proper accounting for organization expenses? Where should organization expenses be placed on the balance sheet?

Question **21–2.** What are the entries to record the declaration and payment of a cash dividend? a stock dividend? What are the three dates to be noted when a dividend is declared? When should the dividend liability be set up?

Question **21–3.** What are the effects upon the net worth of a corporation of (1) a cash dividend, and (2) a stock dividend?

Question **21–4.** Why are stock dividends paid?

Question **21–5.** Dividends have not been paid on the $100,000.00 7 % cumulative preferred stock of the J. C. Calmer Corporation for three years. Should this information appear on the balance sheet? If so, in what manner?

Question **21–6.** May dividends be paid from capital surplus?

Question **21–7.** Distinguish among unissued stock, issued stock, reacquired stock, and treasury stock. Is treasury stock issued stock?

Question **21–8.** One hundred shares of treasury stock, par value $100.00 per share, are purchased by a corporation on the open market. The following entry is made:

Treasury Stock	10,000.00	
Cash		6,000.00
Gain on Purchase of Treasury Stock		4,000.00

Do you approve? Why? If you disapprove, what would your entry be?

Question **21–9.** One hundred shares of treasury stock, par value $100.00 per share, are purchased for $9,000.00 and later resold for $10,000.00. Has a profit of $1,000.00 been earned? Explain clearly.

Question **21–10.** How should treasury stock be shown on the balance sheet?

Question **21–11.** In what three ways may the term "reserve account" be interpreted?

Question **21–12.** Interpret each of the following reserve accounts so that you may know whether the item represents surplus, is a valuation account for some asset, or represents a liability:

Reserve for Accrued Management Compensation
Reserve for Bad Debts
Reserve for Contingencies
Reserve for Depreciation

Reserve for Employees' Saving Accounts
Reserve for Federal Income Taxes
Reserve for General Corporate Purposes
Reserve for Pending Litigation
Reserve for Retirement of Preferred Stock
Reserve for Property and Other Taxes Payable
Reserve for Deferred Interest Income
Reserve for Unfilled Magazine Subscriptions

Question **21–13.** What is meant by an appropriation of surplus? What is the purpose of such an appropriation? Are assets reserved? What disposition is ultimately made of the balance in an appropriated surplus account? Explain clearly.

Question **21–14.** What is the importance of the statement of surplus? According to modern accounting thought, what kind of information should be placed in the statement of surplus?

PROBLEMS

Problem **21–1.** The Borodax Corporation was organized on July 1, 19__, with an authorized capital stock consisting of 5,000 shares 6% cumulative preferred stock and 20,000 shares common stock, all stock of $100.00 par value. Over the next six months the following transactions occurred:

(1) Sold 3,000 shares preferred stock for cash, $300,000.00.
(2) Sold 500 shares preferred stock for cash, $55,000.00.
(3) Sold 5,000 shares common stock for cash, $500,000.00.
(4) Sold 10,000 shares common stock for $1,050,000.00 on terms of 20% down, and the balance payable in two equal installments, October 1 and December 1.
(5) All installment payments were collected on the subscription contracts for 9,500 shares of common stock.
(6) On one subscription contract for 400 shares of common stock, 60% of the subscription price was collected; an extension until February 1 was given for the payment of the balance due.
(7) On one subscription contract for 100 shares of common stock, only the down payment of 20% was collected. This contract was declared forfeited with no refund to the defaulting subscriber.
(8) Organization expenses were paid, $5,000.00.
(9) Net income for the period July 1 — December 31 amounted to $50,000.00. (Debit Cash.)

Required:

(1) Make the entries to record the above transactions. Post to a T-account ledger.
(2) Prepare a balance sheet, December 31, 19__.

Problem **21–2.** Following is the condensed trial balance of the John P. Belmont Corporation on December 31, 19__:

Cash	$200,000.00	
Accounts Receivable	40,000.00	
Notes Receivable	50,000.00	
Inventory	230,000.00	
Plant and Equipment	200,000.00	
Treasury Stock, 300 shares	30,000.00	
Accounts Payable		$ 54,000.00
Cash Dividend Payable		6,000.00
Stock Dividend Payable		100,000.00
Reserve for Contingencies		50,000.00
Reserve for Depreciation		50,000.00
Reserve for Notes Receivable Discounted		50,000.00
Reserve for Taxes Payable		60,000.00
Common Stock, $100.00 par		180,000.00
Earned Surplus		200,000.00
	$750,000.00	$750,000.00

Required:

(1) Prepare a balance sheet, December 31, 19__.

(2) If the $30,000.00 balance in the Treasury Stock account represented the *cost* of 400 shares of stock, how would the balance sheet be altered?

(3) If the $30,000.00 balance in the Treasury Stock account represented the *cost* of 200 shares of stock, how would the balance sheet be altered?

Problem **21–3.** The AB Company has capital stock outstanding of

Preferred Stock, 7% cumulative, nonparticipating, par $100.00	$100,000.00
Common Stock, par $100.00	100,000.00

It is the policy of the AB Company to declare dividends only once a year, December 31, at which time the results of the year are known. What are the maximum dividends payable to each class of stock if surplus at the end of the year is

(1) $10,000.00?

(2) $14,000.00?

(3) $20,000.00?

(4) $ 4,000.00 in the first year, and   }   Assume directors to declare
     $15,000.00 in the second year, and } the maximum dividend pos-
     $18,000.00 in the third year?   } sible in each of these years.

What would be the maximum dividends payable if the preferred stock had been

(1) Cumulative and participating?

(2) Noncumulative and nonparticipating?

Problem **21–4.** No dividend has yet been paid by the Bishop Furniture Company, Inc., in the calendar year of 19__. On the basis of the following balance sheet, dated December 31, 19___, what dividend policy would you recommend to directors of the company?

Cash	$ 4,000.00	Accounts Payable	$ 40,000.00
Notes Receivable	10,000.00	Capital Stock, $100.00 par	100,000.00
Accounts Receivable	80,000.00	Surplus	60,000.00
Merchandise	50,000.00		
Miscellaneous Equipment	16,000.00		
Building	35,000.00		
Land	5,000.00		
	$200,000.00		$200,000.00

Problem 21-5. Following is the tentative condensed balance sheet of the Gidlew Machine Tool Company on December 31, 19___:

Cash	$ 403,000.00	Accounts Payable	$ 150,000.00
U.S. Bonds	99,000.00	Customers Deposits on	
Accounts Receivable	144,000.00	Machines Ordered	104,000.00
Inventories	669,000.00	Preferred Stock, 6% Cu-	
Plant and Equipment (net)	587,000.00	mulative, $100.00 par	100,000.00
Deferred Charges	44,000.00	Common Stock, $2.00 par	200,000.00
		Capital Surplus	336,000.00
		Earned Surplus	1,056,000.00
	$1,946,000.00		$1,946,000.00

This balance sheet did not reflect the following transactions:

Dec. 29 — A cash dividend of $1.00 per share was declared on the common stock.

30 — A cash dividend of 1½% was declared on the preferred stock. With this declaration, all dividends on the preferred stock were up to date.

31 — A stock dividend of 100,000 shares of common stock was declared. Sold 100,000 shares of common stock for cash at $15.00 per share.

These transactions were part of a general program to raise funds for needed capital expenditures, the company having operated at capacity for a number of years.

Required:

Prepare a new balance sheet giving effect to these transactions. Show total liabilities, and the total, also, for net worth.

Problem 21-6. The Y & M Transit Company is in the process of being liquidated. On December 31, 19___, the balance sheet of the company was:

Cash	$1,700,000.00	7% Preferred Stock, $100.00 par	$ 500,000.00
		Common Stock, $100.00 par	1,000,000.00
		Earned Surplus	200,000.00
	$1,700,000.00		$1,700,000.00

Dividends on the cumulative preferred stock were in arrears in the amount of $35.00 per share.

Required:

(1) How should the cash of $1,700,000.00 be distributed?

(2) If the company had cash of $1,500,000.00, and no surplus, how should the cash be distributed?

(3) If the company had cash of $1,300,000.00, and an earned deficit of $200,000.00, how should the cash be distributed?

Problem **21–7.** The Wilson Steamship Company, operating a number of passenger and freight services, was capitalized at $1,000,000.00 (common stock of $100.00 par). In an endeavor to contract the area over which it operated, the company was able to sell one of its lines for a cash consideration of $150,000.00. The properties sold were carried on the books at $120,000.00. The net assets of the company after consummation of the sale were $1,125,000.00, including cash of $320,000.00. Since the cash on hand was much in excess of expected future cash requirements, directors of the company decided to disburse to stockholders all the cash received from the sale of the line mentioned above.

By means of journal entries show how you would recommend that the distribution be made.

Problem **21–8.** The Illinois Glass Company called for redemption on January 1, 1951, its entire issue of outstanding 7 % preferred stock in the par value of $1,000,000.00. The price to be paid on redemption was 120 per share plus the dividend for the quarter ending December 31, 1950.

Required:

(1) What entry should be made on the books of the corporation to record the redemption of the preferred stock?

(2) What mention, if any, would you make on the balance sheet of December 31, 1950, regarding the redemption of the preferred stock?

Problem **21–9.** In 1952 the American Tri-Central Corporation sold for cash 57,143 shares of $1.00 par value common stock as follows:

To Norman J. Harrick, president:
    20,000 shares at $1.25

To stockholders:
    20,000 shares at $1.50

To underwriters:

17,143 shares. The underwriter sold these shares to the general public at $1.62½. The underwriter's commission was $0.25 on each share sold to stockholders and $0.37½ on each share sold to the general public.

Prior to the sale of these shares the company's condensed balance sheet was presented as follows:

Cash	$ 1,571.00	Accounts Payable, etc.	$ 4,825.00
Inventories	27,291.00	Reserve for Depreciation	10,000.00
Accounts Receivable	2,735.00	Common Stock, par $1.00	400,000.00
Fixed Assets	21,167.00	Capital Surplus	309,694.00
Intangibles	322,265.00		
Other Assets	71,337.00		
Earned Deficit	278,153.00		
	$724,519.00		$724,519.00

Required:

(1) Make the entries to record the sale of 57,143 shares of stock.

(2) Prepare a balance sheet, in good form, giving effect to the sale of these shares.

Problem **21–10**. John A. Martin owned several long-term options on prospective oil-producing properties. For the purpose of exercising the options and commencing development of the properties involved, Mr. Martin and associates organized the Martin Oil Company with an authorized capital stock of 250,000 shares of $1.00 par value common stock.

The first 50,000 shares were issued at par to Mr. Martin in payment of his options which were transferred to the company. (Mr. Martin had originally paid $10,000.00 for these options.) At a later date 27,413 shares were sold for $79,767.00, netting the company $65,187.00, after deduction of commissions to salesmen and brokers, $11,965.00, and selling expenses, $2,615.00.

Required:

(1) How should the above transactions be recorded on the books of the Martin Oil Company?

(2) Prepare a balance sheet of the company.

Problem **21–11.** Paul A. Keen surrendered his mining properties to the Arizona Copper Company for 100,000 shares of the company's common stock of $1.00 par value. He later donated 10 % of his stock to the company. What entries should be made upon the books of the corporation?

Problem **21–12.** On January 31, 1939, the Interstate Department Stores, Inc., purchased 1,720 shares of its $100.00 par value preferred stock at a cost of $122,419.40. In accordance with charter provisions of the company, these shares were acquired for the purpose of retirement. What entry should be made?

Problem **21–13.** From the following information prepare a statement of surplus (segregating earned surplus from capital surplus) for the Holland Bakery Company for the year ending December 31, 1952:

Earned surplus, December 31, 1951	$ 11,206.00
Capital surplus, December 31, 1951	245,029.00
Net income for 1952	27,178.00
Premium paid on redemption of preferred stock	10,000.00
Discount on purchase of common stock for treasury (par $50,000.00, cost, $45,000.00)	5,000.00
Dividends paid on preferred stock for 1952	7,000.00
25% stock dividend	25,000.00

Problem **21–14.** A corporation purchased $50,000.00 of its par value common stock on the open market at a cost of $38,000.00. At a later date this stock was sold for $48,000.00. How should the difference of $10,000.00 be reflected on the books? Discuss in a manner which reflects your knowledge of the theory behind this question.

Problem **21–15.** The Knox-Eddy Corporation was organized on October 31, 19__, with an authorized capital stock consisting of 10,000 shares 7% preferred stock, $100.00 par, and 100,000 shares common stock, $20.00 par.

During November and December the following transactions occurred:

(1) Sold 1,000 shares preferred stock at par for cash.
(2) Sold 10,000 shares common stock at par for cash.
(3) Sold 1,000 shares preferred stock at a price of 104 for cash.
(4) Sold 15,000 shares common stock at a price of 22 for cash.
(5) Received subscriptions for 1,000 shares preferred stock at 110.
(6) Received subscriptions for 10,000 shares common stock at 25.
(7) Assets of the Sparks Equipment Company are purchased: land, $50,000.00, building, $250,000.00, fixtures and equipment, $60,000.00, inventory, $140,000.00. These assets were paid for by the issuance of 5,000 shares of preferred stock.
(8) A 60% cash collection was made on all of the shares subscribed for in transaction #5.
(9) All of the subscriptions in transaction #6 were collected.
(10) A stockholder, who obtained his stock in transaction #4, is urgently in need of funds. The corporation acquires from him for cash 1,000 shares of common stock at a price of 20.
(11) A 40% cash collection is made on subscriptions covering 900 shares of preferred stock (originally subscribed for in transaction #5).
(12) Checks totaling $5,000.00 are given to five individuals in payment of costs which they incurred in the organization of the Knox-Eddy Corporation.

Required:

(1) Record the above transactions in journal entry form.
(2) Post to a T-account ledger.
(3) Prepare a balance sheet, December 31, 19__. The assets need not be classified. The net worth section, however, should be presented in detail.

Problem **21–16.** On December 31, 1951, the after-closing trial balance of Collins & Co., Inc., was:

Cash	$ 18,000.00	
Accounts Receivable	75,000.00	
Reserve for Bad Debts		$ 5,000.00
Merchandise	81,000.00	
Fixed Assets	70,000.00	
Reserve for Depreciation		7,000.00
Accounts Payable		48,000.00
Common Stock		100,000.00
Preferred Stock, 7%		50,000.00
Earned Surplus.		34,000.00
	$244,000.00	$244,000.00

The authorized capital stock of the corporation was preferred stock, $100,000.00, and common stock, $200,000.00, all stock being of $100.00 par value.

As of January 2, 1952, the assets and liabilities of the partnership of Dow & Smith were purchased by issuing common stock for the net assets acquired. The purchase was made at proper values:

	Per Dow & Smith Books	Fair Appraised Values
Cash	$ 2,000.00	$ 2,000.00
Accounts Receivable	18,000.00	17,000.00
Merchandise	15,000.00	20,000.00
Fixed Assets	20,000.00	20,000.00
	$55,000.00	
Accounts Payable	$12,000.00	12,000.00

	P & L Ratios		
S. A. Dow, Capital	60%	. . . .	25,000.00
C. M. Smith, Capital	40%	. . . .	18,000.00
			$55,000.00

During 1952 the following transactions also occurred:

(1) $50,000.00 par value preferred stock was sold at par, and $40,000.00 cash collected in part payment of these subscriptions. The balance due on these subscriptions of $10,000.00 was considered collectible.

(2) The corporation purchased 270 shares of its own common stock on the open market at a total cost of $22,000.00 cash.

(3) Sales on account, $200,000.00.

(4) Collections on accounts receivable, $225,000.00.

(5) Purchases on account, $150,000.00.

(6) Paid accounts payable, $180,000.00.

(7) Expenses paid, $45,000.00; expenses incurred but not yet paid, $5,000.00.

(8) Worthless accounts receivable, not written off by December 31, 1952, amounted to $4,000.00. Bad debts expense for the year was estimated at $3,000.00.

(9) A cash dividend of 7 % was declared and paid on the preferred stock.

(10) A cash dividend of 3 % was declared on the common stock. This dividend was payable January 10, 1953.

Required:

(1) Enter above data in general ledger.

(2) Prepare a balance sheet, December 31, 1952. The inventory on this date was $131,000.00.

(3) Prepare a statement of earned surplus for the year 1952.

Problem 21-17. The balance sheet of the Dale Corporation on December 31, 19__, was:

Assets

Cash		$ 35,000.00
Accounts Receivable	$95,000.00	
Reserve for Bad Debts	5,000.00	90,000.00
Merchandise		120,000.00
Machinery	$60,000.00	
Reserve for Depreciation	10,000.00	50,000.00
Prepaid Expenses		5,000.00
		$300,000.00

Liabilities and Net Worth

Accounts Payable	$ 20,000.00
7% Preferred Stock, $100.00 par (Authorized, $200,000.00) . .	100,000.00
Common Stock, $100.00 par (Authorized, $300,000.00)	100,000.00
Earned Surplus.	50,000.00
Capital Surplus	30,000.00
	$300,000.00

During the next calendar year the following transactions occurred:

(1) 250 shares of preferred stock were subscribed for at 110. Collections of $17,500.00 were made on these subscriptions. Of these collections 100 shares were paid in full. The balances due on stock subscriptions were considered good.

(2) 50 shares of Dale Corporation common stock were received at par in payment of an accounts receivable against which the reserve for bad debts had been established.

(3) Sale of merchandise on account, $300,000.00.

(4) Purchase of merchandise on account, $250,000.00.

(5) Collections on accounts receivable were $290,000.00.

(6) Paid accounts payable, $200,000.00.

(7) Paid operating expenses, $60,000.00.

(8) Depreciation expense for the year was $5,000.00.

(9) At the end of the year the amount of prepaid expenses was $12,000.00.

(10) A cash dividend of 7 % was declared and paid on the preferred stock.

(11) A stock dividend of 20 % was declared and paid on the common stock out of earned surplus.

(12) A cash dividend of 5 % was declared on the common stock. This dividend was payable in the next accounting period.

Required:

(1) Prepare a balance sheet, December 31, 19___. New inventory of merchandise, $160,000.00.

(2) Prepare a statement of earned surplus.

Problem **21–18.** The General Marine Supply Company was a partnership comprised of L. A. Hall, G. S. Pennington, A. G. Reynolds, and R. T. Sullivan. The partners decided that their respective interests would be better served if the partnership was converted into a corporation of the same business name. The following information presents the real accounts of the partnership at (1) balances found on the books, and (2) fair values for the transfer of these accounts to the corporation:

	Balance Sheet Values	Fair Market Values
Cash	$ 75,623.00	$ 75,623.00
Securities	16,080.00	14,740.00
Accounts Receivable	121,158.00	*
Inventories	172,016.00	184,849.00
Land	25,000.00	50,000.00
Buildings	194,967.00	175,000.00
Machinery, Fixtures, Equipment	120,211.00	75,000.00
Prepaid Expenses	21,215.00	21,215.00
	$746,270.00	

		Balance Sheet Values	Fair Market Values
Reserve for Bad Debts		$ 22,325.00	*
Notes Payable		84,000.00	84,000.00
Accounts Payable		49,307.00	49,307.00
Accrued Liabilities		7,703.00	7,703.00
	P & L Ratios		
L. A. Hall, Capital	25%	129,016.00	
G. S. Pennington, Capital	20%	113,720.00	
A. G. Reynolds, Capital	25%	143,804.00	
R. T. Sullivan, Capital	30%	196,395.00	
		$746,270.00	

* The accounts receivable are to be revalued by increasing the Reserve for Bad Debts to $40,000.00.

The General Marine Supply Company, accordingly, was organized as a corporation with an authorized capitalization of $250,000.00 cumulative convertible 7 % preferred stock, and $500,000.00 common stock, all stock to be voting stock and of $100.00 par value.

Preliminary to the actual transfer of the assets and liabilities to the corporation, and issuance of stock certificates, partners' capital accounts were to be rounded off to the nearest even hundreds of dollars. To accomplish this partners were to pay in or receive cash in the proper amounts.

The assets and liabilities of the partnership were acquired by the corporation at their fair market values. In exchange for the net assets acquired, the corporation issued $50,000.00 of preferred stock to each of the four partners and common stock to complete the settlements. The balance of the unissued preferred stock was sold to the four partners at a price of $100.00 per share. Of this amount one fourth of the purchase price was immediately received in cash; the balance was payable in three equal annual installments, the first of these installments to be payable one year from date.

The four old partners, now stockholders, almost immediately discovered that they had failed to place any part of the net worth of the partnership in the Surplus account of the corporation and that, because of this failure, directors were precluded from declaring dividends on the preferred and common stocks of the company. To overcome this current difficulty, the four common stockholders decided to donate 20 % of their common stock to the corporation for the specified purpose of creating a surplus out of which dividends might be paid immediately. (In the state in which the General Marine Supply Company was located, this action was legal.) The amount of the donation, roughly, was equal to the undisbursed earnings of the partnership.

The donation was made as agreed; whereupon directors declared an initial quarterly cash dividend on the preferred stock, and a cash dividend of 2 % on the common stock.

Required:

(1) Make the journal entries to record the above information. Post to the ledger. (The books of the partnership were converted to the use of the corporation.)

(2) Prepare a balance sheet giving effect to the foregoing transactions.

Chapter 22

CORPORATIONS: NO-PAR VALUE STOCK — MISCELLANEOUS PROBLEMS OF CAPITAL STOCK

Most states permit corporations to sell stock of no par value, although some states specify that the selling price shall not be less than a certain minimum price, say $5.00 per share. Subject to this kind of statutory restriction, no-par stock may be sold at any price. Irrespective, therefore, of the price at which it is sold, no-par stock issued upon the full payment of stock subscriptions is fully paid stock. The stockholder is free of liability of any kind. Each share of no-par stock, besides being fully paid, participates equally in dividend distributions and in the assets of the corporation in the event of dissolution.

In some states it is required by statutory enactment that, in lieu of a par value, all no-par value stock must have a certain "stated" or declared value. Section 2 of the Business Corporations Law of Pennsylvania defines stated value as follows:

Stated capital means, at any particular time, the sum of the par value of all shares then issued having a par value, the consideration received by a business corporation for all shares then issued without par value, except such part thereof as may have been allocated otherwise than to stated capital in a manner permitted by this act, and such other amounts as may have been transferred to the stated capital account of the corporation, whether from the issue of shares as a share dividend, or otherwise, minus such formal reductions from such sum as may have been effected in a manner permitted by this act.

The accounting for no-par stock with a stated value is the same as that for stock with a par value. In other words, stated value takes the place of par value in the accounts. The preferred and common stocks of the Gillette Safety Razor Company are examples of stocks without par value and which have stated values per share; each of these stocks has a stated value of $7.50 per share.

ACCOUNTING FOR NO-PAR STOCK

Since laws of the various states relative to no-par stock vary widely, one should be familiar with the laws of the state of incorporation when framing entries to recognize specific no-par stock accounting transactions.

In general, however, accounting for no-par stock is relatively simple. There are no accounts for

Authorized capital stock	Discount on stock
Unissued stock	Premium on stock

Where no-par stock is immediately paid for in full, the credit is to a capital stock account for the amount of cash received. If the stock is sold on time, the credit is to a capital stock subscribed account for the amount of the subscriptions.

Example:

The Y Corporation is organized July 1, 1950, with an authorized capital stock of 10,000 shares of no-par common stock. The stock is sold as follows:

July 1 — 3,000 shares are sold at $20.00 per share. These shares were immediately paid for in cash.

July 10 — 2,000 shares are sold at $25.00 per share. These shares were immediately paid for in cash.

July 20 — 4,000 shares are sold at $30.00 per share. These shares were subscribed for on July 20, and paid for on July 31.

The entries for these transactions would be:

1950

July 1	Cash	60,000.00	
	Common Stock		60,000.00
	To record cash sale of 3,000 shares of no-par stock at $20.00.		

July 10	Cash	50,000.00	
	Common Stock		50,000.00
	To record cash sale of 2,000 shares of no-par stock at $25.00.		

July 20	Subscriptions Receivable	120,000.00	
	Common Stock Subscribed		120,000.00
	To record subscriptions to 4,000 shares of no-par stock at $30.00.		

July 31	Cash	120,000.00	
	Subscriptions Receivable		120,000.00
	To record collection of stock subscriptions.		

July 31	Common Stock Subscribed	120,000.00	
	Common Stock		120,000.00
	To record issuance of stock certificates covering 4,000 shares, paid for in full today.		

After these entries have been posted, the capital stock account on July 31 will be

COMMON STOCK (Authorized 10,000 no-par shares)

				1950 July	1	3,000 shares		.	60,000.00
					10	2,000 "			50,000.00
					31	4,000 "			120,000.00

Each share of the 9,000 shares of outstanding no-par common stock represents a $25.56 proprietary claim, irrespective of the amount which that share contributed to the capital of the corporation.

PURCHASES OF NO-PAR TREASURY STOCK

In recording the purchase of no-par treasury stock, practice is not uniform. Treasury Stock is variously debited with

The actual issuing price.
The average issuing price.
The stated value per share or, in the absence of a stated value, with some selected uniform value per share.
The cost of the stock purchased.

In all of these cases, however, there is general agreement that the Treasury Stock account should be kept in a manner to show the number of shares corresponding to the valuation used.

If theory with respect to the purchase of par value treasury stock is sound, it is logical for the same theory to be applied to the purchase of no-par value treasury stock. The basic assumption in both cases is that the purchase of treasury stock, par or no-par, results in a reduction of the *capital* invested in the corporation. In terms of accounts this means a reduction in capital stock, or capital stock and capital surplus. To illustrate:

Example 1:

The Y Corporation has a capital stock account of $230,000.00, representing 10,000 shares of no-par value, and an earned surplus account of $100,000.00. One thousand shares of treasury stock are purchased at a cost of $23,000.00 and later resold for $25,000.00. The entries would be

Treasury Stock 23,000.00
    Cash 23,000.00
To record purchase of 1,000 shares of no-par treasury
stock at 23.

Cash	25,000.00	
Treasury Stock		23,000.00
Capital Surplus		2,000.00

To record sale of 1,000 shares of no-par treasury stock
at 25.

Example 2:

The Y Corporation has a capital stock account of $230,000.00, representing 10,000 shares of no-par value, and an earned surplus account of $100,000.00. One thousand shares of treasury stock are purchased at a cost of $20,000.00 and later resold for $25,000.00. The entries would be

Treasury Stock	23,000.00	
Capital Surplus		3,000.00
Cash		20,000.00

To record purchase of 1,000 shares of no-par treasury
stock at 20.

Cash	25,000.00	
Treasury Stock		23,000.00
Capital Surplus		2,000.00

To record sale of 1,000 shares of no-par treasury stock
at 25.

Example 3:

The Y Corporation has a capital stock account of $230,000.00, representing 10,000 shares of no-par value, and an earned surplus account of $100,000.00. One thousand shares of treasury stock are purchased at a cost of $25,000.00 and later resold for $20,000.00. The entries would be

Treasury Stock	23,000.00	
Capital Surplus	2,000.00	
Cash		25,000.00

To record purchase of 1,000 shares of no-par treasury
stock at 25.

Cash	20,000.00	
Capital Surplus	3,000.00	
Treasury Stock		23,000.00

To record sale of 1,000 shares of no-par treasury stock
at 20.

In order to avoid a debit balance in the Capital Surplus account, some accountants would prefer to debit Earned Surplus instead, basing their decision primarily upon expediency rather than accounting theory.

Example 4:

The Y Corporation has a capital stock account of $100,000.00, representing 10,000 shares of no-par value, stated value $10.00 per share, a capital surplus of $130,000.00, and an earned surplus of $100,000.00. One thousand shares of treasury stock are purchased at a cost of $25,000.00 and later resold for $30,000.00. The entries would be

```
Treasury Stock  . . . . . . . . . . . . . . . . . .    10,000.00
Capital Surplus  . . . . . . . . . . . . . . . . .     15,000.00
    Cash . . . . . . . . . . . . . . . . . . . . . .                 25,000.00
To record purchase of 1,000 shares of no-par treasury
stock (stated value $10.00 per share) at 25.


Cash . . . . . . . . . . . . . . . . . . . . . . .     30,000.00
    Treasury Stock  . . . . . . . . . . . . . . .                    10,000.00
    Capital Surplus  . . . . . . . . . . . . . . .                   20,000.00
To record sale of 1,000 shares of no-par treasury stock
(stated value $10.00 per share) at 30.
```

In all of these entries, the average original issue price remained constant. Should the average issue price of shares change, it would be possible for the Treasury Stock account to appear on the books at varying values per share. For the date on which a balance sheet is to be prepared, all treasury shares should be adjusted to the same value per share, i.e., average price of all shares issued to date, with offsetting adjustments to Capital Surplus.

The theory and basis of the accounting discussed and illustrated above have been stated. At the present time there is a very marked tendency in modern accounting practice to record treasury shares at their *cost of acquisition*. Montgomery, in his *Auditing Theory and Practice*, goes so far as to consider this the method in common use today. Under this philosophy of accounting, Treasury Stock on the balance sheet would be handled as a deduction from the total of capital stock and all surplus balances.

One basis for this accounting is legal in nature (see page 469). The American Accounting Association endorses this treatment of treasury stock by stating: "The outlay for reacquired shares of capital stock, provided the shares are reissuable, should be shown on the balance sheet as an unallocated reduction of capital stock and surplus, and any consequent restriction on surplus distributions should be disclosed."

To illustrate the accounting for treasury stock when it is recorded at cost of acquisition, the entries for the data of Example 4, above, would be

```
Treasury Stock  . . . . . . . . . . . . . . . . . .    25,000.00
    Cash . . . . . . . . . . . . . . . . . . . . . .                 25,000.00
To record purchase of 1,000 shares of no-par treasury
stock at 25.
```

```
Cash . . . . . . . . . . . . . . . . . . . . . .   30,000.00
    Treasury Stock  . . . . . . . . . . . . . .              25,000.00
    Capital Surplus . . . . . . . . . . . . . .               5,000.00
To record sale of 1,000 shares of no-par treasury stock
at 30.
```

DONATED NO-PAR TREASURY STOCK

The Y Corporation has a capital stock account of $230,000.00, representing 10,000 shares of no par value, and an earned surplus account of $100,000.00. One thousand shares of treasury stock are donated. The entry would be

```
Treasury Stock  . . . . . . . . . . . . . . . . .  23,000.00
    Capital Surplus . . . . . . . . . . . . . . .              23,000.00
To record donation of 1,000 shares of no-par treasury
stock at average issue price of 23.
```

If the stock were of a stated value of $10.00 per share, the entry would be

```
Treasury Stock  . . . . . . . . . . . . . . . . .  10,000.00
    Capital Surplus . . . . . . . . . . . . . . .              10,000.00
To record donation of 1,000 shares of no-par treasury
stock at stated value of $10.00 per share.
```

On the sale of these treasury shares, the difference between the cash received and the balance of the Treasury Stock account would be placed in Capital Surplus.

In view of their difficulties in finding a satisfactory value for shares of donated treasury stock, some accountants have advocated the use of a nominal valuation of $1.00 per share. This value, although arbitrary, has been advanced as a usable and conservative substitute which is especially serviceable in those cases where there is the probability of water existing in the original issue of capital stock. Some accountants, indeed, would go even further. They would not even make an entry for donated treasury stock of no-par value; they would only make a memorandum notation of the donation in the Treasury Stock account. The use of a nominal value per share, however, at least has the advantage of inserting treasury stock into the trial balance. This not only prevents the possibility of overlooking donated treasury stock when statements are being prepared but compels attention to both the stock and the capital surplus which is related to it.

DIVIDENDS ON NO-PAR STOCK

Accounting for cash dividends on no-par stock is similar to that for par value stock. The amount of the dividend liability on no-par stock is the number of shares entitled to participate in the dividend multiplied by the amount of the cash dividend per share, which is always stated in the dividend declaration.

The declaration of a stock dividend payable in no-par stock raises the problem of what amount to transfer from Surplus to Capital Stock. The board of directors in their declaration of dividend should fix this amount by stating the number of shares represented by the stock dividend and the value applicable to each.

If the directors specify the number of shares represented by the dividend but fail to indicate the amount to be transferred from Surplus, one of the following procedures may be used to determine the amount:

(1) Number of dividend shares × "stated value" of each no-par share,

or better,

$$(2) \quad \frac{\text{Number of dividend shares}}{\text{Number of shares outstanding before dividend}} \times \begin{array}{l}\text{Balance in}\\ \text{capital stock}\\ \text{account be-}\\ \text{fore dividend}\end{array}$$

NO-PAR STOCK ON THE BALANCE SHEET

No-par stock may be shown on the balance sheet in the following manner:

Common Stock, no par:

Authorized	11,000 shares		
Less unissued	1,000 shares		
Issued	10,000 shares	$230,000.00	
Less Treasury Stock	2,000 shares	46,000.00	
Issued and outstanding	8,000 shares		$184,000.00

The following example shows how treasury stock is handled when it is interpreted as an unallocated deduction relating to the sum of capital stock and surplus. The illustration is taken from the balance sheet of Pratt & Lambert, Inc., December 31, 1944:

Capital Stock and Surplus:

Capital stock of Pratt & Lambert, Inc. — authorized, 375,000 shares of no-par value; issued, 202,500 shares	$3,450,000.00
Capital surplus	65,520.56
Earned surplus	3,183,792.00
	$6,699,312.56
Less capital stock reacquired — 6,427 shares at cost	121,101.93
Remainder — capital stock and surplus	$6,578,210.63

VALUE

The "value" of a share of stock may mean any one of three values:

(1) Par value.

(2) Market value.

(3) Book value. This is the book value of the net assets behind each share of stock. From the standpoint of the common stockholders, the book value of a share of common stock is the amount which each outstanding share of common stock would receive if the business were liquidated and each asset converted into cash at balance sheet values.

On December 31, 1940, for example, the common stock of The American Sugar Refining Company had a par value of $100.00, a market value of $14.75, and a book value of $122.54. On the same date the no-par common stock (stated value $40.00) of the Eastman Kodak Company had a market value of $139.00, and a book value of $72.61. The calculation of this particular book value may be illustrated thus:

Example:

6% Cumulative Preferred Stock, par $100.00:	
Outstanding 61,657 shares	$ 6,165,700.00
Common Stock, no-par, stated value $40.00:	
Outstanding 2,476,013 shares	99,040,520.00
Paid-in Surplus	19,273,502.00
Earned Surplus	38,697,282.00
Reserve for Contingencies	22,772,317.00
Net Worth	$185,949,321.00
Less net worth allocated to preferred stock:	
61,657 × $100.00	6,165,700.00
Net worth allocated to common stock	$179,783,621.00
	÷
Number of common shares outstanding	2,476,013
Book value per share of common stock	$72.61

EARNINGS PER SHARE OF COMMON STOCK

The most widely used method for the calculation of earnings per share of common stock is the following:

$$\frac{\text{Net income for period after deduction of preferred dividends}}{\text{Number of shares outstanding at end of period}}$$

The earnings per share of common stock of the Eastman Kodak Company for the year 1940 were $7.96, calculated as follows:

Net income for 1940	$20,076,739.00
Less dividends on preferred stock for one year:	
6% × $6,165,700.00	369,942.00
Net income applicable to common stock	$19,706,797.00
	÷
Number of common shares outstanding	2,476,013
Earnings per share of common stock	$7.96

PURCHASED TREASURY STOCK: ACCOUNTING FROM THE LEGAL STANDPOINT

The accounting technique, which has been described in Chapters 21 and 22 for transactions involving the acquisition of treasury stock through purchase, is that which is generally used in practice. From the standpoint of the law, however, there is ample ground to justify a very different method of accounting for treasury stock which is purchased.

The law regards the legal capital of a corporation as a trust fund for the benefit of creditors, or as a "representation" of capital relied upon by creditors, and operating as a fraud upon them if the representation is false.[1]

---

[1] *Smith* v. *Dana* (77 Conn. 543). The amount credited to capital stock "constitutes a fund set apart and devoted to the corporate uses and the security of the creditors . . . [and] its dedication is irrevocable, and it must ever remain a sum held in trust for creditors, unless some judicial or other process authorized by legislation intervenes."

Upton v. *Tribilock* (91 U. S. 45, 47). ". . . the capital stock . . . is a fund for the payment of its [the corporation's] debts. It is a trust fund, of which the directors are trustees. . . . The capital paid in . . . is a fund which the trustees cannot squander or give away."

Topken, Loring, and Schwartz v. *Schwartz* (249 N. Y. 206 [1928]). ". . . the capital of a corporation is held in trust for its creditors, so that any agreement to purchase stock from a stockholder, which may result in the impairment of capital will not be enforced, or will be considered illegal if the rights of creditors are affected."

Hospes, et al. v. *Northwestern Manufacturing and Car Company* (48 Minn. 174, 50 N. W. 1117). ". . . the capital of a corporation is the basis of its credit. . . . They [creditors] have a right to assume that it has paid in capital to the amount which it represents itself as having; and if they give it credit on the faith of that representation, and if the representation is false, it is a fraud upon them."

Note: The "trust fund" doctrine as enunciated by these and other cases is subject to certain unfavorable criticisms. (1) There is no factual trust relationship between a corporation and its creditors. (2) Capital stock is not a fund, nor does a corporation segregate assets in an amount equal to its capital stock. (3) The trust fund doctrine is not necessary for the protection of creditors; their interests are well provided for through other well-known avenues of legal redress.

Basically the "trust fund" theory can only mean that there must be no intentional impairment of the capital represented by capital stock, and that claims of creditors take precedence over those of stockholders. Moreover, the courts of the United

It follows, therefore, that, from this point of view

(1) Treasury stock cannot legally result in diminution of the "capital fund" of a company because the capital of a corporation cannot be reduced except by due process of law.

(2) Since this fund (capital stock) must be kept inviolate, the only net worth against which treasury stock can be applied must be surplus, and that therefore the amount of treasury stock purchasable is limited to the amount of the credit balance in the Surplus account. Recent statutes of the various states lean heavily in the direction of this principle.[2]

From the legal point of view, therefore, the accounting for treasury stock (both par and no-par stock) which is acquired by the process of purchase should be patterned after the following entries:

States have not been unanimous in their endorsement of the "trust fund" theory; in *MacDonald* v. *Williams* (174 U. S. 397 [1899]), for instance, the court held that the "trust fund" theory did not apply to solvent corporations.

[2] Section 8 of the Florida corporation act of 1928 contains the provision that ". . . no such corporation shall purchase its own shares of capital stock except from the surplus of its assets over its liabilities including capital."

Section 6 of the business corporation act of Illinois, passed in 1933, reads:

"A corporation shall have power to purchase, take, receive, or otherwise acquire, hold, own, pledge, transfer, or otherwise dispose of its own shares, provided that it shall not purchase, either directly or indirectly, its own shares when its net assets are less than the sum of its stated capital, its paid-in surplus, any surplus arising from unrealized appreciation in value or revaluation of its assets and any surplus arising from surrender to the corporation of any of its shares, or when by so doing its net assets would be reduced below such sum."

Louisiana, in Section 23 of its business corporation act of 1928, holds that "unless the articles otherwise provide, a corporation may purchase its own shares of any class issued by it, but only out of surplus available for dividends."

Under subdivision 7 of Section 30 of the annotated code of Maryland, 1924, it is provided that ". . . no . . . corporation shall purchase any shares of its own stock unless the assets of the corporation remaining immediately after such purchase shall be not less than the debts of the corporation plus the amount of its issued capital stock."

The Michigan and Delaware corporation laws (Section 10-H and Section 19, respectively) provide that ". . . no corporation shall use its funds or property for the purchase of its own shares of capital stock when such use would cause any impairment of the capital of the corporation." (These sections do not prevent a corporation from redeeming its preferred stock by purchase and charging same to Capital Stock and Surplus. See Section 37 for Michigan and Section 27 for Delaware.)

The New York penal code, Section 664, states:

"A director of a stock corporation, who concurs in any vote or act of the directors of such corporation, or any of them, by which it is intended: . . .

5. To apply any portion of the funds of such corporation, except surplus, directly or indirectly, to the purchase of shares of its own stock,

is guilty of a misdemeanor."

Colorado, Delaware, Indiana, Michigan, Missouri, Nevada, Pennsylvania, Rhode Island, and West Virginia provide that the purchase of treasury stock must not impair the capital of a corporation. California, North Dakota, Ohio, and Oklahoma hold that treasury stock may be acquired only out of surplus.

For an extended discussion of this general question the student is referred to the *Journal of Accountancy*, September, 1933, pp. 171–199, for an excellent article entitled "Treasury Stock and the Courts" by L. L. Briggs.

For par value stock

Treasury Stock	10,000.00	
Capital Surplus	476.00	
Cash		10,476.00

To record purchase of 100 shares of common stock
($100.00 par) at cost of $10,476.00.

Earned Surplus.	10,476.00	
Earned Surplus Restricted by Cost of Treasury Stock		10,476.00

To reserve earned surplus in an amount equal to the
cost of treasury stock purchased.

For no-par value stock

Treasury Stock	10,476.00	
Cash		10,476.00

To record purchase of 100 shares of common stock, no-
par value, at cost of $10,476.00.

Earned Surplus.	10,476.00	
Earned Surplus Restricted by Cost of Treasury Stock		10,476.00

To reserve earned surplus in an amount equal to the
cost of treasury stock purchased.

After these entries have been posted, the balance remaining in
the Earned Surplus account will be equal to the maximum price that
can legally be paid in new purchases of treasury stock. Another result of these entries is to reduce the amount of earned surplus which
is available for dividends.

When the treasury stock is sold, the restricted surplus should be
returned to Earned Surplus.

QUESTIONS

Question **22–1.** Describe no-par stock, and its advantages.

Question **22–2.** How would you record (1) the authorization of a no-par
stock issue? (2) the sale of the stock for cash but at varying prices?

Question **22–3.** What value should be placed upon no-par treasury
stock which has been donated or purchased? Explain.

Question **22–4.** When a stock dividend is declared in no-par stock explain how the credit to Capital Stock account is determined.

Question **22–5.** Explain three concepts of value with reference to stock.

Question **22–6.** Is it possible for dividends to be legally paid to no-par
stockholders from any part of their original capital contributions?

PROBLEMS

Problem **22–1.** A corporation was organized with an authorized capital
stock of 100,000 shares of no-par common stock. Subscriptions to capital
stock were received: April 1, for 31,000 shares at $20.00 per share; May 1,

for 30,000 shares at $30.00 per share. The subscriptions were payable 50 % down and 50 % in six months. The subscriptions due on October 1 were paid in full. Those due on November 1 were paid in full except for the amount due on 1,000 shares of stock; a 60-day extension was granted for the payment of this installment.

Required:

(1) Record these transactions in journal entry form.

(2) What is the balance sheet of the corporation at the close of business November 1? Disregard any profit or loss from operations.

Problem 22-2. In 1940 the Seiberling Rubber Company sold 28,000 shares of its $2.50 cumulative convertible prior preferred stock, without par value, at a price of $50.00 per share. What entry should be made to record the sale of these shares?

Problem 22-3. On December 20, 1937, the Ruberoid Company paid dividends on its outstanding capital stock of $0.15 in cash, and $1.40 per share in 4 % notes due December 20, 1940. Before payment of these dividends, the balance sheet of the company was approximately as follows:

Assets	$17,331,631.00	Liabilities	$ 1,109,226.00
		Capital Stock, 397,806	
		shares of no-par value	13,034,164.00
		Surplus	3,188,241.00
	$17,331,631.00		$17,331,631.00

What entry should be made to record the dividends paid on December 20, 1937?

Problem 22-4. The condensed balance sheet of the Crest Wax Company on December 31, 19—, is as follows:

Assets	$327,000.00	Liabilities	$ 17,000.00
		Reserve for Contingencies	50,000.00
		7% Cumulative Preferred	
		Stock, $100.00 par.	100,000.00
		Common Stock, $100.00 par	100,000.00
		Surplus	60,000.00
	$327,000.00		$327,000.00

All dividends on the preferred stock have been paid in full to date. In the event of liquidation, the preferred stock is entitled to a value of $100.00 per share.

Required:

(1) Find the book value per share of common stock.

(2) Find the book value per share of common stock, assuming dividends on the preferred stock to be in arrears $21.00 per share.

Problem **22–5.** The condensed balance sheet of the F. C. Wayne Company on December 31, 19___, is:

Miscellaneous Assets. . . .	$452,000.00	Accounts Payable	$ 20,000.00
Treasury Stock, 300 shares		Reserve for Depreciation .	50,000.00
Common Stock	30,000.00	Reserve for Contingencies .	10,000.00
		Reserve for Income Taxes .	12,000.00
		Reserve for Dividends Payable	15,000.00
		Preferred Stock, 7% Cumulative, $100.00 par	100,000.00
		Common Stock, $100.00 par	200,000.00
		Earned Surplus	75,000.00
	$482,000.00		$482,000.00

What is the book value per share of the common stock? In the event of liquidation the preferred stock is entitled to $100.00 per share. There are no dividends in arrears.

Problem **22–6.** The Y Corporation has a capital stock outstanding of $123,000.00, representing 100,000 shares of no-par common stock. Surplus is currently $20,000.00.

The following transactions occur and are recorded by the entries stated:

(1) 1,000 shares of its own stock are donated to the corporation and resold for $1,500.00.

Treasury Stock	1,230.00	
Capital Surplus		1,230.00
Cash	1,500.00	
Treasury Stock		1,230.00
Capital Surplus		270.00

(2) 1,000 shares of its own stock are purchased for $1,000.00 and resold for $1,100.00.

Treasury Stock	1,230.00	
Cash		1,000.00
Contingent Surplus		230.00
Contingent Surplus	130.00	
Cash	1,100.00	
Treasury Stock		1,230.00
Contingent Surplus	100.00	
Capital Surplus		100.00

(3) 1,000 shares of its own stock are purchased for $1,300.00 and ~~sold~~ for $1,360.00.

Treasury Stock	1,230.00	
Capital Surplus	70.00	
Cash . . . . :		1,300.00
Cash	1,360.00	
Treasury Stock		1,230.00
Capital Surplus		130.00

Do you agree with the entries above? If not, explain how you would have constructed them.

Problem **22–7.** Following is the condensed balance sheet of Kerr & Brown, Inc., on a certain date:

Cash	$ 100,000.00	Current Liabilities . . .	$ 250,000.00
Noncash Current Assets .	400,000.00	Common Stock, $100.00	
Fixed Assets (net)	800,000.00	par	800,000.00
Other Assets	300,000.00	Earned Surplus	550,000.00
	$1,600,000.00		$1,600,000.00

The following transactions occurred in the order indicated:

(1) Part of the surplus was capitalized by the payment of a stock dividend of 25 %.
(2) Stockholders donated 10 % of their shares to the company.
(3) The book value per share of outstanding stock was determined and the donated stock was sold at a price equal to this book value.
(4) 1,000 shares of its own stock were acquired by Kerr & Brown, Inc., at a cost of $140,000.00.
(5) 600 shares of treasury stock were sold for $16,000.00 more than their cost.
(6) 400 shares of treasury stock were sold for $75,000.00.
(7) A cash dividend of 6 % was declared on the outstanding common stock.

Required:

(1) Make journal entries to record the foregoing transactions.
(2) Prepare a new balance sheet giving effect to these transactions

Problem **22–8.** The after-closing trial balance of Bailey & Wood, Inc., on December 31, 1952, was as follows:

Cash	$ 50,802.00	
Notes Receivable	30,000.00	
Notes Receivable Discounted.		$ 12,000.00
Accounts Receivable	101,018.00	
Merchandise	160,011.00	
Fixed Assets	201,142.00	
Reserve for Depreciation		32,912.00
Prepaid Expenses	21,010.00	
Accounts Payable		60,410.00
Preferred Stock, 6%, $100.00 par		100,000.00
Common Stock, no-par, 20,000 shares		187,055.00
Earned Surplus.		130,607.00
Capital Surplus		40,999.00
	$563,983.00	$563,983.00

During 1953 these transactions occurred in the following order:

(1) 1,000 shares of the company's own common stock was purchased in the open market at a cash cost of $10,780.00.
(2) Sales of merchandise on account, $360,000.00.
(3) Collections from customers were $347,018.00. And, in addition, all notes receivable were paid.
(4) Purchases of merchandise on account, $200,000.00.
(5) Paid accounts payable, $250,000.00.
(6) Paid expenses, $40,000.00.
(7) A reserve of $16,000.00 was created against outstanding 1952 accounts receivable.
(8) Estimated uncollectible 1953 accounts receivable, $9,000.00.
(9) Depreciation expense for 1953 was $20,000.00.
(10) All of the treasury stock was sold for $20,011.00 cash.
(11) A stock dividend of one share for each five shares outstanding was declared and paid on the common stock out of earned surplus.
(12) A cash dividend of $6.00 per share was paid on the preferred stock.
(13) A cash dividend of $2.00 per share was declared on the common stock, payable January 20, 1954.

Required:

(1) Prepare a balance sheet, December 31, 1953. New inventory, $114,000.00.
(2) Prepare a statement of earned surplus for the year 1953.

Problem **22–9.** On July 1, 1950, Brookes & Company is organized with an authorized capitalization of

8 % preferred stock, par value $100.00, 1,000 shares
Common stock, no-par value, 1,000 shares

The following transactions occurred on the dates named:

1950

July   1 — 500 shares of preferred stock are subscribed for at par. A 50 % down payment is received with the balance payable in quarterly installments of $5,000.00 each.

725 shares of common stock are subscribed for. Payment is immediately received as follows:

| Merchandise | $20,762.00 | Furniture and Fixtures. . | $2,049.00 |
| Accounts Receivable . . | 11,431.00 | Land . . . . | 4,250.00 |

July 30 — 100 shares of preferred stock are sold for cash at $110.00 per share.

Aug. 1 — 25 shares of common stock are issued to the organizers of the corporation and attorneys, in payment of organization costs, $1,200.00.

Aug. 15 — 250 shares of common stock are issued in payment of a building worth $12,500.00.

Oct.   1 — $5,000.00 cash is received as quarterly payment on preferred stock subscriptions.

Nov.   1 — The stock issued to organizers on August 1 is reacquired by a cash payment of $2,000.00.

Dec. 31 — Sales of merchandise on account to date, $100,000.00.
Purchases of merchandise on account to date, $105,000.00.
Collections on accounts receivable, $90,000.00.
Payments on accounts payable, $58,000.00.
Operating expenses paid, $35,000.00.

Dec. 31 — Cash dividends are declared: 4 % on the preferred stock, $5.00 on the common stock.

Required:

(1) Make journal entries to record above transactions.

(2) Post to a T-account ledger.

(3) Prepare a balance sheet, December 31, 1950. New inventory, $68,088.00.

Problem **22–10.** A corporation has, among other accounts,

6% Preferred Stock, par $100.00	$ 500,000.00
Common Stock, par $100.00	1,000,000.00
Treasury Stock, Common, 1,000 shares	100,000.00
Earned Surplus	110,000.00
Capital Surplus	20,000.00

The capital surplus was created by the purchase of the treasury stock.

Directors of the corporation declare cash dividends of 6 % on the preferred stock, and 5 % on the common stock.

From the legal point of view comment on the propriety of these dividend declarations.

Chapter 23

THE VOUCHER SYSTEM — PETTY CASH

WHY THE VOUCHER SYSTEM IS USED

Up to this point in our exposition of accounting method, transactions with creditors have been handled in two ways:

(1) Merchandise purchases have been recorded immediately upon receipt of invoice.

(2) Bills for supplies and services have been recorded only when paid.

This procedure is not satisfactory when there is delay in the payment of nonmerchandise obligations. Expenditures may not be debited to the operations of the month to which they apply. This is because the month in which an expenditure is paid is not necessarily the month which should be charged with the expenditure. From the standpoint of correct accounting, however, it is clear that expenditures should be debited to the operations of the months to which they belong rather than be debited against the operations of the months in which they happen to be paid. One of the chief advantages of the voucher system is that it incorporates expenditures of every description in the books of the proper month.

OPERATION OF THE VOUCHER SYSTEM

The routine of the voucher system is described by the following steps:

(1) When an invoice is received from a creditor it is checked for validity, for the receipt of the items named, and for its mathematical correctness. When the invoice has been found correct, it is ready to be "vouchered."

(2) The invoice is copied upon the following voucher form:

Voucher No._____

BELL & BELL, INC.
Pittsburgh, Penna.

PAYABLE TO (Creditor's name)   Date _____

          Terms _____

(Address)   Due _____

(Description of invoice)

Approved by

		Entered	
Purchasing Department	Auditor		Treasurer

Note: Instead of copying the invoice, an alternative method is to fasten the invoice to the face of the voucher.

(3) The reverse side of the voucher form is then filled out:

Account No.	Debit	Amount		
350	Material Purchases			**Voucher No.** _____
360	Freight In			(Creditor's name)
380	Direct Labor			
420	Factory Salaries			
430	Factory Supplies			
440	Heat, Light, Power			Amount of Invoice $
450	Indirect Labor			Cash Discount $
470	Misc. Factory Expense			Net Amount $
501	Advertising			
520	Delivery Expense			Due for Payment
560	Misc. Selling Expense			Paid by Check No.
580	Sales Salaries			Date
590	Traveling Expense			
601	Admin. Salaries			
640	Misc. General Expense			
650	Office Supplies			
660	Postage			
	Total			

(Fold on dotted line)

(4) Upon approval, first by the purchasing department, then by the auditor, the voucher goes to the bookkeeper for formal entry in the voucher register. Vouchers, being numbered consecutively, are entered in numerical sequence.

(5) The voucher is filed in the unpaid voucher file according to the date it is due for payment. The invoice, if not attached to the voucher, is filed alphabetically, the voucher number being noted upon it.

(6) When the date of payment arrives, the voucher is removed from the unpaid voucher file and passed to the treasurer for his signature approving payment of the voucher. When this approval has been obtained:

(a) The cashier prepares a check.

(b) The check number is recorded on the voucher.

(c) The check is given to the treasurer for signature.

(d) The check is mailed.

(e) The voucher is sent to the bookkeeper who (i) records the disbursement in the cash payments book and (ii) makes a memorandum of the payment in the "date paid" column of the voucher register.

(f) The voucher is filed with other paid vouchers. Vouchers may be filed numerically but, since the voucher register records vouchers in numerical sequence, it is better that the vouchers be filed alphabetically; this method of filing is especially desirable when invoices are attached to the voucher folder. The numerical sequence, however, is often preferred in the interest of easier audits.

VOUCHER REGISTER

The voucher register is essentially a multicolumn purchases book in which invoices from *all* creditors are recorded. In its most complete form the voucher register is used for the original entry of expenditures of every kind. In the latter respect, however, it should be understood that entries in the voucher register are for specific liabilities of known amounts which are expected to be paid in the reasonably near future. Material and expense invoices will be vouchered immediately but not an item like accrued taxes. Taxes will be recorded in the voucher register only in the month of payment.

The voucher register illustrated on pages 482–483 may be considered typical.

Attention is directed to the following points:

(1) At the end of the month, only column totals are posted to the general ledger. The figures in parentheses are ledger folio references. The accounts in the miscellaneous column are posted individually.

(2) The Vouchers Payable account is a controlling account which replaces the Accounts Payable account on the general ledger. No subsidiary ledger, however, is maintained for Vouchers Payable. Instead, the details of the balance of the Vouchers Payable account are the unpaid items of the voucher register. A monthly reconciliation should be made to see that the sum of the unpaid items in the voucher register is equal to the balance of the Vouchers Payable account in the general ledger. This balance should also, of course, be the sum of the items in the unpaid voucher file. The reconciliation schedule of a particular date should be retained at least until the next schedule is completed.

The number of distribution columns which should be included in a voucher register is primarily dependent upon the requirements of the business which is to use the voucher register. Some businesses, obviously, will require more elaborate columnar records than others. It is sufficient to say that as many columns should be used as may be necessary. Each column, however, should justify its existence by a reasonable amount of use.

A very useful layout of the distribution columns of a voucher register is illustrated on page 486. One column is employed for each *general class* of expenditure; the detailed accounts to be debited are indicated by account numbers placed opposite related amounts.[1] While each item of a column may be separately posted, greater speed will ordinarily be made if postings are made from a summarization of details below the total of each column. This is illustrated in the example. Postings are indicated by √ marks inasmuch as accounts are filed by account number in the general ledger.

This type of voucher register has special applicability to circumstances wherein the accounts of a business include controlling accounts for each general class of expenditure. For instance, if controlling accounts were kept for manufacturing expense, selling expense, and general expense, respectively, only column totals for these items in the voucher register would be posted to the general ledger. The "Summary of Totals," as such, would not be prepared; instead, the bookkeeper in charge of the subsidiary expense ledgers

---

[1] The accounts and account numbers used in this illustration are taken from the numerical chart of accounts on pages 644 to 647.

VOUCHER REGISTER

Line No.	Date	Voucher No.	Creditor	Paid Date	Check No.	Credit — Vouchers Payable	Debit — Administrative Salaries	Debit — Advertising	Debit — Delivery Expense	Debit — Freight In	Debit — General Expense	Line No.
1	1950 Feb. 2	54	Weld & Company			406 00						1
2	3	55	Postmaster	Feb. 3	60	25 00						2
3	5	56	Bell Telephone Company	Feb. 10	84	23 60						3
4	6	57	Terry Specialties, Inc.			212 10						4
5	9	58	Royal Super Service Station	Feb. 14	91	19 47			19 47			5
6	10	59	Black Manufacturing Co.			27 02						6
7	12	60	Underwood Typewriter Co.	Feb. 12	89	12 50					12 50	7
8	13	61	Black Manufacturing Co.			602 15						8
9	14	62	Payroll	Feb. 14	92–109	1,217 50	450 00		62 50			9
10	16	63	Royal Super Service Station			17 20			17 20			10
11	18	64	The Daily News			52 00		52 00				11
12	19	65	Gilbert & Son			614 17						12
13	20	66	Chesapeake & Ohio Railway	Feb. 20	110	11 04				11 04		13
14	23	67	Royal Super Service Station	Feb. 25	111	29 02			29 02			14
15	25	68	First National Bank			500 00						15
16	26	69	Heyer Lettergraph Co.			35 00						16
17	27	70	Selby Office Supply Co.			29 45						17
18	28	71	Royal Super Service Station			28 14			28 14			18
19	28	72	George Tener	Feb. 28	112	214 02						19
20	28	73	Payroll	Feb. 28	113–130	1,229 60	450 00		62 50			20
21												21
22						5,304 98	900 00	52 00	218 83	11 04	12 50	22
23						(57)	(4)	(5)	(10)	(14)	(21)	23
24												24
25												25

482

VOUCHER REGISTER

DEBIT

Line No.	Miscellaneous			Traveling Expense	Selling Expense Miscellaneous	Sales Salaries	Purchases	Postage	Office Supplies	Labor (Misc.)	Line No.
	Name of Account	L.F.	Amount								
1											1
2							406 00	25 00			2
3	Telephone and Telegraph	49	23 60								3
4							212 10				4
5							27 02				5
6											6
7											7
8							602 15			205 00	8
9						500 00					9
10											10
11							614 17				11
12											12
13											13
14											14
15	Notes Payable	28	500 00								15
16	Office Equipment	31	35 00						29 45		16
17											17
18											18
19					214 02		500 00					19
20											217 10	20
21												21
22			558 60	214 02		1,000 00	1,861 44	25 00	29 45	422 10	22
23											23
24				(50)		(41)	(37)	(36)	(32)	(27)	24
25											25

would post the individual entries in the control columns to each of the expense accounts named.

The subsidiary expense ledgers may be kept in either of two forms: (1) in the usual account form, or (2) in the form of a single sheet which may be ruled as follows:

Account No. 700 SELLING EXPENSE Month of ———— 19—

$ ————

Voucher or Journal Page, No.	701 Advertising	710 Commissions	720 Delivery Expense	730 Depreciation Expense	740 Freight Out	760 Miscellaneous Selling Expense	780 Sales Salaries	790 Traveling Expense
TOTALS								

VOUCHER

Line No.	Date		Voucher No.	Creditor	Paid		Credit						
					Date	Check No.	Acct. No.	√	Vouchers Payable		Acct. No.	√	Material Purchases
1	1950 Feb.	3	114	White Supply Company					1,947	82			
2		5	115	Lewisohn & Company	Feb. 14	3124			16,247	20	425		16,247 20
3		6	116	Bell Telephone Company	Feb. 10	3070			112	10			
4		6	117	Chesapeake & Ohio Railway	Feb. 6	3049			687	02	450		687 02
5		10	118	Sundry Salesmen	Feb. 10	3071–9			800	46			
6		12	119	Lowman & Hanford					126	20			
7		13	120	City Treasurer					1,284	10			
8		14	121	Main Office Payroll	Feb. 14	3130–90			13,120	00			
9		14	122	Factory Payroll	Feb. 14	3191–4294			34,939	82			
10													
11													
12		14	123	Western Union Telegraph Company	Feb. 20	4318			145	10			
13		14	124	Berle & Son					18,746	27	425		18,746 27
14		16	125	First National Bank	Feb. 16	4310			10,100	00			
15													
16		18	126	Conway Hardware Company					3,814	20			
17		19	127	Times-Tribune Company					1,100	00			
18		20	128	Republic Iron and Steel Company	Feb. 24	4319			28,889	40	426		28,889 40
19		23	129	Segal-Simmons, Inc.					1,214	10			
20		24	130	Central Garage Company					299	25			
21		25	131	International Nickel Company					26,042	21	427		26,042 21
22		25	132	Sundry Salesmen	Feb. 25	4322			720	21			
23		26	133	Times-Tribune Company					910	00			
24		27	134	Segal-Simmons, Inc.					370	00			
25		28	135	The Nold Company					8,476	20	425		8,476 20
26		28	136	Main Office. Payroll	Feb. 28	4330–89			12,900	00			
27		28	137	Factory Payroll	Feb. 28	4390–5524			34,485	89			
28													
29													
30		28	138	Petty Cash	Feb. 28	5525			45	06			
31													
32							140	√	217,522	61			99,088 30
33													
34				Summary of Totals							425	√	43,469 67
35											426	√	28,889 40
36											427	√	26,042 21
37											450	√	687 02
38													
39													
40													99,088 30

REGISTER.

DEBIT															**LINE No.**
Acct. No.	√	Direct Labor	Acct. No.	√	Manufacturing Expense	Acct. No.	√	Selling Expense	Acct. No.	√	General Expense	Acct. No.	√	Miscellaneous	
															1
			670		1,947 82										2
									884		112 10				3
															4
						790		800 46							5
															6
									850		126 20				7
			690		1,040 00				880		244 10				8
501		9,876 29	620		1,800 00	780		4,200 00	801		7,120 00				9
502		6,414 80	650		11,820 14										10
503		6,828 59													11
															12
									884		145 10				13
												130		10,000 00	14
												1050		100 00	15
															16
			630		3,814 20	701		1,100 00							17
															18
			630		1,214 10										19
						720		299 25							20
															21
															22
						790		720 21							23
			630		370 00	701		910 00							24
															25
															26
			620		1,500 00	780		4,300 00	801		7,100 00				27
501		10,046 00	650		12,010 50										28
502		7,001 10													29
503		5,428 29				790		15 00	860		30 06				30
															31
															32
		45,595 07			35,516 76			12,344 92			14,877 56			10,100 00	33
501	√	19,922 29	620	√	3,300 00	701	√	2,010 00	801	√	14,220 00	130	√	10,000 00	34
502	√	13,415 90	630	√	5,398 30	720	√	299 25	850	√	126 20	1050	√	100 00	35
503	√	12,256 88	650	√	23,830 64	780	√	8,500 00	860	√	30 06				36
			670	√	1,947 82	790	√	1,535 67	880	√	244 10				37
			690	√	1,040 00				884	√	257 20				38
															39
		45,595 07			35,516 76			12,344 92			14,877 56			10,100 00	40

THE CHECK REGISTER

The check register is the name given to the cash payments book under the voucher system. All disbursements are made by check.

The check register is relatively simple in form for the reason that all payments are charged to one account — Vouchers Payable.

CHECK REGISTER

Date	Check No.	Payee	Voucher No.	Debit	Credit	
				Vouchers Payable	Purchases Discounts	Cash

Occasionally it may be advisable to include an additional debit column in the voucher register. This column would care for occasional miscellaneous debits not covered by vouchers and checks, such as bank service fees and similar charges.

PARTIAL PAYMENTS

If, at the time of original entry, it is definitely intended that an invoice is to be paid in installments, a separate voucher should be made out for each installment. But if a payment on account is to be made against the amount of a voucher already recorded on the books, the original voucher should be canceled and two new vouchers issued in its place, one for the part to be paid, the other for the part to remain unpaid.

RETURNED PURCHASES AND ALLOWANCES

If it is necessary to record a credit memorandum received after a voucher has been recorded, the original voucher should be canceled and a new voucher issued for the reduced amount.[2] The new voucher would be recorded in the voucher register as follows:

---

[2] An alternative method is to record the credit memorandum in red ink immediately above the line on which the original voucher is recorded. The amount of the

CREDIT: Vouchers Payable . . . . . $ 900.00   (Amount of new voucher)

DEBIT: Vouchers Payable . . . . . 1,000.00   (Amount of old voucher)

CREDIT: Returned Purchases and Al-
      lowances . . . . 100.00   (Amount of credit memorandum)

The latter two items would be entered in the "Miscellaneous Accounts Debited" column of the voucher register. The figure for $100.00 would be circled, or placed in parentheses, to indicate a credit.

The example on page 490 illustrates the proper recording of credit memorandums and partial payments in the voucher register.

PAYMENT OF VOUCHER BY NOTE

When a voucher is paid by the issuance of a promissory note, the discharge of the voucher liability is recorded by an entry in the general journal:

Vouchers Payable . . . . xxx xx
    Notes Payable . . . .   xxx xx
    To record payment of voucher #__ by 60-day note.

When this entry has been made, the unpaid voucher should be removed from the unpaid voucher file and marked "paid by note, see journal, page —" and filed in the paid voucher file. In the "paid" column of the voucher register suitable notation should be made indicating that the voucher in question has been discharged by note payable rather than by check. (This sentence, incidentally, emphasizes the importance of suitable notation in the "paid" column of the voucher register whenever a debit is made to the Vouchers Payable account.)

Later, when the note is to be paid, a new voucher will be prepared and recorded in the voucher register; the debit in this case will be to Notes Payable.

INDEX OF CREDITORS

If it is desired to have a record of the amount of business done with each creditor (vouchers being filed numerically), a memoran-

---

voucher will then be understood to be the difference between the red ink and the black ink entries. (The credit must also be deducted from the amount shown on the unpaid voucher.) This method cannot be used if the voucher register has been footed and closed.

At the end of the month the black ink total of the Vouchers Payable column will be posted to the credit of the Vouchers Payable account; the red ink total will be posted to the debit of the Vouchers Payable account. The black ink total of the Purchases column will be posted to the debit of the Purchases account; the red ink total of the Purchases column will be posted to the credit of the Returned Purchases and Allowances account.

VOUCHER REGISTER

Date	Voucher No.	Creditor	Explanation	PAID Date	PAID Check No.	CREDIT Vouchers Payable	CREDIT Purchases	DEBIT Miscellaneous Amount	DEBIT Miscellaneous Name of Account
1950 Mar. 10	179	Bendix-Page, Inc.	2/10, n/60.	See Vo. #187		1,000 00	1,000 00		
15	180	Edie & Son	$10,000 invoice payable in 5 monthly installments, beginning April 1.			2,000 00			
15	181	Edie & Son				2,000 00			
15	182	Edie & Son				2,000 00			
15	183	Edie & Son				2,000 00			
15	184	Edie & Son				2,000 00		10,000 00	Machinery
16	185	The Nold Co.	To cancel Vo. #135	Mar. 15		5,000 00		8,476 20	Vouchers Payable
16	186	The Nold Co.	" " "		7017	3,476 20			
17	187	Bendix-Page, Inc.	To cancel Vo. #179			900 00		1,000 00	Vouchers Payable
								(100 00)	Returned Purchases and Allowances

Note: In the "Paid" column on the line where voucher #135 was originally entered should be written "See Vouchers #185–186."

dum card file can be maintained for creditors. The type of card shown below would be used:

ELSON & YOUNG
1202 Market St.,
Chicago 3, Ill.

DATE	VOUCHER No.	AMOUNT	DATE	VOUCHER No.	AMOUNT	DATE	VOUCHER No.	AMOUNT

If such a card file [3] is much used, it is probably better to maintain a formal accounts payable subsidiary ledger in full detail.

INSTALLING A VOUCHER SYSTEM

This may be accomplished in either of two ways:

(1) Debit all bills on the books, when paid, to Accounts Payable.

Each new bill received is put through the regular system of voucher routine. These bills, when paid, are debited to Vouchers Payable.

Under this procedure full employment of the voucher system is delayed until the old accounts payable are completely eliminated. The change-over is gradual.

(2) Prepare a voucher for each unpaid bill on the books. Enter these vouchers in the voucher register. These vouchers are distributed into the miscellaneous column of the voucher register and there debited to Accounts Payable. This debit cancels the credit balance in the Accounts Payable account. *All* bills, when paid, are debited to Vouchers Payable.

This method effects an immediate change-over to the voucher system.

ADVANTAGES OF THE VOUCHER SYSTEM

(1) Expenditures are recorded in the month to which they belong.

(2) Proper authorization is necessary to the entry and payment

---

[3] In place of a card file, some concerns prepare a carbon copy of the voucher. The original is filed numerically, the carbon alphabetically. Still other concerns find the alphabetical file of invoices sufficient as an informal creditors' ledger.

of each creditor's invoice.   Responsibility for each step is definitely fixed.[4]

(3) Each voucher payment is supported by a permanent detailed record.

(4) The prompt payment of bills, with benefit of discount privilege, is facilitated.

(5) The check register is a simple three-column cash payments book.

(6) There is no subsidiary accounts payable ledger.   There are fewer postings.   New accounts, often representing but a transaction or two, are handled with a minimum of bookkeeping labor.

DISADVANTAGES OF THE VOUCHER SYSTEM

(1) Much work is added if
    (a) Invoices are copied upon the voucher form.[5]
    (b) A card index for creditors is maintained.

(2) The voucher register is an awkward arrangement for the handling of
    (a) Corrections of original entries.
    (b) Purchase returns and allowances.
    (c) Regular or irregular installment payments.

(3) No creditor accounts are maintained; their reference value is lost.

PETTY CASH

Most businesses object to the issuance of vouchers and checks for petty expenditures.   Hence they establish a small cash fund out of which petty expenses are paid in cash.   The "imprest system" of handling the petty cash fund operates in the following manner:

July 1 Petty Cash	50.00	
Vouchers Payable.		50.00
To establish petty cash fund of $50.00.		
Vouchers Payable.	50.00	
Cash		50.00
To record payment of petty cash voucher.		

---

[4] This principle is sometimes extended to entries intended for the general journal. Each journal entry is prepared upon a form designed for that purpose; each entry must be audited by an employee, and signed by another, before it can be entered on the books.   Frequently these "journal vouchers" constitute the general journal itself.   Posted vouchers are conveniently filed in a post binder.

[5] Some concerns eliminate formal vouchers and use the voucher register as an accounts payable or invoice register.   Invoices are consecutively numbered and entered in this register, debited to Accounts Payable when paid, and filed alphabetically for permanent reference.   Each invoice is approved before entry, and the check is audited by a responsible employee before being passed for signature.

During the month minor expense bills are paid in cash out of this fund. Each disbursement of petty cash is supported by a receipt, petty cash voucher, or other memorandum evidencing the propriety of the payment.

The disbursements of petty cash may be recorded in a memorandum petty cash disbursements book, one form of which is shown on page 494.

At the end of the month the disbursements of petty cash are summarized as follows:

> $20.00 for postage
> 14.83 for freight and express bills
>   5.00 for carfare
>
> ————
>
> $39.83

In order to replenish the petty cash fund, a check is drawn in favor of the petty cashier. The accounting entries are

```
July 31   Freight In . . . . . . . . . . . . . . . . . . . . .   14.83
          General Expense. . . . . . . . . . . . . . . . .       5.00
          Postage  . . . . . . . . . . . . . . . . . . . . .    20.00
              Vouchers Payable . . . . . . . . . . . . . .               39.83
          To record voucher for replenishment of petty cash fund
          for disbursements made during month of July.


          Vouchers Payable . . . . . . . . . . . . . . . . .    39.83
              Cash  . . . . . . . . . . . . . . . . . . . .              39.83
          To record payment of petty cash voucher.  (One check
          and one voucher thus cover a great many small dis-
          bursements.)
```

It will be noticed that the summarized expense accounts responsible for the diminution of petty cash are debited in recording the replenishment of the fund. They are debited because they are the expenses which make the general cash disbursement necessary.

The petty cash fund should at least be replenished on the last day of each month in order to place the disbursements of petty cash in the accounts of the proper month. It should be understood, however, that replenishment may be made at any time the fund runs low. Too frequent replenishment may be avoided by having the amount of the petty cash fund commensurate with the ordinary needs of the business.

It is not to be inferred from the above discussion that the imprest system of petty cash is limited to businesses which use the full voucher system. Where the voucher register is not used and where disbursements are distributed to accounts from the cash payments book, the imprest system of petty cash would operate as follows:

PETTY CASH DISBURSEMENTS RECORD

PERIOD: FROM ———— To ————

DATE	PAYEE	EXPLANATION	AMOUNT OF PAYMENT	FREIGHT IN	GENERAL EXPENSE	OFFICE SUPPLIES	POSTAGE	MISCELLANEOUS	
								Amount	Account

July 1	Petty Cash	50.00	
	Cash		50.00
	To establish petty cash fund of $50.00.		
July 31	Freight In	14.83	
	General Expense.	5.00	
	Postage	20.00	
	Cash		39.83
	To reimburse the petty cash fund for payments made during the month of July.		

Under either method of the imprest system the balance of the Petty Cash account in the general ledger will not change unless the amount of the petty cash fund is actually increased or decreased.

Under the nonimprest method of handling petty cash, the Petty Cash account is debited for *all* cash placed into the petty cash fund and is credited for *all* disbursements of petty cash. Checks to replenish the petty cash fund are for round amounts rather than for specific vouchers. The summary of disbursements of petty cash is recorded in the journal at least on the last day of each month; or, in lieu of this entry, postings may be made direct from the petty cash disbursements book. Under this method of accounting for petty cash, it is obvious that there will be frequent changes in the balance of the Petty Cash account in the general ledger. Under the non-imprest system of handling petty cash, the accounting entries would be

July 1	Petty Cash	50.00	
	Vouchers Payable		50.00
	To establish petty cash fund of $50.00.		
	Vouchers Payable	50.00	
	Cash		50.00
	To record payment of petty cash voucher.		
July 31	Freight In	14.83	
	General Expense.	5.00	
	Postage	20.00	
	Petty Cash		39.83
	To record disbursements of petty cash in July.		
	Petty Cash	40.00	
	Vouchers Payable		40.00
	To record voucher for replenishment of petty cash fund.		
	Vouchers Payable	40.00	
	Cash		40.00
	To record payment of petty cash voucher.		

As a general rule, the imprest system of petty cash is to be preferred over the nonimprest or "round amounts" system of petty cash.

QUESTIONS

Question **23–1.** Describe, in reasonable detail, the routine of the voucher system.

Question **23–2.** How would you determine the total amount owed to a designated creditor at a given date?

Question **23–3.** On January 31, 19__, the Vouchers Payable account in the general ledger has a balance of $12,427.02. How would you proceed to obtain a detailed proof of this figure? What steps would you take should the reconciliation be found "out of balance"?

Question **23–4.** Describe briefly two types of voucher register. Explain what postings are made from each type.

Question **23–5.** How would you handle a cash purchase under the voucher system?

Question **23–6.** Explain how a purchase return or allowance would be handled on the voucher register.

Question **23–7.** Explain how a Returned Purchases and Allowances account on the general ledger may be provided for under the voucher system.

Question **23–8.** You are unable to meet the payment of $6,414.87 for the invoice of the William O. McKay Company due today. You pay $2,414.87 cash, and give a 60-day, 6% note for the balance. How should this be recorded in the voucher register?

Question **23–9.** What is the purpose of a voucher register index? Why not keep a regular ledger of formal accounts instead?

Question **23–10.** How would you proceed to install a voucher system in a set of books?

Question **23–11.** Enumerate the advantages and disadvantages of the voucher system.

Question **23–12.** A company objects to the "red tape" of the voucher system. It recognizes, however, that there are certain advantages to be gained by its use, and it inquires, accordingly, if it is not possible to obtain these advantages without attendant "red tape." What would you answer?

Question **23–13.** Explain how the imprest system of petty cash operates.

Question **23–14.** Why should the petty cash fund be reimbursed on the last day of every month? How large should the petty cash fund be?

Question **23–15.** Assuming the imprest system of petty cash to be in use, interpret the entries in the following account:

PETTY CASH

1950 July	1 15		CP1 CP2	25 75	00 00	1950 Aug.	1		CR3	50	00

PROBLEMS

Problem **23–1.** The Union Sales Company began business on July 1, 19__. The voucher register was one of its books of original entry and contained columns for:

Date	Purchases
In Favor Of	Freight In
Voucher No.	Miscellaneous Sales Expense
Date Paid	Miscellaneous General Expense
Check No.	Utilities Expense
Vouchers Payable	Sundry

The condensed transactions of the company for the month of July were as follows:

1 — Sold 1,000 shares of no-par capital stock (entire authorized issue) for cash, $101,874.00.

2 — Paid rent for July to Perry Realty Company, $500.00.

3 — Bought merchandise on account from Hale & Company, $8,746.00. Paid Southern Railway for freight on this purchase, $111.00.

5 — Gave Lee R. Hancock, salesman, a travel advance of $500.00 cash.

6 — Purchased office fixtures and equipment on account from Kline & Dameron, Inc., $3,784.00.

7 — A bill for advertising in the *Daily News* is paid, $604.00.

8 — Bought office supplies on account from Dewey & Willkie, Inc., $129.00. (Debit Miscellaneous General Expense.)

10 — Bought merchandise on account from A. J. Hardin, $6,480.00. Paid Southern Railway for freight on this purchase, $48.00.

11 — An air conditioning unit is purchased for cash from York & Co., $1,850.00. Paid Southern Railway for freight, $70.00; and paid York & Co. for installation charges, $80.00.

12 — Bought merchandise on account from L. J. Reed & Company, $14,050.00. Paid Southern Railway for freight on this purchase, $174.00.

14 — Returned $746.00 of the merchandise purchased on July 3 from Hale & Company.

15 — Established a petty cash fund of $100.00. Drew check in favor of Elmo S. Treize, cashier.

17 — Gave Kline & Dameron, Inc., a check for $1,784.00 as part payment of their bill of July 6.

18 — A bill from the Otis Elevator Company for its monthly service charge is received, $10.00.

19 — Bought merchandise on account from the Charles A. Burton Co., $12,801.00.

20 — Paid the L. J. Reed Company for bill of July 12, $14,050.00, less 2% cash discount.

21 — Gave a 10-day note in favor of Hale & Company in payment of balance due on bill of July 3, $8,000.00.

22 — Bought merchandise on account from Hale & Company, $7,-410.00.

24 — A credit memorandum is received from the Charles A. Burton Co. to apply on bill of July 19, $301.00.

26 — Reimbursed petty cash for postage, $50.00.

27 — Bill of the Bell Telephone Company for July is received, $30.00.

28 — Bought merchandise on account from the L. J. Reed Company, $11,026.00. Paid Southern Railway for freight on this purchase, $99.00. Freight terms on this purchase were f.o.b. destination.

29 — A bill for gas, electricity, and other utility services is received from Southern Public Service Corporation, $204.00.

31 — Paid note payable of July 21, $8,000.00.

31 — Sales on account for July amounted to $40,166.00. Collections on accounts receivable amounted to $20,000.00.

31 — The payroll for July was sales salaries, $3,000.00, general salaries, $5,000.00. After deduction of $80.00 for social security taxes and $1,200.00 for income taxes withheld, the payroll was paid by drawing one check for $6,720.00 in favor of Elmo S. Treize, cashier. The check was cashed at the bank; and employees were paid currency and coin in payroll envelopes.

Social security taxes on the payroll, chargeable to the employer, total $320.00. These taxes are due for payment in October and January.

Required:

(1) Enter the above transactions in books of original entry, post to a T-account ledger, then take a trial balance.

(2) Prepare a profit and loss statement for July. The inventory of merchandise on hand July 31, 19__, was estimated at $32,000.00. For the purpose of this problem depreciation expense may be disregarded.

(3) Prepare a balance sheet, July 31, 19__. Include reconciliation schedule for vouchers payable.

Problem **23–2.** The following books of original entry are to be opened for the business of Henry J. Monroe, Inc.:

Cash receipts book   Sales book
Check register   Voucher register
Journal

The voucher register will have distributive columns for:

Advertising	Postage
Freight In	Purchases
General Expense	Sales Salaries
Office Supplies	Miscellaneous

The general ledger accounts to be opened are

Cash	Sales
Accounts Receivable	Returned Sales and Allowances
Inventory	Sales Discounts
Automobiles	Purchases
Reserve for Depreciation —	Purchases Discounts
Automobiles	Freight In
Fixtures and Equipment	Advertising
Reserve for Depreciation —	Automobile Expense
Fixtures and Equipment	Sales Salaries
Vouchers Payable	Traveling Expense
Notes Payable	General Salaries
Common Stock	Office Supplies
Earned Surplus	Postage
	Rent
	Stationery and Printing

A subsidiary ledger for accounts receivable will be carried.

Unless otherwise specified, merchandise transactions are due net on the tenth of the month following date of purchase or sale. The following transactions are to be recorded in the books of Henry J. Monroe, Inc.:

January

2 — All of the authorized 1,000 shares of no-par common stock were issued to Henry J. Monroe, and associates, for cash, $25,000.00, merchandise, $5,000.00.

2 — Paid rent for January to M. C. Millian, $200.00.

3 — Purchased merchandise from Frank & Company, Inc., $3,200.00.

3 — Bought fixtures and equipment from the General Office Equipment Company, $3,000.00, payable net on March 10.

4 — Purchased office supplies on account from Howell's, Inc., $285.00.

4 — Postage stamps are bought for cash, $50.00.

5 — Merchandise is purchased from The Taylor Company, $4,000.00, 3/10, n/30.

5 — Telegrams are sent to a selected list of prospective customers; paid Western Union Telegraph Company, $110.00. Charge Advertising.

5 — A bill is received from the Quality Print Shop for printing, $200.00.

5 — Purchased a Lincoln car, a special job for the needs of the busi-

ness, from the Detroit-Lincoln Company, price, $4,700.00, payable $1,700.00 cash, the balance in four monthly payments.

6 — Sale to Lancaster & Son, $8,000.00, 3/10, 2/20, n/60.

6 — Bill is received from Business Conditions, Inc., for their service for one year, $150.00.

8 — Merchandise purchase from Henry E. Skaggs, $5,000.00, 2/10, n/30.

8 — Paid Grace Steamship Company for freight on above invoice, $110.00.

9 — Paid Quality Print Shop bill of January 5.

10 — Purchased merchandise from The Taylor Company, $3,800.00.

10 — Paid the Darby Transfer Company for freight and cartage on the Taylor merchandise, $87.00.

10 — Telephone bill is received, $18.50.

10 — Paid bill of Business Conditions, Inc.

11 — Merchandise purchase from Ray & Ray, Inc., $4,000.00.

12 — Paid The Taylor Company, $4,000.00, less 3%, for bill of January 5.

15 — Purchased merchandise from Davis & Son, $6,000.00.

15 — Paid Grace Steamship Company for freight on above two purchases, $490.00.

16 — Merchandise is purchased from the Asiatic Importers' Agency under terms of sight draft bill of lading $2,900.00.

17 — Sale of merchandise to Chester & Company, Inc., $11,000.00, 2/10, n/30.

18 — Postage stamps are purchased, and paid, $10.00.

18 — Paid Henry E. Skaggs for bill of January 8. The bill was paid without deduction for cash discount.

19 — Cash is received from Lancaster & Son, $8,000.00, less 2%, for invoice of January 6.

20 — Bill is received for advertising in *Vogue Buyers' Journal*, $1,500.00.

20 — Accepted a 10-day draft, dated today, in favor of Davis & Son, $6,000.00, covering purchase of January 15.

22 — Sales to Central Trading Company, $7,000.00, and to Chester & Company, Inc., $1,000.00.

23 — A purchase credit memorandum, dated January 22, is received from Ray & Ray, Inc., $1,700.00.

24 — Purchased merchandise from Frank & Company, $4,000.00, 2/10, n/30.

24 — Sale to H. J. Glenn, $10,000.00.

25 — Cash is received from Chester & Company, Inc., $11,000.00 less 2%, in payment of invoice of January 17.

26 — A credit memorandum, dated January 20, is received from Henry E. Skaggs for $100.00 representing cash discount which we failed to deduct in our check of January 18.

27 — Office supplies are purchased on account from Howell's, Inc., $115.00.

27 — Paid Frank & Company, $4,000.00 less 2 %, for bill of January 24.

29 — A credit memorandum is issued, in favor of Lancaster & Son, for merchandise returned, $2,000.00. A check is issued in payment less cash discount deduction of 2 %.

30 — The Davis & Son draft of January 20 is paid.

30 — Paid $2,800.00 on The Taylor Company bill of January 10.

31 — A bill is received from the Standard Garage for gasoline, oil, and sundry items, $65.00.

31 — Traveling expenses are paid, $1,000.00 (seven checks).

31 — The payroll for January is paid:

Sales Salaries	$3,000.00
General Salaries	1,000.00
	$4,000.00
Less Withholding Income Tax	562.00
	$3,438.00
Less Social Security Taxes	40.00
Cash disbursed	$3,398.00

Required:

(1) Take a general ledger trial balance.

(2) Prepare a profit and loss statement for the month of January. Inventory, January 31, 19__, $11,004.00. Annual depreciation rates are Lincoln automobile, 20 %, fixtures, 10 %. Accrued social security taxes on employer, $160.00.

(3) Prepare a balance sheet, January 31, 19__.

(4) Prepare a schedule of accounts receivable.

(5) Prepare a schedule of vouchers payable.

Problem **23–3.** A machine is carried on the books at a cost of $10,300.00 and a depreciation reserve of $7,000.00. The machine is traded in for $2,600.00 on the cash purchase of a larger and improved model costing $15,000.00.

How should this purchase be recorded in the voucher register?

Problem **23–4.** On March 1, 19__, a petty cash fund of $200.00 was established. On March 31, 19__, the petty cashier reported the following petty cash disbursements for the month:

Freight in	$ 34.73
Miscellaneous expense	26.16
Postage	75.00
Traveling expense	5.44
	$141.33

Required:

(1) What entry, or entries, should be made in replenishing the petty

cash fund under the imprest system of handling petty cash? Assume that a full voucher system is in use.

(2) If another check were issued in order to increase the amount of the petty cash fund by $50.00, what entry should be made?

Problem 23–5. On December 31, 19—, you make a count of the petty cash fund of a certain corporation with the following results:

Coin	$ 10.85
Currency	200.00
Express bills paid	13.84
Freight bills paid	22.46
Postage stamps on hand	15.68
Receipt covering payment made to a customer for merchandise returned	12.17
Receipt covering donation made to Red Cross	25.00
	$300.00

Required:

(1) What entry should be made if the petty cash fund is to be reimbursed? The imprest system of petty cash, and a voucher register, is in use.

(2) What entry should be made if the petty cash fund were reimbursed with a check for $100.00 under the nonimprest or round-amounts system of petty cash?

Problem 23–6. On February 28, 19—, the petty cash fund consisted of vouchers and cash as follows:

Vouchers:	
Car and taxi fare for cashier	$ 7.80
Freight-in bills	63.74
Postage	25.00
Ten sets of office keys	12.00
Tickets for Chamber of Commerce luncheon	5.00
	$113.54
Cash	86.46
	$200.00

What entry should be made to reimburse the petty cash fund?

Problem 23–7. A petty cash fund of $100.00 is established. The fund is stolen. The fund is re-established at $50.00. What entry should be made for each of these transactions?

Problem **23–8.** On July 1, 19__, a company established a petty cash fund of $100.00. During July disbursements from this fund were as follows:

Telegram	$ 1.50
Freight bill on purchases	4.72
Postage	5.00
Office supplies	1.40
Express on purchases	2.10
Carfare	1.00
Postage	5.00
Freight bill	4.16
12 rolls crepe paper streamers for window display purposes	1.20
Carfare	1.00
Traveling expense	2.50
Freight bill	3.71
Postage due on incoming mail	.12
Freight bill	6.62
Carfare	1.00
Postage	10.00
Donation	5.00
Freight bill	1.19
Placards for advertising department . .	3.50
Freight bill	4.79
Telegram	.97
Carfare	1.00
	$67.48

Required:

(1) Make the entry to establish the petty cash fund on July 1.

(2) Make the entry on July 31 to reimburse the fund.

(3) Assume that on July 31 it was desired to cut the petty cash fund down to $75.00. What entry should be made when the fund is reimbursed?

Chapter 24

MANUFACTURING OPERATIONS

A trading or merchandising business, such as a department store, sells essentially the same product that it buys. The merchandise is purchased ready for resale. A manufacturing business, on the other hand, manufactures the product which it offers for sale.

To the latter type of business, manufacturing costs are of prime importance. The control of business operations is rendered conspicuously insecure without the information which manufacturing costs provide. Full knowledge of manufacturing costs is an essential prerequisite to intelligent and effective operating control. "Without cost data the financial control is inadequate and insecure, production control is unintelligent, and marketing operations lack one of their most important guides." [1]

ELEMENTS OF MANUFACTURING COSTS

Three elements comprise manufacturing costs: direct (or raw) materials, direct labor, and manufacturing expenses.

Direct materials include "those materials which enter directly into the manufacture of the product so that they can be plainly identified with it; such materials can be treated as a direct cost of the product, and the amount chargeable to the product for them is easily ascertainable. Materials which are used in small quantities only, so that the precise quantity used in any one article would be somewhat difficult to measure, are often not regarded as direct material costs, because the computation of the amount of cost would be more trouble than it is worth." [2]

Direct labor is factory labor which can be traced directly to the product and the cost of which it is worth while to determine. Direct labor may be hand labor or that expended with the aid of machines.

Manufacturing expenses are all costs of manufacture other than direct materials and direct labor.

---

[1] T. H. Sanders, *Cost Accounting for Control*, McGraw-Hill Book Company, Inc., p. 3.

[2] *Ibid.*, p. 57.

ACCOUNTING FOR MANUFACTURING OPERATIONS

Two plans are in general use. In one the inventory accounts are brought up to date at the end of the annual accounting period. This plan, the method of "periodic inventory," is generally used by trading concerns. It is the method which has been steadily used in this text up to the present point. In the second plan the inventory accounts are kept up to date continuously. This plan is called the method of "perpetual inventory."

Whether the method of periodic inventory or that of perpetual inventory is used, a manufacturing business will generally have three inventories in place of the single inventory account which is usual for most concerns. These three inventories are

(1) *Raw materials*. Raw materials are direct materials as defined on page 504.

(2) *Work in process*. This is the inventory of partly manufactured goods, i.e., those still in the manufacturing process.

(3) *Finished goods*. These are manufactured goods, finished, and ready for sale.

This chapter will discuss manufacturing accounting under the plan of periodic inventory. Chapter 25 will discuss manufacturing accounting under the plan of perpetual inventory.

MANUFACTURING ACCOUNTING UNDER THE PLAN OF PERIODIC INVENTORY

The plan of periodic inventory is used primarily by small manufacturing companies and by manufacturing businesses which manufacture a standard type of product.

Manufacturing accounting under the plan of periodic inventory is probably best described by the procedure of setting forth a representative set of entries. The entries below are those of the Conant Manufacturing Company whose profit and loss statement appears on page 510.

Purchases	22,000.00	
Vouchers Payable		22,000.00
To record purchases of raw materials.		

Direct Labor	27,000.00	
Factory Repairs	400.00	
Heat, Light, and Power	1,100.00	
Indirect Labor	9,000.00	
Miscellaneous Factory Expense.	500.00	
Vouchers Payable		38,000.00
To record liability for factory payroll, and distribution of payroll to cost accounts.		

Factory Repairs	1,000.00	
Factory Supplies	1,200.00	
Heat, Light, and Power	3,200.00	
Insurance	600.00	
Miscellaneous Factory Expense.	1,600.00	
Taxes	2,000.00	
Vouchers Payable		9,600.00
To record manufacturing expense invoices.		
Advertising Expense	3,000.00	
Delivery Expense	2,800.00	
Insurance Expense	200.00	
Miscellaneous Selling Expense	2,000.00	
Traveling Expenses	4,000.00	
Vouchers Payable		12,000.00
To record selling expense invoices, etc.		
Miscellaneous General Expense	1,800.00	
Office Supplies	1,000.00	
Vouchers Payable		2,800.00
To record general expense invoices.		
Sales Salaries	8,000.00	
General Salaries	7,000.00	
Vouchers Payable		15,000.00
To record nonfactory payroll.		

Before the placement of adjusting and closing entries on the books a trial balance would be taken. The trial balance of the Conant Manufacturing Company appears in the first pair of columns of the manufacturing work sheet on page 512.

Adjusting and Closing Entries

Depreciation Expense — Building	1,500.00	
Depreciation Expense — Mach. & Equipment	2,400.00	
Depreciation Expense — Tools	500.00	
Reserve for Depreciation — Buildings		1,500.00
Reserve for Depreciation — Mach. & Equip. . . .		2,400.00
Tools		500.00
To record depreciation expense on factory fixed assets.		
Depreciation Expense — Office Equipment.	200.00	
Reserve for Depreciation — Office Equipment . .		200.00
To record depreciation expense on nonfactory fixed assets.		
Manufacturing	12,000.00	
Raw Materials		12,000.00
To transfer January 1 inventory of raw materials to Manufacturing account.		

Note: The Manufacturing account is used for the purpose of assembling all manufacturing costs in one account.

Manufacturing	21,000.00	
Purchases Discounts	1,000.00	
Purchases		22,000.00
To transfer net cost of purchased raw materials to Manufacturing account.		

Raw Materials	14,000.00	
Manufacturing		14,000.00

To record new inventory of raw materials on December 31, 19—.

Manufacturing	7,000.00	
Work in Process		7,000.00

To transfer January 1 inventory of work in process to Manufacturing account.

Manufacturing Expense	25,000.00	
Depreciation Expense — Buildings		1,500.00
Depreciation Expense — Mach. & Equip.		2,400.00
Depreciation Expense — Tools		500.00
Factory Repairs		1,400.00
Factory Supplies		1,200.00
Heat, Light, and Power		4,300.00
Indirect Labor		9,000.00
Insurance		600.00
Miscellaneous Factory Expense.		2,100.00
Taxes		2,000.00

To close detailed manufacturing expenses into one summary account.

Manufacturing	52,000.00	
Direct Labor		27,000.00
Manufacturing Expense		25,000.00

To transfer balances of latter two accounts to Manufacturing account

Work in Process	8,000.00	
Manufacturing		8,000.00

To record new inventory of work in process on December 31, 19—.

Cost of Sales	10,000.00	
Finished Goods.		10,000.00

To transfer January 1 inventory of finished goods to Cost of Sales.

Cost of Sales	70,000.00	
Manufacturing		70,000.00

To transfer balance of Manufacturing account to Cost of Sales. This balance represents the cost of the finished goods manufactured during the period.

Finished Goods.	18,000.00	
Cost of Sales		18,000.00

To record new inventory of finished goods on December 31, 19—.

Profit and Loss	62,000.00	
Cost of Sales		62,000.00

To transfer cost of merchandise sold during period to Profit and Loss.

From this point on, the accounting is identical with that for the ordinary trading concern.

The manufacturing entries above may possibly be made more clear by a diagrammatic presentation of the flow of information from account to account. In the diagram on page 508 the balances of the several accounts are transferred to the account, or accounts, to which the arrows point.

Manufacturing

Raw Materials

| 12,000.00 | 12,000.00 ⟶ 12,000.00 | |
| 14,000.00 | ⟵ | 14,000.00 |

Purchases

| 22,000.00 | 22,000.00 ⟶ 22,000.00 | |

Purchases Discounts

| 1,000.00 | 1,000.00 ⟶ | 1,000.00 |

Work in Process

| 7,000.00 | 7,000.00 ⟶ 7,000.00 | |
| 8,000.00 | ⟵ | 8,000.00 |

Direct Labor

| 27,000.00 | 27,000.00 ⟶ 27,000.00 | |

Deprec. Exp. — Bldgs.

| 1,500.00 | 1,500.00 |

Deprec. Exp. — Mach.

| 2,400.00 | 2,400.00 |

Deprec. Exp. — Tools

| 500.00 | 500.00 |

Factory Repairs

| 1,400.00 | 1,400.00 |

Factory Supplies

| 1,200.00 | 1,200.00 |

Manufacturing Expense

- - ⟶ | 25,000.00 | 25,000.00 ⟶ 25,000.00 |

Heat, Light, Power

| 4,300.00 | 4,300.00 |

Cost of Sales

| 70,000.00 ⟶ 70,000.00 | |
| 93,000.00 | 93,000.00 |

Indirect Labor

| 9,000.00 | 9,000.00 |

Insurance

| 600.00 | 600.00 |

Finished Goods

10,000.00	10,000.00 ⟶ 10,000.00	
18,000.00	⟵	18,000.00
		62,000.00

Misc. Factory Expense

| 2,100.00 | 2,100.00 |

| 80,000.00 | 80,000.00 |

Taxes

| 2,000.00 | 2,000.00 |

WORK SHEET

The work sheet for a manufacturing company operating under the plan of periodic inventory differs from the conventional work sheet in only one essential respect: the addition of two columns to care for all elements of manufacturing cost. These columns incorporate the detail which is to be included in the Manufacturing account on the books. The debit balance of the Manufacturing columns represents the cost of goods manufactured during the period and is transferred to the debit Cost of Sales column. The debit balance of the Cost of Sales columns, together with the totals of the Selling Expense and the General Expense columns, is transferred to the debit Profit and Loss column. The credit balance of the Profit and Loss columns, representing the net income of the period, is transferred to the credit Balance Sheet column as an addition to Earned Surplus.

Attention should be carefully directed to the manner in which the new inventories are recorded in the manufacturing work sheet. The new raw materials inventory of $14,000.00 is recorded by a

DEBIT in the balance sheet column, and a
CREDIT in the manufacturing column.

The new work in process inventory of $8,000.00 is recorded by a

DEBIT in the balance sheet column, and a
CREDIT in the manufacturing column.

The new finished goods inventory of $18,000.00 is recorded by a

DEBIT in the balance sheet column, and a
CREDIT in the cost of sales column.

FINANCIAL STATEMENTS

The financial statements to be prepared from the work sheet of the Conant Manufacturing Company are shown on pages 510 and 511. The profit and loss statement is shown in detail. An alternative statement of profit and loss might have been prepared in which cost of sales would be shown as simply $62,000.00, all details of this figure being omitted from the statement proper. The details of cost of goods manufactured and sold would be shown in a separate schedule or statement. Manufacturing expenses, also, might be placed in a separate schedule.

Conant Manufacturing Company

PROFIT AND LOSS STATEMENT

YEAR ENDING DECEMBER 31, 19—

Gross Sales				$110,000.00
Less Sales Discounts				3,000.00
Net Sales				$107,000.00

Cost of Sales:

Finished Goods, January 1, 19—			$10,000.00	
Cost of Goods Manufactured in 19—:				
Work in Process, January 1, 19—.		$ 7,000.00		
Raw Materials Consumed:				
Raw Materials, January 1, 19—	$12,000.00			
Purchases $22,000.00				
Less Purchases				
Discounts . . . 1,000.00	21,000.00			
	$33,000.00			
Raw Materials, December 31, 19—.	14,000.00	19,000.00		
Direct Labor		27,000.00		

Manufacturing Expenses:

Depreciation Expense:				
Buildings	$ 1,500.00			
Mach. & Equipment	2,400.00			
Tools	500.00			
Factory Repairs	1,400.00			
Factory Supplies	1,200.00			
Heat, Light, & Power	4,300.00			
Indirect Labor	9,000.00			
Insurance	600.00			
Miscellaneous Factory Expense.	2,100.00			
Taxes	2,000.00	25,000.00		
		$78,000.00		
Work in Process, December 31, 19—		8,000.00	70,000.00	
			$80,000.00	
Finished Goods, December 31, 19—			18,000.00	62,000.00
Gross Profit				$ 45,000.00

Selling Expenses:

Advertising Expense			$ 3,000.00	
Delivery Expense			2,800.00	
Insurance Expense			200.00	
Miscellaneous Selling Expense			2,000.00	
Sales Salaries			8,000.00	
Traveling Expense			4,000.00	$20,000.00

General Expenses:

Depreciation Expense — Office Equipment. . .	$ 200.00		
Miscellaneous General Expense	1,800.00		
Office Supplies	1,000.00		
General Salaries	7,000.00	10,000.00	30,000.00

Net Profit from Operations . . . . $ 15,000.00

Conant Manufacturing Company

BALANCE SHEET, DECEMBER 31, 19__

Assets

Current Assets:

Cash	$ 20,000.00
Accounts Receivable	37,500.00
Finished Goods.	18,000.00
Work in Process	8,000.00
Raw Materials	14,000.00
	$ 97,500.00

Fixed Assets:	Cost	Reserve for Depreciation	Net Book Value	
Buildings	$30,000.00	$ 4,500.00	$25,500.00	
Machinery	24,000.00	7,200.00	16,800.00	
Tools	2,000.00		2,000.00	
Office Equipment	2,000.00	600.00	1,400.00	
	$58,000.00	$12,300.00	$45,700.00	45,700.00
				$143,200.00

Liabilities and Net Worth

Current Liabilities:

Accounts Payable	$ 20,000.00

Net Worth:

Common Stock, $100.00 par	$100,000.00	
Earned Surplus.	23,200.00	123,200.00
		$143,200.00

CONANT MANU–

Work Sheet Year

	TRIAL BALANCE		ADJUSTMENTS		TRIAL BALANCE AFTER ADJUSTMENT	
	Debit	Credit	Debit	Credit	Debit	Credit
Cash	20,000.00				20,000.00	
Accounts Receivable.	37,500.00				37,500.00	
Finished Goods.	10,000.00				10,000.00	
Work in Process.	7,000.00				7,000.00	
Raw Materials.	12,000.00				12,000.00	
Buildings.	30,000.00				30,000.00	
Reserve for Depreciation – Buildings		3,000.00		(A) 1,500.00		4,500.00
Machinery.	24,000.00				24,000.00	
Reserve for Depreciation – Mach. & Eq.		4,800.00		(B) 2,400.00		7,200.00
Tools.	2,500.00			(C) 500.00	2,000.00	
Office Equipment	2,000.00				2,000.00	
Reserve for Depreciation – Office Eq.		400.00		(D) 200.00		600.00
Accounts Payable		20,000.00				20,000.00
Capital Stock – Common		100,000.00				100,000.00
Earned Surplus		8,200.00				8,200.00
Sales.		110,000.00				110,000.00
Sales Discounts.	3,000.00				3,000.00	
Purchases.	22,000.00				22,000.00	
Purchases Discounts.		1,000.00				1,000.00
Direct Labor	27,000.00				27,000.00	
Manufacturing Expenses						
Depreciation Expense – Buildings . .			(A) 1,500.00		1,500.00	
Depreciation Expense – Mach. & Equip.			(B) 2,400.00		2,400.00	
Depreciation Expense – Tools			(C) 500.00		500.00	
Factory Repairs.	1,400.00				1,400.00	
Factory Supplies	1,200.00				1,200.00	
Heat, Light, & Power	4,300.00				4,300.00	
Indirect Labor	9,000.00				9,000.00	
Insurance.	600.00				600.00	
Miscellaneous Factory Expense. . . .	2,100.00				2,100.00	
Taxes.	2,000.00				2,000.00	
Selling Expenses						
Advertising Expense.	3,000.00				3,000.00	
Delivery Expense	2,800.00				2,800.00	
Insurance.	200.00				200.00	
Miscellaneous Selling Expense. . . .	2,000.00				2,000.00	
Sales Salaries	8,000.00				8,000.00	
Traveling Expenses	4,000.00				4,000.00	
General Expenses						
Depreciation Expense – Office Equip.			(D) 200.00		200.00	
Miscellaneous General Expense. . . .	1,800.00				1,800.00	
General Salaries	7,000.00				7,000.00	
Office Supplies.	1,000.00				1,000.00	
	247,400.00	247,400.00	4,600.00	4,600.00	251,500.00	251,500.00
Cost of Goods Manufactured – To Cost of Sales	. . . .	. . . .	. . . .	. . . .	. . . .	. . . .
Cost of Sales – To Profit and Loss .	. . . .	. . . .	. . . .	. . . .	. . . .	. . . .
Net Income – To Surplus.	. . . .	. . . .	. . . .	. . . .	. . . .	. . . .

FACTURING COMPANY

Ending December 31, 19___

MANUFACTURING		COST OF SALES		PROFIT AND LOSS		BALANCE SHEET	
Debit	Credit	Debit	Credit	Debit	Credit	Debit	Credit
						20,000.00	
						37,500.00	
		10,000.00	18,000.00			18,000.00	
7,000.00	8,000.00					8,000.00	
12,000.00	14,000.00					14,000.00	
						30,000.00	
							4,500.00
						24,000.00	
							7,200.00
						2,000.00	
						2,000.00	
							600.00
							20,000.00
							100,000.00
							8,200.00
					110,000.00		
				3,000.00			
22,000.00							
	1,000.00						
27,000.00							
1,500.00							
2,400.00							
500.00							
1,400.00							
1,200.00							
4,300.00							
9,000.00							
600.00							
2,100.00							
2,000.00							
				3,000.00			
				2,800.00			
				200.00			
				2,000.00			
				8,000.00			
				4,000.00			
				200.00			
				1,800.00			
				7,000.00			
				1,000.00			
	70,000.00	70,000.00					
93,000.00	93,000.00						
. . . .	. . . .		62,000.00	62,000.00			
		80,000.00	80,000.00				
. . . .	. . . .	. . . .	. . . .	15,000.00			15,000.00
				110,000.00	110,000.00	155,500.00	155,500.00

QUESTIONS

Question **24–1.** Define the three elements which comprise manufacturing costs.

Question **24–2.** How is the cost of sales figure determined under the plan of periodic inventory?

Question **24–3.** By means of journal entries describe the technique of manufacturing accounting under the plan of periodic inventory. Explanations may be omitted.

Question **24–4.** What is the function of the Manufacturing account (not the Work in Process account) when accounts are kept under the plan of periodic inventory?

Question **24–5.** The cost of finished goods manufactured is, according to some writers, directly comparable to the purchases of a trading concern. Do you agree? Explain briefly.

PROBLEMS

Problem **24–1.** The accounting of the Wilson Manufacturing Company embraced the plan of periodic inventory. On January 1, 1950, the condensed trial balance of the company was as follows:

Cash	$ 30,000.00	
Accounts Receivable	25,000.00	
Finished Goods	25,000.00	
Work in Process	23,000.00	
Raw Materials	15,000.00	
Factory Fixed Assets	60,000.00	
Reserve for Depreciation		$ 6,000.00
Vouchers Payable		47,000.00
Common Stock, $100.00 par		100,000.00
Surplus		25,000.00
	$178,000.00	$178,000.00

The condensed transactions of the company for the year 1950 were as follows:

(1) Finished goods were sold on account, $148,000.00.
(2) Collections on accounts receivable amounted to $141,000.00.
(3) Purchased raw materials on account for $66,000.00.
(4) Cash disbursed to creditors in payment of raw material purchases amounted to $60,000.00.
(5) The payroll for the year amounted to $44,000.00 and was paid in cash. Of this amount $30,000.00 was for direct labor and $14,000.00 was for indirect labor.
(6) Miscellaneous general factory expenses were paid, $8,000.00.

(7) Depreciation expense on factory fixed assets amounted to $6,000.00 for the year.

(8) General expenses were paid, $29,000.00.

Required:

(1) Prepare entries to record the above transactions.

(2) Post to a T-account ledger.

(3) Take off a trial balance.

(4) Prepare a profit and loss statement for the year 1950. Inventories on December 31, 1950, were finished goods, $34,000.00, work in process, $16,000.00, and raw materials, $22,000.00.

Of the total manufacturing expense incurred in 1950, $3,000.00 was applicable to the production of 1951. This prepaid expense was not a part of any of the foregoing inventory valuations.

(5) Prepare a balance sheet, December 31, 1950.

(6) Prepare, and post, all entries to close the books for 1950.

Problem 24-2. Following is the condensed trial balance after adjustment of the Robbins Manufacturing Company on December 31, 19__:

Cash	$ 40,000.00	
Accounts Receivable	30,000.00	
Finished Goods.	24,000.00	
Work in Process	40,000.00	
Raw Materials	20,000.00	
Factory Fixed Assets	40,000.00	
Reserve for Depreciation		$ 10,000.00
Vouchers Payable		22,000.00
Common Stock, $100.00 par		100,000.00
Surplus		28,000.00
Sales		240,000.00
Purchases	60,000.00	
Direct Labor	65,000.00	
Indirect Labor	15,000.00	
Miscellaneous Manufacturing Expense	8,000.00	
Depreciation Expense — Factory	4,000.00	
Selling Expense	30,000.00	
General Expense	24,000.00	
	$400,000.00	$400,000.00

The new inventories on December 31, 19__, were finished goods, $30,000.00, work in process, $20,000.00, and raw materials, $32,000.00.

Required:

(1) Prepare a ten-column manufacturing work sheet.

(2) Prepare a profit and loss statement for the year.

(3) Prepare a balance sheet, December 31, 19__.

Problem 24-3. Following is the condensed and adjusted trial balance of the Mann Manufacturing Company on December 31, 19__:

Cash	$ 40,000.00	
Accounts Receivable	25,000.00	
Finished Goods.	26,000.00	
Work in Process	23,000.00	
Raw Materials	22,000.00	
Factory Fixed Assets	40,000.00	
Reserve for Depreciation — Factory Fixed Assets.		$ 12,000.00
Nonfactory Fixed Assets	10,000.00	
Reserve for Depreciation — Nonfactory Fixed Assets		3,000.00
Vouchers Payable		30,000.00
Common Stock, $100.00 par		100,000.00
Surplus		30,000.00
Sales		261,000.00
Purchases	80,000.00	
Direct Labor	75,000.00	
Indirect Labor	20,000.00	
Miscellaneous Manufacturing Expense	11,000.00	
Depreciation Expense — Factory	4,000.00	
Selling Expense	33,000.00	
General Expense	26,000.00	
Depreciation Expense — General	1,000.00	
	$436,000.00	$436,000.00

The new inventories on December 31, 19—, were finished goods, $30,000.00, work in process, $37,000.00, and raw materials, $35,000.00.

Required:

(1) Prepare a ten-column manufacturing work sheet.

(2) Prepare a profit and loss statement for the year. Show detail.

Problem **24–4.** On December 31, 19—, the condensed trial balance of the Nash Manufacturing Company was

Cash	$ 33,000.00	
Accounts Receivable	44,000.00	
Finished Goods.	29,000.00	
Work in Process	27,000.00	
Raw Materials	18,000.00	
Factory Equipment	60,000.00	
Reserve for Depreciation — Factory Equipment .		$ 18,000.00
Office Equipment	10,000.00	
Reserve for Depreciation — Office Equipment . .		2,000.00
Land	6,000.00	
Vouchers Payable		22,000.00
Common Stock, $100.00 par		100,000.00
Surplus		60,000.00
Sales		214,000.00
Purchases	70,000.00	
Direct Labor	36,000.00	
Indirect Labor	14,000.00	
General Factory Expense	9,000.00	
Selling Expense	36,000.00	
General Expense	24,000.00	
	$416,000.00	$416,000.00

This trial balance does not reflect the following information:

(1) Depreciation expense on factory equipment, $6,000.00.
(2) Depreciation expense on office equipment, $1,000.00.
(3) Vendor's invoice for raw materials, $10,000.00. Although the materials are on hand and included in the new inventory, the invoice has not been recorded.
(4) New inventories: finished goods, $40,000.00, work in process, $20,000.00, and raw materials, $26,000.00.

Required:

(1) Prepare a manufacturing work sheet.
(2) Draw up a detailed statement of profit and loss for the year.
(3) Prepare a balance sheet, December 31, 19___.

Problem **24–5.** The condensed trial balance of the Malone Manufacturing Company on December 31, 19___, was

Cash	$ 78,000.00	
Notes Receivable	30,000.00	
Notes Receivable Discounted		$ 10,000.00
Accounts Receivable	83,000.00	
Finished Goods.	32,000.00	
Work in Process	30,000.00	
Raw Materials	20,000.00	
Factory Equipment	84,000.00	
Reserve for Depreciation — Factory Equipment .		8,000.00
Office Equipment	10,000.00	
Reserve for Depreciation — Office Equipment . .		1,000.00
Vouchers Payable		45,000.00
Common Stock, $100.00 par		200,000.00
Surplus		100,000.00
Sales		200,000.00
Purchases	82,000.00	
Freight In	5,000.00	
Direct Labor	45,000.00	
Indirect Labor	11,000.00	
General Factory Expense	10,000.00	
Advertising	10,000.00	
Sales Salaries	22,000.00	
General Salaries	12,000.00	
	$564,000.00	$564,000.00

Supplementary Information

(1) Depreciation expense, factory equipment, $8,000.00.
(2) Depreciation expense, office equipment, $1,000.00.
(3) Accrued payroll: direct labor, $5,000.00, indirect labor, $3,000.00, and general salaries, $4,000.00.
(4) Prepaid advertising, $3,000.00.
(5) New inventories: finished goods, $44,000.00, work in process, $15,000.00, and raw materials, $28,000.00.

Required:

    (1) Prepare a manufacturing work sheet.

    (2) Draw up a detailed statement of profit and loss for the year.

    (3) Prepare a balance sheet, December 31, 19__.

Problem **24–6.** Following is the condensed trial balance of the Marks Manufacturing Company on December 31, 19__:

Cash	$ 50,000.00	
Accounts Receivable	48,000.00	
Finished Goods	30,000.00	
Work in Process	50,000.00	
Raw Materials	25,000.00	
Factory Fixed Assets	90,000.00	
Reserve for Depreciation — Factory Fixed Assets.		$ 15,000.00
Salesmen's Automobiles	20,000.00	
Reserve for Depreciation — Salesmen's Automobiles		10,000.00
Vouchers Payable		17,000.00
Debenture Bonds Payable		100,000.00
Common Stock, $100.00 par		100,000.00
Surplus		80,000.00
Sales		300,000.00
Purchases	100,000.00	
Freight In	5,000.00	
Direct Labor	50,000.00	
Indirect Labor	29,000.00	
Repairs to Machinery	6,000.00	
Taxes on Factory Assets	1,000.00	
Depreciation Expense — Factory	9,000.00	
Depreciation Expense — Salesmen's Automobiles	5,000.00	
Advertising	12,000.00	
Salesmen's Salaries	20,000.00	
Traveling Expense	10,000.00	
General Expenses	12,000.00	
General Salaries	46,000.00	
Bond Interest Expense	4,000.00	
	$622,000.00	$622,000.00

The following information is supplementary to the trial balance:

    (1) Accounts receivable of $1,000.00 are worthless and should be written off.

    (2) There is on hand an unpaid and unrecorded advertising bill, $3,000.00.

    (3) Accrued bond interest, $2,000.00.

    (4) Income taxes are estimated at $5,000.00.

    (5) New inventories: finished goods, $62,000.00, work in process, $60,000.00, and raw materials, $40,000.00.

Required:

    (1) Prepare a manufacturing work sheet.

    (2) Draw up a profit and loss statement for the year.

    (3) Prepare a balance sheet, December 31, 19__.

Problem **24-7.** Following is the trial balance of the Redway Manufacturing Company on December 31, 19__:

Cash	$ 80,000.00	
Notes Receivable	20,000.00	
Accounts Receivable	49,000.00	
Finished Goods	33,600.00	
Work in Process	56,000.00	
Raw Materials	28,000.00	
Factory Equipment	100,000.00	
Reserve for Depreciation — Factory Equipment		$ 20,000.00
Nonfactory Equipment	25,000.00	
Reserve for Depreciation — Nonfactory Equipment		8,000.00
Investment in Redway Sales Co., Inc.	50,000.00	
Notes Payable		100,000.00
Vouchers Payable		25,300.00
Common Stock, $100.00 par		100,000.00
Surplus		200,000.00
Sales		300,000.00
Purchases	120,000.00	
Purchases Discounts		2,000.00
Freight In	6,000.00	
Direct Labor	48,000.00	
Depreciation Expense — Factory Equipment	10,000.00	
Heat, Light, Power	6,000.00	
Indirect Labor	20,000.00	
Machinery Repairs	6,000.00	
Salaries of Factory Foremen	10,000.00	
Taxes Expense, factory	1,800.00	
Advertising	9,000.00	
Salesmen's Salaries	30,000.00	
Traveling Expense	8,000.00	
Depreciation Expense, nonfactory	2,000.00	
General Office Expense	10,000.00	
General Office Salaries	31,000.00	
Office Supplies Expense	3,400.00	
Taxes, nonfactory	500.00	
Dividend Income		8,000.00
	$763,300.00	$763,300.00

The following information has not been placed on the books:

(1) Accrued interest on notes receivable, $300.00.
(2) Bad debts, estimated at 1% of sales.
(3) Accrued interest on notes payable, $1,000.00.
(4) Income taxes, estimated at $10,000.00.
(5) Directors have just declared a stock dividend of $100%.
(6) New inventories: finished goods, $70,000.00, work in process, $50,000.00, raw materials, $42,000.00, and office supplies, $1,000.00.

Required:

(1) Prepare a manufacturing work sheet.
(2) Prepare a profit and loss statement for the year.
(3) Prepare a balance sheet, December 31, 19__.

Problem **24–8.** Following is the trial balance of the Case Manufacturing Company on December 31, 19__:

Cash	$ 70,000.00	
Accounts Receivable	100,000.00	
Finished Goods	50,000.00	
Work in Process	10,000.00	
Raw Materials	20,000.00	
Machinery and Equipment	100,000.00	
Reserve for Depreciation — Machinery and Equipment		$ 30,000.00
Delivery Equipment	20,000.00	
Reserve for Depreciation — Delivery Equipment		10,000.00
Office Equipment	12,000.00	
Reserve for Depreciation — Office Equipment		5,000.00
Accounts Payable		60,000.00
Notes Payable		10,000.00
Dividends Payable		30,000.00
Common Stock, $100.00 par		200,000.00
Surplus		24,000.00
Sales		557,000.00
Sales Discounts	4,000.00	
Purchases	200,000.00	
Purchases Discounts		3,000.00
Freight In	5,000.00	
Direct Labor	60,000.00	
Depreciation Expense — Machinery and Equipment	10,000.00	
Indirect Labor	80,000.00	
Machinery Repairs	12,000.00	
Small Tools Expense	3,000.00	
Advertising	30,000.00	
Depreciation Expense — Delivery Equipment	5,000.00	
Miscellaneous Expense — Delivery Equipment	3,000.00	
Sales Salaries	50,000.00	
Traveling Expense	20,000.00	
Depreciation Expense — Office Equipment	1,000.00	
General Office Expense	20,000.00	
Office Salaries	34,000.00	
Taxes Expense (to be apportioned: 60% factory, 20% selling, and 20% general)	10,000.00	
	$929,000.00	$929,000.00

Required:

(1) Prepare a ten-column manufacturing work sheet. New inventories are finished goods, $70,000.00, work in process, $21,000.00, and raw materials, $25,000.00.

(2) Draw up a profit and loss statement for the year.

(3) Prepare a balance sheet, December 31, 19__.

Problem **24–9.** Following is the trial balance of the Concord Manufacturing Company on December 31, 19__:

Cash	$ 192,000.00	
Accounts Receivable	260,000.00	
Finished Goods	212,000.00	
Work in Process	100,000.00	

Raw Materials	60,000.00	
Marketable Securities	244,000.00	
Office Equipment	78,000.00	
Reserve for Depreciation — Office Equipment		$ 30,000.00
Factory Equipment	200,000.00	
Reserve for Depreciation — Factory Equipment . . .		40,000.00
Dies, Patterns, Jigs	100,000.00	
Goodwill	250,000.00	
Notes Payable		100,000.00
Accounts Payable		300,000.00
Common Stock, 100,000 shares no-par		1,024,000.00
Surplus		200,000.00
Sales		1,270,000.00
Purchases	400,000.00	
Freight In	13,000.00	
Direct Labor	257,000.00	
Depreciation Expense — Factory Equipment	20,000.00	
Factory Rent	100,000.00	
Insurance Expense — Factory Assets	4,000.00	
Miscellaneous Factory Expense	246,000.00	
Advertising Expense.	45,000.00	
Miscellaneous Selling Expense	16,000.00	
Sales Salaries	50,000.00	
Traveling Expense	25,000.00	
Depreciation Expense — Office Equipment	7,000.00	
General Office Expense	42,000.00	
Office Salaries	43,000.00	
	$2,964,000.00	$2,964,000.00

Required:

(1) Prepare a ten-column manufacturing work sheet. New inventories are raw materials, $52,000.00, work in process, $150,000.00, finished goods, $118,000.00.

(2) Draw up a profit and loss statement for the year.

(3) Prepare a balance sheet, December 31, 19__.

Problem 24–10. From the following information, and from information which you may discover, prepare the detailed profit and loss statement of the Wilcox Gear Works for the year 1955:

Direct Labor	$ 50,000.00
Finished Goods, January 1, 1955	25,000.00
Finished Goods, December 31, 1955	30,000.00
General Expenses	10,000.00
Gross Profit	64,000.00
Manufacturing Expenses	40,000.00
Purchases of Raw Materials	60,000.00
Raw Materials, January 1, 1955	35,000.00
Raw Materials, December 31, 1955	15,000.00
Sales	220,000.00
Selling Expenses	30,000.00
Work in Process, January 1, 1955	30,000.00

Problem 24–11. On December 31, 1950, the trial balance of the Jersey

Electric Company, after giving effect to adjusting entries (except inventories), was as follows:

Cash	$ 21,960.00	
Accounts Receivable	44,160.00	
Reserve for Bad Debts		$ 2,840.00
Finished Goods	17,080.00	
Work in Process	12,932.00	
Raw Materials	18,544.00	
Prepaid Insurance	524.00	
Factory Building	73,200.00	
Reserve for Depreciation — Factory Building		11,224.00
Machinery	48,000.00	
Reserve for Depreciation — Machinery		19,520.00
Delivery Equipment	14,600.00	
Reserve for Depreciation — Delivery Equipment		8,540.00
Furniture and Fixtures	4,148.00	
Reserve for Depreciation — Furniture and Fixtures		1,760.00
Land	25,000.00	
Accrued Payroll		4,100.00
Dividend Payable		6,000.00
Vouchers Payable		20,770.00
Common Stock, 10,000 shares no-par		120,612.00
Surplus		56,703.00
Sales		248,880.00
Returned Sales and Allowances	1,560.00	
Sales Discounts	3,660.00	
Purchases	75,030.00	
Returned Purchases and Allowances		1,830.00
Purchases Discounts		2,928.00
Freight In	800.00	
Direct Labor	48,200.00	
Depreciation Expense — Building	1,464.00	
Depreciation Expense — Machinery	4,880.00	
Factory Repairs	5,390.00	
Factory Supplies	2,750.00	
Heat, Light, and Power	2,574.00	
Indirect Labor	20,740.00	
Insurance Expense (factory)	610.00	
Miscellaneous Factory Expense	2,196.00	
Taxes (factory)	1,537.00	
Advertising	7,320.00	
Depreciation Expense — Delivery Equipment	3,650.00	
Salesmen's Salaries	14,600.00	
Traveling Expense	7,808.00	
Bad Debts	3,250.00	
Depreciation Expense — Furniture and Fixtures	414.00	
Office Expense	1,510.00	
Office Salaries	15,616.00	
	$505,707.00	$505,707.00

Required:

(1) Prepare a ten-column manufacturing work sheet. New inventories: raw materials, $8,052.00, work in process, $9,860.00, finished goods, $14,620.00.

(2) Draw up a profit and loss statement for the year 1950.

(3) Prepare a balance sheet, December 31, 1950.

Problem **24–12.** On December 31, 19__, the trial balance, before adjustment, of the Indiana Sales Company was:

Cash	$ 201,500.00	
Accounts Receivable	80,000.00	
Finished Goods	60,000.00	
Work in Process	40,000.00	
Raw Materials	70,000.00	
Prepaid Insurance	2,500.00	
Building	100,000.00	
Reserve for Depreciation — Building		$ 20,000.00
Machinery	90,000.00	
Reserve for Depreciation — Machinery		15,000.00
Office Equipment	10,000.00	
Reserve for Depreciation — Office Equipment		1,000.00
Land	10,000.00	
Accounts Payable		50,000.00
Common Stock, $100.00 par		500,000.00
Surplus		100,000.00
Sales		500,000.00
Sales Discounts	7,000.00	
Purchases	300,000.00	
Purchases Discounts		5,000.00
Freight In	5,000.00	
Direct Labor	100,000.00	
Heat, Light, and Power	25,000.00	
Indirect Labor	20,000.00	
Miscellaneous Factory Supplies	6,000.00	
Machinery Repairs	8,000.00	
Advertising	3,000.00	
Sales Salaries	20,000.00	
Traveling Expense	2,000.00	
General Expense	7,000.00	
Office Salaries	24,000.00	
	$1,191,000.00	$1,191,000.00

Supplementary Information

(1) Inventories on December 31, 19__, were finished goods, $62,000.00, work in process, $90,000.00, and raw materials, $100,000.00.

(2) Prepaid expenses on December 31, 19__, amounted to prepaid insurance, $500.00, factory supplies, $1,000.00.

(3) Annual depreciation rates: buildings, 5%, machinery, 10%, and office equipment, 10%.

(4) $1,000.00 of the Heat, Light, and Power account is to be handled as a general nonfactory expense.

(5) Accrued property taxes on December 31, 19__, amounted to $4,000.00. Of this amount, 1/4 was chargeable as a general expense, and 3/4 as a factory expense.

Required:

(1) Prepare a ten-column manufacturing work sheet.

(2) Draw up a profit and loss statement for the year.

(3) Prepare a balance sheet, December 31, 19__.

Problem 24-13. Following is the unadjusted trial balance of the Maine Manufacturing Company on December 31, 19__:

Cash	$ 28,000.00	
Accounts Receivable	225,600.00	
Reserve for Bad Debts		$ 1,211.00
Finished Goods	85,000.00	
Work in Process	24,400.00	
Raw Materials	28,000.00	
Factory Building	250,000.00	
Reserve for Depreciation — Factory Building.		74,000.00
Land	30,000.00	
Machinery and Equipment	133,000.00	
Reserve for Depreciation — Machinery and Equipment		22,000.00
Office Equipment	19,000.00	
Reserve for Depreciation — Office Equipment		6,000.00
Accounts Payable		164,000.00
Common Stock, $100.00 par		400,000.00
Treasury Stock	40,000.00	
Surplus		113,989.00
Sales		865,000.00
Sales Discounts	8,000.00	
Purchases	203,000.00	
Purchases Discounts.		6,000.00
Advertising Expense.	40,000.00	
Direct Labor	202,000.00	
Factory Repairs	26,000.00	
General Office Expense	34,000.00	
Indirect Labor	78,000.00	
Miscellaneous Factory Expense	56,000.00	
Office Salaries	30,000.00	
Sales Salaries	51,000.00	
Taxes (80% to factory, 20% to general)	40,000.00	
Traveling Expense	18,000.00	
Interest Expense	3,200.00	
	$1,652,200.00	$1,652,200.00

The following additional information should be considered:

(1) Inventories, December 31, 19__: finished goods, $88,000.00, work in process, $10,000.00, raw materials, $42,000.00.

(2) Accrued payroll: direct labor, $3,100.00, indirect labor, $1,000.00, sales salaries, $3,000.00, and office salaries, $2,000.00.

(3) Annual depreciation rates: factory building, 3%, machinery and equipment, $12\frac{1}{2}\%$, and office equipment, 10%.

(4) Operations should be charged with $20,000.00 as a provision to cover estimated uncollectible accounts receivable.

(5) A 5% cash dividend has been declared to stock of record December 31, 19__, payable January 20, 19__.

Required:

 (1) Prepare a manufacturing work sheet.
 (2) Draw up a profit and loss statement for 19___:
 (3) Prepare a balance sheet, December 31, 19___.

 Problem 24–14. The trial balance of the Gordon-Frentz Manufacturing Company on December 31, 19___, was as follows:

Cash	$ 32,000.00	
Accounts Receivable	26,000.00	
Reserve for Bad Debts		$ 260.00
Finished Goods.	14,000.00	
Work in Process	10,600.00	
Raw Materials	15,200.00	
Factory Building	60,000.00	
Reserve for Depreciation — Factory Building		8,000.00
Machinery and Equipment	40,000.00	
Reserve for Depreciation — Machinery and Equipment		12,000.00
Automobiles	12,000.00	
Reserve for Depreciation — Automobiles		4,000.00
Office Equipment	5,000.00	
Reserve for Depreciation — Office Equipment		1,000.00
Land	10,000.00	
Dividends Payable		5,000.00
Vouchers Payable		18,710.00
Common Stock, $100.00 par		100,000.00
Surplus		36,000.00
Sales		208,000.00
Returned Sales and Allowances	1,200.00	
Sales Discounts	3,000.00	
Purchases	61,500.00	
Returned Purchases and Allowances		1,500.00
Purchases Discounts		2,400.00
Freight In	640.00	
Direct Labor	38,000.00	
Factory Repairs	4,420.00	
Factory Supplies Expense	2,200.00	
Heat, Light, Power	2,110.00	
Indirect Labor	15,310.00	
Insurance (factory)	930.00	
Miscellaneous Factory Expense	1,800.00	
Taxes (factory)	1,260.00	
Advertising Expense	6,000.00	
Salesmen's Salaries	12,000.00	
Traveling Expense	6,400.00	
Bad Debts Expense	1,000.00	
Office Expense	1,500.00	
Office Salaries	12,800.00	
	$396,870.00	$396,870.00

Supplementary Information

 (1) New inventories December 31, 19___: raw materials, $6,600.00, work in process, $8,000.00, finished goods, $12,000.00.
 (2) Annual depreciation rates: automobiles, 25 %, factory building, 2 %,

office equipment, 10%, machinery and equipment, 10%. Depreciation expense on automobiles is to be apportioned 30% to manufacturing and 70% to selling.

(3) Accrued factory payroll: direct labor, $2,000.00, indirect labor, $1,360.00.

(4) The amount of prepaid insurance expense on December 31, 19—, is $430.00.

Required:

(1) Prepare a manufacturing work sheet.

(2) Draw up a profit and loss statement for the year. The detail for Cost of Sales may be shown in a separate supporting schedule in which should appear the cost of goods manufactured and sold.

(3) Prepare a balance sheet, December 31, 19—.

Chapter 25

MANUFACTURING OPERATIONS (Continued)

MANUFACTURING ACCOUNTING UNDER THE PLAN OF PERPETUAL INVENTORY

For a manufacturing concern the plan of periodic inventory often has important weaknesses:

(1) It does not tell how much inventory should be on hand.

(2) It does not provide for adequate control of stock.

(3) It does not provide for the allocation of raw materials to products, operations, or departments.

(4) The cost of each kind or type of product is not known.

(5) The valuation of inventories of partly manufactured products and finished goods is difficult. Estimates must usually be resorted to.

(6) Monthly financial statements become impracticable because of the time and expense involved in taking and evaluating physical inventories.

The plan of perpetual inventory is intended to circumvent these weaknesses. Manufacturing accounting under the method of perpetual inventory will be discussed in this chapter.

MATERIALS PURCHASED

Direct materials are ordinarily given the name of "raw materials" in manufacturing accounting. The raw materials of one company may be the finished product of another. To a company manufacturing woolen cloth, raw wool would represent raw materials, and the manufactured woolen cloth would represent the finished product. To a company manufacturing men's clothing, the woolen cloth would represent raw materials; and the completed suits would represent the finished product.

All raw material purchases are debited to the Raw Materials (inventory) account from the voucher register. This account is a controlling account, the details of which are kept in a subsidiary ledger; one ledger page — or rather, card — is kept for each kind of raw material. After entry on the voucher register, a purchase invoice for raw materials is recorded in the subsidiary raw materials ledger, one page of which might appear as follows:

Article X

Unit _____
Maximum **700**
Minimum **200**

RECEIVED					ISSUED					ON HAND	
Date	Ref.	Quantity	Price	Amount	Date	Req. No.	Quantity	Price	Amount	Date	Quantity
1950					1950					1950	
Jan. 2	PO 1	1,000	50¢	500 00	Jan. 7	10	400	50¢	200 00	Jan. 2	1,000
					14	28	410	50¢	205 00	7	600
										14	190
15	PO 19	400	50¢	200 00	21	42	360	50¢	180 00	15	590
										21	230
25	PO 31	500	50¢	250 00	28	51	400	50¢	200 00	25	730
										28	330
				950 00					785 00		
Feb. 1	Balance	330	50¢	165 00						Feb. 1	330

528

RAW MATERIALS USED

All materials needed for production are withdrawn from the raw materials inventory by written requisition. These withdrawals are recorded in a raw materials requisition register, illustrated below:

RAW MATERIALS
REQUISITION REGISTER

DATE	REQUISITION No.	AMOUNT	DATE	REQUISITION No.	AMOUNT

At the end of the month, the total raw material disbursements are made the basis of a journal entry: [1]

```
Work in Process . . . . . . . . . . . . . . . . . . . .    xxx xx
      Raw Materials . . . . . . . . . . . . . . . . . .           xxx xx
To charge work in process with value of raw materials con-
sumed.
```

During the month, the withdrawals of material, as evidenced by requisitions, will have been entered on the appropriate cards of the subsidiary raw materials ledger. After all additions and withdrawals have been recorded,[2] each inventory card will represent the quantity and value of the product remaining on hand. The sum of the values on the inventory cards at the end of the month should equal the balance of the Raw Materials inventory account on the general ledger. The value represented by each card will be the beginning inventory value increased or decreased by the difference between the dollar totals of the "Received" and "Issued" columns (see illustration on page 528).

FACTORY SUPPLIES

When the investment in factory supplies warrants, the control over factory supplies should be as exacting as that for raw materials. Factory supplies, as received, would be debited to Factory Supplies

---

[1] This entry may be made separately as above, or it may be made part of a compound entry in which Work in Process is charged with materials, labor, and manufacturing expense all at the same time. The compound entry on page 532 includes the entry above.

[2] Additions are recorded at purchase cost plus transportation; withdrawals are recorded at actual cost or at average cost. The average cost, when used, is generally ascertained monthly.

(inventory) and issued on the authority of written requisitions. At the end of the month, the total requisitions would be made the basis of the following entry:

Factory Supplies (expense). . . . .   xxx xx
      Factory Supplies (inventory) . . . .   xxx xx
To record factory supplies used up in production.

LABOR

The labor of each man is recorded daily on a labor report, one form of which (condensed) is as follows:

		PRODUCTION ORDER No.				ACCOUNT No.					TOTAL
Sunday											Hours
Monday											"
Tuesday											"
Wednesday											"
Thursday											"
Friday											"
Saturday											"
TOTAL HOURS											Hours
WAGE RATE											Rate
AMOUNTS	$				$					$	WAGE

LABOR REPORT

Name _____   No. _____

Week Ending _____

DEBIT

At the end of the payroll period the labor reports are summarized, after which the dollar totals of the several columns are recorded in the payroll distribution register (see page 531).

The totals of the several columns of the payroll distribution register provide the amount of the payroll and its distribution to cost accounts. Direct Labor, for example, will be debited with the sum

PAYROLL DISTRIBUTION REGISTER

WEEK ENDING

EM- PLOYEE NO.	WAGE	PRODUCTION ORDER No.	DEBIT																			ACCOUNT No.
1																						
2																						
3																						
4																						
5																						
6																						
7																						
8																						
9																						
10																						
11																						
12																						
13																						
14																						
15																						
16																						
17																						
18																						
19																						
20																						
TOTAL PAYROLL																						

of the totals of the "Production Order No." columns. The sum of the "Account No." columns is the amount of the indirect labor of the payroll; this total, however, would not as a general rule be debited to the Indirect Labor account. This is because some indirect labor should be charged to Factory Repairs, some to Heat, Light, and Power, some to Indirect Labor, some to Miscellaneous Factory Expense, and some to other accounts. Each "Account No." on the payroll distribution register represents, therefore, an account to which indirect labor may be charged. In distributing the indirect labor of the payroll the totals of the Account No. columns will be debited to the specific accounts which these columns represent.

At the end of the payroll period the totals of the payroll distribution register will be recorded in the voucher register in the following manner:

Direct Labor	xxx xx	
Manufacturing Expense	xxx xx	
Vouchers Payable		xxx xx

To record factory payroll liability and distribution of payroll to cost accounts.

In the entry Manufacturing Expense is a controlling account. The detailed expense accounts are carried in a subsidiary manufacturing expense ledger.

When the last day of the payroll period does not coincide with the last day of the accounting period, care should be taken to distribute the accrued payroll to the cost accounts of the current period.

WORK IN PROCESS

Into this account are placed *all* manufacturing costs. On the books this is expressed by one summary entry made at the end of each month:

Work in Process	xxx xx	
Raw Materials [3]		xxx xx
Direct Labor		xxx xx
Manufacturing Expense		xxx xx

To charge work in process with raw materials, direct labor, and manufacturing expense consumed during month of _____.

The amount of the credit to Raw Materials is the total of raw material requisitions as recorded in the raw materials requisition register for the period; the credit to Direct Labor is the amount of the debit balance in the Direct Labor account; and the credit to Manufacturing Expense is obtained from the summary of manufacturing expense distributed (see page 536).

---

[3] See footnote page 529.

PRODUCTION ORDER

Description _____   No. _____

_____   Date _____

For _____   Due _____

Units _____

MATERIALS			DIRECT LABOR			MANUFACTURING EXPENSE		
Date	Requisition No.	Amount	Date	Employee No.	Amount	Date	Ref.	Amount

SUMMARY

Materials...................... $_____

Direct Labor................. _____

Manufacturing Expense........ _____

TOTAL COST OF GOODS MANUFACTURED ON THIS ORDER.... $_____

_____ units finished at unit cost of _____

Work in Process is an inventory controlling account. Supporting the Work in Process account are various production orders, one production order being issued for each lot of merchandise in the process of manufacture. Each production order is charged with the raw materials, direct labor, and manufacturing expense which are applicable to it. At the end of the month the sum of the cumulative costs of the unfinished production orders should equal the balance of the Work in Process account as it appears in the end-of-the-month balance sheet.

In form a production order may appear as shown on page 533.

The amount of raw material to be charged to each production order is obtained from information on the raw material requisitions.

The amount of labor charged to each order is obtained from the payroll distribution register.

Manufacturing expense is charged to each order according to some predetermined method of expense allocation. This is further explained in the Manufacturing Expense section of this chapter (see page 536).

FINISHED GOODS

During the operating period it is usual for certain manufacturing orders (i.e., production orders) to be completed. The completed production which is represented by these orders is an accretion to the inventory of finished goods. At the end of the month a summary of completed production orders is prepared and made the basis of the following entry:

```
Finished Goods . . . . . . . . . . . . . . . . . . . . .   xxx xx
    Work in Process  . . . . . . . . . . . . . . . . .           xxx xx
    To transfer completed production to inventory of finished
    goods.
```

The Finished Goods inventory account, like Raw Materials, and Work in Process inventories, is a controlling account. A subsidiary ledger, similar to that for raw materials, is maintained; one account, or card, is kept for each kind or type of finished article. Additions to stock, and withdrawals, are recorded in the same way that additions and withdrawals to the stock of raw materials are recorded. The sources of entry are:

For additions to stock: Completed production orders.
For deductions from stock: Sales invoices.

After all entries have been made, each card represents the amount of inventory remaining on hand for that particular finished product.[4]

---

[4] As a general principle, book inventories should be verified, at least once a year, by comparison with physical inventories.

The sum of the detailed values for finished goods should equal the balance in the Finished Goods controlling account on the general ledger.

At the end of the month the finished goods which have been withdrawn from stock, and sold, are recorded thus:

```
Cost of Sales . . . . . . . . . . . . . . . . . . . . . .   xxx xx
    Finished Goods . . . . . . . . . . . . . . . . . .           xxx xx
    To record cost of manufactured product sold.
```

This entry is prepared from a summary of manufactured product sold, ruled somewhat as follows:

MANUFACTURED PRODUCT SOLD

MONTH OF_____ 19__

PRODUCTION ORDER No.	COST	PRODUCTION ORDER No.	COST

or it may be drawn from a special Cost of Sales column in the sales book. A Cost of Sales column means, of course, that each sales invoice is individually "costed" and recorded in the following type of sales book:

SALES BOOK

DATE	INVOICE No.	DEBIT ACCOUNT OF	L.F.	AMOUNT	COST OF SALES

MANUFACTURING EXPENSE

Manufacturing expenses represent all manufacturing costs except direct materials and direct labor. The equitable apportionment of these costs to the product is often a difficult problem. A widely used procedure is to relate the total manufacturing expense to the total direct labor, and to apply this ratio in the distribution of manufacturing expense to the product. For instance, if it is estimated that the total manufacturing expense for a period will be $35,000.00, and that the total direct labor will be $50,000.00, the burden rate for the period will be 70%; a job, then, with a direct labor cost of $80.00 would be charged $56.00 for manufacturing expense.

There are other methods for the distribution of manufacturing expense. These methods are described in any standard text on cost accounting.

At the end of the month a summary of the total manufacturing expense charged to production orders during the month is prepared:

SUMMARY OF MANUFACTURING EXPENSE DISTRIBUTED

MONTH OF_____ 19__

PRODUCTION ORDER No.	MANUFACTURING EXPENSE	PRODUCTION ORDER No.	MANUFACTURING EXPENSE

The total manufacturing expense of this report is made the basis of the following entry:

Work in Process . . . .   xxx xx
    Manufacturing Expense [5] . . . .   xxx xx
To charge work in process with manufacturing expense absorbed by operations.

If manufacturing expense is distributed to production as a fixed percentage of direct labor, then the monetary values of this journal entry can be established by simply applying the percentage against the amount of direct labor for the month.

The account with Manufacturing Expense will have a large

---

[5] This entry is incorporated in the compound entry given on page 532.

If the company has not maintained a controlling account for manufacturing expenses, a preliminary entry is necessary before either of the above entries may be made. All individual manufacturing expense accounts should be transferred to one summary account called Manufacturing Expense.

credit balance until the end of the year, when all of the individual manufacturing expense accounts will be closed to the one summary account, Manufacturing Expense. In constructing interim financial statements throughout the year, the difference between the total of the individual manufacturing expense accounts on the books, and the credit balance in the Manufacturing Expense account, may be placed on the profit and loss statement as other income or other expense, as the case may be.

(Some accountants would handle these differences as adjustments of Cost of Sales; still other accountants would handle them as deferred items for placement on the balance sheet.)

UNDER- OR OVERABSORBED MANUFACTURING EXPENSE

It follows from the above section that the Manufacturing Expense account may have a balance at the end of the accounting period. What should be done with this balance?

Example:

As of January 1, 19__, the management of the X Manufacturing Company estimated that direct labor costs for the next twelve months would amount to $50,000.00, and manufacturing expenses, $35,000.00. These estimates called for a burden distribution rate of 70%, i.e., a predetermined burden rate of 70% to be used in costing individual manufacturing orders throughout the year.

At the end of the year it was found that direct labor actually amounted to $48,000.00, and manufacturing expense, $35,316.00. The amount of manufacturing expense applied to production during the year was therefore 70% of $48,000.00, or $33,600.00. This was recorded by the entry

```
Work in Process . . . . . . . . . . . . . . . . .    33,600.00
    Manufacturing Expense . . . . . . . . . . . .                33,600.00
    To debit work in process with manufacturing expense.
```

On December 31, 19__, therefore, the Manufacturing Expense account was as follows:

MANUFACTURING EXPENSE

35,316.00	33,600.00

In this example the debit balance of the Manufacturing Expense account indicates an underabsorption of manufacturing expense. If the balance of the account had been credit, the balance would have indicated an overabsorption of manufacturing expense. The balance of the account, whether debit or credit, may be due to

(1) The fact that, although operations have been normal, the burden rate in use has been incorrect. This, in turn, may be due to the fact that actual expenses have exceeded estimated expenses, or vice versa; or it may be due to the fact that the distribution base was estimated incorrectly.

(2) The fact that operations have been in excess of, or less than, normal.

Theoretically, any unabsorbed or overabsorbed balance in the Manufacturing Expense account should be distributed to the manufacturing costs of the year. Difficulties arise, however, when the attempt is made to apply this theory to practice. It is upon the basis of expediency, therefore, that accountants have generally sanctioned the practice of transferring any balance in the Manufacturing Expense account to profit and loss as other income or other expense or, alternatively, to the Cost of Sales account. The transfer to profit and loss is especially appropriate if the balance of the Manufacturing Expense account is small as, indeed, it should be if the distribution rate has been correctly calculated and if manufacturing operations have materialized about as expected.

When the unabsorbed or overabsorbed balance is large enough to have a significant bearing upon the detailed accuracy of financial statements, the difference between actual manufacturing expense and manufacturing expense applied should be spread over the year's manufacturing costs by proration to cost of sales and inventories. However, if the difference is large because of idle plant rather than because of fundamental error in predetermined burden rates, the difference should be transferred directly to Profit and Loss for placement in the other-income-and-expense section of the statement of profit and loss. This treatment allows the cost of goods manufactured and sold to be shown at costs which are the normal or budgeted costs.

Under this theory it is logical, in the preparation of monthly profit and loss statements, to show under- or overapplied manufacturing expense in the other-income-and-expense section of the profit and loss statement.

SUMMARY

Manufacturing accounting under the plan of perpetual inventory may be summarized by presenting a representative set of entries. The entries below are those of the Manchester Manufacturing Company whose profit and loss statement appears on page 540.

Raw Materials . . . . 　123,000.00
　　Vouchers Payable . . . . 　　　　　　　123,000.00
To record purchases of direct materials, net, after deduction
of purchases discounts.

Direct Labor . . . . 　100,000.00
Manufacturing Expense (control) . . . . 　30,000.00
　　Vouchers Payable . . . . 　　　　　　　130,000.00
To record liability for payroll, and to record distribution of
payroll to cost accounts.

Manufacturing Expense (control) . . . . 　23,500.00
　　Vouchers Payable . . . . 　　　　　　　23,500.00
To record invoices for manufacturing expenses.

Manufacturing Expense (control) . . . . 　58,500.00
　　Reserve for Depreciation — Buildings . . . . 　　　　　　　7,500.00
　　Reserve for Depreciation — Factory Equipment　. . . 　　　　　　　51,000.00
To record depreciation expense on factory assets.

Depreciation Expense — Delivery Equipment　. . . . . . 　7,500.00
　　Reserve for Depreciation — Delivery Equipment　. . . 　　　　　　　7,500.00
To record depreciation expense on delivery equipment.

Depreciation Expense — Furniture and Fixtures . . . . . . 　6,000.00
　　Reserve for Depreciation — Furniture and Fixtures　. . 　　　　　　　6,000.00
To record depreciation expense on furniture and fixtures.

Vouchers Payable . . . . 　806,500.00
　　Cash　. . . . . 　　　　　　　806,500.00
To record payment of vouchers payable.

Work in Process . . . . 　128,000.00
　　Raw Materials . . . . 　　　　　　　128,000.00
To record raw materials withdrawn from inventory for use in
production.

Work in Process　. . . . . 　100,000.00
　　Direct Labor . . . . 　　　　　　　100,000.00
To charge production with direct labor.

Work in Process　. . . . . 　110,000.00
　　Manufacturing Expense (control) . . . . 　　　　　　　110,000.00
To debit Work in Process for manufacturing expense charged
to production.

Unabsorbed Manufacturing Expense　. . . . . 　2,000.00
　　Manufacturing Expense (control) . . . . 　　　　　　　2,000.00
To write off unabsorbed debit balance in Manufacturing Expense. (The debit member of this entry, in turn, will be
closed to Profit and Loss.)

Finished Goods . . . . 　328,000.00
　　Work in Process　. . . . . 　　　　　　　328,000.00
To record transfer of completed production to inventory of
finished goods.

Cost of Sales . . . . 　363,000.00
　　Finished Goods . . . . 　　　　　　　363,000.00
To record merchandise withdrawn from finished goods inventory, and sold.

At this point a trial balance would be taken. This trial balance appears in the first pair of columns of the manufacturing work sheet on page 542. Note that Cost of Sales appears in this trial balance.

From this point on, the closing entries to be placed on the books would be identical with those for an ordinary trading concern.

It is possible to apply the basic pattern of perpetual inventory accounting to the merchandising transactions of a trading business.[6] This practice, however, is not common.

PROFIT AND LOSS STATEMENT

The profit and loss statement to be prepared from the work sheet of the Manchester Manufacturing Company is as follows:

Manchester Manufacturing Company

PROFIT AND LOSS STATEMENT
FOR THE YEAR ENDING DECEMBER 31, 1950

Gross Sales		$625,000.00
Less Returned Sales and Allowances	$ 20,000.00	
Sales Discounts	5,000.00	25,000.00
Net Sales		$600,000.00
Cost of Sales		363,000.00
Gross Profit		$237,000.00

---

[6] When this is done, the merchandise accounting of a trading business would be somewhat as follows:

(1) At the beginning of the accounting period the balance of the Merchandise account would be the cost value of the merchandise actually on hand as per physical count.

(2) Purchases of merchandise during a period would be debited to the Merchandise account when the purchases book is posted.

(3) At the end of the accounting period, the balance of the Freight In account would be transferred to the Merchandise account.

(4) At the end of the accounting period the following entry for cost of sales is made:

Cost of Sales	xxx xx	
Merchandise		xxx xx

To record cost of merchandise sold; and to leave the Merchandise account with a balance equal to the actual inventory on hand.

After this entry has been posted, the balance of the Merchandise account will be the cost value of the inventory of merchandise on hand at the end of the accounting period. The credit member of this entry is an amount sufficient to reduce the balance of the Merchandise account to the actual value of inventory currently on hand. This value is the cost value of a physical count of inventory.

(5) The balance of the Cost of Sales account is closed to Profit and Loss.

Selling Expenses:
Advertising Expense	$ 15,000.00	
Delivery Expense	14,000.00	
Depreciation Expense — Delivery Equipment	7,500.00	
Insurance	1,000.00	
Miscellaneous Expense	10,000.00	
Sales Salaries	40,000.00	
Traveling Expense	20,000.00	
	$107,500.00	

General Expenses:
Bad Debts Expense	$ 3,500.00		
Depreciation Expense — Office Equipment.	6,000.00		
General Salaries	35,000.00		
Insurance	200.00		
Miscellaneous Expense	8,800.00		
Office Supplies	6,000.00	59,500.00	167,000.00

Net Profit from Operations		$ 70,000.00
Other Income:		
Dividend Income	$ 7,000.00	
Interest Income	5,000.00	12,000.00
		$ 82,000.00

Other Expense:
Unabsorbed Manufacturing Expense	2,000.00

Net Income before Income Taxes	$ 80,000.00
Provision for Income Taxes	20,000.00
Net Income	$ 60,000.00

If detail for the cost of sales is desired, a supporting schedule may be used, thus:

Manchester Manufacturing Company

COST OF SALES FOR THE YEAR ENDING DECEMBER 31, 1950

Finished Goods, January 1, 1950		$120,000.00
Cost of Goods Manufactured in 1950:		
Work in Process, January 1, 1950.	$ 40,000.00	
Raw Materials Consumed	128,000.00	
Direct Labor	100,000.00	
Manufacturing Expense	110,000.00	
	$378,000.00	
Work in Process, December 31, 1950	50,000.00	328,000.00
		$448,000.00
Finished Goods, December 31, 1950		85,000.00
		$363,000.00

Manchester Manufacturing Company

Work Sheet, Year Ending December 31, 1950

	Trial Balance		Profit and Loss		Balance Sheet	
Cash	102,000.00				102,000.00	
Accounts Receivable	100,000.00				100,000.00	
Finished Goods	85,000.00				85,000.00	
Work in Process	50,000.00				50,000.00	
Raw Materials	15,000.00				15,000.00	
Corporate Stocks and Bonds	200,000.00				200,000.00	
Building	300,000.00				300,000.00	
Reserve for Depreciation — Building		37,500.00				37,500.00
Delivery Equipment	30,000.00				30,000.00	
Reserve for Depreciation — Delivery Equipment		17,500.00				17,500.00
Factory Equipment	510,000.00				510,000.00	
Reserve for Depreciation — Factory Equipment		171,000.00				171,000.00
Office Equipment	60,000.00				60,000.00	
Reserve for Depreciation — Office Equipment		22,000.00				22,000.00
Land	100,000.00				100,000.00	
Vouchers Payable		80,000.00				80,000.00
Income Taxes Payable		20,000.00				20,000.00
Common Stock		1,000,000.00				1,000,000.00
Surplus		144,000.00				144,000.00
Sales		625,000.00		625,000.00		
Returned Sales and Allowances	20,000.00		20,000.00			
Sales Discounts	5,000.00		5,000.00			
Cost of Sales	363,000.00		363,000.00			
Advertising	15,000.00		15,000.00			
Delivery Expense	14,000.00		14,000.00			
Depreciation Expense — Delivery Equipment	7,500.00		7,500.00			
Insurance (Selling)	1,000.00		1,000.00			
Miscellaneous Selling Expense	10,000.00		10,000.00			
Sales Salaries	40,000.00		40,000.00			
Traveling Expense	20,000.00		20,000.00			
Bad Debts Expense	3,500.00		3,500.00			
Depreciation Expense — Office Equipment	6,000.00		6,000.00			
General Salaries	35,000.00		35,000.00			
Insurance (General)	200.00		200.00			
Miscellaneous General Expense	8,800.00		8,800.00			
Office Supplies	6,000.00		6,000.00			
Dividend Income		7,000.00		7,000.00		
Interest Income		5,000.00		5,000.00		
Unabsorbed Manufacturing Expense	2,000.00		2,000.00			
Provision for Income Taxes	20,000.00		20,000.00			
	2,129,000.00	2,129,000.00				
Net Income to Surplus			60,000.00			60,000.00
			637,000.00	637,000.00	1,552,000.00	1,552,000.00

Referring to the cost of sales schedule on page 541, the figures for

Raw Materials Consumed
Direct Labor, and
Manufacturing Expense

are obtained from the debit side of the Work in Process account at the end of the accounting year.

When interim statements of profit and loss are prepared, the account with Direct Labor should be interpreted as part of the debit side of the Work in Process account. With respect to manufacturing expenses, as previously pointed out, the difference between the total of the individual manufacturing expense accounts and the credit balance of the Manufacturing Expense account may be placed in the other income or other expense sections of the profit and loss statement, as the case may be.

QUESTIONS

Question **25-1.** What are the weaknesses of manufacturing accounting as carried on under the plan of periodic inventory?

Question **25-2.** By means of journal entries describe the technique of manufacturing accounting under the plan of perpetual inventory. Explanations may be omitted.

Question **25-3.** How is the cost of sales figure determined under the plan of perpetual inventory?

Question **25-4.** From the description in this chapter of manufacturing accounts kept under the perpetual inventory system, state what controlling accounts are maintained. What are the sources of entries made in (1) these controlling accounts, and (2) their related subsidiary ledgers?

Question **25-5.** At the end of the year the summary account with Manufacturing Expense has a debit balance of $2,814.66.
(1) Explain this balance.
(2) What disposition should be made of it when the books are closed?
(3) If this were the balance on October 31, what disposition should be made of it when the October 31 statements are prepared?

Question **25-6.** A company operates under the plan of perpetual inventory. Should it ever take physical inventory? If so, why should the book inventory be maintained?

Question **25-7.** What is the factual source upon which debits or credits are made to the accounts indicated:

Debits to Raw Materials for
    (1) Raw materials purchases
Credits to Raw Materials for
    (2) Raw materials placed into production
Debits to Work in Process for
    (3) Raw materials used
    (4) Direct labor
    (5) Manufacturing expense
Credits to Work in Process for
    (6) Completed production
Debits to Finished Goods for
    (7) Additions to stock
Credits to Finished Goods for
    (8) Deductions from stock

PROBLEMS

Problem **25–1.** The condensed balance sheet of the Wales Manufacturing Company on January 1, 19__, was:

Cash	$ 55,000.00	Vouchers Payable	$ 52,000.00
Finished Goods	12,000.00	Common Stock, $100.00 par	100,000.00
Work in Process	20,000.00	Surplus	10,000.00
Raw Materials	10,000.00		
Machinery and Equipment	65,000.00		
	$162,000.00		$162,000.00

The company operated under the system of perpetual inventory. During the year 19__ the condensed transactions of the company were as follows:

    (1) Purchased raw materials on account, $45,000.00.
    (2) Miscellaneous general factory expenses paid, $4,000.00.
    (3) Depreciation expense on machinery and equipment, $6,000.00.
    (4) The payroll for the year, which was paid in cash, amounted to $33,000.00. Of this amount, $23,000.00 was for direct labor and $10,000.00 was for indirect labor.
    (5) The raw materials requisition register showed a total of $40,000.00 of raw materials drawn from stock and placed into production during the year.
    (6) The summary of completed production orders showed that the total cost value of finished product manufactured during the year was $80,000.00.
    (7) The summary of manufacturing expense distributed showed a total of $19,600.00 manufacturing expense charged to production orders during the year.
    (8) Finished goods were sold on account for $100,000.00. The sum-

mary of finished product sold showed that $67,000.00 of finished goods was withdrawn from stock for purpose of sale.

(9) Cash received from customers amounted to $75,000.00.

(10) Cash payments to creditors for raw material purchases amounted to $50,000.00.

(11) General expenses of administration were paid, $22,000.00.

Required:

(1) Prepare entries to record the above information on the books of the company. Post to a T-account ledger.

(2) Draw off a trial balance.

(3) Prepare a profit and loss statement for the year.

(4) Prepare a balance sheet, December 31, 19__.

(5) Prepare and post closing entries.

Problem 25-2. On January 1, 19__, the trial balance of the Lewis Manufacturing Company was

Cash	$ 470,000.00	
Accounts Receivable	300,000.00	
Finished Goods	150,000.00	
Work in Process	250,000.00	
Raw Materials	130,000.00	
Machinery and Equipment	980.000.00	
Reserve for Depreciation — Machinery and Equipment		$ 280,000.00
Office Equipment	120,000.00	
Reserve for Depreciation — Office Equipment		20,000.00
Vouchers Payable		600,000.00
Common Stock, $100.00 par		1,000,000.00
Surplus		500,000.00
	$2,400,000.00	$2,400,000.00

The Lewis Manufacturing Company operated under the plan of perpetual inventory.

The following condensed transactions occurred during the month of January:

(1) Purchased raw materials on account, $56,000.00.

(2) Paid general factory expenses, $5,000.00.

(3) Depreciation expense on machinery and equipment amounted to $8,000.00.

(4) Depreciation expense on office equipment amounted to $1,000.00.

(5) Payroll for the month paid: direct labor, $30,000.00, indirect labor, $11,000.00.

(6) Raw materials drawn from stock, $50,000.00.

(7) Production orders completed during the month, $100,000.00.

(8) Manufacturing expenses charged to production orders totaled $24,000.00.

(9) Sales on account, $130,000.00. The cost value of the finished goods withdrawn from stock for purpose of sale was $80,000.00.

(10) Collections on accounts receivable, $110,000.00.

(11) Miscellaneous creditor payments, $65,000.00.
(12) Selling expenses paid, $18,000.00.
(13) General expenses paid, $14,000.00.
(14) Factory taxes paid, $1,000.00.

Required:

(1) Enter the above transactions in a T-account ledger.
(2) Draw off a trial balance, January 31, 19—.
(3) Prepare a profit and loss statement for the month of January.
(4) Prepare a balance sheet, January 31, 19—.

Problem **25–3.** The Goodrich Manufacturing Company operates under the plan of perpetual inventory. Except as required by the additional information below, all necessary entries have been made preliminary to the preparation of the adjusted trial balance on December 31, 19—, i.e., inventory entries for the first eleven months of the year are already on the books. Subject to the foregoing, the trial balance of the company on December 31, 19—, is as follows:

Cash	$ 81,000.00	
Accounts Receivable	58,000.00	
Raw Materials	20,000.00	
Work in Process		$ 15,000.00
Finished Goods	23,000.00	
Factory Fixed Assets	80,000.00	
Reserve for Depreciation		10,000.00
Vouchers Payable		40,000.00
Notes Payable		30,000.00
Common Stock, $100.00 par		100,000.00
Surplus		70,000.00
Sales		300,000.00
Cost of Sales	180,000.00	
Direct Labor	30,000.00	
Indirect Labor	28,000.00	
Depreciation Expense — Factory Fixed Assets	6,000.00	
Miscellaneous Factory Expense	34,000.00	
Manufacturing Expense		61,000.00
Selling Expense	32,000.00	
General Expense	27,000.00	
	$599,000.00	$626,000.00

The following additional information has not yet been posted to the ledger:

(1) In the December voucher register, the column for purchases of raw materials shows a total of $27,000.00. All other columns of the voucher register have been posted.
(2) The Raw Materials Requisition Register for December shows a total of $13,000.00.
(3) The Summary of Manufacturing Expense Distributed shows a total of $9,000.00.

(4) The Summary of Completed Production Orders for December shows a total of $27,000.00.

(5) The Cost of Sales column in the sales book for December shows a total of $20,000.00.

Required:

(1) Prepare a profit and loss statement for the year.

(2) Prepare a balance sheet, December 31, 19__.

(3) Make the entries to close the books.

Problem **25–4.** The McCormick Manufacturing Company operates under the plan of perpetual inventory. On December 31, 19__, the trial balance of the company was:

Cash	$ 80,000.00	
Accounts Receivable	70,000.00	
Notes Receivable	90,000.00	
Notes Receivable Discounted		$ 23,000.00
Finished Goods.	30,000.00	
Work in Process	28,000.00	
Raw Materials	33,000.00	
Factory Fixed Assets	100,000.00	
Reserve for Depreciation		20,000.00
Accounts Payable		50,000.00
Notes Payable		20,000.00
Common Stock, 20,000 shares no-par		209,000.00
Surplus		70,000.00
Sales		300,000.00
Cost of Sales	200,000.00	
Direct Labor	70,000.00	70,000.00
Indirect Labor	28,000.00	
General Factory Expense	36,000.00	
Depreciation Expense — Factory Fixed Assets . .	8,000.00	
Manufacturing Expense		70,000.00
Selling Expense	24,000.00	
General Expense	35,000.00	
	—————	—————
	$832,000.00	$832,000.00

The total of the debit side of the Raw Materials inventory account was $102,000.00, and total credits were $69,000.00. At the beginning of the year the balance of the account was $20,000.00.

At the beginning of the year the balance of the Work in Process account was $24,000.00.

The total of the debit side of the Finished Goods inventory account was $230,000.00, and total credits were $200,000.00. At the beginning of the year the balance of the account was $25,000.00.

Required:

(1) Prepare a detailed profit and loss statement for the year. The cost of goods manufactured may be shown as a separate schedule.

(2) Prepare a balance sheet, December 31, 19__.

Chapter 26

DEPRECIATION

DEFINITION

As time goes on, the fixed assets of a business lose their dollar value because of a decline in the amount of service still to be received from them. A piece of machinery may last for years but, eventually, its usefulness will come to an end.[1] Its dollar value will be gone because its service value will have expired. The machine will have been used up in operations just as surely as the power which operated the machine has been used up. As stated on page 284, the investment will have been converted into expense. The term "depreciation" is used to describe the decline which occurs in the dollar value of an asset because of shrinkage in the amount of services receivable.[2] After depreciation has been recorded, the reduced dollar value of a fixed asset reflects the reduced amount of service yet to be derived from it. By "value" here is meant book value or going-concern value — *not* market value or value as established by an engineer in measuring the efficiency of an asset.

This definition of depreciation should be fixed firmly in mind because a loss or shrinkage in value from any other point of view is not depreciation. Acceptance of this definition may be facilitated if it is realized that fixed assets are fundamentally nothing more than long-term prepaid expense accounts.

Depreciation, it should be further observed, applies only to tangible assets. Land is generally considered an exception. However, the fertility of land may be reduced because of cultivation and, where this is the case and the loss is not restored through the use of fertilizers, even land may be said to depreciate in cases in which the utility of the land depends upon its fertility.

Some of the merchandise of an inventory is sometimes found to have deteriorated in value. This deterioration is depreciation. Accountants, however, have generally preferred to handle this par-

---

[1] "All machinery is on an irresistible march to the junk heap, and its progress, while it may be delayed, cannot be prevented by repairs." — Henry Rand Hatfield, *Accounting: Its Principles and Problems*, D. Appleton and Company, 1927, p. 130.

[2] "Broadly speaking, depreciation is the loss not restored by current maintenance, which is due to all the factors causing the ultimate retirement of the property. These factors embrace wear and tear, decay, inadequacy, and obsolescence." — *Lindheimer et al.* v. *Illinois Bell Telephone Co.* 292 U.S. 151 (1934).

ticular loss of value as a problem of inventory valuation rather than as a problem which affects the depreciation expense account.

CAUSES OF DEPRECIATION

Depreciation commonly occurs through the "wear and tear" to which a fixed asset is subject by operations, and to the deterioration in value which comes with the passage of time (age). Engines, typewriters, dispersion dryers, bookkeeping machines, planes, pneumatic tools, and so on, are subject to this physical depreciation. Assets which depreciate physically do not usually change in size; exceptions exist, however, as may be witnessed by the reduction in size of an abrasive stone as it is used up. In all of these cases, however, the asset undergoes a more or less steady diminution in value because of a reduction in the amount of services receivable. Finally, the asset must be retired because it is no longer useful.

Aside from wear, tear, and decay, depreciation may be caused by

(1) *Obsolescence.* Improvements and inventions may make existing equipment unprofitable for further use, or they may shorten the period of profitable employment. As the necessity for the premature retirement of an asset is converted from possibility into actuality, the amount of depreciation expense per accounting period is increased as the estimate of the useful life of the asset is reduced.

(2) *Inadequacy.* Premature depreciation may be forced upon an asset because of the fact that it is no longer able to meet the requirements of a growing volume of business. The demand for service exceeds the ability of the asset to deliver it. The asset, although serviceable for a smaller volume of output, must be retired in favor of a new asset of greater capacity.

(3) *Cessation of demand.* The value of a fixed asset may disappear because the market for the product produced by the fixed asset has vanished.

NECESSITY FOR RECORDING DEPRECIATION

Depreciable fixed assets, in reality, are merely long-term prepaid expense accounts. The investment in them is *used up* over their life period and, as it is used up, the investment is converted into periodic depreciation expense.

Accurate cost and profit figures require the recording of all direct and indirect expenses in the books of account. Depreciation is one of these expenses. Depreciation expense must be recorded because it is one of the costs which are incurred in the production of periodic income. Depreciation is a real expense of doing business; it represents the consumption of value just as surely as does cash which is disbursed for advertising.

If depreciation were not recognized upon the books, the net income of a business would be overstated and depreciable assets would appear on the balance sheet at values greater than their true values. Errors of this kind constitute serious misrepresentations of fact.

In summary the following reasons may be advanced for the recognition of depreciation:

(1) Net income will be stated more accurately if the profit and loss statement for a period includes a reasonable figure for the expense of depreciation.

(2) Since depreciation expense is one of the costs incurred in the operation of a business, it must be recorded because it is one of the costs of producing business income.

(3) Maintenance of the integrity of invested capital is an essential prerequisite to the realization of profits, i.e., there can be no profit unless invested capital is maintained unimpaired. Provision for depreciation expense is necessary to guard against an impairment of capital which might occur through policies of management predicated upon income statements wherein net incomes are overstated by exclusion of the expense of depreciation.

(4) The balance sheet will be more accurate if the values for depreciable fixed assets are stated so as to give effect to depreciation.

(5) It has been legally established that, unless provision has been made for depreciation expense, the disbursement of all the "profits" of a company as dividends to stockholders is an illegal procedure because of the impairment of capital which is caused by such disbursement.

The leading case upholding the validity of an annual charge to profit and loss for the expense of depreciation is *City of Knoxville* v. *Knoxville Water Company* (212 U. S. 1 [1909]).

THE AMOUNT OF DEPRECIATION

In establishing the amount of depreciation expense to be charged to operations over the period represented by the useful life of an asset, three factors must be considered:

(1) Original cost of the asset, including all costs originally expended to make the asset available for service. Such costs include freight on the depreciable asset, installation costs, and so on.

(2) The estimated net realizable scrap value of the asset at the end of its expected period of useful life.

(3) The estimated service life of the asset. This life may be expressed in terms of

      (a) Units of time, as days, months, years.

      (b) Units of hours, as total operating hours.

      (c) Units of production, as total estimated physical output.

The estimated service life of an asset is naturally affected by the policy of repairs and renewals. Depreciation will be less rapid where depreciable assets are maintained in a state of good repair. The policy of repairs and renewals may thus, in one sense, be looked upon as one of the determinants of estimated useful life in the third factor above. The life of any depreciable asset will be longer under a program of sound maintenance. The cost of maintenance, further, should be one of the considerations entering into the original decision to buy or not to buy a particular fixed asset.

The difference between original cost and scrap value (the first and second factors above) is the total depreciable value of an asset. It is the amount of depreciation expense which should be charged to profit and loss over the life of the asset.

As a practical matter it may be remarked, parenthetically, that the scrap value of an asset is often disregarded in calculating the amount of depreciation.

The allocation of total depreciation expense to individual accounting periods is considered at length in the sections which follow.

RECORDING DEPRECIATION ON THE BOOKS

To record the expense of depreciation, and to record the diminution in the book value of an asset, the following type of entry may be made each accounting period:

Depreciation Expense — Buildings	xxx xx	
Depreciation Expense — Machinery	xxx xx	
Depreciation Expense — Equipment	xxx xx	
Buildings		xxx xx
Machinery		xxx xx
Equipment		xxx xx
To record depreciation on buildings, machinery, and equipment.		

After posting, the balances of the asset accounts will represent the new depreciated values. While this practice of "writing down" assets may be accepted, it is generally considered better accounting to set up the credits to assets on account of depreciation in separate reserve accounts, thus:

Depreciation Expense — Buildings	xxx xx	
Reserve for Depreciation — Buildings		xxx xx
To record depreciation on buildings.		

```
Depreciation Expense — Machinery  . . . . . . . . . . .  xxx xx
     Reserve for Depreciation — Machinery  . . . . . . .         xxx xx
To record depreciation on machinery.

Depreciation Expense — Equipment  . . . . . . . . . .  xxx xx
     Reserve for Depreciation — Equipment  . . . . . . .         xxx xx
To record depreciation on equipment.
```

This accounting procedure has several advantages over the method of writing down assets directly:

(1) The cost of the asset is preserved. This is of advantage in determining the amount of the depreciation charge for each accounting period and aids in the preparation of a more informative balance sheet.

(2) The use of a reserve for depreciation account lends emphasis to the fact that the provision for depreciation is an estimate.

Each reserve for depreciation account is a separate account for the placement of credits which would otherwise be made direct to the related asset account. Each reserve for depreciation account is a measure of the cumulative depreciation which has been written off against the asset since the beginning of its service life. The reader of the balance sheet is informed to what extent the asset has been depreciated on the books — 10%, 50%, 90%, or what not — and permitted thereby to judge personally, within the limits of his knowledge, the adequacy or inadequacy of the amount of the reserve for depreciation.

(3) Credits for accrued depreciation and credits for assets sold or otherwise retired from service are clearly separated.

It is customary to carry a separate depreciation expense account, and a separate reserve for depreciation account, for each class of assets. This is done because of the variances in rates of depreciation between different assets; and because, also, it facilitates apportionment of depreciation expense to departments, operations, or products.

The reserve for depreciation account is sometimes called allowance for depreciation. This title, while more appropriate, is not, however, very widely used.

The function of an account which represents an asset subject to depreciation is to show original cost. The function of the related reserve for depreciation account is to show the cumulative depreciation which has taken place in the asset since the date of its acquisition. The reserve account is a measure of the amount of *shrinkage* which has occurred in the gross value of an asset to date. The difference between an asset account and its related reserve for depreciation account is the book value, or present value, of the asset.

ALLOCATION OF DEPRECIATION EXPENSE TO EACH ACCOUNTING PERIOD

The proper journal entries for recording depreciation expense have just been described. Our next concern is the problem of how much depreciation expense to apportion to each accounting period. Just what constitutes a fair periodic charge for depreciation, in a given case, is not always easy to state. The rate of depreciation varies with different assets and with the conditions under which they operate. Further, the amount of depreciation expense for any particular period is necessarily an estimated amount — the best estimate possible, of course, but nevertheless always an estimate. This is so because, with the single exception of original cost, each factor entering into the determination of the amount of depreciation expense is, in itself, an estimate. It is therefore impossible to state with exactness just how much an asset has depreciated in any given period; an approximation only can be made. Our main concern with the amount of the provision for depreciation expense in any given accounting period is that the amount be adequate. It is better to set aside too much depreciation than not enough, for this is at least insurance against overstatement of profits and their unwarranted disbursement, as well as insurance against unknowing impairment of capital through inadequate provision for the expense of depreciation.

It should be recognized that, although an asset may remain at full efficiency for a rather long period of time without noticeable deterioration of value, nevertheless it is proper to charge periods in which the asset remains at full efficiency with depreciation expense inasmuch as these periods contribute to the ultimate necessity of retiring the asset from service.

Various methods have been developed for allocating depreciation expense to accounting periods. In general, they fall into four groups:

(1) The amount of depreciation expense is the same from period to period.

(2) The amount of depreciation expense decreases from period to period.

(3) The amount of depreciation expense increases from period to period.

(4) The amount of depreciation expense is proportionate to periodic operating activity.

There are many specific methods to represent groups (2), (3), and (4). The selection, in a given case, of one or another of the many methods which are available is dependent upon a decision as to which method best represents the conditions of the case under consideration. The selection should be carefully made because the accuracy of the profit and loss statement and the balance sheet is directly affected thereby.

Adherence to some method of allocating depreciation expense to each accounting period is important because it provides a systematic plan for the proper recognition of depreciation on the books. It is unquestionably better *to have some plan than no plan at all.*

Some of the more familiar methods for establishing the periodic charge to depreciation expense will now be described.

METHODS FOR ESTABLISHING THE PERIODIC CHARGE TO DEPRECIATION

The illustrations which are given below rest on the following symbols and factual data:

Factual Data Used in Illustrative Problems

C = Cost	$10,600.00.
S = Scrap Value	$600.00.
n = Estimated Life	10 years, or 50,000 working hours, or 300,000 units of production.
D = Amount of Depreciation per Period	To be computed.
r = Rate of Depreciation	Various. See problems.

I. *The amount of depreciation expense is the same from period to period*

This, the "straight-line method," is widely used. It is simple and easy to apply. The periodic charge for depreciation expense is arrived at through use of the following formula:

$$D = \frac{C - S}{n} = \frac{\$10,600.00 - \$600.00}{10} = \$1,000.00$$

The following table shows the application of this formula:

Year	Debit Depreciation Expense	Credit Reserve for Depreciation	Amount of Reserve for Depreciation	Book Value of Asset at End of Year
				$10,600.00
1	$ 1,000.00	$ 1,000.00	$ 1,000.00	9,600.00
2	1,000.00	1,000.00	2,000.00	8,600.00
3	1,000.00	1,000.00	3,000.00	7,600.00
4	1,000.00	1,000.00	4,000.00	6,600.00
5	1,000.00	1,000.00	5,000.00	5,600.00
6	1,000.00	1,000.00	6,000.00	4,600.00
7	1,000.00	1,000.00	7,000.00	3,600.00
8	1,000.00	1,000.00	8,000.00	2,600.00
9	1,000.00	1,000.00	9,000.00	1,600.00
10	1,000.00	1,000.00	10,000.00	600.00
	$10,000.00	$10,000.00		

II. *The amount of depreciation expense decreases from period to period*

Case (1):

A uniform depreciation rate is applied to the diminishing value of the asset. The rate to be used is determined by the formula:

$$r = 1 - \sqrt[n]{S \div C} = 1 - \sqrt[10]{600.00 \div 10,600.00} = 24.9614\%$$

The following table shows the application of this method of depreciation:

Year	Debit Depreciation Expense	Credit Reserve for Depreciation	Amount of Reserve for Depreciation	Book Value of Asset at End of Year
				$10,600.00
1	$ 2,645.91	$ 2,645.91	$ 2,645.91	7,954.09
2	1,985.45	1,985.45	4,631.36	5,968.64
3	1,489.86	1,489.86	6,121.22	4,478.78
4	1,117.97	1,117.97	7,239.19	3,360.81
5	838.91	838.91	8,078.10	2,521.90
6	629.50	629.50	8,707.60	1,892.40
7	472.37	472.37	9,179.97	1,420.03
8	354.46	354.46	9,534.43	1,065.57
9	265.98	265.98	9,800.41	799.59
10	199.59	199.59	10,000.00	600.00
	$10,000.00	$10,000.00		

Case (2):

Diminishing rates are applied to original cost. No formula is used to determine the rates; they are more or less arbitrarily selected. This method, avoiding complex mathematical formulas, gives satisfactory results provided reasonable care is used in the selection of rates. The following table develops this method of depreciation:

Year	Rate Selected	Debit Depreciation Expense	Credit Reserve for Depreciation	Amount of Reserve for Depreciation	Book Value of Asset at End of Year
					$10,600.00
1	13.49%	$ 1,429.90	$ 1,429.90	$ 1,429.90	9,170.10
2	12.85	1,362.10	1,362.10	2,792.00	7,808.00
3	12.00	1,272.00	1,272.00	4,064.00	6,536.00
4	11.00	1,166.00	1,166.00	5,230.00	5,370.00
5	10.00	1,060.00	1,060.00	6,290.00	4,310.00
6	9.00	954.00	954.00	7,244.00	3,356.00
7	8.00	848.00	848.00	8,092.00	2,508.00
8	7.00	742.00	742.00	8,834.00	1,766.00
9	6.00	636.00	636.00	9,470.00	1,130.00
10	5.00	530.00	530.00	10,000.00	600.00
	94.34%	$10,000.00	$10,000.00		

Case (3):

Diminishing rates, expressed fractionally, are applied to the total depreciable value. Determination of the fractional rate to be used each year may be made as follows:

(a) Obtain the sum of the year's digits:

$$1 + 2 + 3 + 4 + 5 + 6 + 7 + 8 + 9 + 10 = 55$$

(b) The first year's depreciation will be $^{10}/_{55}$ of $10,000.00; the second year's depreciation will be $^9/_{55}$ of $10,000.00; the third year's depreciation will be $^8/_{55}$ of $10,000.00; and so on.

The following table shows the application of this "reducing fraction" method of depreciation:

Year	Fraction	Debit Depreciation Expense	Credit Reserve for Depreciation	Amount of Reserve for Depreciation	Book Value of Asset at End of Year
					$10,600.00
1	10/55	$ 1,818.18	$ 1,818.18	$ 1,818.18	8,781.82
2	9/55	1,636.36	1,636.36	3,454.54	7,145.46
3	8/55	1,454.55	1,454.55	4,909.09	5,690.91
4	7/55	1,272.73	1,272.73	6,181.82	4,418.18
5	6/55	1,090.91	1,090.91	7,272.73	3,327.27
6	5/55	909.09	909.09	8,181.82	2,418.18
7	4/55	727.27	727.27	8,909.09	1,690.91
8	3/55	545.45	545.45	9,454.54	1,145.46
9	2/55	363.64	363.64	9,818.18	781.82
10	1/55	181.82	181.82	10,000.00	600.00
	55/55	$10,000.00	$10,000.00		

It will be observed that the annual charge for depreciation expense decreases rapidly and that the difference between the charges for depreciation in the early and late years is large. A more gradual decline, and a more uniform distribution of depreciation expense, may be obtained by using some figure greater than 1, say 16, as the numerator of the fraction for the last year. In this case, the table for depreciation would be as follows:

Year	Fraction	Debit Depreciation Expense	Credit Reserve for Depreciation	Amount of Reserve for Depreciation	Book Value of Asset at End of Year
					$10,600.00
1	25/205	$ 1,219.51	$ 1,219.51	$ 1,219.51	9,380.49
2	24/205	1,170.73	1,170.73	2,390.24	8,209.76
3	23/205	1,121.95	1,121.95	3,512.19	7,087.81
4	22/205	1,073.17	1,073.17	4,585.36	6,014.64
5	21/205	1,024.39	1,024.39	5,609.75	4,990.25
6	20/205	975.61	975.61	6,585.36	4,014.64
7	19/205	926.83	926.83	7,512.19	3,087.81
8	18/205	878.05	878.05	8,390.24	2,209.76
9	17/205	829.27	829.27	9,219.51	1,380.49
10	16/205	780.49	780.49	10,000.00	600.00
	205/205	$10,000.00	$10,000.00		

III. *The amount of depreciation expense increases from period to period*

Under this method increasing rates are applied to original cost, or to the total depreciable value. If the order in which the rates and fractions of Cases 2 and 3 of the preceding section are reversed, the debits to depreciation expense will also be reversed. The amount of depreciation will then increase from period to period.

The effect of an increasing periodic charge for depreciation expense is, of course, a lower charge to revenue in early years and a higher charge to revenue in later years. Since maintenance expense also tends to increase from year to year, the combination of increasing periodic charges for both depreciation and maintenance so heavily favors early years at the expense of later ones that an increasing periodic charge for depreciation expense must be seriously objected to as a method which is not sufficiently conservative.

IV. *The amount of depreciation expense is made proportionate to periodic operating activity*

This method is based upon the assumption that depreciation expense varies according to the use made of the asset. It is well to qualify this assumption with the statement that the relationship is not inflexibly directly proportionate. An increase, for instance, of 100% in the operating hours of a machine in one period as compared with an earlier period does not necessarily mean that the amount of depreciation expense has also been increased 100%. It is basically true, however, that depreciation expense is greater, in some degree at least, for periods of greater activity than for periods of lesser activity.

Case (1):

The periodic depreciation charge is based upon the number of hours the asset has been used. In applying this method, it is necessary to estimate the total life of the asset in terms of working hours, and then to divide the total depreciation expense by the total working hours to arrive at the estimated depreciation expense per hour. In any given period, the depreciation expense will be the product obtained by multiplying operating hours by the depreciation expense per hour. By formula, the rate per hour is determined:

$$r = \frac{C - S}{n} = \frac{\$10,600.00 - \$600.00}{50,000} = \$0.20 \text{ per hour}$$

The following table shows the application of this "working hours" method of depreciation:

Year	Hours Operated	Debit Depreciation Expense	Credit Reserve for Depreciation	Amount of Reserve for Depreciation	Book Value of Asset at End of Year
					$10,600.00
1	4,212	$ 842.40	$ 842.40	$ 842.40	9,757.60
2	5,628	1,125.60	1,125.60	1,968.00	8,632.00
3	7,042	1,408.40	1,408.40	3,376.40	7,223.60
4	4,879	975.80	975.80	4,352.20	6,247.80
5	5,632	1,126.40	1,126.40	5,478.60	5,121.40
6	5,948	1,189.60	1,189.60	6,668.20	3,931 80
7	3,422	684.40	684.40	7,352.60	3,247.40
8	4,217	843.40	843.40	8,196.00	2,404.00
9	4,068	813.60	813.60	9,009.60	1,590.40
10	4,952	990.40	990.40	10,000.00	600.00
	50,000	$10,000.00	$10,000.00		

Case (2):

The periodic depreciation charge is based upon the number of units of production. In applying this method, it is necessary to estimate the total life of the asset in terms of units of production, and then to divide the total depreciation expense by the total units of production to arrive at the estimated depreciation expense per unit of production. In any given period, the depreciation expense will be the product obtained by multiplying the production of that period by the depreciation expense per unit of production. By formula the depreciation expense per unit is determined thus:

$$r = \frac{C - S}{n} = \frac{\$10,600.00 - \$600.00}{300,000} = \$0.03\frac{1}{3} \text{ per unit of production}$$

The following table shows the application of this "production" method of providing for depreciation:

Year	Units Produced	Debit Depreciation Expense	Credit Reserve for Depreciation	Amount of Reserve for Depreciation	Book Value of Asset at End of Year
					$10,600.00
1	25,287	$ 842.90	$ 842.90	$ 842.90	9,757.10
2	33,813	1,127.10	1,127.10	1,970.00	8,630.00
3	45,237	1,507.90	1,507.90	3,477.90	7,122.10
4	28,974	965.80	965.80	4,443.70	6,156.30
5	34,380	1,146.00	1,146.00	5,589.70	5,010.30
6	35,988	1,199.60	1,199.60	6,789.30	3,810.70
7	18,987	632.90	632.90	7,422.20	3,177.80
8	24,564	818.80	818.80	8,241.00	2,359.00
9	23,658	788.60	788.60	9,029.60	1,570.40
10	29,112	970.40	970.40	10,000.00	600.00
	300,000	$10,000.00	$10,000.00		

COMPOSITE RATE METHOD

The fixed assets of a business are usually divided into major groups such as, for example, machinery, furniture and fixtures, and so on. Each of these groups may contain many individual units, between which there may exist significant variations in regard to their several life expectancies. When the units of a group are numerous, the ascertainment of the amount of depreciation expense for a given accounting period may well become complex as well as more expensive. In their attempt to circumvent this consequence some firms determine the amount of their periodic provision for depreciation expense by a method which is called the "composite rate method." This method is essentially an average rate of depreciation applied to a fixed asset group; fundamentally, however, the method is an expression of one of the basic methods of depreciation-expense determination already described in this chapter. Description of the composite rate method of depreciation will not be made in this chapter inasmuch as the method may be more conveniently described following introduction and exposition of the plant ledger. Consideration and illustration of the composite rate method will therefore be deferred to Chapter 27.

DEPRECIATION IS BASED UPON COST

The foregoing examples give emphasis to an important principle of accounting: that depreciation is based upon original cost. It should be apparent that the maximum value that can be surrendered by an asset through depreciation cannot be more than the amount of the investment in the asset.

There are some who hold that depreciation expense should be based upon replacement cost if that cost is higher than original cost.

Public utilities have entertained this view and have given it support, especially for rate-making purposes. From the standpoint of the profit and loss statement, and the balance sheet, the practice of recording depreciation expense upon the basis of replacement cost is to be condemned for a number of reasons:

(1) Total expenses will be overstated.
(2) Net profits will be understated.
(3) Balance sheets will not be correct because of understatement of assets and net worth.
(4) If it is logical to depreciate an asset on the basis of replacement cost when that cost is in excess of original cost, it is equally logical to depreciate an asset on the basis of replacement cost when that cost is less than original cost. Analysis of this view compels the conclusion that both positions are untenable.

INFORMATION ON DEPRECIATION RATES

The depreciation rate which is to be applied to an asset, or class of assets, requires careful selection. If past experience is inadequate to suggest the rate to be used, outside sources, such as the following, may be referred to:

(1) The manufacturer of the asset to be depreciated.
(2) The experience of other businesses employing depreciable assets of like kind.
(3) Trade associations.
(4) Bureau of Internal Revenue, Bulletin "F" on depreciation studies (1942).
(5) Reputable publishers of income tax guides.
(6) *Accountants' Handbook* (1943).

POSITION OF THE RESERVE FOR DEPRECIATION ON THE BALANCE SHEET

The present value of any depreciable asset is found in two accounts, the asset account and its related reserve for depreciation account. The difference between the two accounts is the net value, i.e., net book value, of the asset. On the balance sheet it follows that each reserve for depreciation account will be deducted from its related asset account, thus:

Machinery	$100,000.00	
Less Reserve for Depreciation	35,000.00	$65,000.00
Delivery Equipment	$ 20,000.00	
Less Reserve for Depreciation	11,000.00	9,000.00

The advantages of this arrangement are several:

(1) Original cost is given for each class of asset.

(2) Each reserve for depreciation account measures, up to the date of the balance sheet, the cumulative impairment of original asset value which has taken place because of depreciation.

(3) Since the provision for depreciation is clearly shown, the reader of the balance sheet is allowed to judge for himself the adequacy of the reserve for depreciation.

Occasionally there may be found the practice of consolidating all depreciation reserve accounts into one Reserve for Depreciation account. The objections to this practice, on the books as well as on the balance sheet, may be briefly stated:

(1) There is no way of determining the book value of each class of assets.

(2) There is no way of judging the adequacy of the cumulative amount of depreciation reserved against each class of assets.

(3) It is difficult to compare actual depreciation of individual assets with that included in the consolidated provision.

MEANING OF THE RESERVE FOR DEPRECIATION

The reserve for depreciation is an account which measures the cumulative shrinkage in the book value of an asset because of depreciation. The reserve for depreciation is not a fund; nor is it purchasing power for the replacement of depreciated assets with new. The reserve for depreciation account, however, does signify the amount of other assets which must have been brought into the business through the channel of realized gross revenues (sales, and other gross incomes) to compensate for the loss of capital sustained by the expense of depreciation. These "other assets" are not normally segregated nor do they constitute a depreciation fund. These assets, even though currently on hand, may not be in a form liquid enough to serve as the direct means of replacing old assets with new. These comments will be made more clear in the following illustration.

ILLUSTRATION

Let us assume that the condensed balance sheet of Ray L. Jackson on January 1, 1941, was

Assets		*Net Worth*	
Cash	$ 10,000.00	Ray L. Jackson, Capital . .	$100,000.00
Other Current Assets . . .	70,000.00		
Fixed Assets (at cost) . . .	20,000.00		
	$100,000.00		$100,000.00

The fixed assets have a life expectancy of ten years.

Let us assume, further, that the condensed profit and loss statement of Mr. Jackson for the ten-year period, January 1, 1941, to December 31, 1950, was as follows:

Sales (for cash)	$1,000,000.00
Cost of Sales (paid in cash)	500,000.00
Gross Profit	$ 500,000.00
Expenses (paid in cash)	380,000.00
Net Profit (before depreciation)	$ 120,000.00
Less Depreciation Expense	20,000.00
Net Profit (after depreciation)	$ 100,000.00

With profits being realized in cash, and assuming no balance sheet changes other than those to recognize profits and depreciation, the condensed balance sheet of Mr. Jackson on December 31, 1950, would be

Ray L. Jackson

BALANCE SHEET, DECEMBER 31, 1950

Assets			*Net Worth*	
Cash		$130,000.00	Ray L. Jackson, Capital . .	$200,000.00
Other Current Assets . . .		70,000.00		
Fixed Assets . .	$20,000.00			
Less Reserve for Depreciation . . .	20,000.00			
		$200,000.00		$200,000.00

Cash has increased from $10,000.00 to $130,000.00, the net increase of $120,000.00 being received through the channel of sales of merchandise. From the standpoint of proprietorship, $20,000.00 of the new assets brought into the business by the $120,000.00 profits (before depreciation) of the ten-year period operate only to make good the $20,000.00 of capital lost through depreciation; the balance, $100,000.00, is net gain, or capital increment. In this example the assets which make good the loss of capital suffered through depreciation are, on December 31, 1950, in the form of cash. This cash, like any cash, may be used for any proper business purpose; and, specifically, it *may* be used to purchase new fixed assets with which to make replacement of those worn out.

Suppose, however, that the new assets of $120,000.00 brought into the business had been used to buy farm land. The balance sheet would then have been:

Ray L. Jackson

BALANCE SHEET, DECEMBER 31, 1950

Assets		*Net Worth*	
Cash	$ 10,000.00	Ray L. Jackson, Capital . .	$200,000.00
Other Current Assets . . .	70,000.00		
Farm Land	120,000.00		
Fixed Assets . . $20,000.00			
Less Reserve for Depreciation . . . 20,000.00			
	$200,000.00		$200,000.00

Although profits and capital remain at the same figures as before, the balance sheet of Mr. Jackson is radically changed. Mr. Jackson has $200,000.00 worth of assets, $20,000.00 of which are new assets replacing the loss of capital through depreciation. But, although they serve as compensatory capital, these assets are not in cash or even its immediate equivalent; they exist in the form of farm land. Yet new fixed assets, when purchased, must be paid for in cash, or a liability incurred for them. In this particular case Mr. Jackson has a difficult replacement problem because of his lack of available cash.

The "moral" of this second case is plain: the prudent business-man will not only make provision for depreciation expense but he also will be careful to see that cash is on hand when depreciable assets require replacement. He must plan to that end. If he desires, cash or securities may be set aside in a separate "fund for the purchase of fixed assets" to insure that liquid assets will be on hand at the time the replacement of fixed assets is necessary. This is a financing problem, however, and one which is not related to the problem of depreciation. But whether or not a business establishes a fund for the purchase of fixed assets, its general liquidity should be planned so as to be commensurate with expected future cash requirements. This calls for careful *management of cash*. This management, in turn, requires a clear appreciation of the fact that the cash position of a business is not related to the policy of depreciation.

The above discussion has assumed that the fixed asset which is being depreciated must ultimately be replaced. Actual replacement will be made, of course, only if the purchase of new fixed assets is deemed to be worth while. To purchase or not is a question of business policy and a question which, having been decided by the management of a business, will be incorporated in its program of financial administration.

RETIRING DEPRECIABLE ASSETS

If an asset subject to depreciation is retired from service by sale or otherwise, the depreciation which has accrued since the books were last closed should be debited to Depreciation Expense and credited to the Reserve for Depreciation. The difference between the new book value and the price received for the asset is the gain or loss on retirement.

Example:

A machine, costing $10,600.00, is depreciated on a straight-line basis (estimated life ten years, estimated scrap value $600.00). At the end of eight years the machine is retired from service and sold for $1,500.00. The entries to record the retirement are:

Depreciation Expense — Machinery	1,000.00	
Reserve for Depreciation — Machinery		1,000.00
To record depreciation expense of the eighth year.		

Cash	1,500.00	
Machinery		1,500.00
To record cash received.		

Reserve for Depreciation — Machinery	8,000.00	
Loss on Retirement of Capital Assets	1,100.00	
Machinery		9,100.00
To record retirement of machine from service.		

If the asset had been sold for $3,000.00, the latter two entries would have been modified to read:

Cash	3,000.00	
Machinery		3,000.00
To record cash received.		

Reserve for Depreciation — Machinery	8,000.00	
Machinery		7,600.00
Gain on Retirement of Capital Assets		400.00
To record retirement of machine from service.		

The accounts "Loss on Retirement of Capital Assets" and "Gain on Retirement of Capital Assets" require brief consideration. Losses and gains realized on the retirement of capital assets may be due to the use of incorrect rates of depreciation in past accounting periods, to changes in the market values of assets retired, to obsolescence, and so on. In line with recent advanced accounting thought, these losses and gains should be transferred to the comprehensive income account with Profit and Loss rather than to the account with Earned Surplus. The transfer to Profit and Loss is especially appropriate in those cases where the amounts of nominal elements are small; and where losses and gains on the retirement of fixed assets represent a constant activity as is the case in most large manufacturing companies.

QUESTIONS

Question **26–1.** Define depreciation. What are its causes? Why should it be recorded?

Question **26–2.** The fertility of a plot of land has decreased because of intensive cultivation over several years. Does this constitute depreciation?

Question **26–3.** The Harding Realty Company has a plot of land which it originally intended to subdivide and sell for residence purposes. The establishment of an incinerator, coal and wood yards, etc., in the vicinity materially injured the attractiveness of the company's holdings. Disposal of the property can now be made only at a loss. Is this depreciation?

Question **26–4.** It is sometimes said that a reserve for depreciation should not exceed 50%–60% of the cost of the asset because the asset would not be economically serviceable if it were depreciated beyond that point. An asset which has been written down more than 50% cannot be considered to be a "going" proposition. A plant or asset cannot be efficiently operated if it is more than half worn out. Do you agree? Explain.

Question **26–5.** Why is it desirable to have separate depreciation expense accounts and separate reserve for depreciation accounts?

Question **26–6.** Explain the considerations that would govern you in deciding how much depreciation to allocate to each accounting period. Your explanation should include the exposition of several methods of computing periodic depreciation.

Question **26–7.** Would you depreciate an automobile on the basis of mileage, or life, or both? Would you depreciate equipment for punching out automobile frames on the basis of life, or production, or both?

Question **26–8.** An investment of $100,000.00 is made by X in a certain type of depreciable asset which is expected to yield total profits of $250,000.00 over a ten-year period. X instructs his bookkeeper to write off depreciation expense for each accounting period in proportion to the profits earned. Would you, as an accountant, support these instructions? Why?

Question **26–9.** As a general rule, would you recommend (1) a straight-line method of depreciation, or (2) an increasing periodic charge for depreciation, or (3) a decreasing periodic charge for depreciation, or (4) a uniform periodic charge for plant expense comprising both depreciation and plant maintenance? Give reasons for your answer. What effect will these several methods have upon cost?

Question **26–10.** Alden College recently completed the construction of a new commerce building with funds which had been donated to it. Should depreciation expense for this building be deducted in the annual operating report of the college?

Question **26–11.** In the case of the *United Railways and Electric Company of Baltimore* v. *West et al.*, a part of the majority opinion of the supreme court of the United States was as follows:

"The utility is entitled to see that from earnings the value of the property invested is kept unimpaired, so that at the end of any given term of years the original investment remains as it was at the beginning. . . . This naturally calls for expenditure equal to the cost of worn out equipment at the time of replacement; and this, for all practical purposes, means present value. It is the settled rule of this court that the rate base is present value, and it would be wholly illogical to adopt a different rule for depreciation."

Do you agree with the opinion of the court? Explain.

Public utilities adherents have often claimed that depreciation for profit and loss purposes and depreciation for rate-making purposes are two different things. Discuss.

Question **26–12.** Explain how you would proceed to establish the depreciation rates to be used against the assets of a newly established firm in the television industry.

Question **26–13.** Explain fully the meaning of the reserve for depreciation.

Question **26–14.** What disposition should be made ultimately of the balance of the reserve for depreciation account? Is this disposition affected by the decision which directors make in deciding to replace, or not to replace, worn out fixed assets? Does the credit balance in the reserve for depreciation account imply that funds are on hand for the purchase of fixed assets?

Question **26–15.** Explain two common ways of accounting for gains and losses realized on the retirement of depreciable assets. Discuss both and indicate which method you believe to be best.

Question **26–16.** *The Wall Street Journal* of February 24, 1933, credited Mr. C. F. Sise, president of the Bell Telephone Company of Canada, with the following statement at a meeting of stockholders: "Our plans for the current year do not contemplate construction to an amount in excess of the funds which will be provided by our depreciation and other reserves, so that any financing which we may undertake will be for the purpose of wiping out these bonds." Discuss Mr. Sise's statement.

PROBLEMS

Problem **26–1.** A heavy duty truck was purchased new on January 1, 19__, for $3,700.00. It was estimated that the truck would have a residual value of about $100.00 at the end of its useful life, which was expected to be about 4 years, or 80,000 miles, whichever came first. On December 31 of the first year, the truck

(a) Was 95 % efficient.
(b) Had a market value of $3,000.00.
(c) Had been operated 25,000 miles.

What should be the amount of depreciation expense in the first year?

Problem **26–2.** A machine is purchased for $8,000.00. It is estimated that, at the end of its expected service life of three years, the residual or trade-in value of the machine will be $500.00. You are required to prepare the depreciation entries that would be made under each of several depreciation methods. The following additional information is furnished.

(a) Production:	in first year	= 16,000 units
	in second year	= 14,000 "
	in third year	= 20,000 "

50,000 units

(b) Working hours:	in first year	= 10,000
	in second year	= 9,200
	in third year	= 10,800

30,000

(c) The proper percentage to use under the diminishing value method is 60.315%.

Problem **26–3.** The following data apply to a unit of machinery purchased January 1, 19__:

Cost: $20,000.00
Scrap value: to be disregarded, the amount being negligible
Estimated life: 4 years

Production:	first year	= 80,000 units
	second year	= 120,000 "
	third year	= 140,000 "
	fourth year	= 160,000 "

500,000 units

Working hours:	first year	= 1,700
	second year	= 2,000
	third year	= 2,100
	fourth year	= 2,200

8,000

Required:

Prepare schedules of depreciation showing the amount of annual depreciation expense under each of the following methods: (a) straight line; (b) unit production; (c) working hours; (d) sum of life periods; (e) fixed percentage of diminishing value. In the application of this method assume a scrap value of $1.00. (The fourth root of .00005 is .084008955.)

Problem 26-4. The consolidated balance sheet of. Standard Brands Incorporated as of December 31, 1932, included the following:

Capital Assets:
Land, Buildings, Machinery, and Equipment, including Delivery Equipment. $46,354,507.27
Less Reserve for Depreciation 25,296,407.38

Capital Assets — Less Depreciation $21,058,099.89

Discuss the acceptability of this presentation of capital assets.

Problem 26-5. The 1932 annual report of the U. S. Industrial Alcohol Company contained the following

"Stockholders at an annual and special meeting called for April 20 will be asked to approve a plan for the reduction of stated capital to $3,738,460 from $22,584,000, creating a capital surplus of $18,846,140, which will be transferred to property reserves for the purpose of reducing net book value of fixed assets to $1.

"As future depreciation charges will be eliminated, a 'reserve for replacement' account will be set up in 1933 by a direct monthly charge against income to provide for replacement of productive facilities. In 1933 it is believed this charge will be $300,000 compared with a charge of approximately $900,000 for depreciation for 1932."

Discuss.

Problem 26-6. A machine costing $6,000.00 is depreciated at the annual rate of 20 % (estimated scrap value, $250.00). At the end of three years the machine is sold for cash, $1,500.00.

With respect to this machine what entries should be placed on the books in the third year?

Problem 26-7. At the end of six years a machine which originally cost $10,300.00 has been depreciated $6,000.00. At the end of the seventh year this machine is traded in for $2,600.00 on the cash purchase of a larger and improved model costing $15,000.00. Show all entries required in the seventh year.

Problem 26-8. Exactly five years ago, certain bookkeeping equipment was purchased at a cost of $3,300.00. The equipment was estimated to have a residual value of $300.00. It was depreciated at the annual rate of 10 %.

Today, July 1, 19__, the above equipment is traded in on new equipment costing $4,000.00. A trade-in allowance of $1,000.00 is received on the old equipment, the balance of the purchase price being paid in cash. The new bookkeeping equipment is to be depreciated at the annual rate of 15 %.

Required:

Make all entries for this year affecting depreciation expense, the asset account, and the reserve for depreciation. Books are closed on a calendar year basis.

Problem **26–9.** The balance sheet of the Blank Company on January 1, 19__, is:

Cash	$ 60,000.00	Common Stock, $100.00 par	$200,000.00
Machinery and Equipment	40,000.00	Surplus	50,000.00
Other Assets	150,000.00		
	$250,000.00		$250,000.00

The profit and loss statement for the ensuing twelve months is:

Sales		$200,000.00
Cost of Sales		100,000.00
Gross Profit		$100,000.00
Cash Expenses	$76,000.00	
Depreciation Expense	4,000.00	80,000.00
Net Profit from Operations		$ 20,000.00

Required:

(1) Assuming that all business is transacted for cash, and that there are no changes in the balance sheet other than those to recognize the operating statement, construct the balance sheet for December 31, 19__.

(2) Suppose the company adopted the policy of investing all cash in excess of a balance of $50,000.00 in investments of one kind or another, including fixed assets. Discuss this policy from the long-run point of view.

Chapter 27

DEPRECIATION (Continued)

PLANT LEDGERS

The Machinery account in the general ledger may represent scores of machines. The Machinery account is therefore a controlling account, the details of which should be found in a subsidiary (plant) ledger. Similarly, each fixed asset account on the general ledger is a controlling account supported by a subsidiary ledger to supply full information on individual units. Buildings and land should be carried in separate accounts; one is depreciable, the other not.

Each subsidiary plant ledger should have a separate card, or page, for each individual asset. A typical form for this purpose follows on page 571.

The reverse side of this form, shown on page 572, may be used for additional information.

The advantages of a well-kept plant ledger are several:

(1) Complete information on each unit of plant is maintained.

(2) The total depreciation expense for a period is the sum of the depreciation charges on the plant cards. This provides maximum accuracy in the total depreciation expense figure for any given period.

(3) Correct depreciation expense figures make possible more accurate profit and loss statements and balance sheets.

(4) Plant ledgers which are classified according to product, department, division, etc., facilitate proper distribution of depreciation expense, and the compilation of accurate cost information.

(5) Plant cards provide information with respect to

    (a) The distribution of equipment within a plant.

    (b) Equipment available for use, transfer, retirement.

    (c) The operating history of each unit. The relative cost of operating each machine will be recorded in written form. Facts are provided for improved policies of depreciation, repairs, and replacement.

Name Hoist with Trolley, Yale Electric Chain

Description 4 Ton, A.C., Lift: Standard = 15 ft.; Maximum = 45 ft.

Serial Number

Bought from Carleton Supply Company

Our Tag Number M 181

Location Dept. 7

Estimated Life 10 years

Rate 10 %

Total Estimated Depreciation $ 1,220.00

Remarks

DATE	DESCRIPTION	REF.	AMOUNT		CUMU-LATIVE COST	
1950						
Jan. 1	Cost	CP2	1,000	00	1,000	00
4	Freight	CP3	20	00	1,020	00
31	Installation	CP5	250	00	1,270	00

		MEMORANDA				
			Depreciation Reserve		Book Value	
Date	Item		Debit	Credit		
1960						
Dec. 31	Deprec.			122.00	1,148	00

571

Date	Remarks	Ref.	Amount	Cumulative Amount

(6) Dependable information is available for tax and insurance purposes.[1]

The sum of the total cost figures on the plant cards should equal the balance in the related controlling account; and the sum of the accumulated depreciation figures on the cards should equal the balance in the related reserve for depreciation account.

DEPRECIATION EXPENSE AND THE COMPOSITE RATE METHOD

Many firms feel that the computation of depreciation expense for each depreciable unit and the entries to be made on each plant card is too expensive a procedure. They recommend that the year's depreciation expense be computed upon the balance in each plant controlling account as of January 1; or that it be the sum of computations made against the balances in the various plant accounts for the length of time the balances remain unchanged. These methods are simple and easy to use. Whether or not they provide acceptable depreciation expense figures depends upon circumstances; an example, using the straight-line method of depreciation, will illustrate.

Example:

At the end of a certain year the Machinery account has a balance of $25,000.00. This balance represents the cost of five machines variously acquired throughout the year as follows:

MACHINERY

19—	
Jan. 1	7,000.00
Mar. 1	5,000.00
Aug. 1	4,000.00
Sept. 1	6,000.00
Oct. 1	3,000.00

The straight-line depreciation rates which apply to each machine follow:

---

[1] In Treasury Decision 4422 (1934) it is provided that "the deduction for depreciation in respect of any depreciable property for any taxable year shall be limited to such ratable amount as may reasonably be considered necessary to recover during the remaining useful life of the property the unrecovered cost or other basis. The burden of proof will rest upon the taxpayer to sustain the deduction claimed. Therefore, taxpayers must furnish full and complete information with respect to the cost or other basis of the assets in respect of which depreciation is claimed, their age, condition, and remaining useful life, the portion of their cost or other basis which has been recovered through depreciation allowances for prior taxable years, and such other information as the Commissioner [of Internal Revenue] may require in substantiation of the deduction claimed."

$$
\left.
\begin{array}{l}
\text{Machine \#1 ($7,000.00) = 10\%} \\
\text{\#2 ($5,000.00) = 9\%} \\
\text{\#3 ($4,000.00) = 11\%} \\
\text{\#4 ($6,000.00) = 8\%} \\
\text{\#5 ($3,000.00) = 12\%}
\end{array}
\right\} \text{Average = 10\%}
$$

The total depreciation expense for the year, assuming no residual value for the asset, will be one of the following amounts:

Case (1):

The depreciation expense is the sum of the depreciation charges as they appear on the individual cards, thus:

Machine	Bought	Cost	Rate	Depreciation Expense	Book Value
#1	Jan. 1	$7,000.00	10%	$ 700.00	$6,300.00
#2	Mar. 1	5,000.00	9%	375.00	4,625.00
#3	Aug. 1	4,000.00	11%	183.33	3,816.67
#4	Sept. 1	6,000.00	8%	160.00	5,840.00
#5	Oct. 1	3,000.00	12%	90.00	2,910.00
				$1,508.33	

Case (2):

The depreciation expense is computed by applying the average depreciation rate against the balance of the asset account at the beginning of the period:

$$10\% \text{ of } \$7,000.00 = \$700.00$$

Case (3):

The depreciation expense is computed by applying the average depreciation rate against the changing balances of the asset account throughout the period:

$$
\begin{array}{lll}
10\% \text{ of } \$ 7,000.00 \text{ for} & 2 \text{ months} = & \$ 116.67 \\
10\% \text{ of } \$12,000.00 \text{ for} & 5 \text{ months} = & 500.00 \\
10\% \text{ of } \$16,000.00 \text{ for} & 1 \text{ month} = & 133.33 \\
10\% \text{ of } \$22,000.00 \text{ for} & 1 \text{ month} = & 183.33 \\
10\% \text{ of } \$25,000.00 \text{ for} & 3 \text{ months} = & 625.00 \\
& 12 \text{ months} = & \$1,558.33
\end{array}
$$

Of the three computations, the first is the most accurate. The second is clearly inadequate, but the third gives almost as great accuracy as the first. In Case (3) the accuracy is due to the fact that, in this specific example, the simple average of 10% happens also to be statistically representative. The simple average is not, however, an average which is always statistically acceptable; for this reason it is, as a general rule, basically better to use a weighted average rather than a simple arithmetic average. Using a weighted average of 9.72% (total annual depreciation, $2,430.00, divided by total cost, $25,000.00), the depreciation expense in the above example would be

9.72% of $ 7,000.00 for	2 months	= $	113.40
9.72% of $12,000.00 for	5 months	=	486.00
9.72% of $16,000.00 for	1 month	=	129.60
9.72% of $22,000.00 for	1 month	=	178.20
9.72% of $25,000.00 for	3 months	=	607.50
	12 months	=	$1,514.70

The method used in Case (2) will give satisfactory results when the balance in the asset account remains fairly constant throughout an accounting period and when a representative composite depreciation rate is used. In both Case (2) and Case (3) it is possible to depreciate individual assets in excess of 100%, but in Case (1) this is not possible. Obviously, the choice of method in a given case depends upon the facility with which an acceptable depreciation figure can be prepared at reasonable cost. The computation of depreciation on individual units, however, conforms to best accounting theory.

To solve a depreciation problem which deals with a specific unit, it is obvious that the depreciation rate to be used should not be the composite rate of the asset group of which the unit is a part but the rate which is specifically applicable to that unit.

PROPERTY EXPENDITURES

Expenditures are more or less regularly required on behalf of fixed assets in order to maintain, or increase, operating efficiency and life. These expenditures may be classified as

(1) Ordinary repairs more or less regularly required.
(2) Extraordinary repairs which in turn may be classified as
    (a) Renewals and replacements.
    (b) Betterments.

Accounting for property expenditures will now be considered

ORDINARY REPAIRS

Expenditures for ordinary repairs should be charged to operations as regular expenses of doing business.

If it is desired to equalize the periodic expense for ordinary repairs, an estimate of the total amount of such expense, over the life of the asset, divided by the years of useful life, will provide the annual average charge for ordinary repairs. At the end of each accounting period the following entry should be made:

Maintenance Expense . . . . xxx xx
    Reserve for Maintenance Expense . . . .   xxx xx

Maintenance expenditures, as incurred, are charged to the Reserve for Maintenance.

The accuracy of this policy is dependent upon the accuracy with which total maintenance expenses and useful life are estimated. It is important to observe that any balance in the Reserve for Maintenance account should always at least represent the amount of depreciation unrecovered by failure to make normal maintenance expenditures. Conservatism would suggest that the actual balance should be somewhat in excess of this minimum.

The statements above suggest that the periodic charge for depreciation expense is not normally affected by current, or ordinary, repairs. This is correct, because, as previously pointed out, the policy of a business with respect to repairs and renewals is in itself one of the factors which enter into the establishment of the periodic depreciation charge. Depreciation expense thus represents the loss *not* taken care of by maintenance.

EXTRAORDINARY REPAIRS

Special scrutiny should be given to major repair jobs because such expenditures may represent something more than just expense. The property may be actually improved through the investment of additional value. Where this is the case, part or all of the expenditure may be charged to a real account instead of to an expense account. Examples of such expenditures are

   (1) Overhauling the motor of an automobile.
   (2) Relining a furnace or kiln.
   (3) Replacing a cedar shingle roof with a copper one.
   (4) Laying silent composition flooring over an old floor.
   (5) Improving the acoustics of an auditorium.
   (6) Remodeling and modernizing a building.

These examples illustrate the point that major repairs actually increase the value of an asset — that is, enough new value has been put into the property to make good part or all of the depreciation of earlier periods. Where this is the case, the expenditure should be recorded on the books in a manner to show the increase in value, thus:

Reserve for Depreciation . . . . xxx xx
    Cash . . . .   xxx xx

Occasionally it is possible for an expenditure of this general type to more than offset all accrued depreciation and actually to make the asset more valuable than it was originally. Where this is the case, the expenditure should be appropriately distributed to the

Reserve for Depreciation account for the cancellation of accrued depreciation to date on the asset.

Asset (or Betterments) account for the value added in excess of original cost. The amount should be accurately established.

Maintenance Expense account for such remaining part of the total expenditure as cannot be debited to the two accounts above.

If major repairs increase the book value of property, of if they increase the period of useful life, the depreciation charges for succeeding periods should be revised accordingly.

Example:

$7,250.00	Original cost (Estimated life 10 years, estimated scrap value, $250.00.)
4,200.00	Six years' depreciation
$3,050.00	Book value at end of 6 years
2,800.00	New value invested in asset through major repairs in January of 7th year.
$5,850.00	New book value
300.00	New estimate of ultimate scrap value
$5,550.00	New value to be depreciated

If the original estimate of useful life is still to be accepted as correct, the subsequent periodic depreciation charges will be $5,550.00 ÷ 4 = $1,387.50 instead of the $700.00 figure in previous use. If it is considered that the asset now has a probable service life remaining of 7 years, instead of 4, because of the repairs made, the annual depreciation charge will be $5,550.00 ÷ 7 = $792.86.

RENEWALS, REPLACEMENT OF PARTS

Renewals, or replacements, although constituting "extraordinary repairs" and therefore governed by the principles which apply to such repairs, nevertheless present questions interesting enough to warrant special attention to them.

(1) When is it proper to capitalize such expenditures?

(2) Should the excess of cost over book value of the part replaced be capitalized?

(3) Should the excess of cost over original cost be capitalized?

(4) When a part is replaced, how is the related reserve for depreciation account affected?

Such questions are not easily answered. Capitalization is dependent upon knowing whether or not the asset has, in fact, become more valuable than before. Certainly no objection should be raised against capitalizing at least a reasonable amount where it is indisputably certain that the expenditure has resulted in an increase in the operating efficiency of the asset. The amount to be capitalized is naturally a problem in itself. A good working rule is to recognize that since a new part has going value only when it is functioning as one of the units of the whole mechanism, the amount to be capitalized should be limited to the excess of renewal cost over original cost of the part replaced.

Two methods of handling renewal and replacement expenditures are presented herewith. The following facts are given:

MACHINE #1 (10-year life; scrap value, $600.00)		RESERVE FOR DEPRECIATION	
10,600.00			4,000.00

At the end of the fourth year of life it is found necessary to replace the grinding unit (original cost $2,500.00) of this machine with a new unit costing $2,750.00.

Method (1):

Loss on Retirement of Capital Assets	1,500.00	
Reserve for Depreciation — Machinery	1,000.00	
Machinery		2,500.00

To remove book value of grinding unit from accounts; original cost of unit, $2,500.00; 4 years' depreciation, $1,000.00.

Machinery	2,750.00	
Cash		2,750.00

To record purchase of new grinding unit.

The balance of the reserve for depreciation account is ordinarily intended to measure the *theoretical* but not actual physical impairment of value which has taken place in an asset because of depreciation. From this point of view, which is the usual view in commercial accounting, Method (1) is correct accounting.

Method (2):

If the balance of the reserve for depreciation account is regularly intended to measure the *actual physical* depreciation of an asset, then the proper entries for the replacement would be

Reserve for Depreciation — Machinery	2,500.00	
Machinery		2,500.00

To clear machinery account of original cost of grinding unit.

Machinery	2,750.00	
Cash		2,750.00

To record purchase of new grinding unit.

The full cost of the part replaced is debited to the reserve for depreciation account on the theory that, since the reserve represents the actual deterioration in value due to depreciation to date, a part of this reserve must represent 100% depreciation of the grinding unit, or $2,500.00. In other words, at the end of four years, the complete machine is estimated as having depreciated $4,000.00; $2,500.00 of this figure is represented by the complete depreciation of the grinding unit now being replaced. On the basis of this accounting the amount of annual depreciation expense for subsequent years would be ($10,850.00 — $600.00 — $1,500.00) ÷ 6 = $1,458.33.

The accounting represented by Method (2) is rarely found in practice. Accountants generally prefer to abide by accounting theory, i.e., that the balance of the reserve for depreciation account shall be a measure of the amount of theoretical depreciation to date.

CAPITAL AND REVENUE EXPENDITURES

A commentary on repairs, replacements, renewals, betterments, etc., would not be complete unless attention had been directed to the importance of correct distribution of plant expenditures between expense and capital. If an expenditure is capitalized instead of being charged to expense, the profits of the business for the period are overstated, as are also the assets and net worth. On the other hand, if expenditures are charged to expense instead of being capitalized, the profits are understated as are also the assets and net worth. Financial statements will therefore be seriously in error when the accounting for property expenditures has not been correct. Where there is doubt as to the correct placement of an expenditure, it is conservative practice to charge the expenditure to expense.

Many companies follow a policy of refusing to capitalize an expenditure amounting to less than a minimum figure, say $25.00, $50.00, or $100.00. Larger amounts are carefully analyzed. Practical considerations indicate that a conservative policy of this kind has much to recommend it.

HOW OFTEN SHOULD DEPRECIATION EXPENSE BE RECORDED?

The purpose of this question is to focus attention upon the statistical accuracy of accounts when depreciation expense is frequently recorded and later offset in whole, or in part, by maintenance expenditures. The following example will illustrate the point to which attention is directed.

A machine costing $12,000.00, purchased new on January 1, is estimated to depreciate $100.00 per month. The following monthly entries are made on the books:

```
Jan. 31 Depreciation Expense — Machinery  . . . . . .   100.00
            Reserve for Depreciation — Machinery  . . .            100.00

Feb. 28 Depreciation Expense — Machinery  . . . . . .   100.00
            Reserve for Depreciation — Machinery  . . .            100.00

Mar. 31 Depreciation Expense — Machinery  . . . . .   100.00
            Reserve for Depreciation — Machinery  . . .            100.00
```

There were no expenditures for maintenance during the months of January, February, and March.

During April, $500.00 is expended for maintenance and it is ascertained that, after this expenditure, the machinery is restored to its original value. The following entry records the effect of this expenditure:

```
Maintenance Expense . . . . . . . . . . . . . . . . . .   200.00
Reserve for Depreciation — Machinery  . . . . . . . .   300.00
    Cash  . . . . . . . . . . . . . . . . . . . . . . .            500.00
```

When this entry has been posted, the ledger will show:

MACHINERY	DEPRECIATION EXPENSE — MACHINERY	MAINTENANCE EXPENSE	RESERVE FOR DEPRE-CIATION — MACHINERY
12,000.00	300.00	200.00	300.00 300.00

These accounts state that the plant expense for the four months' period consists of Depreciation Expense, $300.00, and Maintenance Expense, $200.00. But this is false. The asset on April 30 has the same value as it did on January 1; therefore there has been no depreciation. But it *is* true that it cost $500.00 maintenance expense to keep the machinery at its original value. In order to have the books accord with these facts, the following correction entry must be made:

```
Maintenance Expense . . . . . . . . . . . . . . . . .   300.00
    Depreciation Expense — Machinery  . . . . . . . .            300.00
```

The difficulty which is illustrated by this example may be avoided by recording depreciation but once, that is, at the end of the accounting period. For cost purposes, however, this may not always be desirable. In either case, the accounts at the end of the period should be examined to see that they show correct amounts for each kind of plant expense.

The graph below illustrates the principles which have just been discussed; 100 represents original value, the down-curves loss in value because of depreciation, and the up-curves value restored through maintenance. The problem is to present the correct entries for each of the three years on account of depreciation, maintenance, and major repairs.

Entries:

1st year:	Depreciation Expense	30.00	
	Reserve for Depreciation		30.00
	Maintenance Expense	30.00	
	Cash		30.00
2d year:	Depreciation Expense	0	
	Reserve for Depreciation		0
	Maintenance Expense	50.00	
	Cash		50.00
3d year:	Reserve for Depreciation	30.00	
	Maintenance Expense	70.00	
	Cash		100.00

One caution is in order. The discussion of this section has purposefully used an illustration which is somewhat factitious. In the reality of business, expenditures for maintenance never restore completely *all* of the original value of an asset. Maintenance expenditures may postpone the date of death of an asset but they cannot defer death indefinitely. Therefore some depreciation expense is constantly being incurred.

MAINTENANCE WITHOUT DEPRECIATION

The preceding section endeavored to illustrate the theory that it is possible for all the property expense of an accounting period to consist of maintenance expense only, there being no depreciation. The policy of maintenance without depreciation is claimed by its advocates to have special applicability to large aggregates of properties. The manner of operation is illustrated by the following hypothetical example:

The Royal Transit Company owns 100 Ford 5-passenger sedans which are being used as taxicabs. Each taxicab has an estimated life of four years. The ledger shows the following information:

FORD TAXICABS

Jan. 1, 1946 (25 cabs)	17,500.00	Dec. 31, 1949, Balance	70,000.00
Jan. 1, 1947 (25 cabs)	17,500.00		
Jan. 1, 1948 (25 cabs)	17,500.00		
Jan. 1, 1949 (25 cabs)	17,500.00		
	70,000.00		70,000.00
Jan. 1, 1950, Balance	70,000.00		

RESERVE FOR DEPRECIATION — FORD TAXICABS

Dec. 31, 1949, Balance	43,750.00	Dec. 31, 1946	4,375.00
		Dec. 31, 1947	8,750.00
		Dec. 31, 1948	13,125.00
		Dec. 31, 1949	17,500.00
	43,750.00		43,750.00
		Jan. 1, 1950, Balance	43,750.00

On December 31, 1949, the taxicab fleet has a book value of $26,250.00; and the taxicabs purchased January 1, 1946, are 100% depreciated.

On January 1, 1950, the taxicabs which have been depreciated completely are replaced by 25 new taxicabs costing the same as those replaced, $17,500.00. On December 31, 1950, the following information is available:

(1) During the year 1950 the taxicabs purchased:

Jan. 1, 1947, depreciated	$ 4,375.00
Jan. 1, 1948, depreciated	4,375.00
Jan. 1, 1949, depreciated	4,375.00
Jan. 1, 1950, depreciated	4,375.00
A total depreciation of	$17,500.00

(2) The loss in value due to depreciation, $17,500.00, has been

completely offset by the value added through the purchase of 25 new taxicabs, $17,500.00.

(3) The value of the property at the end of the year is therefore the same as it was at the beginning of the year:

Value January 1, 1950	$26,250.00
New taxicabs purchased	17,500.00
	$43,750.00
Loss through depreciation	17,500.00
Value December 31, 1950	$26,250.00

Therefore, although individual units have depreciated, for *the property as a whole* there has been no depreciation because the value of the property at the end of the year is the same as the value of the property at the beginning of the year. The $17,500.00 expenditure on January 1, 1950, is an expenditure for maintenance — i.e., the cost of preventing further depreciation on *the property as a whole* — and not an expenditure to be capitalized.

The conditions which admit applicability of a policy of maintenance without depreciation are, admittedly, of comparative rareness. The following summary may prove helpful in deciding whether or not such a policy has applicability to a given case:

(1) Its greatest applicability is to a property consisting of many similar units, frequently replaced. At best, such setups are uncommon.

(2) In a given accounting period the value lost through depreciation of individual units is offset by the addition of new property of equal value. Usually this status is reached only after a rather long period of gradual acquisition of the individual units.

(3) To maintain unimpaired the investment in a property consisting of many units is, practically speaking, so difficult as to make the likelihood of such a setup extremely improbable. The possibility of obsolescence enhances the improbability of no depreciation.

In this respect it is to be doubted that, in practice, there are actual cases which even approximate the arbitrary conditions of the taxicab illustration. Especially is it unlikely that maintenance expenditures will be so regular in amount from period to period as to completely obviate the necessity of any provision in the accounts for accrued depreciation.

With reference to a single asset unit it is clear that, over the long run, maintenance alone will not prevent depreciation. Ultimately the unit must be retired because it is no longer serviceable.

Maintenance without depreciation is sometimes claimed to apply to the field of railroad accounting. It is claimed that after a railroad has reached a certain size (i.e., "normal" or "economical" size), further expansion is no longer necessary or, in fact, even desirable. The road has arrived at the size best fitted to serve the territory it traverses. This point may be considered to have been reached when the book value of the property equals, roughly, 50% of the original cost of all the present units; and when subsequent additions of value to the property as a whole will approximately offset the total depreciation expense on individual units. A larger property investment is not needed; all that is necessary is that the present "right size" be kept intact and efficient. The property is maintained through repairs and replacements. For the property as a whole there is no depreciation.

DEPRECIATION VERSUS APPRECIATION

Depreciation is the loss in value of an asset which is caused by the several factors which will ultimately cause the asset to be retired. Depreciation is always the deterioration of the original investment which has been placed into an asset. The depreciation of fixed assets is an expense which very definitely has *no* relationship to the varying market values which fixed assets may command from time to time.

It is often argued that the necessity of recording depreciation expense is obviated when the increase in market value of depreciable property equals, or more than equals, the depreciation expense which would otherwise be recorded for the period.

Those who entertain this view do so mistakenly. It is not correct to offset depreciation expense against a rise in market value because

(1) Depreciation is an actual expense of doing business; it cannot be avoided. A rise in market value, on the other hand, is not an actual profit because the profit, so called, is not a realized profit. It would be thoroughly unsound to offset an actual expense against a contingent gain — a gain which is, at best, quite unrelated to regular operations. To cancel items which are dissimilar in character and which have no relationship to each other is wholly illogical. It would be just as proper to offset the increase in value of stocks and bonds against the expense of taxes.

(2) A rise in market value does not prevent wear and tear upon a property.

(3) The cancellation, in whole or in part, of depreciation expense against market appreciation would cause much variance in the cost records of a company from period to period. The usefulness of these records would be unfavorably affected.

(4) Depreciation expense cannot be avoided. Unrecorded depreciation expense means heavier absorption of depreciation expense on the records of later years.

(5) If profits are to be correctly shown, and if capital is to be maintained, the provision for depreciation is imperative. A rise in market value may never be realized.

(6) A decline in market value does not normally increase the provision for depreciation because the value of an asset to a business does not move up and down in sympathy with market movements. There is a clear line of demarcation between market movements and the fact of depreciation.

DEPRECIATION: ADJUSTMENT FOR REVISION OF ORIGINAL ESTIMATES

Occasionally, one or more of the factors of depreciation may be incorrectly estimated. For instance, if it is later found that an asset will, in all likelihood, have a longer service life than originally estimated, several ways of handling the problem are open:

(1) The old rate may be continued until (a) the asset is discarded, or (b) the asset is 100% depreciated, no depreciation being taken thereafter.

Advantage of this method:

Continues temporarily the comparability of costs.

Disadvantages of this method:

(a) The permanent comparability of present costs with later costs is weakened. Future costs will be understated.

(b) The costs which appear upon the books, both present and future costs, are not the real costs. Nor are the book profits the real profits.

(2) The amount of each subsequent periodic depreciation charge will be the remaining depreciable value divided by the remaining years of useful life.

Disadvantages of this method:

(a) Although this method distributes a depreciation charge to every period, and is, therefore, probably better than the first method, the charge is not the correct charge that should be made to each period for depreciation expense.

(b) Future costs and future profits will not be correct. Cost comparisons will be made less useful.

(3) The periodic depreciation charge should be recalculated in the light of the new information available. For example,

$10,600.00 = Original cost
   600.00 = Estimated scrap value

$10,000.00 = Amount to be depreciated over estimated life of ten years

$ 6,000.00 = Six years' depreciation (straight-line method)
$ 4,600.00 = Book value at end of six years

At this point, it is estimated that the asset will have a total useful life of 12½ years. The periodic depreciation charge is therefore revised to read

$$\$10,000.00 \div 12\frac{1}{2} = \$800.00$$

The reserve for depreciation account should be adjusted so that it will show the balance that would have been there had the depreciation charges for the first 6 years been correct, thus:

Reserve for Depreciation 1,200.00
    Depreciation Adjustment — Prior Years 1,200.00
To correct excessive charge to depreciation for past 6 years. Explanation:
Depreciation recorded in 6 years $6,000.00
Depreciation that should have been recorded:
   6 × $800.00 . . . .   4,800.00

Excess depreciation recorded $1,200.00

From this point on, each accounting period will be charged with the correct depreciation expense of $800.00.

Advantages of this method:

  (a) Subsequent depreciation costs are correct. Each period stands its fair share of depreciation expense.

  (b) Book figures on costs and net profits are correct in so far as the factor of depreciation expense is concerned.

  (c) Assets are correctly valued. Surplus is correct.

Similar adjustments are in order whenever error is found in any of the other factors of depreciation. The governing principle of such adjustments should always be to see that the books show costs and values as they actually are.[2]

---

[2] A number of court decisions strongly support the rule that error in past depreciation rates is not, per se, reason for modification of the true depreciation rates of future periods. Among these decisions see *Galveston Electric Co.* v. *Galveston* (258 U. S. 388 [1922]); *Public Utility Commissioners* v. *New York Telephone Co.* (271 U. S. 23 [1926]); and *Smith* v. *Illinois Bell Telephone Co.* (282 U. S. 133 [1930]).

QUESTIONS

Question **27–1.** What are the functions of a plant ledger? Explain fully.

Question **27–2.** Explain how you would compute the annual depreciation expense for 100 units of various kinds of machinery, all carried in the same machinery account.

Question **27–3.** When repairs and renewals are difficult to estimate, and to differentiate as they occur, would you approve of a policy of increasing the annual charge for depreciation by an amount sufficient to provide for all costs of repairs and renewals, and of charging actual expenditures to the reserve for depreciation account as they occur?

Question **27–4.** The policy of the J. F. Drain Company has been to set up the cost of renewals separately from depreciation expense. In order to distribute the expense of renewals over the periods which have made such renewal costs necessary, the company follows the practice of charging each accounting period with an equal amount. This amount is determined by dividing the total estimated renewals expense by the number of years of expected life for the asset. The yearly entry is similar to that for depreciation:

```
Renewals Expense. . . . . . . . . . . . . . . . . . . . .  xxx xx
     Reserve for Renewals Expense . . . . . . . . . . .      xxx xx
```

Renewal expenditures, as incurred, are charged direct to the reserve.

Do you approve of the company's practice? Why? Is the reserve account real or nominal? How should the reserve for renewals account be placed on the balance sheet if there is a credit balance in the account? If there is a debit balance?

Question **27–5.** What is meant by expenditures for capital and expenditures for revenue?

Question **27–6.** From the standpoint of the financial statements, explain why correct accounting for property expenditures is important.

Question **27–7.** The Gaylord Corporation incurred a heavy expense in connection with the installation and arrangement of equipment and machinery preparatory to operations in a new building. Later on it was ascertained that the new layout was not entirely satisfactory and that a further rearrangement of equipment would be necessary if maximum factory efficiency were to be attained. The expenditures necessary to carry out this rearrangement proved almost as large as the original installation expenditures. Should these new costs be capitalized? Give reasons in support of your answer.

Question **27–8.** What is the effect upon the statistical accuracy of accounts where depreciation is recorded monthly, and where, from time to time, maintenance overcomes earlier depreciation?

Question **27–9.** The directors of the Cotton Textile Company are informed by their comptroller that the property of the company has been 60% depreciated; that since the property could not be efficiently operated if it were depreciated beyond 60%, and since future maintenance is intended to prevent the possibility of further depreciation, that it will be proper, therefore, to omit the customary charge for depreciation expense in the future reports of the company. The comptroller requests that the directors pass a resolution to this effect. As a director of the company, how would you react to this proposal?

Question **27–10.** The Whanger Utility Corporation establishes its periodic provision for depreciation expense on the following basis: 9% of gross revenues, less maintenance expenditures. Occasionally maintenance exceeds the 9% provision; in this case the credit is taken up on the books as miscellaneous income. Discuss.

Question **27–11.** A piece of property (land and building) has a market value greatly in excess of cost. It is proposed therefore to make no provision for depreciation expense this year on the grounds that the rise in market value more than offsets the amount that would otherwise be set aside as depreciation expense. Do you approve? Explain.

Question **27–12.** The directors of the Aromet Manufacturing Company instruct you to charge the current year's operations with a depreciation charge equivalent to 50% of that which would be made without these instructions. The directors justify their directions by explaining that, first, the value of the land on which the company's properties are located has increased sufficiently to more than offset the proposed 50% reduction in the depreciation charge, and, second, the operating profits of the company are not large enough to absorb the usual charge for depreciation. Discuss.

Question **27–13.** An asset, 100% depreciated, is expected to have a further useful life of about 5 years. Would this affect the books? How?

Question **27–14.** Are the following statements true or false? Why?

(1) Depreciation is a sum of money set aside to provide for the replacement of an asset.
(2) Depreciation is always a provision set aside out of profits.
(3) Depreciation is a means of providing for the replacement of an asset when worn out.
(4) Depreciation implies that the asset is less efficient.
(5) Depreciation is not an actual expense if the asset to which it refers is maintained in continuous first-class operating condition.
(6) The amount of depreciation expense for a particular period can never be accurately computed.

(7) Depreciation expense should be computed upon the cost of replacement.

(8) Instead of charging periodic operations with provisions for depreciation expense which may be either too small or too large, it is better to wait until the fact and exact amount of depreciation is known definitely, at which time an adequate charge to surplus may be made.

(9) A credit to the reserve for depreciation account is exactly similar in principle to a credit made to the account with prepaid rent.

(10) The reserve for depreciation should be established on the principle that the amount finally accumulated in the account should be equal to the replacement cost of the asset.

(11) More depreciation should be charged off in prosperous years than in poor years.

(12) Depreciation is never affected by changes in the rate of production.

(13) Depreciation represents an appropriation of the profits of a business.

(14) Depreciation is a provision that must be made in order to provide for the replacement of the asset when retired from service.

(15) The reserve for depreciation measures the shrinkage in the book value of an asset because of depreciation.

(16) The reserve for depreciation is a fund with which new fixed assets may be purchased.

Question **27–15.** Company A began business in 1946 and at that time purchased a number of X-type machines at a cost of $3,000.00 each. Company B entered the same productive field in 1950 but its X-type machines cost $4,500.00 each, due to the higher prices prevailing at that time. Except for certain very minor improvements, the X-type machines of Company B were identical with those of Company A. The life of an X-type machine was estimated at ten years.

From the standpoint of cost, as it is determined by depreciation expense, do both companies have the same production costs? Explain.

If sales prices are based on cost, on what cost will Company A base its sales price? Company B? Why?

Competitively, which company is better situated? On what cost will the companies establish sales prices if competition is exceedingly keen? If competition is not keen?

Question **27–16.** The Annual Report of the Pillsbury Flour Mills, Incorporated, for 1933 stated that "provision has been made for depreciation and maintenance of fixed plants by charging to operations a sum annually equal to 5.8 % of the gross book value of the plants, excluding land, and adding to the reserve for depreciation the excess of such sum over the amount actually expended for repairs and replacements. This depreciation policy has been in effect since 1923." Discuss.

PROBLEMS

Problem **27–1.** The Red Line Transportation Company has purchased the following new motor busses:

	Approximate Life	Depreciation Rates
6 @ $10,000.00	7 years	14%
4 @ $ 6,000.00	6 "	16⅔%
10 @ $ 4,000.00	5 "	20%

The average cost of these motor busses is $6,200.00, and the average life, 5.8 years.

What is the amount of depreciation expense for the first year? What is the journal entry?

At the end of the third year, two of the $4,000.00 busses are retired from service. What entry should be made?

For the purpose of this problem residual values may be disregarded.

Problem **27–2.** Certain factory equipment was purchased on January 1, 1948, at a cost of $10,000.00. The estimated life of this equipment was ten years. On December 31, 1953, the equipment was traded in on new equipment costing $12,000.00. A cash payment of $9,000.00 completed the deal. What entries should be made to record the exchange?

Problem **27–3.** The Wayne Manufacturing Company depreciated its factory equipment at the annual composite group rate of 10%. On December 31, 1954, its factory equipment appeared on the books as follows:

FACTORY EQUIPMENT

	Unit	Life	
Jan. 1, 1950	A	5 years	3,000.00
Jan. 1, 1950	B	10 "	5,000.00
Jan. 1, 1950	C	15 "	12,000.00

RESERVE FOR DEPRECIATION — FACTORY EQUIPMENT

Dec. 31, 1950	2,000.00
Dec. 31, 1951	2,000.00
Dec. 31, 1952	2,000.00
Dec. 31, 1953	2,000.00
Dec. 31, 1954	2,000.00

Required:

(1) Unit A was retired from service on December 31, 1954. What is the entry?

(2) If unit A had been retired from service on December 31, 1953, what entry should have been made?

Problem **27–4.** An asset, costing $7,500.00 new, was estimated to have a serviceable life of 10 years and an estimated residual value of $300.00. No depreciation expense was recorded for nearly 5 years. At the end of the fifth year it is decided that the books should be adjusted to show the correct depreciated value of the asset. What entries should be made?

Problem **27–5.** The Emerson Manufacturing Company bought a machine on January 1, 1945, for $5,000.00. (Expected life, 10 years, scrap value, $200.00.) On January 1, 1953, a major repair of $2,040.00 is made on this machine. It is expected that the effect of this repair will be to extend the life of the machine an additional three years.

What entry should be made to record the disbursement of $2,040.00? What should be the depreciation expense entry for the year 1953?

Problem **27–6.** The Service Manufacturing Company bought a machine on January 1, 1944, for $2,500.00. (Expected life, 10 years, scrap value, $100.00.) On January 1, 1950, it is found that the machine will last but two years more.

Should any entry be made on account of this change in estimated life? If so, what? What should be the depreciation expense entry for the year 1950?

Problem **27–7.** What entries should be made each year in connection with the Machinery account and the following related information?

January 1, 1943 — A machine is purchased for cash at a cost of $10,200.00 (Estimated life, 10 years; scrap value, $200.00.)

January 1, 1948 — It is expected that the machine will last three more years from today.

January 1, 1949 — A major repair of $1,000.00 is made. This cash repair greatly improved the operating efficiency of the machine although it did not affect its estimated life.

December 31, 1950 — The machine is sold for cash, $500.00.

Problem **27–8.** On January 1, 1950, the cash balance of a company was $100,000.00, an amount normally needed to meet the usual requirements of business. During 1950 the capital disbursements of the company amounted to $60,000.00, depreciation expense was $25,000.00, and net profits (realized in cash) were $100,000.00.

On December 31, 1950, the capitalization of the company was common stock, $1,000,000.00, and surplus, $250,000.00.

On the basis of this information and assuming no dividends to have yet been paid in 1950, how much may the company prudently declare as dividends on December 31, 1950?

Problem **27–9.** On January 1 of this year Ness & Company purchased a certain type of machine for $7,350.00. The expected life of the machine was three years, no estimated scrap value. On December 31, after only one year's service, the machine was retired in favor of a new machine costing $8,870.00. No depreciation expense had been recorded during the year. Considerable disagreement has been aroused with respect to the proper accounting for the retirement of the machine. You have been called in to state which, if any, of the following entries are correct, and why.

Assistant bookkeeper:

Depreciation Expense	7,350.00	
Machinery		7,350.00
Machinery	8,870.00	
Cash		8,870.00

Head bookkeeper:

Depreciation Expense	2,450.00	
Loss on Retirement of Capital Assets	4,900.00	
Machinery		7,350.00
Machinery	8,870.00	
Cash		8,870.00

Comptroller:

| Maintenance Expense . . . . | 8,870.00 | |
| Cash . . . . | | 8,870.00 |

For maintenance of productivity and earning capacity of machinery.

Office Manager:

Maintenance Expense	7,350.00	
Machinery	1,520.00	
Cash		8,870.00

On the theory that it took $7,350.00 to maintain the capital value represented by the old machine. The balance constitutes additional capital investment.

Problem 27–10. The Durox Manufacturing Company prepared the following condensed trial balance on December 31, 1950:

Cash	$20,000.00	
Machinery	15,000.00	
Reserve for Depreciation — Machinery		$ 5,000.00
Other Assets (nondepreciable)	30,000.00	
Accounts Payable		4,000.00
Common Stock, $100.00 par		50,000.00
Surplus.		6,000.00
	$65,000.00	$65,000.00

The machinery was purchased on January 1, 1946, and subsequently depreciated on the straight-line method. On January 1, 1951, the efficiency of the machinery on hand was much improved by important repairs costing $2,000.00. It was estimated that the life of the machinery was extended an additional five years by these repairs.

Required:

(1) Make the entries in 1951 affecting depreciation expense and the reserve for depreciation accounts.

(2) Prepare a balance sheet, December 31, 1951. The profit and loss statement for 1951 showed a net income of $10,000.00. All business was transacted on a cash basis. No dividends were paid during the year. Except for net income, no entries were made in the Surplus account in 1951. For the purpose of this requirement, assume that the values for "other assets" and "accounts payable" remain unchanged.

Chapter 28

OBSOLESCENCE AND DEPLETION

Obsolescence has already been referred to as one of the causes of depreciation. It is one of the components of the estimate of useful life and, as such, it is one of the factors establishing the amount of the periodic charge for depreciation. The inclusion, however, of obsolescence as one of the determinants of periodic depreciation carries with it the implication that obsolescence is, per se, a definitely known and measurable factor. Usually, though, this is not the case. Obsolescence is generally a very uncertain consideration. It is commonly quite difficult to state whether or not obsolescence actually will occur and still more difficult to specify *when*. Obsolescence may occur suddenly, unexpectedly; it may occur in the near future, in the distant future, or at any point between; it may never occur at all. It follows, therefore, that obsolescence normally exercises little practical weight in the determination of the periodic charge for depreciation expense.

PROVISION FOR OBSOLESCENCE

When the factor of obsolescence becomes a consideration real enough to compel revision of original estimates of useful life, provision for obsolescence should be made by increasing the periodic charge for depreciation. The amount by which former charges for depreciation have been inadequate should be made a special debit to profit and loss.[1]

---

[1] The report of Rolls-Royce of America, Inc., for the year ending December 31, 1930, showed a charge as follows:

Special Depreciation due to Obsolescence and loss on sale of
    Machinery, Equipment and Current Assets $1,054,962.45

In explanation of this charge, the company stated, in its annual report:

". . . the English Rolls-Royce Company has announced and put on the market abroad the Phantom II chassis, . . . and your company was confronted under its contract with the English Company with the necessity of producing this chassis in America.

". . . it was decided that . . . it would be unwise for the American Company to expend the necessary amount of money to provide the special tools and equipment to build this chassis at its Springfield works.

"Therefore, it has been arranged to import the Phantom II chassis. . . .

"This policy has made it advisable to write off during the past year a substantial proportion of the special tools and equipment at Springfield."

Should a provision for obsolescence be made when there is no certainty that obsolescence will occur and even less certainty as to the time when obsolescence will occur? It would be possible, of course, to provide for obsolescence separately from depreciation, thus:

```
Obsolescence Expense . . . . . . . . . . . . . . . . . . .   xxx xx
        Reserve for Obsolescence  . . . . . . . . . . . . .            xxx xx
```

There are serious objections, however, to an entry of this kind:

(1) The accounting period would be charged with an expense which is not known to be an actual expense.

(2) Total expenses, and costs, would be overstated; profits would be understated. Balance sheet values for fixed assets would be understated.

(3) In order to reflect dependable and usable information, the books should reflect facts in so far as they are determinable. They should not include as costs items which are not known to be costs.

Occasionally a management may wish to recognize the possibility of obsolescence and yet oppose its recognition in the accounts through charges to operations. This desire to "play safe," and yet avoid inaccurate accounting may be satisfied by "earmarking" a part of the surplus account:

```
Surplus . . . . . . . . . . . . . . . . . . . . . . . . .   xxx xx
        Reserve for Obsolescence  . . . . . . . . . . . .            xxx xx
        (or)
        Reserve for Contingencies . . . . . . . . . . . .            xxx xx
```

It is for the management to decide the frequency of this entry, and the amount, or amounts, to be earmarked. The important thing to note about an entry of this kind is that a part of surplus has been set aside and "tagged," so to speak, as provision for the contingency of obsolescence. The amount which is set aside is still true surplus; but it is not free surplus in the sense that it is available for dividends.

If, later on, it is decided that the provision for obsolescence is no longer required, the appropriation may be transferred back to Surplus and again be made available for dividends.

DEPLETION

Wasting assets, such as oil wells and mineral deposits, lose their value with the continuance of extractive operations. For example,

(1) The value of an oil well is steadily lessened as oil is withdrawn.

(2) A coal mine becomes less and less valuable as coal is mined.

(3) Forest land loses value as timber is cut.

The term "depletion" is applied to this special type of exhaustion of capital value.

Depletion is not depreciation. The difference between depletion and depreciation may be brought out by the following comparison:

Depletion	*Depreciation*
(1) Depletion measures the exhaustion of the investment in a natural resource.	(1) Depreciation measures the exhaustion of the investment in plant and equipment.
(2) Depletion occurs only when and if extractive operations are carried on.	(2) Depreciation occurs whether or not operations are carried on.
(3) An asset subject to depletion is one which is directly consumed.	(3) An asset subject to depreciation is one which is indirectly consumed, i.e., the consumption of value is not physical but, instead, is a consumption of service value.
(4) An asset subject to depletion becomes quantitatively less as it is mined or cut.	(4) An asset subject to depreciation does not necessarily become smaller in size as it loses value. Commonly the asset remains physically as large as ever.
(5) An asset subject to depletion, as a practical matter, cannot usually be replaced directly. It is not usually intended that the extracted asset shall be replaced inasmuch as the object of extractive operations is to remove oil, coal, gas, etc., for the purpose of profitable sale.	(5) An asset subject to depreciation may usually be replaced without difficulty. Replacement of machines, automobiles, etc., is usually intended.
(6) The asset which has been extracted is the stock in trade of the enterprise and, as such, is intended for sale.	(6) An asset which is subject to depreciation is not intended for sale. It is not stock in trade but a fixed asset of the business.

From this comparison it should be clear that depletion and depreciation are terms which represent two distinct kinds of capital value impairment. Depletion and depreciation, therefore, are always separately accounted for on the books.

IMPORTANCE OF RECORDING DEPLETION

In order to determine the profit of an enterprise employing wasting assets, not only must out-of-pocket expenses of operation be deducted from revenues but also a figure which represents the depletion of assets. This is necessary because a part of the sales price represents a return of some of the capital invested in the depletive asset; for example, a part of each dollar received from the sale of oil represents a partial return of the money invested in the property containing the oil. A part of the original investment in the well has been recovered in the sales price. Depletion, then, must be recorded as one of the *revenue costs* of a period. The profit realized from extractive operations is the sales price minus the full cost value of the extracted product sold and minus, also, general operating expenses. The provision for depletion is a part of this "full cost value" and, as such, must be recognized in determining the true income of a period.

The following reasons summarize the importance of providing for the cost of depletion:

(1) The balance sheet and the profit and loss statement cannot be correct without an adequate provision being made for depletion.

(2) A provision for depletion is necessary to guard against an impairment of capital which might occur through policies predicated upon income statements wherein net incomes are overstated by exclusion of the provision for depletion.

(3) Dividends paid from profits are distinguished from dividends paid from capital.

(4) A charge for depletion for a mining company parallels a charge for purchases for a merchandising concern, and the raw material cost of the finished product of a manufacturing concern. Depletion, for a business engaged in extractive operations, is the same kind of revenue cost as purchases for a concern engaged in nonextractive operations.

Parenthetically it should be stated that usually, as a practical matter, the residual value of an asset is disregarded in calculating the amount of depletion.

The amount of the depletion provision for a particular accounting period is obtained by multiplying the number of units extracted during that period by the depletion charge per unit.

Example:

John A. Briggs bought a piece of coal land for $90,000.00, the purchase price representing

1,000,000 tons of coal at 8¢	$80,000.00
Value of surface land.	10,000.00
	$90,000.00

An additional expenditure of $20,000.00 for preliminary development work was necessary before actual mining operations could be got under way. In the first year of operations, 30,000 tons of coal were mined. What was the depletion charge for the year?

Solution:

Original cost of property	$ 90,000.00
Preliminary developmental work	20,000.00
	$110,000.00
Less residual value (surface value)	10,000.00
Total depletion	$100,000.00

Depletion rate per ton:
$100,000.00 ÷ 1,000,000 = $0.10
Amount of depletion provision for first year:
30,000 × $0.10   = $3,000.00

RECORDING DEPLETION ON THE BOOKS

The amount of the periodic provision for depletion is recorded on the books in the following manner:

Depletion Expense	3,000.00	
Reserve for Depletion		3,000.00

To record provision for depletion:
30,000 tons of coal at $0.10 = $3,000.00

In any given case the provision for depletion expense depends upon the number of units produced and the amount of cost assigned to each depletion unit. The monetary depletion unit, in turn, is wholly dependent for its accuracy upon the accuracy of the factors which have entered into its calculation. Of prime importance in this respect are ore reserves. If the original estimate of an ore reserve should be revised at a later date, the cost per depletion unit, as a matter of theory, should be changed to correspond. A revision of the cost per depletion unit would involve not only a change in the calculation of current income but adjustment of the reserve for depletion through a special debit or credit to the comprehensive income account with profit and loss. As a practical matter, however, the cost per depletion unit should be revised only when a significant change is made in the original estimate of ore reserves, and when current information indicates that the revised estimate will be one of long serviceability.

DEPLETION AND THE FINANCIAL STATEMENTS

The book value of a property subject to depletion is found by taking the difference between the book cost of a depletive property and the balance of the related reserve for depletion account. Like the reserve for depreciation, the reserve for depletion is a valuation account. On the balance sheet the reserve for depletion account should be deducted from the asset to which it relates, thus:

Mining Property	$110,000.00	
Less Reserve for Depletion.	3,000.00	$107,000.00

Since the periodic provision for depletion expense parallels the periodic charge for purchases for a trading or manufacturing concern, it is proper that depletion be handled like purchases when statements are being prepared, and the books closed. The value of the closing inventory is the sum of depletion and mining costs allocable to the quantity of product represented by the new inventory. To illustrate, consider the following problem and profit and loss statement.

ILLUSTRATIVE PROBLEM

The Federal Coal Company purchased a coal property for $210,000.00. The estimated commercially recoverable tonnage was 1,000,000 tons.

After the property was no longer usable for mining operations, the land was estimated to be worth $10,000.00.

The company erected mine buildings costing $25,000.00, estimated life, 12½ years, no scrap value.

In the first year of operations 100,000 tons of coal were mined, 80,000 tons were sold for $150,000.00, and 20,000 tons were on hand at the end of the year.

Wages and other mining costs paid in cash amounted to $77,-500.00 for the year. Selling and general expenses were $20,000.00, and $30,000.00, respectively.

Prepare a profit and loss statement for the first year.

Solution:

Federal Coal Company

PROFIT AND LOSS STATEMENT FOR YEAR 19—

Sales, 80,000 tons		$150,000.00
Cost of Sales:		
Inventory, January 1, 19—	$ none	
Cost of 100,000 tons mined in 19—:		

Depletion Expense:

100,000 × $0.20	$20,000.00		
Depreciation Expense	2,500.00		
Wages and Other Mining Costs	77,500.00	100,000.00	
		$100,000.00	
Inventory, December 31, 19___, 20,000 tons:			
20,000/100,000 × $100,000.00		20,000.00	80,000.00
Gross Profit			$ 70,000.00
Selling Expenses		$ 20,000.00	
General Expenses		30,000.00	50,000.00
Net Profit from Operations			$ 20,000.00

In general outline this profit and loss statement is similar to one which might be prepared for a manufacturing company operating under the plan of periodic inventory. The student will observe, particularly, that depletion is substituted for raw material purchases, and that the ending inventory is valued at cost. This cost is based on the production costs of the year, i.e., the ending inventory of 20,000 tons is 20% of the production of the year and is valued, accordingly, at 20% of the year's cost of $100,000.00 of producing 100,000 tons.

The student should also observe that in this statement depreciation expense is computed on the reasoning that since 10% of the mine has been depleted, 10% of the cost of the mine buildings has been used up accordingly. On the other hand, had the mine buildings possessed an estimated life of 5 years, it would have been conservative accounting to establish the depreciation expense figure for the first year at 1/5 of $25,000.00, or $5,000.00. It is proper to write off depreciation proportionate to production in those cases where the life of the mine promises to be less than that of the depreciable asset.

MEANING OF THE RESERVE FOR DEPLETION

The reserve for depreciation measures the cumulative shrinkage in the book value of an asset because of depreciation. It is not a fund nor is it purchasing power. It does signify, however, the amount of other assets which must have been brought into the business by realized revenues to compensate for the loss of capital through depreciation.

Similarly, the reserve for depletion measures the cumulative shrinkage in the book value of a wasting asset because of depletion. It is not a fund nor is it purchasing power. The reserve for depletion, however, does signify the amount of other assets which must have been brought into the business by realized revenues (sales) to compensate for the exhaustion of capital as expressed by the provision for depletion expense. Should the correct accounting loss of a business for a period be in excess of the provision for depletion, there is not even any recovery of capital to compensate for that lost through depletion.

Since it is only a measure of the cumulative shrinkage in the book value of an asset because of depletion, the reserve for depletion has no connection whatsoever with the ability of a business to purchase new properties as the old properties are exhausted by extractive operations. If new properties are to be purchased, it is the responsibility of management to administer assets so that liquid purchasing power will be on hand when needed. This is a problem of asset management. The cash position of a business is not related to the policy of depletion or to the reserve for depletion account.

DIVIDENDS AND THE RESERVE FOR DEPLETION

If an enterprise does not find itself able to utilize effectively the new assets which have been received in the stream of revenue transactions, inclusive of new assets which compensate for the capital lost through depletion, and if, also, there is more liquid working capital on hand than is needed, there is no objection to dividend disbursements "out of capital" in amounts whose total does not exceed the balance of the Reserve for Depletion account. If these disbursements are made, the distributions to stockholders should be labeled as dividends from capital in order to advise recipients of the real source of their dividends. This is but to say that, in computing the amount of dividends which may be paid by a company which employs wasting assets, it is not necessary to consider depletion. In other words, the maximum dividend payable at any specific date is an amount equal to the sum of earned surplus and the difference between the balance of the reserve for depletion account, and the cumulative total of dividends already paid out of capital. This latter total is the balance of the account described below, Capital Returned to Stockholders.

In accounting for dividends which are legally paid out of capital rather than income, such dividends should be debited not to the Reserve for Depletion account but to an account titled Capital Returned to Stockholders. This account, or one of similar title, would appear in the balance sheet as a deduction from Capital Stock; it would function as a valuation account for the investment represented by Capital Stock. The balance of this account must not be allowed to exceed the balance of the Reserve for Depletion account. The balance of the Reserve for Depletion account is not disturbed by accounting which reflects the return of capital to stockholders. This account continues to function, as it should, as a true valuation account for the depletive asset to which it relates.

Assets equal to the amount of provisions for depletion are legally distributable. Otherwise it would be obligatory for managements to maintain intact the capitals of their enterprises until their wasting assets were completely exhausted and final liquidation commenced. Unneeded funds could not be returned to those whose funds were invested in the enterprise. Such withholding might be unnecessary and unjust. At the discretion of managements, therefore, the laws of the several states permit dividend distributions not only of profits but of assets equal to the amounts of charges for depletion as well. Creditors are not presumed to be injured by capital distributions of this kind because they are expected to be familiar with the nature of a wasting enterprise, with the risks attaching to it, and to govern their own actions accordingly.

QUESTIONS

Question 28–1. Distinguish between depreciation, obsolescence, and depletion. Explain briefly the accounting recognition that should be given to each, and why.

Question 28–2. The fertility of a plot of land has decreased because of intensive cultivation over several years. Is this depreciation or depletion?

Question 28–3. The Radio Equipment Company has purchased a new and improved piece of equipment for $17,500.00. Engineers estimate that the equipment will be serviceable for 15 years, assuming reasonable maintenance. Inasmuch as the company, in its past experience, has had to replace many comparable units much oftener than every 15 years, because of the rapidity of invention and improvement in the radio industry, the company is somewhat in doubt as to the advisability of depreciating its new purchase on the basis of a 15-year life, although it is conceded that the radio industry is now more stable than it has ever been in the past, and that future improvements and inventions are likely to come at a much slower pace than heretofore. What would you suggest?

Question 28–4. Are assets such as goodwill, leases, patent rights, franchises, etc., subject to depreciation, or depletion? Explain.

Question 28–5. Explain how the periodic charge for depletion is determined.

Question 28–6. Discuss the reserve for depletion from the standpoint of (1) replacement of assets, (2) dividends.

PROBLEMS

Problem **28–1.** The Valley Coal Company bought a piece of coal land, estimated to contain 1,400,000 tons of coal, for $150,000.00. The surface land was estimated to have a value of $7,000.00 after the cessation of mining operations.

The company expended $11,000.00 in developmental costs.

In the first year of operations, 42,000 tons of coal were mined and sold, total gross income from the sale of coal was $49,000.00, and expenses other than depletion were

Direct labor	$22,500.00
Depreciation expense on mine fixed assets	500.00
Selling expenses	7,000.00
General expenses	5,000.00

Required:

(1) What was the company's net income in the first year of operations?

(2) What is the maximum dividend payable from the operations of the first year?

Problem **28–2.** Referring to the Valley Coal Company of Problem 28–1, in the second year of operations 60,000 tons of coal were mined, 55,000 tons were sold for $73,000.00, direct labor was $38,040.00, depreciation expense on mine fixed assets was $840.00, selling expenses were $7,030.00, and general expenses were $14,027.00.

Required:

(1) Prepare a profit and loss statement covering operations of the second year.

(2) Assuming no dividends to have been paid in the first year of operations, what is the maximum dividend payable by the company at the end of the second year?

Problem **28–3.** The Antlers Coal Company purchased a coal property for $235,000.00. The coal reserves of this property were estimated at 1,000,000 tons. No residual value was deemed to be present in the property after mining operations were concluded.

Before active mining operations were commenced, the company incurred developmental costs of $15,000.00. Mine buildings were erected at a cost of $16,000.00, estimated life 8 years, no scrap value.

In the first year of operations 100,000 tons of coal were mined, 90,000 tons were sold for $180,000.00, and 10,000 tons were on hand at the end of the year. Direct labor amounted to $70,000.00 and other cash mining expenses to $23,000.00. Selling expenses were $19,000.00, and general expenses, $28,000.00.

Required:

Prepare a profit and loss statement covering the first year of operations

Problem **28–4.** The Penn Timber Company was the owner of 1,560,-000,000 board feet of timber of which 1,200,000,000 was considered merchantable. The cost of the property was $1,560,000.00.

In the first year of operations 60,000,000 feet were sold. Inventories, being negligible, were disregarded in the company's accounting.

Required:

Make the depletion entry for the first year.

Problem **28–5.** A company acquired a 100% interest in a certain oil property for a cash consideration of $400,000.00. In addition the company expended $75,288.96 for oil well equipment, the salvage value of which was reasonably estimated to be not more than $2,000.00. The property on which the well was located had an estimated reserve of 1,000,000 barrels of oil.

The first year's production was 286,733 barrels of oil.

What accounting should be placed on the company's books to record the exhaustion of capital value in the first year?

Problem **28–6.** The Yonkers Coal Company had a net worth consisting solely of common stock, $500,000.00, at the beginning of a certain fiscal year. Assets were current assets. A coal property was purchased out of current assets at a cost of $235,714.00. This property was estimated to have coal reserves of 2,000,000 tons, and an ultimate residual value of $10,000.00.

The company paid cash developmental costs of $17,286.00; and purchased fixed assets for use in mining operations at a cash cost of $12,000.00.

Statistics on the first year of operations were as follows:

Mined:	60,000 tons
Sold:	55,000 tons for $72,000.00
Inventory, December 31, 19__:	5,000 tons

Depreciation expense on mine fixed assets	$ 1,200.00
Cash expenses:	
Mine labor	26,414.00
Miscellaneous mine costs	8,692.00
Selling expenses	12,000.00
General expenses	8,000.00

Required:

(1) Prepare a profit and loss statement for the first year of operations.

(2) Directors declare the maximum dividends legally payable out of the operations of the first year. What entry should be made?

(3) Prepare a balance sheet, December 31, 19__.

Problem **28–7.** The Fairmont Coal Corporation bought the coal property of the Valley Coal Company (see Problem 28–1) for a cash consideration of $150,000.00. This purchase was made on December 31 of the first year of operations for the latter company.

In the opinion of the Fairmont Coal Corporation, the estimated recoverable commercial tonnage of the mine was 1,000,000 tons: this estimate made allowance for the tonnage which had already been extracted by the Valley Coal Company.

The Fairmont Coal Corporation invested an additional $10,000.00 in developmental work, and $5,000.00 in mine buildings. The buildings were calculated to last for 10 years, which was also the estimated life of the mine. It was estimated that, after exhaustion of the mine property, the residual value of the land would be $10,000.00, and that of the buildings, nothing.

In its first year of operations the Fairmont Coal Corporation mined 110,000 tons of coal and sold 100,000 tons. Mine operating costs paid in cash were $104,687.00; general and selling expenses paid in cash amounted to $14,000.00. Coal sales were $166,000.00.

Required:

Prepare a profit and loss statement of the Fairmont Coal Corporation covering the first year of operations for this company.

Problem **28–8.** The Yandell Lumber Company is the owner of a tract of timber. Subject to the condition of the market, this timber is cut and manufactured into lumber. The following accounts were included in the company's balance sheet of December 31, 1949:

Timber land (uncut timber 1,694,000,000 feet)	$3,388,000.00
Plant and main line railroad (adequate for 10 years with normal replacements).	854,000.00
Miscellaneous equipment (adequate for 10 years with normal replacements).	535,640.00
Logging-railroad spurs (available for logging 300,000,000 feet)	172,900.00

During 1950 the Yandell Lumber Company manufactured 120,000,000 feet which it sold for $3,494,400.00. Logging, manufacturing labor, and expenses amounted to $2,630,708.00. Selling and general expenses were $390,492.00; interest expense was $54,630.00. All of these expenses were paid in cash or liabilities were incurred therefor.

Required:

Prepare a profit and loss statement for the year 1950. Inventories, being negligible, may be disregarded for the purpose of this problem.

Problem **28–9.** The Bretz Corporation purchased a coal property for $370,000.00. The property was estimated to contain 3,000,000 tons of commercially recoverable coal, and to have an ultimate residual value of $25,000.00.

The company immediately expended an additional $30,000.00 in developmental costs.

The following figures describe the operations of the first two years:

	1st Year	2nd Year
Mined	100,000 tons	128,560 tons
Sold 98,000 tons for	$120,604.00	
Sold 125,360 tons for		$160,755.00
Cash mining expenses	$ 45,112.00	$ 76,004.00
Depreciation expense on mine assets	566.00	800.00
Selling expenses	$ 10,001.00	$ 14,078.00
General expenses	14,200.00	28,072.00

Required:

(1) Prepare a profit and loss statement for each year.

(2) Prepare a balance sheet at the end of the second year. Assume that no dividends were paid in either year, that capital stock was $400,000.00, that surplus was the net income or loss from two years' operations, that liabilities were $60,780.00, and that depreciable mine assets were originally costed at $16,000.00. The balance sheet should show as much detail as the information of the problem will permit; assets which cannot be definitely described may be labeled "miscellaneous assets."

(3) If, at the end of the second year, the company paid out the maximum dividend legally distributable out of the operations of the two years, what entry should be made? Assume this transaction to take place after the balance sheet of requirement #2.

Chapter 29

BONDS PAYABLE AND BONDS RECEIVABLE

BONDS PAYABLE

A corporation desiring additional capital may procure funds in three different ways:

(1) By sale of stock.
(2) By accumulation of profits.
(3) By borrowing.

If the corporation decides to borrow money, it may do so in two ways:

(1) By a short-term loan procured from a bank or other lender.
(2) By a long-term loan procured from individual, corporate, or institutional investors.

The latter type of borrowing is evidenced by formal notes payable called bonds.

Definition of a Bond. — A corporate bond may be defined as a written promise, under seal, to pay a specified sum of money, usually $1,000.00, at a fixed time in the future, usually more than ten years after the promise is made, and is usually one of a series of similar bonds all carrying interest at a fixed rate, and all covered by a so-called deed of trust, or mortgage, in which the corporation's property may be, in whole or in part, mortgaged to the trustee for the benefit of all the bondholders.[1]

Characteristics of a Bond. — A bond is a formal promise to pay and, as such, is a direct liability of the issuing corporation. Interest is payable at definite specified dates, January 1 and July 1 of each year, for example. Bond issues are created by formal authorization of the stockholders or the board of directors; and in their actual issuance the bonds must, of course, accord with the provisions of state law as well as with the charter and bylaws of the corporation.

Bonds are either

(1) *Unsecured,* in which case they rest upon the general credit of

---

[1] Adapted from C. W. Gerstenberg, *Financial Organization and Management,* Prentice-Hall, Inc., p. 185.

the issuing corporation. Such bonds are commonly known as debenture bonds.

(2) *Secured,* in which case the security may be
    (a) Real estate. Example: First Mortgage Bond.
    (b) Personal property, such as machinery, equipment, rolling stock, negotiable securities, etc. Examples: Equipment Trust Bonds and Collateral Trust Bonds.

The total bond issue is divided into units of $100.00, $500.00, or $1,000.00, each unit representing one bond; the usual unit, however, is $1,000.00. Collectively, the bondholders are represented by a trustee, usually a bank or trust company, appointed by the corporation. The deed of trust between the corporation and the trustee details the rights of bondholders, the obligations of the corporation, and the property (if any) pledged to the trustee for the benefit of all the bondholders. The trustee, in addition, authenticates (certifies) each bond as being a bond issued under the deed of trust.

Bonds may also be classified as

(1) *Coupon bonds.* Interest is represented by interest coupons which are detached by the bondholder as they come due, and deposited with a bank for collection.

The transfer of ownership of a coupon bond is accomplished by delivery.

(2) *Registered bonds.* The bondholder's name is registered with the corporation. Interest and principal payments, as they come due, are paid to the bondholder by check.

Ownership of a registered bond is transferred by assignment, and by registry of the transfer on the books of the corporation.

Coupon bonds are sometimes registered as to principal only.

There are many kinds of bonds, and bond provisions, and, since it is beyond the compass of this text to consider these matters in the detail which they deserve, the student is referred to a suitable text upon corporation finance for their full description and exposition.

Accounting for Bonds Payable. — Some of the more common accounting problems for bonds payable are illustrated in the pages which follow. For convenience the entries are presented in journal entry form.

The Bonds Are Issued at Par. — On January 1, 1950, the X Corporation sells $100,000.00 of its 10-year 6% bonds at par. Principal due January 1, 1960. Interest payable January 1 and July 1.

Cash 100,000.00
    Bonds Payable 100,000.00
To record sale at par of $100,000.00, 10-year, 6%
bonds, due January 1, 1960.

If the bonds had been subscribed for under an installment plan of payment, the accounting would parallel the accounting for stock sold under similar terms.

No bookkeeping entry is necessary to record unissued or unsubscribed bonds. For informational purposes, however, it is well to place a memorandum of the amount of the authorized issue on the title line of the Bonds Payable account.

The Bonds Are Sold at Par between Interest Dates. — If the X Corporation had sold $90,000.00 of its bonds on January 1, 1950, and $10,000.00 on May 1, 1950, the accounting would have been

```
Jan. 1  Cash  . . . . . . . . . . . . . . . . . .  90,000.00
            Bonds Payable . . . . . . . . . . . .             90,000.00
            To record sale of $90,000.00 par value bonds at
            100.

May 1  Cash  . . . . . . . . . . . . . . . . . .  10,200.00
            Bonds Payable . . . . . . . . . . . .             10,000.00
            Interest Expense . . . . . . . . . . .                200.00
            To record sale of $10,000.00 par value bonds
            at 100, and 4 months' accrued interest.
```

When bonds are sold between interest-payment dates, they are sold at a price, plus accrued interest.

In lieu of the credit to Interest Expense for $200.00, an equally appropriate credit would have been one to the Interest Payable account.

When the X Corporation pays the interest due on July 1, 1950, the entry will be

```
July 1  Interest Expense  . . . . . . . . . . . . . . .  3,000.00
            Cash . . . . . . . . . . . . . . . . .             3,000.00
            To record semiannual payment of interest on 6%
            bonds of 1960.
```

When these several entries have been posted, the Interest Expense account will be

INTEREST EXPENSE	
3,000.00	200.00

The new balance of the Interest Expense account is the correct interest expense for the period January 1 to July 1.

The Bonds Are Sold at a Discount. — On January 1, 1950, the X Corporation sells $100,000.00 of its bonds at 97.

```
Cash  . . . . . . . . . . . . . . . . . . . .   97,000.00
Bond Discount . . . . . . . . . . . . . . . .    3,000.00
     Bonds Payable . . . . . . . . . . . . . .                100,000.00
To record sale of $100,000.00 par value bonds at 97.
```

The Bonds Are Sold at a Premium. — On January 1, 1950, the X Corporation sells $100,000.00 of its bonds at a price of 102.

```
Cash  . . . . . . . . . . . . . . . . . . . .  102,000.00
     Bonds Payable . . . . . . . . . . . . . .                100,000.00
     Bond Premium . . . . . . . . . . . . . .                   2,000.00
To record sale of $100,000.00 par value bonds at 102.
```

Bond Interest. — When the X Corporation sold its bonds at 97, it received net cash of $97,000.00, but covenanted to pay $100,000.00 on January 1, 1960. The difference of $3,000.00 is a further cost of procuring capital; it is, in other words, additional interest expense. Consequently, the total annual interest expense is

$$6\% \text{ on } \$100,000.00 = \$6,000.00$$
$$\tfrac{1}{10} \text{ of } \$3,000.00 = 300.00$$
$$\overline{\phantom{6\% \text{ on } \$100,0}\$6,300.00}$$

In order to debit each accounting period with an interest expense of $6,300.00, the following entries are made:

```
1950
July  1   Interest Expense . . . . . . . . . . . . .   3,000.00
               Cash  . . . . . . . . . . . . . . . .                3,000.00
          To record semiannual payment of interest on
          6% bonds of 1960.

Dec. 31   Interest Expense . . . . . . . . . . . . .   3,000.00
               Accrued Interest Payable . . . . . . .                3,000.00
          To record 6 months' accrual of interest on 6%
          bonds of 1960.

Dec. 31   Interest Expense . . . . . . . . . . . . .     300.00
               Bond Discount . . . . . . . . . . . .                  300.00
          To write off 1/10 of bond discount to 1950.
```

If the books are operated on the monthly accrual basis of accounting in order to facilitate the preparation of interim statements, $\frac{1}{12}$ of the $300.00 annual discount expense may be written off each month.

In the case where the X Corporation floated its bond issue for more than par, i.e., $102,000.00, the extra $2,000.00 would represent a reduction of the cost of procuring capital, and to that extent it reduces the total interest expense. The annual interest charge, in this case, is therefore

$$6\% \text{ on } \$100,000.00 \;\; = \$6,000.00$$
$$\text{Less } \tfrac{1}{10} \text{ of } \$2,000.00 \;= \;\; 200.00$$

$$\$5,800.00$$

The following interest entries for 1950 illustrate the required accounting for each year:

July 1	Interest Expense	3,000.00	
	Cash		3,000.00
	To record semiannual payment of interest on 6% bonds of 1960.		
Dec. 31	Interest Expense	3,000.00	
	Accrued Interest Payable		3,000.00
	To record 6 months' accrual of interest on 6% bonds of 1960.		
Dec. 31	Bond Premium	200.00	
	Interest Expense		200.00
	To write off $\tfrac{1}{10}$ of bond premium as a credit to the interest expense account of 1950.		

At the end of ten years both the Bond Discount and the Bond Premium accounts will have been written off, leaving only the $100,000.00 liability for the bonds. This write-off process is called "amortization" of bond discount, or premium, as the case may be. The method of amortization illustrated in the entries above is called the straight-line method of amortization.

On the balance sheet, discount on bonds payable may be shown as a deferred expense, and bond premium as a deferred credit. However, if the accounting liability for the bonds is to be shown exactly, it would be better to show these two accounts as valuation accounts, thus:

Bonds Payable	$100,000.00	
Less Unamortized Bond Discount.	3,000.00	$ 97,000.00

and

Bonds Payable	$100,000.00	
Plus Unamortized Bond Premium	1,800.00	$101,800.00

This method of evaluating bonds payable on the balance sheet reflects the theory that it is sound accounting to currently evaluate a liability, payable at a future date, at its present discounted value.

From the "practical" standpoint, however, the liability of a company for its bonds payable is the par value of the bonds which are outstanding. This value is normally considered to be the company's liability, regardless of the price which the company may have received for its bonds. If the balance sheet is prepared with this understanding in mind — and this is the general practice of commercial accounting — it follows that unamortized bond discount will be carried as a deferred charge and bond premium as a deferred credit, and that bonds payable will be carried as a liability equal to their par value. This method of presenting bond discount, bond premium, and bonds payable on the balance sheet is essentially a relinquishment of accounting theory in favor of financial expediency.

Bond Expenses. — The flotation of an issue of securities involves certain costs such as, for example, legal fees, printing and engraving expenses, and so on. Although these expenditures represent costs in the procurement of capital, bond expenses cannot, strictly speaking, be considered as true interest costs. In theory, bond expenses should be accounted for as deferred charges to be written off to profit and loss on a straight-line basis over the periods in which the bonds are outstanding. In practice, however, bond expenses are generally written off in the period of their incurrence as an extraordinary charge against income.

The Bonds Are Paid at Maturity. — On January 1, 1960, the X Corporation redeems in full its $100,000.00 of bonds payable.

Bonds Payable	100,000.00	
Bond Interest Payable	3,000.00	
Cash		103,000.00

To record redemption of 6% bonds payable, due today, and payment of 6 months' accrued interest.

Sinking Funds. — A bond contract often contains a provision to the effect that the borrowing corporation will periodically deposit with the trustee of the bond issue a sum of money which, accumulating at compound interest, will be sufficient to retire either all or a part of the entire bond issue at maturity, or which will retire a part of the bond issue before it is legally due for payment. For instance, assuming that the sinking fund is to be large enough to retire the entire bond issue at maturity and, assuming further, that the sinking fund is to increase at the rate of $10,000.00 per year,

At the end of the	The corporation will deposit	Interest earned by trustee on moneys deposited with him (Assume rate of 6%)	Amount of fund
1st year	$10,000.00		$ 10,000.00
2nd year	9,400.00	$ 600.00	20,000.00
3rd year	8,800.00	1,200.00	30,000.00
4th year	8,200.00	1,800.00	40,000.00
5th year	7,600.00	2,400.00	50,000.00
6th year	7,000.00	3,000.00	60,000.00
7th year	6,400.00	3,600.00	70,000.00
8th year	5,800.00	4,200.00	80,000.00
9th year	5,200.00	4,800.00	90,000.00
10th year	4,600.00	5,400.00	100,000.00

Accounting entries are relatively simple.

(1) When cash is deposited with the trustee:

Sinking Fund Cash with Trustee . . . .   xxx xx
     Cash   . . . .   xxx xx

(2) When the trustee reports the investment of sinking fund cash:

Sinking Fund Investments (at cost) . . . .   xxx xx
     Sinking Fund Cash with Trustee . . . .   xxx xx

(3) When the trustee reports income earned:

Sinking Fund Cash with Trustee . . . .   xxx xx
     Sinking Fund Income . . . .   xxx xx

(4) When the trustee reports expenses incurred:

Sinking Fund Expenses. . . . .   xxx xx
     Sinking Fund Cash with Trustee . . . .   xxx xx

(5) When the bonds are paid at maturity:

Bonds Payable 100,000.00
     Sinking Fund Cash with Trustee 100,000.00

Alternatively, the bond contract might call for the payment of equal annual installments to the trustee. These payments, accumulating at compound interest, would become an amount sufficient to retire the bond issue at maturity. Under these conditions the operation of the fund would be as follows:

At the end of the	The corporation will deposit	Interest earned by trustee on moneys deposited with him (Assume rate of 6%)	Amount of fund
1st year	$7,586.80		$ 7,586.80
2nd year	7,586.80	$ 455.21	15,628.81
3rd year	7,586.80	937.73	24,153.34
4th year	7,586.80	1,449.20	33,189.34
5th year	7,586.80	1,991.36	42,767.50
6th year	7,586.80	2,566.05	52,920.35
7th year	7,586.80	3,175.22	63,682.37
8th year	7,586.80	3,820.94	75,090.11
9th year	7,586.80	4,505.41	87,182.32
10th year	7,586.80	5,230.94	100,000.06

In actual practice, sinking fund provisions vary widely. The following sinking fund provisions, for example, illustrate this diversity:

INTERTYPE CORPORATION, 3¾% DEBENTURE BONDS, ISSUED JUNE 15, 1938, AND DUE JUNE 15, 1948

Sinking Fund: payable annually from May 1, 1944 to 1947, inclusive, of sufficient money to redeem at 100 and accrued interest to June 15 of such year, $200,000 principal amount of debentures. Moneys paid into sinking fund are to be applied to redemption of debentures on next succeeding June 15. Debentures may be called for sinking fund at par.

GREAT NORTHERN RAILWAY COMPANY, 3⅛% GENERAL MORTGAGE BONDS, SERIES N AND O, ISSUED JULY 1, 1945, AND DUE JANUARY 1, 1990 AND JANUARY 1, 2000

Sinking Fund: the Company will pay to the Trustee annually on July 1 of each year, commencing with the year 1947, for so long as any of the Series N or O bonds are outstanding in the hands of the public, the sum of $375,000, or the Company's net income (as defined by the accounting classifications of the Interstate Commerce Commission at the time in force) for the year ending on the preceding December 31, whichever is the lesser.

On the balance sheet a sinking fund should be shown as a noncurrent investment account. However, to the extent that sinking fund securities are bonds of the depositing corporation to be retired by the sinking fund, the sinking fund is a deduction from bonds payable. It is not good accounting to consider as an asset a corporation's ownership of its own securities.

Sinking Fund Reserves. — An indenture, besides requiring a corporation to establish a sinking fund, may oftentimes stipulate that a sinking fund reserve shall be established as well. The purpose of such a provision is to prevent an unnecessary depletion of the working capital of a corporation. For example, if a corporation which is required to make a yearly cash payment to the trustee of its sinking fund follows the policy of paying out all, or nearly all, its profits in cash dividends, the ultimate consequence may well be an impairment of cash and working capital, to the detriment of the company's operations, and to the detriment of the bondholders from two standpoints: (1) inability of the company to continue the required sinking fund deposits, and (2) impairment of the worth of their investments in the company's bonds.

This possibility is guarded against by compelling the corporation to retain in the business profits equal to the amount of the sinking fund. Each year it must make the following entry:

```
Surplus . . . . . . . . . . . . . . . . . . . . . . . .   10,000.00
     Reserve for Sinking Fund . . . . . . . . . . . .              10,000.00
To record yearly appropriation of surplus per agreement
with trustee.
```

At the end of each year, therefore, the balance in the Reserve for Sinking Fund account is equal to the balance in the Sinking Fund account.

At maturity, after the bonds have been paid, the sinking fund reserve is no longer needed or required; hence the profits which have been reserved are transferred back to free surplus, thus:

Reserve for Sinking Fund. 100,000.00
    Surplus. 100,000.00
To record transfer of sinking fund reserve to unap-
propriated surplus, the bonds having been paid off.

While a bond contract may call for a sinking fund and a sinking fund reserve it may, on the other hand, call only for a reserve without accompanying fund. The reserve would receive some such title as Reserve for Bonds Payable, and credits would be made to the account as specified in the bond contract. These annual credits to the reserve would be offset by debits to Earned Surplus (although some bond contracts specify Profit and Loss).

Obviously provisions like these increase the security of bonds and increase their attractiveness to the investor.

TREASURY BONDS

Treasury bonds are those which have been issued and later reacquired by the issuing corporation. Since bonds payable may be originally sold below par with no liability attaching to purchasers for the discount, there is no need for a corporation to distinguish between reacquired bonds and treasury bonds on its books.

When a corporation comes into possession of its own bonds of issue, and the bonds are canceled, the debit is to Bonds Payable for the par value of the bonds. If the reacquired bonds are not canceled, the debit is to the Treasury Bonds account. A separate account with Treasury Bonds is generally maintained for statistical reasons. Debits and credits to the Treasury Bond account should always be made for the par value of the bonds involved.

When treasury bonds are acquired in advance of their maturity date, their book value should be cleared from the accounts. The accounting for the purchase of treasury bonds may be summarized in the following manner:

DEBIT   the Treasury Bonds account for the par value of the bonds acquired.

DEBIT   the Bond Interest Payable account for the accrued interest, if any, on the bonds acquired.

DEBIT   the Bond Premium account for the unamortized bond premium applicable to the bonds acquired. For example, if 10% of the outstanding bonds payable are acquired as treasury bonds, then 10% of the balance of the Bond Premium account should be written off.

CREDIT   the Bond Discount account for the unamortized bond discount applicable to the bonds acquired. For example, if 10% of the outstanding bonds payable are acquired as treasury bonds, then 10% of the balance of the Bond Discount account should be written off.

CREDIT   Cash for the amount of cash disbursed.

DEBIT   Loss on Purchase of Treasury Bonds.

(or)

CREDIT   Gain on Purchase of Treasury Bonds, for the loss or gain incurred on the acquisition of treasury bonds. The figure for loss or gain is the difference between the credit to Cash and the consolidated net debit to the first four accounts named in this summary.

Bonds on the Balance Sheet. — When a corporation comes into ownership of its own bonds payable and these bonds are canceled, it is obvious that the liability of the corporation is reduced by an amount equal to the par value of the bonds canceled. On the balance sheet, therefore, it is sufficient that the liability for bonds payable be shown at the figure which represents the corporation's net liability to the outside world; mention of the amount of bonds canceled is not necessary.

Bonds which are not canceled should be shown as a separate item on the balance sheet. Since these bonds result, temporarily at least, in a reduction of bond indebtedness, they should be deducted from the Bonds Payable account, thus:

Bonds Payable:
Authorized $1,000,000.00
Less Treasury Bonds 150,000.00 $850,000.00

In this presentation unissued bonds may be included as treasury bonds.

It is important that treasury bonds available for sale be separately presented on the balance sheet. It would be unsatisfactory to show all bonds in the balance sheet as merely "Bonds Payable . . . $850,000.00" because to do so would conceal the fact that another $150,000.00 of bonds can be issued by the corporation. This is information of essential import to bondholder and stockholder alike.

BONDS RECEIVABLE

Short-Term Investments. — Bonds which are purchased for temporary investment are easily accounted for. They are recorded on the books at full purchase cost (including commissions, tax, etc.). When sold, the cost of the bonds sold should be cleared from the

Bond account with the gain or loss on sale credited to Bond Gain, or Bond Loss, account, as the case may be.

Long-Term Bond Investments. — The accounting for bonds purchased for permanent investment is more complex. The balance of this chapter will be devoted to this phase of bond ownership.

The Bonds Are Purchased at Par. — Assume that on January 1, 1950, an investor purchased $10,000.00 par value Arthur & Company 5½% bonds of 1960 at a price of 100.

Bonds	10,000.00	
Cash		10,000.00

To record purchase of $10,000.00 Arthur & Company 5½% bonds of 1960 at par.[2]

The Bonds Are Purchased at Less than Par. — Assume that the above bonds had been purchased at a price of 80. The entry would be at cost:

Bonds	8,000.00	
Cash		8,000.00

To record purchase of $10,000.00 Arthur & Company 5½% bonds of 1960 at 80.

By way of introduction to the entries which are made subsequent to purchase, the student should understand that when the bonds mature January 1, 1960, the investor will have received the following total income on his investment:

10 years' interest at $550.00 per year	$5,500.00
Difference between purchase price and price received for bonds at maturity ($10,000.00 — 8,000.00).	2,000.00
Total return on capital invested, i.e., interest earned	$7,500.00

Consequently, the average interest return per year is

$$5\tfrac{1}{2}\% \text{ on } \$10,000.00 = \$550.00$$
$$\tfrac{1}{10} \text{ of } \$2,000.00 = \ \ 200.00$$
$$\overline{\hspace{2cm}}$$
$$\$750.00$$

In order, therefore, to credit each period with its correct bond interest income, the following entries should be made each year:

---

[2] If the bonds had been purchased between interest dates, accrued interest would have been purchased as well. For instance, if the bonds had been purchased February 1, 1950, at 100, the entry would have been

Bonds	10,000.00	
Interest Income	45.83	
Cash		10,045.83

To record purchase of $10,000.00 Arthur & Company 5½% bonds of 1960 at 100, and accrued interest.

```
July  1  Cash . . . . . . . . . . . . . . . . . . . . . .   275.00
              Interest Income . . . . . . . . . . . . .              275.00
           To record receipt of semiannual interest on Arthur
           & Company 5½% bonds of 1960.


Dec. 31  Accrued Interest Receivable . . . . . . . . . .   275.00
              Interest Income . . . . . . . . . . . . .              275.00
           To record 6 months' accrual of interest on Arthur
           & Company 5½% bonds of 1960.


Dec. 31  Bonds. . . . . . . . . . . . . . . . . . . . . .   200.00
              Interest Income . . . . . . . . . . . . .              200.00
           To amortize ⅒ of bond discount.
```

It follows, therefore, that the book value of the bonds at the end of each year will be

December 31

1950	$ 8,200.00
1951	8,400.00
1952	8,600.00
1953	8,800.00
1954	9,000.00
1955	9,200.00
1956	9,400.00
1957	9,600.00
1958	9,800.00
1959	10,000.00

On January 1, 1960, when the bonds are redeemed, the entry will be simply

```
Cash . . . . . . . . . . . . . . . . . . . . . . . .   10,275.00
     Interest Income . . . . . . . . . . . . . . . .              275.00
     Bonds . . . . . . . . . . . . . . . . . . . . .           10,000.00
To record redemption of Arthur & Company 5½%
bonds due today, and interest.
```

The Bonds Are Purchased at More than Par. — If the Arthur & Company bonds had been purchased at 104, the entry on January 1, 1950, would have been

```
Bonds . . . . . . . . . . . . . . . . . . . . . . .   10,400.00
     Cash . . . . . . . . . . . . . . . . . . . . .            10,400.00
To record purchase of $10,000.00 Arthur & Company
5½% bonds of 1960 at 104.
```

In order to credit each period with its correct bond interest income which, on an annual basis, is

```
          5½% on $10,000.00 . . . . . . . . . . .   $550.00
          Less ⅒ of $400.00 . . . . . . . . . . .     40.00
                                                    _____
                                                    $510.00
```

the following entries should be made each year:

```
July  1  Cash . . . . . . . . . . . . . . . . . . . . . . . . .    275.00
             Interest Income . . . . . . . . . . . . . .                    275.00
             To record receipt of semiannual interest on Arthur
             & Company 5½% bonds of 1960.

Dec. 31  Accrued Interest Receivable . . . . . . . . . .    275.00
             Interest Income . . . . . . . . . . . . . .                    275.00
             To record 6 months' accrual of interest on Arthur
             & Company 5½% bonds of 1960.

Dec. 31  Interest Income . . . . . . . . . . . . . . . .    40.00
             Bonds. . . . . . . . . . . . . . . . . . . . . .                40.00
             To amortize ⅒ of bond premium.
```

The book value of the bonds at the end of each year will be

December 31

1950	$10,360.00
1951	10,320.00
1952	10,280.00
1953	10,240.00
1954	10,200.00
1955	10,160.00
1956	10,120.00
1957	10,080.00
1958	10,040.00
1959	10,000.00

When the bonds are redeemed January 1, 1960, the entry will be

```
Cash . . . . . . . . . . . . . . . . . . . . . . . . . . .    10,275.00
    Interest Income . . . . . . . . . . . . . . . . . . .                    275.00
    Bonds . . . . . . . . . . . . . . . . . . . . . . . .                10,000.00
    To record redemption of Arthur & Company 5½%
bonds due today, and interest.
```

QUESTIONS

Question **29-1.** Essentially, how does a bond differ from a share of stock?

Question **29-2.** From an accounting standpoint, is the indenture agreement of a bond issue important? Explain.

Question **29-3.** Some accountants use the following entry to record a newly authorized bond issue:

```
Unissued Bonds . . . . . . . . . . . . . . . . . . . . . .    xxx xx
    Bonds Payable . . . . . . . . . . . . . . . . . . . .                xxx xx
```

Do you approve? Why?

Question **29-4.** If it is decided to carry Bond Discount and Expense as a deferred charge on the balance sheet, should it be combined with the other deferred charges to form a single balance sheet item? Explain.

Question **29–5.** Would it be proper to consolidate the Bond Premium account with the Capital Surplus account, and to pay dividends therefrom?

Question **29–6.** What is the purpose of a sinking fund? a sinking fund reserve? What kind of accounts are sinking fund and sinking fund reserve accounts — asset, liability, or net worth accounts? How does a sinking fund operate?

Question **29–7.** Would you approve an item on the balance sheet which read "Cash . . . . $104,000.00" when $60,000.00 of this amount represents cash on deposit with the sinking fund trustee?

Question **29–8.** When bonds payable have been redeemed, explain what disposition should be made of the reserve for sinking fund account.

Question **29–9.** How is income earned by the trustee to be recognized on the books of the corporation which issued the bonds? When and why should this income be recognized?

Question **29–10.** Define treasury bonds. Is it permissible to show treasury bonds as an asset on the balance sheet?

Question **29–11.** When bonds are reacquired by the issuing corporation, what considerations must be borne in mind in constructing the entries to record such acquisition?

Question **29–12.** "When the issuing corporation acquires some of its own bonds as a temporary investment of working capital, the accounting (as of the date of acquisition) should be simply

Bonds Payable in Treasury (at par)	xxx xx	
Interest Expense (for accrued interest to date)	xx xx	
Cash		xxx xx

Any difference between par and the purchase price of the reacquired bonds should be debited or credited to Surplus. If the bonds are purchased below par it is probably better that the discount be credited to a special surplus account named Contingent Surplus Arising through Purchase of Our Bonds Payable below Par."

Do you agree with the foregoing accounting recommendation? Why?

Question **29–13.** To what extent should bonds payable be described and detailed in the balance sheet? Explain.

PROBLEMS

Problem **29–1.** On January 1, 1950, the L. C. Barrett Corporation sold $1,000,000.00 of its 10-year 6 % debenture bonds at a price of 100. Interest was payable January 1 and July 1.

Required:

(1) Make the entry to record the sale of the bonds.

(2) If the bonds, dated January 1, 1950, had been actually sold on January 10, 1950, what should be the entry of sale?

(3) If the bonds had been sold on January 1, 1950, at a price of 96, what should be the entry of sale?

Problem 29-2. On January 7, 1950, the Denny-Sanford Corporation sold a 10-year 6% bond issue of $1,000,000.00 at a price of 96. The bonds were dated January 1, 1950; interest was payable January 1 and July 1. The bonds were callable at 100 on and after January 1, 1955.

On January 1, 1955, the corporation redeemed the entire issue of bonds at the call price of 100.

Required:

(1) Make the entry to record the sale of the bonds.

(2) Make the entry to record the redemption of the bonds.

Problem 29-3. On June 3, 1950, the Krory Stores Corporation redeemed its 15-year 5% debenture bonds due May 1, 1958, in the par value of $10,000,000.00. The price paid was par plus a premium of 4%.

Required:

Make the entry to record the redemption of the bonds.

Problem 29-4. On January 1, 1950, the Baker-Hall Company sold an issue of $1,000,000.00 6% 10-year bonds, dated January 1, 1950, at a price of 97½. Interest was payable January 1 and July 1.

On January 1, 1952, the company purchased $100,000.00 of its own bonds in the open market at a price of 99.

The balance of the bonds, $900,000.00, was paid off on January 1, 1960.

Required:

(1) Make all entries required to be placed on the books up to and including January 1, 1952.

(2) Make the entry to record the redemption of the bonds.

Problem 29-5. On January 1, 1950, the Boles Iron Works issued $1,000,000.00 par value 6% bonds, dated January 1, 1950, and due January 1, 1960; interest was payable semiannually. Net proceeds on the sale of the bond issue amounted to $951,428.58.

Interest was paid regularly on the bonds, but no amortization of bond discount was placed on the books until March 31, 1953. On this date the company purchased $12,000.00 par value of its own bonds at a price of 96.

Required:

(1) What entry, or entries, should be placed on the books to bring the amortization of discount up to date?

(2) What entry should be made to record the purchase of the bonds?

Problem **29–6.** The Staley Electric Company, on January 1, 19__, sold $5,000,000.00 of its 6% 20-year debenture bonds, interest payable January 1 and July 1, realizing net cash of $4,638,957.00.

Required:

(1) Make the entry to record the sale of the bonds.

(2) Make the entries to record the first and fortieth interest payments.

(3) Make the entries to record the first and twentieth annual amortizations of bond discount.

(4) Record the payment of the bonds at maturity.

Problem **29–7.** The condensed balance sheet of the Farrine Hardware Company on December 31, 1950, was:

Land	$ 10,000.00	Common Stock, $100.00 par	$150,000.00
Building (new)	100,000.00	Surplus	50,000.00
Other Assets	90,000.00		
	$200,000.00		$200,000.00

In 1951 the company placed a mortgage of $40,000.00 on its real estate. The mortgage was dated January 1, 1951, was due in 20 years, and carried interest at the annual rate of 7%, interest payable January 1 and July 1. The mortgage bonds were actually sold as follows:

> $25,000.00 on January 1, 1951, at a price of 100
> $15,000.00 on April 1, 1951, for cash proceeds of $13,578.00, not including collection of accrued interest

On January 1, 1953, the company had more cash on hand than was needed for working capital requirements. The mortgage bonds, accordingly, were paid off in full at an average price of 99.

Required:

Present the balance sheet of the company on January 1, 1953, after giving effect to the payment of the bonds. Assume that the annual rate of depreciation on the building was 5%, that the consolidated net income for 1951 and 1952 was $25,000.00, and that no entries were made in the Surplus account other than to record periodic net income. Include cash with "Other Assets" on the balance sheet.

Problem **29–8.** On March 1, 1950, the Madison Building Corporation sold $1,000,000.00 of its 6% mortgage bonds at a price of 90. The bonds were dated January 1, 1950, and were due in 10 years. Interest on the bonds was payable January 1 and July 1. An annual cash deposit of $100,000.00 in the sinking fund and a sinking fund reserve of similar amount were requirements of the bond indenture.

Required:

Frame all entries which should be made on the books of the Madison Building Corporation in connection with the above bond issue up to, and including, December 31, 1951. For the purpose of this problem, the interest earned on the sinking fund investment may be disregarded.

Problem **29–9.** The Hale & Starret Company had the following condensed balance sheet on December 31, 1948:

Bond Discount	$ 465,237.00	Accounts Payable. . . .	$ 1,636,279.00
Other Assets	20,092,809.00	First Mortgage 6% Bonds	
		due December 31, 1958	6,000,000.00
		Common Stock	12,000,000.00
		Surplus	921,767.00
	$20,558,046.00		$20,558,046.00

On January 1, 1950, the company purchased $97,000.00 of its bonds at a cost of $920.00 each.

Required:

Frame the entry to record the purchase of the treasury bonds.

Problem **29–10.** On March 1, 1950, Mr. Raymond C. King purchased a 6 % $1,000.00 bond of the Detroit-Leland Corporation at a cost of $940.00. Interest on this bond was payable January 1 and July 1.

On June 1, 1950, Mr. King sold his bond at a price of $990.00.

Required:

Make the entries of March 1 and June 1, 1950.

Problem **29–11.** On January 31, 1950, Mr. Dale E. Harris purchased $10,000.00 par value Denny-Sanford Corporation bonds at a price of 97. (See Problem 29–2 for a description of these bonds.) Mr. Harris made his purchase with the intention of holding the bonds until their maturity.

On January 1, 1955, the corporation redeemed the entire issue of bonds at their call price of 100.

Required:

(1) Frame the entry to record the purchase of the bonds.

(2) Frame the entries to be made July 1, 1950, December 31, 1950, and January 1, 1955. Record amortization on basis of whole years only.

Problem **29–12.** On March 1, 1950, the First State Bank purchased as a long-term investment $10,000.00 par value Baker-Hall Company bonds at a price of 97½. (See Problem 29–4 for a further description of these bonds.)

On June 30, 1952, the bank decided to make a change in its investment portfolio. Accordingly, it sold the Baker-Hall bonds in the market at a price of 100.

Required:

Make all entries up to and including June 30, 1952.

Problem **29–13.** On August 1, 1950, Bond Investments, Incorporated, purchased $10,000.00 par value Scott Chemical Company convertible 5 % bonds at 74. These bonds were due April 1, 1958; interest was payable April 1 and October 1.

Required:

Assuming that these bonds were purchased for the purpose of short-term investment, show all entries up to, and including, December 31, 1950.

Problem 29-14. Assume that the bonds of Problem 29-13 were purchased as a long-term investment. Under these conditions, what entries should be made up to, and including, December 31, 1950?

Chapter 30

THE PROFIT AND LOSS STATEMENT

The profit and loss statement is one of the two principal statements of accounting. In essence, it is a well-organized report upon the events of an accounting period in so far as gains, costs, and losses are concerned. The difference between the totals for gains and for costs and losses is net income. For many years the profit and loss statement was looked upon as a statement whose importance was not as great as that of the balance sheet. Indeed, the profit and loss statement was simply a statement of supplementary importance.

In recent years, however, the profit and loss statement has replaced the balance sheet as "the dominant statement of accounting." Today, more than ever before, the interest of businessmen and investors centers increasingly upon the earnings of an enterprise and decreasingly upon the fixed, historical values of the balance sheet. Investors, for example, are more interested than ever before in the income aspects of their investments. They are interested not only from the standpoint of the direct yields which they receive in the form of interest and dividends but also because the current worth of their investments is largely determined by the earnings which underlie the securities they own. This interest is one which, succinctly stated, regards performance rather than periodic financial position as the primary test of the success of business enterprise. Balance sheets simply couple one performance period to another.

The primary function of the profit and loss statement is to report the amount of net income which has been earned by a business over an accounting period and to report, also, the elements which have entered into the earning of net income. In the preparation of a statement which fulfills this primary function, a thorough understanding of a correct definition of net income is a cardinal prerequisite.

The profit and loss statement explains the operating progress of a business from one balance sheet date to another. It portrays the income-earning ability of a business. And it constantly emphasizes the importance of controlling the elements which enter into the earning of income. Men must be controlled, funds must be controlled, and the test of business management is how well the results are controlled. It is through the profit and loss statement that appraisals of progress may be made and conclusions drawn. The profit and loss statement is an indispensable tool of management and of those to whom management is responsible.

To be thoroughly effective, the profit and loss statement and its complementary statement, the balance sheet, depend upon a well-organized system of accounts in the general ledger. The general ledger is the central and controlling record of an accounting system. In it finally come to rest all transactions, either in detail or in summary. A successful system of accounts, in turn, requires properly planned and executed business papers containing the basic information of all transactions, functional journals for the recording of this information, and satisfactory subsidiary records for the support of the accounts in the general ledger.

With emphasis having shifted from the balance sheet to the profit and loss statement, it is apparent that the responsibility of the accountant has been accentuated sharply. More than ever before it is his obligation to set forth the amount of net income on the profit and loss statement as accurately as expert ability will allow. The profit and loss statement must be adequately informative, it must be inclusive, and it must conform to the consistent usage of sound principles of accounting.

THE CONTENT AND ORGANIZATION OF THE PROFIT AND LOSS STATEMENT

An effective profit and loss statement should be organized so that major types of information stand clearly revealed. The amount of supplementary detail to be included depends primarily upon the purpose which the statement is to serve. Suffice it to say that enough information should be included to permit the analysis of an income statement to be worth while.

The principal divisions of a profit and loss statement, in the order of their presentation on the statement itself, are the following:

Net Sales
Cost of Sales
Gross Profit
Selling Expenses
General Expenses
Net Profit from Operations
Other Income
Other Expense
Special Income Credits (sometimes called Additions to Income)

Special Income Debits (sometimes called Deductions from Income)
Net Income before Income Taxes
Provision for Income Taxes
Net Income

The profit and loss statement may be prepared in full detail, as illustrated on page 540, or it may be condensed by having separate schedules to support each major type of information, thus:

Manchester Manufacturing Company

PROFIT AND LOSS STATEMENT

YEAR ENDING DECEMBER 31, 1950

Net Sales (after returns, and sales discounts)		$600,000.00
Cost of Sales (Schedule 1)		365,000.00
Gross Profit		$235,000.00
Selling Expenses (Schedule 2)	$107,500.00	
General Expenses (Schedule 3)	59,500.00	167,000.00
Net Profit from Operations		$ 68,000.00
Other Income (Schedule 4)		12,000.00
		$ 80,000.00
Provision for Income Taxes		20,000.00
Net Income		$ 60,000.00

SCHEDULE 1

Manchester Manufacturing Company

STATEMENT OF COST OF GOODS MANUFACTURED AND SOLD

YEAR ENDING DECEMBER 31, 1950

Finished Goods, January 1, 1950		$120,000.00
Cost of Goods Manufactured during 1950:		
Work in Process, January 1, 1950	$ 40,000.00	
Raw Materials Consumed	128,000.00	
Direct Labor	100,000.00	
Manufacturing Expenses	110,000.00	
	$378,000.00	
Work in Process, December 31, 1950	50,000.00	328,000.00
		$448,000.00
Finished Goods, December 31, 1950		85,000.00
		$363,000.00
Add Underabsorbed Manufacturing Expense		2,000.00
Cost of Sales		$365,000.00

SCHEDULE 2

Manchester Manufacturing Company

SELLING EXPENSES

YEAR ENDING DECEMBER 31, 1950

Advertising Expense	$ 15,000.00
Delivery Expense	14,000.00
Depreciation Expense — Delivery Equipment	7,500.00
Insurance Expense	1,000.00
Miscellaneous Selling Expense	10,000.00
Sales Salaries	40,000.00
Traveling Expense	20,000.00
Total	$107,500.00

SCHEDULE 3

Manchester Manufacturing Company

GENERAL EXPENSES

YEAR ENDING DECEMBER 31, 1950

Bad Debts	$ 3,500.00
Depreciation Expense — Office Equipment	6,000.00
General Salaries	35,000.00
Insurance Expense	200.00
Miscellaneous Expense	8,800.00
Office Supplies	6,000.00
Total	$59,500.00

SCHEDULE 4

Manchester Manufacturing Company

OTHER INCOME

YEAR ENDING DECEMBER 31, 1950

Dividend Income	$ 7,000.00
Interest Income	5,000.00
	$12,000.00

Percentage analysis, if desired, may be made a part of the profit and loss statement. Each item of the statement is expressed as a per cent of net sales, which is taken as 100%. This is illustrated in the comparative profit and loss statement on page 634. In addition each expense group may be analyzed in the following manner:

SCHEDULE 2

Manchester Manufacturing Company

SELLING EXPENSES

YEAR ENDING DECEMBER 31, 1950

	Amount	Per cent of Selling Expense	Per cent of Sales
Advertising Expense	$ 15,000.00	13.95%	2.50%
Delivery Expense	14,000.00	13.02	2.33
Depreciation Expense — Delivery Equipment .	7,500.00	6.98	1.25
Insurance Expense	1,000.00	.93	0.17
Miscellaneous Selling Expense	10,000.00	9.30	1.67
Sales Salaries	40,000.00	37.21	6.67
Traveling Expense	20,000.00	18.61	3.33
	$107,500.00	100.00%	17.92%

In the statement of manufacturing, the cost of goods manufactured is taken as 100% when manufacturing costs are made the subject of percentage analysis.

For control purposes in connection with interim statements, a very useful type of percentage analysis compares the percentages of a current month with the percentages which represent cumulative figures of the year to date.

Some of the definite responsibilities of the profit and loss statement are

(1) To have a proper heading:
Name of Firm
Statement of Profit and Loss
Period Covered ————

(2) To show the true net income of a period from regular operations.

(3) To make known the profitability of:
Products
Departments
Divisions
Branches
Companies, and so on
as far as it is practicable to do so.

This information may be presented by means of multicolumn statements or by a single summary statement supported by subsidiary schedules.

(4) To group expenses by responsible authority. Some concerns

attempt a further analysis by dividing each expense group into two parts, one part representing controllable expenses, the other noncontrollable expenses. This is a commendable type of analysis, but its value is limited by the fact that serviceable lines of demarcation between fixed and variable expenses cannot always be established.

(5) To charge each kind of income with all costs, direct and indirect, which apply to it.

(6) To exhibit uniformity as to
    (a) Layout, which, in turn, should be logical.
    (b) Terminology. The meaning of each term should be clear.
    (c) The content of each section and sectional subdivision.
    (d) The period covered. This is important for comparative purposes.

THE PROFIT AND LOSS STATEMENT AND SURPLUS STATEMENT COMBINED

To obtain a full review of the transactions of an accounting period, two statements are necessary:

(1) The profit and loss statement, which is a report upon the amount of net income earned by a business over an accounting period. This income is the net income which remains after the consolidation of *all* of the gains and losses of a period.

(2) The surplus statement, which is a report upon the changes in net worth as represented by the surplus account. These changes include changes which are not explained by the statement of profit and loss.

These two statements are very often combined into one single statement of income-and-earned surplus. After the net income of a period has been set forth, the statement is concluded by a section containing a complete reconciliation of earned surplus.

A condensed consolidated statement of profit and loss, and surplus, for the Manchester Manufacturing Company for the year 1950 would be as follows:

Manchester Manufacturing Company

CONSOLIDATED STATEMENT OF PROFIT AND LOSS AND EARNED SURPLUS,
YEAR ENDING DECEMBER 31, 1950

Net Sales (after returns, and sales discounts)	$600,000.00
Cost of Sales	365,000.00
Gross Profit	$235,000.00

Selling Expenses	$107,500.00	
General Expenses	59,500.00	167,000.00
Net Profit from Operations		$ 68,000.00
Other Income		12,000.00
		$ 80,000.00
Other Expenses		xxx xx
		$ 80,000.00
Special Income Credits:		
Gain on Securities Sold		10,000.00
		$ 90,000.00
Special Income Debits:		
Additional Income Tax — Prior Years		3,000.00
Net Income before Income Taxes		$ 87,000.00
Provision for Income Taxes		20,000.00
Net Income		$ 67,000.00
Surplus, January 1, 1950		217,000.00
		$284,000.00
Less Cash dividends declared during 1950		80,000.00
Surplus, December 31, 1950		$204,000.00

This statement constitutes a full explanation of the change in net worth, as measured by the account with Earned Surplus, from January 1, 1950, to December 31, 1950.

Although the consolidated statement of profit-and-loss-and-surplus was prepared in condensed form, the statement might have been presented so as to include a full measure of detail. This detail could be shown directly on the comprehensive statement of income or it could be presented in the form of supporting schedules as illustrated on page 626.

Where extraneous gains and losses, including adjustments of profits of prior periods, are included in a current comprehensive statement of profit and loss, it is of the utmost importance to distinguish between

> Net profit from operations, and
> Net income.

This distinction is necessary in order to distinguish clearly between income from operations and that which is the result of all transactions.

The present trend in both the theory and the practice of accounting is toward the objective of making income accounts and income statements *fully inclusive*. Under this philosophy *all* of the gains, costs, and losses of a period are placed in the current account with

Profit and Loss and in the current statement of profit and loss. Thus *net income* is understandably set forth as that net income which remains after all nominal elements have been taken into account. This concept of net income is logical and tenable; it is the businessman's understanding of net income; and it harmonizes, also, with the following more formal definition of net income:

The amount of net income earned by a business over a given period of time is the excess of net worth at the end of the period over the net worth at the beginning of the period excluding, however, any increases in realized net worth which have occurred during the period because of investments or donations of capital; and making allowance, further, for any distributions of earned or invested capital.

Net income in the accounts of a corporation is the change in earned surplus for an accounting period, after proper allowances are made for dividends.

Under this philosophy of net income, the only entries which would be made in the Earned Surplus account would be those for:

The net income of a period.
The net loss of a period.
Dividends declared out of earnings.
Transfers to or from earned surplus reserves.

FORM OF THE PROFIT AND LOSS STATEMENT

Throughout this book the pattern of the profit and loss statement has followed one standard design. This is the pattern preponderantly favored by both educators and practicing accountants. It is fair to ask, however, if the form of the profit and loss statement has reached its peak development and, if it has not, to ask what opportunities exist for improvement. In this connection the 1942 statement of income of the United States Steel Corporation is of interest:

Sales and Revenues:

Sales and revenues	$1,861,940,280
Interest, dividends and other	4,011,412
Total	$1,865,951,692

Costs:

Employment costs:	
Wages and salaries	$ 725,750,899
Social security taxes	24,245,901
Payments for pensions	32,664,901
	$ 782,661,701
Purchased products and services	648,401,343
Depletion and depreciation	91,765,371
Amortization of emergency facilities	31,962,146

Loss on sales of fixed assets	4,434,013
Special war costs	25,000,000
Interest and other costs on long-term debt	6,153,392
State, local and miscellaneous taxes	48,255,157
Estimated Federal taxes on income	155,500,000
Total	$1,794,133,123
Income.	$ 71,818,569

The 1942 income statements of General Motors Corporation, the Standard Oil Company of New Jersey, and the United Aircraft Corporation, among others, were constructed in a manner similar to the statement of the United States Steel Corporation.

Is the income statement of the United States Steel Corporation an improvement? Some accountants strongly support this type of statement. They favor it on the grounds that all incomes and costs stand on the same level, i.e., they attach to the enterprise as a whole. Irrespective of individual reactions and attitudes, the statements of the United States Steel Corporation and other companies suggest strongly that profit and loss statements in their conventional form very often leave something to be desired. These new statements of income may be characterized as being evolutionary and exploratory in nature. Without question they are examples of the pressures which exist for the improvement of financial statements. This pressure was further illustrated by the income statements of the United States Steel Corporation for 1943 and 1944:

	1944	*1943*
Products and Services Sold	$2,082,186,895	$1,972,344,751
Costs:		
Employment Costs:		
Wages and salaries	$ 902,162,021	$ 853,266,896
Social Security taxes	21,995,708	26,012,577
Payments for pensions	33,074,986	33,650,490
	$ 957,232,715	$ 912,929,963
Products and Services Bought	792,901,582	706,763,355
Wear and Exhaustion of Facilities:		
Depletion and depreciation	$ 81,083,380	$ 85,163,300
Amortization of emergency facilities	56,765,012	43,652,882
Loss on sales of plant and equipment	1,149,183	5,192,125
	$ 138,997,575	$ 134,008,307
War Costs Included Above Applicable to and Provided for in Prior Years	(3,517,648)	(1,123,261)
Estimated Additional Costs Applicable to This Period Arising Out of War	25,000,000	25,000,000
Interest and Other Costs on Long-Term Debt. . .	4,979,675	6,251,462

State, Local, and Miscellaneous Taxes	40,801,715	41,566,379
Estimated Federal Taxes on Income	65,000,000	84,316,804
Total	$2,021,395,614	$1,909,713,009
Income	$ 60,791,281	$ 62,631,742

For the layman the profit and loss statement is frequently made more informative by the abandonment of conventional accounting terms and the substitution of such titles as

> This Is What We Took In
> This Is What We Expended
> This Is What We Had Left

and so on.

In this book the discussion of new forms of the profit and loss statement must be limited to remarks of an introductory nature. The prime purpose of this section is to suggest the wisdom of an open mind for student, educator, and practicing accountant in constructing and appraising the form of the profit and loss statement. In the intelligent use of the income statements of today, it is eminently proper to regard them as steppingstones for the better statements of tomorrow.

COMPARATIVE PROFIT AND LOSS STATEMENTS

Comparative profit and loss statements are especially useful for purposes of financial analysis. Trends and changes are revealed. The following is a simple two-year comparison:

Manchester Manufacturing Company

COMPARATIVE PROFIT AND LOSS STATEMENT

FOR THE YEARS ENDING DECEMBER 31, 1950, AND 1949

	1950	%	1949	%	+ Increase − Decrease
Gross Sales	$625,000.00	104.17	$588,000.00	105.00	+ $37,000.00
Less Returned Sales, etc.	25,000.00	4.17	28,000.00	5.00	− 3,000.00
Net Sales	$600,000.00	100.00	$560,000.00	100.00	+ $40,000.00
Cost of Sales	365,000.00	60.83	353,000.00	63.04	+ 12,000.00
Gross Profit	$235,000.00	39.17	$207,000.00	36.96	+ $28,000.00
Selling Expenses:					
Advertising Expense	$ 15,000.00	2.50	$ 9,000.00	1.61	+ $ 6,000.00
Delivery Expense	14,000.00	2.33	11,000.00	1.96	+ 3,000.00
Depreciation — Delivery Equipment	7,500.00	1.25	7,500.00	1.34	
Insurance	1,000.00	.17	1,000.00	.18	
Miscellaneous	10,000.00	1.67	10,000.00	1.79	
Sales Salaries	40,000.00	6.67	39,000.00	6.96	+ 1,000.00
Traveling Expense	20,000.00	3.33	22,000.00	3.93	− 2,000.00
Total Selling Expense	$107,500.00	17.92	$ 99,500.00	17.77	+ $ 8,000.00
General Expenses:					
Bad Debts Expense	$ 3,500.00	.58	$ 6,800.00	1.21	− $ 3,300.00
Depreciation — Office Equipment	6,000.00	1.00	6,000.00	1.07	
General Salaries	35,000.00	5.84	33,000.00	5.89	+ 2,000.00
Insurance	200.00	.03	200.00	.04	
Miscellaneous Expense	8,800.00	1.47	8,000.00	1.43	+ 800.00
Office Supplies	6,000.00	1.00	5,000.00	.89	+ 1,000.00
Total General Expense	$ 59,500.00	9.92	$ 59,000.00	10.53	+ $ 500.00
Total Operating Expenses	$167,000.00	27.84	$158,500.00	28.30	+ $ 8,500.00
Net Profit from Operations	$ 68,000.00	11.33	$ 48,500.00	8.66	+ $19,500.00
Other Income:					
Dividend Income	$ 7,000.00	1.17			+ $ 7,000.00
Interest Income	5,000.00	.83	$ 5,000.00	.89	
Total Other Income	$ 12,000.00	2.00	$ 5,000.00	.89	+ $ 7,000.00
Net Income before Income Taxes	$ 80,000.00	13.33	$ 53,500.00	9.55	+ $26,500.00
Provision for Income Taxes	20,000.00	3.33	10,000.00	1.78	+ 10,000.00
Net Income	$ 60,000.00	10.00	$ 43,500.00	7.77	+ $16,600.00

Analysis of these statements reveals that 1950 was a better year than 1949. For instance:

Net sales increased from . . . . $560,000.00 to $600,000.00
    an increase of . . . . $ 40,000.00 or 7.14%.

Gross profits increased from . . . . $207,000.00 to $235,000.00
    an increase of . . . . $ 28,000.00 or 13.53%.
    This increase is more than the percentage increase in
    sales. This is due to an increase in the rate of gross
    profit from . . . .   36.96% to 39.17%.

Selling expenses increased from	$ 99,500.00 to $107,500.00	
an increase of	$ 8,000.00 or 8.04%.	
Related to sales, however, the increase is nominal . . .	17.77% to 17.92%.	
General expenses increased from.	$ 59,000.00 to $59,500.00	
an increase of	$ 500.00 or 0.85%.	
Related to sales, however, they decreased from	10.53% to 9.92%.	
Net profit from operations increased from	$ 48,500.00 to $68,000.00	
an increase of	$ 19,500.00 or 40.21%.	
Related to sales, an increase of [1]	8.66% to 11.33%.	
Although income taxes increased from	$ 10,000.00 to $20,000.00	
an increase of	$ 10,000.00 or 100%.	
Net income after income taxes increased from	$ 43,500.00 to $60,000.00	
an increase of	$ 16,500.00 or 37.93%.	
Related to sales net income increased from	7.77% to 10.00%.	

Analyses which apply to the operations of several years reveal favorable or unfavorable tendencies. The receivership into which the Paramount-Publix Corporation was placed in 1933 came as no surprise to those who had observed the steady rise in fixed charges of the corporation over the period 1929–1932. In 1932 interest charges were approximately 40% of total receipts as compared with a former ratio of about 20%.

Many companies furnish comparative statements for two or more years. The 1936 annual report of the American Sugar Refining Company went so far as to present comparative profit and loss statements for the years 1911 to 1936, and also balance sheets as of the end of each year. In a similar manner the 1940 annual report of the Caterpillar Tractor Company included comparative statements for the years 1926 to 1940. The 1944 annual report of the Monsanto Chemical Company included comparative financial statements for the years 1935 to 1944. The 1944 annual report of the United States Steel Corporation included comparative condensed statements of income for the years 1902 to 1944.

Interim Reports. — To improve the comparability of interim financial statements, some companies use an accounting year of 13 months divided into 28 days each. Each month has 24 business days and 4 Sundays. Interim financial reports are prepared for each 28-day period. Among the companies which use the 13-month year are Best Foods, Inc., Corning Glass Works, Eastman Kodak Company, The Kroger Grocery & Baking Company, and Sears, Roebuck & Company.

A very useful kind of interim report is the profit and loss statement which gives in one column the figures for the current month and, in the second column, cumulative figures for the year to date.

---

[1] The difference between 100% and the per cent of net operating profit is the "operating ratio" of a company.

These cumulative statements are very useful to a business which is operating under a budget. The control of operations is made more intelligent by comparisons of actual figures with those of the budget.

Another very useful kind of interim report for comparative purposes is used by the Commonwealth & Southern Corporation. This company prepares monthly not only a profit and loss statement for the month but also a profit and loss statement for the twelve months ending with the current month. The current month is compared with last month and with the current month of one year ago. The current twelve-month cumulative statement is compared with the cumulative twelve-month statements for preceding months. By these several comparisons the corporation is kept constantly informed not only with respect to current changes but with respect to directional tendencies in secular trend as well.

ITEMS NOT EASILY CLASSIFIED

The proper placement of items on the statement of profit and loss is not always an easy matter. Some of these "doubtful" items are presented below, together with comment for their recommended classification.

Bad Debts. — Bad debts can arise only as the result of a credit business. Bad debt losses are costs of extending credit; therefore they are expenses of the credit department. Whether the credit department is to be classified as selling or as general administrative depends upon which of these two divisions of a business is charged with the responsibility of credit administration. As a general rule, bad debts are classified as a general expense.

Containers. — If a product is delivered to the purchaser in the container into which it was placed by the manufacturing process, the cost of the container is a manufacturing expense. Otherwise boxes, cartons, cases, containers, packages, and so on, are selling expenses.

Depreciation. — Depreciation expense on assets used by the factory should be classified as manufacturing expense; depreciation on assets used by the sales department should be classified as selling expense; and depreciation on assets used for general administrative purposes should be classified as general expense.

Freight In. — Freight paid on merchandise increases the cost of merchandise. It is an addition to cost of sales and to the cost value of merchandise inventory. If freight is paid on selling or general expense items, then the freight also is a selling or general expense. Freight paid on fixed assets is an addition to the cost of these assets.

Manufacturing companies often find it difficult to allocate freight in to purchases. This is especially likely to be the case when perpetual inventory records are kept. They often find it practical therefore to handle freight in as an item of manufacturing expense, or to handle it according to the principles embodied in the next paragraph.

Trading concerns sometimes handle freight on merchandise in the following manner:

(1) All payments for freight on merchandise are debited to an asset account called Merchandise Freight.

(2) At the end of the accounting period, an entry is made:

Cost of Sales . . . .   xxx xx
    Merchandise Freight . . . .   xxx xx
To debit Cost of Sales with freight applicable to merchandise
sold.

The amount transferred is computed by applying the ratio

$$\frac{\text{Transportation charges paid on beginning inventory and purchases}}{\text{Beginning inventory plus purchases}}$$

to the invoice cost of merchandise sold.

Freight Out. — Disbursements made for freight paid on sales should be classified as

(1) Deductions from sales if the selling price f.o.b. destination is more than the selling price f.o.b. shipping point.

(2) Selling expenses in all other cases.

Income Taxes. — Income taxes are levied on a calendar or fiscal year basis. They are not an *expense* of operations but, rather, a coerced appropriation of net income in favor of the state or federal government, the cash payment of the liability being obligatory. When the books are being closed at the end of the accounting year, income taxes should be recorded by an entry of the following type:

Provision for Income Taxes . . . .   xxx xx
    Income Taxes Payable . . . .   xxx xx
To record estimated liability for income taxes for year 19__.

On the profit and loss statement income taxes should be shown as follows:

Net Income before Income Taxes . . . . $xxx xx
Less Provision for Income Taxes . . . .   xxx xx

Net Income . . . . $xxx xx

Interest. — Interest is a payment for the use of capital. Because it is peculiarly financial in nature, accountants have generally allocated interest expense to the "other expense" group, and interest income to the "other income" group, of the statement of profit and loss.

Profits and Losses on Fixed Assets. — Profits or losses arising through the sale or retirement of fixed assets should be placed in the accounts "Gain on Retirement of Capital Assets" or "Loss on Retirement of Capital Assets." It is general accounting practice to close these two accounts to current Profit and Loss when

(1) Transactions involving fixed asset retirements are fairly common.

(2) The total net loss or net gain on the fixed asset retirements of a period are fairly uniform from period to period.

(3) And the amount of net loss or gain is small and of minor importance.

When transactions involving the sale or retirement of fixed assets have been infrequent, and the loss or gain has been significant, past accounting practice has favored the placement of these "extraordinary losses or gains" directly in the account with Earned Surplus. The present trend in accounting practice, however, is to carry *all* losses and gains arising out of the sale or retirement of fixed assets as special debits or credits to the comprehensive income account with current Profit and Loss. This practice is in harmony with modern accounting theory that the income account of a business should be fully inclusive.

Profits and Losses on Security Sales. — Profits realized by the sale of securities which have been classed as a part of the working capital of a business should be classified as other income on the statement of profit and loss. Losses, conversely, should be classified as other expense.

The problem of classification is not so clear with respect to profits which have been realized by the sale of securities not classified as current assets. Where the profits are concomitants of sales made more or less regularly from period to period, the sales would seem to constitute a miscellaneous, regular activity of business operation. In this kind of circumstance it would appear proper to regard security profits as other income, and to regard security losses as other expense.

On the other hand, changes in the investment portfolio of a business may be so infrequent as to preclude their classification as components of "regular business" operations. In such cases the profits and losses on security sales should be placed in separate accounts like Gain on Sales of Securities, or Loss on Sales of Securities. These two accounts would be handled as special income credits or debits on the comprehensive statement of profit and loss, and would be closed into the account with current Profit and Loss. If less modern accounting practice is to be followed, and such gains and losses are considered as direct credits and debits to surplus, these items should be transferred to the account with Earned Surplus.

Purchases Discounts. — Accountants have classified purchases discounts as

(1)　Direct deductions from purchases, or as
(2)　Other income.

From the standpoint of sound accounting principle, only the first of these classifications is correct. The considerations which are advanced in support of both classifications are set forth in the following section.

Sales Discounts. — Accounting practice has produced three classifications for sales discounts. These classifications are as follows:

(1)　Sales discounts are a deduction from sales. Argument in favor of this view is as follows:

The sale price of an article is normally established at that point where, after cash discounts have been provided for, enough revenue will remain to cover all costs and, in addition, yield a profit. The real selling price is the cash price — the amount which will settle the invoice. It would be illogical to state that merchandise is one price if paid for within ten days, but another price if paid for within sixty days. The cash price is fundamental. Anything over the cash price is a charge for the privilege of credit. Merchandise, alone, at the date of purchase, has but one price — the cash price. It follows, therefore, that the correct measure of net sales in the profit and loss statement is the yardstick of translation into cash.

In similar fashion, the measure of net purchases is the cash price for purchases, i.e., purchases less purchases discounts. That purchases discounts are reductions of the cost of merchandise should be especially apparent where Company A offers an article for sale at a price of $1,000.00 net, and Company B offers the same article at a price of $1,000.00, less 2 % cash discount. In this kind of case the purchase should unquestionably be made from Company B.

From the standpoint of accounting principle, the only correct handling of cash discounts is the deduction of sales discounts from sales, and the deduction of purchases discounts from purchases.

The two classifications of cash discounts given below are frequently met in practice. They rest, however, on relatively weak theoretical grounds.

(2) Sales discounts are other expense, and purchases discounts are other income. Argument in favor of this view of cash discounts is as follows:

(a) Cash discounts are attributes of capital. They are offered in order to increase the productivity of working capital. They are taken for the same reason. To the vendor, sales discounts not taken are gains of adequate capital — enough capital to finance credit sales. Purchases discounts not taken are, on the other hand, costs of not having enough capital. From all points of view, therefore, cash discounts are financial considerations.

Objection: If purchases discounts are nonoperating incomes it follows, in consequence, that income of this kind may be realized whenever a bill for merchandise is paid, less proper deduction for cash discount. This is to say that income may be earned not only by the sale of goods but also by their purchase. The truth, of course, is that income can be realized *only* by the *sale* of merchandise.

(b) Cash discounts are interest considerations. Through them the seller is enabled to obtain the use of cash capital much sooner than would otherwise be possible. Cash discounts are interest fees which compensate the seller for furnishing capital for 30, 60, 90 days, or whatever the period may be, to the purchaser.

Objection: This argument can be only partially true because a discount of 2 % taken at the end of 10 days, when the full credit term is 30 days, gives the seller his money 20 days earlier; 2 % for 20 days is interest at the rate of 36 % per year. Obviously, only that part of 36 % which is equal to the current interest rate on money can be considered as interest for capital advanced to the buyer.

(3) As an operating expense. Argument in favor of this view is as follows:

Cash discounts are inducements to pay promptly. They are offered in order to minimize bad debt losses and the expenses of credit administration (investigation, supervision, collection, etc.).

Customers are expected to take their cash discounts; those who do not are singled out for special attention by the credit management. This is especially the case when all invoices are payable, less discount, by the tenth of the month following date of invoice — a practice which, by the way, is widely used.

Cash discounts are therefore direct instrumentalities of the credit division of a business. Discounts taken by customers are expenses of the credit department. In turn, if the credit department is a part of the sales department, cash discounts are selling expenses; otherwise, they are general administrative expenses.

SALES TAXES

In many states a sales tax is levied on retail sales. The collection is made by the retailer who, in turn, remits periodically to the State Treasurer.

Since his role is that of a tax collector, the retailer should not allow his collections of sales taxes to be credited to income accounts nor his remittances of sales taxes to be debited to expense accounts. Sales taxes should be accounted for as follows:

Cash (or) Accounts Receivable	10,200.00	
Sales		10,000.00
Liability for Sales Tax		200.00

To record sales of $10,000.00, and liability for 2% sales tax.

If, for any given period, the amount paid to the State Treasurer is the amount of sales tax collections, the disbursement will be recorded simply:

Liability for Sales Tax	xxx xx	
Cash		xxx xx

To record remittance of sales tax collections to State Treasurer.

If the amount to be remitted to the State Treasurer is a certain percentage of net sales, the check will differ from the amount of sales tax actually collected from customers. This will be the case because of such reasons as no tax on small sales, no tax on nonmerchandise sales, failure to collect some sales taxes, and possible varying rates of sales tax on individual retail sales. For any given period any difference between the amount of sales tax remitted to the State Treasurer and the amount of sales tax collections is an item of expense or gain to the retail merchant.

An alternative "businessman's" method of accounting for sales taxes is that of crediting Sales with the total of sales and sales taxes. At the end of the accounting period, Sales is debited and Liability for Sales Tax credited for the amount required to be remitted to the State Treasurer. Discrepancies between collections and payments are absorbed in the Sales account.

SOCIAL SECURITY TAXES

Social security taxes are (1) old-age benefit taxes and (2) unemployment compensation taxes. They are calculated on the wages and salaries *actually paid* during an accounting period.

Federal old-age benefit taxes apply to the first $3,000.00 of the wages and salaries of each employee engaged in a nonexempt industry. The rates prescribed in the original Federal Insurance Contributions Act are 2% for the years 1944 and 1945, 2½% for the years 1946, 1947, and 1948, and 3% thereafter. These rates are assessed against the payroll base; and the amount so determined is an assessment against both the employer and the employee. The tax levied upon employees must be withheld from the wages paid. The tax withheld plus his own tax must be paid by the employer to his local collector of internal revenue in the month following the close of a calendar quarter. (The prescribed rates of tax may be changed by Congress. In 1944 and 1945, for example, Congress enacted special legislation to the effect that the rate for each of these years should be 1% and not 2%.)

Unemployment compensation taxes of 3%, payable each January 31 for the preceding calendar year, are assessed against employers of eight or more individuals. It is a tax applicable to the first $3,000.00 paid to an employee. The liability for federal tax may be reduced by a credit equal to the amount of unemployment compensation taxes paid to a state up to 90% of the gross amount of federal tax. Thus, in effect, the rate of federal tax becomes 0.3% of the payroll base, and the state tax, 2.7%.

To illustrate the basic accounting involved, assume that social security taxes are to be recorded for the month of December, 1944, on a payroll of $25,000.00, of which $20,000.00 is taxable. Federal taxes will be calculated at the rates prescribed in the original Federal Insurance Contributions Act. The state unemployment compensation tax is 2.7% on employers and 2% on employees. The journal entry would be as follows:

```
Wages Expense..........................   25,000.00
Federal Social Security Taxes ..............     460.00
     2% × $20,000.00 = $400.00
     .3% × $20,000.00 =   60.00
State Unemployment Compensation Taxes.........     540.00
     2.7% × $20,000.00 = $540.00
          Federal Social Security Taxes Payable .....            860.00
               4% × $20,000.00 = $800.00
               .3% × $20,000.00 =   60.00
          State Unemployment Compensation Taxes Payable          940.00
               2.7% × $20,000.00 = $540.00
               2% × $20,000.00 =   400.00
          Wages Payable .....................       24,200.00
To record December payroll and social security taxes.

Wages Payable ............................   24,200.00
     Cash .................................            24,200.00
To record payment of payroll.
```

On the profit and loss statement social security taxes should receive the same accounting classification as the wages and salaries to which they apply. A tax on direct labor would be an increase in the direct cost of that labor; a tax on indirect labor would be a manufacturing expense; a tax on wages and salaries of the sales department would be a selling expense; and a tax on wages and salaries of the general office would be a general expense.

While this theory of classification is sound, some accountants feel that satisfactory results are attainable by the simple alternative of classifying all social security taxes into two kinds of overhead expense. Under this alternative, social security taxes applicable to the factory would be a manufacturing expense, and those applicable to nonfactory operations would be a general administrative expense.

Miscellaneous. — Circumstances sometimes alter the placement of an expense. For instance, traveling expenses of salesmen are selling expenses, whereas traveling expenses of company auditors are general administrative expenses, and traveling expenses of the purchasing agent are purchasing department expenses (if this classification of expense is maintained).

Still other expenses are distributable to two or more expense groups. In such cases the expenses should be apportioned to the groups upon a basis deemed to be equitable. As an example of expense apportionment consider personal property taxes; these should be allocated to manufacturing, selling, and general administrative, according to the ratios of personal property valuations within each hf these divisions of the business. It is clear that the apportionment of an expense must be reasonably accurate or it will not be worth while.

CLASSIFICATION OF ACCOUNTS

The preparation and organization of financial statements, and the assembly of detail incident thereto, may be greatly expedited by proper organization of the accounts of a business. Naturally, one of the important requisites of any accounting system is that the accounts should provide all necessary detail. Correlative to this requisite is the necessity that, in the recording of this detail, each account stand for a definite purpose and have accounting treatment from period to period consistent with the purpose of the account when first established.

Where the accounts of a business are relatively few in number, they are sometimes arranged alphabetically. Statements can be quickly prepared from the trial balance of an alphabetical ledger by insertion of account balances in a previously prepared form of statement which may be printed or typed. If printed forms are not used, pro forma (i.e., outline) statements may be quickly made up by using the statements of earlier periods as master models.

Where many accounts are required, however, some other arrangement of the ledger is desirable. Usually the accounts are arranged so that the order of real accounts in the ledger is parallel to the order of items on the balance sheet; and the order of nominal accounts is parallel to the order in which nominal accounts appear in the statement of profit and loss. When the accounts of a ledger are arranged in this manner it is usual to number the accounts and to refer to the accounts by number rather than by name. In the ledger the accounts would be arrayed in numerical sequence. In this respect loose-leaf ledgers are of special convenience. With regard to the books of original entry, and vouchers, there is obvious convenience in referring to accounts by number rather than by name. An example of account classification and organization is afforded by the following illustration of a numerical system of accounts:

ASSETS: 1–99

    CURRENT ASSETS: 1–49

        1: Cash
        2: Petty Cash
        5: Notes Receivable
        6: Notes Receivable Discounted
        7: Accounts Receivable
        8: Reserve for Bad Debts
      10: Finished Goods
      20: Work in Process
      30: Raw Materials
      40: Accrued Income Receivable
      45: Prepaid Expenses

    INVESTMENTS: 50–59

      51: Bonds
      53: Common Stocks
      55: Mortgages
      57: Preferred Stock
      59: Real Estate

    FIXED ASSETS: 60–79

      61: Buildings
      62: Reserve for Depreciation of Buildings
      63: Delivery Equipment
      64: Reserve for Depreciation of Delivery Equipment
      65: Furniture and Fixtures
      66: Reserve for Depreciation of Furniture and Fixtures
      67: Jigs, Fixtures, Equipment
      68: Reserve for Depreciation of Jigs, Fixtures, Equipment

69: Land
71: Machinery
72: Reserve for Depreciation of Machinery
73: Office Machines
74: Reserve for Depreciation of Office Machines
75: Tools

INTANGIBLES: 80–89

81: Copyrights
83: Patterns
84: Patents
85: Trademarks
87: Goodwill

OTHER ASSETS: 90–99

95: Organization Expense

LIABILITIES: 100–199

CURRENT LIABILITIES: 100–159

100: Income Taxes Payable
105: Withholding Income Taxes Payable
110: Social Security Taxes Payable
120: Payroll
130: Accrued Expenses
135: Dividends Payable on Common Stock
140: Notes Payable
150: Vouchers Payable
155: Deferred Income

OTHER LIABILITIES: 160–179

FIXED LIABILITIES: 180–199

190: Bonds Payable
191: Bond Discount
192: Bond Premium

NET WORTH: 200–299

CAPITAL STOCK: 200–249

200: Capital Stock — Preferred
225: Capital Stock — Common

SURPLUS: 250–299

250: Capital Surplus
275: Earned Surplus

OPERATING INCOME: 300–399

     300: Sales
     325: Returned Sales and Allowances
     350: Cost of Sales

MANUFACTURING: 400–699

     425: Purchases
     450: Freight In
     475: Returned Purchases and Allowances
     501: Direct Labor
     600: Manufacturing Expense Control
          610: Depreciation Expense — Buildings
          611: Depreciation Expense — Jigs, Fixtures, Equipment
          612: Depreciation Expense — Machinery
          613: Depreciation Expense — Tools
          620: Factory Repairs
          630: Factory Salaries
          640: Factory Supplies
          650: Heat, Light, Power
          660: Indirect Labor
          670: Insurance
          680: Miscellaneous Factory Expense
          690: Taxes

SELLING EXPENSES: 700–799

     700: Selling Expense Control
          701: Advertising
          710: Commissions
          720: Delivery Expense
          730: Depreciation Expense — Delivery Equipment
          740: Freight Out
          750: Insurance
          760: Miscellaneous Selling Expense
          780: Sales Salaries
          790: Traveling Expense

GENERAL EXPENSES: 800–899

     800: General Expense Control
          801: Administrative Salaries
          810: Bad Debts Expense

820: Depreciation Expense — Furniture and Fixtures

821: Depreciation Expense — Office Machines

830: Insurance

840: Miscellaneous General Expense

850: Office Supplies

860: Postage

870: Stationery and Printing

880: Taxes

884: Telephone and Telegraph

OTHER INCOMES: 900–999

925: Interest Income

OTHER EXPENSES: 1000–1099

1025: Interest Expense

SPECIAL INCOME CREDITS: 1100–1199

SPECIAL INCOME DEBITS: 1200–1299

CLEARING AND SUMMARY ACCOUNTS: 1300–1399

1350: Manufacturing

1399: Profit and Loss

When the accounts of a ledger are arranged in the order in which they appear on the balance sheet and the profit and loss statement, it is obvious that the arrangement greatly facilitates preparation of the financial statements. In the chart of accounts illustrated above, certain account numbers in each group were not used; this was done in order to permit proper placement in the ledger of such new accounts as may be required to be opened in the future.

In the foregoing numerical account arrangement, manufacturing expenses were of the 600 series, selling expenses were of the 700 series, and general expenses were of the 800 series. Within each series the expense accounts were arranged both alphabetically and numerically.

For another illustration of a system of accounts see pages 765–768.

Where the accounts of a business are very numerous, the accounts may be arranged according to the principle illustrated in the following numerical arrangement:

600: Manufacturing Expense Control
      610: Depreciation Expense — Buildings
      611: Depreciation Expense — Jigs, Fixtures, Equipment
      612: Depreciation Expense — Machinery
      613: Depreciation Expense — Tools
      620: Factory Repairs
      630: Factory Salaries
      640: Factory Supplies
      650: Heat, Light, Power
      660: Indirect Labor
      670: Insurance
      680: Miscellaneous Factory Expense
      690: Taxes

700: Selling Expense Control
      714: Depreciation Expense — Delivery Equipment
      730: Sales Salaries
      731: Commissions
      765: Advertising
      770: Insurance
      780: Miscellaneous Selling Expense
      794: Delivery Expense
      795: Freight Out
      796: Traveling Expense

800: General Expense Control
      812: Depreciation Expense — Office Machines
      815: Depreciation Expense — Furniture and Fixtures
      825: Bad Debts Expense
      830: Administrative Salaries
      840: Office Supplies
      841: Postage
      842: Stationery and Printing
      870: Insurance
      880: Miscellaneous General Expense
      890: Taxes
      892: Telephone and Telegraph

In this numerical arrangement of the accounts, similar items have similar numbers, 630 representing Factory Salaries, 730 Sales Salaries, and 830 Administrative Salaries, the "30" of each number indicating salaries.

It is apparent even from this brief discussion of account classification that the accounts of a ledger may be arranged according to various plans. Whatever classification may be adopted in a particular case, the classification should at least have the twin objectives of minimizing the burden of bookkeeping labor as much as possible and also of providing correct data for the expeditious preparation of profit and loss statements and balance sheets. Professor Kester has summed up the problem of account classification by stating that "in general any classification of accounts is good which serves well its intended use."

QUESTIONS

Question **30–1.** What are some of the major functions of a profit and loss statement? Explain why these functions are important.

Question **30–2.** The United States Rubber Company has factories, branches, and five main sales divisions: (1) clothing, (2) footwear, (3) mechanical goods, (4) tires, (5) drug sundries. What major types of information would you expect to find on the company's profit and loss statement?

Question **30–3.** To what expense group would you allocate these items?

(1) Freight paid on returned sales.
(2) Freight paid on returned purchases.
(3) The cost of kegs in which nails are shipped.
(4) The returnable carboy in which sulphuric acid is shipped.
(5) Storage on goods kept in a public warehouse.
(6) Provision for uncollectible accounts.
(7) Cost of operating an electric sign.
(8) Wages of janitors and watchmen.
(9) Christmas gifts to purchasing agents.
(10) Merchandise purchased from X for $1,050.00 although the same identical merchandise could have been obtained from other sources for $1,000.00. The purchase was made from X because X is an excellent customer of the company.
(11) Cost of trip to legislature to protest against proposed sales tax.
(12) Federal income tax.
(13) Expenses for research purposes.
(14) Interest paid on funds borrowed to meet seasonal increase in inventory.

Question **30–4.** Explain how cash discounts may be handled in the profit and loss statement. State your preference and why.

Question **30–5.** Some firms allow their customers cash discounts provided bills are paid by the tenth of the month following date of invoice. What is your opinion of this kind of discount policy?

Question **30–6.** (1) Do you think that sales or purchases discounts not taken should be recognized on the books? Why? (2) What accounting would your recommend for discounts received on nonmerchandise bills?

Question **30–7.** Should telephone and telegraph expense be apportioned to more than one expense group? If so, how?

Question **30–8.** What principles should govern the establishment of a good system of accounts?

Question **30–9.** What information would you be interested in obtaining from an examination of several comparative profit and loss statements? What information, other than that given in the text, can you draw from the comparative profit and loss statement of the Manchester Manufacturing Company?

Question **30–10.** "The real profit of a company can only be known by converting all assets to cash and liquidating all liabilities." Discuss.

Question **30–11.** "A rise in value is not a profit." Is this true? Discuss.

Question **30–12.** (1) During 1931, 1932, and 1933, many large corporations purchased their own obligations in the open market at considerable discounts. Should these profits have been included in statements of profit and loss? Explain. (2) If a company sells securities from its own investment portfolio, should the gains or losses realized on such sales be included in the statement of profit and loss? If so, where should they be placed on the statement of profit and loss? If they are not to be included in the statement of profit and loss explain what disposition should be made of them and why.

PROBLEMS

Problem **30–1.** The condensed operating statements of The Royal Candy Company for the years 1950 and 1949 are as follows:

	1950	1949
Gross Sales	$240,000.00	$115,000.00
Less Returned Sales and Allowances	40,000.00	15,000.00
Net Sales	$200,000.00	$100,000.00
Cost of Sales	116,000.00	60,000.00
Gross Profit	$ 84,000.00	$ 40,000.00
Selling Expenses:		
Advertising	$ 10,000.00	$ 2,000.00
Commissions	6,000.00	3,000.00
Delivery Expense	4,000.00	2,500.00
Miscellaneous Selling Expense	4,000.00	1,500.00

Sales Salaries	12,000.00	8,000.00
Traveling Expense	5,000.00	3,000.00
Total Selling Expenses	$ 41,000.00	$ 20,000.00

General Administrative Expenses:

Administrative Salaries	$ 12,000.00	$ 9,000.00
Bad Debts	3,800.00	1,000.00
Depreciation	1,500.00	1,500.00
Miscellaneous General Expense	3,700.00	2,000.00
Office Supplies	3,000.00	1,600.00
Taxes	1,000.00	900.00
Total General Administrative Expenses . . .	$ 25,000.00	$ 16,000.00
Total Operating Expenses	$ 66,000.00	$ 36,000.00
Net Profit from Operations	$ 18,000.00	$ 4,000.00

What are your conclusions with respect to the operations of the two years?

Problem **30–2.** On December 31, 1950, Howard A. Teele prepared the following statements:

PROFIT AND LOSS STATEMENT

Sales		$43,656.00
Cost of Sales		24,061.00
Gross Profit		$19,595.00
Expenses:		
Advertising . .	$ 3,020.00	
Freight In . .	750.00	
General Expense	1,822.00	
General Salaries	12,001.00	
Insurance . . .	360.00	
Sales Taxes . .	642.00	18,595.00
Net Profit		$ 1,000.00

BALANCE SHEET

Cash	$ 5,201.00
Accounts Receivable	10,162.00
Merchandise	4,604.00
Fixtures and Equipment . .	2,000.00
5% Bonds	4,000.00
	$25,967.00
Accounts Payable	$ 5,420.00
Howard A. Teele, Capital . .	20,547.00
	$25,967.00

When examining these statements on March 1, 1951, you find that they did not include provision for the following items existing as of December 31, 1950:

(1) Unpaid advertising bill, $106.00.
(2) Prepaid insurance, $200.00.
(3) Office supplies inventory, $322.00.
(4) Unpaid salaries, $2,004.00.
(5) Depreciation expense for 1950 on fixtures and equipment, $200.00.
(6) Six months' accrued bond interest.
(7) Consumers' sales tax of 2 % has been included in the credit to Sales. Three fourths of the year's sales tax has been remitted to the State Treasurer; the remaining one fourth is due for payment not later than January 31, 1951.

(8) Unrecorded merchandise invoice, $80.00. This merchandise was not included in the new inventory.

Required:

(1) Prepare a corrected profit and loss statement for 1950, in good form.

(2) Prepare a corrected balance sheet, December 31, 1950, in good form.

(3) Frame the entry, or entries, to correct the books on March 1, 1951.

Problem **30-3.** From the information below, prepare the profit and loss statement of the Barr Manufacturing Company for the year ending December 31, 19___. Special care should be taken with respect to form and detail. Use a supporting schedule for the cost of goods manufactured and sold.

Advertising	$ 250,000.00
Building Repairs	11,000.00
Commissions Earned	7,000.00
Depreciation Expense:	
Factory Building	28,000.00
Machinery and Tools	44,000.00
Miscellaneous Equipment	101,000.00
Office Equipment	10,000.00
Salesmen's Cars	7,000.00
Direct Labor	3,000.00
Factory Superintendence	79,000.00
Factory Supplies (expense)	84,000.00
Finished Goods, January 1, 19___	164,000.00
Finished Goods, December 31, 19___	85,000.00
Freight Out	10,000.00
Gain on Capital Assets Sold	1,200.00
General Manufacturing Expense	173,000.00
General Miscellaneous Expense	200,000.00
General Office Salaries	500,000.00
Goods in Process, January 1, 19___	100,000.00
Goods in Process, December 31, 19___	123,000.00
Heat, Fuel, and Boiler Expense	36,000.00
Indirect Labor	126,000.00
Insurance on Factory Building	8,000.00
Insurance on Finished Goods	15,000.00
Insurance on Goods in Process	18,000.00
Insurance on Machinery and Equipment	21,000.00
Insurance on Office Equipment	1,200.00
Insurance on Raw Materials and Supplies	15,000.00
Insurance on Salesmen's Cars	10,000.00
Interest Expense	3,000.00
Interest Income	14,000.00
Light and Power	54,000.00
Machinery Repairs	25,000.00
Purchases	1,218,000.00
Purchases Discounts	12,000.00
Purchases Returns and Allowances	20,000.00
Raw Materials, January, 1 19___	24,000.00
Raw Materials, December 31, 19___	25,000.00
Rent Income	5,000.00
Sales	5,000,000.00

Sales Discounts	45,000.00
Sales Salaries	900,000.00
Taxes (factory)	189,000.00
Transportation In	55,000.00
Traveling Expense	150,000.00

Problem **30–4.** The books of J. C. Tresler were closed on December 31, 1949. One month later his trial balance was:

Cash	$ 413.36	
Accounts Receivable	371.45	
Merchandise	7,547.25	
Furniture and Fixtures	9,585.43	
Reserve for Depreciation — Furniture and Fixtures		$ 1,448.37
Inventory of Sales Supplies	300.00	
Accounts Payable		3,823.03
Notes Payable		5,500.00
Sales Tax Liability		47.03
J. C. Tresler, Capital		7,666.04
Sales		3,153.11
Purchases	2,494.42	
Purchases Discounts		25.64
Freight In	24.50	
Advertising	87.14	
Cash Short Expense	30.11	
General Expense	459.44	
Rent Expense	90.00	
Salaries and Wages	354.68	
Selling Expense	18.82	
Taxes Expense		127.61
Utilities Expense	14.23	
	$21,790.83	$21,790.83

On further examination you find the following information:

(1) The cash includes a bad check for $10.00.

(2) Fixed assets are estimated to depreciate at the annual rate of 8 %.

(3) The monthly rent bill is $135.00, payable in advance on the 20th of each month. On January 20, 1950, the bookkeeper debited the rent check to the General Expense account. On January 1, 1950, the amount of prepaid rent was $90.00; this prepayment is the balance which appears in the Rent Expense account of the trial balance.

(4) The notes payable of $5,500.00 carry 10 % running interest. One month's interest has accrued on these notes.

(5) The credit in the Sales Tax Liability account represents collection of sales tax from customers during January. You ascertain that Mr. Tresler's liability to the State Treasurer is 2 % sales tax on all sales. This sum is required to be paid in February.

(6) The credit balance in the Taxes Expense account represents the liability of Mr. Tresler on January 1, 1950, for

Personal property taxes for 1949	$118.64
Social security taxes for December, 1949 . .	8.97
	$127.61

On January 17, 1950, when these taxes were paid, the debit was made to General Expense.

(7) The liability of Mr. Tresler for social security and unemployment taxes for January is 4% of his payroll for the month.

(8) January bills for light, water, and gas are $80.53. You find that these bills were paid February 10.

(9) There is on hand an unpaid bill for wrapping paper, twine, etc. (chargeable to Selling Expense) for $8.28. These supplies were all used up in January.

(10) Inventories on hand January 31, 1950, are estimated at merchandise, $7,834.07, and sales supplies, $250.00.

Required:

(1) Prepare a profit and loss statement for the month of January, 1950.
(2) Prepare a balance sheet, January 31, 1950.

Problem **30–5.** Following is the trial balance of the Pendleton Manufacturing Company on December 31, 19—:

Accounts Receivable	$ 28,000.00	
Accrued Payroll		$ 3,360.00
Advertising	6,000.00	
Automobiles	12,000.00	
Cash	40,000.00	
Common Stock, $100.00 par		100,000.00
Depreciation Expense — Automobiles (factory). .	900.00	
Depreciation Expense — Automobiles (selling) . .	2,100.00	
Depreciation Expense — Factory Building . . .	1,200.00	
Depreciation Expense — Machinery	4,000.00	
Depreciation Expense — Office Equipment. . . .	340.00	
Direct Labor	40,000.00	
Dividends Payable		5,000.00
Factory Building	60,000.00	
Factory Repairs	4,420.00	
Factory Supplies (expense)	2,200.00	
Finished Goods.	14,000.00	
Freight In	640.00	
Heat, Light, and Power	2,110.00	
Income Taxes Payable		7,000.00
Indirect Labor	17,000.00	
Insurance Expense (factory)	500.00	
Land	20,000.00	
Machinery	40,000.00	
Miscellaneous Factory Expense.	1,800.00	
Office Equipment	3,400.00	
Office Expense	1,200.00	
Office Salaries	12,800.00	
Prepaid Insurance	430.00	
Property Taxes (factory)	1,260.00	
Provision for Income Taxes	7,000.00	

Purchases (of raw materials)	61,500.00	
Purchases Discounts		2,400.00
Raw materials	15,200.00	
Reserve for Depreciation — Automobiles		7,000.00
Reserve for Depreciation — Factory Building . .		9,200.00
Reserve for Depreciation — Machinery		16,000.00
Reserve for Depreciation — Office Equipment . .		1,440.00
Returned Purchases and Allowances		1,500.00
Returned Sales and Allowances	1,200.00	
Sales		214,000.00
Sales Discounts	3,000.00	
Salesmen's Salaries	12,500.00	
Social Security Taxes	3,000.00	
Social Security Taxes Payable		2,400.00
Surplus (earned)		50,000.00
Traveling Expense	6,000.00	
Vouchers Payable		16,000.00
Withholding Income Taxes Payable		1,000.00
Work in Process	10,600.00	
	$436,300.00	$436,300.00

Required:

(1) Prepare a well-organized profit and loss statement for 1950. If desired, the cost of sales section of the profit and loss statement may be supported by a detailed schedule covering the cost of goods manufactured and sold. Social security taxes should be apportioned: 70% factory, 15% selling, and 15% general.

The new inventories on December 31, 1950, were raw materials, $6,600.00, goods in process, $8,000.00, and finished goods, $12,000.00.

(2) Prepare a balance sheet, December 31, 1950.

Problem **30–6.** Before allowance of 6% interest on loans, and 8% interest on partners' capitals, the condensed trial balance of A and B for the year ending December 31, 19—, was

Miscellaneous Assets	$203,000.00	
Revenues		$ 45,000.00
Expenses	42,000.00	
B — Loan Payable		50,000.00
A — Capital		100,000.00
B — Capital		50,000.00
	$245,000.00	$245,000.00

The firm had commenced business at the beginning of the year with $100,000.00 of capital from A; and $50,000.00 of capital, and a $50,000.00 loan, from B. Profits and losses were to be shared: A, 60%, B, 40%.

Although B had pledged $70,000.00 of capital, he actually invested only $50,000.00. It was mutually agreed that he was to be charged 10% interest on the amount of his deficiency of $20,000.00. This charge has not been placed on the books.

Required:

(1) Prepare a profit and loss statement for the year. Your statement should be carefully constructed and adequately detailed.

(2) Prepare a balance sheet, December 31, 19—. The only accounts of partners to be placed in the balance sheet are capital and loan accounts.

(3) Is the net income, or net loss, of your profit and loss statement one which has actually been *realized*? Explain why you do, or do not, think so.

Problem **30–7.** On December 31, 1950, the ledger of Robert L. Hardister, a merchant, showed Taxes Expense with a balance of $8,256.00, and Taxes Payable, $5,200.00. These accounts were detailed as follows:

TAXES EXPENSE

1950		
Mar. 15	Income tax for 1949	2,400.00
May 1	Property tax	3,156.00
Jan. to	Twelve sales tax re-	
Dec.	mittances to State	
	Treasurer	2,700.00

TAXES PAYABLE

1949		
Dec. 31	Estimated accrued property taxes for eight months . .	2,000.00
Dec. 31	Sales tax for December 1949	200.00
Dec. 31	Provision for 1949 income tax	3,000.00

The bookkeeper debited all disbursements for taxes of any kind to the Taxes Expense account. The disbursement on May 1, 1950, for $3,156.00 covered property taxes for the tax year, May 1, 1949, to April 30, 1950. On May 1, 1949, the payment for property taxes was $3,000.00. The tax bill for the year ending April 30, 1951, is estimated at $3,396.00

Sales taxes collected, or debited to accounts receivable, were credited to the Sales account as a matter of bookkeeping convenience. The total sales tax collected from or debited to customers in any given month was remitted by Mr. Hardister to the State Treasurer by the 20th of the next succeeding month. December, 1950, sales taxes of $225.00 were remitted to the State Treasurer on January 15, 1951. The offsetting debit for the credit of $200.00 in the Taxes Payable account was the Sales account.

Due to the fact that operations for 1950 had resulted in a small net loss, no income tax was expected to be payable for the year 1950.

Required:

(1) What should be the amount of Taxes Expense on the profit and loss statement of Mr. Hardister for the year 1950?

(2) What adjusting entries, if any, should be placed on the books?

Problem **30–8.** The partnership of Taylor & Webster commenced business on January 1, 19__. Six months later, June 30, 19__, the trial balance of their books was:

Cash	$ 68,901.00	
Notes Receivable	21,511.00	
Accounts Receivable	50,231.00	
Bonds (at cost).	42,114.00	
Merchandise	34,352.00	
Office Fixtures and Equipment	10,000.00	
Building	80,000.00	
Land	14,000 00	
Notes Payable		$ 25,000.00
Accounts Payable		66,204.00
Mortgage Payable		70,000.00
Thomas Taylor, Loan		25,000.00
Thomas Taylor, Capital		80,000.00
Thomas Taylor, Drawing	2,900.00	
W. C. Webster, Capital		50,000.00
W. C. Webster, Drawing	4,200.00	
Sales		228,856.00
Returned Sales	1,849.00	
Sales Discounts	2,979.00	
Purchases	133,810.00	
Purchases Discounts		3,517.00
Freight In	5,414.00	
Advertising	7,150.00	
General Expense	9,746.00	
Insurance Expense	1,960.00	
Salaries and Wages	43,520.00	
Selling Expense	9,633.00	
Supplies	5,540.00	
Taxes	1,200.00	
Interest Earned		5,850.00
Interest Expense	3,417.00	
	$554,427.00	$554,427.00

Additional Information

(1) The accounts receivable are considered to be fully collectible.

(2) The balance of the Advertising account includes $150.00, a cash deposit on an advertising contract applicable to the next six months' period.

(3) The Bonds account represents a short-term investment in $42,-000.00 par value 5% American Telephone & Telegraph Company's Debenture Bonds due 1960, interest payable January 1 and July 1.

(4) Annual depreciation rates have been fixed at office fixtures and equipment, 10%, building, 2½%.

(5) The balance of the Insurance Expense account represents
    (a) A three-year fire insurance policy on buildings, effective January 1 of the current year; premium, $1,356.00.

    (b) A one-year fire insurance policy on personal property, effective April 1 of the current period; premium, $604.00.

(6) Six months' interest on the mortgage at the annual rate of 5% is due and payable July 1.

(7) The Notes Payable account represents a nine-month note with interest at the annual rate of 8%, and dated January 1 of the current year. One quarterly payment of interest was made on this note on April 1.

(8) Notes receivable consist of the following three notes:

Dated	Amount	Term	Interest
February 1	$ 6,000.00	6 months	6%
May 1	4,728.00	90 days	6%
June 15	10,783.00	60 days	6%

(9) One of the purchase invoices for merchandise bought on account and recorded on the books on June 29 was incorrectly priced. The correct amount of the invoice is $710.00 instead of $920.00. The merchandise represented by this invoice has been included in the new inventory at $920.00.

(10) The inventory of merchandise on hand June 30 is $58,520.00.

(11) There are accrued salaries and wages of $1,480.00, payable in July.

(12) There are supplies on hand of $640.00.

(13) The balance of $1,200.00 in the Taxes account is applicable to the current calendar year.

(14) Partners are authorized to draw $300.00 per month. Excess withdrawals, as of June 30 and December 31, are subject to a flat penalty of 10%.

(15) Both partners agreed originally to capital investments of $80,-000.00 each. Any capital deficiency, it was further agreed, should be assessed six months' interest at the annual rate of 8%, assessment to be applied against capital deficiencies existing on June 30 and December 31 of each calendar year.

Required:

    (1) Prepare a twelve-column work sheet.

    (2) Prepare a profit and loss statement for the half-year to date.

    (3) Prepare a balance sheet, June 30, 19__.

Problem 30–9. The trial balance of the Buck Manufacturing Company on December 31, 1950, was as follows:

Cash	$ 100,775.00	
Notes Receivable	120,000.00	
Notes Receivable Discounted		$ 100,000.00
Accounts Receivable	250,000.00	
Reserve for Bad Debts		10,000.00
Finished Goods	90,000.00	
Work in Process	78,000.00	
Raw Materials	116,000.00	
Bonds (cost, as of January 1, 1950)	70,000.00	
Buildings	240,000.00	
Reserve for Depreciation — Buildings		20,000.00

Delivery Equipment.	36,000.00	
Reserve for Depreciation — Delivery Equipment		13,000.00
Furniture, Fixtures and Equipment	24,000.00	
Reserve for Depreciation — Furniture, Fixtures, and Equipment		7,000.00
Jigs, Fixtures, and Factory Equipment	80,000.00	
Reserve for Depreciation — Jigs, Fixtures, and Factory Equipment		20,000.00
Land	42,000.00	
Machinery	460,000.00	
Reserve for Depreciation — Machinery		160,000.00
Tools	52,000.00	
Notes Payable		25,000.00
Social Security Taxes Payable		15,875.00
Vouchers Payable		112,000.00
Common Stock, $100.00 par		840,000.00
Treasury Stock	40,000.00	
Surplus		228,000.00
Dividends Paid	36,000.00	
Sales		2,200,000.00
Returned Sales and Allowances	20,000.00	
Sales Discounts	25,000.00	
Purchases	1,000,000.00	
Returned Purchases and Allowances		20,000.00
Purchases Discounts.		45,600.00
Freight In	15,000.00	
Direct Labor	288,000.00	
Factory Insurance	11,000.00	
Factory Repairs	6,000.00	
Factory Supplies	30,000.00	
Heat, Light, and Power	90,000.00	
Indirect Labor	76,000.00	
Miscellaneous Factory Expense	50,000.00	
Property Taxes (factory).	8,000.00	
Social Security Taxes (factory)	17,400.00	
Advertising	20,000.00	
Delivery Equipment Expense	40,000.00	
Sales Salaries and Commissions	57,600.00	
Traveling Expense	50,000.00	
Warehouse Expense	12,000.00	
General Salaries	144,000.00	
Insurance Expense (nonfactory)	1,500.00	
Miscellaneous General Expense	4,000.00	
Office Supplies Expense	8,000.00	
Postage	800.00	
Property Taxes (nonfactory)	1,000.00	
Social Security Taxes (nonfactory)	9,700.00	
Telephone and Telegraph	1,200.00	
Interest Income.		6,500.00
Interest Expense	2,000.00	
	$3,822,975.00	**$3,822,975.00**

Supplementary Information

Accruals:
Interest earned on notes receivable		$ 100.00
Interest unpaid on notes payable		250.00

Accrued payroll December 31, 1950:

Direct labor	$12,000.00	
Indirect labor	4,000.00	
Sales salaries	2,400.00	
General salaries	6,000.00	24,400.00

From this accrued payroll there was required to be withheld from employees' pay checks $225.00 for social security taxes, and $5,000.00 for income taxes. The Buck Manufacturing Company was liable for an additional $900.00 of social security taxes on this payroll ($600.00 factory, $300.00 nonfactory).

Bad debts were estimated at 1% of net sales.

Annual depreciation rates:

Building	5%	Jigs, fixtures, and factory equipment		20%
Delivery equipment	33⅓%	Machinery		10%
Furniture, fixtures, and equipment	10%	Tools		25%

Inventories, December 31, 1950:

Raw materials	$120,000.00
Work in process	60,000.00
Finished goods	100,000.00

Prepaid expenses:

Unexpired factory insurance premiums	$ 1,000.00
Inventory of factory supplies.	1,250.00

Miscellaneous:

The expense for heat, light, and power should be distributed 90% to factory, and 10% to general administrative expense.

The delivery equipment is used for both factory and sales purposes, 40% and 60%, respectively.

Nonfactory insurance expense and property taxes should be distributed 80% to selling and 20% to general administrative. Nonfactory social security taxes should be prorated 30% to selling and 70% to general administrative.

Warehouse expense should be allocated 50% to factory and 50% to selling.

The account receivable of F. W. Conway is uncollectible, $1,000.00.

The Bond account represents a long-term investment in $100,000.00 par value Valadium Corporation 5% bonds, due January 1, 1958. Interest on these bonds is payable January 1 and July 1.

Estimated liability for commissions to salesmen who have exceeded their sales quotas for the year is $20,000.00 (no deduction for social security taxes).

A cash dividend of 1½% was declared December 20, 1950, payable January 10, 1951, to stock of record December 31, 1950.

The company's liability for income taxes was estimated at $50,000.00.

Required:

(1) Prepare a work sheet, incorporating columns for adjustments, manufacturing, cost of sales, selling expenses, general expenses, profit and loss, and balance sheet.

(2) Prepare a profit and loss statement for 1950, supported by schedules for

> Cost of goods manufactured and sold
> Manufacturing expenses
> Selling expenses
> General expenses

(3) Prepare a balance sheet, December 31, 1950.

(4) Prepare a statement of surplus for the year 1950.

Chapter 31

THE BALANCE SHEET

The profit and loss statement is a statement which reports and explains the income of a business over a period of time. The balance sheet, on the other hand, is a statement of financial condition as of a specific date. The balance sheet incorporates, and significantly so, the results of past transactions; it is a statement of financial condition produced by the operations of a period. It incorporates the profit and loss statement as all, or part of, the explanation of the increase or decrease in net worth.

In summary we may say that the balance sheet marks the end of a period of performance. It shows the effectiveness of this period of performance in terms of the financial results achieved: assets and equities are marshaled as to amount and kind and for appraisal of their relationships to each other.

THE CONTENT AND ORGANIZATION OF THE BALANCE SHEET

The balance sheet is a statement of the assets and equities of a business. If these items are properly arranged, as they should be, the balance sheet will emphasize certain major types of information. Detail may be added, in greater or lesser degree, either by inclusion in the statement itself, or by means of supplementary schedules. The amount of detail to be included, and the manner of presenting it, is dependent upon the purpose of the balance sheet. For instance,

For the management: a master balance sheet supported by detailed schedules for purposes of operating control.

For credit purposes: a statement detailed as to current assets and current liabilities but probably condensed in other respects.

For stockholders and potential stockholders, and for bondholders and potential bondholders: a statement with sufficient detail to permit adequate appraisal of proprietary and bond equities.

For long-term financing: a statement giving significant detail as to long-time values, i.e., fixed assets.

For public purposes, such as filing with the Secretary of the State of Massachusetts: a condensed statement.

661

Whatever the purpose of the balance sheet, detail commensurate with that purpose should always be presented.

The principal divisions of the balance sheet, in order of their presentation on the statement itself, are the following:

Assets	*Liabilities and Net Worth*
Current Assets	Current Liabilities
Long-Term Investments	Other Liabilities
Fixed Assets	Long-Term Liabilities
Intangibles	Net Worth

The ability of a company to pay its debts is of universal interest. The above order of items on the balance sheet is arranged to conform to that interest. Cash is first, with other assets following in the order of their convertibility into cash. On the liability side, the obligations which must be paid first are listed first, and those which are payable later are listed in the order of their probable liquidation.

This "current-to-fixed" order for balance sheet items is widely used. Sometimes the reverse order is employed but this is not common. The order of arrangement, in any case, should be logical and in harmony with the purpose of the balance sheet. The "current-to-fixed" order is usually to be preferred because, in the words of R. H. Montgomery, "as long as the auditor has no practicable method of restricting the ultimate use of the balance sheet which he submits, he is forced to assume that in every case the balance sheet may be submitted to credit grantors." [1] This is an assumption which has general application.

Some of the definite responsibilities of the balance sheet are

(1) A proper heading:

> Name of Firm
> Balance Sheet
> Date

(2) The inclusion of all assets, liabilities, and proprietary claims. These should be presented in the way which best explains financial condition. There should also be included information such as, for example, lawsuits, contingent liabilities, valuation bases, maturity dates of fixed liabilities, etc. Information of this kind may be presented in the form of footnotes to the balance sheet, or as memoranda in the body of the balance sheet proper.

(3) Adequate detail [2] and orderly presentation. Assets and lia-

---

[1] *Auditing Theory and Practice*, The Ronald Press, 5th ed., p. 79.

[2] The published balance sheet of the United States Trust Company of New York for December 31, 1932, showed assets of $98,663,846.17. Of this total, stock and bond investments constituted $27,696,555.00. This latter figure was completely itemized. Similar detail attended the balance sheets, December 31, 1945, of the Tri-Continental Corporation, and of The Lehman Corporation.

bilities should be logically arranged and grouped and a total shown for each group. Relationships should be clearly apparent. On the liability side of the balance sheet grand totals should be shown for liability and proprietary items.

(4) Correct valuations. The basis of valuation, if other than cost, should be stated.

(5) Uniformity as to
  (a) Layout
  (b) Terminology
  (c) The content matter of each account and section
  (d) Date when it is desired to make comparisons over several periods. It is preferable to compare a December 31 balance sheet with another December 31 balance sheet, etc.

ITEMS NOT EASILY CLASSIFIED[3]

Accounts with Officers and Employees. — Because of the special character of these debts, accounts with officers and employees should appear as a separate item on the balance sheet. They may be included in the current asset group if payable within one year.

Cash in Closed Banks. — Cash in closed banks should not be placed in the current asset group. Realization is usually partial and long delayed. It would be better to class this asset as a deferred accounts receivable.

Cash in Sinking Fund. — If sinking fund cash is subject to the control of the depositing company, it is a current asset. If it is not subject to the control of the company, it should follow the current asset group as a separate item.

Credit Balances in Customers' Accounts. — Credit balances in customers' accounts are subject to payment in cash and should be shown on the balance sheet as current liabilities.

Debit Balances in Creditors' Accounts. — Debit balances in creditors' accounts are current assets because they are subject to current collection in cash.

Deferred Expenses. — In its broad concept, deferred expenses are those expenditures not entirely chargeable as expenses of the operations of a current period, the unconsumed portions of which will be written off to the expense accounts of future periods. In this sense even depreciable fixed assets are deferred expenses.

---

[3] In this connection two articles by Anson Herrick will be found both readable and stimulating: "What Should Be Included in Current Assets?" *Journal of Accountancy*, January, 1932; and "Current Assets and Liabilities," *Journal of Accountancy*, November, 1933.

In its narrow concept, deferred expenses are divisible into (1) prepaid expenses and (2) deferred charges. Prepaid expenses are assets; they are inventories of expense commodities or services receivable. Deferred charges are expenditures which will be written off against the revenues of two or more operating periods on a more or less *arbitrary* basis. Examples of deferred charges are experimental costs, rearrangement of factory layout, and the like.

The balance sheet should clearly distinguish between prepaid expenses and deferred charges. With respect to their classification, prepaid expenses should be classed as current assets if these expenses represent advance applications of cash — disbursements which would otherwise have to be made in the next accounting period. True prepaid expenses are as much a part of the working capital cycle as inventories.

Deferred charges, if any, should be shown as a final grouping on the asset side of the balance sheet. As a matter of fact, deferred charges (narrowly defined) are not assets at all. However, they are sometimes admitted to the balance sheet on grounds no better than the questionable one of expediency.

Deferred Incomes. — As a matter of custom, deferred incomes are commonly shown on the balance sheet as a separate class of liability. However, deferred incomes are properly includible with the current liabilities of a balance sheet. There is no doubt that unearned income which, to become earned income, will require the use of current assets is a current liability. Unfilled subscriptions to *The Saturday Evening Post* are an example of deferred income which is properly classified as a current liability by The Curtis Publishing Company. Unredeemed tickets for transportation are another example of deferred income which is an undisputed current liability.

It is also proper for deferred incomes, which require only the passage of time to become earned income, to be classed as a current liability. Rent collected in advance is an example. This liability will be liquidated by the process of making available for tenant occupancy the premises specified in the contract of rental. Such availability involves consumption of current assets for purposes of insurance, taxes, and other costs of ownership. Deferred rent income is an obvious component of working capital.

Deferred interest income is a current liability only if it represents interest collected in advance. Otherwise, deferred interest income on notes receivable is a valuation account and should be deducted from notes receivable on the balance sheet. Where large values are involved, as for banks, finance and insurance companies, this is preferred accounting. Where small values are involved, the theory also applies; however, if the values are not of significant proportion, tolerance is warranted if the notes receivable of a business are shown as a current asset and the nominal amount of deferred interest income is shown as a current liability.

Investments. — Investments in securities are current assets or investments. (See Stocks and Bonds, below.) Investments in real estate and other nonliquid assets should not be combined with stock and bond investments but should be shown as a separate group labeled "nonliquid investments" to precede the fixed asset group of the balance sheet.

Sinking Fund Bonds. — A contractual sinking fund under the control of a trustee is an asset to the depositing corporation. On the balance sheet this asset should follow the current asset group as a separate classification.

If, however, the trustee has used all, or part of, the fund to acquire bonds of the issue for which he is trustee, the bonds so acquired should be shown as an offset to the liability represented by the Bonds Payable account. The practical effect of the trustee's acquisition is to reduce the corporation's indebtedness to the outside world.

Stocks and Bonds. — If bonds mature within one yeas, or if securities are intended to be sold within one year, the bonds and stocks should be classified as current assets. On the other hand, if it is not probable that the securities, in the normal course of business, will be converted into cash within one year, they should be classified as investments. In other words, unless the nature of an investment and the purpose of the investment are such as to indicate its early conversion into cash, the investment should *not* be classified as a current asset. It is important that stock and bond investments be correctly classified on the balance sheet for the reason that an incorrect classification will result in an incorrect presentation of working capital.

On the balance sheet stock and bond *investments* should follow the current assets and, where circumstances demand, they should be subdivided into liquid and nonliquid investments.

Miscellaneous. — Other balance sheet items often incorrectly classified are: bond premium and discount; depreciation, depletion, and other valuation reserves; organization expense; stock premium and discount; treasury stock and bonds. The balance sheet aspects of these items have been discussed in earlier chapters of this text.

Circumstances are material to problems of balance sheet classification. For instance, real estate employed in a manufacturing business is a fixed asset, whereas for a concern whose major activity is the purchase and sale of real estate, the latter will represent stock in trade. An automobile is a fixed asset for most concerns; yet to automobile dealers, automobiles represent merchandise inventory and should be shown as properly labeled current assets. It follows, therefore, that proper interpretation is a necessary prerequisite to the proper classification of an item on the balance sheet.

COMPARATIVE BALANCE SHEETS

Balance sheet analysis, like profit and loss statement analysis, is often productive of significant information, and especially so if several consecutive balance sheets are compared. The following example is a two-year comparative balance sheet of the Manchester Manufacturing Company:

Manchester Manufacturing Company

COMPARATIVE BALANCE SHEETS FOR DECEMBER 31, 1950 AND 1949

Assets

	1950	%	1949	%	+ Increase − Decrease
Current Assets:					
Cash	$ 102,000.00	7.82	$ 60,000.00	4.67	+ $ 42,000.00
Accounts Receivable	100,000.00	7.67	130,000.00	10.12	− 30,000.00
Finished Goods	85,000.00	6.52	120,000.00	9.35	− 35,000.00
Work in Process	50,000.00	3.83	40,000.00	3.12	+ 10,000.00
Raw Materials	15,000.00	1.15	20,000.00	1.56	− 5,000.00
Total Current Assets	$ 352,000.00	26.99	$ 370,000.00	28.82	− $ 18,000.00
Investments:					
Government Bonds			$ 100,000.00	7.78	− $100,000.00
Corporate Stocks and Bonds . .	$ 200,000.00	15.34			+ 200,000.00
Total Investments	$ 200,000.00	15.34	$ 100,000.00	7.78	+ $100,000.00
Fixed Assets:					
Buildings	$ 300,000.00		$ 300,000.00		
Reserve for Depreciation . .	37,500.00		30,000.00		
	$ 262,500.00	20.13	$ 270,000.00	21.03	− $ 7,500.00
Delivery Equipment	$ 30,000.00		$ 30,000.00		
Reserve for Depreciation . .	17,500.00		10,000.00		
	$ 12,500.00	.96	$ 20,000.00	1.56	− 7,500.00
Factory Equipment	$ 510,000.00		$ 500,000.00		
Reserve for Depreciation . .	171,000.00		120,000.00		
	$ 339,000.00	26.00	$ 380,000.00	29.59	− 41,000.00
Office Equipment	$ 60,000.00		$ 60,000.00		
Reserve for Depreciation . .	22,000.00		16,000.00		
	$ 38,000.00	2.91	$ 44,000.00	3.43	− 6,000.00
Land	$ 100,000.00	7.67	$ 100,000.00	7.79	
Total Fixed Assets	$ 752,000.00	57.67	$ 814,000.00	63.40	− $ 62,000.00
Total Assets	$1,304,000.00	100.00	$1,284,000.00	100.00	+ $ 20,000.00

Liabilities and Net Worth

	1950	%	1949	%	+ Increase − Decrease
Current Liabilities:					
Vouchers Payable	$ 80,000.00	6.14	$ 147,000.00	11.45	− $ 67,000.00
Income Taxes Payable	20,000.00	1.53	10 000.00	.78	+ 10,000.00
Dividends Payable			10,000.00	.78	− 10,000.00
Total Current Liabilities. .	$ 100,000.00	7.67	$ 167,000.00	13.01	− $ 67,000.00
Net Worth:					
Common Stock, $100.00 par . . .	$1,000,000.00	76.69	$ 900,000.00	70.09	+ $100,000.00
Surplus	204,000.00	15.64	217,000.00	16.90	− 13,000.00
Total Net Worth	$1,204,000.00	92.33	$1,117,000.00	86.99	+ $ 87,000.00
Total Liabilities and Net Worth .	$1,304,000.00	100.00	$1,284,000.00	100.00	+ $ 20,000.00

In addition to the analysis above, each balance sheet group may be further analyzed, thus:

	1950	%	1949	%
Current Assets:				
Cash	$102,000.00	28.98	$ 60,000.00	16.22
Accounts Receivable	100,000.00	28.41	130,000.00	35.13
Finished Goods	85,000.00	24.15	120,000.00	32.44
Work in Process	50,000.00	14.20	40,000.00	10.81
Raw Materials	15,000.00	4.26	20,000.00	5.40
Total Current Assets	$352,000.00	100.00	$370,000.00	100.00

RATIOS

The comparative balance sheet of the Manchester Manufacturing Company permits certain obvious comparisons of 1950 percentages with those of 1949. In addition to these comparisons, there are certain others which are important enough to warrant special attention. Some of these use balance sheet data only, and some use data from both the balance sheet and the profit and loss statement. Some of the more common of these other comparisons are discussed and illustrated below. The figures which are used are taken from the financial statements of the Manchester Manufacturing Company.

CURRENT RATIO

This ratio occupies high rank as a test of current condition. Credit analysts usually feel that a company should have $2 of current assets for each $1 of current liabilities. A 2 to 1 ratio, however, should not be considered an inflexible standard. This is because a satisfactory current ratio for one company may not be a satisfactory current ratio for another. A 2 to 1 ratio for a company in the restaurant business would generally indicate excellent condition, whereas a 2 to 1 ratio for a piano manufacturer would ordinarily indicate poor current financial condition. A satisfactory current ratio in the piano industry would be about 5 to 1. This high ratio in the piano industry is required because of the large amount of capital invested in noncash current assets, especially inventories, and because it takes so long to convert inventories into cash.

The standard for a current ratio is therefore dependent upon the rapidity with which noncash current assets are converted into cash. If the turnover (conversion) is slow, the standard for the current ratio is high; if the turnover is high, the standard is low.

The current ratio is computed as follows:

$$\frac{\text{Current assets}}{\text{Current liabilities}} = \begin{cases} 1949 = \dfrac{370,000.00}{167,000.00} = 2.22 \\[2ex] 1950 = \dfrac{352,000.00}{100,000.00} = 3.52 \end{cases}$$

Should current assets in general, and merchandise inventory in particular, increase over a period of time, the usual result would be a reduction in the current ratio. The current ratio would be reduced because an increase in inventory and receivables is usually accompanied by a concurrent increase in current liabilities. Contrariwise, should current assets in general, and merchandise inventory in particular, decrease over a period of time, the usual result would be an increase in the current ratio. The current ratio would be higher because a decrease in inventory and receivables is usually accompanied by a concurrent decrease in current liabilities. As these items are converted into cash, the cash received is used to reduce current liabilities, thus causing an immediate improvement in the current ratio.

These ratios were obtained by using the items which constitute working capital, i.e., current assets and current liabilities. Current assets are "cash, and other assets which, within the next twelve months of normal business operations, are intended to be (a) converted into cash or (b) used up in the production of income." This definition emphasizes the fact that current assets are acquired with the primary purpose and intention of near-term conversion into cash. More broadly it shows that current assets involve tests for purpose, intention, convertibility into cash, or their utilization for income-producing purposes.

Some accountants, however, would define current assets as "cash and other assets which will be converted into cash within one year in the normal operation of the business; and also any other assets that might readily be converted into cash without jeopardizing the affairs of the business." Under this definition readily marketable securities, whether held for the long or the short term, would be classed as current assets. On this basis the current ratios of the Manchester Manufacturing Company would be

$$\frac{\text{Current assets}}{\text{Current liabilities}} = \begin{cases} 1949 = \dfrac{470,000.00}{167,000.00} = 2.81 \\[2ex] 1950 = \dfrac{552,000.00}{100,000.00} = 5.52 \end{cases}$$

ACID TEST RATIO

The significance of the current ratio is dependent upon the liquidity of its components. If accounts receivable have increased because collections have slowed down, if accounts receivable have increasingly been converted into notes receivable instead of being collected, and if the inventory is of such nature that the rate of its conversion into cash is slow, then the result of all this is a current ratio with certain unwelcome implications. This is true even though the current ratio is a high one, and "improved" over earlier ratios.

If a company has $300,000.00 in current assets and $100,000.00 in current liabilities, the current ratio is 3 to 1 and apparently favorable. But if inventory represents $250,000.00 of the current assets, and six months or more are required to convert the inventory into cash, the company in reality has but $50,000.00 of funds available for the payment of $100,000.00 of current liabilities. The original estimate of the ability of the company to pay its current debts must therefore be significantly revised.

The "acid test" ratio of a company's current position is a ratio which relates only cash and its immediate equivalent to the current liabilities, thus:

$$\frac{\text{Cash} + \text{Receivables} + \text{Marketable securities}}{\text{Current liabilities}} = \begin{cases} 1949 = \dfrac{290,000.00}{167,000.00} = 1.74 \\[2ex] 1950 = \dfrac{402,000.00}{100,000.00} = 4.02 \end{cases}$$

A 1 to 1 ratio is generally considered favorable.

RATIO OF ACCOUNTS RECEIVABLE TO NET SALES

To test the efficacy of a company's collection policy, the following ratio may be employed:

$$\frac{\text{Accounts receivable}}{\text{Net sales}} = \begin{cases} 1949 = \dfrac{130,000.00}{560,000.00} = 23.21\% \\[2mm] 1950 = \dfrac{100,000.00}{600,000.00} = 16.67\% \end{cases}$$

Net sales is used as the denominator provided the ratio of credit sales to total sales is relatively constant.

These percentages can be converted into the average number of days' sales uncollected:

1949 = 23.21 % of 365 (days in year) = 84.7 days
1950 = 16.67 % of 365 (days in year) = 60.8 days

These days also represent, approximately, the average collection period for accounts receivable provided the figures for trade debtors for 1949 and 1950 represent the average amount of accounts receivable outstanding for those years. Greater accuracy will be obtained in these day-figures if accounts receivable are related to credit sales.

RATIO OF ACCOUNTS PAYABLE TO NET PURCHASES

This ratio is applicable to a trading concern. It is designed to test the manner in which a business takes care of its own trade obligations for merchandise. The ratio gives the per cent of the net merchandise purchases which are unpaid at the end of the accounting period, thus:

$$\frac{\text{Accounts payable for merchandise}}{\text{Net merchandise purchases}} = \%$$

This percentage may be converted into days as in the preceding section.

When notes payable represent merchandise obligations, the amount of outstanding notes payable should be added to the numerator of the above fraction for greater accuracy in the final percentage.

To ascertain if a company is taking its purchases discounts, the following calculation may be made:

Merchandise accounts payable, January 1, 19__	$xxx xx
Add merchandise purchases in 19__	xxx xx
	$xxx xx
Less merchandise accounts payable, December 31, 19__	xxx xx
Accounts payable paid in 19__	$xxx xx
Average purchase discount rate	%
Purchases discounts available in 19__	$xxx xx
Purchases discounts taken in 19__	xxx xx

MERCHANDISE TURNOVER

The control of inventory is one of the important problems of management. The inventory must be large enough to fill satisfactorily the orders of customers. On the other hand, the inventory must not be too large. This is important in order to avoid tying up too much capital in inventory and to minimize the cost of inventory depreciation and obsolescence.

One measure for testing the sales efficiency of a business is that of merchandise turnover.

Merchandise turnover may be defined as a ratio which shows how many times a period the merchandise inventory has been converted into sales. Each merchandise turnover represents one gross profit; hence the normal favorable interpretation given to an increasing rate of inventory turnover. Capital is more profitably employed. A business which requires an inventory of $50,000.00 to support a sales volume of $100,000.00 is obviously better managed, and relatively more profitable, than one which, in the same line of business, requires an inventory of $100,000.00 for the same volume of sales.

The ratio for merchandise turnover is computed as follows:

$$\frac{\text{Cost of sales}}{\text{Average inventory of finished goods}} = \begin{cases} 1949 = \dfrac{353,000.00}{(130,000.00 + 120,000.00) \div 2} = 2.82 \\[2ex] 1950 = \dfrac{365,000.00}{(120,000.00 + 85,000.00) \div 2} = 3.56 \end{cases}$$

The converse of the above ratios, wl.en multiplied by 365, shows that the inventory of finished goods on December 31, 1949, was equivalent to 129 days' sales as compared with 102 days' sales for the inventory of finished goods on December 31, 1950.

In lieu of the ratio of merchandise turnover, a rough measure of the merchandising efficiency of a business will be afforded by a comparison of sales with the value of the average amount of inventory. The ratio of sales to inventory, however, is a very rough test. Among other things, the numerator of the ratio is stated at selling price (cost + gross profit), whereas the average inventory is stated at cost. The ratio of sales to inventory may be used as a substitute for the ratio of cost of sales to inventory when the figure for cost of sales is not available. When so used, however, the ratio should be regarded as only a rough approximation.

WORKING CAPITAL

Closely akin to the current ratio are the computations for working capital and working capital turnover. Working capital may be defined as the excess of current assets over current liabilities. Adequate working capital is a well-recognized requisite for business success; but "adequate" working capital, like the current ratio, varies between businesses and industries. A baking corporation with a sales volume of $1,000,000.00 per year, and all on a cash basis, would require relatively little working capital; a retail furniture store, on the other hand, with a sales volume of $1,000,000.00, and liberal terms of credit, would require a relatively large amount of working capital.

The following ratio is a test of the productivity of working capital:

$$\frac{\text{Sales}}{\text{Average working capital}} = \begin{cases} 1949 = \dfrac{560,000.00}{(217,000.00 + 203,000.00) \div 2} = 2.67 \\ 1950 = \dfrac{600,000.00}{(203,000.00 + 252,000.00) \div 2} = 2.64 \end{cases}$$

A larger volume of sales per dollar of working capital indicates more intensive use of capital. A business which transacts a sales volume per year of $1,000,000.00 on a working capital of $250,000.00 is, obviously, a better managed business than a similar one which requires $500,000.00 of working capital to support the same sales volume.

A decrease in working capital may not be an ominous sign. If the decrease is due to reduction of indebtedness, or is due to the transfer of funds to more profitable employment, the decrease is understandable. Increases or decreases in the amount of working capital require, in all cases, careful interpretation before conclusions are drawn.[4]

There is some difference between a business which has current assets of $100,000.00 and current liabilities of $98,000.00, or working capital of $2,000.00; and another business which has current assets of $10,000.00 and current liabilities of $8,000.00, and also working capital of $2,000.00. A working capital balance does not always tell the whole story. Some analysts, therefore, feel that the ratio for productivity of working capital will be more meaningful if it is altered to mean "sales divided by average gross current assets."

---

[4] The following interesting statement by Thomas F. Woodlock, with respect to working capital, appeared in the *Wall Street Journal* of March 30, 1933:

"From the earliest days of corporation reporting to the public, the integrity of net profits has been the all-important thing. It may be of interest to our analysts of today to know that thirty years ago, when 'industrials' began to occupy the main space in the stock list, the maintenance or otherwise of 'net working capital' from year to year was regarded as a rough and ready test of the integrity of the reported net profits. It was not a bad test for those days — and perhaps not so very bad for these!"

RATIO OF FIXED ASSETS TO TOTAL ASSETS

This ratio is computed as follows:

$$\frac{\text{Fixed assets}}{\text{Total assets}} = \begin{cases} 1949 = \dfrac{814,000.00}{1,284,000.00} = 63.40\% \\[2ex] 1950 = \dfrac{752,000.00}{1,304,000.00} = 57.67\% \end{cases}$$

This ratio is designed to show what part of the total assets employed in a business is represented by fixed assets. At times an increasing ratio of fixed assets to total assets may signify an unfavorable tendency to overinvestment in fixed assets. To ascertain whether or not fixed assets are maintaining their former rate of productivity, net operating profit or net sales should be related to fixed assets, and comparisons made for two or more periods.

RATIO OF SALES TO FIXED ASSETS

The productivity of an increasing investment in fixed assets may be tested by ascertaining whether or not the increased investment has been compensated for by an increased volume of business. For example,

$$\frac{\text{Net sales}}{\text{Fixed assets}} = \begin{cases} 1949 = \dfrac{560,000.00}{814,000.00} = 68.80\% \\[2ex] 1950 = \dfrac{600,000.00}{752,000.00} = 79.05\% \end{cases}$$

These percentages mean that for each dollar invested in fixed assets in 1949 the dollar volume of sales was $0.6880; in 1950 the dollar volume rose to $0.7905.

NET WORTH RATIO

This ratio is computed as follows:

$$\frac{\text{Net worth}}{\text{Total assets}} = \begin{cases} 1949 = \dfrac{1,117,000.00}{1,284,000.00} = 86.99\% \\[2ex] 1950 = \dfrac{1,204,000.00}{1,304,000.00} = 92.33\% \end{cases}$$

An increase in this ratio over several accounting periods is an indication of a strengthening proprietary interest. A decreasing ratio signifies that creditors are contributing a larger proportion of the funds used in the business. An increasing amount of debt is ordinarily to be construed as an unfavorable omen, and especially so if the debt continues to rise over a considerable period of time.

RATIO OF NET INCOME TO NET WORTH

This ratio measures the earning power of invested capital. It is therefore a very important ratio. It is computed as follows:

$$\frac{\text{Net income}}{\text{Net worth January 1}} = \begin{cases} 1949 = \dfrac{43,500.00}{1,038,000.00} = 4.19\% \\[2ex] 1950 = \dfrac{60,000.00}{1,117,000.00} = 5.13\% \end{cases}$$

If a company does not operate on a calendar year basis, the denominator of the above ratio should be the net worth at the beginning of the fiscal period.

If greater accuracy is required, the denominator of the above ratio should be the average amount of net worth for the period in which the net income is earned.

RATIOS: THEIR FURTHER CONSIDERATION

The ratios which have been presented in the preceding pages are not, by any means, all of the ratios which are available to the business analyst. The ratios which have been given, however, are among the most important. A description of other ratios may be found in standard texts on business finance and advanced accounting and also in the *Accountants' Handbook* and the *Financial Handbook*.

Financial analysis, it should be pointed out, is not a matter of routine procedure. Ratios, averages, and amounts have their value when they are used intelligently. Discrimination and standards are necessary. Due recognition must also be given to other factors which bear upon accounting results such as, for instance,

General business conditions
The business cycle
Business conditions within the industry
Growth curves of industry and company
Factors peculiar to the company being analyzed

There is no substitute for sound judgment. And sound judgment in financial analysis, as in any other kind of analysis, depends upon the assembly and careful appraisal of all factors which have a bearing upon the problem at hand.

THE MANCHESTER MANUFACTURING COMPANY

It is now in order to continue the analysis of the Manchester Manufacturing Company which was begun on page 634. The following is a summary of further information with respect to the affairs of the company:

Current assets with which to meet each dollar of current liabilities have increased from . . . . $2.22 to $3.52

Cash, and its immediate equivalent, when related to each dollar of current liabilities, has increased from $1.74 to $4.02

Cash alone has increased from . . . . $60,000.00 to $102,000.00
which, in itself, is more than enough to pay all of the current liabilities on December 31, 1950, of $100,000.00.

Accounts receivable have decreased from . . . . . . $130,000.00 to $100,000.00
a decrease (in terms of sales) of . . . .   23.21% to 16.67%.
This decrease reflects the improved collections of the year, the average time necessary to collect accounts being reduced from . . . .   84.7 days to 60.8 days.

Finished goods inventory decreased from . . . . . . $120,000.00 to $85,000.00
a decrease of . . . . $35,000.00, or 29.17%,
although sales increased . . . . $40,000.00, or 7.14%.
This reflects the improvement in merchandise turnover from . . . .   2.82 to 3.56

Working capital has increased from . . . . $203,000.00 to $252,000.00
an increase of . . . . $49,000.00, or 24.14%,
and concomitant with an increase in the investment in marketable securities from . . . . $100,000.00 to $200,000.00.
The productivity of working capital has been maintained at a rate almost identical with that of 1949, working capital turnover declining negligibly from   2.67 to 2.64.

Fixed assets have declined from . . . . $814,000.00 to $752,000.00
a decrease of . . . . $62,000.00, or 7.62%,
although sales increased . . . . $40,000.00, or 7.14%.
In terms of sales, the productivity of each dollar invested in fixed assets increased from . . . . . . $0.6880 to $0.7905
Related to total assets, fixed assets have declined from . . . .   63.40% to 57.67%.

Fixed assets, further,
(1) Appear to be in the right proportion to each other, and to total assets.
(2) Exhibit no tendency toward overinvestment.
(3) Appear to have adequate depreciation reserves.
(4) Offer no financial problem of replacement. The company has $200,000.00 in corporate stocks and bonds, readily marketable, and which are not included in working capital. On the other hand, no significant capital expenditures appear to be required for 1951.

All values are tangible values.

The liabilities of the company have been reduced from   13.01% to 7.67%
of all assets employed in the business. Creditors therefore have a smaller interest in the company.

Net worth has increased from . . . . $1,117,000.00 to $1,204,000.00,
although the book value of each share of common stock has decreased from . . . . $124.11 to $120.40.
This decrease is due to the sale of $100,000.00 of capital stock at par.

The rate of return on capital, as measured by net income, increased from . . . .   4.19% to 5.13%.

STATEMENT OF SOURCE AND APPLICATION OF FUNDS

The variation of items in the 1950 balance sheet of the Manchester Manufacturing Company from their status in 1949 is given by the "increase-decrease" column of the comparative balance sheet. If these changes are properly analyzed and classified, an interesting summary of the flow of funds within the business for 1950 may be had. This summary is usually called a statement of source and application of funds and, as the name implies, shows

(1) The sources from which new funds were obtained.
(2) The uses to which these funds were put.

The term "funds" is generally defined as being working capital. Thus the statement of source and application of funds is a statement which describes the ebb and flow of working capital for a business.

There are several sources from which funds may be derived:

(1) Decreases in assets, i.e., realization of assets in whole or in part
(2) Increases in liabilities
(3) Increase in capital investment
(4) Profits

The funds of a business

(1) May be used to purchase additional assets.
(2) May be used to reduce liabilities.
(3) May be used to reduce the capital investment.
(4) May be used up by losses.

From the standpoint of the comparative balance sheet, and the application-of-funds work sheet (pages 680–681), the excess of debits over credits in an account for a period of time represents an application of funds, whereas an excess of credits over debits represents a source of funds.

The items of the increase-decrease column of the comparative balance sheet (and the second pair of columns on the work sheet on page 680) may be gathered together and a summary prepared to show that the Manchester Manufacturing Company

Obtained funds from the following sources:		*and*	*Used them for the following purposes:*	
(1) Sale of government bonds	$100,000.00		(1) To purchase corporate stocks and bonds . .	$200,000.00
(2) Sale of common stock .	100,000.00		(2) To reduce surplus . . .	13,000.00
(3) Reduction of fixed assets	62,000.00		(3) To increase working capital	49,000.00
	$262,000.00			$262,000.00

This summary is a simple statement of source and application of funds. It is interesting if from no other aspect than to show that the management of the Manchester Manufacturing Company actually had available to it a far larger amount of new funds than is indicated by the net income figure of $60,000.00 on the profit and loss statement for 1950. This summary is also interesting because it tells what disposition was made of the new funds of $262,000.00.

The foregoing summary, however, is not accurate. Certain corrections are necessary because

(1) The reduction of fixed assets by $62,000.00 really represents

Funds received through operations of business to compensate for the capital used up through depreciation	$72,000.00
Less additional investment in factory equipment.	10,000.00
	$62,000.00

(2) The reduction of surplus by $13,000.00 represents

Dividends declared in 1950	$73,000.00
Less net income for 1950	60,000.00
	$13,000.00

By including this information the summary on page 676 may be revised. Corrected, it will show that the Manchester Manufacturing Company

Obtained funds from the following sources:		*and*	*Used them for the following purposes:*	
(1) Sale of government bonds	$100,000.00		(1) To purchase corporate stocks and bonds . .	$200,000.00
(2) Sale of common stock .	100,000.00		(2) To purchase factory equipment	10,000.00
(3) Operations of the business	132,000.00		(3) To pay dividends . . .	73,000.00
			(4) To increase working capital	49,000.00
	$332,000.00			$332,000.00

This summary may be recast so as to constitute a formal financial statement. A statement of this kind, prepared from the work sheet on page 680, would be as follows:

Manchester Manufacturing Company

STATEMENT OF SOURCE AND APPLICATION OF FUNDS
YEAR ENDING DECEMBER 31, 1950

Funds Were Provided by:

The sale of government bonds for.			$100,000.00
The sale of common stock for			100,000.00
Operations of the business:			
Net income as per statement of profit and loss		$ 60,000.00	
Add noncash charges to Profit and Loss:			
Depreciation Expense — Building	$ 7,500.00		
Depreciation Expense — Delivery Equipment	7,500.00		
Depreciation Expense — Factory Equipment	51,000.00		
Depreciation Expense — Office Equipment	6,000.00	72,000.00	132,000.00
			$332,000.00

Funds Were Applied to:

The purchase of corporate stocks and bonds	$200,000.00	
The purchase of factory equipment	10,000.00	
The payment of dividends	73,000.00	283,000.00
Increase in Working Capital (Schedule 1)		$ 49,000.00

SCHEDULE 1

Manchester Manufacturing Company

SCHEDULE OF WORKING CAPITAL
DECEMBER 31, 1950, AND DECEMBER 31, 1949

	December 31 1950	December 31 1949	Working Capital Increase	Working Capital Decrease
Cash	$102,000.00	$ 60,000.00	$ 42,000.00	
Accounts Receivable	100,000.00	130,000.00		$ 30,000.00
Finished Goods	85,000.00	120,000.00		35,000.00
Work in Process	50,000.00	40,000.00	10,000.00	
Raw Materials	15,000.00	20,000.00		5,000.00
Total Current Assets	$352,000.00	$370,000.00		
Vouchers Payable	$ 80,000.00	$147,000.00	67,000.00	
Income Taxes Payable	20,000.00	10,000.00		10,000.00
Dividends Payable		10,000.00	10,000.00	
Total Current Liabilities	$100,000.00	$167,000.00		
Working capital	$252,000.00	$203,000.00		
Increase in working capital				49,000.00
			$129,000.00	$129,000.00

Because it provides a condensed description of the flow of funds within a business, the statement of source and application of funds is a valuable adjunct to the balance sheet and the statement of profit and loss. The statement of source and application of funds is a regular part of the annual reports of some corporations, among them being the Caterpillar Tractor Company, the Consolidated Gas Company of New York, the Gardner-Denver Company, the Rustless Iron & Steel Company, and the United States Steel Corporation.

For the development of the statement of source and application of funds in its relation to more complex accounting situations, refer to the author's *Intermediate Accounting*.

APPLICATION OF FUNDS WORK

	BALANCE SHEET December 31				YEAR'S EXCESS			
	1950		1949		Debits		Credits	
Cash	102,000	00	60,000	00	42,000	00		
Accounts Receivable	100,000	00	130,000	00			30,000	00
Finished Goods	85,000	00	120,000	00			35,000	00
Work in Process	50,000	00	40,000	00	10,000	00		
Raw Materials	15,000	00	20,000	00			5,000	00
Government Bonds			100,000	00			100,000	00
Corporate Stocks and Bonds	200,000	00			200,000	00		
Building.	300,000	00	300,000	00				
Delivery Equipment	30,000	00	30,000	00				
Factory Equipment	510,000	00	500,000	00	10,000	00		
Office Equipment	60,000	00	60,000	00				
Land	100,000	00	100,000	00				
. . . .	1,552,000	00	1 460, 00	00				
. . . .								
Vouchers Payable	80,000	00	147,000	00	67,000	00		
Income Taxes Payable	20,000	00	10,000	00			10,000	00
Dividends Payable			10,000	00	10,000	00		
Rsv. for Deprec. — Building	37,500	00	30,000	00			7,500	00
Rsv. for Deprec. — Delivery Equipment .	17,500	00	10,000	00			7,500	00
Rsv. for Deprec. — Factory Equipment .	171,000	00	120,000	00			51,000	00
Rsv. for Deprec. — Office Equipment . .	22,000	00	16,000	00			6,000	00
Common Stock.	1,000,000	00	900,000	00			100,000	00
Surplus	204,000	00	217,000	00	13,000	00		
. . . .	1,552,000	00	1,460,000	00				
Profits per Books								
Profits — Noncash charges to Profit and Loss:								
Depreciation Expense — Building . . .								
Depreciation Expense — Delivery Equipment								
Depreciation Expense — Factory Equipment								
Depreciation Expense — Office Equipment								
Payment of dividends								
. . . .								
Increase of working capital								
. . . .								
. . . .					352,000	00	352,000	00
. . . .								

Question **31–7.** Explain why the current ratio may be deceptive as a measure of a company's debt-paying ability.

Question **31–8.** The following ratios are in addition to those given in the chapter. What is the purpose of each of these ratios?

Inventory December 31	÷ Net purchases
Net income	÷ Total assets
Operating profit	÷ Net worth
Net income (before interest)	÷ Interest charges
Funded debt	÷ Fixed assets
Finished goods inventory	÷ Cost to manufacture for period
Average finished goods inventory	÷ Cost of sales
Materials consumed	÷ Average materials inventory
Cost of sales + operating expenses	÷ Sales

Question **31–9.** Name ten financial ratios, and state what each is intended to measure. (In your answer to this question do not include any of the ratios in the preceding question.)

Question **31–10.** You are one of the statisticians of the Goodrich Investment Service of New York City. At 9.00 A.M. you receive a telegram from one of your clients in Manhattan, Kansas, requesting an opinion by 12.00 M. on the American Cyanamid Company. Outline the financial analysis you would make in framing your reply.

Question **31–11.** One of your clients is considering the purchase of the Hale Department Stores Company, a chain of 20 stores operating in 20 towns spread over 5 states. You are asked to make an examination of the Hale Department Stores Company and to prepare a report which will be of material assistance to your client in deciding whether or not to make the purchase.

In outline form, describe the examination program you would pursue and the report you would prepare for your client.

PROBLEMS

Problem **31–1.** The condensed balance sheets of The Royal Candy Company for the dates indicated are as follows:

	December 31	
Assets	1950	1949
Cash	$ 11,000.00	$ 28,000.00
Accounts Receivable	40,000.00	25,000.00
Notes Receivable		20,000.00
Merchandise	38,000.00	20,000.00
Stocks and Bonds (short term, readily marketable)	20,000.00	5,000.00
Total Current Assets	$109,000.00	$ 98,000.00
Land	$ 10,000.00	$ 10,000.00

Depreciable Fixed Assets	60,000.00	60,000.00
Reserve for Depreciation — Fixed Assets	(24,000.00)	(18,000.00)
Total Fixed Assets	$ 46,000.00	$ 52,000.00
	$155,000.00	$150,000.00

Liabilities and Net Worth

Vouchers Payable	$ 30,000.00	$ 25,000.00
Notes Payable		20,000.00
Wages and Salaries Payable		5,000.00
Total Current Liabilities	$ 30,000.00	$ 50,000.00
Common Stock, $100.00 par	$100,000.00	$ 80,000.00
(*Note:* The additional $20,000.00 of stock was issued December 20, 1950.)		
Surplus	25,000.00	20,000.00
	$125,000.00	$100,000.00
	$155,000.00	$150,000.00

Required:

(1) Using the above comparative balance sheets and, where required, the comparative profit and loss statements on page 650, calculate the following ratios:

    (a) Current ratio for 1950 and 1949.

    (b) Acid test ratios for 1950 and 1949.

    (c) Ratio of accounts receivable to net sales for 1950 and 1949. How old are the accounts receivable at the end of each year?

    (d) Ratio of merchandise turnover for 1950.

    (e) Ratio showing productivity (as measured by sales) of working capital for 1950 and 1949.

    (f) Ratio of fixed assets to total assets for 1950 and 1949.

    (g) Ratio of sales to fixed assets for 1950 and 1949.

    (h) Ratio showing productivity (as measured by sales) of the net investment in the business for 1950 and 1949.

    (i) Net worth ratio for 1950 and 1949.

    (j) Ratio of net income to net worth for 1950 and 1949. On January 1, 1949, the capital stock was $80,000.00 and the surplus, $16,000.00.

(2) What are your conclusions with respect to the balance sheets of the two dates in question?

Problem **31–2.** The following items and information were used in preparing the certified balance sheet of Shearer & Company, Inc., December 31, 1955:

Accounts Payable	$ 4,920.00	$ 121,022.00
Accounts Receivable (including $8,000.00 of employees' accounts receivable)	154,076.00	1,076.00

Accrued Expenses Payable		15,609.00
6% Bonds Payable, due in annual installments of		
$25,000.00 beginning January 1, 1956		250,000.00
Capital Surplus		39,631.00
Cash	115,905.00	
Common Stock, $100.00 par		500,000.00
Deferred Rent Income		3,468.00
Discount on Bonds Payable	5,000.00	
Dividends Payable on Preferred Stock		4,000.00
Earned Surplus		46,109.00
Experimental and Research Costs	72,062.00	
Finished Goods, at cost*	36,014.00	
Goodwill	50,000.00	
Land	25,000.00	
Notes Payable		50,000.00
Notes Receivable	60,000.00	
Notes Receivable Discounted		35,000.00
Organization Expense	7,210.00	
Patents	40,000.00	
Plant, Machinery, and Equipment	412,513.00	
Preferred Stock, 8% Cumulative, $100.00 par		100,000.00
Prepaid Advertising	1,588.00	
Prepaid Insurance.	3,670.00	
Raw Materials†	31,011.00	
Reserve for Contingencies		10,000.00
Reserve for Depreciation		88,088.00
Reserve for Uncollectible Accounts		12,074.00
Stocks and Corporation Bonds, at cost‡	84,016.00	
Treasury Stock, Common§	30,000.00	
U.S. Government Bonds, at amortized cost	99,020.00	
Work in Process, at cost	44,072.00	
	$1,276,077.00	$1,276,077.00

*Market value, $40,000.00.
†Market value, $25,028.00.
‡Market value, $72,844.00. These stocks and bonds were short-term investments.
§Acquired at cost of $25,000.00, difference of $5,000.00 being credited to earned surplus.

Required:

Prepare a balance sheet in good form, including proper classification of items. Prepaid expenses should be classified as current assets. All of the accounts of the trial balance above are balance sheet accounts. The U.S. Government bonds are long-term investments. The Accounts Payable item of $4,920.00 represents accounts payable with debit balances; and the Accounts Receivable item of $1,076.00 represents accounts receivable with credit balances.

Problem **31–3.** From the following information, prepare a classified balance sheet of the Union Carbide and Carbon Corporation as of December 31, 1940:

Debit Accounts

Land, Buildings, Machinery, and Equipment	$290,574,237.68
Patents, Trademarks, and Goodwill	1.00
Cash	78,566,746.51
Affiliated Domestic and Foreign Companies	4,643,935.60
Raw Materials	23,803,350.56
Receivables (after Reserve for Doubtful Accounts)	
Trade Notes and Accounts	24,616,754.65
Other Notes and Accounts	2,074,054.04
Finished Goods	14,384,518.51
Prepaid Insurance, Taxes, etc.	2,308,174.70
Marketable Securities (Cost or Market, whichever lower)	2,737,741.03
Work in Process	12,044,169.02
Other Securities (classify as Investments)	1,341,125.84
Net Current Assets Located outside United States and Canada . . .	11,377,652.69
	$468,472,461.83

Credit Accounts

Reserve for Depreciation	$103,802,932.55
Earned Surplus	95,648,684.98
Bond Interest Payable	250,000.00
Accounts Payable	12,025,275.98
Taxes (Including Income Taxes)	25,736,782.18
Capital Stock, 9,277,788 shares of no par value	192,879,842.43
Other Accrued Liabilities	1,170,602.71
Dividend Payable January 1, 1941	6,958,341.00
Fifteen-Year, 2½% Sinking Fund Debentures, due September 1, 1953	30,000,000.00
	$468,472,461.83

(1) Inventories are valued at cost or market, whichever is lower.
(2) Of the $30,000,000.00 of debenture bonds outstanding, a $900,-000.00 installment was due within one year of December 31, 1940.

Problem **31-4.** The Jackson Cut-Rate Drug Company began operations on January 20, 1950. On December 31, 1950, the bookkeeper of the company prepared the following trial balance:

Cash	$ 1,706.68	
Cash Deposit with E. R. Squibb & Sons	100.00	
Cash Deposits with Utilities	75.00	
Accounts Receivable	391.04	
Fixtures and Equipment	9,852.26	
Remodeling Expense	1,845.70	
Organization Expense	141.80	
Accounts Payable		$ 3,675.91
Notes Payable		5,000.00
Common Stock, $10.00 par		10,000.00
Capital Surplus		2,000.00
Sales		36,665.03
Purchases	32,331.03	
Purchases Discounts		289.47
Freight and Express on Purchases	185.12	
Advertising Expense	2,132.66	
General Expense	1,147.72	

Interest Expense	357.33
Rent Expense	1,500.00
Salaries and Wages	4,205.41
Sales Tax Expense	631.24
Utilities Expense	1,027.42

$57,630.41	$57,630.41

The following information, which is obtained by you from various sources, is available for adjusting and closing the books:

(1) The inventory of merchandise on December 31, 1950, is $6,760.24.

(2) Rent is payable monthly in advance, $125.00 on the 20th of each month.

(3) During the year various kinds of supplies were purchased and debited to General Expense. On December 31, 1950, the inventory of supplies on hand is $300.00.

(4) The cash of $1,706.68 includes $12.00 of bad checks. These checks are considered worthless.

(5) There are unrecorded general expense bills on hand amounting to $31.93.

(6) Depreciation on fixtures and equipment should be computed at the rate of 8% per year.

(7) Remodeling Expense is a deferred charge. The balance of $1,845.70 should be written off to profit and loss at the rate of 10% per year.

(8) An accounts receivable claim against the Gilbert Drug Company for $114.88 has been compromised for $50.00. On January 10, 1951, a check for $50.00 was received from the Gilbert Drug Company in full settlement of their account.

(9) The notes payable consist of one note in favor of the Guaranty National Bank for $3,000.00, dated October 20, 1950, and due January 20, 1951, with interest at 8%. This interest has not been recorded on the books. The other note payable, $2,000.00, is for funds advanced by the largest stockholder. For the time being, the funds have been advanced without interest cost to the Jackson Cut-Rate Drug Company.

(10) Unrecorded and unpaid taxes for 1950 amount to $85.00.

(11) The unrecorded and unpaid utility bills (water, light, gas, etc.) for December, 1950, amount to $88.29.

(12) Organization expense is to be carried to the balance sheet as an asset.

(13) During 1950 the sales taxes collected from customers have been included in the credit to Sales. The monthly sales tax remittances to the State Treasurer have been debited to Sales Tax Expense. On December 31, 1950, there was a sales tax of $87.68 due to the State Treasurer for the sales tax collected on December sales.

(14) The company is liable for social security taxes on its payroll.

(For the purpose of this problem the liability for social security taxes may be taken to be 1 % of the payroll for old age, and 3 % for unemployment.) This unrecorded liability is payable early in 1951.

Required:

(1) Prepare a profit and loss statement for the period ending December 31, 1950.

(2) Prepare a balance sheet, December 31, 1950.

Problem **31–5.** Following is the adjusted trial balance of the Wilson Manufacturing Company on December 31, 19—:

Cash	$ 73,000.00	
Accounts Receivable	55,000.00	
Reserve for Bad Debts		$ 3,000.00
Notes Receivable	40,000.00	
Notes Receivable Discounted		13,000.00
Finished Goods	22,000.00	
Work in Process	17,000.00	
Raw Materials	33,000.00	
Office Equipment	20,000.00	
Reserve for Depreciation — Office Equipment		7,000.00
Machinery and Equipment	135,000.00	
Reserve for Depreciation — Machinery and Equipment		25,000.00
Buildings	100,000.00	
Reserve for Depreciation — Buildings		20,000.00
Land	30,000.00	
Patents	50,000.00	
Trademarks and Tradenames	25,000.00	
Factory Supplies	7,000.00	
Office Supplies	6,000.00	
Accounts Payable		50,000.00
Notes Payable		30,000.00
Income Tax Liability		12,000.00
Cash Dividend Payable		2,000.00
Mortgage Payable (due in 5 years)		25,000.00
Common Stock, $100.00 par		100,000.00
Stock Dividend Payable		100,000.00
Surplus		220,000.00
Sales		376,000.00
Sales Discounts	6,000.00	
Purchases	105,000.00	
Purchases Discounts		5,000.00
Freight In	3,000.00	
Direct Labor	80,000.00	
Depreciation Expense — Machinery and Equipment	13,000.00	
Depreciation Expense — Building (apportion 90% to factory)	5,000.00	
Factory Supplies Expense	12,000.00	
Factory Superintendence	7,000.00	
Heat, Light, and Power	10,000.00	
Indirect Labor	10,000.00	
Maintenance and Repairs	8,000.00	
Miscellaneous Factory Expense	2,000.00	
Taxes (apportion 90% to factory)	5,000.00	
Advertising Expense	16,000.00	

Freight Out	1,000.00	
Miscellaneous Sales Expense	4,000.00	
Sales Salaries	20,000.00	
Traveling Expense	6,000.00	
Depreciation Expense — Office Equipment.	2,000.00	
General Office Salaries	25,000.00	
Miscellaneous Office Expense.	3,000.00	
Office Supplies Expense	5,000.00	
Interest Expense	3,000.00	
Interest Income		2,000.00
Cost of Exhibit at World's Fair	14,000.00	
Provision for Income Taxes	12,000.00	
	$990,000.00	$990,000.00

Required:

(1) Prepare a well-organized profit and loss statement for the year. New inventories are finished goods, $37,000.00, work in process, $20,000.00, raw materials, $38,000.00.

(2) Prepare a balance sheet, December 31, 19___.

Problem **31–6.** For the year ending December 31, 19___, the Mannen-Bell Company had an average inventory of $22,000.00, sales of $80,000.00, and a gross profit of 45%. For the following twelve-month period, the company planned a 20% increase in sales, a 50% increase in the rate of merchandise turnover, and a gross profit percentage of 50%.

What inventory did the company plan to carry?

Problem **31–7.** In a certain year, the A. B. Cummins Corporation had sales of $100,000.00, cost of sales, $60,000.00, expenses of $30,000.00, and an average inventory of $20,000.00.

What would the profit and loss statement of the company have been if, for the year,

The physical volume of sales had been 20% greater?

Selling prices were 5% less per unit?

The rate of merchandise turnover had been increased to 3.5 without, however, increasing the investment in inventory?

Problem **31–8.** At the beginning of an accounting period, the merchandise inventory of a company was $17,300.00. At the end of the period the inventory was $22,700.00. The profit and loss statement for the period showed that

The rate of merchandise turnover was 4.2.

Purchases amounted to 106% of the cost of sales.

Freight in amounted to $360.00.

The ratio of gross profit to sales was 30%.

Selling expenses were 15% of sales.

General expenses were 5% of sales.

Required:

Prepare a detailed profit and loss statement for the period.

Problem **31–9.** With respect to Problem 31–8, the vice-president suggested that it might be advantageous for the company to plan operations for the next accounting period as follows:

Carry the same average inventory as in the preceding period.

Have a merchandise turnover of 5.0.

Assuming unit costs to continue unchanged, reduce selling prices by 10%.

Plan for the same expense, in dollars, as was incurred in the previous year.

Required:

Prepare the company's profit and loss statement for the new year according to the plan of the vice-president. Should the proposed suggestions be followed?

Problem **31–10.** For 1950 certain statistics of the Benway Company were

Sales	$136,740.00
Inventory, January 1, 1950	24,989.00
Inventory, December 31, 1950	16,033.00
Cost of sales	82,044.00
Selling and general expenses	42,726.00
Accounts Receivable	41,022.00

Required:

(1) How many days will it take to collect the accounts receivable?

(2) On the basis of a 4.0 ratio for the productivity of working capital, how much net working capital is employed?

(3) It is suggested that a 10% reduction in selling prices for 1951 will result in a merchandise turnover of 5.0 per year, and an increase in expenses of $2,000.00. Would the company make more or less money in 1951 by employment of this plan? Prove by setting up two profit and loss statements, one showing normal expected results, the other showing results under the proposed plan.

Problem **31–11.** The condensed balance sheets of Freeman & Company on December 31, 1950 and 1949, were:

	1950	*1949*
Cash	$ 2,600,000.00	$ 2,200,000.00
Accounts Receivable	1,200,000.00	700,000.00
Inventories	5,600,000.00	5,700,000.00
Current Assets	$ 9,400,000.00	$ 8,600,000.00
Investments	2,700,000.00	1,700,000.00
Lands and Leaseholds	1,000,000.00	1,400,000.00
Plant and Equipment (net)	5,000,000.00	3,600,000.00
	$18,100,000.00	$15,300,000.00

Accounts Payable	$ 2,900,000.00	$ 1,900,000.00
Taxes Payable	700,000.00	400,000.00
Bonds Payable		2,000,000.00
Common Stock	10,000,000.00	7,000,000.00
Surplus	4,500,000.00	4,000,000.00
	$18,100,000.00	$15,300,000.00

The amount of net income for 1950, after depreciation expense of $500,000.00, was $2,500,000.00. Dividends paid during the year amounted to $2,000,000.00.

Required:

(1) Prepare a statement of source and application of funds.

(2) Prepare a supplementary schedule of working capital.

Problem 31–12. The condensed balance sheets of the Layton Sales Company on December 31, 1950 and 1949, were:

	1950	1949
Cash	$2,700,000.00	$2,200,000.00
Accounts Receivable	1,800,000.00	2,000,000.00
Inventories	1,600,000.00	1,000,000.00
Securities	1,000,000.00	
Land	100,000.00	100,000.00
Plant and Equipment (after reserves for depreciation: 1950, $200,000.00, 1949, $100,000.00)	1,000,000.00	1,100,000.00
Goodwill		1,000,000.00
	$8,200,000.00	$7,400,000.00

Accounts Payable	$1,000,000.00	$1,200,000.00
Accrued Taxes	500,000.00	200,000.00
Bonds Payable		1,000,000.00
Preferred Stock, $100.00 par		1,000,000.00
Common Stock, $100.00 par	5,000,000.00	2,000,000.00
Surplus	1,700,000.00	2,000,000.00
	$8,200,000.00	$7,400,000.00

Net income for 1950 was shown by the profit and loss statement to be $1,200,000.00. Depreciation expense was $300,000.00. Dividends paid during 1950 amounted to $500,000.00. Goodwill in the amount of $1,000,-000.00 was written off during 1950 by a direct debit to Surplus.

Required:

(1) Prepare a statement of source and application of funds.

(2) Prepare a supplementary schedule of working capital.

Problem 31–13. The following comparative statements are taken from the annual reports of the Chrysler Corporation for the years indicated. Analyze these statements in significant detail. Prepare a written report on the financial progress exhibited by the company over the eight-year period.

Chrysler Corporation

COMPARATIVE INCOME STATEMENTS

(*In Millions of Dollars*)

	1940	1939	1938	1937	1936	1935	1934	1933
Sales	$745	$550	$413	$770	$667	$517	$362	$239
Cost of Sales	634	460	352	662	546	431	319	202
Gross Profit	$111	$ 90	$ 61	$108	$121	$ 86	$ 43	$ 37
Expenses	50	45	39	45	45	42	32	23
Net Profit	$ 61	$ 45	$ 22	$ 63	$ 76	$ 44	$ 11	$ 14
Taxes	23	8	3	12	14	9	2	2
Net Income	$ 38	$ 37	$ 19	$ 51	$ 62	$ 35	$ 9	$ 12

Chrysler Corporation

COMPARATIVE BALANCE SHEETS

(*In Millions of Dollars*)

	1940	1939	1938	1937	1936	1935	1934	1933
Cash	$109	$ 73	$ 70	$ 35	$ 47	$ 57	$ 31	$ 12
Accounts Receivable, etc.	26	17	17	28	32	22	18	28
Inventories	59	55	47	50	61	49	38	35
Current Assets	$194	$145	$134	$113	$140	$128	$ 87	$ 75
Property, Plant, & Equipment	$110	$115	$119	$116	$118	$115	$129	$129
Reserve for Depreciation	46	48	49	50	57	61	69	68
	$ 64	$ 67	$ 70	$ 66	$ 61	$ 54	$ 60	$ 61
Other Assets	10	10	8	10	10	12	12	12
Total Assets	$268	$222	$212	$189	$211	$194	$159	$148
Accounts Payable, etc.	$ 79	$ 51	$ 56	$ 39	$ 75	$ 62	$ 38	$ 21
6% Debenture Bonds						5	30	40
Misc. Liabilities and Reserves	25	15	15	19	12	15	15	5
Total Liabilities	$104	$ 66	$ 71	$ 58	$ 87	$ 82	$ 73	$ 66
Common Stock	$ 22	$ 22	$ 22	$ 22	$ 22	$ 22	$ 22	$ 22
Surplus	142	134	119	109	102	90	64	60
Net Worth	$164	$156	$141	$131	$124	$112	$ 86	$ 82
	$268	$222	$212	$189	$211	$194	$159	$148

Approximately four million shares of common stock were outstanding over the eight-year period.

Problem **31-14.** From the following comparative financial statements, prepare an analysis of the progress of The Penford Corporation over the years 1948–1953.

The Penford Corporation

COMPARATIVE INCOME STATEMENTS

	1953	*1952*	*1951*	*1950*	*1949*	*1948*
Sales	$13,369,344	$10,403,281	$11,690,058	$16,011,103	$19,061,556	$16,417,750
Cost of Sales	8,823,767	6,970,198	7,890,789	11,047,661	13,343,089	11,820,780
Gross Profit	$ 4,545,577	$ 3,433,083	$ 3,799,269	$ 4,963,442	$ 5,718,467	$ 4,596,970
Depreciation Expense	$ 678,068	$ 664,941	$ 625,869	$ 607,208	$ 631,694	$ 647,063
Other Operating Expenses	2,056,504	1,886,752	2,218,297	2,430,915	2,563,037	2,059,495
	$ 2,734,572	$ 2,551,693	$ 2,844,166	$ 3,038,123	$ 3,194,731	$ 2,706,558
Net Profit From Operations	$ 1,811,005	$ 881,390	$ 955,103	$ 1,925,319	$ 2,523,736	$ 1,890,412
Add Miscellaneous Income	470,542	212,672	364,400	283,640	294,120	79,381
Less Interest on Funded Debt					50,003	153,986
	$ 2,281,547	$ 1,094,062	$ 1,319,503	$ 2,208,959	$ 2,767,853	$ 1,815,807
Federal Income Taxes	661,648	284,456	316,680	397,612	498,213	272,371
Net Income	$ 1,619,899	$ 809,606	$ 1,002,823	$ 1,811,347	$ 2,269,640	$ 1,543,436

The Penford Corporation

COMPARATIVE BALANCE SHEETS

Assets	1953	1952	1951	1950	1949	1948
Cash	$ 313,375	$ 603,223	$ 302,504	$ 333,834	$ 443,163	$ 520,787
Demand Loans	425,000	950,000	100,000	900,000	900,000	600,000
U.S. and Other Securities	3,063,000	1,635,000	1,725,500	1,000,000	1,000,000	1,000,000
Accounts and Notes Receivable	490,682	379,416	473,128	641,812	908,545	901,330
Other Accounts Receivable	76,638	67,755	53,183	88,837	654,780	380,951
Inventories	1,869,504	1,555,894	2,114,599	2,708,239	2,900,695	2,943,099
Total Current Assets	$ 6,238,199	$ 5,191,288	$ 4,768,914	$ 5,672,722	$ 6,807,183	$ 6,346,176
Land, Buildings, Machinery, etc.	$11,167,207	$11,345,669	$11,873,832	$11,822,486	$11,760,614	$12,264,823
Reserve for Depreciation	5,498,025	5,033,366	4,865,385	4,288,842	3,790,470	3,337,823
	$ 5,669,182	$ 6,312,303	$ 7,008,447	$ 7,533,644	$ 7,970,144	$ 8,927,000
Miscellaneous Investments and Advances	$ 986,828	$ 1,008,738	$ 1,048,435	$ 634,613	$ 729,202	$ 547,063
Prepaid Expenses	162,408	188,192	284,706	256,049	251,801	269,505
Goodwill	1	1	1	1	1	1
Total Assets	$13,056,618	$12,700,522	$13,110,503	14,097,029	$15,758,331	$16,089,745
Liabilities and Net Worth						
Accounts Payable	$ 196,226	$ 87,307	$ 278,602	$ 209,335	$ 337,952	$ 487,246
Accrued Taxes and Miscellaneous	440,211	321,622	336,905	466,510	528,470	470,087
Total Current Liabilities	$ 636,437	$ 408,929	$ 615,507	$ 675,845	$ 866,422	$ 957,333
Bonds Due December 1, 1953				895,984	873,802	1,970,305
Reserves and Unearned Income	424,809	413,871	710,707			405,462
Capital Stock Preferred					2,566,800	2,889,500
Capital Stock Common (no-par)	4,481,394	4,800,437	4,800,437	5,714,699	5,714,699	5,714,699
Surplus	7,513,978	7,077,285	6,983,852	6,810,501	5,736,608	4,152,446
Total of Liabilities and Net Worth	$13,056,618	$12,700,522	$13,110,503	$14,097,029	$15,758,331	$16,089,745
Shares of Common Stock Outstanding	390,000	400,000	400,000	424,965	424,965	424,965

Problem **31–15.**

Allen Equipment Company

CURRENT POSITION

As of December 31, 1950, Mr. Allen, of the Allen Equipment Company, was very much interested in having the balance sheet of his company reflect as strong a liquid position as possible. The following condensed excerpt of current position is taken from the preliminary statement of financial condition as prepared by Mr. Allen's bookkeeper:

Cash	$46,027.14	
Accounts Receivable	12,014.66	
Merchandise	24,927.81	
Other Current Assets	17,979.63	$100,949.24
Accounts Payable	$47,723.32	
Other Current Liabilities	7,311.89	$ 55,035.21

After examination of these figures, Mr. Allen decided that it would be possible to show a much stronger current position. He directed the elimination of merchandise and accounts payable of $821.17, which amount represented an order of rubber packing and miscellaneous supplies from the Rainbow Packing Company. The merchandise represented by this order was not yet on hand, nor had an invoice been received to cover it. Nevertheless the bill of lading in Mr. Allen's possession proved that the shipment was in transit.

Mr. Allen directed his cashier to prepare checks in payment of $39,-288.08 of the accounts payable, and told his bookkeeper to adjust the December 31 balance sheet so as to reflect the new status of financial condition.

The checks, properly prepared and signed, were not immediately despatched, for Mr. Allen instructed the cashier to hold them in his desk, temporarily, until he, Mr. Allen, authorized their mailing.

As an independent accountant, would you have prepared and certified to a balance sheet which incorporated the adjustments which Mr. Allen directed? Why or why not? Discuss fully.

Problem **31–16.** Submit an intelligent criticism of the following balance sheet:

Western Electric Company, Incorporated

BALANCE SHEET, DECEMBER 31, 1940

Assets

Plant at Cost	
Land	$ 9,384,410
Buildings, Service Equipment and Machinery	115,708,101
Small Tools, Furniture and Fixtures	14,319,512
Total Plant	139,412,023

Investments

Subsidiary and Associated Companies		47,727,492
Realty, Including Sales Contracts and Mortgages Receivable, at Cost less Reserve of $890,295		2,334,510
Other, at Cost less Reserve of $11,903		1,094,944
Total Investments		51,156,946
Deferred Receivables less Reserve of $45,556		933,054
Prepaid Insurance and Rent		366,066

Current Assets

Advances to Suppliers		150,804
Merchandise at the Lower of Cost or Market		
Raw Materials and Supplies		7,533,532
In Process		20,621,191
Completed		22,113,738
Total Merchandise.		50,268,461

Receivables

Notes			239,467
Accounts			
Bell Telephone Companies			34,169,804
Subsidiary and Associated Companies			1,436,508
Other Customers		$2,589,331	
Employees		47,153	
		2,636,484	
Less Reserve		13,797	2,622,687
Total Receivables			38,468,466

Marketable Securities at the Lower of Cost or Market

United States Government		3,000,000
Municipals		1,543,728
Total Marketable Securities (Value at Market $4,583,003)		4,543,728
Cash and Deposits		10,648,482
Total Current Assets		104,079,941
Grand Total		295,948,030

Liabilities

Capital and Surplus

Capital (Represented by 6,000,000 shares, without Par Value, Authorized and Outstanding)

Cash Paid in by Stockholders		$141,000,000
From Surplus		1,500,000
		142,500,000
Surplus.		24,333,039
Total Capital and Surplus		166,833,039

Reserves

Depreciation of Plant		78,355,110
Employment Stabilization		3,273,649
Equalization of Development		4,408,842
Workmen's Compensation		250,000
Other Self-Insured Risks		237,348
Total Reserves		86,524,949

Notes Payable to Trustee of Pension Fund   11,509,521
Deferred Credits   1,150,304
Current and Accrued Liabilities
  Accrued Taxes and Interest   13,423,889
  Accounts Payable
    Pay Rolls and Suppliers   9,256,261
    Subsidiary and Associated Companies   1,501,011
    Other   2,736,528
  Drafts Payable   3,012,528
                                                    ————————

      Total Current and Accrued Liabilities   29,930,217

         Grand Total   295,948,030

Contingent Liabilities — Notes Guaranteed . . . . $ 1,429,744

Problem **31–17.**

ALLIED CHEMICAL & DYE CORPORATION: I

ADEQUACY OF FINANCIAL STATEMENTS

During 1932 and 1933 the Committee on Stock List of the New York Stock Exchange engaged in extended correspondence with the Allied Chemical & Dye Corporation in an effort to induce the corporation to submit more informative financial reports. The 1932 balance sheet and income statement were among the reports criticized by the Committee. These reports follow:

Allied Chemical & Dye Corporation

CONSOLIDATED GENERAL BALANCE SHEET, DECEMBER 31, 1932

Assets

Property account:
  Real Estate, Plants, Equipment, Mines, etc. $222,990,044.37

Investments:
  Bonds and Stocks of Other Companies $12,535,809.92
  Sundry 156,700.21   12,692,510.13

Current assets:
  Cash $25,883,392.78
  U. S. Government and Other Marketable Securi-
    ties [4] 92,404,341.36
  Accounts and Notes Receivable 9,721,719.65
  Inventories [4] 22,645,245.29   150,654,699.08

Deferred charges:
  Prepaid Taxes, Insurance, etc. 892,884.71

[4] President Weber's Annual Report stated:

"The policy of valuing inventories at the end of the year on a basis of cost or market, whichever was lower, has been continued.

"U. S. Government and other marketable securities are stated at cost. The difference between cost and market value is amply provided for in the general contingency reserves created for the protection of the Company's assets and operations."

Other assets:

Patents, Processes, Trade-Marks, Goodwill, etc.		21,305,942.61
		$408,536,080.90

Liabilities

Current liabilities:

Accounts Payable	$ 1,827,846.87	
Wages Accrued	180,906.83	
Dividends Payable	4,289,417.75	$ 6,298,171.45

Reserves:

Depreciation, Obsolescence, etc.	$129,257,567.42	
General Contingencies [5]	55,887,867.30	
Taxes	1,731,371.86	
Insurance	2,269,316.42	
Sundry	2,347,675.43	191,493,798.43

Capital stock:

Preferred Stock, Par $100 per Share		
Issued 392,849 Shares	$ 39,284,900.00	
Common Stock, without par value, basis $5 per Share		
Issued 2,401,288 Shares	12,006,440.00	51,291,340.00

Surplus — December 31, 1932:

Capital Surplus	$ 61,752,335.00	
Further Surplus	97,700,436.02	159,452,771.02
		$408,536,080.90

Allied Chemical & Dye Corporation

Consolidated Income Account

Year Ended December 31, 1932

Gross Income after provision for depreciation, obsolescence, all state and local taxes, repairs and renewals	$12,730,108.80
Federal Taxes	1,288,919.28
Net Income	$11,441,189.52

Surplus Account

Surplus at December 31, 1931	$165,169,252.50	
Net Income year 1932	11,441,189.52	$176,610,442.02

---

[5] In its Annual Report for the year ending December 31, 1931, the corporation stated:

"With a realization that the world-wide economic readjustment now being experienced may be attended by a continuance of disturbed business conditions, it has been deemed advisable to transfer $40,000,000 from surplus to contingency reserves for the purpose of amply protecting the Company's operations and assets against future contingencies."

Dividends:
   Cash — Preferred . . . . $ 2,749,943.00
              Common 14,407,728.00   17,157,671.00

Surplus at December 31, 1932 . . . . $159,452,771.02

The advances of the Committee on Stock List were not kindly received. The corporation was markedly disinclined to adopt the reforms which were urged upon it, its general defense being that the publication of the information requested would be damaging to the corporation in the conduct of its business and not in the best interest of its stockholders.

The Committee on Stock List recognized that "the special nature of the business of the corporation might lend some justification to this viewpoint." The Committee proceeded carefully and considerately, and the changes which it finally requested were those which, to the Committee, were essential to the protection of the investor and yet could not be demonstrated as being harmful to the business of the company.

You are requested to study the financial statements of the Allied Chemical & Dye Corporation. If the controversy between the Exchange and the corporation had been referred to you for adjudication, what changes in the corporation's reports, if any, would you have insisted upon, giving due regard for the interests involved, and for the principles of good accounting?

ALLIED CHEMICAL & DYE CORPORATION: II

ADEQUACY OF FINANCIAL STATEMENTS (*continued*)

The following information was not officially reported by the Allied Chemical & Dye Corporation but was elicited by the New York Stock Exchange, and by the annual meeting of the corporation's stockholders, April 24, 1933.

With respect to the item "U. S. Government and Other Marketable Securities" on the 1932 balance sheet of the company, it was ascertained that

(1) Their market value was about $28,000,000 less than cost.[6]

(2) Included therein were "substantial" holdings of the company's own preferred and common stocks. In its letter of May 26, 1933, to President Weber, the Exchange stated that "it appears from your letter to the governing committee that holdings of your own stock constitute the most important item of the so-called 'other marketable securities.'"

The Exchange continued:

". . . While custom has, in some instances, sanctioned the inclusion of a corporation's own stock among its assets, this cannot be justified unless

---

[6] In answer to Stockholder James W. Gerard's question at the annual meeting of stockholders, April 24, 1933. The presiding officer stated that "the reserves which have been provided are ample to take care of this depreciation."

the facts are fully disclosed. Furthermore, under the existing conditions, there is no justification for including such holdings among current assets.

"In the financial reports of your company since 1929, there has been no indication either in the balance sheet or in income or surplus accounts which would lead stockholders to believe that your company had purchased either its own preferred or common stocks. On the contrary, the statement of surplus against which you have annually charged the amount of dividends paid has shown a deduction from surplus equal to the current rate of dividend on the entire amount of preferred and common stock which was issued and supposedly outstanding in the hands of the public. This form of statement tended to make stockholders believe that your company had not purchased its own shares.

"The above described method of reporting the dividends paid by your company necessarily casts doubt upon the validity of the income statement of your company. When this fact was pointed out to you, you stated that the amount of these dividends had not been included in the income account because a corresponding sum had simultaneously been credited to an unspecified reserve account.

"This explanation of the manner in which the dividends on stock held by the company had been included in your financial statements does not solve the problem. If it is improper for a corporation to increase its income by including therein dividends on its own stock (and this, of course, would be particularly true where the dividends paid were not fully earned, as was the case with your company in 1932, according to the published reports for that year), it is equally improper for a corporation to credit such dividends to some reserve account without disclosing the relevant facts to stockholders."

With respect to the content of the "U. S. Government and Other Marketable Securities" item, Mr. H. F. Atherton, secretary of the Allied Chemical & Dye Corporation, wrote the Exchange as follows under date of May 24, 1933:

". . . The fact is that about $20,000,000 of U. S. government securities are included. It had been rumored that the balance of the item represents a speculative trading account, largely affecting the company's earnings. The fact is that it consists practically entirely of the securities of six companies. Of these holdings the chief are substantial holdings of the company's preferred and common stock. The others are in the main holdings in other companies which are related to this company's operations, and for this reason we consider that it would be contrary to the best interests of our stockholders to publish the list of these holdings. All these securities have been held for years; there have been no sales of any of them at any time, except that in 1931 the company decreased its holdings in one other company by less than 20% and in another by less than 15%. None of these securities are current assets in the sense that the company contemplates cashing them in the near future, but only in the sense they are in fact readily marketable. The company has never speculated in the security markets and never will under the present management."

Referring to the income account of the company, the Exchange commented, in its letter of May 26, 1933, as follows:

". . . Since you do not disclose the amount of your annual appropriation for depreciation, or obsolescence, it is possible to increase or decrease these at pleasure. It has also been developed at our hearings that income from securities and the above mentioned dividends upon your own reacquired stock, as well as non-recurrent items, such as a large tax refund, may have been credited more or less directly to reserves. Within wide limits, therefore, the lack of information as to details of your income account makes it possible for the management of your company to vary the reported income up or down, at pleasure, and makes it impossible to compare intelligently the income account of one year with that of another. We do not say that this great power has been abused. We do say that it ought not to exist. After considering these facts, the Governing Committee concluded that the income account of your company, as it has been reported in the past, amounts to nothing more than a statement of an arbitrary amount which the management and directors of your company have elected to call 'income.'"

The financial statements of Allied Chemical & Dye Corporation are published once each year. In an effort to increase the number of releases each year, the Committee on Stock List wrote the corporation under date of June 23, 1932, as follows:

". . . As a suggestion, rather than a request, we ask you to consider again the matter of the publication of either quarterly income statements or the quarterly publication of an income statement for the preceding twelve months. We have reviewed the reply of the secretary of your company to Mr. Whitney's letter of October 8, 1931, requesting the publication of such statements; but it is not clear to us how twelve months' statements published quarterly can possibly be misleading."

Does the Allied Chemical & Dye Corporation, by listing its securities on the New York Stock Exchange, assume an obligation to provide present and prospective stockholders with "reasonable" information about the affairs of the company? Do the 1932 statements furnish such "reasonable" information?

To your mind, how should the item "U. S. Government and Other Marketable Securities" have been presented on the balance sheet? Explain carefully and in detail. What is the inference to be drawn from the company's handling of this item on its balance sheet of December 31, 1932?

Are dividends on reacquired stock credits to income, or to reserves? What is "income"? Do you agree that the position of the Exchange with respect to the adequacy of the corporation's income account is well taken? Why?

Discuss the request of the Exchange for interim reports. Are such reports difficult to compile? Are they likely to be misleading, or to be competitively injurious to the corporation? Should the company be asked to prepare and release such statements? Why? What is your opinion of twelve months' income statements released quarterly?

Prepare a summary of the changes which you would make in the official 1932 financial statements of the Allied Chemical & Dye Corporation.

Chapter 32

VALUATION

Just as the income statement and the balance sheet are the fundamental statements of accounting, so is valuation the fundamental component of each of these statements. The income statement and balance sheet, obviously, can be correct only if their constituent values are correct. Valuation is the heart of the statement of income. It is also the heart of the balance sheet.

The problem of valuation is always present. When assets are acquired there is the problem of valuation as of the date of acquisition. At the end of each accounting period there is the problem of revaluation. Wealth is not a static thing; it is dynamic, a thing of life. The values of business are changing so constantly that each new balance sheet is a balance sheet of new values.

The problem of valuation is so broad and complex that its full consideration is precluded in a text on elementary accounting. Only an introduction can be attempted in this book. Valuation, as discussed in this chapter, will be valuation presented from the standpoint of a going concern.

The problem of valuation initially requires a careful segregation of expenditures into those for capital and revenue purposes. Expenditures which are mistakenly capitalized result in an overstatement of net income, and an inflation of the asset values of the balance sheet. Expenditures which are improperly debited to expense result in an understatement of net income and asset values.[1] Correct classification of expenditures is the cornerstone of sound valuation accounting. No expenditure should be capitalized unless there is positive assurance of the present existence of value. When there is doubt as to the classification of an expenditure, it is conservative to debit the expenditure to expense.

All assets should be recorded at cost on their dates of acquisition. On successive balance sheet dates current assets should be valued upon the basis of their expected normal convertibility into cash, and fixed assets should be valued at cost less adequate cumulative depreciation or depletion to date. Other assets, such as intangibles, should be valued at conservative cost — in some cases original cost

---

[1] Capital and revenue expenditures were discussed at length in Chapter 27, page 579.

less amortization to date, in other cases at original cost without deduction for amortization. In all cases, however, the individual values of the assets (and liabilities) of each balance sheet should be established in conformity with sound principles of accounting.

When assets are sold or otherwise retired from service, their book values should be cleared from the accounts.

Assets which cannot be valued satisfactorily on financial statements may be referred to through the use of footnotes.

The problems of valuation which follow are discussed in the order in which the accounts appear on the balance sheet.

CURRENT ASSETS

As a general rule current assets should be valued at their expected convertibility into cash in the normal operations of business. Within the framework of this general rule is included the specific rule of cost or market, whichever is lower. This rule enjoys favor as a conservative rule for the valuation of certain current assets.

CASH

Cash includes:

Money
Undeposited checks of current date
Checking accounts
Bank drafts
Express and postal money orders

Cash which is restricted, such as savings accounts, time deposits, or a trustee sinking fund, should not be included in the general cash expected to be used for the payment of current liabilities. Dishonored checks should not be included in the general cash of a business; on dishonor these checks should be debited to accounts receivable.

ACCOUNTS RECEIVABLE

The value of accounts receivable should be face value less an adequate provision for uncollectible accounts. The remainder represents the approximate amount of cash which should be realized on the collection of outstanding accounts receivable. If the cash value of accounts receivable is to be shown more accurately, a further deduction from accounts receivable should be made to cover the amount of sales discounts which are yet available to customers with unpaid accounts. Accounts receivable would then appear on the balance sheet in the following manner:

Accounts Receivable		$106,000.00	
Less Reserve for Bad Debts	$6,000.00		
Reserve for Sales Discounts . .	1,000.00	7,000.00	$99,000.00

From this it follows that if it is logical to deduct available sales discounts from accounts receivable it is logical, also, for available purchases discounts to be deducted from accounts payable (on the liability side of the balance sheet).

The accounting which underlies the use of reserves for cash discounts in the valuation of accounts receivable and accounts payable is described in the author's *Intermediate Accounting*.

NOTES RECEIVABLE

Notes receivable should be valued at face value. Past-due and dishonored notes should not be included under this heading but should be classified separately and valued at face value less adequate reserve for uncollectibility.

MARKETABLE SECURITIES HELD AS SHORT-TERM INVESTMENTS

Stocks and bonds purchased as short-term investments of working capital should be recorded at cost. Cost includes brokerage fees, taxes, and other costs incidental to purchase. The valuation of these securities at later dates is a problem in itself. Complexities are engendered which are similar in nature to those encountered in the valuation of merchandise inventory. Valuation may be at (1) cost, (2) cost or market, whichever is lower, or (3) market. The comments which are made on pages 706–712 with respect to these methods of valuation for merchandise inventory apply also to securities purchased as short-term investments.

As a general rule accountants prefer the first two methods. Shrinkages in market values below the cost of marketable securities should be recognized by the establishment of adequate reserves out of current profit and loss. On the balance sheet marketable securities should be accompanied by a memorandum indicating the valuation base employed and, where cost is the base, by a notation as to the current market value of the securities, thus:

Stocks and bonds, at cost (market value, $110,000.00) $100,000.00

As a general rule the dollar balance of an account representing securities is not affected by the receipt of either a cash or a stock dividend.

Stocks and bonds may be purchased at various prices. When securities are sold their cost should be cleared from the proper stock or bond account, as the case may be. If a sold security cannot be identified as belonging to a specific purchase and therefore as belonging to part, or all, of a specific cost, the accounting should proceed on the assumption that the first securities sold were the first securities purchased.

MERCHANDISE INVENTORY

The valuation of merchandise inventory is one of the most important of valuation problems as well as one of the most complex. That this is so will be clear after a careful examination of the following condensation of methods for the valuation of merchandise inventory.

I. *Valuation at cost*

What is cost? There are several answers to this question:

(1) Each item of inventory is valued at last invoice cost. For example,

```
1950 purchases of article A:
          January 2   2,000 @ $1.00 = $2,000.00
          June 1      2,200 @  1.25 =  2,750.00
          October 1     800 @  1.50 =  1,200.00
December 31 (1950) inventory:
          Quantity  = 1,000 units
          Valuation = 1,000 @ $1.50 = $1,500.00
```

This method is subject to the criticism that the last invoice price may not be a price which is representative of the entire inventory.

(2) Each item of inventory is valued at actual invoice cost, thus:

```
December 31 inventory:
      Quantity = 1,000 units which, upon analysis,
                 represent
                 100 units of January 2 purchase
                 200 units of June 1 purchase
                 700 units of October 1 purchase

                 1,000

      Valuation =     100 @ $1.00 = $  100.00
                      200 @ $1.25 =    250.00
                      700 @ $1.50 =  1,050.00

                                   $1,400.00
```

In theory this method is the perfect way of "costing" an inventory. In practice, however, the theory is often found to be impracticable because of the expense involved and because of the difficulty of associating each item of inventory with a particular purchase.

(3) Each item of inventory is valued at average cost:

December 31 inventory:
                    Quantity = 1,000 units
                    Valuation = 1,000 @ $1.25 (simple average cost)   = $1,250.00
                                                    (or)
                                       = 1,000 @ $1.19 (weighted average cost) = $1,190.00

(4) Each item of inventory is valued upon a "first-in, first-out" basis. It is assumed that the inventory on hand represents the last merchandise purchased, thus:

December 31 inventory:
                    Quantity = 1,000 units
                    Valuation =   800 @ $1.50 (October 1 purchase)   = $1,200.00
                                       200 @ $1.25 (June 1 purchase)   =   250.00
                                                                                                 ——————
                                                                                                 $1,450.00

Thus, in this brief exposition, valuation of inventory "at cost" may mean any one of the following valuations: [2]

(a) $1,500.00   (c) $1,250.00   (d) $1,450.00
(b)   1,400.00   1,190.00

The effect of the use of each of these several cost valuations upon the balance sheet, and upon the net income figure of the statement of profit and loss, should be clear.

In each of these methods of inventory valuation, "cost" is interpreted to mean invoice cost plus transportation charges paid by the purchaser up to the time that the goods have been received in his place of business. In the interest of accounting consistency, and to conform with sound accounting theory, purchases discounts should be deducted in arriving at the cost of a merchandise inventory.

II. *Valuation at cost or market, whichever is lower*

This method for the valuation of inventory is widely used. The term "market" means the current replacement cost of the inventory on hand. For tax purposes the Treasury Department defines market value as follows: "Under ordinary circumstances 'market' means the current bid price prevailing at the date of the inventory for the particular merchandise in the volume in which [it is] usually purchased by the taxpayer."

Under this method, if the inventory has a market value in excess of cost, the inventory is valued at cost. The inventory is not valued at market value because to do so would bring an unrealized profit on the books. A profit can actually be realized only through a transaction of sale.

If the inventory has a market value less than cost, the inventory

———————————
[2] Reference to texts on advanced accounting and on auditing will disclose additional methods of inventory valuation "at cost."

is valued at market value. The shrinkage in value is taken up as a loss of the current accounting period although, to be sure, the loss is an unrealized one. The loss is included as one of the costs of current income purely as a matter of financial conservatism.

Under the rule of cost or market, whichever is lower, the value of the inventory is obtained by applying the rule to *each item of inventory*, thus:

	Cost	Market	Value of Inventory
Article A	$1,400.00	$1,500.00	$1,400.00
Article B	2,000.00	1,700.00	1,700.00
Value of inventory			$3,100.00

From the standpoint of the balance sheet, valuation of the inventory at cost or market, whichever is lower, is conservative valuation. From the standpoint of the operating statement, however, the use of a value which is less than cost will not give correct gross profit information:

PROFIT AND LOSS STATEMENT

	With Inventory Valued at	
	Cost	Market
Sales	$100,000.00	$100,000.00
Cost of sales:		
Purchases	90,000.00	90,000.00
December 31 inventory:		
At cost	30,000.00	
At cost or market, whichever is lower		25,000.00
Cost of sales	$ 60,000.00	$ 65,000.00
Gross Profit	$ 40,000.00	$ 35,000.00

The following statement would seem to be a better representation of what has occurred:

Sales		$100,000.00
Cost of Sales:		
Purchases	$90,000.00	
December 31 inventory at cost	30,000.00	60,000.00
Gross Profit		$ 40,000.00
Operating Expenses		29,000.00
Net Profit from Operations		$ 11,000.00

Other Expense:
  Shrinkage in value of inventory as measured by
    replacement cost 5,000.00

Net Income . . . . $ 6,000.00

Under the cost or market rule, inventory on the balance sheet will
be valued at

(1) Lower than cost if replacement cost is less than actual cost.
     This lower valuation is assumed to represent the lower
     cash convertibility of the merchandise on hand.[3]
(2) Cost, if cost is less than market. This valuation, as previous-
     ly stated, is conservative; but, on the other hand, it is
     not representative in cases where the market value is
     higher than the cost value. It would seem that if current
     assets are to be stated in the balance sheet at their ex-
     pected cash values, that if merchandise inventory has a
     replacement value greater than cost value, and that if this
     appreciation is expected to be realized, some mention of
     the increased valuation should be made, thus:

Assets:
  Merchandise inventory at cost (market value, $38,000.00) . . $30,000.00
                   (or)
Assets:
  Merchandise inventory at cost $30,000.00
        Add unrealized profit. 8,000.00

           Market value $38,000.00
Net Worth:
  Unrealized surplus arising from appreciation of
     merchandise inventory   . . . . $ 8,000.00

The $8,000.00 figures may be regarded purely as balance sheet
memoranda. But, if desired, they may be incorporated in the books
in the form of memoranda accounts.

III. *Retail method of inventory*

Valuation of inventory under this method is as follows:

	At Cost	At Retail
January 1 inventory	$18,000.00	$ 26,000.00
Purchases	47,200.00	72,000.00

[3] An interesting editorial appeared in the *Journal of Accountancy*, Vol. 53, No. 3
(March, 1932), pp. 161–164, on the matter of inventory valuation. ". . . If he [the
accountant] feels that the inventory, when there is a demand for that inventory, will
surely have a greater value than at present, he has at least logic on his side when he
advocates departure from the generally estimable principle of cost-or-market-whichever-
is-lower."

Freight In	1,800.00	
Markups (in addition to original markup)		2,000.00
Total merchandise to be accounted for . . .	$67,000.00	$100,000.00
	(Cost is 67% of retail.)	
Sales		$ 60,000.00
Markdowns (made during period of established selling prices)		4,000.00
Sales at intended retail		$ 64,000.00
December 31 inventory at retail		$ 36,000.00
December 31 inventory at cost (67% of $36,000.00) .	$24,120.00	

The following conditions are necessary to the successful use of the retail method of inventory:

(1) Accurate information must be maintained for

Purchases at cost and at retail
Other merchandise costs
Additional markups

Sales
Markdowns

(2) This information must be maintained by departments, or sections if the rate of markup varies for these departments, or sections. Inventories, accordingly, are determined for each department, or section.

(3) The rate of markup should be uniform within a section, department, or store, as the case may be.

(4) A physical inventory should be taken periodically.

IV. *Valuation of inventories for manufacturing companies*

As a general rule,

Raw materials are valued at (1) cost, or (2) cost or market, whichever is lower.

Work in process is valued at cost as represented by the detailed cost sheets embracing work in process.

Finished goods are valued at (1) cost, or (2) cost or market, whichever is lower.

This section may well conclude with the sentence with which it began: *The valuation of merchandise inventory is one of the most important of valuation problems as well as one of the most complex.* In addition it may be said that the mere mechanics of the problem of inventory valuation is often an expensive process as well.

Parenthetically, it may be in order to comment on the matter of interim financial statements and the inventories which form a part of these statements. Interim financial statements, of course, are prepared directly from work sheets; the books are not closed. The accuracy of interim statements, no less so than annual statements, is greatly dependent upon the valuation which is placed upon the item of inventory. Naturally, this valuation should be established on the basis of an actual physical count of the inventory at the end of each interim period. However, managements are often satisfied to have these statements based on estimated inventories rather than on actual physical inventories. This is because estimated inventories involve less expense and because the estimated values are believed to approximate closely the real values involved. But after the ledger has accumulated its data for twelve months and the books are being formally closed for the year, the closing should always be strictly on the basis of exact data, and inventory values resting on physical count *must* be used.

One final word is necessary. The merchandise which is being valued must be owned by the business on whose accounts and statements the merchandise is to appear as an asset. Only merchandise on hand and in transit to which the purchaser has title should be the subject of valuation; all other merchandise (like consignment merchandise on hand, or purchases in transit f.o.b. destination, for example) should be excluded. It is important for the accountant to be well acquainted with the law of sales relating to the times at which title passes in order for merchandise and merchandise liabilities to be evaluated correctly.

As a general rule, it may be said that title to merchandise passes when the parties intend it to pass. If their intention is not clear, recourse may be had to rules established for the purpose of determining the times at which titles pass. These detailed rules are found in the Uniform Sales Act, Sections 17–22. The Uniform Sales Act has been adopted by New York and more than twenty-five other states. Important excerpts from the Uniform Sales Act follow:

Sec. **18.** (1) Where there is a contract to sell specific or ascertained goods, the property in them is transferred to the buyer at such time as the parties intend it to be transferred.

(2) For the purpose of ascertaining the intention of the parties, regard shall be had to the terms of the contract, the conduct of the parties, usages of trade and the circumstances of the case.

Sec. **19.** Rule 4. (1) Where there is a contract to sell unascertained or future goods by description, and goods of that description and in a deliverable state are unconditionally appropriated to the contract, either by the seller with the assent of the buyer, or by the buyer with the assent of the seller, the property in the goods thereupon passes to the buyer. Such assent may be expressed or implied, and may be given either before or after the appropriation is made.

(2) Where, in pursuance of a contract to sell, the seller delivers the goods to the buyer, or to a carrier or other bailee (whether named by the buyer or not) for the purpose of transmission to or holding for the buyer, he is presumed to have unconditionally appropriated the goods to the contract, except in the cases provided for in the next rule and in Section 101. This presumption is applicable although by the terms of the contract the buyer is to pay the price before receiving delivery of the goods, and the goods are marked with the words collect on delivery or their equivalent.

Rule 5. If the contract to sell requires the seller to deliver the goods to the buyer, or at a particular place, or to pay the freight or costs of transportation to the buyer, or to a particular place, the property does not pass until the goods have been delivered to the buyer or reached the place agreed upon.

SUPPLIES

Office and factory supplies should be valued at cost as applied to a physical inventory of usable supplies.

LONG–TERM INVESTMENTS

SECURITIES

As a general rule, stocks purchased for long-term investment should be valued at cost, and bonds at amortized cost. If the bonds were purchased at a price below par, their value on the balance sheet should be cost plus discount amortized to date. If they were purchased at a price above par, their value on the balance sheet should be cost minus premium amortized to date. If the information is important, market values of securities carried as long-term investments may be referred to through the use of footnotes.

As a general rule, market values may be disregarded. However, if market values are significantly less than cost, a special surplus reserve may be established as a precautionary measure. Gains or losses realized on the disposal of securities carried as long-term investments should be placed in the comprehensive income account with profit and loss.

In certain cases the investment of one corporation in the stock of another corporation may be an investment large enough to represent a controlling interest. The relation of parent company and subsidiary will then exist. In such cases the investment may be carried on the books of the parent company (1) at cost, or (2) at cost, plus the parent company's share of the profits of the subsidiary company, and minus the parent company's share of the losses of the subsidiary, and minus the parent company's share of cash dividends declared. The profits, losses, and dividends here referred to are the profits, losses, and dividends of the subsidiary company after the date on which the parent company acquired its controlling interest in the subsidiary company. When the balance sheet of the parent company is prepared, however, it is desirable for the actual assets and liabilities of the subsidiary company, and their attendant values, to be substituted for the value of the stock investment account on the books of the parent company. In more formal language, it is necessary to prepare a consolidated balance sheet. With respect to income, it is necessary to prepare a consolidated profit and loss statement.

The preparation of consolidated financial statements is beyond the compass of this book. This is a topic for treatment in the field of advanced accounting.

SINKING FUND WITH TRUSTEE

This account should be:

Debited with	*Credited with*
All deposits made with the trustee.	Disbursements made by the trustee to retire bonds of issue.
Dividends or interest received by the trustee.	Losses on sales of sinking fund securities by the trustee.
Profits on sales of sinking fund securities by the trustee.	Trustee expenses paid out of sinking fund moneys.

FIXED ASSETS

As a general rule fixed assets should be valued at cost less cumulative depreciation, depletion, or amortization to date. Cost includes

(1) Cost of acquisition:

> Invoice cost
> Freight and cartage
> Sales and excise taxes
> All costs incurred for the purpose of making the fixed asset ready for use (installation costs, running-in costs, etc.)

(2) Cost of later capital additions

In arriving at proper accounting valuations for fixed assets, due regard should be given to the philosophy that fixed assets really represent long-term prepaid expenses, and that periodic provisions for depreciation, depletion, or amortization are made to reflect the portions of these prepayments which have been converted into expense during the periods in question.

At any given date, an inventory of the items of a particular class of fixed assets, stated at their individual costs, should agree with the balance of the fixed asset account on the general ledger.

When an asset is sold, or otherwise retired from service, the book value of the asset should be cleared from the accounts.

Appreciation in the value of fixed assets is not usually recognized in the accounts. This rule, while conservative, is not entirely inflexible. Appreciation may be recognized in the accounts if it is "permanent" and if it is based on proper appraisal. The resulting surplus should be segregated in a special, properly titled surplus account, such as Appraisal Surplus. In succeeding accounting periods, the charges to operations for depreciation, depletion, or amortization should continue to be on the basis of original cost.

BUILDINGS

Buildings should be recorded on the books at cost. This cost includes all reasonable expenditures incurred up to the date on which the building is ready for occupancy. Cost includes

Architects' fees
Building permit

Insurance paid during period
of construction
Subsequent improvements

On the balance sheet buildings should appear at cost less cumulative depreciation to date.

LAND

Land should be valued at cost. This includes cost of purchase and expenditures for permanent improvements, such as:

Commissions
Draining, filling, grading
Paving

Sidewalks
Title fees
Water and sewer assessments

As a general rule land does not depreciate. Hence it should always appear in the balance sheet at cost.

The market price for land, at times, may differ widely from cost. Market values, however, are generally not admitted to the balance sheet. Variances of market values from costs represent unrealized gains or losses.

TOOLS

Tools should be valued on the balance sheet at depreciated cost. This valuation may be arrived at by either of the two following methods:

(1) New tools are debited to an asset account, Tools, and their value written off in 2, 3, or 4 years. The credit may be to the Tools account, or to the Reserve for Depreciation — Tools account.

(2) New tools are debited to an asset account, Tools. At the end of the year a physical inventory of tools is taken and valued at cost, or estimated depreciated cost. The Tools account is written down to the new valuation, the write-down constituting an offset debit to Depreciation Expense — Tools.

INTANGIBLES

Intangible assets may be defined as a special class of immaterial fixed assets of which brands, copyrights, formulas, franchises, goodwill, patents, and trade-marks are leading examples. The chief common characteristics of intangible assets are

(1) They are usually directly related to the future earnings of a business.

(2) Their value is generally dependent upon the "going-concern" concept of business enterprise. They attach to the enterprise as a whole. Although exceptions exist, like copyrights and patents, intangible assets evince a tendency to be inseparable from the business which owns them. Goodwill is an outstanding example.

The test of the value of intangibles is earning power. To clothe intangibles with accounting value a business should have earning power large enough to cover satisfactorily not only its net tangible assets but its intangibles as well. Thus, intangible assets should be capitalized only when they have a genuine present value defensible by the test of earnings yet to be realized. When so capitalized, debits to intangible asset accounts may include reasonable costs to purchase, develop, and defend.

Intangibles of definite life should be amortized over their commercial useful life by periodic charges to operations. There is a tendency on the part of some accountants to value intangibles of indefinite life at cost, with never any deduction for amortization. However, accounting valuations for intangible assets of definite and indefinite lives are warranted only by the test of the present existence of future earning power.

The investiture of intangible assets with significant account balances raises practical problems of accounting valuations. At best, many of the valuations attending the intangible assets of actual business are characterized by transience and uncertainty. In the interest of financial conservatism, many companies have written off their intangible assets. Lump sum write-offs of the values of intangible assets should be made by special debits to the comprehensive income account with current profit and loss. Credits are generally made to the asset accounts involved rather than to accounts with valuation reserves.

Many companies carry their intangible assets at a value of $1.00.[4]

In no case is there warrant for the retention of an accounting valuation for an intangible whose commercial value has expired.

COPYRIGHTS

Copyrights have a legal life of twenty-eight years with privilege of renewal for a similar period. Because copyright revenues generally last only a few years, the copyright cost should be written off in proportion to gross revenues as nearly as it is possible to do so. Some companies go so far as to write off the entire cost against the gross revenue of the first year.

GOODWILL

Goodwill exists when the net income of a specific business unit is greater than the normal rate of return expected for the general business or industry of which the specific unit is a part. Goodwill is the valuation placed upon this extra earning power.

Goodwill may also be defined as follows: When a specific business

---

[4] In its Annual Report of 1933, the Commercial Solvents Corporation stated that "the Corporation makes it a practice not to attribute on its books any value to intangible assets. . . ."

The New York Times stated, January 15, 1933, that Radio Corporation of America, in its first twelve years of existence, appropriated 55.6% of its net income (before write-downs) to write down "various capital accounts, such as patents, contracts, goodwill, inventories, plant and equipment, and other tangible and intangible assets." Total write-down over the twelve-year period, out of earnings, amounted to $52,695,730. Additional write-downs, out of capital, amounted to $31,130,360.

The Bell Aircraft Corporation balance sheet of December 31, 1941, carried "Airplane Design Rights, Drawings, and Patents" at the significant but nominal valuation of $1.00.

The following are representative companies which carry their intangibles at $1.00:

Archer-Daniels-Midland Company	Oliver Farm Equipment Company
Armstrong Cork Company	Pittsburgh Plate Glass Company
Brown Shoe Company, Inc.	Union Carbide and Carbon Corporation
Liggett & Myers Tobacco Company	U.S. Steel Corporation
May Department Stores Company	White Sewing Machine Corporation
Nunn-Bush Shoe Company	Yale & Towne Manufacturing Company

unit has a value over and above the fair value of its net assets (excluding goodwill), the difference is goodwill.

Reasons advanced for the existence of goodwill include the following:

Efficient and courteous organization
Favorable customer attitude and buying habits
Location
Monopoly
Quality of merchandise and service
Possession of special privileges
Reputation for fair dealing

When these factors, singly or in combination, result in the realization of earnings greater than normal, goodwill exists. (It should be observed, however, that location is a factor in goodwill only when the value of location is not reflected in the value of the land.) The real test of the existence of goodwill, to repeat, is the ability of a specific business unit to earn a rate of return greater than "normal" for this general type of business.

It is a well-established principle of accounting that goodwill should not appear on the books of a business unless it has been purchased.

There are several ways of determining the purchase price (i.e., valuation) of goodwill. In all of them there is the fundamental assumption that the goodwill will continue for the benefit of future operations. Four methods for the determination of goodwill are

I. *Arbitrary sum for goodwill*

   Examples:

   (a) Purchase price of business (round amount) $100,000.00
        Net assets 94,814.00

        Goodwill . . . . $ 5,186.00

   (b) Purchase price of business $100,814.00
        Net assets 94,814.00

        Goodwill (round amount) . . . . $ 6,000.00

II. *Goodwill is x years' purchase of the average profits of a business for a period of years which are deemed representative of future periods*

   Example:

   $10,000.00 Average yearly profits
            3 Years' profits purchased

   $30,000.00 Goodwill

III. *Goodwill is x years' purchase of amount by which average profits exceed "normal" profits for that type of business*

Example:

$80,000.00 Invested capital

$10,000.00 Average profit (12½%)
  8,000.00 "Normal" profit expected from this type of business, i.e., 10%

$ 2,000.00 Excess profits
        10 Years for which these excess profits may be reasonably expected
           to continue

$20,000.00 Goodwill

IV. *Goodwill equals excess profits capitalized at "normal" rate of return*

Example:

$80,000.00 Invested capital

$10,000.00 Average profit (12½%)
  8,000.00 "Normal" profit expected from this type of business, i.e., 10%

$ 2,000.00 Excess profits
   ÷
   10%   "Normal" rate of return

$20,000.00 Goodwill

In this example the rate of 10% means that the excess profits are expected to continue indefinitely because the business is expected to continue to earn a total income of $10,000.00 per annum indefinitely. The excess income, then, is viewed as a perpetuity.

If the business continues to earn $10,000.00 annually, the purchaser will earn 10% on his capital investment of $100,000.00. He will earn the normal rate of return. Furthermore, if the business continues to earn just 10%, and if 10% continues to be the normal rate of return, there will be no more excess profits for this business.

If, under other conditions, the permanence of goodwill was doubtful because of doubt as to the length of the period for which the excess profits might continue to be earned, the additional risk involved would be compensated for by using a higher rate for the capitalization of excess profits. If a rate of 20% were used, goodwill would be $2,000.00 ÷ 20% = $10,000.00. If 25% were used, goodwill would be $2,000.00 ÷ 25% = $8,000.00. These rates make allowance for the unusual risk inherent in assuming the perpetuity of the differential income of $2,000.00.

A businessman would be likely to explain the use of the 20 % rate as indicating that the excess profits promise to be short-lived, i.e., five years, and the 25 % rate as indicating a probable life of four years. He is also very likely to state that the excess profits being purchased are those for five years, for four years, or for the number of years indicated by the rate used for the capitalization of excess earnings.

The first and second methods are not to be recommended. They disregard the fundamental upon which goodwill rests, i.e., earning power in excess of normal. The third and fourth methods represent more reasonable approaches to the problem of the valuation of goodwill. It should be borne in mind, however, that the goodwill figure which is finally agreed upon by buyer and seller is usually a compromise of judgment, computation, and bargaining. Some corporations write off goodwill, either in one lump sum, or by periodic charges to surplus over several periods.[5] Goodwill is written off because of the fluctuations in value to which goodwill is subject, and also because of public inclination to discount heavily the valuations placed upon goodwill items in balance sheets. The specific justification generally advanced for write-offs of goodwill is the factor of financial conservatism. Many companies carry goodwill on their books at a nominal valuation of $1.00.[6]

As a matter of sound accounting theory, the investment in true goodwill is a revenue cost of future excess income. Goodwill should be amortized systematically by regular charges to the profit and loss accounts of future accounting periods, i.e., those periods for which excess profits were purchased. For an extended discussion of goodwill accounting, the student is referred to Chapter 20 of the author's *Intermediate Accounting*.

LEASEHOLDS

A leasehold is a contractual right to the occupancy of specified realty for a stated period of time.

In the ordinary lease agreement, where the contract calls for

---

[5] Typical in this respect is the Chrysler Corporation which, in 1931, reduced its goodwill from $25,000,000.00 to $1.00. Similarly, in 1935, the Borden Company reduced its goodwill from $7,000,000.00 to $1.00.

[6] Among these are the following:

American Commercial Alcohol Corporation	First National Stores, Inc.
The Borden Company	Liquid Carbonic Corporation
Borg-Warner Corporation	Nash Motors Company
Canada Dry Ginger Ale, Incorporated	National Tea Company
Chrysler Corporation	E. R. Squibb & Sons
Curtiss-Wright Corporation	F. W. Woolworth Company
Dixie-Vortex Company	

certain periodic payments of rent, no value should be given to the leasehold for purposes of the balance sheet. This is because no actual investment of capital has been made. If, however, the lessee has paid, say $5,000.00, for the right to occupy property for five years, with no further payment required, it is clear that the expenditure is a payment in advance of the rent for the entire five-year period. The expenditure is an asset, prepaid rent, one fifth of which should be written off each year to Rent Expense, thus:

Rent Expense	1,000.00	
Leasehold (or) Prepaid Rent		1,000.00

To write off $\frac{1}{5}$ of leasehold cost against income of this year.

This accounting represents "straight-line" amortization of the investment in the leasehold. Assuming the original payment to have been made January 1, 1950, the valuation of the leasehold at the end of each accounting period will be

December 31, 1950	$4,000.00
December 31, 1951	3,000.00
December 31, 1952	2,000.00
December 31, 1953	1,000.00
December 31, 1954	0.00

Assets constructed on leased property by the lessee should be written off in equal annual installments over the period of their commercial life. The maximum write-off period, however, is the period from the date of completion of construction to the date on which the lease expires.

PATENTS

Patents should be recorded on the books at cost. Cost includes

Purchase price	Fees (attorney and federal)
Developmental expenditures	Cost of legal defense

Patents have a definite life of seventeen years without privilege of renewal. They should be amortized by writing off at least $\frac{1}{17}$ of their cost each year to the operating account, Patents Expense, or Amortization of Patents. However, if a patent has a commercial life of less than seventeen years, the write-offs should be proportionately greater. Ideally, the cost of a patent should be written off in proportion to the annual gross incomes earned on the patent.

On the balance sheet patents should be carried at cost, less adequate amortization to date. Many companies, however, prefer to carry patents at some nominal valuation like $1.00.[7]

---

[7] These companies include P. Lorillard Company, Monsanto Chemical Company, Packard Motor Car Company, Underwood Elliott Fisher Company, U.S. Steel Corporation, and the Westinghouse Electric Corporation.

TRADE-MARKS

This asset should be valued at cost to purchase, develop, and defend. Because its legal life is without limit, a trade-mark is the permanent and exclusive property of its owner. Valuation of a trade-mark may therefore remain continuously at cost (i.e., without deduction for amortization). Many concerns, however, write off such values as a matter of conservatism, or carry them at a nominal valuation.[8] In no case is there warrant for the retention of an accounting valuation for a trade-mark whose commercial value has expired.

LIABILITIES

Liabilities are usually placed in the balance sheet at the cash values of the considerations which will be given to discharge them. To this general rule minor modifications are sometimes made. These modifications, covering such items as accounts payable, bonds payable, and deferred incomes, are discussed in the author's *Intermediate Accounting*.

A balance sheet should include all known liabilities at proper accounting valuations. Liabilities should be classified correctly and a total shown for all of them.

Contingent liabilities should be recognized by short-extending them or by mention in footnotes to the balance sheet.

VALUATION AND THE PROBLEM OF NET WORTH

The designation "watered stock" is applied to capital stock which has been issued for overvalued assets. The consequence of an overissue of stock is an overstatement of net worth. More generally, "water" may be stated to be present whenever the net worth of a business is overstated. This overstatement may be due to the fact that maintenance expenditures have been stinted, that depreciation charges have been inadequate, that revenue charges have been capitalized, or that liabilities have been understated or even omitted. Fundamentally, however, defective *valuation* is the cause of an overstatement of net worth.

The converse of an overstatement of net worth is an understatement of net worth. When the net worth of a business is understated, the amount of the understatement constitutes a "secret reserve." This secret reserve may be caused by original undervaluation of properties, or it may be due to the fact that capital expenditures have been charged to revenue, or that depreciation charges have been excessive, or that assets have been written down too rapidly or

---

[8] *Ibid.*

omitted, or that liabilities have been overstated. But, again, defective *valuation* is the cause of an understatement of net worth.

The history of finance is replete with cases which illustrate overstatements and understatements of net worth. Fundamentally, however, there is no good reason why the net worth of a business should not be stated as accurately as human ability will permit. A true presentment of net worth, in turn, is dependent upon complete observance of the principles of correct valuation. Thus, again, it may be stated that *valuation* is the heart of financial statements and, further, that *valuation* is *the* constituent element of net income and net worth.

QUESTIONS

Question **32–1.** (1) Explain why the problem of valuation is important. (2) What is the interest of the profit and loss statement in the problem of valuation? (3) What are the general principles of valuation?

Question **32–2.** Define, and explain the importance of, capital and revenue expenditures.

Question **32–3.** Professor Kester, in discussing the valuation of short-term investments, says that "since realizable value is the information desired, valuation at market, whether lower or higher than cost, is the only proper basis for use on the balance sheet." — (*Advanced Accounting*, p. 176.) Discuss.

Question **32–4.** Discuss the propriety of charging the Goodwill account with (1) discount on stock and (2) the cost of an intensive advertising campaign.

Question **32–5.** For balance sheet purposes, how would you value the following?

(1) Bonds held as investments.
(2) An apartment building which cost $100,000.00 to construct, not including $2,100.00 spent in razing the previously existing structure.
(3) Land is purchased for $20,000.00 for promotion as a realty development. Before the land is ready for sale, it is necessary to spend $10,000.00 for improvements such as grading, sidewalks, etc. Interest, amounting to $350.00, is paid on money borrowed, temporarily, for the work of improvement. After approximately one year's work, the property is ready for the market. The estimated sale value of the property is $60,000.00.
(4) Land is donated by a city to a company upon condition that the company maintain certain standards of operation for a period of five years. The land has a market value of $11,000.00.

(5) A corporation constructs a new building which is financed, in part, by the sale of $1,000,000.00 first-mortgage bonds at 90. The corporation charges the discount to the Buildings account.

(6) A leasehold, originally executed for 10 years, and costing $25,-000.00, has 4 years yet to run.

(7) A machine has an invoice cost of $1,000.00. Freight paid on the machine amounts to $50.00, and installation costs, $200.00.

(8) After 6 months it is decided to replace the foundation of the above machine with a better one. The old base is taken out and a new one installed. Total cost of this work, $364.00.

(9) A company manufactures certain equipment for its own use at a cost of $1,198.15. If the company had purchased this equipment on the open market, the cost would have been $2,000.00.

(10) The factory layout of the X corporation is altered for the purpose of providing a more efficient flow of work. The cost of this work is $7,500.00.

(11) A neon advertising sign is purchased at a cost of $600.00.

(12) A building, in the process of construction, is damaged by a violent storm. Because of this fact, total construction costs are increased 25 %.

Question **32–6.** Describe several methods for the valuation of merchandise inventory. Give your opinion of each method.

Question **32–7.** A company values its merchandise inventory at expected selling price multiplied by its cost of sales ratio for the year. What is your opinion of the company's valuation?

Question **32–8.** The Fairchild Pictures Corporation released 30 new pictures last year. How would you have valued the pictures in the corporation's film inventory of December 31?

Question **32–9.** On the balance sheet how would you show the value of the assets related to the following credit accounts:

Marginal account with broker
Mortgage on real estate
Notes Receivable Discounted
Reserve for Bad Debts
Reserve for Depletion
Reserve for Depreciation
Reserve for Sales Discounts Offered
Reserve for Decline in Value of Merchandise Inventory
Reserve for Decline in Value of Short-Term Investments
Reserve for Decline in Value of Long-Term Investments

Question **32–10.** You purchase an automobile billed to you as follows:

One V-8, Model 40, Standard, 5-window coupe.	$790.00
Freight	42.50
Bumpers	15.00
Tire and Tube	19.60

Gas, Oil, and Lubrication	5.89
Tax Reimbursed Manufacturer	14.89
Interest and Insurance	50.17
License	15.40
	$953.45

How should this invoice be recorded?

Question **32–11.** What are secret reserves? How are they created? Can they be justified? Explain fully.

PROBLEMS

Problem **32–1.** On an auditor's count and examination, the cash of the Knox & Wills Corporation was detailed as follows:

Balance of Cash account on books	$19,364.00
Coin and currency on hand	500.00
Unrecorded and undeposited customers' checks on hand	1,204.00
Postage stamps	100.00
Balance of bank account at First National Bank as per bank statement	20,412.00
Advance made to president of Knox & Wills Corporation, but covered by his check on hand dated three months from now .	500.00
Checks issued but not yet cleared through the bank	2,148.00

Required:

How should the cash appear on the balance sheet?

Problem **32–2.** The accounts receivable control of Hastings & Robbins, Inc., shows a balance of $121,476.09, including a $10,000.00 cash advance made to the Tyler Foundry Company on a contract for $50,000.00 covering certain items to be fabricated by the latter company for Hastings & Robbins, Inc.

How should accounts receivable be shown on the balance sheet?

Problem **32–3.** The purchase of a machine was covered by an invoice detailed as follows:

Machine, model XXZ4	$7,500.00
Sales tax	150.00
	$7,650.00

(1) The machine was paid for by check after taking a cash discount of 4%.

(2) The purchaser paid freight charges on the machine amounting to $250.00. Installation costs were $650.00.

Required:

What is the cost of this machine for balance sheet purposes?

Problem **32–4.** The L. C. Coleman Company handles one product only. The following condensed information is given to you for the year 1950:

January 1, 1950 inventory:
> Quantity = 1,500 units
> Valuation = $30,000.00 (at cost)
>   = $27,000.00 (at replacement cost)

Purchases for 1950:

2,000 units	@ $18.40 =	$36,800.00
2,200 units	@ $23.00 =	50,600.00
800 units	@ $27.60 =	22,080.00
		$109,480.00

December 31, 1950 inventory:
> Quantity   = 1,000 units
> Replacement cost per unit = $28.00

Required:

(1) Give five valuations of inventory at cost.

(2) Prepare a profit and loss statement for 1950. (Sales, $125,000.00, operating expenses, $18,000.00.)

(3) Prepare a balance sheet presentation of inventory.

(4) Assume that the replacement cost of the inventory on December 31, 1950, was $22.00 per unit. How would you have answered the two preceding requirements?

Problem **32–5.** The debit side of one of the bond accounts of The Eastern Investment Corporation, an investment trust, appears below:

WILEY CORPORATION 6% DEBENTURES OF 1960

1948	Par	Cost
Jan. 2	10,000.00	9,500.00
Apr. 1	20,000.00	18,000.00
July 1	50,000.00	40,000.00

On October 1, 1948, the trust sold $50,000.00 par value of these bonds at a price of 85.

What entry should be made to record the sale of these bonds? What cost value should be placed on the remaining Wiley Corporation bonds in the company's portfolio?

Problem **32–6.** The Elliott-Dern Corporation classified its account with Investment Securities as part of working capital. During a certain calendar year this account was as follows:

INVESTMENT SECURITIES

	Shares				Shares		
Jan. 1	1,000	Delco, Inc.	12,000.00	June 10	500	Delco, Inc.	10,000.00
	800	Lee Drug Co.	40,000.00	July 1	500	Lee Drug Co.	35,000.00
Apr. 10	1,000	Du Barry Radio	20,000.00	Nov. 10	1,000	Du Barry Radio	14,000.00
July 17	200	Lee Drug Co.	12,000.00	20	400	Lee Drug Co.	30,000.00
Oct. 29	1,000	Elliott-Dern Corp.	100,000.00				
Dec. 31	1,500	Delco, Inc.	22,000.00				

The bookkeeper of the Elliott-Dern Corporation debited the account with Investment Securities for the cost of all securities purchased, and credited it with the sales price of all securities sold.

On December 31, 19__, market values were in excess of the cost of all shares remaining in the company's inventory of securities.

Required:

(1) What journal entry should be made to adjust properly the balance of the Investment Securities account?

(2) How should investment securities be shown in the balance sheet?

Problem 32–7. The cost of the factory equipment of the James Manufacturing Company was $250,000.00. At a later date the company rearranged the layout of its equipment in order to reduce production costs. The cost of this work of rearrangement was $42,000.00.

How should this expenditure be accounted for? How should it be reflected in the periodic statements?

Problem 32–8. The Office Equipment account of the Coleman Manufacturing Company has a current balance of $12,476.00, and the related reserve for depreciation account a balance of $4,080.00.

These balances do not give effect to the following transaction:

Three calculating machines have just been traded in on the cash purchase of three new calculating machines costing $450.00 each. A trade-in allowance of $25.00 was received on each old machine. The old machines were originally purchased at a cost of $400.00 each, had an original estimated life of 5 years, and were actually used for $4\frac{1}{2}$ years.

Required:

How should the office equipment account be shown on the balance sheet?

Problem 32–9. The net earnings of the W. T. Nash Company for the past five years have been, in order, $16,044.00, $14,090.00, $17,102.00, $18,538.00, and $16,016.00.

Over these five years the average amount of net capital employed in the business was $150,000.00.

Required:

Accepting 8 % as a normal rate of return on invested capital, what is the goodwill of this company worth on a 25 % basis?

Problem 32–10. The condensed balance sheet of the Zee Company is

Assets	$150,000.00	Liabilities	$ 20,000.00
		Common Stock, $100.00 par	100,000.00
		Surplus	30,000.00
	$150,000.00		$150,000.00

For the past three years, the net income of the company has been $11,000.00, $15,000.00, and $13,000.00, respectively.

If average earnings in excess of an 8 % normal return on capital are to be capitalized at 20 %, what is the goodwill of this company worth?

In each of the past three years the net worth of the company has been substantially the amount shown in the above balance sheet.

Problem **32–11.** The Lowman Company reports the following figures:

	Net Income	Average Net Worth (Excluding goodwill)
1944	$ 7,000.00	$100,000.00
1945	15,000.00	100,000.00
1946	12,000.00	106,000.00
1947	6,000.00	110,000.00
1948	7,000.00	109,000.00
1949	11,000.00	115,000.00
1950	16,000.00	120,000.00

The Lowman Company receives favorably a proposal by the Field Company looking toward the purchase of the Lowman Company. You are requested to place an estimate on the value of the goodwill, if any, of the Lowman Company. A normal rate of return in this line of business is 7 %.

Problem **32–12.** The following items are taken from the 1940 annual reports of the companies named:

The Borden Company:

Trade-marks, Patents and Goodwill $1.00

Commercial Solvents Corporation:

Fixed Assets:
Land, buildings and equipment acquired prior to
    December 31, 1932 — at cost $7,035,210.35
Less Reserves for depreciation and reduction of
    assets charged against earnings and earned
    surplus prior to that date 7,035,209.35   1.00

Land, buildings and equipment acquired subse-
    quent to December 31, 1932 at cost to Cor-
    poration or subsidiaries or at book values of
    predecessor companies $5,603,737.60
Less Reserves for depreciation and
    reduction of assets provided
    at or prior to acquisition . . $ 510,047.29
     Reserves for depreciation
    charged against earnings since
    date of acquisition or installa-
    tion 1,270,439.62   1,780,486.91   3,823,250.69

Goodwill and patents 1.00

Goodyear Tire & Rubber Company:

Goodwill, Patents and Trade-marks 1.00

May Department Stores Company:

Fixed Assets:
Land, buildings and leaseholds, on the basis of cost less depreciation and amortization of $10,124,956.43 . . . . $26,400,923.40
Established amount of leases acquired subsequent to organization
of the Company ($871,411.03 on the basis of original amount
of $3,017,700.00 less amortization of $2,146,288.97) 1.00
Furniture, fixtures and equipment ($4,502,483.10 on the basis of
cost less depreciation) 1.00
Delivery equipment ($181,247.63 on the basis of cost less depreci-
ation) 1.00
Goodwill, trade-names, etc. 1.00

Nunn-Bush Shoe Company:

Lasts, Dies and Patterns, Trade-marks and Goodwill 1.00

Oliver Farm Equipment Company:

Patents, Designs, Trade-marks, and Goodwill 1.00

White Sewing Machine Corporation:

Installment Accounts Receivable — Old 1.00
Patents and Goodwill. 1.00

F. W. Woolworth Company:

Goodwill 1.00

Discuss and intelligently criticize the valuation policies which are reflected in the above balance sheet excerpts.

Problem **32–13.**

Bonwit Teller & Company (17 B.T.A. 1019)

CLASSIFICATION OF EXPENDITURE

Bonwit Teller & Company is a corporation with its principal place of
business at 721 Fifth Avenue, New York City. It deals in feminine apparel.

Bonwit Teller & Company was a lessee of a building on the northeast
corner of Fifth Avenue and Thirty-eighth Street. In 1922 the company
sublet its entire interest in the building to the Primrose Silk Company for a
rental substantially more than that which Bonwit Teller & Company was
obligated to pay to its own lessor.

For effecting this transaction Bonwit Teller & Company paid a brokerage fee of $20,000; the company deducted this payment from its report of
income for 1922. The deduction, however, was disallowed by the Commissioner of Internal Revenue, who stated that the expenditure should have
been capitalized. The decision of the Commissioner was confirmed by the
United States Board of Tax Appeals, October 18, 1929, which nevertheless
admitted that "the question [was] not free from difficulty."

How do you believe the above expenditure should have been accounted
for?

Problem **32–14.**

Stern Brothers

DEFERRED CHARGES

For many years Stern Brothers, a department store in New York City, was located on leased property on Twenty-third Street. With the decline of Twenty-third Street as a shopping center the company began to find its own location increasingly less desirable and less profitable; it therefore began to seek a new location for its store. The company eventually obtained a location on Forty-second Street which it found desirable and on which it obtained a lease for twenty years.

The company moved into its Forty-second Street premises about 15 months in advance of the expiration of its lease on Twenty-third Street. The company continued, however, to make the payments which were required by the contract of lease on its old premises. These payments, rent, taxes, and sundry other items, together with $88,072.08 of equipment abandoned at the old location, totaled $520,164.56. This total amount was recorded by the company as a deferred charge to future operations with 10 % of this amount being charged off annually thereafter to profit and loss.

Do you approve of this accounting of Stern Brothers? Explain.

Problem **32–15.**

Atwater Kent Manufacturing Company (16 B.T.A. 881)

EXCESS COST OF BUILDING

The Atwater Kent Manufacturing Company was a Pennsylvania corporation with its principal office in Philadelphia, Pennsylvania. Until 1923 its business was the manufacture and sale of radio parts; in that year it began to assemble and sell complete radio sets under the Atwater Kent name. To carry out this plan it was necessary to make additions to plant and equipment.

The radio business is, to a large extent, seasonal, the fall and winter months being the most productive ones. For this reason the company was anxious to have the first unit of its proposed four-unit plant ready for occupancy not later than October 1, 1923, so as to be able to secure the fall trade of that year.

The first unit of plant was completed and ready for occupancy October 1, 1923. Under ordinary conditions two or three months longer would have been required for completion. The excess cost of the construction of the plant, due to the effort to complete it by October 1, was reported by Ballinger & Company, contractors, to be

Additional cost of structural steel	$12,300.00
Bonuses or overtime pay for labor	15,500.00
Additional sums paid to subcontractors	27,900.00
Architect's fee of 10% of total	5,570.00
	$61,270.00

In its income tax return for the year 1923 the Atwater Kent Manufacturing Company deducted from gross income as an expense of that year the sum of $61,270.00, which it claimed was a sum paid for early occupancy of its new plant. The Commissioner of Internal Revenue disallowed the deduction.

On appeal, the company stated that "it paid this excess cost solely for the use of its plant from October 1 to November 15, 1923, and that at November 15 the value represented by the expenditure was gone; that on and after December 1, 1923, the building was worth no more than if it had been completed within the usual time, and that the excess amount paid for early completion is a direct charge against its profits for the year 1923." It contended that "it is entitled to the deduction of the amount either as an ordinary and necessary expense of doing business in 1923, or as depreciation sustained within the year 1923."

Regarding the company's contentions, the United States Board of Tax Appeals stated:

"We think it is clear that the entire cost of the building erected in 1923 was an amount paid for new buildings within the meaning of section 215 (a) of the Revenue Act of 1921, and is specifically excluded from the deductions allowable in computing net income. The fact that the cost of construction under the circumstances was in excess of the amount that would have been paid out for the construction of the building in ordinary course, does not change the character of the expenditure.

"The petitioner further contends that the excess cost for early completion was a direct charge against profits for 1923, since such excess cost was paid in order that profitable operations could be carried on in the building during October and November of 1923. Granted that such operations were profitable, there is no proof that the profits of the year have any direct relation to the excess cost of early completion. On the ground of indefiniteness, the contention must be and is denied.

"The amount of the deduction on account of depreciation allowable in any taxable year must be determined with regard to the actual 'wear and tear' of the thing used. There is nothing to indicate that the petitioner's plant here was put to any harder usage or that it actually sustained any greater depreciation in the year 1923 than in the following years. We can not say that the petitioner used up in the year 1923 all of the additional cost of constructing the plant in that year, or that no further profits from this additional cost came to the petitioner after the end of the year 1923."

With reference to this last point the Atwater Kent Manufacturing Company cited Mandel Brothers, 4 B.T.A. 341, where the Board held that an expenditure made by a taxpayer to a prior tenant for possession of the premises for a specific period of two years preceding the time that the taxpayer would have come into possession in his own right afforded no benefits beyond the two-year period and therefore should be amortized ratably over the two-year period.

In your opinion how should the excess expenditure of $61,270.00 have been accounted for?

Is the expenditure a capital expenditure or is it a charge against revenue? In the latter case, should the charge be booked as a debit to the cost of sales, as an ordinary expense of doing business, or as depreciation expense? Discuss.

Problem **32–16.**

Worth & Stafford

VALUATION OF REAL ESTATE

The firm of Worth & Stafford, located on the south water-front district of Seattle, has been engaged in a general marine repair business for many years. Early in 1949 it acquired, through purchase, the business of one of its smaller competitors, the Elliott Marine Repair Works. Worth & Stafford continued the operation of both businesses for the balance of 1949 and well into 1950. In that year, however, the company's volume of business contracted sharply in common with all other companies in the same line of business.

Because of the unpromising outlook for general business conditions, and also because both its units of plant were operating unprofitably, it was decided in the latter part of 1950 to consolidate all activities in the main Worth & Stafford plant to secure greater operating efficiency. All personal, usable property of the Elliott works was accordingly transferred to the main plant until such time as the Elliott plant could profitably be reopened.

During 1951 and 1952 the building on the Elliott property was used as a garage for the automobile equipment of Worth & Stafford. This conversion involved no new expense to the company.

In the preparation of the December 31, 1952, balance sheet, the question arose as to the proper valuation of the Elliott property on this statement. The land represented an investment of $40,000, and the building, $55,000. Losses of Worth & Stafford had been heavy in both 1951 and 1952, and the outlook for business in 1953 was exceedingly unfavorable. In the opinion of Mr. Stafford it was doubtful if the Elliott property would ever be returned to its former use by Worth & Stafford.

In view of the stagnant market for industrial real estate, sale of the Elliott property was out of the question, except possibly at heavy sacrifice. It was probable, therefore, that the Elliott property would have to be carried as a frozen investment for a long period of time.

It was the expectation of Mr. Stafford that, for lack of other more productive use, the Elliott building would probably be continued in service as a garage for the storage and repair of Worth & Stafford automobiles, although a building for this purpose could have been erected as a cost of not over $10,000.

How should the Elliott property be valued on the December 31, 1952, balance sheet of Worth & Stafford? Explain what new accounting, if any, you would recommend in connection with this valuation.

APPENDIXES

A. Practice Sets
B. Private Ledger

APPENDIX A

PRACTICE SETS

Practice Set No. 1: Single Proprietorship
Practice Set No. 2: Partnership
Practice Set No. 3: Manufacturing Corporation

Practice Set No. 4: Single Proprietorship
Practice Set No. 5: Partnership
Practice Set No. 6: Manufacturing Corporation

Six practice sets are presented on pages 735–829. Two sets cover the businesses of single proprietorships, two sets cover partnership businesses, and two sets cover manufacturing corporations operating under the plan of periodic inventory. Practice Set No. 1 may be used alternatively with Practice Set No. 4; for example, one set may be used in the first semester and the other set may be used when the introductory course is repeated in the second semester. Practice Set No. 2, similarly, may be used alternatively with Practice Set No. 5; and Practice Set No. 3 with Practice Set No. 6.

The accounting period for each practice set is two months. The current year should be used in all dates.

Unless otherwise indicated, purchases and sales of merchandise are on credit and are due for payment on the 10th of the month following date of invoice, less cash discounts of 2% for purchases and 1% for sales. Cash sales and cash purchases take regular cash discounts; C.O.D.'s and sight drafts are net, no cash discount. Exceptions from these terms are stated in the text. Unless otherwise stated, "purchase" and "sale" transactions are transactions for the purchase and sale of merchandise, respectively.

New pages should be used each month for the books of original entry. In the general journal, skip one line between entries.

Henry J. Franklin

PRACTICE SET NO. 1: SINGLE PROPRIETORSHIP

Practice Set No. 1 will employ the following books of original entry: sales book, purchases book, cash receipts book, cash payments book, and journal. The general ledger accounts will be as follows:

Current Assets:
Cash
Accounts Receivable (control)
Reserve for Bad Debts
Notes Receivable

Merchandise
William A. Phelps, Travel Advance
Harold W. Spear, Travel Advance
Prepaid Expenses

Fixed Assets:

Office Equipment
Reserve for Depreciation — Office Equipment

Current Liabilities:

Accounts Payable (control)
Notes Payable
Social Security Taxes Payable
Withholding Income Taxes Payable

Net Worth:

Henry J. Franklin, Capital
Henry J. Franklin, Personal
Profit and Loss

Profit and Loss:

Sales
Returned Sales and Allowances
Sales Discounts
Cost of Sales
Purchases
Returned Purchases and Allowances
Purchases Discounts
Freight In
Advertising
Delivery Expense
Sales Salaries
Traveling Expense
Bad Debts Expense
Depreciation Expense — Office Equipment
General Expense
General Salaries
Insurance Expense
Office Supplies Expense
Rent
Social Security Taxes
Utilities Expense (To this account charge bills for water, electricity, gas, and telephone.)
Interest Expense

NOVEMBER 2

Henry J. Franklin began business with an investment of cash $12,-000.00.

Paid November rent to the Globe Building Company, $250.00.

November 3

Paid $2,000.00 to the Standard Office Equipment Company for sundry items of office equipment (furniture, safe, filing cabinets, etc.).

Paid $47.12 to Drake & Stone, Inc., for sundry office supplies, books, stationery, etc.

Purchased for cash one typewriter, one adding machine, and one cash register, from the Carter Office Machines Company, $280.00.

November 4

Purchase from Bell & Bennett, $178.97.
Purchase from Clark & Son, $633.92.
Purchase from Cox & Cox, $612.00.
Paid Bell Telephone Company bill, $10.50.
Paid for postage stamps, $5.00.

November 5

Sale to William Boyd, $600.00.
Sale to C. H. Brooks & Company, $387.00.
Purchase from F. M. Dent & Company, $601.00.
Paid freight on purchase from Cox & Cox, $10.11.

November 6

Cash sale to Burley & Son, $737.00, net.
Cash purchase from Cox & Cox, $614.00, less 2%.
Paid Cox & Cox invoice of November 4, $612.00, less 2%.
Paid White & Bollard for one year's fire insurance premium on merchandise inventory, $36.00.

November 7

Sale to William Boyd, $421.00.
Sale to C. H. Brooks & Company, $301.00.
General expenses are paid, $24.25.

November 9

Paid Clark & Son invoice of November 4, $633.92, less 2%.
Purchase from Cox & Cox, $724.00.
Issued credit memorandum to William Boyd for merchandise returned from shipment of November 7, $21.00.

November 10

Cash is received from C. H. Brooks & Company in payment of invoice of November 5, $387.00, net.

Traveling expenses are paid, $48.14.

Paid F. M. Dent & Company invoice of November 5, $610.00 (an overpayment of $9.00), no discount.

November 11

Cash sale to William Boyd, $648.00, net.
Purchase from Cox & Cox, $323.02.
Purchase from F. M. Dent & Company, $310.00. (Terms on this purchase, 5/10, n/30.)

November 12

Sale to D. J. Conley, $826.50, terms net.
Purchase from Bell & Bennett, $565.16.
Invoice is received from Clark & Son covering purchase of merchandise, $560.00, and prepaid freight, $20.00. The freight terms on this merchandise were f.o.b. shipping point.
Paid general expenses, $20.16.

November 13

Purchase from Bell & Bennett, $511.42.
Paid New York Central Railroad for freight on Bell & Bennett shipments of November 12 and 13, $17.36.
An advertising bill of the *Empire Times* is paid, $75.10.

November 14

Paid Cox & Cox invoice of November 9, $724.00, less 2%.
A credit memorandum is received from Bell & Bennett for merchandise returned (originally billed November 12), $29.62.
A credit memorandum is received from F. M. Dent & Company acknowledging our overpayment of $9.00 on November 10.
The payroll for the first half of the month is: general salaries, $250.00, sales salaries, $100.00. Cash of $306.00 is disbursed; $3.50 is withheld from payroll checks to cover deductions for social security taxes of 1%, and $40.50 is withheld to cover deductions for income taxes. (The payroll is paid today; November 15 is Sunday.)

November 16

Merchandise is sold to Stanwood's, Inc., $788.00; shipment is made today with sight draft bill of lading attached. (Record this transaction as per common business practice as described on pages 274–275.)
Purchase from F. M. Dent & Company, $979.22.
Issued credit memorandum to William Boyd for merchandise returned (originally billed November 7), $12.10.

November 17

Paid Bell & Bennett invoice of November 4, $178.97, net.
Paid freight on purchase of November 16, $21.16.
Traveling expenses are paid, $72.64.
Paid Cox & Cox invoice of November 11, $323.02, less 2%.
Sale to William Boyd, $684.50.

November 18

Cash is withdrawn by Mr. Franklin for personal use, $50.00.

Drew check favor Clark & Son in payment of invoice of November 12, less 2%.

Sales invoice to D. J. Conley for merchandise, $1,019.70, and for freight prepaid today, $8.26. Terms on this shipment were 2/10, 1/20, n/30, and f.o.b. shipping point.

November 20

Sale to C. H. Brooks & Company, $640.00.

Purchase from Cox & Cox, $1,346.60.

Paid City Delivery Service, Inc., for delivery expenses, $54.70.

November 21

Purchase from Bell & Bennett, $730.10.

Purchase from Cox & Cox, $750.00.

Paid F. M. Dent & Company invoice of November 11, $310.00, net.

Issued credit memorandum to C. H. Brooks & Company for merchandise returned from invoice of November 7, $12.04.

November 23

Sale to Stanwood's, Inc., $347.00.

The Empire National Bank credits our account for collection of our sight draft of November 16 on Stanwood's, Inc., $788.00.

November 24

At our request, a credit memorandum is received from F. M. Dent & Company for cash discount not taken by us on our payment of November 21, $15.50.

Sale to the Raymond Sales Company, $726.15.

Drew check in favor of Bell & Bennett:

$565.16   Invoice November 12

29.62   Credit memorandum November 14

$535.54

10.71   2% discount

$524.83   Amount of check

November 25

Sale to D. J. Conley, $1,219.00.

Purchase from F. M. Dent & Company, $618.17.

Cash purchase from Judson & Ray, Inc., $113.00, less 5%.

November 26

Sale to C. H. Brooks & Company, $471.03.
Drew check in favor of F. M. Dent & Company:

	$979.22	Invoice November 16
	19.58	2% discount
	$959.64	
$ 9.00		Credit memorandum November 14
15.50		Credit memorandum November 24
	24.50	
	$935.14	Amount of check (*Note:* Has the amount of the check been calculated correctly?)

November 27

Sale to Fraser & Nelson, Inc., $537.14.
Received check from D. J. Conley, in payment of our invoice of November 18 as follows:

$1,019.70	Merchandise
20.39	2% discount
$ 999.31	
8.26	Prepaid freight
$1,007.57	Amount of check

Issued credit memorandum to D. J. Conley for merchandise returned by him from shipment of November 25, $25.25.

November 28

Sale to D. J. Conley, $874.31, terms net.
Sale to Stanwood's, Inc., $211.05.
Bill for electricity and gas is paid, $27.40.
Paid City Delivery Service, Inc., for delivery expenses, $40.21.

November 30

Purchase from Clark & Son, $871.69.
Received a thirty-day, noninterest-bearing, note, dated today, from William Boyd, $987.90. This note covers the balance due on our invoices of November 5 and 7.

The payroll for the second half of the month is: general salaries, $250.00, sales salaries, $200.00. Cash of $391.50 is disbursed; $4.50 is withheld to cover deductions for social security taxes of 1%, and $54.00 is withheld for income taxes.

After the books have been posted, compare your trial balance with the following:

Henry J. Franklin

TRIAL BALANCE, NOVEMBER 30, 19—

Cash	$ 5,688.07	
Accounts Receivable	6,800.39	
Notes Receivable	987.90	
Office Equipment	2,280.00	
Accounts Payable		$ 4,827.98
Social Security Taxes Payable		8.00
Withholding Income Taxes Payable		94.50
Henry J. Franklin, Capital		12,000.00
Henry J. Franklin, Personal	50.00	
Sales		11,438.38
Returned Sales and Allowances	70.39	
Sales Discounts	20.39	
Purchases	11,042.27	
Returned Purchases and Allowances		29.62
Purchases Discounts		120.78
Freight In	68.63	
Advertising	75.10	
Delivery Expense	94.91	
Sales Salaries	300.00	
Traveling Expense	120.78	
General Expense	49.41	
General Salaries	500.00	
Insurance Expense	36.00	
Office Supplies Expense	47.12	
Rent	250.00	
Utilities Expense	37.90	
	$28,519.26	$28,519.26

Record this trial balance on an 8-, 10-, or 12-column work sheet. Then place adjusting entries on the work sheet to cover the following items:

(1) Bad debts are estimated at ½ % of net sales (after sales discounts).

(2) Office equipment is to be depreciated at the rate of 10 % per annum.

(3) Social security taxes accrued on the November payroll are 1 % old-age benefit tax, and 3 % unemployment tax. These are taxes charged against the employer. They do not include taxes withheld from the wage and salary checks of employees.

(4) One month's insurance premium has expired. (For the purpose of this practice set, adjusting entries for expense prepayments may all be debited to the single account Prepaid Expenses.)

After these adjustments have been recorded, complete the work sheet. The inventory of merchandise on November 30, 19—, is estimated at $1,500.00.

Prepare a profit and loss statement for the month of November.

Prepare a balance sheet as of November 30, 19—.

Do not close the books.

December 1

Paid December rent to the Globe Building Company, $250.00.

Checks are drawn for $100.00 each in favor of William A. Phelps, and Harold W. Spear, salesmen, as advances for traveling expenses.

Received check from Stanwood's, Inc., in payment of invoice of November 23, $347.00, less 1%.

December 2

Sale to C. H. Brooks & Company, $719.95.

Purchase from Bell & Bennett, $341.00.

Paid freight on above purchase, $8.61.

December 3

Received check from C. H. Brooks & Company for invoice of November 26, $471.03, less 1%.

Postage stamps are purchased, $10.00.

Paid $70.00 to the Community Chest Fund.

December 4

Sale to D. J. Conley, $518.13.

Sale to Stanwood's, Inc., $425.70.

Purchase from F. M. Dent & Company, $899.11.

December 5

Paid Bell Telephone Company bill, $12.88.

Merchandise is taken from stock by Mr. Franklin for personal use, $50.00.

December 7

Sale to William Boyd, $232.12.

Received check from Fraser & Nelson, Inc., $537.14, less 1%, for invoice of November 27.

C. H. Brooks & Company notifies us of an error in the computation of our invoice of December 2. The notice is found to be correct. A credit memorandum is sent the company for the amount of the overcharge, $18.00.

December 8

Purchase from Clark & Son, $196.86.

November 30 statements from creditors are found to be correct. Checks are mailed to creditors in settlement of all November 30 balances, less 2%. Analysis of the F. M. Dent & Company account shows that its invoice of November 5, which we paid net, should have been discounted 2%. This additional discount is deducted in today's check.

December 9

Sale to Fraser & Nelson, Inc., $402.20.

Cash purchase from J. S. Bache & Company, $32.13, less 5%.

A credit memorandum is received from Bell & Bennett for merchandise returned from our purchase of December 2, $44.07.

December 10

Sale to Howard Coburn & Company, $381.70.

Purchase from Cox & Cox, $1,258.41.

Paid New York Central Railroad for freight on Cox & Cox purchase, $22.77.

Traveling expenses are paid, $38.10.

December 11

Purchase from F. M. Dent & Company, $2,558.40.

Received check from Stanwood's, Inc., $211.05, less 1%, for invoice of November 28.

Received check from D. J. Conley in payment of the balance of his account on November 30, less 2%. A debit memorandum is mailed to D. J. Conley for discount not allowed; 1% cash discount is allowed on invoice of November 25, other items net.

Paid City Delivery Service, Inc., for delivery expenses, $31.00.

December 12

Sale to William Boyd, $660.00.

General expenses are paid, $28.10.

December 14

Sale to C. H. Brooks & Company, $704.02.

An extra 1% cash discount for payment within 5 days is offered by F. M. Dent & Company on its invoice of December 11. Check is drawn in payment, less 3%.

Mailed credit memorandum for $20.00 to William Boyd as an allowance on merchandise sold December 7.

December 15

Purchase from Bell & Bennett, $796.40.

Paid New York Central Railroad for freight on this purchase, $15.62.

Sale to D. J. Conley, $798.77. Freight of $10.88 is prepaid on this invoice whose freight terms were f.o.b. shipping point.

Funds are borrowed today from the Empire National Bank on our $1,000.00 note, dated today, for sixty days, without interest. Bank rate 6%.

The payroll for the first half of the month is: general salaries, $250.00, sales salaries, $300.00. After deduction of 1% for social security taxes, and $66.00 for income taxes, the payroll is paid in cash.

December 16

Merchandise is shipped C.O.D. express to Edgar Ames & Company, $49.20.

Purchase from Cox & Cox, $673.20.

$300.00 cash and a thirty-day note without interest, dated today, are received from William Boyd for the balance of his account receivable to date.

December 17

Sale to Fraser & Nelson, Inc., $938.60.

Sale to the Raymond Sales Company, $211.04.

Received check from C. H. Brooks & Company for the balance of its account on November 30, $928.96, net.

December 18

Sale to Harold & Elton, $622.14.

Purchase from Clark & Son, $803.12.

Drew check in favor Cox & Cox for bill of December 10, $1,258.41, less 2%.

December 19

Paid City Delivery Service, Inc., for delivery expenses, $31.74.

Paid advertising bill from the *Empire Times*, $60.00.

Invoice covering prepaid freight is received from Clark & Son, $24.14, covering shipment of December 18. Freight terms on this shipment were f.o.b. shipping point.

December 21

Purchase from F. M. Dent & Company, $1,204.69.

Received check from Raymond Sales Company in payment of November 24 invoice, $726.15, net, and December 17 invoice, $211.04, less 1%.

Cash purchase from Judson & Ray, Inc., $87.50, less 5%.

Paid Drake & Stone, Inc., for sundry office supplies, $30.14.

December 22

Cash sale to Burley & Son, $80.00, net.

Paid freight on F. M. Dent & Company purchase of December 21, $22.48. Freight terms on this purchase were f.o.b. destination.

A sixty-day draft, dated December 18, is received from Harold & Elton in settlement of invoice of that date.

December 23

Sale to D. J. Conley, $300.10.

Merchandise is shipped C.O.D. parcel post to Howard Healey, $27.70.

Purchase from Bell & Bennett, $616.00.

Henry J. Franklin withdraws $100.00 cash for personal use.

December 24

Sale to Harold & Elton, $521.24.

Sale to Stanwood's, Inc., $179.17.

Remittance is received today on C.O.D. shipment of December 16.

DECEMBER 26

Issued credit memorandum to Raymond Sales Company for merchandise returned from shipment of December 17, $129.72.

Invoice covering prepaid freight is received from Bell & Bennett, $11.00, covering shipment of December 23. Freight terms on this shipment were f.o.b. destination.

DECEMBER 28

Sale to C. H. Brooks & Company, $463.10.

Purchase from Cox & Cox, $519.80.

At its request, drew check favor the Raymond Sales Company to cover our credit memorandum of December 26. (Deduct 1% discount.)

DECEMBER 29

Sale to Howard Coburn & Company, $200.85.

Gas, electricity, and water bills are paid, $41.10.

Paid City Delivery Service, Inc., for delivery expenses, $14.20.

DECEMBER 30

William A. Phelps and Harold W. Spear, salesmen, submit their traveling expense reports for December, $73.44 and $69.70, respectively. Checks are received for the unexpended portions of their travel advances.

A check for $700.00 is received from William Boyd as part payment of his note of November 30, due today. A ten-day extension is given to Mr. Boyd in which to pay the balance of $287.90.

General expenses are paid, $37.44.

DECEMBER 31

Sale to the Raymond Sales Company, $415.80.

The payroll for the second half of the month is: general salaries, $250.00, sales salaries, $300.00. After deduction of 1% for social security taxes, and $66.00 for income taxes, the payroll is paid in cash.

After the books have been posted, draw off a trial balance. (The correct balance for Cash is $3,446.98.) Record this trial balance on an 8-, 10-, or 12-column work sheet. Then place adjusting entries on the work sheet to cover the following items:

(1) Bad debts, estimated at ½% of net sales (after sales discounts).

(2) Office equipment, to be depreciated at the rate of 10% per annum.

(3) Accrual of social security taxes on the payroll.

(4) Unexpired insurance.

(5) Prepaid interest on notes payable.

After these adjustments have been recorded, complete the work sheet. The inventory of merchandise on December 31, 19—, by actual count and valuation is $4,874.12.

Prepare a profit and loss statement for the two months ending with December 31, 19—.

Prepare a balance sheet as of December 31, 19—.

Record adjusting entries on the books. Close the books. Record reversing entries.

Reconcile the cash account. The bank statement received from the Empire National Bank as of December 31, 19__, was as follows:

		DEBITS			DEPOSITS	BALANCE
Dec. 1	Balance					5,688.07
1		250.00	100.00	100.00	343.53	5,581.60
3		8.61			466.32	6,039.31
4		10.00				6,029.31
7					531.77	6,561.08
9		12.88	2,054.67			4,493.53
10		1,216.69				3,276.84
11		854.26	593.79	30.52	3,045.61	4,843.88
12		22.77	31.00			4,790.11
14		38.10				4,752.01
15		28.10			990.00	5,713.91
16		15.62				5,698.29
17		2,481.65	10.88	478.50	1,228.96	3,956.22
19		1,233.24				2,722.98
22		83.12	60.00			2,579.86
23		31.74	22.48			2,525.64
24					1,064.28	3,589.92
26		30.14				3,559.78
30		41.10				3,518.68
31		14.20	478.50	37.44	756.86	3,745.40

Franklin & Graham

PRACTICE SET NO. 2: PARTNERSHIP

The partnership of Franklin & Graham was formed on January 1, 19__, for the purpose of continuing and expanding the business heretofore operated solely by Mr. Henry J. Franklin. The articles of partnership provided, among other things, that

(1) The capital of each partner shall be $12,000.00. It was mutually agreed that the form and value of each partner's capital contribution should be as follows:

Henry J. Franklin:

Cash $3,073.15
Accounts Receivable:
    C. H. Brooks & Company $1,869.07
    Howard Coburn & Company 582.55
    C.O.D.'s — Howard Healey 27.70
    D. J. Conley 1,673.83
    Fraser & Nelson, Inc. 1,340.80
    Harold & Elton. 521.24
    Raymond Sales Company 415.80
    Stanwood's, Inc. 604.87

                                 $7,035.86

Reserve for Bad Debts 100.02 6,935.84

Notes Receivable (noninterest-bearing):
Nov. 30 William Boyd, due Jan. 9. . . . . $ 287.90
Dec. 16 William Boyd, due Jan. 15 . . . . . . 1,256.62
Dec. 22 Harold & Elton, due Feb. 20 . . . . . 622.14 2,166.66

Inventory 4,874.12
Prepaid Insurance (premium for 10 months on mer-
chandise inventory) 30.00
Prepaid Interest (discount on notes payable) 7.50
Office Equipment $2,280.00
Reserve for Depreciation 38.00 2,242.00

Accounts Payable:
Bell & Bennett $1,709.33
Clark & Son 1,024.12
Cox & Cox 1,193.00
F. M. Dent & Company 2,081.32 6,007.77

Notes Payable, dated December 15, due in 60 days,
noninterest-bearing 1,000.00
Social Security Taxes Payable (relating to payrolls
of November and December). 95.00
Withholding Income Taxes Payable (relating to payrolls of November and December) 226.50

William F. Graham:
Building $12,000.00
Land 3,000.00
Mortgage Payable on real estate, due 10 years from
now, interest at 6% per annum, payable February
1 and August 1 . . . . 5,000.00
And cash to make up the balance.

(2) Salaries, chargeable as business expenses, shall be:

Henry J. Franklin . . . . $250.00 per month
William F. Graham . . . . $150.00 per month

(3) In addition to salaries, partners shall be permitted to make drawings against profits at the average rate of $100.00 per month. Drawings in
excess of this average may be made only by mutual consent. Excess drawings, however, shall be charged interest at the rate of 12% per annum.

(4) Interest at the rate of 6% per annum shall be allowed on the average
balance of each partner's capital account. When the average capital of a
partner during an accounting period is less than his minimum required investment, his drawing account shall be charged with interest computed
against his deficiency at the rate of 12% per annum.

(5) Interest charged to a partner's drawing account because of sections 3 or 4 shall not be made the base of further charges for interest in the
same accounting period.

(6) The profit and loss ratio of the partners shall be equal.

(7) The accounting period shall be the calendar year unless the partners mutually agree upon a shorter period.

Credit and cash discount terms for merchandise transactions will be the same as those for Practice Set No. 1. Sales and purchases transactions, in this practice set, have been purposely grouped so as to occur on the last two days of each week. This has been done in order to expedite the student's recording of such transactions. With similar intent, personal accounts have been limited to those used in Practice Set No. 1.

The following books of original entry will be employed: sales book, returned sales and allowances book, purchases book, returned purchases and allowances book, cash receipts book, cash payments book, and journal. The general ledger accounts will be as follows:

Current Assets:

Cash
Stocks and Bonds
Notes Receivable
Notes Receivable Discounted
Interest Receivable
Accounts Receivable
Reserve for Bad Debts
Inventory
Prepaid Expenses (Sundry)
Prepaid Insurance
Prepaid Interest
William A. Phelps, Travel Advance
Harold W. Spear, Travel Advance

Fixed Assets:

Building
Reserve for Depreciation — Building
Delivery Equipment
Reserve for Depreciation — Delivery Equipment
Office Equipment
Reserve for Depreciation — Office Equipment
Land

Current Liabilities:

Accounts Payable
Interest Payable
Property Taxes Payable
Social Security Taxes Payable
Withholding Income Taxes Payable
Notes Payable

Fixed Liabilities:

Mortgage Payable

Net Worth:

Henry J. Franklin, Capital
Henry J. Franklin, Personal

William F. Graham, Capital
William F. Graham, Personal
Profit and Loss

Profit and Loss:

Sales
Returned Sales and Allowances
Sales Discounts
Cost of Sales
Purchases
Returned Purchases and Allowances
Purchases Discounts
Freight In
Advertising
Delivery Expense
Depreciation Expense — Delivery Equipment
Miscellaneous Sales Expense
Sales Salaries
Traveling Expense
Bad Debts
Depreciation Expense — Building
Depreciation Expense — Office Equipment
General Expense
General Salaries
Insurance Expense
Office Supplies
Partners' Salaries
Property Taxes
Social Security Taxes
Utilities Expense
Interest Income
Interest Expense

The accounts of the general ledger are arranged in the order in which they appear on the balance sheet and the profit and loss statement, respectively.

The books of Franklin & Graham are to be kept on the accrual basis of accounting, as described in Chapters 14 and 15.

JANUARY 1

The partnership of Franklin & Graham began business with the assets and liabilities described in the partnership agreement.

Purchases from:

Bell & Bennett	$200.45
Cox & Cox	785.01

Paid freight on these purchases, Check No. 1, $14.32.

JANUARY 2

Sales to:

Invoice

#1	William Boyd	$872.11
2	C. H. Brooks & Company	433.44
3	Burley & Son (shipment made sight draft). . . .	825.44
4	Raymond Sales Company	671.52

Paid Bell Telephone Company bill, Check No. 2, $14.76.

Check No. 3 in payment of bill in favor of White & Bollard for fire insurance premiums on building, three-year premium, $194.40; office equipment, one-year premium, $24.00.

JANUARY 4

A freight bill, covering the merchandise shipped to the Raymond Sales Company on January 2, is paid by Check No. 4, $12.60. This merchandise was shipped freight prepaid although it was mutually agreed that buyer and seller would each stand one half of the freight charges.

Checks No. 5 and No. 6 are drawn for $100.00 each in favor of William A. Phelps, and Harold W. Spear, salesmen, as advances for traveling expenses.

JANUARY 5

Received check from Fraser & Nelson, Inc., in payment of December account, $1,340.80, less 1%.

The Harold & Elton sixty-day draft (note receivable) for $622.14, and dated December 22, is discounted at the Empire National Bank. Bank rate 6%.

JANUARY 6

Paid general expenses, Check No. 7, $18.74.

Paid advertising bill from the *Empire Times*, Check No. 8, $96.27.

Paid City Delivery Service, Inc., for delivery expenses, Check No. 9, $30.17.

JANUARY 7

Received check from Stanwood's, Inc., in payment of December account, $604.87, less 1%.

Received check from Harold & Elton in payment of December account, $521.24, less 1%.

JANUARY 8

Purchases from:

Bell & Bennett	$810.88
Clark & Son	710.11
Cox & Cox	688.74
F. M. Dent & Company	673.12

Paid freight on these four purchases, Check No. 10, $41.26. The freight terms on the Clark purchase were f.o.b. destination; the freight on this purchase amounted to $12.04.

Received credit memorandum from Bell & Bennett for merchandise returned from our purchase of January 1, $36.17.

JANUARY 9

Sales to:

Invoice

#5	C. H. Brooks & Company	$343.50
6	D. J. Conley	925.68
7	Harold & Elton	736.04
8	Stanwood's, Inc.	882.56

Cash sale, invoice #9, to Lasser & Co., $100.14, less 1%.

Received cash from William Boyd for balance due on his note of November 30, $287.90.

December 31 statements from merchandise creditors are found to be in agreement with our accounts. Checks No. 11–14 are mailed to creditors in settlement of all December accounts, less cash discounts of 2%. All accounts payable balances on December 31 were for merchandise, except for the two following accounts:

CLARK & SON

	Dec.	8 Mdse.	196.86
		18 Mdse.	803.12
		19 Frt.	24.14

F. M. DENT & CO.

Dec. 21 Frt.	22.48	Dec.	4 Mdse.	899.11
			21 Mdse.	1,204.69

JANUARY 11

Received check from C. H. Brooks & Company in payment of December account, $1,869.07, less 1%.

Received check from D. J. Conley in payment of December account:

$ 518.13	December 4 invoice for merchandise
798.77	December 15 invoice for merchandise
10.88	December 15 freight
300.10	December 23 invoice for merchandise
45.95	Cash discount not allowed on remittance of December 11
$1,673.83	
16.74	1% discount
$1,657.09	Amount of check (Is the calculation correct? If not, credit D. J. Conley for the proper amount when the check is recorded.)

January 12

Issued credit memorandum #1 to William Boyd for merchandise returned from sale of January 2, $25.60.

Social security taxes for the months of November and December are paid. The old-age benefit check, No. 15, in favor of the Collector of Internal Revenue, covers the 1 % tax withheld from the wages and salaries ($1,900.00) of employees in November and December; and an additional 1 % levied against the employer. The remittance for unemployment insurance is a tax levied against the employer; the amount of this tax is 3 % of wages and salaries of employees in November and December. This remittance is mailed in two checks: Check No. 16 to the State Treasurer for 90 % of the tax, and Check No. 17 to the Collector of Internal Revenue for 10 % of the tax.

January 13

The Empire National Bank credits our account for collection of our sight draft of January 2 on Burley & Son, $825.44.

Received postal money order in payment of C.O.D. shipment to Howard Healey on December 23, $27.70.

January 14

Traveling expenses of Mr. Franklin are paid, Check No. 18, $62.71.

Issued Check No. 19 for $1,000.00 to James Bennett & Company in payment of 100 shares of the common stock of the Allen Refining Corporation.

Received check from Howard Coburn & Company in payment of December account, $582.55, less 1 %. The discount is not allowed since the last date for discount was January 10. A debit memorandum covering the discount not allowed is mailed to Howard Coburn & Company.

January 15

Purchases from:

Bell & Bennett	$632.97
Cox & Cox	384.18
F. M. Dent & Company	426.51

Paid freight on these purchases, Check No. 20, $24.01.

The payroll for the first half of the month is: partners' salaries, $200.00, sales salaries, $300.00, general salaries, $250.00. After deduction of 1 % for social security taxes on the wages and salaries of *employees*, and $82.00 for income taxes, the payroll is paid by Checks No. 21–28. (Mr. Franklin and Mr. Graham receive Checks No. 21 and 22, $200.00.)

Real-estate taxes for the year ending last December 31 are paid, Check No. 29, $601.32.

JANUARY 16

Sales to:

Invoice

#10	Burley & Son (terms, sight draft)	$ 725.76
11	C. G. Watkins (C.O.D. express)	9.19
12	D. J. Conley	1,142.06
13	Fraser & Nelson, Inc.	816.70
14	Stanwood's, Inc.	388.64

Paid City Delivery Service, Inc., Check No. 30, $28.01.

Issued credit memorandum #2 to D. J. Conley for merchandise returned from sale of January 9, $13.64.

JANUARY 18

Received check for $5.73 from Howard Coburn & Company for cash discount not allowed on its remittance of January 14. The check should have been $5.83; the company is notified by telephone.

Received check for $256.62 from William Boyd to apply on his note for $1,256.62, due January 15. Mr. Boyd requests, and is granted, an extension until January 25 to make payment on the balance due.

JANUARY 19

Received check for $12.04 from Clark & Son covering freight on their shipment of January 8.

Issued Check No. 31 to William F. Graham for personal use, $100.00.

Paid for postage stamps, Check No. 32, $10.00.

JANUARY 20

Received credit memorandum from Cox & Cox as an allowance on our purchase of January 15, $25.00.

Issued credit memorandum #3 to D. J. Conley for merchandise returned from sale of January 9, $15.44.

Issued credit memorandum #4 to Burley & Son for merchandise returned from sale of January 2, $91.32. Issued Check No. 33 in payment. This merchandise was returned by Burley & Son freight collect; paid this freight bill as our expense, Check No. 34, $5.01.

JANUARY 21

The Empire National Bank credits our account for collection of our sight draft of January 16 on Burley & Son, $725.76.

10¢ in stamps is received from Howard Coburn & Company to take up shortage in its remittance of January 18; also 57¢ in stamps from D. J. Conley for shortage in his remittance of January 11. The stamps are sold to Mr. Franklin for cash.

General expenses are paid, Check No. 35, $28.16.

Paid City Delivery Service, Inc., Check No. 36, $32.90.

JANUARY 22

Purchases from:

Bell & Bennett	$ 612.56
Clark & Son	627.20
F. M. Dent & Company	1,096.72

Paid freight on the Bennett and Dent purchases, Check No. 37, $20.08.

JANUARY 23

Sales to:

Invoice

#15	William Boyd (sight draft)	$ 314.20
16	C. H. Brooks & Company	527.55
17	Howard Coburn & Company	1,365.28
18	D. J. Conley	336.37
19	Fraser & Nelson, Inc.	601.59
20	Raymond Sales Company	813.28

Cash sale, invoice #21, to Ray & Son, $362.41, less 1%.

JANUARY 25

Received debit memorandum from Clark & Son for prepaid freight on shipment of January 22, $16.11. Freight terms on this shipment were f.o.b. shipping point.

Received credit memorandum from F. M. Dent & Company for merchandise returned from purchase of January 22, $60.33.

Mr. Boyd is unable to make the payment which he had promised to make today for the balance due on his note of December 16. A new note for $1,000.00 with interest at 8%, dated January 15, for thirty days, is executed in place of the old note.

JANUARY 26

Paid Drake & Stone, Inc., for sundry office supplies, Check No. 38, $42.01.

The C.O.D. shipment ($314.20) made to William Boyd on January 23 is refused, apparently because of the sight draft attached. Rather than release the goods on open account, Mr. Franklin instructs the railroad to return the shipment. Credit memorandum #5 is issued to cover the returned merchandise. (Record this credit memorandum in the journal.)

Transportation charges are paid on the returned Boyd merchandise, Check No. 39, $12.09.

JANUARY 27

Gas, electricity, and water bills are paid, Check No. 40, $38.90.

Issued credit memorandum #6 to C. H. Brooks & Company for merchandise returned from sale of January 23, $27.03.

Issued Check No. 41 in favor of the Collector of Internal Revenue for withholding income taxes for the months of November and December, $226.50.

JANUARY 29

Purchases from:

Bell & Bennett	$ 817.71
Clark & Son	840.25
Cox & Cox	792.35
F. M. Dent & Company	1,508.19
Judson & Ray, Inc. (sight draft, honored today)	184.56

Paid freight on these purchases, Check No. 43, $47.20.

JANUARY 30

Sales to:

Invoice

#22	C. H. Brooks & Company	. . . .	$618.67
23	Howard Coburn & Company	. . . .	324.95
24	Raymond Sales Company	. . . .	739.20
25	Willis & Gray (C.O.D. express)	. . . .	47.20

Paid freight on shipment to the Raymond Sales Company, Check No. 44, $16.24. Freight terms on this sale were f.o.b. shipping point.

Cash sale, invoice #26, to R. C. Bales, $188.62, less 1%.

William A. Phelps and Harold W. Spear, salesmen, submit their traveling expense reports for January, $80.21 and $88.14, respectively. Checks No. 45–46 are issued to cover.

The payroll for the second half of the month is partners' salaries, $200.00, sales salaries, $300.00, general salaries, $250.00. After deduction of 1% for social security taxes on the wages and salaries of employees, and $82.00 for income taxes, the payroll is paid by Checks No. 47–54. (January 31 is Sunday.)

After the books have been posted, enter the January trial balance on a work sheet. Complete the work sheet, making proper provision for needed adjustments. In this connection the following items of information should be taken into consideration:

Buildings should be depreciated at 5% per annum on original cost.

Office equipment should be depreciated at 10% per annum on original cost.

Bad debts should be provided for at ½% of net sales (after sales discounts).

Social security taxes imposed on the employer should be accrued at the following rates: 1% on wages and salaries of employees for old-age benefits, and 3% on wages and salaries of employees for unemployment insurance.

The inventory of merchandise on January 31, 19—, is estimated at $5,000.00.

Prepare a profit and loss statement for the month of January.

Prepare a balance sheet as of January 31, 19—.

Do not close the books.

Reconcile the cash account. The bank statement received from the Empire National Bank as of January 31, 19___, was as follows:

		DEBITS		DEPOSITS	BALANCE
Jan. 1				5,198.15	5,198.15
2	14.32				5,183.83
4	14.76	12.60			5,156.47
5	100.00			1,944.76	7,001.23
6	18.74	100.00		1,114.85	7,997.34
7	218.40				7,778.94
8	96.27				7,682.67
9				387.04	8,069.71
11	41.26	1,169.14	1,675.14	3,507.47	8,691.64
12	30.17	1,004.12	2,039.24		5,618.11
13				853.14	6,471.25
14				576.72	7,047.97
15	5.70	38.00	1,000.00		6,004.27
16	24.01	462.50	200.00		5,317.76
18	51.30	62.71			5,203.75
20	601.32	28.01	100.00	274.39	4,748.81
21	5.01	10.00		725.76	5,459.56
22	20.08				5,439.48
23	91.32	28.16	32.90		5,287.10
25				359.46	5,646.56
26	42.01				5,604.55
27	12.09				5,592.46
29	38.90			186.73	5,740.29
30	47.20	184.56	226.50		5,282.03

FEBRUARY 1

(In the entry of transactions for February, new pages should be used for the books of original entry.)

Paid interest on real-estate mortgage, Check No. 55, $150.00.

Bought for cash from the Hood Motor Sales Company one Ford delivery truck with special panel body, Check No. 56, $1,014.92.

Paid for automobile license for the balance of the calendar year, Check No. 57, $22.00.

Paid the Central Insurance Agency for a one-year automobile insurance premium, Check No. 58, $48.00.

Bought for cash two Northern Pacific 6% $1,000.00 par value bonds of 2047 at 100, and accrued interest, Check No. 59. Interest is payable January 1 and July 1. (Record the accrued interest as a debit in the Interest Income account.)

Received cash from William F. Graham as an additional capital investment, $1,500.00.

FEBRUARY 2

Paid Bell Telephone Company bill, Check No. 60, $15.44.

General expenses are paid, Check No. 61, $42.79.

FEBRUARY 3

Issued credit memorandum #7 to the Raymond Sales Company for merchandise returned from sale of January 23, $22.40.

Check No. 62 for $6.25 is mailed in payment of the weekly releases of Barrett's *Analyst* for a thirty-day period. This is a trial subscription to a service which provides news, trade analyses, statistics, advice, etc., to its subscribers and is expected to aid sales administration. The subscription agreement provides that, at the end of thirty days, the above $6.25 may be applied on a regular twelve months' $60.00 subscription.

FEBRUARY 4

Received express money order in payment of C.O.D. shipment to C. G. Watkins, January 16, $9.19.

A 7% note, dated January 10, and due February 10, is received from the Raymond Sales Company in payment of their December account, $415.80. The note is immediately discounted at the Empire National Bank. Bank rate 6%.

FEBRUARY 5

Purchases from:

Bell & Bennett	$684.92
Cox & Cox	582.17
F. M. Dent & Company	374.22
Judson & Ray, Inc. (sight draft, honored today)	102.00

Paid freight on these purchases, Check No. 64, $18.25.

FEBRUARY 6

Sales to:

Invoice

#27	Howard Healey (C.O.D. parcel post)	$ 31.02
28	D. J. Conley	884.16
29	Harold & Elton	524.77
30	Stanwood's, Inc.	400.67

Paid freight on the shipment to D. J. Conley, Check No. 65, $11.09. Freight terms on this sale were f.o.b. shipping point.

FEBRUARY 8

Funds are borrowed from the Empire National Bank on our note for $5,000.00, dated today, for 30 days, without interest. Bank rate 6½%.

Merchandise is withdrawn from stock by Mr. Franklin for his personal use, $200.00 (cost value).

FEBRUARY 9

Received check for $2,201.96 from the Raymond Sales Company in payment of balance due on its January account, less credit memorandum of February 3. (Is the amount of the check correct? If not, credit Raymond Sales Company for the proper amount when the check is recorded.)

Issued Check No. 66 for $164.00 in favor of Empire National Bank. This check is in payment of withholding income taxes for January. The bank is a depositary of the Collector of Internal Revenue.

FEBRUARY 10

Received checks in payment of January accounts: C. H. Brooks & Company, $1,896.13, less 1%, and Howard Coburn & Company, $1,690.23, less 1%.

Received express money order covering C.O.D. shipment to Willis & Gray on January 30, $47.20.

Cash sale to Elliott & Mason, invoice #31, $35.11, less 10%.

January 31 statements from creditors are found to be in agreement with our accounts. Checks No. 67–70 are mailed to creditors in settlement of all January accounts, less cash discounts of 2% on merchandise.

FEBRUARY 11

Received checks in payment of January accounts:

D. J. Conley . . . . $2,375.03, less 1%.
Fraser & Nelson, Inc. . . . . 1,418.29, less 1%.
Stanwood's, Inc. . . . . 1,271.20, less 1%.

We are notified by the Empire National Bank that the Raymond Sales Company note of January 10, due February 10, was not paid. Check No. 71 is issued to take up the note.

Received credit memorandum from Bell & Bennett for merchandise returned from purchase of February 8, $22.10.

FEBRUARY 12

Received two notes from Harold & Elton:

#1: A sixty-day note, dated February 10, for $743.40, in payment of sales invoice of January 9, $736.04, and sixty days' prepaid 6% interest, $7.36.

#2: A thirty-day trade acceptance, dated February 6, in payment of invoice of February 6, $524.77, less 1%. This acceptance does not carry interest.

Purchases from:

Bell & Bennett . . . . $ 841.56
Clark & Son 1,041.00
Cox & Cox 487.22

Paid freight on these purchases, Check No. 72, $20.21.

FEBRUARY 13

Issued Check No. 73 to Empire National Bank in payment of our note payable due today, $1,000.00.

Discounted the Harold & Elton note for $743.40 at the Empire National Bank. Bank rate 6%.

Sales to:

Invoice

#32	Fraser & Nelson, Inc.	$1,051.23
33	Harold & Elton.	801.17
34	Raymond Sales Company	431.77
35	Burley & Son (shipment made sight draft)	150.02

February 15

The payroll for the first half of the month is: partners' salaries, $200.00, sales salaries, $300.00, general salaries, $250.00. After deduction of 1% for social security taxes on the wages and salaries of employees, and $82.00 for income taxes, the payroll is paid by Checks No. 74–81.

Check is received from William Boyd in payment of his note, dated January 15, and interest.

Received from William Boyd, sixty-day 8% note dated February 10 for $846.51 in payment of January account.

February 16

Traveling expenses of Mr. Franklin are paid, Check No. 82, $44.51.

Postage stamps are purchased, Check No. 83, $15.00.

Cash sale to E. A. Herrick, invoice #36, $128.01, less 1%.

February 17

The Empire National Bank credits our account for collection of our sight draft of February 13 on Burley & Son, $150.02.

Paid Drake & Stone, Inc., for sundry office supplies, Check No. 84, $32.63.

February 18

Clark & Son draw a draft on us, dated February 12 and due March 10, to cover their invoice of February 12, $1,041.00, less discount of 2%. The draft is accepted.

A credit memorandum is received from Cox & Cox for merchandise returned from purchase of February 12, $23.49.

February 19

Received postal money order in payment of C.O.D. shipment to Howard Healey, February 6, $31.02.

Purchases from:

Clark & Son	$ 901.42
Cox & Cox	1,208.41
F. M. Dent & Company	865.40
J. S. Bart & Company (sight draft honored today)	48.12 (net)

Paid freight on these four purchases, Check No. 86, $46.28. The freight terms on the Clark purchase were f.o.b. destination; the freight on this purchase amounted to $14.23.

FEBRUARY 20

Sales to:

Invoice

#37	C. H. Brooks & Company	$ 788.50
38	Howard Coburn & Company	1,432.27
39	D. J. Conley	345.11
40	Fraser & Nelson, Inc.	646.80
41	Edgar Ames & Company (C.O.D. express) . .	155.12

Paid City Delivery Service, Inc., Check No. 87, $20.01.

FEBRUARY 22

Paid advertising bill from the *Empire Times*, Check No. 88, $75.19.

Received debit memorandum from Clark & Son for prepaid freight on shipment of February 19, $27.41.   This bill was for extra charges incurred on certain invoice items shipped air express.

FEBRUARY 23

Issued credit memorandum #8 to Fraser & Nelson, Inc., for merchandise returned from sale of February 20, $11.56.

Issued credit memorandum #9 to C. H. Brooks & Company as an allowance on invoice of February 20, $25.00.

General expenses are paid, Check No. 89, $32.48.

The Harold & Elton draft for $622.14, discounted January 5, was due for payment February 20.

FEBRUARY 24

Issued Check No. 90 to William F. Graham for personal use, $100.00.

Gas, electricity, and water bills are paid, Check No. 91, $48.03.

A check, dated February 22, for $419.20 is received from the Raymond Sales Company in payment of its note ($415.80) of January 10, due February 10, and dishonored (see Check No. 71).   The check of the Raymond Sales Company includes interest for 1 month and 12 extra days.

FEBRUARY 25

Paid the Shell Oil Company for a fifty-gallon drum of oil (for the delivery truck), Check No. 92, $34.53.

Burley & Son write in to claim a credit for 1 % cash discount on their purchases of January and February.   Although Burley & Son have been sold on a sight draft basis, they appear to be developing into an excellent customer.   As a goodwill gesture, their claim is allowed, credit memorandum #10 issued, and Check No. 93 to cover, for 1 % cash discount on the following sales invoices:

Invoice

# 3	January 2	$ 825.44
10	January 16	725.76
35	February 13	150.02
		$1,701.22

C/m
\#4   January 20   91.32

$1,609.90

FEBRUARY 26

Purchases from:

Bell & Bennett . . . . $ 381.92
Clark & Son 320.84
F. M. Dent & Company 1,007.32

Paid freight on these purchases, Check No. 94, $19.06.
Cash sale to J. E. Hamlin, invoice \#42, $74.21, less 1 %.

FEBRUARY 27

Sales to:

Invoice
\#43   William Boyd ($500.00 cash is received as down
          payment on this sale) $1,359.97
   44   C. H. Brooks & Company 816.34
   45   Burley & Son 214.60
   46   D. J. Conley 584.31
   47   Stanwood's, Inc. 499.52

William A. Phelps and Harold W. Spear, salesmen, submit their traveling expense reports for February, $80.02, and $71.44, respectively. Checks are received for the unexpended portions of their travel advances.

The payroll for the second half of the month is: partners' salaries, $200.00, sales salaries, $300.00, general salaries, $250.00. After deduction of 1 % for social security taxes on the wages and salaries of employees, and $82.00 for income taxes, the payroll is paid by Checks No. 95–102. (February 28 is Sunday.)

After the books have been posted, enter the February trial balance on a work sheet. (The cash payments book should not be finally closed until the cash account has been reconciled with the bank statement.) Complete the work sheet, making proper provision for needed adjustments. These should follow the pattern for January, making allowance, however, for the following new items of information:

The delivery equipment should be depreciated at $33\frac{1}{3}$ % per annum on original cost.

There is on hand an unrecorded and unpaid expense invoice, dated February 26, from Lander's Garage for gasoline, oil, and minor service on the Ford truck, $21.44.

The inventory of merchandise on February 28, 19__, by actual count and valuation is $4,998.59.

The inventory of office supplies is $20.00; and there is on hand a fifty-gallon drum of automobile oil, $34.53.

Prepare a profit and loss statement for the two months ending February 28, 19__.

Prepare a balance sheet as of February 28, 19__.

In view of the fact that Mr. Franklin and Mr. Graham have received and accepted an attractive offer for the purchase of their business, it is decided to close the books.

The bank statement received from the Empire National Bank as of February 28, 19__, was as follows:

		DEBITS			DEPOSITS	BALANCE
Feb. 1 Balance						5,282.03
1	16.24	200.00	462.50	1,500.00		6,103.29
2	88.14					6,015.15
3	15.44	150.00	1,014.92			4,834.79
4	2,010.00	80.21		427.00		3,171.58
5	18.25	22.00	42.79			3,088.54
6	102.00	11.09				2,975.45
8				4,972.92		7,948.37
10	48.00	2,977.63		5,831.26		10,754.00
11	3,571.33	2,572.77		5,013.88		9,623.78
12	2,150.12	418.23				7,055.43
13	1,000.00	20.21		736.34		6,771.56
15	164.00			1,006.67		7,614.23
16	200.00	462.50				6,951.73
18	6.25	44.51	15.00			6,885.97
19	32.63	46.28				6,807.06
20				307.77		7,114.83
22	20.01					7,094.82
23	48.12	75.19				6,971.51
24				419.20		7,390.71
25	32.48	48.03				7,310.20
26	34.53					7,275.67
27	19.06			73.47		7,330.08
27 Service charge for printing checks			4.02			7,326.06

MARCH 1

Effective today the business of Franklin & Graham is sold to Edison & Fisher, Inc., for a cash consideration of $25,000.00. All of the assets and liabilities of Franklin & Graham, except cash, are transferred to the corporation.

All cash on hand is disbursed to Mr. Franklin and Mr. Graham by Checks No. 103–104.

Blackwell Manufacturing Company, Inc.

PRACTICE SET NO. 3: MANUFACTURING CORPORATION

The partnership of Blackstock & Wellman was a manufacturing enterprise of many years' successful operation. On July 1, 19__, the partners decided to incorporate their business under the name of the Blackwell Manufacturing Company, Inc. The authorized capital stock of the new corporation was as follows:

Preferred stock:
  7% cumulative, nonvoting, 2,500 shares, $100.00 par
Common stock:
  10,000 shares, $100.00 par

Common stock was subscribed for at par as follows:

Robert S. Allen	100 shares
James D. Blackstock	4,000 shares
Sumner H. Wellman	3,500 shares
	7,600 shares

The subscription of Robert S. Allen was paid for in cash. The subscriptions of Mr. Blackstock and Mr. Wellman were paid for by turning over the net assets of the partnership, partnership goodwill of $50,000.00, and cash for the balance. The balance sheet of the partnership on June 30, 19—, was as follows:

Blackstock & Wellman

BALANCE SHEET, JUNE 30, 19—

Assets

Current Assets:

Cash		$ 74,758.18
Petty Cash		100.00
Notes Receivable	$ 42,357.12	
Less Notes Receivable Discounted	22,848.08	19,509.04
Accounts Receivable	$220,416.44	
Less Reserve for Bad Debts	18,223.17	202,193.27
Inventories:		
Finished Goods.	$192,800.37	
Work in Process	65,014.92	
Raw Materials	109,207.46	
Factory Supplies	2,914.66	369,937.41
		$666,497.90

Fixed Assets:

	Gross Value	Reserve for Depreciation	Net Book Value	
Automobiles	$ 26,089.06	$ 8,128.17	$ 17,960.89	
Buildings	122,010.40	31,722.70	90,287.70	
Furniture, Fixtures, and Office Equipment	12,412.84	3,044.28	9,368.56	
Land	40,320.00		40,320.00	
Machinery	137,880.62	38,954.10	98,926.52	
Tools	6,272.14		6,272.14	
	$344,985.06	$81,849.25	$263,135.81	263,135.81
				$929,633.71

Liabilities and Net Worth

Current Liabilities:

Accrued Interest Payable on Mortgage	$ 1,500.00
Accrued Interest Payable on Notes Payable	500.00
Social Security Taxes Payable	5,408.95
Accrued Property Taxes Payable (10 months)	5,417.20
Notes Payable	100,000.00
Accounts Payable	83,821.10
	$196,647.25

Long-Term Debt:

Mortgage Payable on Real Estate, 6%, due in ten years, interest payable January 1 and July 1	50,000.00
Total Liabilities	$246,647.25

Net Worth:

	P & L Ratio		
James E. Blackstock, Capital . . . 60%	$360,571.90		
Sumner H. Wellman, Capital . . . 40%	322,414.56		682,986.46
			$929,633.71

Supporting schedules to the above balance sheet are

NOTES RECEIVABLE:

Date of Note	Maker	Time	Rate of Interest	Amount	Discounted at Metropolitan National Bank on
June 1	Eastern Sales Company	120 days	6%	$22,848.08	June 1
10	Carsten & Earles	30 days		11,376.93	
24	Lewis & Son	60 days		8,132.11	
				$42,357.12	

ACCOUNTS RECEIVABLE:

Berg & Evans	$ 16,481.47
Carsten & Earles	12,232.87
Clemson Bros., Inc.	26,407.25
Dean, Witter & Company	66,865.28
Elliott & Company, Inc.	32,491.12
General Sales Company, Inc..	14,684.99
Harper-Harris Company.	29,238.74
Lewis & Son	22,014.72
	$220,416.44

NOTES PAYABLE:

Date of Note	Payee	Time	Rate of Interest	Amount
May 31	Metropolitan National Bank	120 days	6%	$100,000.00

ACCOUNTS PAYABLE:

Ne Page & Nelson	$12,014.70
Pioneer Supply Company	10,626.09
Rex Metal Works	14,016.72
Sears-Scott, Inc.	8,482.77
Terminal Sales Company	16,422.64
Union Hardware Company	10,418.29
Wallace Equipment Company	11,839.89
	$83,821.10

The following books of original entry are to be employed:

Sales book
Returned sales and allowances book
Voucher register
Cash receipts book

Check register
Notes receivable register
Journal

The Blackwell Manufacturing Company, Inc., adopted the following numbered system of accounts:

REAL ACCOUNTS

Assets:

1   Cash
2   Petty Cash
5   Notes Receivable
6   Notes Receivable Discounted
7   Accounts Receivable
8   Reserve for Bad Debts
10   Finished Goods
20   Work in Process
25   Raw Materials
30   Factory Supplies

40   Interest Receivable
46   Prepaid Insurance
47   Prepaid Taxes, Licenses, Fees

50   Sundry Salesmen — Travel Advances

61   Automobiles
62   Reserve for Depreciation — Automobiles
63   Buildings
64   Reserve for Depreciation — Buildings
65   Furniture, Fixtures, and Office Equipment
66   Reserve for Depreciation — Furniture, Fixtures, and Office Equipment
69   Land
71   Machinery
72   Reserve for Depreciation — Machinery

75   Tools
76   Reserve for Depreciation — Tools

80   Goodwill

90   Organization Expense

Liabilities and Net Worth:

100   Income Taxes Payable
101   Withholding Income Taxes Payable
103   Property Taxes Payable
105   Social Security Taxes Payable
107   Taxes Payable — Miscellaneous
110   Dividends Payable — Preferred stock
111   Dividends Payable — Common Stock

130   Interest Payable — Mortgage
131   Interest Payable — Notes Payable
132   Notes Payable

140   Vouchers Payable

181   Mortgage Payable on Real Estate

200   Preferred Stock
225   Common Stock
250   Capital Surplus
275   Earned Surplus

Nominal Accounts

Operating Income:

300   Sales
325   Returned Sales and Allowances
330   Sales Discounts
350   Cost of Sales

Manufacturing:

450   Freight In
475   Purchases Discounts

501   Direct Labor

600   Manufacturing Expense (summary and distribution account)
610   Depreciation Expense — Buildings
612   Depreciation Expense — Machinery
613   Depreciation Expense — Tools

620 Factory Repairs
640 Factory Supplies
650 Heat, Light, Power
660 Indirect Labor
670 Insurance
680 Miscellaneous Factory Expense
688 Social Security Taxes
689 Taxes, Licenses, Fees

Selling Expenses:

701 Advertising
720 Delivery Expense
730 Depreciation Expense — Automobiles
750 Insurance
760 Miscellaneous Selling Expense
780 Sales Salaries
788 Social Security Taxes
789 Taxes, Licenses, Fees
790 Traveling Expense

General Expenses:

801 Administrative Salaries
810 Bad Debts Expense
820 Depreciation Expense — Buildings
821 Depreciation Expense — Furniture, Fixtures, and Office Equipment
830 Insurance
840 Miscellaneous General Expense
850 Office Supplies
860 Postage
870 Stationery and Printing
888 Social Security Taxes
889 Taxes, Licenses, Fees
894 Telephone and Telegraph

Other Income:

925 Interest Income
950 Miscellaneous Income
975 Scrap Sales

Other Expense:

1025 Interest Expense
1050 Miscellaneous Expense

Special Income Credits: 1100–1199

1150 Recovery on Bad Debt Provisions of Prior Years

Special Income Debits: 1200–1299

Clearing and Summary Accounts: 1300–1399

    1399   Profit and Loss

JULY 1

Before the transactions below are recorded, the student should place on the books the proper opening entries for capital stock from information recited above. Include cash in the journal entry recording the investments of Mr. Blackstock and Mr. Wellman. Fixed assets should be set up at gross values; accrued depreciation as of June 30 should be credited to reserve for depreciation accounts.

The accounts payable, in addition to being entered in the opening journal entry (as vouchers payable), should also be entered in the voucher register, beginning with Ne Page & Nelson as Voucher No. 1, Pioneer Supply Company as Voucher No. 2 and so on. The seven credits to Vouchers Payable should be debited to Account 140, Vouchers Payable, in the distribution columns.

Balances for the eight accounts receivable accounts should be entered in the subsidiary ledger. The three notes receivable should be entered as *memoranda* in the notes receivable register.

The books of the Blackwell Manufacturing Company are to be kept on the monthly accrual basis of accounting, as described in Chapters 15 and 25, adjusting entries being made at the end of each month. Inventories are to be maintained under the perpetual inventory system.

Two controlling accounts will be kept, one for Accounts Receivable, and one for Vouchers Payable.

JULY 1

Voucher No. 8, favor James E. Blackstock, for organization expenses paid by him, $4,203.72. Drew Check No. 1 in payment.

Voucher No. 9, favor State Treasurer, for automobile license plates for next 6 months, $250.02. Drew Check No. 2 in payment.

Voucher No. 10, in favor of sundry salesmen, for traveling advances, $1,200.00. Drew Checks No. 3–9 in payment.

Voucher No. 11, favor John E. Davis, for six months' interest on mortgage, due today, $1,500.00. Drew Check No. 10 in payment.

Voucher No. 12, favor General Insurance Agency, for insurance premiums on

Building (three years)	$1,920.00
Merchandise (one year)	2,520.00
Automobiles (one year)	408.00
Other personal property (one year)	1,200.00
	$6,048.00

July 2

Voucher No. 13, favor Bell Telephone Company, $37.50.

Voucher No. 14, favor Standard Office Supply Company, for office supplies, $308.08.

Voucher No. 15, favor Adams & Buckner, for miscellaneous selling expenses, $111.04.

July 3

Voucher No. 16, favor Pioneer Supply Company, for factory supplies, $906.98.

Issued credit memorandum #1 to Elliott & Company, Inc., for merchandise returned from sale of June 29, $1,260.52.   Cost, $1,109.54.

July 5

Voucher No. 17, favor Central Service Machinery Company, for factory repairs, $983.68.

Voucher No. 18, favor Sears-Scott, Inc., for raw material purchases, $12,010.17.

Voucher No. 19, favor Northern Pacific Railway, for freight on purchases, $112.14.

Check No. 11 to pay Voucher No. 19.

Check No. 12 to pay Voucher No. 12.

Check No. 13 to pay Voucher No. 13.

July 6

Sales to:

Invoice			Cost
#1	Berg & Evans	$10,723.26	$9,014.75
2	Carsten & Earles	7,903.67	6,728.52
3	Dean, Witter & Company	6,990.47	5,766.29
4	Elliott & Company, Inc.	9,048.17	7,680.94
5	Harper-Harris Company	8,164.29	6,722.50

July 8

Voucher No. 20, favor Grebe & Gillette, for miscellaneous general expenses, $74.92.

Voucher No. 21, favor Chase & Chase, for miscellaneous factory expenses, $529.28.

July 9

June 30 statements from creditors are found to be in agreement with our accounts.   Checks No. 14–20 are drawn in payment:

Vo. No. 1	Ne Page & Nelson	$12,014.70, less 2%.
2	Pioneer Supply Company	10,626.09, less 2%.
3	Rex Metal Works	14,016.72, less 2%.
4	Sears-Scott, Inc.	8,482.77, less 3%.

5	Terminal Sales Company	16,422.64, less 2%.
6	Union Hardware Company . . .	10,418.29, less 2%.
7	Wallace Equipment Company . .	11,839.89, less 1%.

Received from Harper-Harris Company, note dated July 10, for thirty days, 6% interest, in payment of June account $29,238.74.

JULY 10

Voucher No. 22, favor Pioneer Supply Company, for factory supplies, $1,008.12.

Received cash from Carsten & Earles for note of June 10 due today, $11,376.93.

Received checks in payment of June accounts receivable:

Berg & Evans.	$16,481.47, less 2%.
Clemson Bros., Inc.	26,407.25, less 2%.
Dean, Witter & Company	66,865.28, less 2%.
General Sales Company	14,684.99, less 2%.
Lewis & Son	22,014.72, less 2%.

JULY 11

Voucher No. 23, favor Wallace Equipment Company, for miscellaneous factory expenses, $432.96.

Check No. 21 to pay Voucher No. 15.

Check No. 22 to pay Voucher No. 17.

JULY 12

Issued credit memorandum #2 to Berg & Evans for merchandise returned from sale of July 6, $783.84. Cost, $650.16.

Raw material purchases from:

Ne Page & Nelson	$12,517.89
Terminal Sales Company	13,062.91

Voucher No. 26, favor Northern Pacific Railway for freight on raw material purchases, $184.13.

Check No. 23 to pay Voucher No. 26.

JULY 13

Sales to:

Invoice			Cost
#6	Clemson Bros., Inc.	$ 4,728.72	$ 4,019.32
7	Dean, Witter & Company	9,583.72	8,126.17
8	General Sales Company, Inc. . .	10,284.63	8,741.93
9	Lewis & Son	12,379.07	10,922.20

JULY 15

Voucher No. 27, favor *Garfield Trade Register*, for advertising, $1,001.18.

Voucher No. 28, favor City Treasurer, for fine imposed on one of our drivers for speeding, $50.00.

Check No. 24 to pay Voucher No. 28.

July 16

Received credit memorandum from Terminal Sales Company for raw materials returned from purchase of July 12, $607.49.

Received from Elliott & Company, Inc., check for $20,000.00; and note for $12,491.12, dated July 10, for thirty days, without interest, in payment of June account.

July 17

Voucher No. 30, in favor of Payroll, for payroll for period July 1 to 15, inclusive. Two days are required for the preparation of the payroll; its distribution is as follows:

501	Direct Labor	$12,011.50
620	Factory Repairs	869.14
650	Heat, Light, Power	152.00
660	Indirect Labor	6,126.23
680	Miscellaneous Factory Expense	591.14
720	Delivery Expense	727.82
780	Sales Salaries	760.00
801	Administrative Salaries	1,015.00
		$22,252.83

From this accrued payroll there were required to be withheld from employees' checks social security taxes of $201.04, and income taxes of $3,112.77.

(On its own account the Blackwell Manufacturing Company was liable for social security taxes on this payroll, $804.16. These taxes will be paid next October and January.)

Drew Check No. 25, in favor of Payroll — Blackwell Manufacturing Company, Inc., in payment of Voucher No. 30.

July 18

Voucher No. 31, favor Lowman, Rand, Inc., for miscellaneous selling expenses, $130.44.

Issued credit memorandum #3 to Lewis & Son for merchandise returned from sale of July 13, $817.47. Cost, $677.88.

July 19

Raw material purchases from:

Rex Metal Works	$35,949.34
Sears-Scott, Inc.	10,432.08

Voucher No. 34, favor Northern Pacific Railway, for freight on purchases, $317.21.

Check No. 26 to pay Voucher No. 34.

July 20

Sales to:

Invoice			Cost
#10	Berg & Evans	$ 6,472.15	$ 5,601.32
11	Carsten & Earles	9,672.70	8,142.79
12	Dean, Witter & Company	12,005.94	10,216.04
13	Elliott & Company, Inc.	7,214.92	6,122.86
14	Lewis & Son	7,069.99	6,009.22

July 22

Voucher No. 35, favor Metropolitan Auto Service, Inc., for automobile repairs, $62.41.

Voucher No. 36, favor Moody & Jackson, for stationery and printing, $386.73.

July 23

Voucher No. 37, favor Pioneer Supply Company, for factory supplies, $1,117.33.

Voucher No. 38, favor Northern Pacific Railway, for freight on the Pioneer purchase, $20.36.

Voucher No. 39, favor George H. Mason Company, for miscellaneous general expense, $153.66.

Check No. 27 to pay Voucher No. 38.

July 24

Received credit memorandum from Sears-Scott, Inc., for raw materials returned from purchase of July 19, $697.10.

Voucher No. 41, favor Central Service Machinery Company, for factory repairs, $788.07.

July 25

Issued credit memorandum #4 to Lewis & Son for merchandise returned from sale of July 13, $569.33. Cost, $467.84.

Voucher No. 42, favor Union Hardware Company, for miscellaneous factory expense, $601.24.

July 26

Raw material purchase from Ne Page & Nelson, $7,687.16.

Voucher No. 44, favor Northern Pacific Railway, for freight on raw material purchases, $39.66.

Check No. 28 to pay Voucher No. 27.

Check No. 29 to pay Voucher No. 36.

Check No. 30 to pay Voucher No. 41.

Check No. 31 to pay Voucher No. 44.

July 27

Sales to:

Invoice			Cost
#15	Berg & Evans	$7,294.16	$6,200.03
16	Carsten & Earles	9,589.04	8,169.76
17	Dean, Witter & Company	8,001.12	6,810.10
18	Elliott & Company, Inc.	9,588.20	7,903.38

July 29

Received from Harper-Harris Company, note dated July 11, due September 11, for $8,164.29, without interest, in payment of invoice of July 6.

Voucher No. 45, favor City Treasurer, for gas, electricity, and water, $1,461.52. Charge $\frac{4}{5}$ to factory, $\frac{1}{5}$ to general administrative expense.

July 30

Voucher No. 46, favor *Garfield Trade Register*, for advertising, $1,487.44.

Voucher No. 47, favor Sterling Oil Company, for gasoline and oil, $362.90.

July 31

Voucher No. 48, in favor of sundry salesmen, for traveling expense reports, $684.99.

Voucher No. 49, favor Western Union Telegraph Company, $129.46.

Voucher No. 50, favor Harris C. Graham, Cashier, to reimburse petty cash as follows:

760	Miscellaneous Selling Expense	$14.02
790	Traveling Expense	9.18
840	Miscellaneous General Expense	12.59
850	Office Supplies	4.83
860	Postage	15.00
870	Stationery and Printing	16.00
		$71.62

The voucher register is kept open until the summary of the payroll for the period July 16 to 31 is ready. The payroll voucher, No. 51, is distributed as follows:

501	Direct Labor	$19,460.46
620	Factory Repairs	1,260.74
650	Heat, Light, Power	152.00
660	Indirect Labor	9,202.37
680	Miscellaneous Factory Expense.	527.28
720	Delivery Expense	801.05
780	Sales Salaries	760.00
801	Administrative Salaries	1,015.00
		$33,178.90

From this accrued payroll there were required to be withheld from employees' checks social security taxes of $288.44, and income taxes of $4,504.83.

(On its own account the Blackwell Manufacturing Company was liable for social security taxes on this payroll, $1,153.76.)

Checks No. 32–38 to pay Voucher No. 48.

Check No. 39 to pay Voucher No. 50.

Of the social security taxes owed as of June 30, $2,163.54 are payable in July. This amount represents withholding taxes for the period April to June. Voucher No. 52 is drawn up, $2,163.54, and it is paid by Check No. 40 (favor Collector of Internal Revenue).

Entries for usual month-end adjustments should now be placed on the books as follows:

(1) Accrued depreciation. Annual depreciation rates to be applied against original cost, i.e., account balances at the beginning of each month are

Automobiles	30%
Buildings (90% to factory, 10% to general administrative expense)	3%
Furniture, Fixtures, and Office Equipment	10%
Machinery	10%
Tools	33⅓%

(2) Accrue for July property taxes. Prorate ⅞ to factory, ⅛ to general administrative expense.

(3) Accrue for July payroll taxes on employer (see July 17 and July 31 payroll information). Apportion to manufacturing, selling, and general administrative expense, in proportion to the distribution of the July payroll over these three groups. These taxes are due for payment in October (old-age benefit tax), and next January (unemployment tax).

(4) Write off July apportionment of prepaid automobile license expense.

(5) Accrue for interest on notes receivable.

(6) Accrue for interest on notes payable and the real-estate mortgage. Calculate interest for one month of 30 days, using the 6% rule.

(7) Expired insurance. Prorate insurance expense on
   Buildings: 90% factory, 10% general administrative.
   Inventory: 50% factory, 50% general administrative.
   Other personal property: 90% factory, 10% general administrative.

(8) Transfer the balances of accounts No. 450, Freight In, and No. 475, Purchases Discounts, to Account No. 25, Raw Materials.

(9) The Raw Materials Requisition Register shows $87,407.24 requisitioned for use in manufacturing operations. Debit Account No. 20, Work in Process, credit Account No. 25, Raw Materials.

(*Note:* In the stores ledger separate account cards are maintained for Freight In and Purchases Discounts. The Freight In account is credited monthly for the amount of freight applicable to raw materials issued; and Purchases Discounts is debited for an amount which will reduce this account card to zero at the end of the month. The credit to Freight In and debit to Purchases Discounts are included in the total of $87,407.24 for the raw materials requisition register.)

(10) The Factory Supplies Requisition Register shows $3,092.91 requisitioned for use in manufacturing operations. Debit Account No. 640, Factory Supplies, credit Account No. 30, Factory Supplies.

(11) Transfer the balance of Account No. 501, Direct Labor, $31,471.96, to Account No. 20, Work in Process.

(12) Overhead has been charged to production orders at the rate of 95 % of direct labor cost. The Summary of Manufacturing Expense Distributed shows a total of $29,898.36. This total is checked and found correct (95 % × $31,471.96 = $29,898.36). Debit Account No. 20, Work in Process, credit Account No. 600, Manufacturing Expense.

(13) The Summary of Completed Production Orders for July totals $137,043.26. Debit Account No. 10, Finished Goods, credited Account No. 20, Work in Process.

(14) Post all books of original entry. The Cost of Sales column in the sales book should be posted as a debit to Account No. 350, Cost of Sales, and as a credit to Account No. 10, Finished Goods.

(15) Prepare

(a) Trial balance, July 31, 19__.
(b) Profit and loss statement for the month of July.
(c) Balance sheet, July 31, 19__, with supporting schedules for accounts receivable and vouchers payable.

August 1

(In the entry of transactions for August, use new pages for the books of original entry.)

Voucher No. 53, favor Bell Telephone Company, $54.11.

Voucher No. 54, favor Moody & Jackson, for printing office and factory forms, $150.00. Apportion ⅔ to factory, ⅓ to general administrative expense.

August 2

Voucher No. 55, favor Chase & Chase, for miscellaneous factory expenses, $412.01.

Voucher No. 56, favor Belmont & Keen, for miscellaneous general expenses, $174.16.

Check No. 41 to pay Voucher No. 51.

August 3

Raw material purchases from:

Ne Page & Nelson	$16,472.81
Terminal Sales Company	8,852.19

Voucher No. 59, favor Northern Pacific Railway, for freight on purchases, $156.72.

Check No. 42 to pay Voucher No. 59.

AUGUST 4

Sales to:

Invoice			Cost
#19	Berg & Evans	$ 7,352.14	$6,280.40
20	Clemson Bros., Inc.	10,322.40	8,825.04
21	Dean, Witter & Company	8,843.04	7,576.29
22	Harper-Harris Company	7,943.50	6,584.19

AUGUST 6

Check No. 43 to pay Voucher No. 53.

Voucher No. 60, favor Central Service Machinery Company, for factory repairs, $188.52.

AUGUST 7

Issued credit memorandum #5 to Clemson Bros., Inc., for merchandise returned from sale of August 4, $919.25.   Cost, $772.36.

Voucher No. 61, favor Pioneer Supply Company, for factory supplies, $801.04.

AUGUST 8

Received from Harper-Harris Company note dated August 4, and due September 10, for $7,943.50, without interest, in payment of invoice of August 4.

Voucher No. 62, favor *Garfield Trade Register*, for advertising, $1,266.47.

AUGUST 9

July 31 statements from creditors are found to be correct.   Checks are drawn in payment as follows:

Check No.	to pay	Voucher No.
44	. . . .	14
45	. . . .	16; 22; 37; all less 2%.
46	. . . .	18; 40; both less 1%.
47	. . . .	20
48	. . . .	21
49	. . . .	23
50	. . . .	24; 43; both less 2%.
51	. . . .	29; less 2%.
52	. . . .	31
53	. . . .	32; less 2%.
54	. . . .	35
55	. . . .	39
56	. . . .	42; less 2%.
57	. . . .	45
58	. . . .	46
59	. . . .	47
60	. . . .	49

Cash is received from Harper-Harris Company for its note of July 10, $29,238.74, and 6% interest.

Cash is received from Elliott & Company, Inc., for its note of July 10, $12,491.12.

August 10

Received checks in payment of July accounts:

Berg & Evans.	$23,705.73, less 2%.
Carsten & Earles, for June account	12,232.87, net.
Clemson Bros., Inc.	4,728.72, less 2%.
Dean, Witter & Company	36,581.25, less 2%.
Elliott & Company, Inc.	24,590.77, net.
General Sales Company, Inc.	10,284.63, less 2%.
Lewis & Son	18,062.26, less 2%.

Raw material purchase from Ne Page & Nelson, $8,001.99.

Voucher No. 64, favor Northern Pacific Railway, for freight on purchases, $41.04.

Check No. 61 to pay Voucher No. 64.

Check No. 62 to Metropolitan National Bank covering income taxes withheld from employees' checks in July, $7,617.60. This bank is an accredited depositary of the Collector of Internal Revenue.

August 11

Sales to:

Invoice			Cost
#23	Carsten & Earles	$ 6,517.84	$ 5,561.15
24	Dean, Witter & Company	12,614.32	10,709.17
25	Elliott & Company, Inc.	7,613.24	6,499.25
26	General Sales Company, Inc.	6,294.73	5,351.15
27	Harper-Harris Company	11,642.16	9,889.46

Voucher No. 66, favor Northern Pacific Railway, $81.02. By agreement this freight bill is to be paid by Harper-Harris Company, for whose account the payment is made by Check No. 63.

August 13

Received credit memorandum from Ne Page & Nelson for raw materials returned from purchase of August 10, $768.46.

Terminal Sales Company offers 1 % extra discount on its bill of August 3 if payment is made within ten days. Check No. 64 to pay Voucher No. 58, less 3 %.

August 14

Voucher No. 68, favor Lowman, Rand, Inc., for miscellaneous selling expenses, $121.19.

Credit is requested by, and granted to, Elliott & Company, Inc., for 2 % sales discount on its remittance of August 10 for $24,590.77. Credit memorandum #6.

Check No. 65 to pay Voucher No. 61, net.

AUGUST 15

Voucher No. 69, favor Pioneer Supply Company, for factory supplies, $837.91.

Voucher No. 70, favor Northern Pacific Railway for freight on Pioneer purchase, $18.77.

Check No. 66 to pay Voucher No. 70.

AUGUST 16

Issued credit memorandum #7 to Elliott & Company, Inc., for merchandise returned from sale of August 11, $205.52. Cost, $173.54.

Voucher No. 71, favor Wallace Equipment Company, for miscellaneous factory expenses, $444.15.

AUGUST 17

Raw material purchases from:

Rex Metal Works	$26,432.07
Sears-Scott, Inc.	19,392.73

Voucher No. 74, favor Northern Pacific Railway, for freight on purchases, $301.18.

Voucher No. 75, in favor of Payroll for payroll for period August 1 to 15, inclusive. Its distribution is as follows:

501	Direct Labor	$15,483.07
620	Factory Repairs	362.17
650	Heat, Light, Power	152.00
660	Indirect Labor	6,366.90
680	Miscellaneous Factory Expense.	614.08
720	Delivery Expense	747.16
780	Sales Salaries	760.00
801	Administrative Salaries	1,102.00
		$25,587.38

From this accrued payroll there were required to be withheld from employees' checks social security taxes of $244.10, and income taxes of $3,701.14.

(On its own account the Blackwell Manufacturing Company was liable for social security taxes on this payroll, $976.40.)

Check No. 67 to pay Voucher No. 74.

Check No. 68 to pay Voucher No. 75.

AUGUST 18

Sales to:

Invoice			Cost
#28	Berg & Evans	$ 9,796.02	$ 8,182.52
29	Clemson Bros., Inc.	8,928.36	7,641.10
30	Elliott & Company	7,356.92	6,065.98
31	Harper-Harris Company	9,429.58	8,074.24

32 Eastern Sales Company, shipment
sent sight draft; cash received
today 12,152.16 10,829.34

August 20

Received an accepted thirty-day time draft from Carsten & Earles for $6,517.84, without interest, dated August 11, covering our shipment of that date.

Voucher No. 76, favor Moody & Jackson for promotional sales catalogues, $400.00.

Voucher No. 77, favor Carr & Wright, for miscellaneous general expenses, $82.64.

August 21

Check No. 69 to pay Voucher No. 62.

Issued credit memorandum #8 to Berg & Evans for merchandise returned from sale of August 18, $534.28. Cost, $425.28.

Voucher No. 78, favor Central Service Machinery Company, for factory repairs, $584.32.

August 22

Voucher No. 79, favor Union Hardware Company, for miscellaneous factory expense, $401.57.

Voucher No. 80, favor Standard Office Supply Company, for office supplies, $277.28.

August 23

Voucher No. 81, favor *Garfield Trade Register*, for advertising, $1,082.26.

Cash is received from Lewis & Son, for their note of June 24, for $8,132.11, due today.

Check No. 70 to pay Voucher No. 78.

August 24

Voucher No. 82, favor Rex Metal Works, for raw material purchases, $11,889.97. (Enter this voucher with knowledge of Voucher No. 83.)

Voucher No. 83, favor Northern Pacific Railway, for freight on purchases, $100.16. In accordance with the terms of purchase, one half of this freight bill is to be paid by Rex Metal Works.

Check No. 71 to pay Voucher No. 83.

August 25

Sales to:

Invoice		Cost
#33	Dean, Witter & Company . . . . $ 9,631.78	$8,063.13
34	Elliott & Company, Inc. 7,042.93	5,946.66
35	General Sales Company, Inc. . . . 8,023.21	6,809.92
36	Lewis & Son 10,082.36	8,450.42

AUGUST 27

Voucher No. 84, favor Pioneer Supply Company, for factory supplies, $1,005.60.

Miscellaneous scrap materials are sold for cash to the Weston Junk Company, $100.00.

Voucher No. 85, favor Union Hardware Company, for shop tools, $352.84.

AUGUST 28

Voucher No. 86, favor Metropolitan Auto Service, Inc., for automobile repairs, $66.07.

One of the delivery trucks, now 26 months old, and originally costing $2,601.10, is traded in on a new model. The trade-in allowance received from the Wilson Motor Company is $500.00. The new truck is delivered today at an invoice cost of $1,748.20.

Check No. 72 to pay Voucher No. 87.

AUGUST 29

Some of the merchandise returned by customers is not considered to be salable as new merchandise of our usual grade. This "returned" merchandise is withdrawn from finished goods stock and sold for cash on invoice #37 to Kenway & Robb for $2,500.00. Cost, $2,544.14.

Voucher No. 88, favor Adams & Buckner, for miscellaneous selling expenses, $141.25.

AUGUST 30

Voucher No. 89, favor City Treasurer, for gas, electricity, and water, $1,138.40. Charge ⅘ to factory, and ⅕ to general administrative expense.

Voucher No. 90, favor Sterling Oil Company, for gasoline and oil, $321.77.

AUGUST 31

Voucher No. 91, in favor of sundry salesmen, for traveling expense reports, $781.29.

Voucher No. 92, favor Western Union Telegraph Company, $101.24.

Voucher No. 93, favor Harris C. Graham, Cashier, to reimburse petty cash as follows:

450	Freight In	$11.07
760	Miscellaneous Selling Expense	12.73
790	Traveling Expense	15.00
840	Miscellaneous General Expense	21.07
850	Office Supplies	4.69
860	Postage	25.00
		$89.56

The payroll voucher, No. 94, for the period August 16 to 31, is distributed as follows:

501	Direct Labor	$16,774.16
620	Factory Repairs	1,842.04
650	Heat, Light, Power	152.00
660	Indirect Labor	8,905.12
680	Miscellaneous Factory Expense	588.01
720	Delivery Expense	798.15
780	Sales Salaries	760.00
801	Administrative Salaries	1,202.00
		$31,021.48

From this accrued payroll there were required to be withheld from employees' checks social security taxes of $254.99, and income taxes of $3,802.74.

(On its own account the Blackwell Manufacturing Company was liable for social security taxes on this payroll, $1,019.96.)

Checks No. 73–79 to pay Voucher No. 91.

Check No. 80 to pay Voucher No. 93.

A bill for 8% interest, for twenty-one days, on $27,165.41, is mailed to Carsten & Earles, covering their overdue account.

Directors declare a 2% cash dividend on the common stock payable October 1 to stock of record, September 15.

Entries for month-end adjustments should now be placed on the books as follows:

(1) Accrued depreciation on fixed assets. Prorate depreciation expense as in July.

(2) Accrue for August property taxes. Prorate $\frac{7}{8}$ to factory, $\frac{1}{8}$ to general administrative expense.

(3) Accrue for August payroll taxes on employer (see August 17 and August 31 payroll information). Apportion to manufacturing, selling, and general administrative expense, in proportion to the distribution of the August payroll over these three groups. These taxes are due for payment in October (old-age benefit tax), and next January (unemployment tax).

(4) Write off August apportionment of prepaid automobile license expense.

(5) Accrue for interest on notes payable and the real-estate mortgage.

(6) Expired insurance. Prorate insurance expense as in July.

(7) According to the revenue acts of the state in which the Blackwell Manufacturing Company, Inc., is located, it is specified that for each year ending June 30 there shall be imposed upon each corporation a franchise tax of $0.125 for each share of outstanding capital stock. Accrue for this tax (July and August) at the annual rate of $0.125 for each share of outstanding stock of the Blackwell Manufacturing Company, Inc.

(8) Transfer the balances of Accounts No. 450, Freight In, and No. 475, Purchases Discounts, to Account No. 25, Raw Materials.

(9) The Raw Materials Requisition Register shows $86,177.17 requisitioned for use in manufacturing operations. Debit Account No. 20, Work in Process, credit Account No. 25, Raw Materials.

(10) The Factory Supplies Requisition Register shows $3,525.74 requisitioned for use in manufacturing operations. Debit Account No. 640, Factory Supplies, credit Account No. 30, Factory Supplies.

(11) Transfer the balance of Account No. 501, Direct Labor, $32,257.23, to Account No. 20, Work in Process.

(12) Overhead has been charged to production orders at the rate of 95 % of direct labor cost. The Summary of Manufacturing Expense Distributed shows a total of $30,644.37. This total is checked and found correct (95 % × $32,257.23 = $30,644.37). Debit Account No. 20, Work in Process, credit Account No. 600, Manufacturing Expense.

(13) The Summary of Completed Production Orders for August totals $134,331.82. Debit Account No. 10, Finished Goods, credit Account No. 20, Work in Process.

(14) Since all June 30 accounts receivable have been collected, directors authorize the transfer of the balance in the Reserve for Bad Debts to Account No. 1150, Recovery on Bad Debt Provisions of Prior Years.

(15) Because the Carsten & Earles account is giving evidence of weakness, the directors authorize a provision, for possible loss in collection, of 10 % of the amount owed by the company.

(16) Post all books of original entry.

(17) Prepare

    (a) Trial balance, August 31, 19___.

    (b) Profit and loss statement for the months of July and August.

    (c) Balance sheet, August 31, 19___, with supporting schedules for accounts receivable and vouchers payable.

If desired, the books of the Blackwell Manufacturing Company may be formally closed. If this is to be done, proceed as follows:

(1) Transfer all individual manufacturing expense accounts to Account No. 600, Manufacturing Expense. Transfer the new balance of Account No. 600, Manufacturing Expense, to Account No. 350, Cost of Sales.

(2) Transfer all nominal accounts, in profit and loss statement order, to Account No. 1399, Profit and Loss.

(3) Transfer the balance of Account No. 1399, Profit and Loss, to Account No. 275, Earned Surplus.

(4) Rule up all closed accounts.

Henry J. Franklin

PRACTICE SET NO. 4: SINGLE PROPRIETORSHIP

Practice Set No. 4 will employ the following books of original entry: sales book, purchases book, cash receipts book, cash payments book, and journal. The general ledger accounts will be as follows:

Current Assets:

Cash
Accounts Receivable (control)
Reserve for Bad Debts
Notes Receivable
Merchandise
William A. Phelps, Travel Advance
Harold W. Spear, Travel Advance
Prepaid Expenses

Fixed Assets:

Office Equipment
Reserve for Depreciation — Office Equipment

Current Liabilities:

Accounts Payable (control)
Notes Payable
Social Security Taxes Payable
Withholding Income Taxes Payable

Net Worth:

Henry J. Franklin, Capital
Henry J. Franklin, Personal
Profit and Loss

Profit and Loss:

Sales
Returned Sales and Allowances
Sales Discounts
Costs of Sales
Purchases
Returned Purchases and Allowances
Purchases Discounts
Freight In
Advertising
Delivery Expense
Sales Salaries
Traveling Expense
Bad Debts Expense
Depreciation Expense — Office Equipment
General Expense
General Salaries
Insurance Expense
Office Supplies Expense
Rent
Social Security Taxes

Utilities Expense (To this account charge bills for water, electricity, gas, and telephone.)

Interest Expense

NOVEMBER 2

Henry J. Franklin began business with an investment of cash, $20,-000.00.

Paid November rent to the Globe Building Company, $300.00.

NOVEMBER 3

Paid $2,000.00 to the Standard Office Equipment Company for sundry items of office equipment (furniture, safe, filing cabinets, etc.).

Paid $58.12 to Drake & Stone, Inc., for sundry office supplies, books, stationery, etc.

Purchased for cash two typewriters, one adding machine, and one cash register from the Carter Office Machines Company, $400.00.

NOVEMBER 4

Purchase from Bell & Bennett, $214.63.

Purchase from Clark & Son, $760.50.

Purchase from Cox & Cox, $762.00.

Paid Bell Telephone Company bill, $15.00.

Paid for postage stamps, $10.00.

NOVEMBER 5

Sale to William Boyd, $750.00.

Sale to C. H. Brooks & Company, $446.40.

Purchase from F. M. Dent & Company, $712.00.

Paid freight on purchase from Cox & Cox, $12.14.

NOVEMBER 6

Cash sale to Burley & Son, $884.00, net.

Cash purchase from Cox & Cox, $744.00, less 2%.

Paid Cox & Cox invoice of November 4, $762.00, less 2%.

Paid White & Bollard for one year's fire insurance premium on merchandise inventory, $48.00.

NOVEMBER 7

Sale to William Boyd, $504.80.

Sale to C. H. Brooks & Company, $328.40.

General expenses are paid, $35.20.

NOVEMBER 9

Paid Clark & Son invoice of November 4, $760.50, less 2%.

Purchase from Cox & Cox, $874.00.

Issued credit memorandum to William Boyd for merchandise returned from shipment of November 7, $28.64.

NOVEMBER 10

Cash is received from C. H. Brooks & Company in payment of invoice of November 5, $446.40, net.

Traveling expenses are paid, $46.80.

Paid F. M. Dent & Company invoice of November 5, $721.00 (an overpayment of $9.00), no discount.

NOVEMBER 11

Cash sale to William Boyd, $784.10, less 1%.

Purchase from Cox & Cox, $412.76.

Purchase from F. M. Dent & Company, $380.00. (Terms on this purchase, net 30 days, no discount.)

NOVEMBER 12

Sale to D. J. Conley, $990.81, terms net.

Purchase from Bell & Bennett, $678.20.

Invoice is received from Clark & Son covering purchase of merchandise, $675.00, and prepaid freight, $25.00. The freight terms on this merchandise were f.o.b. shipping point.

Paid general expenses, $30.76.

NOVEMBER 13

Purchase from Bell & Bennett, $648.90.

Paid New York Central Railroad for freight on Bell & Bennett shipments of November 12 and 13, $22.74.

An advertising bill of the *Empire Times* is paid, $104.00.

Paid City Delivery Service, Inc., for delivery expenses, $36.50.

NOVEMBER 14

Paid Cox & Cox invoice of November 9, $874.00, less 2%.

A credit memorandum is received from Bell & Bennett for merchandise returned (originally billed November 12), $36.80.

A credit memorandum is received from F. M. Dent & Company acknowledging our overpayment of $9.00 on November 10.

The payroll for the first half of the month is general salaries, $300.00, sales salaries, $200.00. Cash of $435.00 is disbursed; $5.00 is withheld from payroll checks to cover deductions for social security taxes of 1%, and $60.00 is withheld to cover deductions for income taxes. (The payroll is paid today; November 15 is Sunday.)

NOVEMBER 16

Merchandise is sold to Stanwood's, Inc., $954.80; shipment is made today with sight draft bill of lading attached. (Record this transaction as per common business practice as described on pages 274–275.)

Purchase from F. M. Dent & Company, $1,204.00.

Issued credit memorandum to William Boyd for merchandise returned (originally billed November 7), $16.40.

NOVEMBER 17

Paid Bell & Bennett invoice of November 4, $214.63, net.
Paid freight on purchase of November 16, $25.20.
Traveling expenses are paid, $86.10.
Paid Cox & Cox invoice of November 11, $412.76, less 2%.
Sale to William Boyd, $811.12.

NOVEMBER 18

Cash is withdrawn by Mr. Franklin for personal use, $100.00.
Drew check favor Clark & Son in payment of invoice of November 12, less 2%.
Sales invoice to D. J. Conley for merchandise, $1,236.52, and for freight prepaid today, $14.20. Terms on shipment were 2/10, 1/20, n/30 and f.o.b. shipping point.

NOVEMBER 20

Sale to C. H. Brooks & Company, $784.00.
Purchase from Cox & Cox, $1,626.74.
Paid City Delivery Service, Inc., for delivery expenses, $35.62.

NOVEMBER 21

Purchase from Bell & Bennett, $876.22.
Purchase from Cox & Cox, $904.00.
Paid F. M. Dent & Company invoice of November 11, $380.00, net.
Issued credit memorandum to C. H. Brooks & Company for merchandise returned from invoice of November 7, $15.44.

NOVEMBER 23

Sale to Stanwood's, Inc., $428.77.
The Empire National Bank credits our account for collection of our sight draft of November 16 on Stanwood's, Inc., $954.80.

NOVEMBER 24

Negotiations with F. M. Dent & Company for an additional 5% trade discount on their invoice of November 11 for $380.00 have been concluded successfully. A credit memorandum for $19.00 is received from F. M. Dent & Company to cover this discount.
Sale to the Raymond Sales Company, $881.20.
Drew check in favor of Bell & Bennett:

$678.20	Invoice November 12
36.80	Credit memorandum November 14
$641.40	
12.83	2% discount
$628.57	Amount of check

NOVEMBER 25

Sale to D. J. Conley, $504.10.

Purchase from F. M. Dent & Company, $742.88.

Cash purchase from Judson & Ray, Inc., $140.00, less 5%.

NOVEMBER 26

Sale to C. H. Brooks & Company, $576.42.

Drew check in favor of F. M. Dent & Company:

$1,204.00	Invoice November 16
24.08	2% discount
$1,179.92	
$ 9.00	Credit memorandum November 14
19.00	Credit memorandum November 24
28.00	
$1,151.92	Amount of check (*Note:* Has the amount of the check been calculated correctly?)

NOVEMBER 27

Sale to Fraser & Nelson, Inc., $654.80.

Received check from D. J. Conley, in payment of our invoice of November 18 as follows:

$1,236.52	Merchandise
24.73	2% discount
$1,211.79	
14.20	Prepaid freight
$1,225.99	Amount of check

Issued credit memorandum to D. J. Conley for merchandise returned by him from shipment of November 25, $30.01.

NOVEMBER 28

Sale to D. J. Conley, $968.20, terms net.

Sale to Stanwood's, Inc., $264.71.

Bill for electricity and gas is paid, $39.60.

NOVEMBER 30

Received a thirty-day, noninterest-bearing note, dated today, from William Boyd, $1,209.76. This note covers the balance due on our invoices of November 5 and 7.

The payroll for the second half of the month is: general salaries, $300.00, sales salaries, $200.00. Cash of $435.00 is disbursed; $5.00 is withheld to cover deductions for social security taxes of 1 %, and $60.00 is withheld for income taxes.

After the books have been posted, compare your trial balance with the following:

Henry J. Franklin

TRIAL BALANCE, NOVEMBER 30, 19—

Cash	$12,599.66	
Accounts Receivable	7,147.08	
Notes Receivable	1,209.76	
Office Equipment	2,400.00	
Accounts Payable		$ 4,798.74
Social Security Taxes Payable		10.00
Withholding Income Taxes Payable		120.00
Henry J. Franklin, Capital		20,000.00
Henry J. Franklin, Personal	100.00	
Sales		12,753.15
Returned Sales and Allowances	90.49	
Sales Discounts	32.57	
Purchases	12,336.83	
Returned Purchases and Allowances		36.80
Purchases Discounts		128.48
Freight In	85.08	
Advertising	104.00	
Delivery Expense	72.12	
Sales Salaries	400.00	
Traveling Expense	132.90	
General Expense	75.96	
General Salaries	600.00	
Insurance Expense	48.00	
Office Supplies Expense	58.12	
Rent	300.00	
Utilities Expense	54.60	
	$37,847.17	$37,847.17

Record this trial balance on the 8-, 10-, or 12-column work sheet. Then place adjusting entries on the work sheet to cover the following items:

(1) Bad debts are estimated at $100.00 for the month.

(2) Office equipment is to be depreciated at the rate of 10 % per annum.

(3) Social security taxes accrued on the November payroll are 1 % old-age benefit tax, and 3 % unemployment tax. These are taxes charged against the employer. They do not include taxes withheld from the wage and salary checks of employees.

(4) One month's insurance premium has expired. (For the purpose of this practice set, adjusting entries for expense prepayments may all be debited to the single account Prepaid Expenses.)

(5) There is on hand a bill, dated November 30, 19—, of the City Delivery Service, Inc., for delivery services rendered, $48.99. (Credit Accounts Payable.)

After these adjustments have been recorded, complete the work sheet.

The inventory of merchandise on November 30, 19__, is estimated at
$2,000.00.

Prepare a profit and loss statement for the month of November.

Prepare a balance sheet as of November 30, 19__.

Do not close the books.

December 1

Paid December rent to the Globe Building Company, $300.00.

Checks are drawn for $200.00 each in favor of William A. Phelps, and
Harold W. Spear, salesmen, as advances for traveling expenses.

Received check from Stanwood's, Inc., in payment of invoice of November 23, $428.77, less 1%.

December 2

Sale to C. H. Brooks & Company, $910.80.

Purchase from Bell & Bennett, $410.00.

Paid freight on above purchase, $8.61.

Paid City Delivery Service, Inc., or bill of November 30, $48.99.

December 3

Received check from C. H. Brooks & Company for invoice of November 26, $576.42, less 1%.

Postage stamps are purchased, $15.00.

Paid $10.00 to the Salvation Army Christmas Relief Fund.

December 4

Sale to D. J. Conley, $621.50.

Sale to Stanwood's, Inc., $512.84.

Purchase from F. M. Dent & Company, $1,078.11.

December 5

Paid Bell Telephone Company bill, $16.40.

Merchandise is taken from stock by Mr. Franklin for personal use,
$50.00.

December 7

Sale to William Boyd, $280.46.

Received check from Fraser & Nelson, Inc., $654.80, less 1%, for invoice of November 27.

C. H. Brooks & Company notifies us of an error in the computation of
our invoice of December 2. The notice is found to be correct. A credit
memorandum is sent the company for the amount of the overcharge, $10.00.

December 8

Purchase from Clark & Son, $246.42.

November 30 statements from creditors are found to be correct. Checks
are mailed to creditors in settlement of all November 30 balances, less 2%.
Analysis of the F. M. Dent & Company account shows that its invoice of

November 5, which we paid net, should have been discounted 2%. This additional discount is deducted in today's check.

DECEMBER 9

Sale to Fraser & Nelson, Inc., $500.64.

Cash purchase from J. S. Bache & Company, $45.60, less 5%.

A credit memorandum is received from Bell & Bennett for merchandise returned from our purchase of December 2, $24.01.

DECEMBER 10

Sale to Howard Coburn & Company, $466.08.

Purchase from Cox & Cox, $1,540.19.

Paid New York Central Railroad for freight on Cox & Cox purchase, $28.33.

Traveling expenses are paid, $76.24.

DECEMBER 11

Purchase from F. M. Dent & Company, $3,091.80.

Received check from Stanwood's, Inc., $264.71, less 1%, for invoice of November 28.

Received check from D. J. Conley in payment of the balance of his account on November 30, less 2%. A debit memorandum is mailed to D. J. Conley for discount not allowed; 1% cash discount is allowed on invoice of November 25, other items net.

Paid City Delivery Service, Inc., for delivery expenses, $41.17.

DECEMBER 12

Sale to William Boyd, $802.00.

General expenses are paid, $36.71.

In order to finance the purchase of a house, Mr. Franklin withdraws $8,000.00 cash from the business.

DECEMBER 14

Sale to C. H. Brooks & Company, $854.28.

An extra 1% cash discount for payment within 5 days is offered by F. M. Dent & Company on its invoice of December 11. Check is drawn in payment, less 3%.

Mailed credit memorandum for $20.00 to William Boyd as an allowance on merchandise sold December 7.

DECEMBER 15

Purchase from Bell & Bennett, $964.72.

Paid New York Central Railroad for freight on this purchase, $19.01.

Sale to D. J. Conley, $985.11. Freight of $18.32 is prepaid on this invoice whose freight terms were f.o.b. shipping point.

Funds are borrowed today from the Empire National Bank on our $1,000.00 note, dated today, for sixty days, without interest. Bank rate 6%.

The payroll for the first half of the month is general salaries, $300.00, sales salaries, $250.00. After deduction of 1 % for social security taxes, and $66.00 for income taxes, the payroll is paid in cash.

DECEMBER 16

Merchandise is shipped C.O.D. express to Edgar Ames & Company, $64.15.

Purchase from Cox & Cox, $807.84.

$300.00 cash and a thirty-day note without interest, dated today, are received from William Boyd for the balance of his account receivable to date.

DECEMBER 17

Sale to Fraser & Nelson, Inc., $1,156.32.

Sale to the Raymond Sales Company, $258.25.

Received check from C. H. Brooks & Company for the balance of its account on November 30, $1,096.96, net.

DECEMBER 18

Sale to Harold & Elton, $746.81.

Purchase from Clark & Son, $973.61.

Drew check in favor Cox & Cox for bill of December 10, $1,540.19, less 2 %.

DECEMBER 19

Paid City Delivery Service, Inc., for delivery expenses, $31.74.

Paid advertising bill from the *Empire Times*, $85.00.

Invoice covering prepaid freight is received from Clark & Son, $30.10, covering shipment of December 18. Freight terms on this shipment were f.o.b. shipping point.

DECEMBER 21

Purchase from F. M. Dent & Company, $1,440.21.

Received check from Raymond Sales Company in payment of November 24 invoice, $881.20, net, and December 17 invoice $258.25, less 1 %.

Cash purchase from Judson & Ray, Inc., $109.60, less 5 %.

Paid Drake & Stone, Inc., for sundry office supplies, $36.41.

DECEMBER 22

Cash sale to Burley & Son, $99.17, net.

Paid freight on F. M. Dent & Company purchase of December 21, $22.48. Freight terms on this purchase were f.o.b. destination.

A sixty-day draft, dated December 18, is received from Harold & Elton in settlement of invoice of that date.

DECEMBER 23

Sale to D. J. Conley, $362.99.

Merchandise is shipped C.O.D. parcel post to Howard Healey, $43.24.

Purchase from Bell & Bennett, $740.69.

Henry J. Franklin withdraws $150.00 cash for personal use.

DECEMBER 24

Sale to Harold & Elton, $632.94.

Sale to Stanwood's, Inc., $220.00.

Remittance is received today on C.O.D. shipment of December 16.

DECEMBER 26

Issued credit memorandum to Raymond Sales Company for merchandise returned from shipment of December 17, $151.16.

Invoice covering prepaid freight is received from Bell & Bennett, $20.01, covering shipment of December 23. Freight terms on this shipment were f.o.b. destination.

A check for $1,000.00 is received from C. H. Brooks & Company to apply on December account. A cash discount of $2\frac{1}{2}\%$ is to be allowed C. H. Brooks & Company.

DECEMBER 28

Sale to C. H. Brooks & Company, $564.61.

Purchase from Cox & Cox, $625.07.

At its request, drew check favor the Raymond Sales Company to cover our credit memorandum of December 26. (Deduct 1% discount.)

DECEMBER 29

Sale to Howard Coburn & Company, $251.12.

Gas, electricity, and water bills are paid, $69.32.

Paid City Delivery Service, Inc., for delivery expenses, $18.50.

DECEMBER 30

William A. Phelps and Harold W. Spear, salesmen, submit their traveling expense reports for December, $108.44 and $92.10, respectively. Checks are received for the unexpended portions of their travel advances.

General expenses are paid, $45.02.

DECEMBER 31

The payroll for the second half of the month is general salaries, $300.00, sales salaries, $400.00. After deduction of 1% for social security taxes, and $84.00 for income taxes, the payroll is paid in cash.

After the books have been posted, draw off a trial balance. (The correct balance for Cash is $1,717.35.) Record this trial balance on an 8-, 10-, or 12-column work sheet. Then place adjusting entries on the work sheet to cover the following items:

(1) Bad debts, estimated at $200.00 for the two months.
(2) Office equipment, to be depreciated at the rate of 10% per annum.
(3) Accrual of social security taxes on the payroll.
(4) Unexpired insurance.
(5) Prepaid interest on notes payable.

After these adjustments have been recorded, complete the work sheet. The inventory of merchandise on December 31, 19__, by actual count and valuation is $6,629.91.

Prepare a profit and loss statement for the two months ending with December 31, 19__.

Prepare a balance sheet as of December 31, 19__.

Record adjusting entries on the books. Close the books. Record reversing entries.

Reconcile the cash account. The bank statement received from the Empire National Bank as of December 31, 19__, was as follows:

		DEBITS			DEPOSITS	BALANCE
Dec. 1	Balance					12,599.66
3		300.00	200.00			12,099.66
4		8.61	200.00		995.14	12,886.19
5		10.00	15.00			12,861.19
8					648.25	13,509.44
9		16.40	48.99			13,444.05
11		713.78	28.33			12,701.94
12		43.32	1,494.62		2,646.50	13,810.50
14		2,480.13	76.24		990.00	12,244.13
15		8,000.00				4,244.13
16		36.71	19.01	18.32		4,170.09
17		2,999.05	41.17	478.50		651.37
18					1,396.96	2,048.33
21		1,509.39				538.94
23		104.12				434.82
24		31.74	36.41		1,300.19	1,666.86
26		22.48				1,644.38
30		18.50	149.65			1,476.23
31		45.02			1,199.46	2,630.67

Franklin & Graham

PRACTICE SET NO. 5: PARTNERSHIP

The partnership of Franklin & Graham was formed on January 1, 19__, for the purpose of continuing and expanding the business heretofore operated solely by Mr. Henry J. Franklin. The articles of partnership provided, among other things, that

(1) Minimum capital investments shall be Henry J. Franklin, $12,-000.00, William F. Graham, $15,000.00. It was mutually agreed that the form and value of each partner's capital contribution should be as follows:

Henry J. Franklin:
Cash . . . . $ 1,176.15
Accounts Receivable:
   C. H. Brooks & Company $1,294.05
   Howard Coburn & Company 717.20
   C.O.D.'s — Howard Healey 43.24

D. J. Conley	2,031.84	
Fraser & Nelson, Inc.	1,656.96	
Harold & Elton	632.94	
Stanwood's, Inc.	732.84	
	$7,109.07	
Reserve for Bad Debts	200.00	6,909.07

Notes Receivable (noninterest-bearing):

Nov. 30 William Boyd, due Dec. 30	$1,209.76	
Dec. 16 William Boyd, due Jan. 15.	1,573.58	
Dec. 18 Harold & Elton, due Feb. 16	746.81	3,530.15

Inventory		6,629.91
Prepaid Insurance (premium for 10 months on merchandise inventory)		40.00
Prepaid Interest (discount on notes payable)		7.50
Office Equipment	$2,400.00	
Reserve for Depreciation	40.00	2,360.00

Accounts Payable:

Bell & Bennett	$2,091.40	
Clark & Son	1,250.13	
Cox & Cox	1,432.91	
F. M. Dent & Company	2,495.84	7,270.28

Notes Payable, dated December 15, due in 60 days, noninterest-bearing		1,000.00
Social Security Taxes Payable (relating to payrolls of November and December)		112.50
Withholding Income Taxes Payable (relating to payrolls of November and December)		270.00

William F. Graham:

Building		$15,000.00
Land		3,000.00
Mortgage Payable on real estate, due 10 years from now, interest at 6% per annum, payable February 1 and August 1		5,000.00

And cash to make up the balance.

(2) Salaries, chargeable as business expenses, shall be:

Henry J. Franklin	$300.00 per month
William F. Graham	200.00 per month

(3) In addition to salaries, partners shall be permitted to make drawings against profits at the average rate of $100.00 per month. Drawings in excess of this average may be made only by mutual consent. Excess drawings, however, shall be charged interest at the rate of 12% per annum.

(4) Interest at the rate of 6% per annum shall be allowed on the average balance of each partner's capital account. When the average capital of a partner during an accounting period is less than his minimum required investment, his drawing account shall be charged with interest computed against his deficiency at the rate of 12% per annum.

(5) Interest charged to a partner's drawing account because of sections 3 or 4 shall not be made the base of further charges for interest in the same accounting period.

(6) The profit and loss ratio of the partners shall be equal.

(7) The accounting period shall be the calendar year unless the partners mutually agree upon a shorter period.

Credit and cash discount terms for merchandise transactions will be the same as those for Practice Set No. 4. Sales and purchases transactions, in this practice set, have been purposely grouped so as to occur on the last two days of each week. This has been done in order to expedite the student's recording of such transactions. With similar intent, personal accounts have been limited to those used in Practice Set No. 4.

The following books of original entry will be employed: sales book, returned sales and allowances book, purchases book, returned purchases and allowances book, cash receipts book, cash payments book, and journal. The general ledger accounts will be:

Current Assets:

    Cash
    Stocks and Bonds
    Notes Receivable.
    Notes Receivable Discounted
    Interest Receivable
    Accounts Receivable
    Reserve for Bad Debts
    Inventory
    Prepaid Expenses (Sundry)
    Prepaid Insurance
    Prepaid Interest
    William A. Phelps, Travel Advance
    Harold W. Spear, Travel Advance

Fixed Assets:

    Building
    Reserve for Depreciation — Building
    Delivery Equipment
    Reserve for Depreciation — Delivery Equipment
    Office Equipment
    Reserve for Depreciation — Office Equipment
    Land

Current Liabilities:

    Accounts Payable
    Interest Payable
    Property Taxes Payable
    Social Security Taxes Payable
    Withholding Income Taxes Payable
    Notes Payable

Fixed Liabilities:

> Mortgage Payable

Net Worth:

> Henry J. Franklin, Capital
> Henry J. Franklin, Personal
> William F. Graham, Capital
> William F. Graham, Personal
> Profit and Loss

Profit and Loss:

> Sales
> Returned Sales and Allowances
> Sales Discounts
> Cost of Sales
> Purchases
> Returned Purchases and Allowances
> Purchases Discounts
> Freight In
> Advertising
> Delivery Expense
> Depreciation Expense — Delivery Equipment
> Miscellaneous Sales Expense
> Sales Salaries
> Traveling Expense
> Bad Debts
> Depreciation Expense — Building
> Depreciation Expense — Office Equipment
> General Expense
> General Salaries
> Insurance Expense
> Office Supplies
> Partners' Salaries
> Property Taxes
> Social Security Taxes
> Utilities Expense
> Interest Income
> Interest Expense

The accounts of the general ledger are arranged in the order in which they appear on the balance sheet and the profit and loss statement, respectively.

The books of Franklin & Graham are to be kept on the accrual basis of accounting, as described in Chapters 14 and 15.

January 1

The partnership of Franklin & Graham began business with the assets and liabilities described in the partnership agreement.

Purchases from:

Bell & Bennett $247.36
Cox & Cox 845.30

Paid freight on these purchases, Check No. 1, $17.67.

JANUARY 2

Sales to:

Invoice

#1	William Boyd	$ 755.00
2	C. H. Brooks & Company	534.81
3	Burley & Son (shipment made sight draft) . .	1,018.64
4	Raymond Sales Company	581.86

Paid Bell Telephone Company bill, Check No. 2, $15.20.

Check No. 3 in payment of bill in favor of White & Bollard for fire insurance premiums on building, three-year premium, $252.00; office equipment, one-year premium, $30.00.

JANUARY 4

A freight bill, covering the merchandise shipped to the Raymond Sales Company on January 2, is paid by Check No. 4, $12.60. This merchandise was shipped freight prepaid although it was mutually agreed that buyer and seller would each stand one half of the freight charges.

Checks No. 5 and No. 6 are drawn for $200.00 each in favor of William A. Phelps, and Harold W. Spear, salesmen, as advances for traveling expenses.

JANUARY 5

Received check from Fraser & Nelson, Inc., in payment of December account, $1,656.96, less 1%.

The Harold & Elton sixty-day draft (note receivable) for $746.81, and dated December 18, is discounted at the Empire National Bank. Bank rate 6%.

JANUARY 6

Paid general expenses, Check No. 7, $22.38.

Paid advertising bill from the *Empire Times*, Check No. 8, $94.12.

Paid City Delivery Service, Inc., for delivery expenses, Check No. 9, $36.02.

JANUARY 7

Received check from Stanwood's, Inc., in payment of December account, $732.84, less 1%.

Received check from Harold & Elton in payment of December account, $632.94, less 1%.

In order to strengthen the cash position of the business, Mr. Graham invests cash, $3,000.00.

JANUARY 8

Purchases from:

Bell & Bennett	$1,000.63
Clark & Son	876.22
Cox & Cox	901.17
F. M. Dent & Company	832.24

Paid freight on these four purchases, Check No. 10, $44.20. The freight terms on the Clark purchase were f.o.b. destination; the freight on this purchase amounted to $13.94.

Received credit memorandum from Bell & Bennett for merchandise returned from our purchase of January 1, $40.02.

JANUARY 9

Sales to:

Invoice

#5	C. H. Brooks & Company	$ 374.80
6	D. J. Conley	1,142.60
7	Harold & Elton.	914.77
8	Stanwood's, Inc.	1,089.08

Cash sale, invoice #9, to Lasser & Co., $311.20, less 1%.

Received cash from William Boyd for balance due on his note of November 30, $1,209.76.

December 31 statements from merchandise creditors are found to be in agreement with our accounts. Checks No. 11–14 are mailed to creditors in settlement of all December accounts, less cash discounts of 2%. All accounts payable balances on December 31 were for merchandise, except for the two following accounts:

CLARK & SON

	Dec.	4 Mdse.	246.42
		18 Mdse.	973.61
		19 Frt.	30.10

F. M. DENT & CO.

Dec. 22 Frt.	22.48	Dec.	4 Mdse.	1,078.11
			21 Mdse.	1,440.21

JANUARY 11

Received check from C. H. Brooks & Company in payment of December account, $1,294.05, less 1%.

Received check from D. J. Conley in payment of December account:

$ 621.50   December 4 invoice for merchandise
985.11   December 15 invoice for merchandise

18.32 December 15 freight
362.99 December 23 invoice for merchandise
43.92 Cash discount not allowed on remittance of December 11.

———
$2,031.84
20.32 1 % discount
———
$2,011.52 Amount of check (Is the calculation correct? If not,
======= credit D. J. Conley for the proper amount when the
check is recorded.)

JANUARY 12

Issued credit memorandum #1 to William Boyd for merchandise returned from sale of January 2, $30.21.

Social security taxes for the months of November and December are paid. The old-age benefit check, No. 15, in favor of the Collector of Internal Revenue, covers the 1 % tax withheld from the wages and salaries ($2,-250.00) of employees in November and December; and an additional 1 % levied against the employer. The remittance for unemployment insurance is a tax levied against the employer; the amount of this tax is 3 % of wages and salaries of employees in November and December. This remittance is mailed in two checks: Check No. 16 to the State Treasurer for 90 % of the tax, and Check No. 17 to the Collector of Internal Revenue for 10 % of the tax.

JANUARY 13

The Empire National Bank credits our account for collection of our sight draft of January 2 on Burley & Son, $1,018.64.

Received postal money order in payment of C.O.D. shipment to Howard Healey on December 2, $43.24.

JANUARY 14

Traveling expenses of Mr. Franklin are paid, Check No. 18, $44.17.

Issued Check No. 19 for $1,000.00 to James Bennett & Company in payment of 100 shares of the common stock of the Central Oil Corporation.

Received check from Howard Coburn & Company in payment of December account, $717.20, less 1 %. The discount is not allowed since the last date for discount was January 10. A debit memorandum covering the discount not allowed is mailed to Howard Coburn & Company.

JANUARY 15

Purchases from:

Bell & Bennett $781.10
Cox & Cox 474.51
F. M. Dent & Company 482.69

Paid freight on these purchases, Check No. 20, $30.23.
The payroll for the first half of the month is: partners' salaries, $250.00,

sales salaries, $300.00, general salaries, $250.00. After deduction of 1% for social security taxes on the wages and salaries of *employees*, and $82.00 for income taxes, the payroll is paid by Checks No. 21–28. (Mr. Franklin and Mr. Graham receive Checks No. 21 and 22, $250.00.)

Real estate taxes for the year ending last December 31 are paid, Check No. 29, $601.32.

JANUARY 16

Sales to:

Invoice

#10	Burley & Son (terms, sight draft)	$ 546.22
11	C. G. Watkins (C.O.D. express)	11.34
12	D. J. Conley	1,410.26
13	Fraser & Nelson, Inc.	884.30
14	Stanwood's, Inc.	479.61

Paid City Delivery Service, Inc., Check No. 30, $26.18.

Issued credit memorandum #2 to D. J. Conley for merchandise returned from sale of January 9, $18.12.

JANUARY 18

Received check for $7.07 from Howard Coburn & Company for cash discount not allowed on its remittance of January 14. The check should have been $7.17; it is decided, however, to allow the extra 10¢ discount rather than incur the cost of collecting this small item.

Received check for $573.58 from William Boyd to apply on his note of December 16 for $1,573.58, due January 15. Mr. Boyd requests, and is granted, an extension until January 25 to make payment on the balance due.

JANUARY 19

Received check for $13.94 from Clark & Son covering freight on their shipment of January 8.

Issued Check No. 31 to William F. Graham for personal use, $100.00.

Paid for postage stamps and stamped envelopes, Check No. 32, $20.00.

JANUARY 20

Received credit memorandum from Cox & Cox as an allowance on our purchase of January 15, $25.00.

Issued credit memorandum #3 to D. J. Conley for merchandise returned from sale of January 2, $15.44.

Issued credit memorandum #4 to Burley & Son for merchandise returned from sale of January 16, $112.42. Issued Check No. 33 in payment. This merchandise was returned by Burley & Son freight collect; paid this freight bill as our expense, Check No. 34, $5.01.

JANUARY 21

The Empire National Bank credits our account for collection of our sight draft of January 16 on Burley & Son, $546.22.

62¢ in stamps is received from D. J. Conley to take up the shortage in his remittance of January 11. The stamps are sold to Mr. Franklin for cash.

General expenses are paid, Check No. 35, $33.52.

Paid City Delivery Service, Inc., Check No. 36, $37.41.

JANUARY 22

Purchases from:

Bell & Bennett . . . . $ 743.61
Clark & Son 801.96
F. M. Dent & Company 1,363.44

Paid freight on the Bennett and Dent purchases, Check No. 37, $20.99.

JANUARY 23

Sales to:

Invoice

#15   William Boyd (sight draft) . . . . $ 264.32
16   C. H. Brooks & Company 660.00
17   Howard Coburn & Company 1,684.76
18   D. J. Conley 301.70
19   Fraser & Nelson, Inc. 742.63
20   Raymond Sales Company 1,003.84

Cash sale, invoice #21, to Ray & Son, $412.16, less 1%.

JANUARY 25

Received debit memorandum from Clark & Son for prepaid freight on shipment of January 22, $20.16. Freight terms on this shipment were f.o.b. shipping point.

Received credit memorandum from F. M. Dent & Company for merchandise returned from purchase of January 22, $72.56.

Mr. Boyd is unable to make the payment which he had promised to make today for the balance due on his note of December 16. A new note for $1,000.00 with interest at 8%, dated January 15, for thirty days, is executed in place of the old note.

JANUARY 26

Paid Drake & Stone, Inc., for sundry office supplies, Check No. 38, $44.20.

The C.O.D. shipment ($264.32) made to William Boyd on January 23 is refused, apparently because of the sight draft attached. Rather than release the goods on open account, Mr. Franklin instructs the railroad to return the shipment. Credit memorandum #5 is issued to cover the returned merchandise. (Record this credit memorandum in the journal.)

Transportation charges are paid on the returned Boyd merchandise, Check No. 39, $15.21.

JANUARY 27

Gas, electricity, and water bills are paid, Check No. 40, $38.90.

Issued credit memorandum #6 to C. H. Brooks & Company for merchandise returned from sale of January 23, $36.01.

Issued Check No. 41 in favor of the Collector of Internal Revenue for withholding income taxes for the months of November and December, $270.00.

JANUARY 29

Purchases from:

Bell & Bennett	$1,009.05
Clark & Son	1,136.87
Cox & Cox	954.36
F. M. Dent & Company	1,861.11
Judson & Ray, Inc. (sight draft, honored today)	164.00

Paid freight on these purchases, Check No. 43, $47.20.

JANUARY 30

Sales to:

Invoice

#22	C. H. Brooks & Company	$640.04
23	Howard Coburn & Company	377.60
24	Raymond Sales Company	912.10
25	Willis & Gray (C.O.D. express)	38.72

Paid freight on shipment to the Raymond Sales Company, Check No. 44, $17.01. Freight terms on this sale were f.o.b. shipping point.

Cash sale, invoice #26, to R. C. Bales, $201.30, less 1%.

William A. Phelps and Harold W. Spear, salesmen, submit their traveling expense reports for January, $84.20 and 85.04, respectively. Checks No. 45–46 are issued to cover.

The payroll for the second half of the month is: partners' salaries, $250.00, sales salaries, $350.00, general salaries, $250.00. After deduction of 1% for social security taxes on the wages and salaries of employees, and $90.00 for income taxes, the payroll is paid by Checks No. 47–54. (January 31 is Sunday.)

After the books have been posted, enter the January trial balance on a work sheet. Complete the work sheet, making proper provision for needed adjustments. In this connection the following items of information should be taken into consideration:

Buildings should be depreciated at 5% per annum on original cost.

Office equipment should be depreciated at 10% per annum on original cost.

Bad debts are estimated at $100.00 for the month.

Social security taxes imposed on the employer should be accrued for at the following rates: 1 % on wages and salaries of employees for old-age benefits, and 3 % on wages and salaries of employees for unemployment insurance.

The inventory of merchandise on January 31, 19—, is estimated at $7,200.00.

Prepare a profit and loss statement for the month of January.

Prepare a balance sheet as of January 31, 19—.

Do not close the books.

Reconcile the cash account. The bank statement received from the Empire National Bank as of January 31, 19—, was as follows:

	DEBITS			DEPOSITS	BALANCE
Jan. 1				3,301.15	3,301.15
4	15.20	17.67			3,268.28
5	12.60			2,381.97	5,637.65
6	200.00	200.00			5,237.65
7	22.38			4,352.12	9,567.39
9	282.00	94.12		1,517.85	10,709.12
11	2,445.47	36.02		3,292.63	11,520.26
12	2,049.57	1,404.25			8,066.44
13	44.20	1,225.73		1,061.88	7,858.39
15	1,000.00			710.03	7,568.42
16	45.00	44.17	462.50		
	250.00	30.23			6,736.52
18	6.75	26.18	20.00	580.65	7,264.24
19	60.75	100.00			7,103.49
20	601.32				6,502.17
22	112.42			560.78	6,950.53
23	37.41	20.99			6,892.13
25	33.52			408.04	7,266.65
26	5.01				7,261.64
27	15.21				7,246.43
29	44.20	38.90			7,163.33
30	17.01	47.20	164.00	199.29	7,134.41

FEBRUARY 1

(In the entry of transactions for February, new pages should be used for the books of original entry.)

Paid interest on real-estate mortgage, Check No. 55, $150.00.

Bought for cash from the Hood Motor Sales Company one Ford delivery truck with special panel body, Check No. 56, $1,220.33.

Paid for automobile license for the balance of the calendar year, Check No. 57, $27.50.

Paid the Central Insurance Agency for a one-year automobile insurance premium, Check No. 58, $48.00.

Bought for cash two Northern Pacific 6 % $1,000.00 par value bonds of 2047 at 100, and accrued interest, Check No. 59. Interest is payable January 1 and July 1. (Record the accrued interest as a debit in the Interest Income account.)

February 2

Paid Bell Telephone Company bill, Check No. 60, $18.29.
General expenses are paid, Check No. 61, $51.84.

February 3

Issued credit memorandum #7 to the Raymond Sales Company for merchandise returned from sale of January 23, $27.48.

Check No. 62 for $6.25 is mailed in payment of the weekly releases of Barrett's *Analyst* for a thirty-day period. This is a trial subscription to a service which provides news, trade analyses, statistics, advice, etc., to its subscribers and is expected to aid sales administration. The subscription agreement provides that, at the end of thirty days, the above $6.25 may be applied on a regular twelve months' $60.00 subscription.

February 4

Received express money order in payment of C.O.D. shipment to C. G. Watkins, January 16, $11.34.

Merchandise is withdrawn from stock by Mr. Franklin for his personal use, $200.00 (cost value).

February 5

Purchases from:

Bell & Bennett	$871.64
Cox & Cox	721.18
F. M. Dent & Company	432.69
Judson & Ray, Inc. (sight draft, honored today)	125.00

Paid freight on these purchases, Check No. 64, $22.61.

February 6

Sales to:

Invoice

#27	Howard Healey (C.O.D. parcel post)	$ 38.28
28	D. J. Conley	1,103.96
29	Harold & Elton	724.33
30	Stanwood's, Inc.	504.60

Paid freight on the shipment to D. J. Conley, Check No. 65, $13.62. Freight terms on this sale were f.o.b. shipping point.

February 8

A 6% note, dated today, and due March 10, is received from the Raymond Sales Company in payment of part of their January account, $1,000.00, less 1%. The note is immediately discounted at the Empire National Bank. Bank rate 6%.

Funds are borrowed from the Empire National Bank on our note for $5,000.00, dated today, for 30 days, without interest. Bank rate 6½%.

FEBRUARY 9

Received check for $1,478.92 from the Raymond Sales Company in payment of balance due on its January account, less credit memorandum of February 3. (Is the amount of the check correct? If not, credit Raymond Sales Company for the proper amount when the check is recorded.)

Issued Check No. 66 for $172.00 in favor of Empire National Bank. This check is in payment of withholding income taxes for January. The bank is a depositary of the Collector of Internal Revenue.

FEBRUARY 10

Received checks in payment of January accounts: C. H. Brooks & Company, $2,173.64, less 1%, and Howard Coburn & Company, $2,062.36, less 1%.

Received express money order covering C.O.D. shipment to Willis & Gray on January 30, $38.72.

Cash sale to Elliott & Mason, invoice #31, $35.11, less 1%.

January 31 statements from creditors are found to be in agreement with our accounts. Checks No. 67–70 are mailed to creditors in settlement of all January accounts, less cash discounts of 2% on merchandise.

FEBRUARY 11

Received checks in payment of January accounts:

D. J. Conley	$2,821.00, less 1%.
Fraser & Nelson, Inc.	1,626.93, less 1%.
Stanwood's, Inc.	1,568.69, less 1%.

Paid Chamber of Commerce dues, Check No. 71, $25.00.

Received credit memorandum from Bell & Bennett for merchandise returned from purchase of February 8, $27.20.

FEBRUARY 12

Received two notes from Harold & Elton:

#1: A sixty-day note, dated February 10, for $923.92, in payment of sales invoice of January 9, $914.77 and 60 days' prepaid 6% interest, $9.15.

#2: A thirty-day trade acceptance, dated February 6, in payment of invoice of February 6, $724.33, less 1%. This acceptance does not carry interest.

Purchases from:

Bell & Bennett	$1,100.68
Clark & Son	807.34
Cox & Cox	564.21

Paid freight on these purchases, Check No. 72, $24.66.

FEBRUARY 13

Issued Check No. 73 to Empire National Bank in payment of our note payable due today, $1,000.00.

Discounted the Harold & Elton note for $923.92 at the Empire National Bank. Bank rate 6%.

Sales to:

Invoice

#32	Fraser & Nelson, Inc.	$1,298.24
33	Harold & Elton	983.40
34	Raymond Sales Company	638.51
35	Burley & Son (shipment made sight draft)	190.17

FEBRUARY 15

The payroll for the first half of the month is: partners' salaries, $250.00, sales salaries, $400.00, general salaries, $250.00. After deduction of 1% for social security taxes on the wages and salaries of employees, and $98.00 for income taxes, the payroll is paid by Checks No. 74–81.

Check is received from William Boyd in payment of his note for $1,000.00, dated January 15, and interest.

Received from William Boyd, sixty-day 8% note dated February 10 for $724.79 in payment of January account.

FEBRUARY 16

Traveling expenses of Mr. Franklin are paid, Check No. 82, $51.17.
Postage stamps are purchased, Check No. 83, $10.00.
Cash sale to E. A. Herrick, invoice #36, $161.15, less 1%.

FEBRUARY 17

The Empire National Bank credits our account for collection of our sight draft of February 13 on Burley & Son, $190.17.

Paid Drake & Stone, Inc., for sundry office supplies, Check No. 84, $40.26.

FEBRUARY 18

Clark & Son draw a draft on us, dated February 12 and due March 10, to cover their invoice of February 12, $807.34, less discount of 2%. The draft is accepted.

A credit memorandum is received from Cox & Cox for merchandise returned from purchase of February 12, $54.25.

FEBRUARY 19

Received postal money order in payment of C.O.D. shipment to Howard Healey, February 6, $38.28.

Purchases from:

Clark & Son	$1,110.78
Cox & Cox	1,504.81
F. M. Dent & Company	1,067.92
J. S. Bart & Company (sight draft honored today)	64.40 (net)

Paid freight on these four purchases, Check No. 86, $46.28. The freight terms on the Clark purchase were f.o.b. destination; the freight on this purchase amounted to $14.23.

FEBRUARY 20

Sales to:

Invoice

#37	C. H. Brooks & Company	$1,073.01
38	Howard Coburn & Company	527.54
39	D. J. Conley	414.76
40	Fraser & Nelson, Inc.	684.72
41	Edgar Ames & Company (C.O.D. express)	68.41

Paid City Delivery Service, Inc., Check No. 87, $20.01.

FEBRUARY 22

Paid advertising bill from the *Empire Times*, Check No. 88, $82.70.

The Harold & Elton draft for $746.81, discounted January 5, was due for payment February 16.

FEBRUARY 23

Issued credit memorandum #8 to Fraser & Nelson, Inc., for merchandise returned from sale of February 20, $24.16.

Issued credit memorandum #9 to C. H. Brooks & Company as an allowance on invoice of February 20, $25.00.

General expenses are paid, Check No. 89, $38.41.

FEBRUARY 24

Issued Check No. 90 to William F. Graham for personal use, $100.00.

Gas, electricity, and water bills are paid, Check No. 91, $51.08.

FEBRUARY 25

Paid the Shell Oil Company for a fifty-gallon drum of oil (for the delivery truck), Check No. 92, $42.11.

Burley & Son write in to claim a credit for 1 % cash discount on their purchases of January and February. Although Burley & Son have been sold only on a sight draft basis, they appear to be developing into an excellent customer. As a goodwill gesture, their claim is allowed, credit memorandum #10 issued, and Check No. 93 to cover, for 1 % cash discount on the net sales made to Burley & Son in the months of January and February to date.

FEBRUARY 26

Purchases from:

Bell & Bennett	$ 471.39
Clark & Son	372.17
F. M. Dent & Company	1,243.03

Paid freight on these purchases, Check No. 94, $20.24.
Cash sale to J. E. Hamlin, invoice #42, $104.21, less 1%.

FEBRUARY 27

Sales to:

Invoice

#43	William Boyd ($500.00 cash is received as down payment on this sale)	$1,320.80
44	C. H. Brooks & Company	996.27
45	Burley & Son	464.25
46	D. J. Conley	726.19
47	Stanwood's, Inc.	598.34

William A. Phelps and Harold W. Spear, salesmen, submit their traveling expense reports for February, $88.62 and $134.17, respectively. Checks are received for the unexpended portions of their travel advances.

The payroll for the second half of the month is: partners' salaries, $250.00, sales salaries, $400.00, general salaries, $250.00. After deduction of 1% for social security taxes on the wages and salaries of employees, and $98.00 for income taxes, the payroll is paid by Checks No. 95–102. (February 28 is Sunday.)

After the books have been posted, enter the February trial balance on a work sheet. (The cash payments book should not be finally closed until the cash account has been reconciled with the bank statement.) Complete the work sheet, making proper provision for needed adjustments. These should follow the pattern for January, making allowance, however, for the following new items of information:

Bad debts for the two months are estimated at $100.00.

The delivery equipment should be depreciated at 33⅓% per annum on original cost.

There is on hand an unrecorded and unpaid expense invoice, dated February 26, from Lander's Garage for gasoline, oil, and minor service on the Ford truck, $22.12. There is also on hand an unrecorded and unpaid expense invoice, dated February 28, from John C. Leonard, certified public accountant, for accounting services rendered, $50.00.

The inventory of merchandise on February 28, 19__, by actual count and valuation is $7,954.18.

The inventory of office supplies is $20.00; and there is on hand a fifty-gallon drum of automobile oil, $42.11.

Prepare a profit and loss statement for the two months ending February 28, 19__.

Prepare a balance sheet as of February 28, 19__.

In view of the fact that Mr. Franklin and Mr. Graham have received and accepted an attractive offer for the purchase of their business, it is decided to close the books.

The bank statement received from the Empire National Bank as of February 28, 19__, was as follows:

		Debits		Deposits	Balance
Feb. 1 Balance					7,134.41
1	270.00	85.04	250.00		6,529.37
2	84.20	504.00	150.00		5,791.17
3	18.29	27.50	1,220.33		4,525.05
4	51.84				4,473.21
5	2,010.00	6.25			2,456.96
6	22.61	13.62			2,420.73
8				5,974.26	8,394.99
9	48.00			1,478.92	9,825.91
10	125.00				9,700.91
11	2,778.91	172.00		4,267.12	11,017.12
12	3,666.90	25.00	4,377.58	5,956.45	8,904.09
13	3,087.33	1,000.00	24.66	915.14	5,707.24
16	250.00	545.50		1,166.21	6,077.95
17	10.00	51.17		190.17	6,206.95
20	46.28	64.40			6,096.27
22	40.26				6,056.01
23	20.01				6,036.00
25	38.41	82.70	100.00		5,814.89
26	51.08			141.45	5,905.26
27	16.43	42.11			5,846.72
27 Service charge (for exchange)			.57		5,846.15

MARCH 1

Effective today the business of Franklin & Graham is sold to Edison & Fisher, Inc., for a cash consideration of $30,000.00. All of the assets and liabilities of Franklin & Graham, except cash, are transferred to the corporation.

All cash on hand is disbursed to Mr. Franklin and Mr. Graham by Checks No. 103–104.

Blackwell Manufacturing Company, Inc.

PRACTICE SET NO. 6: MANUFACTURING CORPORATION

The partnership of Blackstock & Wellman was a manufacturing enterprise of many years' successful operation. On July 1, 19__, the partners decided to incorporate their business under the name of the Blackwell Manufacturing Company, Inc. The authorized capital stock of the new corporation was as follows:

Preferred Stock, 7% cumulative, nonvoting:
3,000 shares, par value $100.00

Common Stock:
10,000 shares no par value

Common stock was subscribed for at a price of $110.00 per share as follows:

Robert S. Allen	500 shares
James D. Blackstock	4,500 shares
Sumner H. Wellman	4,000 shares
	9,000 shares

The subscription of Robert S. Allen was paid for in cash. The subscriptions of Mr. Blackstock and Mr. Wellman were paid for by turning over the net assets of the partnership, and cash for the balance. The balance sheet of the partnership on June 30, 19__, was as follows:

Blackstock & Wellman

BALANCE SHEET, JUNE 30, 19__

Assets

Current Assets:

Cash			$110,974.55
Petty Cash			200.00
Notes Receivable		$ 52,268.77	
Less Notes Receivable Discounted		28,194.53	24,074.24
Accounts Receivable		$269,752.17	
Less Reserve for Bad Debts		22,484.19	247,267.98
Inventories:			
Finished Goods.		$241,916.22	
Work in Process		80,201.18	
Raw Materials		134,762.01	
Factory Supplies		3,796.49	460,675.90
			$843,192.67

Fixed Assets:	Gross Value	Reserve for Depreciation	Net Book Value	
Automobiles	$ 32,234.11	$ 10,034.16	$ 22,199.95	
Buildings	150,000.00	37,500.00	112,500.00	
Furniture, Fixtures, and Office Equipment	15,324.69	3,762.48	11,562.21	
Land	30,000.00		30,000.00	
Machinery	171,414.65	48,001.63	123,413.02	
Tools	10,588.46	2,846.19	7,742.27	
	$409,561.91	$102,144.46	$307,417.45	307,417.45
				$1,150,610.12

Liabilities and Net Worth

Current Liabilities:

Accrued Interest Payable on Mortgage	$	1,500.00
Accrued Interest Payable on Notes Payable		500.00
Social Security Taxes Payable		6,688.19

Accrued Property Taxes Payable (10 months)	10,437.28
Notes Payable	100,000.00
Accounts Payable	103,645.37

$ 222,770.84

Long-Term Debt:
Mortgage Payable on Real Estate, 6%, due in ten years, interest payable January 1 and July 1 . . . . 50,000.00

Total Liabilities . . . . $ 272,770.84

Net Worth:

P & L Ratio

James E. Blackstock, Capital	. . . . 60%	. . . . . $465,979.11	
Sumner H. Wellman, Capital	. . . . 40%	411,860.17	877,839.28

$1,150,610.12

Supporting schedules to the above balance sheet are:

NOTES RECEIVABLE:

Date of Note	Maker	Time	Rate of Interest	Amount	Discounted at Metropolitan National Bank on
June 1	Eastern Sales Company	120 days	6%	$28,194.53	June 1
10	Carsten & Earles	30 days		14,039.44	
24	Lewis & Son	60 days		10,034.80	

$52,268.77

ACCOUNTS RECEIVABLE:

Berg & Evans	$ 20,358.14
Carsten & Earles	15,095.36
Clemson Bros., Inc.	30,324.84
Dean, Witter & Company	82,511.76
Elliott & Company, Inc.	40,094.04
General Sales Company, Inc.	18,121.27
Harper-Harris Company.	36,080.60
Lewis & Son	27,166.16

$269,752.17

NOTES PAYABLE:

Date of Note	Payee	Time	Rate of Interest	Amount
May 31	Metropolitan National Bank	3 months	6%	$100,000.00

ACCOUNTS PAYABLE:

Ne Page & Nelson	$ 14,826.20
Pioneer Supply Company	13,112.69
Rex Metal Works	17,340.77
Sears-Scott, Inc.	10,417.64

Terminal Sales Company 20,256.43
Union Hardware Company 12,744.99
Wallace Equipment Company 14,946.65

$103,645.37

The following books of original entry are to be employed:

Sales book   Check register
Returned sales and allowances book   Notes receivable register
Voucher register   Journal
Cash receipts book

The Blackwell Manufacturing Company, Inc., adopted the following numbered system of accounts:

REAL ACCOUNTS

Assets:

1   Cash
2   Petty Cash
5   Notes Receivable
6   Notes Receivable Discounted
7   Accounts Receivable
8   Reserve for Bad Debts
10 Finished Goods
20 Work in Process
25 Raw Materials
30 Factory Supplies

40 Interest Receivable
46 Prepaid Insurance
47 Prepaid Taxes, Licenses, Fees

50 Sundry Salesmen — Travel Advances

61 Automobiles
62 Reserve for Depreciation — Automobiles
63 Buildings
64 Reserve for Depreciation — Buildings
65 Furniture, Fixtures, and Office Equipment
66 Reserve for Depreciation — Furniture, Fixtures, and Office
        Equipment
69 Land
71 Machinery
72 Reserve for Depreciation — Machinery
75 Tools
76 Reserve for Depreciation — Tools

80   Goodwill

90   Organization Expense

Liabilities and Net Worth:

100   Income Taxes Payable
101   Withholding Income Taxes Payable
103   Property Taxes Payable
105   Social Security Taxes Payable
107   Taxes Payable — Miscellaneous
110   Dividends Payable — Preferred Stock
111   Dividends Payable — Common Stock

130   Interest Payable — Mortgage
131   Interest Payable — Notes Payable
132   Notes Payable

140   Vouchers Payable

181   Mortgage Payable on Real Estate

200   Preferred Stock
225   Common Stock
250   Capital Surplus
275   Earned Surplus

NOMINAL ACCOUNTS

Operating Income:

300   Sales
325   Returned Sales and Allowances
330   Sales Discounts
350   Cost of Sales

Manufacturing:

450   Freight In
475   Purchases Discounts

501   Direct Labor

600   Manufacturing Expense (summary and distribution account)
610   Depreciation Expense — Buildings
612   Depreciation Expense — Machinery
613   Depreciation Expense — Tools
620   Factory Repairs
640   Factory Supplies
650   Heat, Light, Power

660 Indirect Labor
670 Insurance
680 Miscellaneous Factory Expense
688 Social Security Taxes
689 Taxes, Licenses, Fees

Selling Expenses:

701 Advertising
720 Delivery Expense
730 Depreciation Expense — Automobiles
750 Insurance
760 Miscellaneous Selling Expense
780 Sales Salaries
788 Social Security Taxes
789 Taxes, Licenses, Fees
790 Traveling Expense

General Expenses:

801 Administrative Salaries
810 Bad Debts Expense
820 Depreciation Expense — Buildings
821 Depreciation Expense — Furniture, Fixtures, and Office Equipment
830 Insurance
840 Miscellaneous General Expense
850 Office Supplies
860 Postage
870 Stationery and Printing
888 Social Security Taxes
889 Taxes, Licenses, Fees
894 Telephone and Telegraph

Other Income:

925 Interest Income
950 Miscellaneous Income
975 Scrap Sales

Other Expense:

1025 Interest Expense
1050 Miscellaneous Expense

Special Income Credits: 1100–1199

1150 Recovery on Bad Debt Provisions of Prior Years

Special Income Debits: 1200–1299

Clearing and Summary Accounts: 1300–1399

    1399   Profit and Loss

JULY 1

Before the transactions below are recorded, the student should place on the books the proper opening entries for capital stock from information recited above. Include cash in the journal entry recording the investments of Mr. Blackstock and Mr. Wellman. Fixed assets should be set up at gross values; accrued depreciation as of June 30 should be credited to reserve for depreciation accounts.

The accounts payable, in addition to being entered in the opening journal entry (as vouchers payable), should also be entered in the voucher register, beginning with Ne Page & Nelson as Voucher No. 1, Pioneer Supply Company as Voucher No. 2 and so on. The seven credits to Vouchers Payable should be debited to Account 140, Vouchers Payable, in the distribution columns.

Balances for the eight accounts receivable accounts should be entered in the subsidiary ledger. The three notes receivable should be entered as *memoranda* in the notes receivable register.

The books of the Blackwell Manufacturing Company are to be kept on the monthly accrual basis of accounting, as described in Chapters 15 and 25, adjusting entries being made at the end of each month. Inventories are to be maintained under the perpetual inventory system.

Two controlling accounts will be kept, one for Accounts Receivable, and one for Vouchers Payable.

JULY 1

Voucher No. 8, favor James E. Blackstock, for organization expenses paid by him, $5,118.74. Drew Check No. 1 in payment.

Voucher No. 9, favor State Treasurer, for automobile license plates for next 6 months, $308.52. Drew Check No. 2 in payment.

Voucher No. 10, in favor of sundry salesmen, for traveling advances, $2,000.00. Drew Checks No. 3–9 in payment.

Voucher No. 11, favor John E. Davis, for six months' interest on mortgage, due today, $1,500.00. Drew Check No. 10 in payment.

Voucher No. 12, favor General Insurance Agency, for insurance premiums on

Building (three years)	$2,340.00
Merchandise (one year)	3,000.00
Automobiles (one year)	504.00
Other personal property (one year)	1,500.00
	$7,344.00

JULY 2

Voucher No. 13, favor Bell Telephone Company, $46.28.

Voucher No. 14, favor Standard Office Supply Company, for office supplies, $380.17.

Voucher No. 15, favor Adams & Buckner, for miscellaneous selling expenses, $135.79.

JULY 3

Voucher No. 16, favor Pioneer Supply Company, for factory supplies, $1,119.21.

Issued credit memorandum #1 to Elliott & Company, Inc., for merchandise returned from sale of June 29, $1,260.52. Cost, $1,109.54.

JULY 5

Voucher No. 17, favor Central Service Machinery Company, for factory repairs, $1,213.86.

Voucher No. 18, favor Sears-Scott, Inc., for raw material purchases, $14,820.55.

Voucher No. 19, favor Northern Pacific Railway, for freight on purchases, $138.38.

Check No. 11 to pay Voucher No. 19.

Check No. 12 to pay Voucher No. 12.

Check No. 13 to pay Voucher No. 13.

JULY 6

Sales to:

Invoice			Cost
#1	Berg & Evans	$13,232.50	$11,124.20
2	Carsten & Earles	9,753.13	8,312.99
3	Dean, Witter & Company	8,603.09	7,239.80
4	Elliott & Company, Inc.	11,165.44	9,478.28
5	Harper-Harris Company	10,074.73	8,442.37

JULY 8

Voucher No. 20, favor Grebe & Gillette, for miscellaneous general expenses, $88.75.

Voucher No. 21, favor Chase & Chase, for miscellaneous factory expenses, $650.66.

JULY 9

June 30 statements from creditors are found to be in agreement with our accounts. Checks No. 14–20 are drawn in payment:

Vo. No.			
1	Ne Page & Nelson	$14,826.20, less 2%.
2	Pioneer Supply Company	13,112.69, less 2%.
3	Rex Metal Works	17,340.77, less 2%.
4	Sears-Scott, Inc.	10,417.64, less 3%.
5	Terminal Sales Company	20,256.43, less 2%.
6	Union Hardware Company	12,744.99, less 2%.
7	Wallace Equipment Company	14,946.65, less 2%.

Received from Harper-Harris Company, note dated July 10, for thirty days, 6% interest, in payment of June account, $36,080.60.

July 10

Voucher No. 22, favor Pioneer Supply Company, for factory supplies, $1,244.02.

Received cash from Carsten & Earles for note of June 10 due today, $14,039.44.

Received checks in payment of June accounts receivable:

Berg & Evans.	$20,358.14, less 2%.
Clemson Bros., Inc.	30,324.84, less 2%.
Dean, Witter & Company	82,511.76, less 2%.
General Sales Company	18,121.27, less 2%.
Lewis & Son	27,166.16, less 2%.

July 11

Voucher No. 23, favor Wallace Equipment Company, for miscellaneous factory expenses, $531.80.

Check No. 21 to pay Voucher No. 15.

Check No. 22 to pay Voucher No. 17.

July 12

Issued credit memorandum #2 to Berg & Evans for merchandise returned from sale of July 6, $964.26. Cost, $802.30.

Raw material purchases from:

Ne Page & Nelson	**$15,447.08**
Terminal Sales Company	16,119.63

Voucher No. 26, favor Northern Pacific Railway for freight on raw material purchases, $214.88.

Check No. 23 to pay Voucher No. 26.

July 13

Sales to:

Invoice			Cost
#6	Clemson Bros., Inc.	$ 6,035.24	$ 4,759.84
7	Dean, Witter & Company	11,826.31	10,027.69
8	General Sales Company, Inc. . .	12,791.23	10,710.94
9	Lewis & Son	15,277.51	13,177.90

July 15

Voucher No. 27, favor *Garfield Trade Register*, for advertising, $1,223.12.

Voucher No. 28, favor City Treasurer, for fine imposed on one of our drivers for speeding, $50.00.

Check No. 24 to pay Voucher No. 28.

July 16

Received credit memorandum from Terminal Sales Company for raw materials returned from purchase of July 12, $751.64.

Received from Elliott & Company, Inc., check for $30,094.04; and note for $10,000.00, dated July 10, for thirty days, without interest, in payment of June account.

JULY 17

Voucher No. 30, in favor of Payroll, for payroll for period July 1 to 15, inclusive. Two days are required for the preparation of the payroll; its distribution is as follows:

501	Direct Labor	$14,822.19
620	Factory Repairs	1,072.52
650	Heat, Light, Power	188.00
660	Indirect Labor	7,559.77
680	Miscellaneous Factory Expense	729.47
720	Delivery Expense	898.13
780	Sales Salaries	950.00
801	Administrative Salaries	1,300.00
		$27,520.08

From this accrued payroll there were required to be withheld from employees' checks social security taxes of $221.11, and income taxes of $3,811.10.

(On its own account the Blackwell Manufacturing Company was liable for social security taxes on this payroll, $884.44. These taxes will be paid next October and January.)

Drew Check No. 25, in favor of Payroll — Blackwell Manufacturing Company, Inc., in payment of Voucher No. 30.

JULY 18

Voucher No. 31, favor Lowman, Rand, Inc., for miscellaneous selling expenses, $168.24.

Issued credit memorandum #3 to Lewis & Son for merchandise returned from sale of July 13, $1,008.76. Cost, $827.64.

JULY 19

Raw material purchases from:

Rex Metal Works	$44,361.49
Sears-Scott, Inc.	12,875.19

Voucher No. 34, favor Northern Pacific Railway, for freight on purchases, $381.44.

Check No. 26 to pay Voucher No. 34.

JULY 20

Sales to:

Invoice			Cost
#10	Berg & Evans	$ 8,186.63	$ 6,912.03
11	Carsten & Earles	11,936.11	10,048.20
12	Dean, Witter & Company	14,851.33	12,606.59
13	Elliott & Company, Inc.	8,724.37	7,411.38
14	Lewis & Son	9,003.21	7,555.61

July 22

Voucher No. 35, favor Metropolitan Auto Service, Inc., for automobile repairs, $70.51.

Voucher No. 36, favor Moody & Jackson, for stationery and printing, $477.22.

July 23

Voucher No. 37, favor Pioneer Supply Company, for factory supplies, $1,374.79.

Voucher No. 38, favor Northern Pacific Railway, for freight on the Pioneer purchase, $25.12.

Voucher No. 39, favor George H. Mason Company, for miscellaneous general expense, $189.62.

Check No. 27 to pay Voucher No. 38.

July 24

Received credit memorandum from Sears-Scott, Inc., for raw materials returned from purchase of July 19, $860.51.

Voucher No. 41, favor Central Service Machinery Company, for factory repairs, $972.48.

July 25

Issued credit memorandum #4 to Lewis & Son for merchandise returned from sale of July 13, $702.55. Cost, $588.30.

Voucher No. 42, favor Union Hardware Company, for miscellaneous factory expense, $729.59.

July 26

Raw material purchase from Ne Page & Nelson, $9,485.96.

Voucher No. 44, favor Northern Pacific Railway, for freight on raw material purchases, $48.94.

Check No. 28 to pay Voucher No. 27.

Check No. 29 to pay Voucher No. 36.

Check No. 30 to pay Voucher No. 41.

Check No. 31 to pay Voucher No. 44.

July 27

Sales to:

Invoice			Cost
#15	Berg & Evans	$ 9,000.99	$ 7,650.84
16	Carsten & Earles	11,832.88	10,081.48
17	Dean, Witter & Company	10,073.38	8,401.66
18	Elliott & Company, Inc.	12,831.84	9,752.77

July 29

Received from Harper-Harris Company, note dated July 11, due September 11, for $10,074.73, without interest, in payment of invoice of July 6.

Voucher No. 45, favor City Treasurer, for gas, electricity, and water, $1,803.52. Charge ⅘ to factory, ⅕ to general administrative expense.

July 30

Voucher No. 46, favor *Garfield Trade Register*, for advertising, $1,891.04.

Voucher No. 47, favor Sterling Oil Company, for gasoline and oil, $460.88.

July 31

Voucher No. 48, in favor of sundry salesmen, for traveling expense reports, $845.28.

Voucher No. 49, favor Western Union Telegraph Company, $159.75.

Voucher No. 50, favor Harris C. Graham, Cashier, to reimburse petty cash as follows:

760	Miscellaneous Selling Expense	$17.30
790	Traveling Expense	11.33
840	Miscellaneous General Expense	15.54
850	Office Supplies	5.96
860	Postage	25.00
870	Stationery and Printing	20.00
		$95.13

The voucher register is kept open until the summary of the payroll for the period July 16 to 31 is ready. The payroll voucher, No. 51, is distributed as follows:

501	Direct Labor	$22,941.09
620	Factory Repairs	1,555.75
650	Heat, Light, Power	188.00
660	Indirect Labor	11,045.45
680	Miscellaneous Factory Expense	650.66
720	Delivery Expense	988.50
780	Sales Salaries	1,000.00
801	Administrative Salaries	1,500.00
		$39,869.45

From this accrued payroll there were required to be withheld from employees' checks social security taxes of $341.10, and income taxes of $6,030.41.

(On its own account the Blackwell Manufacturing Company was liable for social security taxes on this payroll, $1,364.40.)

Checks No. 32–38 to pay Voucher No. 48.

Check No. 39 to pay Voucher No. 50.

Of the social security taxes owed as of June 30, $2,675.28 are payable in July. This amount represents withholding taxes for the period April to June. Voucher No. 52 is drawn up, $2,675.28, and it is paid by Check No. 40 (favor Collector of Internal Revenue).

Entries for usual month-end adjustments should now be placed on the books as follows:

(1) Accrued depreciation. Annual depreciation rates to be applied against original cost, i.e., account balances at the beginning of each month are

Automobiles 30%
Buildings (90% to factory, 10% to general administrative
    expense) 3%
Furniture, Fixtures, and Office Equipment 10%
Machinery 10%
Tools 33⅓%

(2) Accrue for July property taxes. Prorate ⅞ to factory, ⅛ to general administrative expense.

(3) Accrue for July payroll taxes on employer (see July 17 and July 31 payroll information). Apportion to manufacturing, selling, and general administrative expense, in proportion to the distribution of the July payroll over these three groups. These taxes are due for payment in October (old-age benefit tax), and next January (unemployment tax).

(4) Write off July apportionment of prepaid automobile license expense.

(5) Accrue for interest on notes receivable.

(6) Accrue for interest on notes payable and the real-estate mortgage. Calculate interest for one month of 30 days, using the 6 % rule.

(7) Expired insurance. Prorate insurance expense on

    Buildings: 90 % factory, 10 % general administrative.
    Inventory: 50 % factory, 50 % general administrative.
    Other personal property: 90 % factory, 10 % general administrative.

(8) Transfer the balances of accounts No. 450, Freight In, and No. 475, Purchases Discounts, to Account No. 25, Raw Materials.

(9) The Raw Materials Requisition Register shows $107,860.53 requisitioned for use in manufacturing operations. Debit Account No. 20, Work in Process, credit Account No. 25, Raw Materials.

(*Note:* In the stores ledger separate account cards are maintained for Freight In and Purchases Discounts. The Freight In account is credited monthly for the amount of freight applicable to raw materials issued; and Purchases Discounts is debited for an amount which will reduce this account card to zero at the end of the month. The credit to Freight In and debit to Purchases Discounts are included in the total of $107,860.53 for the raw materials requisition register.)

(10) The Factory Supplies Requisition Register shows $3,816.65 requisitioned for use in manufacturing operations. Debit Account No. 640, Factory Supplies, credit Account No. 30, Factory Supplies.

(11) Transfer the balance of Account No. 501, Direct Labor, $37,763.28, to Account No. 20, Work in Process.

(12) Overhead has been charged to production orders at the rate of 95 % of direct labor cost. The Summary of Manufacturing Expense Distributed shows a total of $35,875.12. This total is checked and found correct

(95% × $37,763.28 = $35,875.12). Debit Account No. 20, Work in Process, credit Account No. 600, Manufacturing Expense.

(13) The Summary of Completed Production Orders for July totals $169,111.38. Debit Account No. 10, Finished Goods, credit Account No. 20, Work in Process.

(14) Post all books of original entry. The Cost of Sales column in the sales book should be posted as a debit to Account No. 350, Cost of Sales, and as a credit to Account No. 10, Finished Goods.

(15) Prepare

    (a) Trial balance, July 31, 19___.

    (b) Profit and loss statement for the month of July.

    (c) Balance sheet, July 31, 19___, with supporting schedules for accounts receivable and vouchers payable.

AUGUST 1

(In the entry of transactions for August, use new pages for the books of original entry.)

Voucher No. 53, favor Bell Telephone Company, $63.11.

Voucher No. 54, favor Moody & Jackson, for printing office and factory forms, $180.00. Apportion 2/3 to factory, 1/3 to general administrative expense.

AUGUST 2

Voucher No. 55, favor Chase & Chase, for miscellaneous factory expenses, $508.42.

Voucher No. 56, favor Belmont & Keen, for miscellaneous general expenses, $208.74.

Check No. 41 to pay Voucher No. 51.

AUGUST 3

Raw material purchases from:

Ne Page & Nelson	$20,327.45
Terminal Sales Company	10,923.60

Voucher No. 59, favor Northern Pacific Railway, for freight on purchases, $193.39.

Check No. 42 to pay Voucher No. 59.

AUGUST 4

Sales to:

Invoice			Cost
#19	Berg & Evans	$ 9,172.54	$ 7,750.01
20	Clemson Bros., Inc.	12,737.84	10,890.01
21	Dean, Witter & Company	10,912.31	9,309.02
22	Harper-Harris Company	9,812.28	8,271.69

AUGUST 6

Check No. 43 to pay Voucher No. 53.

Voucher No. 60, favor Central Service Machinery Company, for factory repairs, $232.64.

AUGUST 7

Issued credit memorandum #5 to Clemson Bros., Inc., for merchandise returned from sale of August 4, $1,134.35. Cost, $937.72.

Voucher No. 61, favor Pioneer Supply Company, for factory supplies, $985.16.

AUGUST 8

Received from Harper-Harris Company note dated August 4, and due September 10, for $9,812.28, without interest, in payment of invoice of August 4.

Voucher No. 62, favor *Garfield Trade Register*, for advertising, $1,562.82.

AUGUST 9

July 31 statements from creditors are found to be correct. Checks are drawn in payment as follows:

Check No.	to pay	Voucher No.
44	. . . .	14
45	. . . .	16; 22; 37; all less 2%.
46	. . . .	18; 40; both less 3%.
47	. . . .	20
48	. . . .	21
49	. . . .	23
50	. . . .	24; 43; both less 2%.
51	. . . .	29; less 2%.
52	. . . .	31
53	. . . .	32; less 2%.
54	. . . .	35
55	. . . .	39
56	. . . .	42; less 2%.
57	. . . .	45
58	. . . .	46
59	. . . .	47
60	. . . .	49

Cash is received from Harper-Harris Company for its note of July 10, $36,080.60, and 6% interest.

Cash is received from Elliott & Company, Inc., for its note of July 10, $10,000.00.

AUGUST 10

Received checks in payment of July accounts:

Berg & Evans.	$29,455.86, less 2%.
Carsten & Earles, for June account	15,095.36, net.
Clemson Bros., Inc.	6,035.24, less 2%.
Dean, Witter & Company	45,354.11, less 2%.

Elliott & Company, Inc.	31,461.13, net.
General Sales Company, Inc.	12,791.23, less 2%.
Lewis & Son	22,569.41, less 2%.

Raw material purchase from Ne Page & Nelson, $9,874.45.

Voucher No. 64, favor Northern Pacific Railway, for freight on purchases, $45.71.

Check No. 61 to pay Voucher No. 64.

Check No. 62 to Metropolitan National Bank covering income taxes withheld from employees' checks in July, $9,841.51. This bank is an accredited depositary of the Collector of Internal Revenue.

AUGUST 11

Sales to:

Invoice			Cost
#23	Carsten & Earles	$ 8,043.01	$ 6,562.47
24	Dean, Witter & Company	15,566.07	13,338.52
25	Elliott & Company, Inc.	9,394.74	8,020.07
26	General Sales Company, Inc. . .	7,767.70	6,403.33
27	Harper-Harris Company	14,366.43	11,203.59

Voucher No. 66, favor Northern Pacific Railway, $99.98. By agreement this freight bill is to be paid by Harper-Harris Company, for whose account the payment is made by Check No. 63.

AUGUST 13

Received credit memorandum from Ne Page & Nelson for raw materials returned from purchase of August 10, $874.24.

Terminal Sales Company offers 1% extra discount on its bill of August 3 if payment is made within ten days. Check No. 64 to pay Voucher No. 58, less 3%.

AUGUST 14

Voucher No. 68, favor Lowman, Rand, Inc., for miscellaneous selling expenses, $147.18.

Credit is requested by, and granted to, Elliott & Company, Inc., for 2% sales discount on its remittance of August 10 for $31,461.13. Credit memorandum #6.

Check No. 65 to pay Voucher No. 61, net.

AUGUST 15

Voucher No. 69, favor Pioneer Supply Company, for factory supplies, $1,058.66.

Voucher No. 70, favor Northern Pacific Railway for freight on Pioneer purchase, $23.16.

Check No. 66 to pay Voucher No. 70.

AUGUST 16

Issued credit memorandum #7 to Elliott & Company, Inc., for merchandise returned from sale of August 11, $246.92. Cost, $201.71.

Voucher No. 71, favor Wallace Equipment Company, for miscellaneous factory expenses, $525.19.

August 17

Raw material purchases from:

Rex Metal Works	$32,617.17
Sears-Scott, Inc.	23,930.63

Voucher No. 74, favor Northern Pacific Railway, for freight on purchases, $355.61.

Voucher No. 75, in favor of Payroll for payroll for period August 1 to 15, inclusive. Its distribution is as follows:

501	Direct Labor	$18,489.11
620	Factory Repairs	446.92
650	Heat, Light, Power	187.57
660	Indirect Labor	8,473.75
680	Miscellaneous Factory Expense.	757.68
720	Delivery Expense	922.00
780	Sales Salaries	950.00
801	Administrative Salaries	1,400.00
		$31,627.03

From this accrued payroll there were required to be withheld from employees' checks social security taxes of $301.16, and income taxes of $5,371.84.

(On its own account the Blackwell Manufacturing Company was liable for social security taxes on this payroll, $1,204.64.)

Check No. 67 to pay Voucher No. 74.

Check No. 68 to pay Voucher No. 75.

August 18

Sales to:

Invoice				Cost
#28	Berg & Evans	$12,088.29	$10,344.03
29	Clemson Bros., Inc.	11,017.60	9,429.12
30	Elliott & Company	9,078.44	7,532.22
31	Harper-Harris Company	11,636.10	9,963.61
32	Eastern Sales Company, shipment sent sight draft; cash received today	14,995.77	13,363.41

August 20

Received an accepted thirty-day time draft from Carsten & Earles for $8,043.01, without interest, dated August 11, covering our shipment of that date.

Voucher No. 76, favor Moody & Jackson, for promotional sales catalogs, $500.00.

Voucher No. 77, favor Carr & Wright, for miscellaneous general expenses, $89.64.

August 21

Check No. 69 to pay Voucher No. 62.

Issued credit memorandum #8 to Berg & Evans for merchandise returned from sale of August 18, $659.30. Cost, $561.82.

Voucher No. 78, favor Central Service Machinery Company, for factory repairs, $722.28.

August 22

Voucher No. 79, favor Union Hardware Company, for miscellaneous factory expense, $493.07.

Voucher No. 80, favor Standard Office Supply Company, for office supplies, $342.16.

August 23

Voucher No. 81, favor *Garfield Trade Register*, for advertising, $1,335.51.

Cash is received from Lewis & Son, for their note of June 24, for $10,-034.80, due today.

Check No. 70 to pay Voucher No. 78.

August 24

Voucher No. 82, favor Rex Metal Works, for raw material purchases, $14,672.22. (Enter this voucher with knowledge of Voucher No. 83.)

Voucher No. 83, favor Northern Pacific Railway, for freight on purchases, $123.60. In accordance with the terms of purchase, one half of this freight bill is to be paid by Rex Metal Works.

Check No. 71 to pay Voucher No. 83.

August 25

Sales to:

Invoice			Cost
#33	Dean, Witter & Company	$11,638.82	$ 9,949.90
34	Elliott & Company, Inc.	8,444.18	7,338.18
35	General Sales Company, Inc. . .	9,900.64	8,444.14
36	Lewis & Son	12,441.63	10,574.62

August 27

Voucher No. 84, favor Pioneer Supply Company, for factory supplies, $1,240.91.

Miscellaneous scrap materials are sold for cash to the Weston Junk Company, $100.00.

Voucher No. 85, favor Union Hardware Company, for shop tools, $435.40.

August 28

Voucher No. 86, favor Metropolitan Auto Service, Inc., for automobile repairs, $81.53.

One of the delivery trucks, now 26 months old, and originally costing

$2,601.10, is traded in on a new model. The trade-in allowance received from the Wilson Motor Company is $600.00. The new truck is delivered today at an invoice cost of $2,300.00.

Check No. 72 to pay Voucher No. 87.

August 29

Some of the merchandise returned by customers is not considered to be salable as new merchandise of our usual grade. This "returned" merchandise is withdrawn from finished goods stock and sold for cash on invoice #37 to Kenway & Robb for $3,000.00. Cost, $3,114.79.

Voucher No. 88, favor Adams & Buckner, for miscellaneous selling expenses, $149.62.

August 30

Voucher No. 89, favor City Treasurer, for gas, electricity, and water, $1,404.81. Charge ⅘ to factory, and ⅕ to general administrative expense.

Voucher No. 90, favor Sterling Oil Company, for gasoline and oil, $404.60.

August 31

Voucher No. 91, in favor of sundry salesmen, for traveling expense reports, $964.11.

Voucher No. 92, favor Western Union Telegraph Company, $122.46.

Voucher No. 93, favor Harris C. Graham, Cashier, to reimburse petty cash as follows:

450	Freight In.	$ 1.32
760	Miscellaneous Selling Expense	15.71
790	Traveling Expense	6.17
840	Miscellaneous General Expense	26.00
850	Office Supplies	5.79
860	Postage	35.00
		$89.99

The payroll voucher No. 94, for the period August 16 to 31, is distributed as follows:

501	Direct Labor	$18,848.31
620	Factory Repairs	1,016.87
650	Heat, Light, Power	188.00
660	Indirect Labor	9,137.92
680	Miscellaneous Factory Expense	725.60
720	Delivery Expense	984.92
780	Sales Salaries	950.00
801	Administrative Salaries	1,500.00
		$33,351.62

From this accrued payroll there were required to be withheld from employees' checks social security taxes of $310.11, and income taxes of $5,684.77.

(On its own account the Blackwell Manufacturing Company was liable for social security taxes on this payroll, $1,240.44.)

Checks No. 73–79 to pay Voucher No. 91.

Check No. 80 to pay Voucher No. 93.

Voucher No. 95, in favor of Metropolitan National Bank, for note payable due today.

Check No. 81 to pay Voucher No. 95.

A bill for 8% interest, for twenty-one days, on $33,522.12, is sent to Carsten & Earles, covering their overdue account.

Directors declare a cash dividend of $2.00 per share on the common stock, payable October 1 to stock of record, September 15.

Entries for month-end adjustments should now be placed on the books as follows:

(1) Accrued depreciation on fixed assets. Prorate depreciation expense as in July.

(2) Accrue for August property taxes. Prorate $7/8$ to factory, $1/8$ to general administrative expense.

(3) Accrue for August payroll taxes on employer (see August 17 and August 31 payroll information). Apportion to manufacturing, selling, and general administrative expense, in proportion to the distribution of the August payroll over these three groups. These taxes are due for payment in October (old-age benefit tax), and next January (unemployment tax).

(4) Write off August apportionment of prepaid automobile license expense.

(5) Accrue for interest on the real-estate mortgage.

(6) Expired insurance. Prorate insurance expense as in July.

(7) According to the revenue acts of the state in which the Blackwell Manufacturing Company, Inc., is located, it is specified that for each year ending June 30 there shall be imposed upon each corporation a franchise tax of $0.139 for each share of outstanding capital stock. Accrue for this tax (July and August) at the annual rate of $0.139 for each share of outstanding stock of the Blackwell Manufacturing Company, Inc.

(8) Transfer the balances of Accounts No. 450, Freight In, and No. 475, Purchases Discounts, to Account No. 25, Raw Materials.

(9) The Raw Materials Requisition Register shows $106,342.63 requisitioned for use in manufacturing operations. Debit Account No. 20, Work in Process, credit Account No. 25, Raw Materials.

(10) The Factory Supplies Requisition Register shows $4,350.76 requisitioned for use in manufacturing operations. Debit Account No. 640, Factory Supplies, credit Account No. 30, Factory Supplies.

(11) Transfer the balance of Account No. 501, Direct Labor, $37,337.42, to Account No. 20, Work in Process.

(12) Overhead has been charged to production orders at the rate of 95% of direct labor cost. The Summary of Manufacturing Expense Distributed

shows a total of $35,470.55. This total is checked and found correct ($95\% \times \$37,337.42 = \$35,470.55$). Debit Account No. 20, Work in Process, credit Account No. 600, Manufacturing Expense.

(13) The Summary of Completed Production Orders for August totals $165,765.44. Debit Account No. 10, Finished Goods, credit Account No. 20, Work in Process.

(14) Since all June 30 accounts receivable have been collected, directors authorize the transfer of the balance in the Reserve for Bad Debts to Account No. 1150, Recovery on Bad Debt Provisions of Prior Years.

(15) Because the Carsten & Earles account is giving evidence of weakness, the directors authorize a provision, for possible loss in collection, of 10 % of the amount owed by the company.

(16) Post all books of original entry.

(17) Prepare

    (a) Trial balance, August 31, 19___.

    (b) Profit and loss statement for the months of July and August.

    (c) Balance sheet, August 31, 19___, with supporting schedules for accounts receivable and vouchers payable.

If desired, the books of the Blackwell Manufacturing Company may be formally closed. If this is to be done, proceed as follows:

(1) Transfer all individual manufacturing expense accounts to Account No. 600, Manufacturing Expense. Transfer the new balance of Account No. 600, Manufacturing Expense, to Account No. 350, Cost of Sales.

(2) Transfer all nominal accounts, in profit and loss statement order, to Account No. 1399, Profit and Loss.

(3) Transfer the balance of Account No. 1399, Profit and Loss, to Account No. 275, Earned Surplus.

(4) Rule up all closed accounts.

APPENDIX B

THE PRIVATE LEDGER

Occasionally a business may be found in which it is desired that certain information be kept confidential as, for instance,

Investment	Management salaries
Loans	Profits

This information may be kept confidential by placing it in a private ledger. This ledger will be represented on the general ledger by an account called Private Ledger. Conversely, the nonconfidential information of the general ledger will be represented on the private ledger by an account called General Ledger. Together, the two ledgers comprise the general ledger.

In brief, the private ledger system operates as follows:

H. L. Schiff has the following balance sheet as of December 31, 1954:

Assets		Liabilities and Net Worth	
Cash	$ 11,000.00	Accounts Payable	$ 25,000.00
Accounts Receivable	35,000.00	*Notes Payable	10,000.00
*Merchandise	10,000.00		
*Fixtures and Equipment	3,000.00	*H. L. Schiff, Capital	74,000.00
*Real Estate	30,000.00		
*Securities	20,000.00		
	$109,000.00		$109,000.00

Mr. Schiff decides to keep the starred items, as well as the profits, in a confidential, or private ledger; and to keep the unstarred (nonconfidential) items in the general ledger. The following entries are made in the general and private journals:

General Journal			Private Journal		
Notes Payable	10,000.00		Merchandise	10,000.00	
H. L. Schiff, Capital	74,000.00		Fixtures and Equipment	3,000.00	
Merchandise		10,000.00	Real Estate	30,000.00	
Fixtures and Equipment		3,000.00	Securities	20,000.00	
Real Estate		30,000.00	General Ledger	21,000.00	
Securities		20,000.00	Notes Payable		10,000.00
Private Ledger		21,000.00	H. L. Schiff, Capital		74,000.00
To transfer first 6 accounts to the private ledger.			To set up accounts transferred from the general ledger.		

The condensed transactions for the year 1955 are:

Deposited in private bank account	$ 500.00
Sales on account	60,000.00
Purchases on account	35,000.00
Expenses paid from general cash account	15,000.00
Expenses paid from private cash account	200.00

Cash paid to merchandise creditors 22,000.00
Cash received from customers 40,000.00
Notes paid 10,000.00
Interest received on securities 1,200.00
Merchandise inventory December 31, 1955 . . . . . . 12,000.00

The following entries record these transactions and also close the books for the year ending December 31, 1955:

GENERAL JOURNAL

Private Ledger . . Cash . . . . For cash turned over to private ledger.	500.00	500.00
Accounts Receivable . . . . . . Sales . . . . To record sales made on account.	60,000,00	60,000.00
Purchases . . . . Accounts Payable . . . . To record purchases made on account.	35,000.00	35,000.00
Expenses . . . . Cash . . . . To record expenses paid.	15,000.00	15,000.00
Accounts Payable . Cash . . . . For payments made to merchandise creditors.	22,000.00	22,000.00
Cash . . . . . . Accounts Receivable . . For cash received from customers.	40,000.00	40,000.00
Private Ledger . . Cash . . . . For cash turned over to private ledger.	10,000.00	10,000.00

PRIVATE JOURNAL

Cash . . . . . . General Ledger To record deposit in private bank account.	500.00	500.00
Expenses . . . . Cash . . . . To record expenses paid.	200.00	200.00
Cash . . . . . . General Ledger To record deposit in private bank account.	10,000.00	10,000.00
Notes Payable . . Cash . . . . For notes paid.	10,000.00	10,000.00

GENERAL JOURNAL

Cash . . . . . .　1,200.00
　　Private Ledger　　　　　1,200.00
For deposit made
today by Mr. Schiff.[1]

Sales . . . . . .　60,000.00
　　Purchases . .　　　　35,000.00
　　Expenses . .　　　　　15,000.00
　　Private Ledger　　　　10,000.00
To close nominal
accounts, same be-
ing transferred to
the private ledger.

PRIVATE JOURNAL

General Ledger . .　1,200.00
　　Interest Income　　　　1,200.00
For interest col-
lected on securities.

Purchases . . . .　35,000.00
Expenses . . . .　15,000.00
General Ledger . .　10,000.00
　　Sales . . . .　　　　60,000.00
To set up accounts
transferred from
general ledger.

(Note: Instead of new accounts being
opened on the private ledger, these three
may be posted directly to the Profit and
Loss account in detail. If this is done, subsequent entries are modified accordingly.)

Cost of Sales . . .　45,000.00
　　Merchandise . ·　　　10,000.00
　　Purchases . .　　　　35,000.00
To close.

Merchandise . . .　12,000.00
　　Cost of Sales .　　　　12,000.00
To set up new in-
ventory.

Profit and Loss . .　33,000.00
　　Cost of Sales .　　　　33,000.00
To close.

Sales . . . . . .　60,000.00
　　Profit and Loss　　　　60,000.00
To close sales ac-
count.

Profit and Loss . .　15,200.00
　　Expenses . .　　　　　15,200.00
To close expenses
into Profit and Loss.

Interest Income .　1,200.00
　　Profit and Loss　　　　1,200.00
To close interest in-
come account.

Profit and Loss . .　13,000.00
　　H. L. Schiff,
　　　Capital . .　　　　　13,000.00
To transfer profit
to H. L. Schiff's
capital account.

---

[1] If the deposit had been made in favor of the private bank account, and not the
general bank account, only one entry would have been made, and that on the private
ledger as follows:

　　　　Cash . . . .　1,200.00
　　　　　Interest Income . . . . . .　　　　1,200.00

Trial balances of the two ledgers, after closing, would be:

GENERAL LEDGER		
Cash	$ 4,700.00	
Accounts Receivable	55,000.00	
Accounts Payable		$38,000.00
Private Ledger		21,700.00
	$59,700.00	$59,700.00

PRIVATE LEDGER		
Cash	$ 300.00	
Fixtures and Equipment	3,000.00	
General Ledger	21,700.00	
Merchandise	12,000.00	
Real Estate	30,000.00	
H. L. Schiff, Capital		$87,000.00
Securities	20,000.00	
	$87,000.00	$87,000.00

A profit and loss statement (prepared from the preclosing trial balances, or from the Profit and Loss account on the private ledger) for the period would be as follows:

H. L. Schiff

PROFIT AND LOSS STATEMENT

YEAR ENDING DECEMBER 31, 1955

Sales			$60,000.00
Cost of Sales:			
Merchandise January 1, 1955		$10,000.00	
Purchases		35,000.00	
		$45,000.00	
Merchandise December 31, 1955		12,000.00	33,000.00
Gross Profit			$27,000.00
Expenses			15,200.00
Net Profit from Operations			$11,800.00
Other Income:			
Interest Income			1,200.00
Net Income			$13,000.00

Together the two ledgers produce the balance sheet:

H. L. Schiff

BALANCE SHEET, DECEMBER 31, 1955

Assets		Liabilities and Net Worth	
Cash	$ 5,000.00	Accounts Payable	$ 38,000.00
Accounts Receivable	55,000.00		
Merchandise	12,000.00	H. L. Schiff, Capital	87,000.00
Fixtures and Equipment	3,000.00		
Real Estate	30,000.00		
Securities	20,000.00		
	$125,000.00		$125,000.00

COMMENTARY

(1) Each ledger has one account whose details are found in the other ledger. One ledger is not subsidiary to the other; rather, it is complementary. Together, the two constitute the general ledger.

(2) The merchandise inventory, an essential determinant of profits, is kept in the private ledger.

(3) The General Ledger account on the private ledger has a debit balance of $21,700.00; this balance means that the general ledger is accountable for $21,700.00 of net assets.

(4) The Private Ledger account on the general ledger has a credit balance of $21,700.00. This balance signifies accountability to the private ledger for $21,700.00 and is, in other words, representative of H. L. Schiff's ownership claim to the net assets on the general ledger.

(5) The general ledger is supported by the usual books of original entry. The private ledger is supported by a private journal, private cash receipts book, and a private cash payments book. A private bank account will also be carried.

(6) The private books of account require but a small amount of bookkeeping labor, whatever is sufficient to record confidential transactions and to close the books. The bulk of bookkeeping labor continues for the general books — the recording of purchases, sales, cash receipts and payments, and so on.

INDEX

(Including brief glossary)